Madrid

timeout.com/madrid

Time Out Digital Ltd
Universal House
251 Tottenham Court Road
London W1T 7AB
United Kingdom
Tel: +44 (0)20 7813 3000
Fax: +44 (0)20 7813 6001
Email: guides@timeout.com
www.timeout.com

Published by Time Out Digital Ltd, a wholly owned subsidiary of Time Out Group Ltd.
Time Out and the Time Out logo are trademarks of Time Out Group Ltd.

© Time Out Group Ltd 2013
Previous editions 1995, 1997, 1999, 2000, 2002, 2004, 2007, 2010.

10 9 8 7 6 5 4 3 2 1

This edition first published in Great Britain in 2013 by Ebury Publishing.
A Random House Group Company
20 Vauxhall Bridge Road, London SW1V 2SA

Random House Australia Pty Ltd 20 Alfred Street, Milsons Point, Sydney, New South Wales 2061, Australia

Random House New Zealand Ltd 18 Poland Road, Glenfield, Auckland 10, New Zealand

Random House South Africa (Pty) Ltd Isle of Houghton, Corner Boundary Road & Carse O'Gowrie,
Houghton 2198, South Africa

Random House UK Limited Reg. No. 954009

Distributed in the US and Latin America by Publishers Group West (1-510-809-3700)

For further distribution details, see www.timeout.com.

ISBN: 978-1-84670-375-1

A CIP catalogue record for this book is available from the British Library.

Printed and bound in Great Britain by Butler Tanner & Dennis, Frome, Somerset.

The Random House Group Limited supports the Forest Stewardship Council® (FSC®), the leading international
forest-certification organisation. Our books carrying the FSC label are printed on FSC-certified paper. FSC is the
only forest-certification scheme supported by the leading environmental organisations, including Greenpeace.
Our paper procurement policy can be found at www.randomhouse.co.uk/environment.

MIX
Paper from
responsible sources
FSC® C023561

Contents

Introduction

Like London, Paris and any other number of capital cities, Madrid has very few residents who can seriously call themselves *madrileño*. At best they're likely to be second generation, and with strong links to the *pueblo* somewhere else in Spain where many of the family still live. Yet the presence of migrants from all over the country helps to make the capital what it is. In short, Madrid offers the best of Spain.

Andalucía may be the birthplace of flamenco, but no other city can match the capital for top-class venues, and sooner or later the best artists all make their way here. Equally, much of the new lease of life injected into flamenco over the past decade has come from musicians living in the capital. The country's premier bullring is also in Madrid, and any aspiring *torero* must make his debut in Las Ventas if he's to establish a name for himself.

The city may be 350 kilometres from the nearest Med beach, and was once no more than a scruffy market town in the middle of an arid plain, but since the beginning of this century it has boasted the best fish and seafood in Europe. The paella matches any in Valencia, while the *bacalao al pil-pil* rivals the finest that San Sebastián can muster. Long unable to provide its own fruit and vegetables, Madrid demands and pays for the choicest pickings, wherever in the country they might come from and at whatever time of year.

In the euphoria of newly democratic Spain at the beginning of the 1980s, when anything and everything seemed possible, Madrid was suddenly full of artists, actors, musicians, filmmakers, writers and dancers – the much-lauded Movida. This outpouring of street-level creativity was encouraged by a city council policy of providing heavy funding for popular arts, with festivals running back-to-back throughout the year. *Madrileño*-in-chief Pedro Almodóvar declared that one of his early movies, the 1982 *Labyrinth of Passions*, was based on the obvious fact that Madrid was now the centre of the world.

Since then, the drug problems of the 1990s, and the recession and political infighting of the early 21st century, have all taken their toll on this bouncy optimism, some grand architectural projects notwithstanding. And yet, the vital bar, café and club society that emerged through the Movida is still with us, and Madrid today offers a greater variety of nightlife than any other European city. Sure, there are challenges aplenty, and prices have risen at the same rate as unemployment, but it is still possible to get caught up in that same uplifting swirl of energy and sense of potential that the city first experienced way back in the '80s.

Sally Davies, Editor

About the Guide

GETTING AROUND

The back of the book contains street maps of Madrid, as well as overview maps of the city and its surroundings. The maps start on page 302; on them are marked the locations of hotels (❶), restaurants (❶), tapas bars (❶) and cafés and bars (❶). The majority of the businesses listed in this guide are located in the areas we've mapped; the grid-square references in the listings refer to these maps.

THE ESSENTIALS

For practical information, including visas, disabled access, emergency numbers, lost property, useful websites and local transport, see Essential Information. It begins on page 276.

THE LISTINGS

Addresses, phone numbers, websites, transport information, hours and prices are all included in our listings, along with selected other facilities. All of these were checked and correct when this book went to press. However, business owners can alter their arrangements at any time, and fluctuating economic conditions can cause prices to change rapidly.

The very best venues in the city, the must-sees and must-dos in every category, have been marked with a red star (★). In the Explore chapters, we've also marked venues with free admission with a FREE symbol.

PHONE NUMBERS

The area code for Madrid is 91. Even if you're in the city, you'll always need to use the code. From outside Spain, dial your country's international access code (00 from the UK, 011 from the US) or a plus symbol, followed by the Spanish country code (34) and the nine-digit number. So, to reach the Prado Museum, dial +34 91 330 28 00. For more on phones, see p291.

FEEDBACK

We welcome feedback on this guide, both on the venues we've included and on any other locations that you'd like to see featured in future editions. Please email us at guides@timeout.com.

Time Out Guides

Founded in 1968, Time Out has grown from humble beginnings into the leading resource for anyone wanting to know what's happening in the world's greatest cities. Alongside our influential weeklies in London, New York, Chicago and Dubai, we publish more than 20 magazines in cities as varied as Beijing and Beirut; a range of travel books, with City Guides joined by the pocket-sized Shortlist series; and an information-packed website. The company remains proudly independent, still owned by Tony Elliott four decades after he launched Time Out London.

Written by local experts and illustrated with original photography, our books also retain their independence. No business has been featured because it has advertised, and all of the restaurants and bars are visited and reviewed anonymously.

ABOUT THE EDITOR

Sally Davies has lived in Spain since 2001, and has edited and contributed to a number of books on the country. She also writes on Spain for a range of publications including The Guardian, Sunday Times, Daily Telegraph and Evening Standard.

A full list of the book's contributors can be found on page 11.

MUSEO THYSSEN-BORNEMISZA

Featuring an eclectic and sprawling collection of art through the ages, and from around the world, the Museo Thyssen is guaranteed to please everyone. *See p46.*

MALASAÑA

Once a playground for junkies, Malasaña is now Madrid's hippest *barrio* – a wonderland of cupcake shops, brunch cafés and achingly cool boutiques. *See p56.*

M30

Chamartín Station

PLAZA DE CASTILLA

AVDA PIO XII

NORTHERN SUBURBS

TETUÁN

Dehesa de la Villa

ARGÜELLES & MONCLOA

M30

Parque del Oeste

CHAMARTÍN

AVDA RAMÓN Y CAJAL

Las Ventas Bullring

AVENIDA DE AMÉRICA

Auditorio Nacional

C/FRANCISCO

Santiago Bernabéu Stadium

C/JOAQUÍN COSTA

C/SERRANO

C/MARÍA DE MOLINA

ÉGARA

PASEO DE LA

C/OR

VERDE

C/RDO. FDEZ VI

C/BRAVO MURILLO

CAL

C/JOS

C/SANTA ENGRACIA

ALES

DEZ

CHAMBERÍ

THE RETIRO
An elegant, classically designed park, containing the only known monument to Satan in the world. See p65.

MUSEO DEL PRADO
The greatest collection of religious art in the world, and an essential stop on any Madrid circuit. See p61.

THE RASTRO
Madrid's famed Sunday market is as much about the buzz it generates as what it has on offer. Get there early for breakfast before the crowds arrive. See p149.

PALACIO REAL
A Bourbon palace with an astonishing 3,000 rooms, many of them (including the impressive armoury) open to public view. See p38.

SALAMANCA & RETIRO

MALASAÑA & CONDE DUQUE

SOL & GRAN VÍA

CHUECA

HUERTAS & SANTA ANA

LOS AUSTRIAS & LA LATINA

RASTRO & LAVAPIÉS

VALLECAS

SOUTHERN SUBURBS

Parque de la Elipa

Parque del Buen Retiro

Campo del Moro

Parque de Tierno Galvan

Centro Cultural Conde Duque

Museo Thyssen

Museo del Prado

Puerta del Sol

Palacio Real

Atocha Station

Centro de Arte Reina Sofía

Vicente Calderón Stadium

Rayo Vallecano Stadium

Planetario

Plaza de España

Plaza Mayor

PLAZA DE COLÓN

PASEO DE RECOLETOS

PASEO DEL PRADO

GRAN VÍA

M30

AVDA DEL MEDITERRÁNEO

CALLE DO...

C/ALCALÁ

C/GOYA

C/VELÁZQUEZ

C/SERRANO

C/PRÍNCIPE DE...

C/FUENCARRAL

C/HORTALEZA

C/ARENAL

C/BAILÉN

C/MAYOR

C/TOLEDO

RONDA DE TOLEDO

HUERTAS

C/ATOCHA

C/PRINCESA

...VELA

PASEO SANTA M...

800 m
800 yds

0

© Copyright Time Out Group 2013

Whenever, wherever you need money...

We get it there in **10 minutes***

1. Arrange for the person sending the money to visit a MoneyGram agent near them. After sending the money, they will give you a reference number.

2. Find your nearest MoneyGram agent at moneygram.com

3. Give the reference number and your ID¨ to the MoneyGram agent.

4. Fill out one simple form to receive your money.

MoneyGram.
money transfer

900 81 16 32   moneygram.com

Time Out Madrid

Editorial
Editor Sally Davies
Deputy Editor Dominic Earle
Listings Editors Matthew Bremner, Sally Davies,
    Mary-Ann Gallagher, Koos Vos
Proofreader Marion Moisy
Indexer Holly Pick

Editorial Director Sarah Guy
Management Accountant Margaret Wright

Design
Senior Designer Kei Ishimaru
Group Commercial Senior Designer Jason Tansley

Picture Desk
Picture Editor Jael Marschner
Deputy Picture Editor Ben Rowe
Freelance Picture Researchers Isidora O'Neill,
    Lizzy Owen

Advertising
Sales Director St John Betteridge
Advertising Sales Charlie Sokol

Marketing
Senior Publishing Brand Manager Luthfa Begum
Head of Circulation Dan Collins

Production
Production Controller Katie Mulhern-Bhudia

Time Out Group
Chairman & Founder Tony Elliott
Chief Executive Officer Aksel Van der Wal
Editor-in-Chief Tim Arthur
UK Chief Commercial Officer David Pepper
International Managing Director Cathy Runciman
Group IT Director Simon Chappell
Group Marketing Director Carolyn Sims

Contributors
Introduction Nick Lyne. **Madrid Today** Simon Hunter. **Seeing the Bulls** Robert Elms. **Movida Movies** Rob Stone.
Diary Harvey Holtom (*In the Frame: Burial of the Sardine* Clayton Maxwell). **Explore** Sally Davies, Harvey Holtom,
Simon Hunter (*Saints and Sinners* Annie Bennett; *Walk, Don't Walk* Clayton Maxwell, *Visions of Hell* Richard
Schweid; *The Quick and the Dead* Michael Jacobs; *Park Life* Nick Rider). **Restaurants** Sally Davies (*Toilet Training*
Simon Hunter). **Tapas** Sally Davies (*Profile: El Mercado de San Miguel* Anna Norman). **Cafés & Bars** Sally Davies
(*In the Frame: Tertulias* Michael Jacobs; *Grape Expectations* Clayton Maxwell). **Shops & Services** Harvey Holtom,
Simon Hunter, Anna Norman. **Hotels** Helen Jones, Danny Wood. **Children** Andrew Wallace. **Film** Sally Davies.
Gay & Lesbian Barry Byrne, Pablo Espinoza, Jimmy Shaw (*Pride and Joy* Simon Hunter, Anna Norman). **Nightlife**
Simon Hunter. **Performing Arts** Mary-Ann Gallagher. **Sport & Fitness** Alex Leith, Mary-Ann Gallagher (*Bath Time*
Clayton Maxwell). **Escapes & Excursions** Sally Davies (*Spires and Tyres* Annie Bennett). **History** Nick Rider.
Architecture Harvey Holtom (*Profile: CaixaForum Madrid* Anna Norman). **Essential Information** Sally Davies.
Additional reviews throughout by Matthew Bremner, Sally Davies, Simon Hunter, Anna Norman, Matt Norman.

The Editor would like to thank Aleix Artigas, Jorge Barrero Manzano, Annie Bennett, Jana Cerdán, Laura Cuenca,
Aurélie Herrou, Simon Hunter, Carlos Menéndez, Tess O'Donovan, Dez Petrie, Paz Sánchez Rubio and Bob Steane.

Maps john@jsgraphics.co.uk

Cover photograph Plaza de Cibeles by Matej Kastelic
Back cover photography Jon Santa Cruz

Photography Page 3 Pavel L Photo and Video/Shutterstock.com; 8 (top), 9 (bottom), 25, 32, 37, 39, 42, 43, 45,
48 (bottom), 50, 53, 54, 55, 62, 67, 71, 78, 80, 81, 83, 88, 89, 90, 91, 93, 96, 97, 108, 109, 112, 116, 117,
119, 122, 123, 127, 132, 133, 134, 136, 146, 147, 150, 151, 155, 157, 160, 164, 165, 166, 167, 174, 176,
177, 178, 184 (bottom), 185, 186, 187, 190, 191, 194, 195, 204, 207, 208, 210, 213, 214, 215, 229, 232,
236, 272, 302/303 Jon Santa Cruz; 8 (bottom), 152 Alberto Loyo/Shutterstock.com; 9 (top), 26, 33, 34, 57, 63
(top, bottom), 64 (bottom), 105, 142, 143, 145, 183, 216, 220 Anna Norman; 12/13 gary718/Shutterstock.com;
14, 40 Victor Torres/Shutterstock.com; 16, 184 (top), 189 (top) Pedro Rufo/Shutterstock.com; 18 Fernando Cortes/
Shutterstock.com; 21 Agencia EFE/Rex Features; 24, 28 Shelly Wall/Shutterstock.com; 29 Jorg Hackemann/
Shutterstock.com; 30/31 S Borisov/Shutterstock.com; 48 (top) rubiphoto/Shutterstock.com; 55, 64 (top) Pedro
Sala/Shutterstock.com; 60, 68 Rafael Ramirez Lee/Shutterstock.com; 63 (top) holbox/Shutterstock.com;
65 S Borisov/Shutterstock.com; 69, 79, 154 Tupungato/Shutterstock.com; 70 Ungor/Shutterstock.com;
72 Carol Garanda/Shutterstock.com; 73 Dmitry Agafontsev/Shutterstock.com; 74 Fernando Blanco Calzada/
Shutterstock.com; 75, 237 Marques/Shutterstock.com; 77 Scott Chasserot; 85 (top) Miguel de Guzman; 86/87
Matías Costa/Nophoto; 94, 95 nito/Shutterstock.com; 95 (top) Cio/Shutterstock.com; 95 (bottom) bonchan/
Shutterstock.com; 103, 106, 107, 111, 114, 115, 121, 128, 138, 180, 200, 275 Karl Blackwell; 124
Markus Mainka/Shutterstock.com; 141 Pedro Rufo/Shutterstock.com; 149 baldovina/Shutterstock.com; 172/173
criben/Shutterstock.com; 179 Nomad Soul/Shutterstock.com; 181 Sony Pics/Everett/Rex Features; 189 Sara
Houlison/Shutterstock.com; 221 C Jimenez/Shutterstock.com; 234 Israel Hervas Bengochea/Shutterstock.com;
238 Richard Semik/Shutterstock.com; 242, 244 aguilarphoto/Shutterstock.com; 243 Ondacaracola/Shutterstock.
com; 245 Tomas1111/Shutterstock.com; 246 Leoks/Shutterstock.com; 250/251 pedrosala/Shutterstock.com;
252 Houlton Archive; 255 Fotowan/Shutterstock.com; 256 De Agostini/Getty Images; 260 Jose Angel Astor Rocha/
Shutterstock.com; 263 Getty Images; 268 Brian Maudsley/Shutterstock.com; 270 JPF/Shutterstock.com; 276/
277 Nanisimova/Shutterstock.com.

The following images were supplied by the featured establishments/artists: 15, 22, 23, 27, 36, 38, 41, 46 (top),
46 (bottom), 49, 55, 58, 66, 84, 85, 131, 137, 144, 156, 169, 179 (bottom), 182, 203, 209, 211 (top), 217,
218, 219, 259, 267.

Madrid Today

Down but by no means out.

TEXT: SIMON HUNTER

Besieged by crippling strikes, constant demonstrations, high unemployment, and swingeing cuts to health care and education, the last few years have been particularly challenging for the Spanish capital, and indeed the rest of the country. With jobless figures at record levels, the housing market still in the doldrums, and local and regional government struggling to find funding, *madrileños* are wearily facing up to the prospect of more hardship ahead, with rising living and transport costs and higher taxes.

When the economic crisis first began to bite in 2008, the city was still enjoying the fruits of the boom years with the completion of major projects such as the Cuatro Torres skyscrapers in the north of the city, the new wing on the Prado Museum, and the Madrid Río park project, built on top of the M-30 ring road (now buried underground in a labyrinth of tunnels). But public discontent over job cuts, corrupt politicians and a dysfunctional democratic system was bubbling under the surface, only to explode spectacularly on 15 May 2011 into an orgy of popular protest with the emergence of the 15M movement, AKA the *indignados*. Madrid marked the epicentre of this extraordinary desire for change, inspiring a movement that swept across the country and the world, even serving as the basis for Occupy Wall Street (a fact often forgotten by the media outside Spain). Spain's football team provided some welcome distraction by winning Euro 2012, but the positivity was short-lived and the outlook is far from rosy.

FROM BOOM TO BUST

Spain's strong economic growth in the first decade of the 21st century, up to the recession, was driven by property prices, which helps to explain why the crash was so dramatic in 2008 as the bottom fell out of the market. The government of José María Aznar laid the groundwork for this housing bubble, while the subsequent government of the Socialist Party's José Rodríguez Zapatero did nothing to slow its expansion. After a reasonably successful first mandate – which saw, among other things, gay marriage legalised and the influence of the Church tempered in schools – Zapatero floundered at the helm, firstly running into trouble owing to his refusal to admit there was a crisis, and then singularly failing to get to grips with it. The result was that the Socialists took a beating at the polls – on a national, regional and local level – painting the political map PP (Partido Popular or Popular Party) blue in 2011. Enter Prime Minister Mariano Rajoy, whose obsession with bringing down the country's deficit has seen austerity measures hit key areas of public spending, such as health and education.

But it's not so much Zapatero and Rajoy who have shaped the Madrid we see today. Former mayor and PP politician Alberto Ruiz Gallardón was the real driving force behind many of the grand urban renewal projects that have come to define the capital, and left large swathes of the city in a state of permanent roadworks for much of the noughties. But while many – in particular the city's taxi drivers – swore and cursed about the disruption this caused, there's now almost unanimous approval for the changes, in particular the €3.5-billion project to move part of the M-30 ring road underground and build the Madrid Río park on top. Locals now have a new park that stretches for ten kilometres along the banks of the Manzanares River, complete with cafés, fountains, bike lanes, skate parks, football pitches, tennis courts and even a BMX track. Once derided as a Pharaoh, due to his apparent desperation to leave his imprint on the city, Gallardón has been lavished with praise for his efforts to modernise Madrid – a city that, unlike Barcelona and Seville, has never had the excuse of an Olympics or Expo to indulge in a spot of cosmetic surgery.

IN FOCUS

Madrid Río project.

IN FOCUS

Madrid on the March

Madrileños are taking to the streets in force.

Due to a shocking lack of transparency, it's often hard to get any meaningful statistics out of any level of Spanish government, be it local, provincial, regional or national. But the politicians are only too keen to get some numbers out there when it suits them. And so it was in early 2013 that the government delegate in Madrid, Cristina Cifuentes, announced that there'd been an average of ten demonstrations a day in the capital during the previous year.

Since Spain threw off the shackles of the Franco dictatorship, its people have been ever more willing to get out on the street and demonstrate. Who could forget the sight of hundreds of thousands of *madrileños*, clutching their umbrellas as they braved the March rain to descend on the capital after the tragic Atocha bombings of 2004? But with all levels of government cutting spending, and record numbers of people out of work, it's clear that the propensity to take to the streets in protest has risen exponentially. The 15M movement sprang up in the wake of the Arab Spring, and has inspired veteran and

newbie activists alike to take to the streets. Even pensioners are getting in on the act, dubbing themselves *perro-yayas* (literally 'dog grandparents'), a play on the *perro-flauta* (dog-and-tin whistle) nickname given to Spain's band of dreadlocked, crusty youth.

But is anyone listening? Certainly the response of the Popular Party government and the police has been heavy-handed, to say the least – riot cops doled out liberal beatings during the Surround Congress protests. But citizen journalism is playing a huge part in these disparate movements, with any such actions quickly uploaded to YouTube. What's more, the fine intentions of the 15M movement – whose views can be summed up as a lament that the politicians no longer represent the people – are gradually being translated into action within the system: 2013 saw the launch of Partido X, a new political party initially made up of 90 key players from the 15M movement that aims to bring power back to the people via 'wikigovernment', referendums, transparency and direct participation in the drawing up of laws.

But Gallardón has recently gone from to hero to villain, thanks to his new role as Justice Minister in Rajoy's government, where his radical proposals for a return to Transition-era abortion policies and the introduction of court fees for citizens have revealed him to be, for many, a wolf in sheep's clothing. When Gallardón stepped down from his role as mayor, his deputy took over – the much-derided Ana Botella, wife of former Prime Minister José María Aznar and object of anger for the city's vibrant gay population, because of past comments she made that were openly hostile to the influential LGBT community in the capital. Her political standing dropped sharply in the wake of the October 2012 Madrid Arena tragedy, when five young Spanish girls were killed in a human crush at a Halloween party at the council-owned and -run venue. The incident highlighted City Hall's lax enforcement of building regulations and health and safety rules, and the revelation that Botella spent the day at a spa just hours after the enormity of the disaster became clear did nothing to sustain her popularity levels.

Along with Gallardón's civic successes, there have been plenty of white elephants too – many related to the city's three consecutive Olympic bids, put forward despite the parlous financial state of the city and region. Among the failed projects is the Caja Mágica sports arena, which has been a major flop, as well as the Peineta Olympic stadium, which is still not complete after years of council dilly-dallying. The Cuatro Torres business park has been underwhelming, to say the least: a massive conference centre due to be built in the shadow of the four towers has now been scrapped, leaving the luxury hotel in the Sacyr Vallehermoso Tower half-empty and the surrounding area woefully underdeveloped.

Such awful municipal mismanagement has even driven *madrileños* to take matters into their own hands, reclaiming public spaces for community centres. Take La Latina, for example, where the council knocked down the local leisure centre in 2009 in order to refurbish it. Unfortunately, though, the money ran out and the site lay untouched. Until, that is, a group of residents took the space over and renamed it El Campo de Cebada, offering cultural and social activities for locals of all ages.

BRICK LANE IN SPAIN

Aside from the cosmetic changes of recent years, there has been a seismic shift in the city's social make-up as well. Walk down any street and you'll hear Spanish being spoken, of course, but the accents are by no means all from Spain; the lilting tones of South America and the mangled grammar of other immigrants are everywhere. You'll hear Romanian, Polish and every other European language, not to mention Chinese, Arabic and a medley of African tongues. Madrid these days seems as multicultural as London, and nowhere is this more evident than in Lavapiés, where countless curry houses – with Bangladeshis out on the street vying for business – make the area feel like Brick Lane (albeit with better weather).

Madrid's immigrants have not had an easy time of it in recent years. With the onset of the economic crisis, the demand for cheap labour for construction projects plummeted and this workforce is getting the feeling that it's no longer wanted. Unlike some other regions, the Spanish capital has opted to implement the government's plans to refuse health care to undocumented immigrants, a slap in the face for a workforce that contributed so much back when times were good.

THE FUTURE

Whichever way you spin it, tough times undoubtedly lie ahead for Spaniards and *madrileños* alike. But, despite chronic funding shortages, the capital continues to move forward in a positive way with the construction of new cycle lanes and a firm commitment to green public transport. And that positivity is also apparent in the *madrileños* themselves, young and old, who refuse to give up. There's an omnipresent spirit at work in this city that stretches from teenaged activists to middle-aged café owners. And it's a spirit that makes all visitors to the Spanish capital feel very, very welcome.

IN FOCUS

Seeing the Bulls

Love it or hate it, the corrida isn't going away any time soon.

For many visitors to Spain the bullfight is a barbaric anachronism, a preening blood sport that's dying out in this modern land. Well, they're right about it being bloody: this isn't a fun day out for the squeamish. But they're wrong on every other count – at least from Madrid's point of view. First off, it isn't a sport. The essence of sport is an even contest where the end result is not predictable. The events in the arena are not a competition, and the end result is always the same – the bulls will die. The harsh reality is that you're watching the ritual slaughter of six animals for sheer entertainment. Closest perhaps to opera, and reviewed in the culture section of most newspapers, this is a theatrical performance, a tragedy, involving a truly wild animal and men in *trajes de luces*, 'suits of lights'. Of course, it isn't fair; it isn't supposed to be. And despite the 2010 ban in Catalonia – as well as the terrible goring of José Tomás, Spain's most celebrated bullfighter, some months earlier – it isn't dying out in Madrid.

Robert Elms is a writer and broadcaster, with a long connection to Spain and its culture.

Ringside Seats

Times, tickets and festivals.

The 25,000-capacity Plaza de Toros de Las Ventas (C/Alcalá 237, 91 356 22 00, www.las-ventas.com) holds corridas every Sunday from March to October, as well as on various public holidays and festivals. The traditional starting time is 7pm, though some kick off as early as 5pm. Tickets for Sunday bullfights can be obtained at *taquillas* (ticket windows) near the main entrance of the bullring or online (*see below*). Prices vary greatly, from around €5 to as much as €150. As a rule of thumb, the nearer the seat is to the arena the pricier the ticket, and any equivalent ticket is cheaper in *sol* (in the sun) than in *sombra* (in the shade).

If you can't get hold of a ticket at the *taquillas*, there are plenty of authorised agents in Madrid, though they charge 20 per cent commission. Try La Taurina (C/Pasaje Matheu s/n, 91 522 92 16) or Localidades Galicia (Plaza del Carmen 1, 91 531 27 32, www.bullfightticketsmadrid.com). There is also an independent online booking service, www.ticketstoros.com, with pages in English. Tickets can then be collected at the TEYCI kiosk, near the main *taquilla*, an hour before the *corrida* begins. You'll need to show your passport or confirmation email if you booked online.

LAS FERIAS

The best time to watch a top-quality *corrida* is during the Feria de San Isidro. For 20 consecutive evenings from mid May to early June, bullfights are held at 7pm, including *novilladas*, *rejones* (on horseback) and *Goyescas* (in period costume). However, it's difficult to get tickets for what is the highlight of the season for bullfighting aficionados. Most tickets for the San Isidro are snapped up way in advance by season ticket holders. Any that are

unclaimed are put on sale five days before the corresponding fight; by law 1,000 tickets for each fight must be put up for sale at 10am on the day of the fight, though huge queues form for these. San Isidro is preceded by the Feria de la Comunidad, which has a number of *novilladas* and a major fight on 2 May. Fights are also held daily during the Feria de Otoño, beginning in late September.

OUTSIDE MADRID

Many towns within easy reach of Madrid stage *corridas* on some Sundays during the season and on their annual saint's day. Many also hold bull fairs, with daily bullfights, during their annual *fiestas*. These small-town fairs often include an *encierro*, in which young bulls are run through the streets first thing in the morning, as in Pamplona's San Fermín. But be warned: bull-running requires a deal of acquired skill, and untrained tourists should be aware that joining in is extremely dangerous. Several have died doing so.

The first bullfights of the year take place during usually freezing February in Valdemorillo, to the north-west of Madrid. Aranjuez holds important bullfighting *ferias* on 30 May and in early September. But August is the cruellest month of the year for the bulls: Chinchón has *novilladas* in its historic Plaza Mayor, and a smaller event takes place in Manzanares el Real. The most spectacular *encierro* close to Madrid is in San Sebastián de los Reyes, while the most prestigious fair is the one in Colmenar Viejo; both in late August. Toledo holds a bullfight on Corpus Christi day. There is more information on these towns in the Escapes & Excursions chapter (*see pp228-249*). Tourist information offices will have information on dates.

IN FOCUS

'On such days, the dreadful danger and the awesome artistry will touch every soul present.'

IN FOCUS

In recent years television has taken the top stars of the ring to new heights, and the leading matadors are among the highest-paid performers in the world. On the big days in the big rings, every seat is sold and the atmosphere is electric. In truth, it isn't really a bullfight – that's a mistranslation of *la corrida*, the bull-running. Any man foolish enough to fight a wild bull would die in seconds. The Iberian fighting bull is arguably the most dangerous animal in the world, and the idea is to control it and then 'dance' with it before dispatching it; to create a fleeting but profound beauty out of the act of slaughter. To the Spanish this is a celebration of death, which in other countries is hidden away, as countless animals die in ignominy in abattoirs. The bull, which has lived a minimum of four years of absolutely natural existence, on the finest pasture Spain can provide, then gets his chance for a day of destiny and maybe even glory in the sun. 'We are going to see the bulls,' they say.

At heart, the Spanish attitude to the *corrida* comes from a profoundly different view of nature. In Britain, for example, nature is a distant green and fluffy thing that has to be protected. In Spain, a land still tied to agriculture, where the sun is too hot and the soil too poor, nature is a powerful, noble adversary, which has to be respected but dominated. And the fighting bull is its greatest champion. Day after day Spain sends her young men (and the occasional woman) out on to the sand (*arena* simply means sand) to enact this elaborate metaphor of man's continuing struggle with nature, to prove that beauty can still be summoned from the beast.

But that doesn't mean that if you go and see a *corrida* it will be any good. Even the superstar matadors don't come with a guarantee, and what they are attempting is a difficult business with a genuinely wild and unpredictable animal. The ideal is that the various stages of this highly technical ritual are played out fluently and smoothly, all grace and style. The bull should be brave and noble, and the men controlled and artistic. The emotional high point should be the *faena*, when the matador is in the ring alone with the bull and the true dance of death occurs. This is where man and animal become almost as one as they pass each other time and again, closer and closer, in a heart-stopping blur of crimson and gold. Then the moment of truth arrives and the great beast should be felled with a single blow from the sword. That's how it should be.

But of course it isn't always, and what is supposed to be elegant and honest can end up brutal and clumsy, unworthy of the poetry and the art. Sometimes the bulls are flawed and weak, other times the matadors cowardly and sloppy.

But then, one blazing afternoon, all the fates will fall into place. A bull, fierce, swift and handsome, will come racing out into a packed *plaza*, hear the crowd gasp, and see the matador straighten. It will charge and charge and the men will work with valour and honour to make sure that its death, and therefore its life, is a memorable one. The extraordinary emotion transmitted from the matador, the man in the gleaming gold, charged with the terrible task of dealing death, will infect the crowd. As he cavorts with the bull, *olés* soft and long will start to emerge, a collective exhalation, as a single man takes the primeval power of this beautiful adversary and slows it to a dream with a few sublime swishes of his cape. Then finally, in frozen silence, he will leap over the horns, his sword straight to the heart and his place in the annals assured.

On such, all too rare, days, the dreadful danger and the awesome artistry will touch every soul present, showing why Spain still clings to this ancient and terrible entertainment as the very soul of its identity, *la fiesta nacional*.

Movida Movies

Join the counterculture club.

TEXT: ROB STONE

The seasonal skies of Madrid that enthralled Goya and Velázquez have been a similar gift to filmmakers. Many foreign epics of the 1960s were made in the studios on the city's outskirts, including Anthony Mann's *El Cid* (1961) and *The Fall of the Roman Empire* (1964), Nicholas Ray's *King of Kings* (1961) and *55 Days at Peking* (1963), and David Lean's *Dr Zhivago* (1965). Recent internationally made films to have employed the city and environs include Milos Forman's *Goya's Ghosts* (2006) and Paul Greengrass's *The Bourne Ultimatum* (2007), the concluding episode of the Euro-tripping, amnesiac spy tale.

But although Madrid makes the top rank alongside such cities as New York, Paris and Tokyo, it is best understood by Spanish filmmakers, who have captured the skies, architecture and contrasts in several classic and modern masterpieces. The creative force of Spanish cinema was especially intense during the Movida, the cultural, sexual and chemical free-for-all that followed Spain's transition to democracy in the 1970s and early '80s – immortalised in the earliest films of Pedro Almodóvar (*pictured above*).

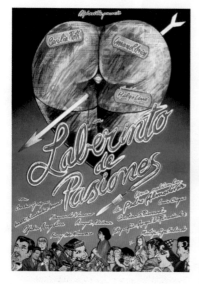

REEL REBELLION

The Movida took its name from a Spanish phrase meaning 'to have a business thing happening', which also doubled as slang for 'a drug transaction'. It was partly an ad hoc translation of British punk. Unlike British punk, however, the Movida was not so much a working-class movement as a drug-fuelled middle-class pretence of bohemian rebellion against the society of the recent past.

Perhaps the most crucial venue for the Movida's cinematic manifestation was the Alphaville (C/Martín de los Heros 14), which more recently changed its name to Golem. This still-thriving cinema opened in 1977 (when Spain's transition to peaceful democracy and public liberty was assured), and immediately established its revolutionary credentials with a week-long festival of Cuban films. Since then, it has continued to feature politically charged cinema, especially of the contemporary German kind. Wim Wenders' *The American Friend* (1977) still holds the record for the longest continuous run, at an impressive 67 weeks. This pales into insignificance, however, alongside the ten years of late-night screenings enjoyed by Almodóvar's *Laberinto de pasiones* (*Labyrinth of Passion*, 1982).

ALMODÓVAR'S EARLY DAYS

Laberinto de pasiones is a melodramatic, absurdist farce about a nymphomaniac called Sexilia (Cecilia Roth), a gay Islamic terrorist named Sadec (Antonio Banderas) and the son of the exiled Shah of Iran (Imanol Arias). Gobsmacked by the film's outrageousness, most international critics failed to notice the romanticism and compassion that Almodóvar clearly felt for those who had so recently been marginalised from Spanish society.

The Movida was also documented in the magazine *La Luna*, in Francisco Umbral's long-running column in *El País* and in TV programmes. There were also alternative music and variety shows presented by Paloma Chamorro and Almodóvar's earliest (and recently reconciled) muse, actress Carmen Maura.

Maura starred with the punk diva Alaska in *Pepi, Luci, Bom y otras chicas del montón* (*Pepi, Luci, Bom and Other Girls Like Mom*, 1980), which was two years in the making on a £20,000 budget raised by Almodóvar from his friends. In this scatological melodrama of female solidarity, Pepi (Maura) and Bom (Alaska) seek to liberate the masochistic Luci (Eva Siva) from her marriage to a policeman who respects her too much to beat her. Luci becomes a groupie for a band of degenerates, which provokes her jealous husband into beating her senseless, thereby resulting in a happy ending. The perverse yet romantic logic of the film was a faithful reflection of its time and audience, many of whom featured in the scenes set in the legendary Rock-Ola nightclub and other venues of the Movida, such as the Alphaville.

THE FALL-OUT

Almodóvar's humour became gradually darker and darker in his later films, when disillusionment with democracy and the repercussions from the drug-fuelled and sex-motivated excesses of the Movida soiled the carefree mood. By the time of *¡Átame!* (*Tie Me Up! Tie Me Down!*, 1989), the director was seeking to reconcile his wayward characters with the more conventional elements of Spain, such as the family unit and fidelity, erstwhile Alphaville and the clubs El Penta (C/Palma 4), La Vía Láctea (C/Velarde 18) and El Sol (C/Jardines 3) remain.

La Bobia bar on the edge of the Rastro (C/San Millán 3), where the opening sequence of *Laberinto* was filmed, is still standing, but now houses a rather dull café. A leisurely walking tour could start from here, after which you could move on up to the Plaza Mayor, where Otto and Ana so narrowly miss each other in Julio Medem's *Los amantes del Círculo Polar* (*Lovers of the Arctic Circle*, 1998), and on to the Plaza de España, where Sofía and Jota collide in Medem's *La ardilla roja* (Red Squirrel, 1993). From here, you can either head up the raucous Gran Vía, so miraculously deserted in Alejandro Amenábar's *Abre los ojos* (*Open Your Eyes*, 1997), or head into the sidestreets surrounding the Ópera district, where Matías meets his cousin Violeta in Fernando Trueba's *Ópera prima* (*First Effort*, 1980). Either route should get you to Callao in time for an *aperitivo* beneath the hoarding of the FNAC superstore (C/Preciados 28), which hosted the advertising for Leo's novel in Almodóvar's *La flor de mi secreto* (*The Flower of My Secret*, 1995), before a stroll to the Sevilla metro station where Antonio, the rogue ETA terrorist, shoots a cop in Imanol Uribe's *Días contados* (*Running Out of Time*, 1994). Enjoy lunch in one of the bars on the Plaza de Colón, close to the María Guerrero Theatre (C/Tamayo y Baus 4) where Becky (Marisa Paredes) performed 'Piensa en mí' in Almodóvar's *Tacones lejanos* (*High Heels*, 1991). Then consider an afternoon shopping in chic Chueca, where Almodóvar filmed *La ley del deseo* (*Law of Desire*, 1987).

because the human cost of the Movida in terms of drug abuse and AIDS was by then so apparent. Drugs had been the main spur to the fantasy nightlife, but by *¿Qué he hecho yo para merecer esto?* (*What Have I Done to Deserve This?*, 1984) the drug-dealing son of glue-sniffing housewife Gloria (Carmen Maura) is warning her not to graduate to hard drugs; and in *¡Átame!*, although the psychopathic Ricky (Antonio Banderas) kidnaps ex-junkie porn star Marina (Victoria Abril), he shows great concern for her returning need. Indeed, a prime motor of the plot of *Todo sobre mi madre* (*All About My Mother*, 1999) is the effort of the female collective to rescue one of their ilk from her addiction, and there is clearly something desperately retrospective about the wish-fulfilment ending of this film, which culminates in the miraculous birth of a child whose immune system holds a cure for AIDS.

REMAINS OF THE DAYS

Sadly, the Rock-Ola nightclub (C/Padre Xifré 5), which featured in *Laberinto de pasiones*, is now a supermarket. Several of the most iconic venues of the Movida have also gone, such as the Carolina discotheque (C/Bravo Murillo 202), which became a clothes shop. Nevertheless, the

Whatever others might have you believe, the Movida is now long gone, being uniquely of its time and therefore rightly defunct. You can still go from bar to bar in Madrid, check out a gig at El Sol, catch something avant-garde at Alphaville, and pretend along with many avid tourists that the Movida is still happening. But resist the pretence – Almodóvar turned 60 in 2009 and, like him, this extraordinary period in Madrid's cultural history is best revisited through his early films.

IN FOCUS

Diary

A plan for all seasons.

Practically all year round, apart from perhaps during the late winter lull (when everybody is worn out and broke from Christmas, New Year and Reyes celebrations) and at the end of summer, anyone coming to the Spanish capital is likely to encounter some sort of arts festival, music festival, *fiesta* or themed film season. There's something here to suit all tastes, but to make sure you catch one you like, it's worth doing a little forward planning.

Events and festivals that receive official sponsorship come under the aegis of either the Ayuntamiento (city council) or the Comunidad de Madrid (regional government), and the influence of politics, inevitably, is felt in culture. Municipal events have looked less tawdry and more upbeat of late, though, and regional cultural policy has managed to maintain a consistently high standard in recent years. Other events, such as the annual photographic extravaganza PHotoEspaña, are independent and still more are semi-independent, functioning with a mix of public and private money.

SPRING

See also p212 **Music Beyond Madrid** for the annual Música Antigua Aranjuez festival.

Festival de Arte Sacro
Various venues. **Information** Tourist offices & 012, www.madrid.org. **Date** Feb/Mar.
This two-month festival of music, dance, theatre, poetry, movies and conferences focuses on the role of religion in art, music, dance and film through the centuries.

Día de la Mujer/Semana de la Mujer
Various venues. Route normally starts at Plaza Jacinto Benavente, Huertas & Santa Ana. Metro Sol or Tirso de Molina. **Information** Dirección General de la Mujer (91 720 62 63). **Date** 8 Mar & surrounding wk.
International Women's Day is celebrated in Madrid with a march, usually from Plaza Jacinto Benavente to the bottom of C/Atocha. Some of the many other related events taking place over the week include short film seasons and concerts.

Teatralia
Various venues. **Information** Tourist offices & 012, www.madrid.org/teatralia. **Date** 3wks Mar.

A regional jamboree of performing arts, including theatre, puppet shows, circus and cinema, as well as workshops and other activities aimed at children and young people.

Semana Santa (Holy Week)
All over Madrid. **Information** Tourist offices & 010, www.esmadrid.com. **Date** wk leading up to Good Friday and Easter weekend (Mar/Apr).
Easter is usually a good time to be in Madrid, as many *madrileños* get out of town for the long weekend, and the weather is usually good. In Madrid and nearby towns, there are many parish processions in which hooded *penitentes* schlep figures of Christ and the Virgin around. Regarded as the most impressive is that of Jesús Nazareno el Pobre from San Pedro El Viejo and around La Latina. All over town there are organ and choral performances in churches.

Fiesta del Trabajo (May Day)
City centre & Casa de Campo. Metro Batán or Lago. **Date** 1 May.
The largest May Day march, attracting upwards of 60,000 people, is organised by the communist-led CCOO and the socialist UGT unions, which converge on Sol. Smaller in scale but quite animated is the anarcho-syndicalist CGT's march from Atocha to Plaza Jacinto Benavente. The anarchist purists

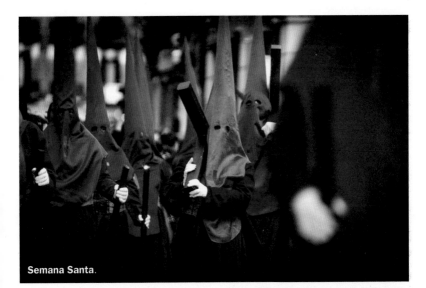

Semana Santa.

CNT/AIT, meanwhile, march up C/Bravo Murillo from Cuatro Caminos. Many of the participants then head to the Casa de Campo where the UGT organises a lively party with stalls run by the *casas regionales*, clubs representing Spain's regions.

Dos de Mayo
District of Malasaña. Metro Bilbao, Noviciado or Tribunal. **Information** Tourist offices & 012, www.somosmalasana.com. **Date** wk of 2 May. **Map** p307 G8.

Commemorating the fateful day in 1808 when the people of Madrid rose up against Napoleon's occupying troops and paid for their audacity by being massacred, 2 May is now the region's official holiday and kick-starts a nearly continuous series of *fiestas* that go on throughout the rest of the spring and summer. Things get going in the Malasaña neighbourhood – named after the uprising's teenage heroine, Manuela Malasaña – in the Plaza Dos de Mayo, where the Monteleón barracks, a main bastion of resistance, then stood. The council attempted to ban festivities in 2004 and since then a neighbourhood association has organised home-spun activities, from kids' workshops to outdoor gigs and a tortilla competition.

★ San Isidro
Plaza Mayor, Los Austrias, & all over Madrid. **Information** Plaza Mayor tourist office & 010, www.esmadrid.com/sanisidro. **Date** 1wk around 15 May.

For six days either side of 15 May, this is the time to see *madrileños* doing what they do best: taking to the streets and having a rollicking good knees-up.

The *fiestas* celebrate San Isidro, Madrid's patron saint, a humble 12th-century labourer and well-digger to whom all manner of miracles are attributed and whose wife, María de la Cabeza, was also canonised, making them the only sainted couple in history. The action centres on the Plaza Mayor, where the *fiestas* are officially declared open and nightly gigs are held (with the odd classical performance thrown in). There is more music in Las Vistillas park; music, theatre, painting workshops and more are put on for kids in the Retiro; classic *zarzuela* arias get an airing in the Conde Duque Cultural Centre; the Auditorium in the Museo de la Ciudad programmes classical music; in the Planetarium there are performances of early, medieval and baroque music; and lovers of

---

**INSIDE TRACK
WHAT'S ON WHEN**

Advanced festival information is scarce as programming tends to be finalised close to the starting date. For details on Ayuntamiento-backed events, call 010 or visit www.madrid.es and www.esmadrid. com; for Comunidad-backed events, call 012 or go to www.madrid.org. See also www.fiestas-de-madrid.com. Otherwise, listings magazines such as *Guía del Ocio* and *Metrópoli* (a supplement of *El Mundo*) provide information on the Friday preceding big events. Spanish speakers should also try www.lanetro. com, a good listings site.

INSIDE TRACK FIESTAS

Fiestas usually celebrate a religious or historical event, though this is really just a pretext for dressing up, getting out and partying, something for which *madrileños* seem to have an innate talent. Dos de Mayo, San Isidro, San Antonio de la Florida and La Paloma are *fiestas* that people take part in with great gusto, and all are normally accompanied by good weather. Not that freezing temperatures or a few drops of rain are an impediment for the thousands who step out for Reyes (Three Kings' Day) and Carnaval.

Spanish Golden Age theatre are catered for in the Plaza de San Andrés. An associated event is the Feria de la Cacharrería, a ceramics market, held in the Plaza de las Comendadoras, close to Conde Duque. Recent additions to the programming are Documenta, a short season of international documentary films; + Arte, a mixed bag of installations, performances, hip hop, electronic music and sanctioned graffiti; and Universimad, a rock festival at the Complutense.

Throughout the week there are also numerous religious ceremonies in various churches. The 15th itself sees a procession of vintage cars in the Castellana. Possibly most fun of all is the traditional *romería* (pilgrimage) at and around the Ermita de San Isidro, in the park of the same name; families in traditional *castizo* garb, looking like something out of a Goya painting, drink from wine skins and stuff themselves with traditional *madrileño* delicacies such as chorizo, morcilla and other offal dishes.

Feria del Libro Antiguo y de Ocasión
Paseo de Recoletos, Salamanca. Metro Banco de España or Colón. **Information** 91 420 34 21. **Date** 2wks May.
This old and second-hand book fair, spanning a week either side of the San Isidro weekend, has been held annually for more than 30 years. Here you may stumble across rare treasures, out-of-print editions or recent remainders. Don't expect much in English.

★ Documenta Madrid
Various venues. **Information** 91 517 98 17, www.documentamadrid.com. **Date** 1wk May.
This popular international documentary film festival, which is organised by the Ayuntamiento de Madrid, celebrated its tenth year in 2013. It consists of one week of screenings, workshops and related activities, in high-profile venues such as Matadero Madrid (also the festival's main office; *see p84*), Cine Doré (the Filmoteca; *see p183*) and Casa de América.

SUMMER

La Feria del Libro (Book Fair)
Parque del Retiro. Metro Atocha or Ibiza. **Information** 91 533 88 36, www.ferialibro madrid.com. **Date** 2wks end May-June. **Map** p313 L11-N14.
First celebrated in 1933, the Book Fair is now a major international event. Hundreds of publishers are present and well-known writers show up to sign copies of their works.

PHotoEspaña.

★ PHotoEspaña

Various venues. **Information** 91 360 13 26,
www.phedigital.com. **Date** June, July.

Every spring/summer since 1998, PHotoEspaña has
swept through Madrid's major museums and galleries, redefining the city as an international photography epicentre. In recent years, the retinue of
photographic stars, many of whom give workshops
and lectures throughout the festival, has included
Nan Goldin, Joel Peter Witkin, Philip Lorca di Corcia
and Paul Graham. PHotoEspaña also transforms
C/Huertas into an outdoor exhibition space and puts
on slide projections in Plaza Santa Ana and at the
Centro Cultural Conde Duque.

★ Suma Flamenca

Various venues. **Information** www.madrid.org/
sumaflamenca. **Date** June.

The month-long Suma Flamenca is Madrid's high-
profile flamenco festival, a feast of music, dance
and intense emotion. The 15 concert venues include
Teatros del Canal (Sala Roja; *see p216*) and the
Centro Cultural Pilar Miró in Plaza Antonio María
Segovia, plus a host of other buildings and theatres.

In the Frame Burial of the Sardine

Festivals don't get much fishier than this.

It doesn't get much weirder. On Ash
Wednesday, the last day of Carnival,
Madrid mourns the death of a sardine.
With Pythonesque absurdity, its scaly
little corpse, dressed in Sunday best,
is sombrely paraded through the streets
of old Madrid by the Alegre Cofradía de
la Sardina (Happy Brotherhood of the
Sardine). They carry its
diminutive coffin from
bar to bar, enjoying a
tongue-in-cheek display
of funereal ceremony
along with their *cañas*.
The route changes
annually, but always
winds up at the Fuente
de los Pajaritos in the
Casa de Campo.

The origins of this
wacky pageant are sadly
unclear. Some say that
it derives from the days
when sardines were sold
in abundance on the last
day before Lent, and that
the ripe little fellow came
to symbolise the many
sacrifices that lay ahead until Easter. The
fish may also have phallic implications, and
its burial could be a harbinger of sexual
abstinence during Lent. Other sources
link it to the reign of Carlos III (1759-88),
when a shipload of rotten sardines arrived
at his court and he ordered that they be
buried immediately.

Despite the ritual's uncertain roots,
Goya's masterful and macabre painting
suggests that the custom was in full swing
by the early 1800s (the precise date of
the painting is unknown). Goya depicts
a frenzied bacchanal of cavorting, masks

and partner-swapping, overseen by a
gruesome death mask. Despite the title
of the painting, no sardines are in sight.

The sardine, its burial and other carnival
merriment were suppressed during the
dictatorship. La Alegre Cofradía, a small
group of high-spirited friends, thought they'd
chance it anyway. One Ash Wednesday
in the early 1950s,
they marched the fish
to the Casa de Campo,
singing and dancing en
route. The police were
summoned by a priest,
who felt this spectacle
to be sacrilegious.
The police found the
entourage to contain
so many venerable old
lawyers, doctors and
journalists, however,
that they simply joined
the throng.

Nowadays, the
Cofradía has more than
90 members and a sister
organisation, La Peña del
Boquerón (Anchovy Club),
for the widows of the dead sardine. The
march usually begins at 6pm, from sardine
HQ at C/Rodrigo de Guevara 4 in La Latina
(you will know the building by the fish on
the door). But be prepared for a mournful
moment, as all of the ornately painted
miniature coffins from previous years are
on display at the Cofradía site, and you will
be expected to pay proper respects to the
dearly departed fish.

*Goya's Burial of the Sardine is found
at the Real Academia de Bellas Artes
de San Fernando (see p210).*

IN FOCUS

Veranos de la Villa.

and in the Centro Cultural Galileo, and fringe venues all over town offer plenty of 'alternative' shows. Also outdoors is a two-screen cinema in the Parque de la Bombilla, down on the Paseo de la Florida.

Verbenas de San Cayetano, San Lorenzo & La Paloma
La Latina & Lavapiés. Metro La Latina. **Information** Tourist offices & www.madrid.es. **Date** 6-15 Aug. **Map** p311 F/G/H14.
Madrid popular culture at its best – the streets and squares of the Lavapiés, Rastro and La Latina neighbourhoods are dolled up with flowers and bunting and the locals don their *castizo* gear for some serious street partying. San Cayetano is first, on 7 August, followed by San Lorenzo on the 10th and La Paloma on the 15th. Daytime sees parades and events for kids; by night there are organ grinders, traditional *chotis* dancing, the aroma of grilled chorizo and *churros*, sangria by the bucketful and a lot of good fun.

AUTUMN

Fiestas del Partido Comunista
Parque Dolores Ibarrubi, San Fernando de Henares. Metro Jarama. **Information** Partido Comunista de España (91 300 49 69, www.fiesta.pce.es). **Date** mid Sept.
Now in the political minority, the Spanish Communist Party still has enough clout to stage this three-day *fiesta*. There are performances by flamenco and rock bands, theatre shows, stalls run by political groups, debates on many political and social issues and lots of regional cuisine in the *casas regionales*.

★ La Noche en Blanco
Various venues. **Information** www.esmadrid. com/lanochenblanco. **Date** Early Sept.
To have '*una noche en blanco*' means to spend a sleepless night, and this is insomniac heaven. In Madrid, as in Paris, Rome, Brussels and Riga, for one night only you can wander from exhibition centre to museum, from fashion show to concert all night long and all for free. See website for venues.

Estampa
Matadero Madrid (see p84). Metro Legazpi. **Information** 91 544 77 27, www.estampa.org. **Date** Mid Oct.
A firm fixture on the arts calendar, Estampa is a well-attended show that brings together galleries and collectors from around the world to exhibit prints and contemporary artworks.

★ Festival de Otoño a Primavera
Various venues. **Information** Comunidad de Madrid (91 720 81 94/3), tourist offices & 012, www.madrid.org. **Date** Nov-June.
Recently expanded and renamed, somewhat clunkily, the 'Autumn to Spring Festival', this event offers somewhere in the region of 60 theatre, dance

San Antonio de la Florida
Ermita de San Antonio de la Florida (see p78). **Information** 91 547 07 22. **Date** 13 June. **Map** p306 A9.
One of the first of the summer's biggest street parties, the San Antonio celebrations can trace their history back a very long way; 13 June is the feast day of San Antonio, the patron saint of seamstresses. Single women used to place 13 pins in the baptismal font of the hermitage. If one stuck to her finger she would marry within a year. The main party, including events for kids, takes place across the Paseo de la Florida, in the Parque de la Bombilla.

★ Orgullo Gay (Gay Pride)
Around Chueca. **Information** www.cogam.org, www.orgullolgtb.org. **Date** 1wk late June/early July.
One week of partying in Chueca, Madrid's gay neighbourhood, and a huge parade on the Saturday that runs from Puerta de Alcalá to Plaza de España. *See also p189* **Pride Without Prejudice.**

★ Veranos de la Villa
Various venues. **Information** 91 758 92 70, http://veranosdelavilla.esmadrid.com. **Date** July/Aug.
As part of the 'Summers in the City' festival, a good selection of top names have appeared at the Centro Cultural Conde Duque and at the Matadero Madrid. Among them are Brazilians Milton Nascimento, Caetano Veloso and Carlinhos Brown, top flamenco artists, Youssou N'Dour and Femi Kuti, Regina Spektor, Jimmy Cliff and Charlotte Gainsbourg. Elsewhere, *zarzuelas* are programmed in both the Centro Cultural de la Villa and in the Sabatini Gardens beside the Royal Palace. The 'Titirilandia' puppet season for kids takes place in the Retiro, while Golden Age or more contemporary theatre productions may be seen outdoors beside the Muralla Árabe

IN FOCUS

and music spectacles, and remains one of the city's major performing arts events. Acts as diverse as the Brodsky Quartet, Ballets Trockadero de Monaco, groups from Rajasthan, La Comédie Française and Eddie Palmieri have all popped up, although in recent years the festival has focused on theatre, with *Tartuffe* and *The Taming of the Shrew* big draws.

WINTER

Feria de Artesanía
Plaza de España. Metro Plaza de España, Sol & Gran Vía. **Information** www.feriade.com. **Date** mid Dec-5 Jan. **Map** p307 E10.
This large and crowded crafts fair is an ideal place to look for original presents and coincides with Christmas, New Year and Reyes.

Navidad (Christmas)
All over Madrid. **Date** 25 Dec.
Less hyped than in northern climes, Christmas begins, very reasonably, in December, and is traditionally less important than Epiphany (Reyes; *see right*). Consequently, you are not reminded of the number of shopping days left until Christmas at every turn. Father Christmas, tinsel, flashing lights and baubles are far more evident than a few decades ago, however; all these trappings, plus lots of other cheap festive junk, are sold in the Christmas market in Plaza Mayor throughout December. The big family blow-out is usually on Noche Buena (Christmas Eve) with shrimps, red cabbage and either roast lamb, sea bream or both. Some families exchange presents on the otherwise fairly quiet Christmas Day, but the big ones are usually saved for 6 January.

Noche Vieja (New Year's Eve)
Puerta del Sol, Sol & Gran Vía. Metro Sol. **Date** 31 Dec. **Map** p311 H11.
New Year's Eve is celebrated with gusto, usually *en familia*, and involves another blow-out meal, litres of cava and the curious tradition of eating 12 grapes as the clock chimes midnight. Ever resourceful, many supermarkets now sell seedless grapes pre-packed in dozens for the occasion. The Puerta del Sol is where thousands throng. Clubs and bars organise parties.

Reyes (Three Kings)
All over Madrid. **Date** 5-6 Jan.
On the evening of 5 January, Noche de Reyes, thousands of children and their parents line up along C/Alcalá to watch the annual *cabalgata* (parade), which is also televised. Dozens of elaborate floats pass by and the riders hurl sweets to the children. Later, most families have a big dinner, and the following day presents await those who have been good. Those who haven't get a piece of coal.

Carnaval
Various venues. **Date** wk of Shrove Tuesday.
Carnival is a very good excuse for dressing up and partying, either in the street or in Madrid's many bars and clubs. It opens in the Plaza Mayor, followed by a parade around old Madrid. On Ash Wednesday, the last day, there is a ribald ceremony during which a fish is carted around to the strains of a marching band, before being interred (*see p27* **In the Frame**).

IN FOCUS

Navidad.

Explore

The Old City

Where hipsters follow in the footsteps of Habsburgs.

The cramped old city, with its narrow medieval streets, contains Madrid's most atmospheric and well-defined *barrios*, as well as its best eating, drinking and nightlife options and many of its landmark buildings. Most visitors spend the bulk of their time here – whether enjoying the Habsburg and Bourbon splendour of Los Austrias and Santa Ana, the laid-back tapas bars of La Latina, the alternative cultural scene of Lavapiés, or the heady nightlife and trendy cafés of Malasaña and Chueca. The heart of the area is the Puerta del Sol, and much of old Madrid converges on this square.

Map p311	**Cafés & Bars** p122
Restaurants p89	**Hotels** p155
Tapas p111	

Plaza Mayor, the heart of Golden Age Madrid, lies south-west of here, along C/Mayor, while two art museums from Madrid's 'Golden Triangle' – the Reina Sofía and the Thyssen-Bornemisza – lie to the east, bordering the Paseo del Prado.

C/Cava Baja.

South of Gran Vía

LOS AUSTRIAS

The oldest part of the city, site of the Muslim town and of most of medieval Madrid, falls between **Plaza de la Cebada**, **Plaza Mayor** and the **Palacio Real**. Even though most of the streets still follow their original medieval lines, this may not be immediately apparent today. Like several other parts of the Old City, this area has been smartened up over the past decade, and is now home to a slew of wine bars and expensive restaurants. Tucked away in side streets are the 12th-century **San Nicolás de los Servitas** and the city's other Mudéjar tower, the 14th-century **San Pedro el Viejo**. If you continue down C/Segovia beneath the viaduct, you'll pass a forlorn fragment of the ninth-century **Muralla Árabe** (Arab wall), the only substantial relic of Madrid's Muslim founders. The area around it, known as the **Parque Emir Mohammed I**, has recently been relandscaped, with the addition of information plaques giving interesting historical information.

Back into town, along C/Mayor is the **Plaza de la Villa**, Madrid's oldest square

EXPLORE

Plaza de la Paja

and home to the city hall, the **Casa de la Villa**. In pre-Habsburg times, the square was also the preferred place of residence for the elite; one such residence, the **Torre de los Lujanes**, can still be seen there. Along with the **Casa de Cisneros**, also on the square, the buildings make up a compendium of the history of the city from provincial town to the imperial capital it was to become.

Despite its ancient beginnings, the area has come to be known as the 'Madrid de los Austrias', after the Habsburgs, although in truth Philip II and his dynasty can scarcely claim responsibility for much of it. The greatest monument they *did* build, however, stands at the area's core: the **Plaza Mayor**, archetypal creation of Castilian baroque (a style that's also known as 'Herreran', after its key architect). On the north side of the *plaza* is the city's main **tourist office**, while at the south side, at the corner of C/Toledo, stand the twin baroque towers of **San Isidro**, perhaps Madrid's most important historic church. Continue down here to reach **La Latina** and the **Rastro** flea market.

To the west of the square, off Calle Cava de San Miguel, lies one of the city's most successful new openings, the **Mercado de San Miguel** (*see p114* **Profile**), a refurbished food market that's become a favoured tapas-munching spot for tourists and upper-class *madrileños*. Just down from here is the peaceful **Plaza del Conde de Barajas**, home to the excellent Taller Puntera leather goods shop. To the east, leading on from the Calle Cava de San Miguel, is the **Arco de los Cuchilleros** (Knifemakers' Arch), which runs from the south-west corner of the square via a spectacular bank of steps leading down through C/Cuchilleros to the **Plaza de la Puerta Cerrada**, the walls of which are decorated with some engaging 1970s murals. From here the **C/Cava Baja**, home to many of the most celebrated *mesones*, temples to Madrid's traditional cuisine, runs south,

leading to the squares (**Plaza de San Andrés**, **Plaza del Humilladero**, **Plaza de la Paja**) that are prime territory for the traditional Sunday La Latina tapas bar crawl (*see below* **Inside Track**).

To the south-east of the square, at the **Plaza de la Provincia**, is another major work in the Herreran style: the squatly proportioned **Palacio de Santa Cruz**, which was the work of several architects between 1629 and 1643. Despite its grand appearance, the palace was originally the court prison, with a dungeon so deep that prisoners had to rub their rags with lard and set them alight to stop themselves from going blind. These days the building has a somewhat more dignified role as the Foreign Ministry. In former times, executions often took place in the Plaza de la Cebada, just a tumbril ride away.

For centuries C/Mayor was Madrid's main thoroughfare. The cross-streets between Mayor and Arenal offer an odd mixture of bookbinders, picture-framers and Galician restaurants. The western end of C/Mayor, near the **Palacio Real**, has several old palaces and runs out west into C/Bailén, connected southwards to a splendid 1930s concrete **viaduct** that offers views of the sierra and the Casa de Campo. The viaduct's

---

INSIDE TRACK
LA LATINA SUNDAYS

La Latina remains a popular Sunday outing for *madrileños* of all stripes. The tradition is to start at El Rastro flea market, and then head to the tapas bars around Cava Baja, Plaza de la Paja, Plaza San Andrés and Calle Humilladero for an aperitif of vermouth and some tapas. The hedonistic, sociable affair continues all day long, with some bars resembling scenes normally associated with late-night antics.

notoriety as a suicide point has led the city authorities to place giant glass panels all along it, giving it a very strange look and feel – without doing much to deter the jumpers.

At the southern end of the viaduct are the hill and park of **Las Vistillas**. The park has more great views and is often used for neighbourhood events, concerts and dances during *fiestas* and in summer. Beyond the park are the river and the elegant arches of the **Puente de Segovia**, a bridge commissioned by Philip II from Juan de Herrera and completed in 1584 to make it easier for the king to get to El Escorial.

FREE Iglesia-Catedral de San Isidro (La Colegiata)

C/Toledo 37 (91 369 20 37). Metro La Latina or Tirso de Molina. **Open** *Sept-July* 7.30am-1pm, 6-9pm daily. **Map** p311 G13.

Still popularly known as La Colegiata, this massive church, built between 1622 and 1633, once formed part of an important Jesuit college attended by many of the Golden Age playwrights. The high-baroque design by Pedro Sánchez was inspired by the quintessential church of the Jesuits, the Gesù in Rome; the façade was completed by Francisco Bautista in 1664. In 1768, after Charles III expelled the Jesuits from Spain, the church was separated from the college, dedicated to San Isidro and altered by Ventura Rodríguez to house the remains of the saint and his wife, which had been brought here from the Capilla de San Isidro (*see p36*). La Colegiata was the city's provisional cathedral for nearly a century, between 1885 and 1993, when the Catedral de la Almudena (*see p37*) was finally finished and inaugurated.

FREE Museo de los Orígenes (Casa de San Isidro)

Plaza de San Andrés 2 (91 366 74 15, www. madrid.es/museosanisidro). Metro La Latina. **Open** *Sept-July* 9.30am-8pm Tue-Sun. *Aug* 9.30am-2.30pm Tue-Fri; 10am-2pm Sat, Sun. **Admission** free. **Map** p311 F13.

Dedicated to the city's patron saint, the well-digger and labourer San Isidro, this museum sits on the spot where he supposedly lived and performed one of his most famous miracles: when his son, Illán, fell into a well, Isidro made the water rise and thus was able to rescue the unfortunate lad. The well – or *a* well, anyway – is preserved inside the house, as is the chapel built in 1663 on the spot where Isidro allegedly died. According to legend, he was originally buried here too. This is, then, a museum that deals in legends as much as in solid artefacts, and the current material on show is a little limited. More interesting are the finds from local archaeological digs, formerly kept in the Museo de Historia and now in the basement here. They include items from lower-Palaeolithic settlements in the area, as well as artefacts from the Roman villas along the Manzanares, and from the Muslim era. Although the museum was recently renamed, it's still popularly known as the Casa de San Isidro.

Plaza Mayor

Metro Sol. **Map** p311 G12.

Plaza Mayor began life in the 15th century as a humble market square, then known as the Plaza del Arrabal ('Square outside the Walls'). In the 1560s, after Madrid was made capital of Spain by Philip II, architect Juan de Herrera drew up plans for it to be completely rebuilt, but the only part constructed

Plaza Mayor.

Walk Royal Madrid

A stroll through medieval and Habsburg Madrid.

DURATION: 45MINS

The 16th-century exteriors that once fronted Madrid's interconnecting squares – Plaza de la Paja, Plaza de la Cruz Verde, Plaza de los Carros – were mostly replaced in the 1800s, but these intimate *plazas* and most of the winding streets of the district of Los Austrias still follow their original Arab and medieval courses, and a

walk around these alleys can still be evocative of the Habsburg city, and the medieval town before it.

From Plaza Mayor, walk down the steps under Arco de Cuchilleros in the SW corner.

Walking down C/Cuchilleros, named after the knifemakers who long ago plied their trade here, look out for the 18th-century **El Sobrino de Botín** (*see p91*) on the left, allegedly the oldest restaurant in the world. Continue across the Puerta Cerrada into C/Cava Baja, and you will be walking along the line of the 12th-century wall, now lined with restaurants and tapas bars.

Cut right up C/Almendro and then take the first right down the narrow Pretíl de Santisteban.

At the end is the pretty C/Nuncio, home to several wine bars. Turn left, and on the Costanilla de San Pedro is the dusty 17th-century church of **San Pedro el Viejo**.

Carry on past San Pedro, left down C/Príncipe de Anglona, and veer left to Plaza de la Paja.

'Straw Square' was the medieval grain and fodder market, and probably marked the most southern point of the Arab wall. Buildings of note that survived 19th-century reconstruction are **San Andrés** church and the **Capillas del Obispo** and **San Isidro**.

Walk up the Costanilla de San Andrés.

On the other side of San Andrés is what appears to be one rambling square.

However, different sections are known by different names. As well as the **Plaza de la Cebada** (Barley Square), which was once the site for public executions, and the **Plaza de San Andrés**, there is the **Plaza de la Puerta de Moros** (Moors' Gate) – site of the gate to the Muslim quarter (or Morería, under Christian rule).

From there, turn right down Carrera de San Francisco.

The dome of **San Francisco el Grande** at the end is seen in some of Goya's skylines.

Right of the church, head along Travesía de las Vistillas to C/Morería, which then winds back over C/Bailén to Plaza de la Morería.

The knot of streets between here and **Plaza de la Paja** and **Puerta de Moros** formed the Morería, to which Madrid's community of Mudéjar Muslims were confined for four centuries. The little **Plaza de la Morería** was the site of the mosque and the courts.

From there follow C/Alamillo to C/Segovia. Cross over and head up through C/Conde, then left at C/Cordón.

This little alley leads round into the **Plaza de la Villa**, with the city hall. It began life as the Arab souk, and was Madrid's main square until the creation of the Plaza Mayor.

Turn right down C/Codo (Elbow Street) to Plaza Conde de Miranda.

Stop off at the 17th-century **Convento de las Carboneras**, where nuns sell own-baked biscuits through a hatch.

EXPLORE

Teatro Real.

immediately was the Casa de la Panadería ('the Bakery'). Finished under the direction of Diego Sillero in 1590, it's typical of the Herreran style, with grey slate roofs, spiky pinnacles and two towers that dominate the square. In the early 1990s, in a move unlikely to be contemplated in most other countries, this historic edifice was decorated with colourful psychadelic murals. The rest of the *plaza* was built by Juan Gómez de Mora for Philip III and completed in 1619, although large sections were destroyed by fire in 1790 and had to be rebuilt. Bullfights, carnivals and all the great ceremonies of imperial Madrid were held here. At its centre is a statue from 1616 of Philip III on horseback by Giambologna and Pietro Tacca, which stood originally in the Casa de Campo and was moved here in the 19th century.

The square is still an important hub, with most Madrid-wide celebrations, such as the Veranos de la Villa or San Isidro festivals, centred here, along with a traditional Christmas fair in December. Best enjoyed on quiet weekday mornings, Plaza Mayor has plenty of pavement cafés from which to contemplate its graceful architecture. On Sunday mornings the *plaza* bustles with a stamp and coin market.

Plaza de la Villa

Metro Ópera or Sol. **Map** p311 F12.
Madrid's oldest square, home to the city's main marketplace in Muslim and early medieval times, contains three noteworthy buildings. Dominant is the Casa de la Villa, or City Hall, designed in Castilian-baroque style by Juan Gómez de Mora in 1630, although not completed until 1695. The façade was also altered by Juan de Villanueva in the 1780s. It contrasts nicely with the Casa de Cisneros, which was built as a palace by a relative of the great Cardinal Cisneros in 1537. Restored in 1910, it now also houses municipal offices. Opposite the Casa de la Villa is the simple Torre de los Lujanes, from the 1460s, where one of Madrid's aristocratic families once resided. It is believed that King Francis I of France was kept prisoner in the tower by Charles V after his capture at the Battle of Pavia in 1525.

★ FREE San Andrés, Capilla del Obispo & Capilla de San Isidro

Plaza de San Andrés 1 (91 365 48 71). Metro La Latina. **Open** 7.45am-1pm, 6-8pm Mon-Thur, Sat; 6-8pm Fri. Open for services only Sun. Capilla del Obispo (guided tour) 10am-12.30pm Tue; 4-5.30pm Thur. **Admission** *Church* free. *Capilla de San Isidro* €2. **Map** p311 E13.
The large church of San Andrés dates from the 16th century, but was badly damaged in the Civil War in 1936 and later rebuilt in a relatively simple style. Attached to it (but with separate entrances) are two of Madrid's most historic early church buildings. The Capilla del Obispo (Bishop's Chapel, 1520-35), with its entrance on Plaza de la Paja, is the best-preserved Gothic building in the city. It contains finely carved tombs and a 1550 altarpiece by Francisco Giralte. It reopened to the public (by guided tour only) in 2010, after being closed for restoration for some 40 years. Further towards Plaza de los Carros is the Capilla de San Isidro, built in 1642-69 by Pedro de la Torre to house the remains of the saint, which were later transferred to the Iglesia-Catedral de San Isidro.

FREE San Pedro el Viejo

Costanilla de San Pedro (91 365 12 84). Metro La Latina. **Open** 6-8pm daily (phone to check). **Admission** free. **Map** p311 F13.
This impressive Mudéjar brick tower dates from the 14th century, although the rest of the church dates from much later, having been rebuilt during the 17th century.

Ópera

The area between Plaza Mayor and the **Palacio Real** is named after the **Teatro Real** opera house at its centre. As well as containing some of the city's most important buildings (the **cathedral** among them), this is one of the most elegant areas of Madrid. A tunnel whisks traffic under the stunning **Plaza de Oriente**, so named because it sits east of the palace, making it one of the most pleasant spots for a coffee. Curiously, Madrid owes this stately square, which seems to complement the Palacio Real ideally, not to the Bourbon monarchs but to Spain's 'non-king', Joseph Bonaparte, who initiated the clearing of the area during his brief reign (1808-13). After his departure it was largely neglected before being laid out in formal style in 1844. During the dictatorship, devotees from all over the country stormed the square for a glimpse of Franco, who addressed his rallies from the palace balcony.

At the square's centre is a fine equestrian statue of King Philip IV that once stood in the courtyard of the Palacio del Buen Retiro. It was made in the 1640s by the Italian sculptor Pietro Tacca, who – on the insistence of the Count-Duke of Olivares – was required to create the first-ever monumental bronze statue featuring a rearing horse, rather than one with four feet on the ground. This remarkable feat was achieved with engineering assistance from Galileo.

On the esplanade between the cathedral and the palace, archaeological excavations have recently been undertaken to unearth the remains of the original Muslim fortress and of the foundations of Philip II's Alcázar, covered over by the building of the later Palacio Real. Some of the discoveries, including impressive Moorish arches, have been open to public view. Behind the palace, the delightful **Campo del Moro** gardens run down towards the Manzanares and the Paseo de la Florida.

Catedral de la Almudena.

Palacio Real. *See p38.*

FREE Campo del Moro

Paseo de la Virgen del Puerto (91 454 88 00). Metro Príncipe Pío. **Open** *Oct-Mar* 10am-5pm Mon-Sat; 9am-6pm Sun. *Apr-Sept* 10am-7pm daily. **Map** p306 C/D11.
This vast garden was named after a Muslim leader in the Middle Ages, Ali Ben Yusut, who attempted to capture the fortress that is now the Palacio Real. Unfortunately, it is only accessible from the Paseo de la Virgen del Puerto side, requiring a fairly long walk down Cuesta de San Vicente or Cuesta de la Vega. As a reward, however, you will see two fine monumental fountains. Nearest the palace is *Los Tritones*, originally made in 1657 for the palace in Aranjuez (*see p243*); the other is *Las Conchas*, designed in the 18th century by Ventura Rodríguez. Both were moved here in the 1890s.

FREE Catedral de la Almudena

C/Bailén 10 (91 542 22 00). Metro Ópera. **Open** 9am-8.30pm daily. **Map** p310 D12.
This is not Spain's most impressive cathedral, and it's something of a miracle that it exists at all. For centuries, Church and State could not agree on whether Madrid should have a cathedral; once they did, it took 110 years to complete it. Work began in 1883 on a neo-Gothic design by the Marqués de Cubas, but this scheme went off course after only the crypt was completed. Another architect, Fernando Chueca Goitia, took over in 1944, and introduced a neoclassical style. Although the cathedral has failed to win much affection over the years, it was finally finished in 1993 and visited by the Pope. The site once contained the church of Santa

Basílica de San Francisco el Grande.

María de la Almudena, formerly the main mosque of Muslim Madrid (the name comes from the Arabic *al mudín*, 'the mill') until it was knocked down by liberal reformers in 1870. One of its more interesting pieces is the 13th-century polychromatic funerary chest of San Isidro.

Palacio Real (Palacio de Oriente)

Plaza de Oriente, C/Bailén (91 454 88 00). Metro Ópera. **Open** *Oct-Mar* 10am-5pm Mon-Sat; 9am-2pm Sun. *Apr-Sept* 9am-7pm daily. **Admission** (with guided tour) €10; €5 reductions; free under-4s. Free to EU citizens Wed & Thur pm. **Credit** AmEx, DC, MC, V. **Map** p311 E11.

Commissioned by Philip V after the earlier Alcázar was lost to a fire in 1734, the Royal Palace is rarely used by the royal family, and many of its 3,000 rooms are open to view. The architects principally responsible for the final design, which reflects the taste of the Spanish Bourbons, were Italian – Giambattista Sacchetti and Francesco Sabatini – with contributions by the Spaniard Ventura Rodríguez. Filippo Juvarra, Philip V's first choice, had planned a palace four times as large, but after his death the project became a little less ambitious. Completed in 1764, the late-baroque palace is built almost entirely of granite and white Colmenar stone, and, surrounded as it is by majestic gardens, contributes to the splendour of the city.

Inside you must follow a fixed route, but are free to set your own pace rather than follow a tour. The entrance into the palace is awe-inspiring: you pass up a truly vast staircase and then through the main state rooms, the Hall of Halbardiers and Hall of Columns, all with soaring ceilings and frescoes by Corrado Giaquinto and Giambattista Tiepolo. In the grand Throne Room there are some fine 17th-century sculptures commissioned by Velázquez, which were

saved from the earlier Alcázar. Other highlights are the extravagantly ornate private apartments of the palace's first resident, Charles III, again decorated by Italians. Particularly striking are the Gasparini Room, the king's dressing room, covered in mosaics and rococo stuccoes by Mattia Gasparini; and the Porcelain Room, its walls covered entirely in porcelain reliefs. A later addition is another giant: the State Dining Room, redesigned for King Alfonso XII in 1880 and still used for official banquets. There are also imposing collections of tapestries, table porcelain, gold and silver plates and finally clocks, a particular passion of the little-admired King Charles IV.

One of the highlights is the Real Armería (Royal Armoury), reached via a separate entrance off the palace courtyard, with a superb collection of ceremonial armour, much of it worn by Charles V and other Habsburgs. Look out, too, for the suits of armour worn by El Cid and his horse – displayed on life-size statues. On the other side of the courtyard, the Royal Pharmacy is also worth a visit. One of the oldest in Europe, it was wholly dedicated to attending to the many ailments of Spain's crowned heads over several centuries. In years to come, an opportunity to view the excavations of the older Alcázar and Muslim fortress beneath the palace will also form part of the visit. The palace is closed to the public when official receptions or ceremonies are due, so it's a good idea to check before visiting. On the first Wednesday of each month the Royal Guard stages a ceremonial Changing of the Guard in the courtyard, at noon. There are tours of the Palace throughout the day. *Photo p37.*

FREE San Nicolás de los Servitas

Plaza San Nicolás (91 559 40 64). Metro Ópera. **Open** 8.30am-1.30pm, 5.30-8pm Mon; 8.30-9am, 6.30-8pm Tue-Sat; 10-10.30am, 6.30-8.30pm Sun. **Map** p311 E12.

The oldest surviving church in Madrid stands a few minutes from Plaza de Oriente. Its 12th-century tower is one of two Mudéjar towers (*see also p36* San Pedro el Viejo), built by Muslim craftsmen living under Christian rule, in the city. Most of the rest of the church was rebuilt later, during the 15th and 16th centuries. There is no entry during mass.

LA LATINA

La Latina – officially the area below Plaza de la Cebada, but many people think of the squares north of here as being part of it – takes its name from the nickname of Beatriz Galindo, teacher of Latin and confidante to Queen Isabella. At the end of the 15th century, she paid for a hospital to be built on the square that bears her name. Its site is now occupied by the **Teatro La Latina**, a stronghold of traditional Spanish entertainment. The district is relatively quiet except during its grand *fiestas*, around the time of **La Paloma** in August.

Basílica de San Francisco el Grande
*Plaza de San Francisco (91 365 38 00). Metro
La Latina.* **Open** 10.30am-12.30pm, 4-6pm Tue-
Fri. Last admission half hour before closing.
Admission (guided tour only) €3; €2 reductions;
free under-4s. **Map** p310 D14.

This huge, multi-tiered church between Puerta
de Toledo and the Palacio Real is difficult to miss.
A monastery on the site, reputedly founded by Saint
Francis of Assisi, was knocked down in 1760;
between 1761 and 1784 Francisco Cabezas and later
Francesco Sabatini built this neoclassical church in
its place. Most challenging was the construction of
the spectacular dome, with a diameter of 33m

(108ft). The dome was restored fairly recently, and
work on the rest of the basilica has also now been
completed. Inside there is an early Goya, *The
Sermon of San Bernardino of Siena* (1781), and several frescoes by other artists.

SOL

The **Puerta del Sol** represents the very heart
of Madrid, both because it contains *kilómetro
cero* (the mark from which distances from the
city are measured) and for its time-honoured role
as chief meeting place. Famously, through the
centuries people have come to Sol to find out

Saints and Sinners

Madrid's church-going public are kept busy all year round.

If you're female and single, you might want
to make a discreet pilgrimage to the **Ermita
de San Antonio de la Florida** (*see p78*)
if you happen to be in Madrid on 13 June.
This is Anthony of Padua's feast day,
a saint whose many attributes
supposedly include the ability
to rustle up boyfriends out
of thin air – for Madrid girls
at least. The tradition was
perhaps started by young
seamstresses, as the
custom is to turn up at the
church with a handful of
pins. The girls queue up to
drop the pins in the font, then
stick their hand into the water.
The test is whether the pins stick
to their hand. If so, love is just
around the corner. It's got to be worth a go.

The **Iglesia de San Antón** on C/Hortaleza,
on the other hand, is dedicated to Saint
Anthony of Egypt, who, like Saint Francis,
had a way with animals. On 17 January,
the people of Madrid commemorate this by
bringing not only their pets, but also farm
animals to the church to be blessed. This
causes something of a livestock bottleneck
in the narrow, busy C/Hortaleza, as dogs,
cats, rabbits, goats, donkeys and pigs wait
to enter the church. Not far away, at the
Iglesia de Santa Pascual on the Paseo
de Recoletos, you might catch sight of a
famous face slinking in or out. The church
contains a figure of Saint Clare, who in
recent times has been appointed the patron
saint of television. Actors, actresses and
stars of reality TV pop in to ask her to help
them get the role that will finally make them
a household name.

Iglesia de Jesús de Medinaceli.

On 27 July, expect to see a very long
queue of people if you are in the vicinity of
the **Convento de la Encarnación** (*see p41*).
The reliquary of this 17th-century convent
contains a phial of blood purportedly
belonging to Pantaleón, the
doctor saint. On his feast day,
the dubious contents of the
phial miraculously liquefy,
which augurs great things
for those who witness the
event. Yet more expectant
queuing goes on every
Friday outside the **Iglesia
de Jesús de Medinaceli** on
Plaza de Jesús. Inside the
church is a statue of Jesus
of Nazareth that had fallen into
the hands of the Moors and was
retrieved against all odds by Trinitarian
monks in the 17th century. Kissing the
foot of the statue is believed to be very
auspicious. In fact, after announcing their
engagement in 2003, one of the first things
Prince Felipe and his wife-to-be Letizia did
was turn up at the church to do just that.

They got married in the **Catedral de la
Almudena**, named after a wooden figure
now to be found in the crypt. When the
Moors arrived in Madrid, they displaced the
Visigoths, who before fleeing hid the statue
in the wall of their fortress, along with two
burning candles. A few centuries later, when
the Christians regained power, the hiding
place was discovered – and guess what?
Those candles were still flickering away.
This happy event has led to a public holiday
on 9 November, something that has kept
Almudena as everybody's favourite saint,
with no further miracles required.

EXPLORE

what's going on. Until the 1830s, the block between C/Correo and C/Esparteros was occupied by the monastery of San Felipe el Real, the steps and cloister of which were, in Habsburg Madrid, one of the recognised *mentideros* – literally 'pits of lies', or gossip-mills – where people came to pick up on the latest news, anecdotes or scurrilous rumours. In a city with no newspapers – but where who was in or out of favour was of primary importance – *mentideros* were a major social institution, and rare was the day when at least one of the great figures of Spanish literature, such as Cervantes, Lope or Quevedo, did not pass by here. The steps of San Felipe were also overlooked by one of the largest brothels of the era, another attraction for men about town. On a more respectable note, the Café Pombo, home to legendary *tertulias* (*see p131* **In the Frame**), stood on the corner of C/Carretas. It is still Madrid's most popular meeting point, particularly the spot by the monument with the symbols of Madrid (a bear and a *madroño* or strawberry tree) at the junction with C/Carmen.

Under the Habsburgs the Puerta del Sol, the main, easternmost gate (*puerta*) of 15th-century Madrid, was surrounded by churches and monasteries. It was rebuilt in its present form in 1854-62. The square's most important building is the **Casa de Correos**, built in 1766 by Jaime Marquet as a post office for Charles III. Today it houses the regional government, the Comunidad de Madrid, but in the Franco era it had much grimmer connotations, as the Interior Ministry and police headquarters. It was altered significantly in 1866, when the large clock tower was added; this is now the building's best-known feature, since it's the clock the whole country sees on New Year's Eve, when revellers crowd into the square to eat their lucky grapes, one for each stroke of midnight. In the 1990s,

the tower developed a precarious incline due to rot in its timbers, but it was rebuilt and unveiled once again in 1998. Sol is also where Napoleon's Egyptian cavalry, the Mamelukes, charged down on the *madrileño* crowd on 2 May 1808, as portrayed in one of Goya's most famous paintings.

The building works that saw Sol bristling with JCBs and ringed with iron fencing for some six years, while the tunnel linking Atocha and Chamartín was being excavated, were finally completed in 2010, leaving the place with a new Cercanías Renfe Sol rail station stop, shiny new dome entrances to the metro, and a new lease of life. A less popular move has been the removal of the iconic Tío Pepe sign from atop the building on the eastern side – rumoured to be earmarked as an Apple Store – but in 2013 a campaign was launched for its reinstatement.

Tucked in the middle of the area between Sol, Arenal, C/Alcalá and Gran Vía is the **Real Monasterio de las Descalzas Reales**, bursting with artworks and a deliciously unexpected oasis amid the traffic and bustle of Sol. At the west side of the area, just above the Plaza de Oriente, is the peaceful and little visited **Convento de la Encarnación**, also worth a look. Just north of that, occupying the site of another convent, is the old 19th-century **Palacio del Senado** (Senate), now made redundant by its back-to-back counterpart in granite and smoked glass by Santiago Goyarre.

Running almost alongside C/Preciados up to Gran Vía is newly pedestrianised but still shabby C/Montera, lined with cheap, dated shops and the main area for street prostitution in the city centre. At the top, parallel with Gran Vía, is C/Caballero de Gracia, with a 19th-century oratory that lays on special Masses for the working girls, many of them Latin American, who operate along the street. While seedy, this

Puerta del Sol. *See p39.*

Real Monasterio de las Descalzas Reales.

area is not generally dangerous, and is heavily policed. Care should be taken when walking around late at night, however, especially if you're on your own.

Convento de la Encarnación

Plaza de la Encarnación 1 (91 547 05 10, information 91 454 88 00). Metro Ópera or Santo Domingo. **Open** 10am-2pm, 4-6.30pm Tue-Sat; 10am-3pm Sun. **Admission** (incl guided tour) €7; €4 reductions; free under-4s. Free to EU citizens Wed & Thur pm. **Map** p307 E11.

Before the Alcázar burned down, this understated convent was its treasury, connected by a concealed passageway. In 1611, it was inaugurated as a monastery by Philip III and his wife Margaret of Austria, and rebuilt to a design by Gómez de Mora. However, much of the original building, including the church, was damaged by fire in 1734 and rebuilt in a classical-baroque style in the 1760s by Ventura Rodríguez. It still contains a community of around 20 nuns, but most of the building is open to the public. Although not as lavishly endowed as the Descalzas Reales, it contains a great many pieces of 17th-century religious art, the most impressive of which is Jusepe Ribera's shimmering *chiaroscuro* portrait of John the Baptist. The Encarnación's most famous and memorable room, however, is the *reliquario* (relics room). In its glass casements are displayed some 1,500 saintly remains, bone fragments and former possessions of saints and martyrs, in extravagantly bejewelled copper, bronze, glass, gold and silver reliquaries. Its prize possession is what purports to be the solidified blood of San Pantaleón, kept inside a glass orb. The blood reportedly liquefies each year from midnight on the eve of his feast day, 27 July (*see p39* **Saints and Sinners**). Note that visits are by guided tour only, and tours leave 30 minutes after the first person signs up; so there's little point turning up as it opens.

Real Monasterio de las Descalzas Reales

Plaza de las Descalzas 3 (information 91 454 88 00). Metro Callao or Sol. **Open** 10am-1pm, 4-5.45pm Tue-Sat; 10am-2pm Sun. **Admission** (by guided tour only) €7; €4 reductions; free under-5s. Free to EU citizens Wed & Thur pm. **Map** p311 G11.

The convent of the Descalzas Reales ('Royal Barefoot Nuns') is the most complete 16th-century building in Madrid and still houses a cloistered community. It was originally built as a palace for Alonso Gutiérrez, treasurer of Charles V, but was converted into a convent in 1556-64 by Antonio Sillero and Juan Bautista de Toledo after Philip II's widowed sister Joanna of Austria decided to become a nun. Founded with royal patronage, the Descalzas became the preferred destination of the many widows, younger daughters and other women of the royal family and high aristocracy of Spain who entered religious orders. Hence it also acquired an extraordinary collection of works of art – paintings, sculptures, tapestries and *objets d'art* – given as bequests by the novices' families. Equally lavish is the baroque decoration of the building itself, belying its sternly austere façade, with a grand painted staircase, frescoed ceilings and 32 chapels, only some of which can be visited.

The largest non-Spanish contingents in its art collection are Italian, with Titian, Bernardino Luini, Angelo Nardi and Sebastiano del Piombo, and Flemish, with Breughel (an *Adoration of the Magi*), Joos Van Cleve and Rubens. The Descalzas is also an exceptional showcase of Spanish baroque religious art, with works by Gaspar Becerra, Zurbarán, Claudio Coello and even a tiny painting attributed to Goya. In addition, as you walk around you can catch glimpses of the nuns' courtyard vegetable garden, which has remained virtually unchanged since the convent was built, and is closed to the public. The monastery was seen by very few until the 1980s,

INSIDE TRACK PICKPOCKETS

Although Madrid isn't a violent city, petty crime such as pickpocketing and bag-snatching is still rife on the metro and buses, as well as in touristy areas such as the Rastro, Retiro park, Puerta del Sol, Plaza Mayor and around the Gran Vía.

To avoid being a vicitim, don't leave your belongings on the back of café chairs or on the ground; keep your hand on top of your bag in the metro; be wary if someone pulls out a map to ask or offer directions – thieves often work in pairs, and this could be a way to distract you; and beware of fake policemen – if someone asks to see your ID, ask to see theirs first.

EXPLORE

when it was restored and partially opened as a museum. It can be visited only with official tours, which leave every 20 minutes and last around 50 minutes. Frustratingly, the guides rarely speak English, there is no printed information about the convent and the paintings are not labelled. Note also that only a limited number of tickets are sold every day, so it's worth arriving early. It is still an enjoyable place to visit, though, for the sheer sumptuousness of its artworks and fittings.

GRAN VÍA

The **Plaza de España**, at the western end of the Gran Vía, is dominated by Franco's bombastic architecture. It is flanked by two classic buildings of the type sponsored by the regime when out to impress: the '50s-modern **Torre Madrid** (1957) and the enormous **Edificio España** of 1948-53. The three statues standing in the middle – of Cervantes, Don Quixote and Sancho Panza – are by Teodoro

Anasagasti and Mateo Inurria, from 1928. The square around them is big, noisy and not a particularly relaxing place to sit.

The Gran Vía itself was created in 1910 by slicing through the Old City so that traffic could easily reach Cibeles from C/Princesa. Intended to be a broad modern boulevard, it got grander still when World War I made neutral Madrid a clearing house for international money. With the economy booming, developers and architects set out to embrace modernity as hard as they could to show that if you wanted something impressive, they could provide it. In the following decades, each generation added its own stamp, and the result is certainly eclectic.

Heading down the Gran Vía, the area north and east of Sol was originally the city's financial district, hence the number of grand edifices owned by banks and insurance companies. Its other great avenue is **C/Alcalá**, which follows the centuries-old main route into Madrid from the east. In the 18th century, when it was lined

Paseo del Arte

The art triumvirate of the Prado, the Thyssen and the Reina Sofía.

Reina Sofía.

In the **Prado** (*see p61*), the **Thyssen** (*see p46*) and the **Reina Sofía** (*see p52*), Madrid has three art palaces that are quite simply world-class. You'll find them dotted along Paseo del Prado, in what has increasingly, and slightly facetiously, come to be known as the 'Golden Triangle'. This formidable trio of museums has made Madrid the world's capital of art for many people in the know, and with extensive revamps of all three museums over the past decade (reckoned to have cost some €150 million in total), this label is only set to stick more firmly.

The city council initiative known as the **Paseo del Arte** ('art stroll') takes advantage of the proximity of the three art collections, promoting the fact that they are barely ten minutes' walk from one another. The idea

echoes Berlin's Museum Island and London's Museum District. The axis that unites the big three – as well as avant-garde newcomer the **CaixaForum** (*see p60*) – is the Paseo del Prado.

Of course, it would be far too tiring to approach the Paseo del Arte as a one-day itinerary – a visit to just one of the three museums is likely to take up several hours, and plenty of energy. The idea is more to familiarise visitors with the area – which is becoming more and more pedestrian-friendly – so that the museums can be understood within a historial, geographical and cultural context, and for visits to then be undertaken at one's leisure.

TICKETS

A joint ticket, the **Paseo del Arte**, gives entry to the Prado, the Reina Sofía and the Thyssen-Bornemisza for €21.60. It is available from the ticket desks at all three museums; after visiting one you can visit the other two at any time in the same calendar year. Each museum also has its own 'friends' tickets, giving unlimited entry for a year, which are more expensive and more widely publicised. A better deal is the €36 annual museum ticket (Tarjeta Anual de Museos Estatales), available from any state-run museum, which gives unlimited entry to all the main museums (except the Thyssen).

by aristocratic palaces, it was described as the grandest street in Europe. It is still pretty impressive today, with a wonderful variety of 19th- to early 20th-century buildings, from the dignified 1882 **Banesto** building (corner of C/Sevilla) to the cautiously modernist **Círculo de Bellas Artes**. There are also fine older constructions along the street, such as the austere neoclassical Finance Ministry, built as the **Aduana**, or customs administration, by Francesco Sabatini between 1761 and 1769, and, alongside it, the **Real Academia de Bellas Artes de San Fernando**. At the point where Alcalá and Gran Vía meet stands Pedro de Ribera's exuberantly baroque church of **San José** (1730-42), with a plaque inside to commemorate the fact that Simón Bolívar was married here in 1802.

Círculo de Bellas Artes

C/Alcalá 42 & C/Marqués de Casa Riera 2 (91 360 54 00, www.circulobellasartes.com). Metro Banco de España. **Open** *Café* 9am-1am Mon-Thur; 9am-3am Fri, Sat; 8am-midnight Sun. *Exhibitions* 11am-2pm, 5-9pm Tue-Sat; 11am-2pm Sun. **Admission** (excl exhibitions) €1. *Exhibitions* €3; €2 reductions; free under-8s. Free to all 2-4pm Mon-Sat. **No credit cards. Map** p312 I11.
The Círculo de Bellas Artes occupies a superb building, designed by Antonio Palacios and completed in 1926. It is a key player in every aspect of the Madrid arts scene: as well as a beautifully airy main floor café, with a gracious pavement terrace, the Círculo offers a plethora of classes, exhibitions, lectures and concerts in its theatre and concert hall, as well as an annual masked ball for carnival. *Photo p45.*

Museo de la Real Academia de Bellas Artes de San Fernando

C/Alcalá 13 (91 524 08 64, www.realacademia bellasartessanfernando.com). Metro Sevilla or Sol. **Open** 10am-3pm Tue-Sun. **Admission** (excluding exhibitions) €5; €2.50 reductions; free under-18s, over-65s. Free to all Wed. *Calcografía Nacional* free. **No credit cards. Map** p311 H11.
This undervisited museum is in fact one of Madrid's most important and oldest permanent artistic institutions (it was founded in 1794). The eclectic collection is partly made up of works of varying quality donated by aspiring members in order to gain admission to the academy. The museum's greatest possessions, though, are its 13 works by Goya, an important figure in the early years of the Academia. They include two major self-portraits; a portrait of his friend, the playwright Moratín; a portrait of Charles IV's hated minister Godoy; and the *Burial of the Sardine*, a carnival scene that foreshadows his later, darker works. Another of the academy's most prized possessions is the Italian mannerist Giuseppe Arcimboldo's *Spring*, a playful, surrealistic portrait of a man made up entirely of flowers. It was one of

Plaza de España.

a series on the four seasons painted for Ferdinand I of Austria in 1563: *Summer* and *Winter* are still in Vienna, but the whereabouts of *Autumn* is unknown. There are also important portraits by Velázquez and Rubens, and several paintings by Zurbarán. Among the later works, the best known are some Picasso engravings and a Juan Gris; the most surprising are the colourful fantasies of Múñoz Degrain and the De Chirico-esque work of Julio Romero de Torres. Look out, too, for Leandro Bassano's superb *La Riva degli Schiavoni.*

The academy also has a valuable collection of plans and drawings, including those of Prado architect Juan de Villanueva, and rare books. In the same building is the Museo de Calcografía Nacional, a similarly priceless collection and archive of engraving and fine printing, which has many of the original plates for the great etching series of Goya.

HUERTAS & SANTA ANA

Spain has more bars and restaurants per capita than any other country in the world, and you can get the impression that most of Madrid's are crowded into the wedge-shaped swathe of streets between Alcalá and C/Atocha. Oddly enough, this clearly defined area has an identity problem, for the authorities can never agree on a name; however, if anyone suggests a pub crawl down Huertas, or a jar in Santa Ana, it will always bring you – and several thousand others on any weekend – to the right place.

This was once the haunt of Madrid's Golden Age literary set (*see p47* **Walk**), which explains the district's rather fussy alternative name of

EXPLORE

www.museothyssen.org

MUSEO THYSSEN-BORNEMISZA
PASEO DEL PRADO, 8
MADRID, SPAIN

Barrio de las Letras ('The District of Letters'). Here were the theatres that provided them with a living, along with whorehouses and low dives for entertainment. It is still the city's most distinctive theatre district. Close by, but not too close, lived the nobles who might have tossed a couple of ducats their way if they buttered them up with a sonnet. Otherwise there were feuds, libellous exchanges and duels to fall back on. A recent tidying up of the area has brought about pedestrianisation of much of Huertas's street, and literary quotes inlaid in bronze underfoot.

Lope de Vega's charming old house, the **Casa-Museo Lope de Vega**, with its tiny garden, is on the street named after his enemy, Miguel Cervantes, the author of *Don Quixote*. Cervantes lived around the corner on C/León, but was buried in the enclosed convent of the **Trinitarias Descalzas** (the 'Barefoot Trinitarians') on C/Lope de Vega, which seems deliberately confusing. Coming upon the massively plain, slab-like brick walls of the Trinitarias amid the Huertas bars is a great surprise, and gives a vivid impression of what old Madrid must have looked like before the great clear-out of religious houses in the 1830s, of which this is a rare survivor.

A reverential nod is in order to the wonderful **Ateneo** library on C/Prado, the literary and philosophical club that became a cultural institution and has been a major centre of discussion and thought at many times in its history, most notably in the years leading up to the Republic of 1931. In the old days, Ateneo members could also find any number of cafés nearby with a suitably literary atmosphere.

The **Carrera de San Jerónimo** borders the north of the district. Once part of the Ceremonial Route of the Habsburg and Bourbon monarchs, today it is one of the centres of official Madrid. On one side is the **Congreso de los Diputados**, Spain's parliament building, while opposite is the **Westin Palace** hotel (*see p160*), where politicians go to mingle and relax. At the bottom of this stretch, where it meets the Paseo del Prado at the last corner of the neighbourhood, is the world-famous **Museo Thyssen-Bornemisza** (*see pp48-49* **Profile**), containing one of the world's most important private collections of 20th-century (and other) art. Head up the hill in the other direction and you'll reach **Lhardy**, the classic Franco-Spanish restaurant founded in 1839 (*see p99*). North of San Jerónimo, behind the Congreso, is the grand 1856 **Teatro de la Zarzuela**, the city's most characterfully distinguished music theatre.

To the south of the Carrera de San Jerónimo, several streets run back towards Huertas proper. On C/Echegaray is the former site of **Los Gabrieles**, until a few years ago a much-loved bar sheathed in perhaps the world's most

photographed wall-to-wall tiles, but which has now been converted into luxury flats. However, all is not lost, as another beautifully tiled bar, **Viva Madrid**, lies just around the corner on C/Manuel Fernández y González 7 (91 429 36 40), while the nearby **Villa Rosa** on C/Nuñez de Arce also has an impressive tiled exterior.

Last, but in no way least, there is the core of the district, **Plaza Santa Ana**. Like Plaza de Oriente, this popular square was bequeathed to Madrid by poor Joseph Bonaparte, who tore down yet another convent to do so. Somebody should thank him: lined by some of the city's most popular bars and pavement terraces, Santa Ana has long been one of Madrid's favourite places for hanging out for an entire afternoon. On the eastern side of the *plaza* is the distinguished **Teatro Español**, on a site that has been a theatre continuously since 1583 when the Corral del Príncipe opened its doors to the *mosqueteros*, a heckling mob whose reactions were so violent, they sometimes forced terrified playwrights to change plots mid-play.

🆓 Casa-Museo Lope de Vega

C/Cervantes 11 (91 429 92 16). Metro Antón Martín. **Open** (by appt only) 10am-3pm Tue-Sun. Closed Aug. **Admission** free. **Map** p312 I12.
Spain's most prolific playwright and poet, Félix Lope de Vega Carpio (1562-1635) spent the last 25 years of his life in this simple, tranquil three-storey house. Oddly enough, the street in which it stands is now named after his arch rival Cervantes (who, confusingly, is buried in a convent on the nearby C/Lope de Vega). The house and charming garden – remarkable survivors from the Golden Age – are the most interesting things to see. The furniture and ornaments are approximations to Lope de Vega's

Círculo de Bellas Artes. *See p43.*

EXPLORE

Barrio de las Letras. *See p45.*

household inventory, rather than the originals. However, even the garden contains the same fruit trees and plants he detailed in his journals. Visits are by guided tour only – call ahead to book.

FREE Museo Colecciones Instituto de Crédito Oficial (ICO)

C/Zorrilla 3 (91 420 12 42, www.fundacionico.es). Metro Banco de España. **Open** 11am-8pm Tue-Sat; 10am-2pm Sun. **Admission** free. **Map** p312 I11.
This small museum is run by the ICO, a state bank. Its collection has three main parts: most important among them is Picasso's *Suite Vollard* series, a milestone in 20th-century prints, dating from 1927 to 1937. There is also a fine selection of modern Spanish sculpture and international painting from the 1980s.

★ Museo Thyssen-Bornemisza

Palacio de Villahermosa, Paseo del Prado 8, Huertas & Santa Ana (91 369 01 51, 91 420 39 44, www.museothyssen.org). Metro Banco de España. **Open** *Permanent collection* 10am-4pm Mon; 10am-7pm Tue-Sun. *Temporary exhibitions*

Sept-mid July 10am-7pm Tue-Sun. Mid July-Aug 10am-11pm daily. **Admission** €9; €6 reductions; free under-12s. Free to all Mon. *Paseo del Arte ticket* €21.60. *Temporary exhibitions* varies. **Credit** AmEx, DC, MC, V. **Map** p312 J12. *See pp48-49* **Profile**.

FREE Palacio del Congreso de los Diputados (Las Cortes)

Carrera de San Jerónimo (91 390 65 25, www.congreso.es). Metro Banco de España or Sevilla. **Open** *Guided tours* 10.30am-12.30pm Sat. Closed Aug. **Admission** free. **Map** p312 I12.
Spain's parliament, the Cortes, was built in 1843-50 by Narciso Pascual y Colomer on the site of a recently demolished monastery, which has led to no end of problems, as the plot is too cramped to accommodate the legislators' ancillary offices. A classical portico gives it a suitably dignified air, but the building is best distinguished by the handsome 1860 bronze lions that guard its entrance. Tourists can only visit on Saturdays, on the popular free guided tours, which cannot be booked in advance. You'll need to wait outside the iron gates on the Carrera de San Jerónimo to join a tour. Tours are on hold until at least mid 2013 while the roof and courtyard undergo renovation.

LAVAPIÉS

South of Sol and the Plaza Mayor is the area traditionally considered the home of Madrid's *castizos*. Castizos are something like London's East End cockneys: rough-diamond chirpy types straight out of a Spanish *My Fair Lady*. Many of them materialise round here in best bib and tucker – cloth caps for the men; long, frilly dresses for the ladies – for the city's summer festivals. Since the end of the 1990s, however, Lavapiés has taken on a new characteristic: as a big recipient of non-Spanish immigration – from China, Pakistan, North and West Africa – it is quickly becoming the city's most multicultural neighbhourhood.

These districts have always been the kind of place where newcomers to the city could find a niche. Historically they were known as the *barrios bajos*, in the double sense of low-lying and full of low life – the closer to the river, the shabbier the surroundings. In imperial Madrid, most of the food brought to the city came in through the **Puerta de Toledo**, and many of the tasks that the upper classes wanted neither to see nor smell, such as slaughtering and tanning, were concentrated here. Consequently, these districts became home to Madrid's first native working class. In the 18th century, the *majos* and *majas* from these streets were admired by the intelligentsia for their caustic wit (for Goya's portraits of them, *see p267* **In the Frame**), sowing the seed for the *castizo* tradition.

Walk Literary Madrid

Exploring the city's Golden Age.

DURATION: 30MINS

The cafés, theatres and churches around Plaza Santa Ana were the centre of literary life during Spain's 16th- and 17th-century Golden Age.

Begin at the junction of C/Atocha with Costanilla de los Desamparados.
C/Atocha 87 was once the printing press where the first edition of *Don Quixote* was published. It is now the **Museo Cervantino**. See the bronze bas-relief of a scene from the book and, above, the head of Cervantes.

Walk up Desamparados and turn right down C/Moratín.
At the **Plazuela de San Juan** is a plaque celebrating poet and playwright Leandro Moratín, born here in 1760.

Turn left up C/Jesús and left again on C/Lope de Vega.
The church ahead of the junction, on the right, is the **Iglesia de Jesús de Medinaceli**, famously a 17th-century centre of rumour and gossip, especially when attended by the great actresses of the time. Up on C/Lope de Vega, on the left, is the **Convento de las Trinitarias**, where Cervantes was buried (his remains have since disappeared). On the anniversary of his death, a mass is held for him and the other great Spanish writers.

Turn right up C/Quevedo.
On the right-hand corner is a plaque marking the house where 17th-century rivals Francisco de Quevedo and Luis de Góngora lived. Quevedo, a satirist, made mincemeat of the hapless and terminally ill poet Góngora in an exchange of verse. He also triumphed posthumously, when the council renamed the street after him, failing to mention Góngora on the plaque. At the end of the street, on C/Cervantes 11, is the **Casa-Museo Lope de Vega** (*see p45*), where Lope de Vega lived and died. No.2 on this street was built on the site of Cervantes' old house.

Turn left, and right down C/León to C/Prado.
At No.21 is the Ateneo library, with an impressive marble staircase, walls lined with portraits of Spain's greatest figures and delightfully antiquated rooms. Back up C/Prado, you arrive at the Plaza Santa Ana, home to the Teatro Español and bars such as the **Cervecería Alemana** (*see*

p125), where writers such as the playwright Ramón del Valle-Inclán and, later, Ernest Hemingway were regulars. The theatre itself sits on the site of one of the great open-air *corral* theatres of the Golden Age.

Facing the theatre, turn left up C/Príncipe.
This street was home to many of the literary haunts of the day, but the only one that remains is **Las Cuevas de Sésamo** at No.7 (*see p195*), worth a visit for the quotes painted on the walls and the printed history the staff will give anyone who's interested.

At Plaza Canalejas turn left down C/Cruz.
C/Victoria on the left has a plaque marking the site of the writers' and politicians' meeting point and subject of Benito Pérez Galdos' eponymous novel, **La Fontana de Oro**. Further up C/Cruz is a mural depicting a reflection of the street, and asking 'Where has the theatre gone? Or is the street the theatre?' The theatre in question is the **Corral de la Cruz**, another open-air theatre that stood on the site.

Turn left down C/Álvarez Gato, through the square and down C/San Sebastián.
What is now a florist in the yard on the corner with C/Huertas used to be the graveyard for the adjacent **Iglesia de San Sebastián**; the ancient olive tree remains a symbol for all literary luminaries buried there. Opposite is a plaque showing the site of the **Fonda de San Sebastián** – favoured hangout of the 18th-century writers.

EXPLORE

Profile Museo Thyssen-Bornemisza

An impressive private collection spanning the centuries.

The private collection of the late Baron Hans-Heinrich Thyssen-Bornemisza is widely considered to be the most important in the world. Consisting of some 800 paintings, it came to Madrid on loan, but in 1993 a purchase agreement was signed with the Spanish state. The Baron's decision to sell was doubtlessly influenced both by his wife, Carmen 'Tita' Cervera, and by the offer to house the collection in the Palacio de Villahermosa, an early 19th-century edifice superbly converted by architect Rafael Moneo at fantastic cost. Thanks to this revamp, involving terracotta-pink walls, marble floors and skylights, it is possible to view the works with near-perfect illumination. In 2004, the museum unveiled its new wing, containing some 200 works from Carmen Cervera's own collection.

The collection was started by the Baron's father in the 1920s but was dispersed among his heirs when he died. The Baron bought back the paintings from his relatives and then expanded the collection, buying up first Old Masters and then contemporary works during the 1960s. The Baron's home in Switzerland only had space for 300 works, leading him to look for a larger home for the collection, most of which may now be seen in Madrid, though some paintings are in the MNAC museum in Barcelona.

THE COLLECTION

Works of art are displayed in chronological order. Beginning on the second floor, you'll find 13th-century paintings, notably by the early Italians, such as Duccio di Buoninsegna. You finish the tour on the ground floor, where Roy Lichtenstein's *Woman in Bath* is on show. Along the way, you'll have seen examples of all the major schools. The collection partly complements the Prado

and Reina Sofía's collections with large holdings of 17th-century Dutch painting, Impressionism, German Expressionism, Russian constructivism, geometric abstraction and Pop Art.

The Thyssen's detractors say the collection is a ragbag of every kind of style. However, one of its great attractions is that, while it is extraordinarily broad in scope, it is recognisably a personal collection that reflects a distinct taste, as seen in the room dedicated to early portraits, with works by Antonello da Messina and Hans Memling. Equally quirky is the section on early North American painting, including the *Presumed Portrait of George Washington's Cook* by Gilbert Stuart and works by American artists who are rarely seen in Europe, among them Thomas Cole, Frederick Remington and Winslow Homer.

The Thyssen also has its share of real masterpieces. Among the Old Masters, the works of Duccio, van Eyck and Petrus Christus stand out. The museum's most famous painting, however, is the great Florentine master Domenico Ghirlandaio's idealised *Portrait of Giovanna Tornabuoni* (1488) in the Portrait Room. Two rooms further on is Vittore Carpaccio's allegorical *Young Knight in a Landscape* (1510), another gem. Among the masters of the Flemish School represented is the *Annunciation* diptych by van Eyck. The Thyssen is also strong in the German Renaissance, with works by Cranach the Elder and Dürer.

From the later 16th century and baroque there are superb paintings, such as Titian's *Saint Jerome in the Wilderness*. There are also representative works by El Greco, Rubens and Tintoretto, and Bernini's *Saint Sebastian*.

The German Expressionists are well represented too, with powerful works by Emil Nolde, Ernst Ludwig Kirchner, Otto Dix, Max Beckmann and Blue Rider group artists Franz Marc and Kandinsky. Also present, on the ground floor, are some more familiar modern masters – Braque, Mondrian, Klee, Max Ernst and Picasso (in the shape of his 1911 *Man with a Clarinet*), among others. The last few rooms focus on the USA, with works by Georgia O'Keeffe and Edward Hopper among others.

THE CARMEN THYSSEN-BORNEMISZA COLLECTION

This extension opened in 2004 and incorporates two adjoining buildings: Nos.19 (the Palacio de Goyeneche) and 21 of the C/Marqués de Cubas. The space exhibits some 220 works of the 300 belonging to the private collection of 'Tita' Cervera, which she has ceded to the Spanish state for an 11-year period. In addition, there is a huge area for temporary shows and the library, restoration workshops and cafeteria have all been enlarged.

Access is from Room 18 on the second floor, which leads straight into rooms with early Italian and Flemish works by the likes of Jan Breughel and van Dyck. Moving on, you will enter a gallery that contains landscapes by Canaletto, Constable, Guardi and van Gogh. In the next room is 18th-century French and Italian painting, and beyond a selection of 19th-century paintings from North America. Downstairs on the first floor you'll find work by North American Impressionists. Two rooms are given over to Gauguin and other post-Impressionists. From then on, you move into German Expressionists, Fauvists and the early 20th-century avant-garde. The collection also contains four Rodin sculptures.

EXPLORE

EXPLORE

Few writers have been as central to the life and culture of Madrid as Ramón Gómez de la Serna, one of the most original and influential Spanish authors of the 20th century. Born in Madrid in 1891, he is best remembered for his near untranslatable literary form known as *greguerías* – brief poetic statements in which words, ideas and objects are brought together in almost stream-of-consciousness fashion ('It is only in botanical gardens that trees carry visiting cards').

On the eastern edge of La Latina is the **Rastro**, Madrid's time-honoured Sunday flea market. It runs all the way down Ribera de Curtidores to the Ronda de Toledo from **Plaza Cascorro**, with its monument honouring a young soldier raised in a nearby orphanage, who volunteered for a suicide mission in Cuba in the 1890s. A true cultural phenomenon, the Rastro is also a district with a strong identity, moulded by centuries of acting as an emporium for goods of all kinds. The market is a social experience more than a shopping destination, but look out for pickpockets.

If, on the other hand, instead of trying to make your way down the Rastro, you head from Plaza Cascorro slightly eastwards down **C/Embajadores**, you will enter Lavapiés proper. Because of the rapid changes in the area, Lavapiés has sometimes been portrayed, in local conversations and the press, as an urban crisis zone to be avoided. This is one of the areas with a high incidence of petty crime, commonly associated with gangs of North African boys

living on the streets, who have especially bad relations with the local Chinese shopkeepers. However, these images have a tendency to get out of proportion: there are places in Lavapiés it's probably best to steer clear of (the small square halfway down Mesón de Paredes, by C/Cabestreros, is the most obvious example), but it would be a shame if this led anyone to avoid the whole neighbourhood, for this web of sloping, winding streets remains one of the most characterful parts of Old Madrid.

Plaza Tirso de Molina, with its statue of the Golden Age dramatist whose name it bears, is the main crossroads between these *barrios bajos* and the city centre proper. It was cleaned up a few years ago and is home to a permanent, fragrant flower market, among other things. From here C/Mesón de Paredes, which is one of the two main arteries of historic Lavapiés (the other is C/Embajadores), winds off down the hill. Along Mesón de Paredes there are still some of Madrid's most historic *tabernas*, but they stand next to shops selling tropical fruit, Moroccan teahouses, halal butchers, African fabric stores and any number of Chinese-owned wholesale stores selling discount jewellery and T-shirts.

Also on Mesón de Paredes, near the bottom by C/Sombrerete, is **La Corrala**, the city's best surviving example of an 1880s courtyard tenement, predictably garnished with freshly washed sheets and underwear billowing from the balconies. After the demolition of Madrid's monasteries in the mid 19th century, many streets in these districts were rebuilt with these distinctive, open-balconied tenements. *Corralas* always faced an inner patio, multiplying noise and lack of privacy, factors of urban life that have luckily rarely bothered Spaniards. The *corrala* has become a characteristic of Madrid life; this one, restored in the 1980s, is used in

Rastro.

Walk Working Madrid

A historic hike through the barrio of Lavapiès.

© Copyright Time Out Group 2013

EXPLORE

DURATION: 30MINS

Atmospheric Lavapiés shows Madrid's past, present and future. Once the Jewish quarter, long the main working-class area and still home to a large gypsy community, it is now the most racially mixed *barrio* in the city. It has acquired an often exaggeratedly bad reputation, but it's generally safe by day.

Begin at Plaza Tirso de Molina.

At its eastern end is the **Teatro Nuevo Apolo**, part art deco and part neo-Mudéjar. On the south side of the *plaza* is the present headquarters of the CNT anarchist workers' union, a reflection of Lavapiés' long-term association with left-wing politics.

Turn down C/Mesón de Paredes.

The street is named after the long-gone inn of Señor Paredes, inventor of the *emparedado* (a type of sandwich). For refreshment today, there is the historic **Taberna de Antonio Sánchez** at No.13 (*see p118*). Mesón de Paredes once boasted all manner of shops, but nowadays these are mostly Chinese-run wholesale shops.

Turn right down C/Abades and left on C/Embajadores.

'Ambassadors' Street' was so named because all Madrid's foreign embassies were moved here during a 17th-century outbreak of the plague. Just by the corner of C/Oso, amid the urban disorder, is the baroque church of **San Cayetano**, built by a variety of architects, including Ribera and

Churriguera, between 1678 and 1761. Despite the many hands involved in its construction, its façade is one of the most finely worked in Madrid. Opposite, a plaque signals the house of the great 18th-century architect Pedro de Ribera.

Turn left at C/Sombrerete.

'Little Hat Street' was named after the hat worn by Portuguese monk Miguel dos Santos when he was paraded through the streets before being hanged in the 16th century. He had been accused of acting as accomplice to chef Gabriel de Espinosa, who claimed to be the missing heir to the Portuguese throne. After the hanging, the hat was left on a muck heap in this street. Where the street becomes the **Plaza Agustín Lara** are the ruins of the 18th-century church/school, **Escuelas Pías de San Fernando**, destroyed in the Civil War. Facing the ruins across from C/Mesón de Paredes is Madrid's most famous *corrala* tenement block (*see p50*).

Continue to Plaza de Lavapiés.

A former stomping ground for the *majos* and *majas* (*see p267* **In the Frame**), and once the centre of the Jewish area, the Plaza has a scruffy appeal. From here runs tree-lined **C/Argumosa**, with its Indian restaurants and pavement cafés.

At the far end, go left into C/Doctor Fourquet.

Home to several galleries, this street leads to C/Santa Isabel and the **Reina Sofía**.

INSIDE TRACK
SQUAT MOVEMENT

Squatting first arose in Madrid and other Spanish cities during the rural exodus of the 1960s and '70s, and was later revived as the *okupa* movement during La Movida Madrileña in the '80s, when thousands of squats were legalised. In the past decade, the movement has been reignited once again, in a highly politicised form and partly in response to house price inflation. In various squatted buildings around Malasaña and, in particular, Lavapiés, grassroots organisations now offer activities such as yoga and film screenings. One of the most famous of these 'social centres' is Patio Maravillas in Malasaña, which runs a bike repair shop, an internet café, English and art classes, concerts and more from its (new) home in Calle de Pez. It started in a building on Calle del Acuerdo – now famous for its exterior graffiti – but the organisation was controversially evicted by police in January 2010.

summer as a setting for a season of *zarzuela* comic operas. A later *corrala*, not easily visible from the street, is at C/Embajadores 60. At the bottom of this area is a dynamic cultural centre, **La Casa Encendida**.

The **Plaza de Lavapiés** is believed to have been the centre of Madrid's medieval Jewish community, expelled, like all others in her dominions, by the pious Queen Isabella in 1492. Today, the recently renovated square has several good cafés and restaurants, as well as the Teatro Valle-Inclán. The narrow, very steep streets between the *plaza* and C/Atocha are more tranquil than those around Mesón de Paredes, and, with boxes of geraniums on virtually every balcony, often strikingly pretty. Despite all the changes in the area, these closely packed streets of old apartments, shops and workshops still convey the essence of a distinctive urban way of life. At the top of the area by C/Atocha is the Filmoteca Española film theatre, in the **Cine Doré** building (*see p183*).

Running away from the south-east corner of the Plaza de Lavapiés is **C/Argumosa**, known as the 'Costa Argumosa', with shops, restaurants and outdoor terrace bars that make a popular summer alternative to the more expensive and hectic places further into town. Argumosa leads towards Atocha and the **Museo Nacional Centro de Arte Reina Sofía** (*see pp54-55* **Profile**). Its opening in 1992 led to the appearance nearby of attractive one-off shops

and galleries, while the Jean Nouvel extension, completed in 2005, and consisting of three buildings around a central *plaza*, is a symbol of modern Madrid. Close by, filling up a big stretch of C/Santa Isabel, is the 17th-century **Convento de Santa Isabel**, sponsored, like the Encarnación, by Margaret of Austria, wife of Philip III, and one of the largest religious houses to escape the liberals' axe in the 1830s.

★ FREE La Casa Encendida
Ronda de Valencia 2 (90 243 03 22, www.lacasa encendida.es). Metro Embajadores. **Open** 10am-9.45pm daily. **Admission** free. *Cinema* €2. **Credit** MC, V. **Map** p312 H15.
This exciting new multidisciplinary centre in a large neo-Mudéjar building was conceived as a space for cultural interchange. Spread over four floors, it offers exhibitions principally by emerging artists working in all genres, but also features cutting-edge performance art and music (including short seasons of video artists) and activities for kids.

★ Museo Nacional Centro de Arte Reina Sofía
Edificio Sabatini *C/Santa Isabel 52.* **Edificio Nouvel** *Plaza del Emperador Carlos V s/n (91 774 10 00, www.museoreinasofia.es). Metro Atocha.* **Open** 10am-9pm Mon, Wed-Sat; 10am-7pm Sun. **Admission** €8; free students, under-18s, over-65s. Free to all 7-9pm Mon, Wed-Sat; 3-7pm Sun. *Paseo del Arte ticket* €21.60. **Credit** DC, MC, V. **Map** p312 J14/15.
See pp54-55 **Profile**.

Puerta de Toledo
Glorieta de la Puerta de Toledo. Metro Puerta de Toledo. **Map** p311 E15.
Slightly swallowed up by traffic at the meeting point of the Old City and the roads in from the south-west, this neoclassical gate was one of the monuments commissioned by Napoleon's brother Joseph in his brief span as King of Spain.

North of Gran Vía
CHUECA

The neighbourhood of Chueca, bounded by Gran Vía, C/Fuencarral and the Paseo de Recoletos, has been through several transformations. In the 18th century, C/Hortaleza was the site of the Recogida, a refuge for 'public sinners', where women could be confined for soliciting on the street or merely on the say-so of a male family member. Release was only possible through marriage or a lifetime tour of duty in a convent. In the 19th century, Chueca became a more respectable, affluent district, but by the 1970s and early '80s it had turned into a shabby area. Since then, though,

EXPLORE

it has undergone a spectacular revival, due, above all, to it becoming the gay centre of Madrid.

The epicentre of the scene is **Plaza de Chueca**; its terraces are packed with crowds on hot summer nights, and the only limitation on the scene is whether the *plaza* can actually hold any more people. On the back of the gay scene, many more restaurants, trendy shops, cafés and clubs have opened up, and **Fuencarral**, the borderline between Chueca and Malasaña, is now the heart of Madrid's club-fashion scene. Many gay venues have acquired a fashionable crossover status among the hip non-gay crowd (to the extent that some gays now find some Chueca clubs too 'diluted'). Whatever, Chueca has established itself as a booming free zone for socialising of all kinds, gay and heterosexual.

The north side of the district, above C/Fernando VI, is not really Chueca proper and is often known as **Alonso Martínez**, after the metro station. It's not so much part of 'gay Chueca' either, although it, too, has many new restaurants and bars. Instead, it's one of the foremost preserves of Madrid's teen scene. Streets such as Fernando VI or C/Campamor and Plaza Santa Bárbara are lined with bars

and clubs catering to a young crowd, and on weekend nights the roads are packed too, with noisy (but safe) crowds of kids. Just west of here are the city's history museum, the **Museo de Historia**, and the **Museo del Romanticismo**.

Towards Recoletos, Chueca also becomes more commercial and more upmarket by day. C/Barquillo is full of hi-fi shops, while C/Almirante and its cross-street C/Conde de Xiquena are important fashion shopping zones. Off Almirante, in C/Tamayo y Baus, is one of Madrid's most important theatres, the **Teatro María Guerrero**.

This area is also part of official Madrid, with the giant **Palacio de Justicia** on C/Bárbara de Braganza. It was formerly the Convento de las Salesas, built in 1750-58 under the patronage of Queen Bárbara, wife of Fernando VI. It has housed law courts since 1870. Its refined classical baroque contrasts nicely with the art nouveau of the **Palacio Longoria**, a few streets away. To the south of Chueca, towards C/Alcalá, there is an isolated relic of Philip II's Madrid, the **Plaza del Rey**, and venerable 1580s **Casa de las Siete Chimeneas**, originally designed by Juan de Herrera, architect of El Escorial.

Museo del Romanticismo. See p56.

EXPLORE

EXPLORE

Profile Museo Nacional Centro de Arte Reina Sofía

Little sister to the Prado and Thyssen, the Reina Sofía has its own share of masterpieces.

Occupying an immense, slab-sided building, the Reina Sofía (*see p52*) boasts an impressive façade with glass-and-steel liftshafts, designed by British architect Ian Ritchie. And since 2005, the museum has just as impressive a rear, in the form of three buildings arranged around a courtyard and covered by a triangular, zinc-and-aluminium roof, the work of French architect Jean Nouvel. This ambitious extension added almost 30,000 square metres to the already vast space in the patio to the south west of the main edifice.

The Reina Sofía's great jewel is still unquestionably *Guernica*, Picasso's impassioned denunciation of war and fascism, a painting that commemorates the destruction in 1937 of the Basque town of Guernica by German bombers that flew in support of Francoist forces in the Spanish Civil War. Certain art historians have seen it more in formal terms, as a reflection on the history of Western painting using elements from the work of the Old Masters. Picasso refused to allow the painting to be exhibited in Spain under the Franco regime, and it was only in 1981 that it was finally brought to Spain from the Museum of Modern Art in New York.

Guernica has been in the Reina Sofía since the museum's official inauguration in 1992, when it was transferred from the Casón del Buen Retiro amid great controversy. The artist had intended the painting to be housed in the Prado – of which the Casón is at least an annexe – and his family bitterly opposed the change of location. There is no question that the acquisition of *Guernica* hugely boosted the prestige of the Reina Sofía. And with the museum's recent revamp, the painting is now displayed under improved lighting and viewing conditions.

The rest of the Reina Sofía's permanent collection, which came mainly from the old Museo Español de Arte Contemporáneo in Moncloa, has been criticised, with many questioning its claim to be an international centre for contemporary art. At best, it is pointed out, it is a reasonable collection of Spanish modern art, with thin coverage of non-Spanish artists. It certainly contains works by practically all the major Spanish artists of the 20th century – Picasso, Dalí, Miró, Julio González, Tàpies, Alfonso Ponce de León and Antonio Saura are all present – but even here there are few major works.

In response, an active acquisitions policy adopted in the 1990s has sought to fill some gaps and to add works by major foreign artists.

With the appointment of new director Manuel Borja-Villel at the start of 2008 came a total reorganisation – completed in 2010 – of the collection. It is no longer organised along linear historial or grand thematic lines, but in a way that interweaves common influences, themes and ideas; so works by Luis Buñuel are now displayed alongside works by Picasso, Goya, Solana and even African art.

THE COLLECTION

The permanent collection, comprising more than 1,000 works, is spread over the first, second and fourth floors of the Sabatini building, while temporary shows are weaved throughout. The ground floor also features Espacio Uno, a space for more cutting-edge work.

The second floor is still the most important, housing Collection 1: Historical Avant-Garde. This includes 'Guernica and the 1930s' in Room 206, with works by Juan Miró, Oskar Schlemmer, Torres García, and, of course, Picasso. Other themes explored on this floor include Modernity, Progress and Decadentism, with works by Picasso and José Gutiérrez Solana; The New Culture in Spain; Dalí, Surrealism and Revolution; Juan Gris; and Cubism, with more works by Picasso, as well as Georges Braque and Sonia Delaunay.

Collection 2: Triumph and Failure of Modernity: the 1950s and 1960s, is on the fourth floor, in Room 405. This section explores themes such as European art after World War II, and the 'End of Painting', with more works by Picasso and Miró.

Collection 3: Paradigm Shift is in Room 104 on the first floor, with works by Yves Klein, Robert Rauschenberg, Eduardo Arroyo and Raymond Hains, mainly from the 1960s and '70s.

FREE **Museo de Historia**

*C/Fuencarral 78 (91 701 18 63, www.
munimadrid.es/museodehistoria). Metro Tribunal.*
Open *Sept-July* 9.30am-8pm Tue-Fri; 10am-2pm
Sat, Sun. *Aug* 9.30am-2.30pm Tue-Fri; 10am-2pm
Sat, Sun. **Admission** free. **Map** p308 H9.
Most of the museum – previously called the Museo
Municipal – has been closed for several years for
renovation work, and no date has been given for its
reopening. At present there is an interesting scale
model of 1830s Madrid in the basement, along with
a handful of drawings of the city. The building itself
boasts an exuberantly ornate entrance by Pedro de
Ribera, one of the finest examples of baroque architecture in Madrid, and worth seeing in itself.

Museo del Romanticismo

*C/San Mateo 13 (91 448 10 45, http://museo
romanticismo.mcu.es). Metro Tribunal.* **Open**
May-Oct 9.30am-8.30pm Tue-Sat; 10am-3pm Sun.
Nov-Apr 9.30am-6.30pm Tue-Sat; 10am-3pm Sun.
Admission €3; €1.50 reductions. Free to all from
2pm Sat. **No credit cards**. **Map** p308 H9.
The Museo del Romanticismo is essentially a reconstruction of a typical aristocratic house of the
Spanish Romantic period (early to mid 19th century);
a charming collection of furniture, paintings, ornaments, early pianos and other pieces that evoke the
time. As well as these objets d'art there are paintings
from the likes of Francisco Goya and Vicente López
Portaña, thousands of prints and lithographs and a
substantial number of antique photographs. There's
also a tearoom with a pretty garden (you don't need
a museum ticket to enter). *Photos p53.*

Sociedad General de Autores y Editores (Palacio Longoria)

C/Fernando VI 4. Metro Alonso Martínez.
Map p308 I8.
Given the extraordinary output of Catalan *mod-
ernista* architects such as Gaudí in Barcelona in the
early 20th century, it is remarkable, to non-Spaniards
at least, that there is not a single example of their
work in Madrid. The only thing at all like it is this
building in Chueca, designed by José Grasés Riera in
1902 as a residence for banker Javier González
Longoria. The voluptuous façade looks as if it was
moulded by an expert in giant cake decoration. It was
once thought that Catalan architecture influenced
Grasés, but Héctor Guimard and French art nouveau
seem to have been a more direct inspiration. The
building is now owned by the Spanish Writers' and
Artists' Association, and is not open to the public.

MALASAÑA & CONDE DUQUE

By day, the neighbourhood of Malasaña, between
C/Fuencarral and San Bernardo, still has a laid-
back neighbourhood feel, with grannies watering
their geraniums on wrought-iron balconies and
idiosyncratic corner shops. By night, though,

this has long been an epicentre of Madrid's bar
culture. Although less showy than Chueca, this
is the city's hipster *barrio*, albeit with a grungy
edge; for Malasaña is still associated with chilled-
out cafés, rock bars and cheap, studenty
socialising – although the tentacles of Old City
gentrification are beginning to take further hold,
with a smattering of new boutiques, cafés and
bars opening up in the area in the past few
years, especially on calle Espíritu Santo.

On 2 May 1808 this area was the centre of
resistance to the French. The name of the district
comes from a 17-year-old seamstress heroine,
Manuela Malasaña, who was shot by the
invaders for carrying concealed weapons (her
scissors) or ammunition to the Spanish troops –
there are various versions of her exploits. The
name of the main square, **Plaza Dos de Mayo**,
also recalls that day. Where the square is today
was then the Monteleón artillery barracks, from
where the artillery captains Daoíz and Velarde
galvanised the resistance of the people. The last
remaining part of the barracks, a gate, stands in
the square with a monument to the two men.

The area gained a tough reputation in the
1980s, when syringes and broken bottles used to
litter the *plaza* and side streets in the mornings,
but urban renovation schemes have been very
successful, and the neighbourhood feels a lot
safer to walk around at night. It is now one of the
centres of the San Isidro festivals in May, hosting
nightly concerts, fairs and outdoor parties.

The streets between Fuencarral and San
Bernardo abound with great cafés, bars and
restaurants. There are also indications – such as
the broad-arched doorways for carriages – that
the 19th-century well-to-do once lived here. One
of the most rewarding streets is **C/San Vicente
Ferrer**, with jewellery shops and a delightful
1920s tile display advertising the long-defunct
pharmacy Laboratorios Juanse. Other old ceramic
signs on the **C/San Andrés** feature a little
boy signalling that his chamber pot is full, and
a dramatic, reclining vamp. C/La Palma and
C/Divino Pastor, with craft and jewellery shops,
are equally worth a stroll. To the north is Glorieta
de Bilbao, site of one of Madrid's best traditional
cafés, the **Café Comercial** (*see p129*).

The atmosphere gets more lively as you
approach the streets near Fuencarral that lead
down to the Gran Vía, such as **Corredera
Baja de San Pablo**. This is an area of cheap
restaurants, wholesale produce dealers in white
aprons, shops selling nothing but light bulbs and
working-class people who have known each other
all their lives. Recent additions are club-style
fashion shops, especially towards or on
C/Fuencarral. This area contains the triangle
(bordered by streets Corredera Baja de San Pablo,
Desengaño and Valverde) recently named as
TriBall by the city council and canny business

EXPLORE

Malasaña.

folk who are looking to create a creative quarter that alludes to New York City's Tribeca. At the corner of the Corredera Baja and C/Ballesta there is an unusual brick church, built by Philip III for his Portuguese subjects in Madrid. Later it was set aside for German Catholic émigrés, and is still known as **San Antonio de los Alemanes**. It is rarely open to visitors. Just a block away along C/Pez, often unnoticed amid the shops, bars and theatres that surround it, is the slab-walled convent of **San Plácido**, another of Madrid's surviving religious houses. Down where C/Fuencarral meets Gran Via is the **Fundación Telefónica** exhibition space. The area west of C/San Bernardo is most commonly known as **Conde Duque** after its finest monument, the **Centro Cultural Conde Duque**. Nearby is the **Museo de Arte Contemporáneo**, and slightly hidden next to it is the **Palacio de Liria**.

FREE Centro Cultural Conde Duque

C/Conde Duque 11 (91 480 04 01, www. munimadrid.es/condeduque). Metro Noviciado or Ventura Rodríguez. **Open** 10am-2pm, 5.30-9pm Tue-Sat; 10.30am-2pm Sun. **Admission** free. **Map** p307 F8.

Housed in a former barracks, built in the 18th century for Philip V's guard by Pedro de Ribera, the magnificently restored Conde Duque is a multipurpose cultural centre. Around a dozen shows, both artistic and historical, are held annually in the two exhibition spaces and the two vast patios. Open-air concerts in summer bring in a range of performers. Also housed here are the city's newspaper and video libraries, as well as the Museo Municipal de Arte Contemporáneo (*see right*), which opened in 2001.

FREE Fundación Telefónica

C/Gran Via 28, entrance at C/Valverde 2 (91 522 66 45, www.fundacion.telefonica.com/ arte_tecnologia). Metro Gran Vía. **Open** 10am-8pm Tue-Sun. **Admission** free. **Map** p307 H11.

Run by Telefónica, the national telephone company, this foundation functions on several levels. The Museo de las Telecomunicaciones is a permanent exhibition illustrating the history of telecommunications. Another large space is used to display selections from Telefónica's permanent collection of Spanish art, including various works by Eduardo Chillida, Luis Fernández, Miró, Picasso and Tàpies, and it also has a permanent show based around post-Civil War Spanish artists of the so-called Madrid and Paris schools, the latter in exile. Temporary exhibitions feature both the arts and technology.

FREE Museo de Arte Contemporáneo

C/Conde Duque 9 & 11 (91 588 58 61). Metro Noviciado. **Open** *Sept-June* 10am-2pm, 5.30-9pm Tue-Sat; 10.30am-2.30pm Sun. *July, Aug* 10am-2pm, 6-9pm Tue-Sat; 10.30am-2pm Sun. **Admission** free. **Map** p307 F8.

The council's contemporary art collection covers painting and graphic work, along with sculpture, photography and drawing. Highlights include work by Eduardo Arroyo, Ouka Lele, Eduardo Úrculo, Jorge Oteiza and Eva Lootz.

FREE Palacio de Liria

C/Princesa 20 (91 547 53 02, www.fundacion casadealba.com). Metro Ventura Rodríguez. **Open** *Guided tours* 10am, 11am, noon Fri. Booking obligatory. Closed July-Oct. **Admission** free. **Map** p307 E8.

This sober, neoclassical palace, completed in 1783 and refurbished in the 1910s by Edwin Lutyens, is still the private property of Spain's premier aristocrat, the Duchess of Alba. The extraordinary collection includes work by Rembrandt, Palma Vecchio, Titian and Rubens, and one of the most important Goyas in private hands: his portrait of an earlier Duchess of Alba in red and white. The Friday guided tours must be booked in advance and in writing. Bookings can be made by email (visitas@fundacioncasadealba. com). The waiting list is several months long.

EXPLORE

The Retiro & Salamanca

Take in some art, then stroll in the park.

EXPLORE

Most visitors encounter the area around the Retiro within the first few days of a trip to the city, seeing as it's home to Madrid's star attraction, the Museo del Prado. The famous art museum – which contains the world's largest and finest collection of Spanish art – is often referred to in relation to the 'Golden Triangle' it forms with the nearby Thyssen-Bornemisza and the Reina Sofía (covered in the Old City chapter). These museums, together with the wide, leafy boulevards of the Paseo del Prado, make up the Paseo del Arte (*see p42*) – the 'art stroll' that has become an even more apt

Map pp308-309 & pp312-313	**Cafés & Bars** p132
Restaurants p109	**Hotels** p166
Tapas p120	

concept with the opening of the postmodern CaixaForum arts centre. To the east of the museum district is the Retiro, a verdant oasis of old-fashioned delights, and a perfect post-museum respite – especially in hot weather. North of here is the *barrio* of Salamanca, an area known for its designer shopping, expensive restaurants and futuristic architecture (along the Paseo de la Castellana). But it's also home to some of the city's most fascinating small museums.

Paseo del Prado.

The Retiro & Around

PASEO DEL PRADO

The most attractive section of Madrid's north–south avenue, and the one that most new arrivals in Madrid first become familiar with, is the oldest: the **Paseo del Prado**, from Atocha up to Plaza de Cibeles. Once an open space between the city wall and the Retiro (*prado* means 'meadow'), it was given its present form between 1775 and 1782, from a design chiefly by José de Hermosilla; it was the most important of Charles III's attempts to give his shabby capital the kind of urbane dignity he had seen in Paris and Italy. The king intended it to be a grand avenue lined by centres of learning and science. It was originally called the Salón del Prado (*see p61* **Walk, Don't Walk**), and the form of the main section, from Cibeles to

CaixaForum Madrid. *See p60.*

Plaza Cánovas del Castillo, was modelled on Piazza Navona in Rome, with three fountains by Ventura Rodríguez: **Cibeles** at the most northerly point, **Neptune** to the south and a smaller figure of **Apollo** in the middle. The southern stretch of the Paseo, tapering down to Atocha, has another statue, the *Four Seasons*, in front of the Museo del Prado. In the 19th century, the Paseo del Prado was the great promenade of Madrid. Virtually the entire population, rich and poor, took a turn along it each evening, to see and be seen, pick up on the latest city gossip, make assignations and show off new clothes.

Despite the traffic, the tree-lined boulevard still has many attractions on and around it, most notably Madrid's 'big three' art museums: the **Museo Thyssen-Bornemisza** (*see p46*), near the statue of Neptune, at the border with Santa Ana; Charles III's **Museo Nacional del Prado** (*see pp62-63* **Profile**), with its new wing on Calle Ruiz de Alarcón; and, at the very bottom, in the south-east corner of Lavapiés, the **Museo Nacional Centro de Arte Reina Sofía** (*see p52*). Together with the cutting-edge **CaixaForum** (*see p275* **Power to the People**), which opened in 2008, these spaces form the Paseo del Arte.

To the left of the Paseo, looking north, streets lead off into Huertas and the Old City, while to the right is the tranquil district of the Retiro. The knot of elegant streets in between the Paseo and the Retiro make up Madrid's most concentrated museum district, with, as well as the Museo del Prado, the **Museo Naval**, the **Bolsa de Comercio de Madrid** and the **Museo Nacional de Artes Decorativas**.

Heading south from here, other highlights include the **Real Jardín Botánico**, on the Paseo del Prado itself; the rows of second-hand bookstalls on the newly pedestrianised **Cuesta de Moyano** (*see below* **Inside Track**) which runs along the southern side of the botanical garden; the magnificently grandiose 1880s **Ministry of Agriculture**, right on Glorieta de Atocha, and designed by Ricardo Velázquez, the same architect who created the delicate exhibition halls inside the Retiro itself; and the landmark 19th-century **Atocha** station.

A few blocks east from here along the (traffic-ridden) Paseo Reina Cristina, a turn right down C/Julián Gayarre leads to the **Real Fábrica de Tapices**. On Julián Gayarre there is also the much rebuilt **Basilica de Atocha** and the odd, often deserted, **Panteón de Hombres Ilustres** containing the elaborate tombs of Spanish politicians of the 19th century.

FREE Bolsa de Comercio de Madrid
Plaza de la Lealtad 1 (91 589 10 20, www. bolsamadrid.es). Metro Banco de España. **Open** (guided tour only) *Individuals* noon Thur. *Groups* 10am Mon-Fri. Closed July. **Admission** free. **Map** p312 J11.
In the same *plaza* as the Hotel Ritz, Madrid's stock exchange is a landmark as well as a business centre. Enrique María Repullés won the competition to design it in 1884, with a neoclassical style chosen to reflect that of the nearby Prado. The building has

INSIDE TRACK
CUESTA DE MOYANO

The Cuesta de Moyano (*see above*) – the hilly pathway linking the Paseo del Prado with the Retiro park – has now been pedestrianised as part of the Plan Especial Prado-Recoletos (*see p84*). Lined with bookstalls, it makes for a lovely, browsing-infused stroll.

EXPLORE

EXPLORE

two distinct areas: one is the trading area; the other, open to the public, houses an exhibition on the market's history. Guided tours last 60 minutes; phone to arrange a visit.

★ CaixaForum Madrid

Paseo del Prado 36 (91 330 73 00, http:// obrasocial.lacaixa.es). Metro Atocha. **Open** 10am-8pm daily. **Admission** €4. **Credit** MC, V. **Map** p312 J13/J14.

Housed in the former Mediodía Electric Power Station, and remodelled by architects Herzog & de Meuron to striking effect, this cutting-edge cultural centre runs a lively programme of events and exhibitions. Contemporary and traditional temporary art exhibitions are run alongside engaging and stimulating music and poetry events, as well as lectures, debates and workshops. Federico Fellini, Fotopres photojournalism and the Fairtrade movement have all been the focus of recent shows. By virtue of its location, CaixaForum can be considered a new addition to the 'Paseo del Arte', sitting as it does inside the 'Golden Triangle' formed by the Prado, Reina Sofia and Thyssen on the Paseo del Prado. If the planned closure of the CosmoCaixa goes ahead, some of the activities will move here. *See also p275* **Power to the People.** *Photo p59.*

FREE Estación de Atocha

Glorieta del Emperador Carlos V. Metro Atocha. **Map** p312 K15.

Madrid's classic wrought-iron and glass main rail station was completed in 1892, to a design by Alberto del Palacio. It remained much the same, gathering a coating of soot, until the 1980s, when Rafael Moneo – he of the Museo Thyssen and Prado extension – gave it a complete renovation in preparation for Spain's golden year of 1992. Entirely new sections were added for the AVE high-speed train to Andalucia and Barcelona, and the *cercanías* local rail network, and an indoor tropical garden was installed in an imaginative blend of old and new.

Museo Nacional de Antropología

C/Alfonso XII 68 (91 539 59 95, http:// mnantropologia.mcu.es). Metro Atocha. **Open** 9.30am-8pm Tue-Sat; 10am-3pm Sun. **Admission** €3; €1.50 students; free under-18s, over-65s. **No credit cards. Map** p312 K15.

This three-storey building between the Retiro and Atocha station houses several levels, each devoted to a specific region or country. The first level has an extensive collection from the Philippines (a former Spanish colony), dominated by a 6m (20ft) dugout canoe. Among the bizarre highlights are a 19th-century Philippine helmet made from a blowfish, shrunken human heads from Peru, and the skeleton

Estación de Atocha.

of Don Agustín Luengo y Capilla, an Extremaduran who stood 2.25m (7ft 4in) tall. Even more enticing is a shrivelled tobacco leaf-skinned mummy, said to have once been in Charles III's royal library. Both are in the annexe to the first level.

Museo Nacional de Artes Decorativas

C/Montalbán 12 (91 532 64 99, http:// mnartesdecorativas.mcu.es). Metro Banco de España. **Open** 9.30am-3pm Tue-Sat; 10am-3pm Sun. **Admission** €3; €1.50 students; free under-18s, over-65s. Free to all Thur pm & all day Sun. **No credit cards. Map** p312 K11.
The Decorative Arts Museum houses more than 15,000 objets d'art, furniture and tapestries from all over Spain, plus many from China. One of the most prized rooms is the fifth-floor tiled kitchen, painstakingly transferred from an 18th-century Valencian palace, whose 1,604 painted tiles depict a domestic scene, with a huddle of servants making

hot chocolate. Also of great interest is the second floor, where the Spanish Baroque pieces are concentrated, among them ceramics from Talavera and Teruel, textiles, gold and silver work and jewellery cases from the Tesoro del Delfín (Treasure of the Grand Dauphin), the rest of which is in the Prado. Elsewhere are 19th-century dolls' houses, antique fans, an ornate 16th-century four-poster bedstead and a Sèvres porcelain jug given to Queen Isabel II by Napoleon III.

★ Museo Nacional del Prado

C/Ruiz de Alarcón 23, off Paseo del Prado (91 330 28 00, 91 330 29 00, www.museodel prado.es). Metro Atocha or Banco de España. **Open** 10am-8pm Mon-Sat; 10am-7pm Sun. **Admission** €14; €3.50 reductions; free under-18s, EU students under 25. Free to all 6-8pm Tue-Sat, 5-7pm Sun. *Paseo del Arte ticket €21.60.* **Credit** AmEx, DC, MC, V. **Map** p312 J12/13. *See pp62-63* **Profile.**

Walk, Don't Walk

The ups and downs of the controversial plan to give the paseos back to the people.

Thanks to Charles III's efforts in the 18th century, the Paseo del Prado was to become the social heart of the city. Charles's idea was for this to become a centre of learning, with the main research institutions for arts and sciences, all open to the public, based here. He had it adorned with statues and fountains, and the area became known as El Salón del Prado. Early photos show women strolling with parasols while men in black bowlers hold ardent discussions. The 19th-century writer Richard Ford effused: 'The Prado, a truly Spanish thing and scene, is unique; and as there is nothing like it in Europe; and oh, wonder! no English on it, fascinates all who passes the Pyrenees.'

Oh, wonder! In time, however, thanks to the invention of the combustion engine, the Paseo del Prado was to become less of a promenade and more of a motorway, with cars speeding through red lights and tour buses blocking the view of the fountains. The controversial **Plan Especial Prado-Recoletos**, however, has sought to remedy this. The team behind the project, headed by Portuguese architect Álvaro Siza, wants to reclaim the Paseo for pedestrians, widening the pavements, planting new trees and reducing traffic lanes. The plan – initiated in 2005, but which only got underway in 2008 – has once again stalled due to political rows and limited funds. But the idea is to create a broad expanse of

walkable promenade that will link the Plaza de Colón and the big three museums (the 'Golden Triangle') to Atocha train station, with minimal interference from passing traffic. So far, the stretch from Colón along Paseo Recoletos to Cibeles is the only part that has been remodelled, along with isolated spots around the Retiro, such as the now-pedestrianised bookstall-lined Cuesta de Moyano. The towering statue of Columbus in the Plaza de Colón has also been moved back to its original spot in the centre of the adjacent roundabout. But the Paseo del Prado itself is still waiting for its facelift.

In fact, the remodelling of the Paseo has been the most contentious and disruptive element of the project. The plan to cut the number of traffic lanes down from 12 to six has sparked intense opposition from right-wing politicians over fears of reduced north–south traffic mobility, and tunnels have also been proposed between Atocha and Cibeles.

Whether or not the controversial tunnel proposal is approved, the eventual completion of the Prado-Recoletos plan will mean that strollers will, at some point in the future, be able to amble leisurely between Madrid's best art museums, and that the fountain-filled Prado 'salon' will be returned to its 19th-century self as Madrid's best place to see and be seen.

EXPLORE

Profile Museo Nacional del Prado

Madrid's flagship museum is now bigger and better than ever.

Housed in a vast neoclassical building begun by Juan de Villanueva for King Charles III in 1785, the Prado is Madrid's best-known attraction. Charles originally wanted to establish a museum of natural sciences, but by the time it opened in 1819, the plan had changed: the Prado was to be a public art museum – one of the world's first – displaying the royal art collection.

The main phases of the Prado's ambitious expansion programme of the past decade have now come to fruition, making the collection more comprehensive than ever before. In 2007, after long delays, the new extension opened, on the site of the San Jerónimo cloisters behind the main building. The highly controversial cube-shaped edifice designed by Rafael Moneo houses the museum's temporary galleries, as well as a huge foyer containing the café-restaurant, information points, a book and gift shop and, on the first floor, the restoration workshops.

Director Miguel Zugaza's action plan for the 2009-2012 period – known as its 'second expansion' – has involved a massive internal reorganisation, with the aim of increasing the number of works displayed by 50 per cent (to around 1,500 works). In 2009, the first step was reached with the opening of 12 new rooms (arranged chronologically) on the ground floor, containing a total of 176 pieces from the museum's 19th-century collection (many moved from El Casón del Buen Retiro).

In spring 2010, a further seven new rooms opened containing newly restored works. Dedicated to Medieval and Renaissance Spanish art, they complete the ground floor collections of the Villanueva building, and significantly expand the museum's displays of 12th- to 16th-century Spanish painting. The plan is ongoing, though somewhat delayed, and more rooms are expected to open.

THE COLLECTION

The Prado embraces art from the 12th to the 20th centuries, and contains the world's largest collection of Spanish works. Its core is still the royal holdings, however, so it reflects royal tastes and political alliances from the 15th to the 17th centuries: court painters Diego de Velázquez and Francisco de Goya are well represented. Political ties with France, Italy and the southern, Catholic Netherlands also assure the

EXPLORE

presence of works by Titian, Rubens and Hieronymous Bosch.

But Spanish monarchs had begun collecting long before this time. By the 1500s, Queen Isabella already had a substantial collection of works by Flemish artists. During the reigns of Emperor Charles V (1519-56) and Philip II (1556-98), Italian and Flemish works continued to dominate. Titian was a favourite of both kings, and the eclectic Philip II also purchased several works by Bosch, among them the triptych *Garden of Earthly Delights* (*see p66* **Visions of Hell**), which he had hanging on his bedroom wall in El Escorial.

Philip IV (1621-65), a major patron of Rubens, is seen as the greatest Habsburg art collector. He was contemptuous of Spanish painters until he saw the work of the young Velázquez, who served him as court painter for nearly 40 years (1623-60). Velázquez also supervised the acquisition of other works, adding some 2,000 paintings by Renaissance and 17th-century masters.

Spain's first Bourbon King, Philip V (1700-46), brought with him one of the museum's most extraordinary possessions, displayed in the basement: the Tesoro del Delfín ('Treasures of the Grand Dauphin') – mostly 16th- and 17th-century Italian objets d'art. The last monarch to add significantly to the royal collection was Charles IV (1788-1808), the employer of Goya, possibly the least respectful court painter who ever lived, as evidenced by his portraits of Charles IV's family.

HIGHLIGHTS AND BASIC FLOOR PLANS

It's impossible to do the Prado justice in a single visit, and we don't suggest you try. Pick up a floor plan when you arrive to help you track down the don't-misses.

The ground floor contains Flemish and Italian works from the 14th to the 16th centuries, including Breughel the Elder's *Triumph of Death* and Bosch's *Garden of Earthly Delights* (Room 56A), as well as Spanish art from the 12th to the 19th centuries, including some of Goya's major works, and in particular his masterpiece *The Third of May* (Room 64; *see also p259* **In the Frame**). The ground-floor central gallery also displays many works from the sculpture collection.

The highlight of the first floor is undoubtedly the Velázquez rooms, in the Central Gallery. Here you'll find the Prado's most famous work, *Las Meninas* (Room 12), which is often described as the finest painting in the world because of its complex interplay of perspectives and realities. Elsewhere on this floor are Italian paintings from the 15th to 18th centuries and Spanish art from the 16th to the 19th centuries, including several works by El Greco, a room dedicated to Joaquín Sorolla (Room 60A), and Goyas from the period 1780 to 1800 (there's an entire room dedicated to Goya on the second floor).

EXPLORE

Puerta de Alcalá.

most impressive monuments built for King Charles III, a massive neoclassical gate designed by his favourite Italian architect, Francesco Sabatini, to provide a grand entrance to the city. It was built between 1769 and 1778, using granite and stone from Colmenar. Possible to miss in daytime traffic, it is hugely impressive at night.

Real Fábrica de Tapices

C/Fuenterrabía 2 (91 434 05 50, www.real fabricadetapices.com). Metro Menéndez Pelayo. **Open** *Guided tours only* 10am-2pm Mon-Fri (last tour approx 1.30pm). Closed Aug. **Admission** €4; €3 reductions; free under-6s. **No credit cards.** **Map** p313 M15.

Goya created some of his freshest images as designs for Madrid's royal tapestry factory, founded in 1721. Originally it was in Chueca, but has been here since 1889. The hand-working skills and techniques used haven't changed, and are evident from the intricate, painstaking work carried out in its two sections – the carpet room and the tapestry room. Goya designs are a mainstay of the work that's done here today (the factory also maintains carpets for royal palaces and the Ritz, as well as undertaking work for private clients). Guided tours are normally in Spanish, but if you call in advance an English-speaking guide can always be arranged.

FREE Museo Naval

Paseo del Prado 5 (91 523 87 89, www.armada. mde.es/museonaval). Metro Banco de España. **Open** 10am-7pm Tue-Sun. **Admission** free. **Map** p312 J11.

Madrid's naval museum contains examples of the booty accumulated by Columbus and other mariners during Spain's period of maritime expansion, and an array of navigational instruments, muskets, guns and naval war paintings. Glass displays enclose primitive weapons, some of which, like the swords lined with sharks' teeth from the Gilbert Islands, promise greater damage than their Western counterparts. The most impressive room is dominated by a huge mural map that traces the routes taken by Spain's intrepid explorers; in front of it are two equally impressive 17th-century giant globes. This same room also holds the museum's most valuable possession: the first known map of the Americas by a European – a parchment paper drawing by royal cartographer Juan de la Cosa, believed to have been made for Ferdinand and Isabella in 1500. Also worth a look is the room occupied by items salvaged between 1991 and 1993 from the *Nao San Diego*, which sank in the China Seas in 1600. You'll need to show a passport or other form of ID to gain entry.

FREE Puerta de Alcalá

Plaza de la Independencia. Metro Retiro. **Map** p308 K11.

A short distance along C/Alcalá from Cibeles, in the middle of another traffic junction, stands one of the

★ Real Jardín Botánico

Plaza de Murillo 2 (91 420 30 17, www.rjb.csic.es). Metro Atocha. **Open** *Nov-Feb* 10am-6pm daily. *Mar, Oct* 10am-7pm daily. *Apr, Sept* 10am-8pm daily. *May-Aug* 10am-9pm daily. **Admission** €3; €1.50 students; free under-10s, over-65s. **No credit cards.** **Map** p312 K13/14.

Madrid's luscious botanical gardens were created for Charles III by Juan de Villanueva and the

Real Jardín Botánico.

EXPLORE

San Jerónimo el Real.

botanist Gómez Ortega in 1781. They sit alongside the Paseo del Prado, just south of the Prado museum, but inside this deep-green glade, with over 30,000 plants from around the world, it's easy to feel that city life has been put on hold. A sign at the entrance asks that you treat the gardens as if they were a museum, but don't feel bad about getting comfortable with a book for a while; it's one of the best spots in Madrid to do so. The building in the middle of the gardens is used as a gallery space.

FREE San Jerónimo el Real

C/Moreto 4 (91 420 30 78). Metro Banco de España. **Open** *Sept-June* 10am-1.30pm, 5-8.30pm daily. *July, Aug* 10am-1pm, 6-8.30pm daily. **Map** p312 K12.

Founded in 1464 and rebuilt for Queen Isabella in 1503, this church near the Retiro was particularly favoured by the Spanish monarchs, and used for state ceremonies. Most of the original building was destroyed during the Napoleonic Wars, and the present church is largely a reconstruction that was undertaken between 1848 and 1883. The cloisters at the side of the church have been taken over for use as galleries by the Prado.

THE RETIRO

When Philip II ruled Madrid, this whole area was just open country, apart from the church of **San Jerónimo** (*see above*) and a few other royal properties. In the 1630s, it was made into gardens – unprecedented in size for the era, at nearly 122 hectares (300 acres) – that became part of the **Palacio del Buen Retiro**, built by the Conde Duque de Olivares for Philip IV to impress the world. Gardeners were brought in from across Europe to create the park and its lake, and to ensure that it would feature shade and flowers throughout a Madrid summer. Charles III first opened sections of the park to the public in 1767, but it was only after the fall of Isabel II in 1868 that the gardens became entirely free to the public. After it became a park, the Retiro acquired most of its many statues, particularly the giant 1902 monument to King Alfonso XII presiding over the lake.

Since it was made open to all, the Retiro has found a very special place in the hearts and habits of the people of Madrid. On a Sunday morning stroll, especially before lunch, you will see multigenerational families watching puppet shows, dog-owners and their hounds, children playing on climbing frames, vendors hawking everything from *barquillos* (traditional wafers) to etchings, palm and tarot readers, buskers from around the world, couples on the lake in hired boats, kids playing football, elderly men involved in leisurely games of *petanca* (boules), cyclists, runners, and a good many bench-sitters who want nothing more than to read the paper. During the week it's much emptier, and it's easier to take a look at some of the 15,000 trees, the rose garden and the park's fine exhibition spaces: the **Palacio de Cristal**, the **Palacio de Velázquez** and the **Casa de Vacas**. Built in the 19th century, they were extensively renovated during the 1980s.

At the southern end of the park is the **Real Observatorio Nacional**, a fine neoclassical building. However, the greatest curiosity of the park is Madrid's monument to Lucifer, in the

EXPLORE

Visions of Hell

The Prado is home to two of the world's finest Last Judgement paintings.

EXPLORE

In Room 56A of the Prado are two of the greatest paintings ever done of the Last Judgement: Pieter Breughel the Elder's *The Triumph of Death* painted in 1562; and *The Garden of Earthly Delights*, the triptych by Hieronymous Bosch (El Bosco in the Spanish), thought to have been completed around 1501. The latter is one of the greatest canvases of all time. And the *Triumph of Death* is no lightweight effort either; even if Breughel had not also been Flemish and an unabashed admirer of Bosch's painting, it would still be a good choice to display near *Earthly Delights*. It is smaller, a single canvas, but imagined in hallucinatory detail that is every bit a counterweight to the Bosch. In it, hundreds of skeletons herd the living into a huge coffin. The humans are terrified, helpless, shoved, pushed and prodded along by skeletons. There is a huge bony horse and astride it is a skeletal general in death's army, huge scythe in one hand, reaping as he tramples through the waves of terrified human beings. A dog feeds on a dead woman's body. The horizon is high on the painting; the whole shocking scene in the foreground fades into dark spectral colours punctuated by pockets of leaping flames.

On the facing wall is Bosch's triptych, two metres high, the centre panel twice the width of the wings, which fold in over it. Painted on the back of the wings, so as to form another scene when they are covering the centre panel, is the third day of creation as described in Genesis. The main triptych depicts our peopled world in its implacable fullness and flesh, its joys and sufferings, all in amazingly modern detail.

The left panel shows the Garden of Eden in its innocence, but even here all is not peace and light, as beasts swallow other beasts, hinting at the savage brute world on which ours is built. In the centre panel is the antediluvian world of the senses – the world as we know it, a variety of human pleasure as modern as television or Hollywood's latest scandal. Sensual romps we have no trouble recognising as our own – the pleasures of the flesh in trysts, threesomes, group gropes, everyone indulging. Beside it, in the last panel, hell itself, Judgement Day, when the former revellers are tied and tortured by ghouls and animals: miserable, dominated, impaled, ensnared and enslaved, their cities burning in the implacable darkness of the last days.

The Garden of Earthly Delights is full of the most modern of physical forms, from a round earth to airships. The power of its images is undimmed across the centuries, and they still resonate to this day.

moment of his fall from heaven. Known as the **Angel Caído** (Fallen Angel), this bizarrely unique statue on the avenue south of the Palacio de Cristal is thought to be the only monument to the devil in the world.

After the death of Philip IV in 1665, little use was made of the Retiro, although the palace gained a new lease of life when the Alcázar burned down in 1734, as it became the primary royal residence in Madrid until the Palacio Real was completed in 1764. However, in 1808 Napoleon's troops made it a barracks, and when the British army arrived in 1812 to fight over Madrid, much of the palace was destroyed.

On the north side of the park, forming a bridge between it and Salamanca, is the grand **Puerta de Alcalá**, still imposing despite being surrounded by the hectic traffic of the Plaza de la Independencia. The districts around and south of the Retiro are in some ways similar to Salamanca, but less emphatically affluent and more mixed.

FREE Centro Cultural Casa de Vacas

Parque del Retiro (91 409 58 19). Metro Retiro.
Open 10am-9pm daily. Times may vary.
Admission free. **Map** p313 L11.
This exhibition space in the Retiro, close to the boating lake, is run by the local council and offers shows on a variety of subjects, ranging from children's books to wildlife photography.

FREE Palacio de Cristal

Parque del Retiro (91 774 10 00). Metro Retiro.
Open *Oct-Mar* 10am-6pm daily. *Apr-Sept* 10am-10pm Mon, Wed-Sat; 11am-6pm Sun. **Admission** free. **Map** p313 M13.
This 1880s glass and wrought-iron construction, which is an outpost of the Reina Sofía, is a lovely, luminous space for viewing art. Shows here often involve large-scale installations, sculpture or pieces specially conceived for the space. *Photo p68.*

FREE Palacio de Velázquez

Parque del Retiro (91 573 62 45). Metro Retiro.
Open *Oct-Mar* 10am-6pm daily. *Apr-Sept* 10am-10pm Mon, Wed-Sat; 11am-6pm Sun. **Admission** free. **Map** p313 M12.
Built by Ricardo Velázquez for a mining exhibition in 1883, this pretty brick and tile building amid the trees of the Retiro is topped by large iron and glass vaults. Another Reina Sofía annexe, its galleries are wonderfully airy and host very good temporary shows. Contemporary dance has also featured.

Real Observatorio Nacional

C/Alfonso XII 3 (91 527 01 07, www.oan.es). Metro Atocha. **Open** *Guided tours* (by appointment only) 4.30pm Fri; noon, 4.30pm Sat; noon Sun. **Admission** €5; free under-3s. **Credit** MC, V. **Map** p313 L15.

The Retiro. *See p65.*

EXPLORE

Palacio de Cristal. *See p67.*

EXPLORE

One of Charles III's scientific institutions, the Observatorio was completed after his death in 1790. Beautifully proportioned, it is Madrid's finest neo-classical building, designed by Juan de Villanueva. It still contains a working telescope, which can only be seen by prior request. One room is also open to the public, as part of a guided tour.

Salamanca & Around

PLAZA DE CIBELES

Midway between the Puerta del Sol and the Retiro, this four-way intersection and its statue signify Madrid to Spaniards as much as the Eiffel Tower or the Empire State Building identify their particular cities. It is surrounded by some of the capital's most prominent buildings: the **Palacio de Cibeles** – formerly the Palacio de Comunicaciones (the main post office), but which has recently been turned into a stunning information centre and exhibition space, **CentroCentro** – the **Banco de España**, the **Palacio Buenavista** (now the Army headquarters) and the Palacio de Linares, which houses the **Casa de América**. The Ventura Rodríguez statue in the middle is of Cybele, Roman goddess of fertility and symbol of natural abundance, on a chariot drawn by lions. The goddess and the fountain around her have traditionally been the gathering point for victorious Real Madrid fans (Atlético supporters head for the fountain of Neptune, by the Thyssen museum) and the place where wins by the Spanish national team have been celebrated.

Banco de España
Plaza de Cibeles. Metro Banco de España.
Map p308 J11.
This grandiose pile on the corner of Calle Alcalá was designed in 1882 by Eduardo Adaro and Severiano Sainz de la Lastra to house the Bank of Spain. The eclectic style was strongly influenced by French Second Empire designs, with a few Viennese touches. The decorative arched window and elaborate clock above the main entrance are best appreciated from a distance. *Photo p70.*

⋏ FREE CentroCentro
Plaza de Cibeles 1 (91 480 00 08, www.centro centro.org). Metro Banco de España. **Open** 10am-8pm Tue-Sun. *Mirador* 10.30am-1.30pm, 4-7pm Tue-Sun. **Admission** free. *Mirador* €2; 50¢ under-12s. Free to all 1st Wed of mth.
Map p308 J11.
This extraordinary construction, which dwarfs the Plaza de Cibeles and is regularly compared to a sand-castle or a wedding cake, was until recently the world's most spectacular post office. It was designed in 1904 by Antonio Palacios and Joaquín Otamendi and completed in 1918, and is the best example of the extravagant style favoured by Madrid's elite at its most expansive. The design was influenced by Viennese art nouveau, but it also features many traditional Spanish touches, with a grand entrance (complete with an oversized revolving door), a Hollywood film-set staircase, soaring ceilings, stunning columns and grand marble floors. In 2011, the building was transformed into a five-storey exhibition space, with a cultural information centre in the main entrance hall. There's a colourful and comfortable reading area, with sofas, beanbags, newspapers

and iPads, and a café, while upstairs are various exhibition halls and the *mirador* – a lookout point with a panoramic view of the city. *Photos p71.*

PASEO DE RECOLETOS

While other cities have rivers cutting through them as navigational points of reference, Madrid has two great avenues: the Gran Vía and its continuation, C/Alcalá, running east–west, and the **Paseo de la Castellana** – which becomes the **Paseo de Recoletos** and the **Paseo del Prado** as it runs north–south. The leg that runs north of Cibeles, Paseo de Recoletos, was mostly added in the 1830s and '40s. The Palacio de Linares, now the **Casa de América**, is perhaps the best preserved of the palaces built by wealthy families after the Restoration. The curiously grand marble palace a little further north on the right, which is now the **Banco Hipotecario**, was once the residence of the Marqués de Salamanca, 19th-century Madrid's huckster-in-chief. It famously had the first flushing toilets in Madrid, an amenity the marquis later offered to residents in his new housing developments.

At the north end of Recoletos, on the right, stands the huge building that houses the **Biblioteca Nacional** and, behind it, the **Museo Arqueológico Nacional**. The most ambitious project of the reign of Isabel II, the building was commissioned in 1865, but only completed in 1892. It overlooks the **Plaza de Colón**, which has recently been remodelled, and whose Columbus statue now sits in the central roundabout. The square houses the **Fernán Gómez** theatre and arts centre (formerly the Centro Cultural de la Villa).

FREE Casa de América

Palacio de Linares, Plaza de Cibeles 2 (91 595 48 00, www.casamerica.es). Metro Banco de España. **Open** 11am-7.30pm Mon-Fri; 11am-3pm Sat. *Guided tours* 11am, noon, 1pm Sun. Closed Aug. **Admission** free. *Guided tour* €7; €4 reductions; free under-12s. **Map** p308 J11.

Housed in the 1872 Palacio de Linares, the Casa de América showcases Latin American art, both by established figures and by emerging talents. It also has the important role of promoting cultural contacts between Spain and South America. As well as this, there are film seasons, music, theatre and talks given by leading writers, film directors, playwrights and political figures. There are also print and video libraries, a good bookshop and a terrace with arts events in summer. *Photo p72.*

FREE Museo del Biblioteca Nacional

Biblioteca Nacional, Paseo de Recoletos 20 (91 580 77 59, www.bne.es). Metro Colón. **Open** 10am-9pm Tue-Sat; 10am-2pm Sun. **Admission** free. **Map** p308 K9/10.

With over three million volumes, Spain's national library has been called the 'Prado of paper'. Among the wealth of printed matter is every work published in Spain since 1716, Greek papyri, Arab, Hebrew and Greek manuscripts, Nebrija's first Spanish grammar, bibles, and drawings by Goya, Velázquez, Rembrandt and many others. Given the precious and fragile nature of the texts, access was limited to scholars, but in 1996 the administration opened this museum to allow the public a glimpse of the library's riches. The displays are conceived as interactive, steering visitors through bibliographical history via multimedia applications including laser shows, videos and holographs.

EXPLORE

Plaza de Cibeles.

Banco de España
See p68.

See p68.

FREE Teatro Fernán Gómez, Centro de Arte

Plaza de Colón 4 (91 436 25 40, http:// teatrofernangomez.esmadrid.com). Metro Colón. **Open** *Exhibitions* 11am-8pm Tue-Fri; 11am-9pm Sat; 11am-2pm Sun. **Admission** *Exhibitions* free. **Map** p308 K9.

Previously called the Centro Cultural de la Villa, the city council's only purpose-built cultural centre has been renamed after the late Spanish actor and director Fernán Gómez, who died in 2007. On offer is a mixed bag of theatre, puppets, opera and *zarzuelas* in the summer, as well as art exhibitions, usually featuring important Hispanic artists.

PASEO DE CASTELLANA

Sights along the Castellana are listed here from bottom to top, south to north. The metro system partly avoids the avenue, but the 27 bus runs up and down the whole stretch, covering the Paseo del Prado, Recoletos and the Castellana.

In 1860, when he designed Madrid's 'extension', Carlos María de Castro took the significant decision, since the Paseo del Prado and Recoletos were already there, to continue along the same route with the main avenue of the new district. Thus the Castellana was born. Until the Republic of 1931 demolished Madrid's old racetrack, the avenue reached only as far as C/Joaquín Costa. Today it snakes away freely northwards, through thickets of office blocks. It also contains, near the junction with C/Juan

Bravo (location of the recently renamed **Museo Arte Público de Madrid**), Madrid's 'beach' of upmarket terrace bars, at the height of fashion in the mid 1990s and still thronged with *pijos* (akin to London's Sloanes). To the east is the Salamanca district, the heart of affluent Madrid and the city's most upscale shopping area.

In the 1970s and '80s, banks and insurance companies vied with each other to commission trendy architects to create corporate showcases along the upper Castellana; see the **Bankinter** building at No.29 and **Bankunión** at No.46. Beyond the latter, the **Museo de Ciencias Naturales** is set back from the road on a grassy hill; further still, on the left, is the Kafka-esque grey bulk of the enormous **Nuevos Ministerios** government complex. Begun in 1932, it contains many government ministries, and is one of the largest projects bequeathed by the Spanish Republic to Madrid. It was designed by a team led by Secundino Zuazo, chief architect of the Gran Madrid plan, in a monolithic '30s rationalist style; then, after the victory of General Franco, the same architect added to the still-unfinished building some curving, traditionalist details more to the taste of the new regime. Inside it has a park-like garden, open to the public.

Beyond that, a huge branch of the Corte Inglés signals your arrival at the **AZCA** complex. The Asociación Zona Comercial A, known to some as 'Little Manhattan', is a glitzy skyscraper development first projected during the Franco regime's industrial heyday in the '60s, but it gained extra vigour in democratic Spain's 1980s boom to become a symbol of Madrid yuppiedom. At its centre is the **Plaza Picasso**, a small park, and amid the office blocks are a chic shopping mall, restaurants and other facilities to make it a self-contained 'workers' city'. At its north end is the **Torre Picasso**, designed by Japanese architect Minoru Yamasaki (also responsible for New York's World Trade Center) in 1988 and, at 157 metres (515 feet), Madrid's tallest building. Beyond it is the circular **Torre Europa**.

A little further up again, opposite each other, are the **Real Madrid** stadium, Estadio Bernabéu, and the **Palacio de Congresos** conference centre. By this time, the view up the Paseo de la Castellana is dominated by the two leaning towers officially known as the **Puerta de Europa** (*photo p73*) at Plaza Castilla. These remarkable smoked-glass blocks, leaning in at 15 degrees off the perpendicular, are perhaps the greatest monument to Spain's 1980s boom. They were begun with finance from the Kuwait Investment Office (the towers are often called the **Torres KIO**) and left unfinished for years after a financial scandal in 1992. With their rather phallic fountain in the middle, they have joined the landmarks of modern Madrid.

EXPLORE

★ FREE Museo Arte Público de Madrid

Paseo de la Castellana 41. Metro Rubén Darío.
Admission free. **Map** p309 L6.

An unconventional museum, this 1970s outdoor space at the junction of the Castellana with C/Juan Bravo was the brainchild of engineers José Antonio Fernández Ordoñez and Julio Martínez Calzón. Designing a bridge across the avenue, they thought the space underneath would be a good art venue, and sculptor Eusebio Sempere convinced fellow artists to donate their work. All the major names in late 20th-century Spanish sculpture are represented – including Pablo Serrano, Miró and Chillida – and much of their work is spectacular, especially the dynamic stainless-steel *Mon per a infants* ('A world for children') by Andreu Alfaro and the cascade by Sempere that forms the museum's centrepiece.

Museo de Ciencias Naturales

C/José Gutiérrez Abascal 2 (91 411 13 28, www.mncn.csic.es). Metro Gregorio Marañón.
Open *Sept-June* 10am-5pm Tue-Fri, Sun; 10am-8pm Sat. *July, Aug* 10am-5pm Tue-Fri, Sun; 10am-3pm Sat. **Admission** €6; €3 reductions; free under-4s, over-65s. **No credit cards.**

The Natural Science Museum occupies two spaces in a huge building overlooking a sloping garden on the Castellana. Much of the north wing is given over to temporary exhibitions, which tend to be hands-on, interactive and fun for kids. Permanently in this wing is 'Mediterranean Nature and Civilisation', a large exhibition of Mediterranean flora and fauna, illustrating the region's biodiversity. The smaller space to the south contains a more old-fashioned presentation of fossils, dinosaurs and geological

CentroCentro. *See p68.*

EXPLORE

Casa de América. See p69.

exhibits. A replica of a diplodocus dominates the two-floor space, surrounded by real skeletons of a glyptodont (giant armadillo) and other extinct animals. The most distinguished skeleton here, though, is that of the *Megatherium americanum*, a bear-like creature from the pleistocene period unearthed in Luján, Argentina, in 1788.

SALAMANCA

In the mid 19th century, as it became evident that Spanish cities needed to expand beyond their old walls, attempts were made to ensure that this happened in an orderly way. Madrid and Barcelona had plans approved for *ensanches* ('extensions'). Carlos María de Castro's 1860 plan for Madrid envisaged the expansion of the city north and east in a regular grid pattern, with restrictions on building height and public open spaces at regular intervals within each block to ensure a healthy, harmonious landscape. The problem, though, was that for a good while few members of Madrid's middle classes seemed to have the money or motivation to invest in such a scheme, and they preferred to stay within the cramped, noisy Old City. That Madrid's *ensanche* got off the ground at all was due to a banker, politician and speculator notorious for his dubious business practices, the Marqués de Salamanca.

The marquis had previously built his own vast residence, now the **Banco Hipotecario**, on Paseo de Recoletos in the 1840s. He spent one of the several fortunes he made and lost in his lifetime building a first line of rectangular blocks along C/Serrano, from C/Goya up to Ramón de la Cruz. However, his ambitions overstretched his resources, the apartments proved expensive for local buyers, and he went terminally bankrupt in 1867. Nevertheless, it is to the rogue Marqués, not the old Castilian university town, that Madrid's smartest *barrio* owes its name.

It was only after the Restoration of 1874 that Madrid's wealthier citizens really began to appreciate the benefits of wider streets and residences with more class than the musty old neighbourhoods could supply. Once the idea caught on, the exodus proceeded apace, and the core of Salamanca was built up by 1900. The wealthiest families of all built individual palaces along the lower stretch of the Paseo de la Castellana, in a wild variety of styles – French imperial, Italian Renaissance, neo-Mudéjar. The block on C/Juan Bravo between Calles Lagasca and Velázquez contains a magnificent example: the neo-baroque palace of the **Marqueses de Amboage**, now the Italian Embassy. From the C/Velázquez side it's possible to see the extraordinarily lush gardens. Other mansions are scattered around the district, tucked in between apartment blocks. Those who couldn't quite afford their own mansion moved into giant apartments in the streets behind. The area has been the centre of conservative, affluent Madrid ever since.

Salamanca is a busy area, with streets that often boom with traffic, and so the best time to explore it is Saturday morning, when the shops are open but traffic has slackened. Streets such as Calles Jorge Juan, Ortega y Gasset, Goya and Juan Bravo yield top designers, art galleries and dealers in wine, silver or superior leather goods.

EXPLORE

Salamanca also has its own social scene, based around C/Juan Bravo, with shiny, smart bars and discos. Towards the east end of C/Goya there is a slightly more affordable shopping area; on the very eastern flank of Salamanca is Madrid's bullring, **Las Ventas**; and south of here is the numismatic **Museo Casa de la Moneda**.

Art buffs are advised to head for the marble tower with sculpture garden at C/Castelló 77, base for the **Fundación Juan March**'s first-rate collection of modern art, which also hosts great contemporary art shows and free classical concerts. For private art galleries, C/Claudio Coello, parallel to C/Serrano, is the city's most elegant centre. At the north end of Serrano is the eclectic **Museo Lázaro Galdiano**.

The blocks of Serrano, Claudio Coello and Lagasca below C/Ortega y Gasset are the oldest part of Salamanca, the first section built up by the Marqués in the 1860s. Streets here are narrower, traffic less intense and shops closer together. There are charming buildings with intriguing details – such as the glass-galleried block on the corner of Claudio Coello and C/Ayala. The block between Claudio Coello and Lagasca on C/Ayala also contains the **Mercado de la Paz**, Salamanca's excellent market.

FREE Fundación Juan March

C/Castelló 77 (91 435 42 40, www.march.es). Metro Núñez de Balboa. **Open** *Mid Sept-June* 11am-8pm Mon-Sat; 10am-2pm Sun. Guided tours in English (by appointment only) 11am-1pm Wed. **Admission** free. **Map** p309 N6.

This cultural foundation, set up by the wealthy financier Juan March in 1955, is one of the most important in Europe. Each year, a couple of major exhibitions are held here, and a decent selection of the foundation's 1,300 works of contemporary Spanish art is also on permanent display.

Museo Arqueológico Nacional

C/Serrano 13 (91 577 79 12, http://man.mcu.es). Metro Serrano. Closed until at least late 2013; see website for details. **Map** p308 K10.
One of Madrid's oldest museums, dating back to 1867, the Museo Arqueológico Nacional shares the same building as the Biblioteca Nacional and Museo del Libro. It is currently undergoing long-term renovations (with no confirmed date for completion). It traces the evolution of human cultures, from prehistoric times up to the 15th century, and the collection of artefacts includes finds from the Iberian, Celtic, Greek, Egyptian, Punic, Roman, Paleochristian, Visigothic and Muslim cultures. Remarkably, the

EXPLORE

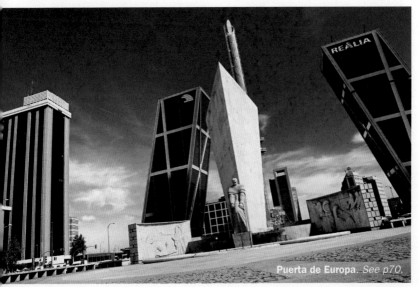

Puerta de Europa. *See p70.*

EXPLORE

The Quick and the Dead

In search of some of Spain's more famous departed.

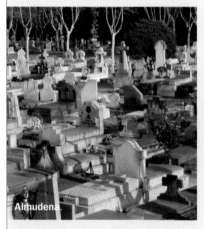

Almudena.

Spanish philosopher Miguel de Unamuno famously wrote that the dead in Spain were never allowed to rest. The truth of this observation will become apparent to anyone who wonders what has happened to the tombs of famous Spaniards who have died in Madrid. Remarkably, the remains of none of the city's outstanding Golden Age figures, including Cervantes, Lope de Vega and Calderón de la Barca, have survived, though there was a brief moment of excitement in 1999 following the discovery of bones wrongly believed to be those of Velázquez and his wife.

Even those Spaniards wealthy enough in the past to have paid for *sepultura perpetua* (others still have their bodies automatically removed from their tombs after ten years) have not been guaranteed a tranquil posthumous life. The expansion and destruction of churches has led to constant transferences of corpses, during the course of which a high proportion of these have been mislaid or misidentified.

In view of this unfortunate situation, a decision was finally taken in 1869 to create what Spain so obviously lacked – a national pantheon for its heroes. The domed late 18th-century **Basílica de San Francisco** was set aside for this purpose, and the remains of Calderón and other famous Spaniards were taken to the church in a triumphant procession involving cannon fire and horse squadrons. But barely had

the corpses had time to recover from their journey than the parishes from where they had come began to reclaim them. In the case of Calderón, the body would be moved several more times before disappearing entirely.

The fiasco of San Francisco did not put an end to the idea of a Spanish pantheon. In the 1890s, next to the then ruined 16th-century Basilica and Monastery of Atocha, the **Panteón de Hombres Ilustres** was built. However, this too proved a failure, and most of the illustrious corpses for whom it was intended were taken away, leaving just the remains of largely forgotten politicians. Today, it's one of Madrid's least visited sites, but worth a look for its inappropriately Italianate architecture, and its splendidly elaborate tombs by Benlliure and other fashionable Spanish sculptors of the period.

While the Panteón de Hombres Ilustres is centrally located, visitors with a love of cemeteries will find themselves travelling to some of the city's poorest outlying districts. The largest of the city's cemeteries is that of the **Almudena**, out to the east (metro García Noblejas), the terrifying scale of which, not to mention the dusty, grim surroundings, gives it a compellingly morbid appeal. Across the road is the comparatively intimate **Civic Cemetery**. Tidied up in the early 1990s following the burial here of the Communist leader Dolores Ibarruri ('La Pasionaria'), this contains the tombs of hundreds of opponents to Franco and the Catholic Church. At the end of the Civil War, numerous Republican prisoners were shot here and thrown into a mass grave.

But the most absorbing of Madrid's cemeteries is the **Sacramental de San Justo**, attached to the cemetery of the Hermitage of San Isidro (bus 17) out west. In a state of poignant neglect, this overgrown, cypress-shaded wasteland is the resting place of some of the more distinguished writers of 19th- and 20th-century Spain, from the romantic Madrid poet Mariano José de Larra to prolific writer and man-about-town Ramón Gómez de la Serna. Luis Buñuel was greatly drawn to this cemetery; his memory of coming across the hair of a woman protruding from a cracked grave here was used by him in his film *The Phantom of Liberty*.

Plaza de Toros de Las Ventas.

great majority of pieces came from excavations carried out within Spain, illustrating the extraordinary continuity and diversity of human settlement in the Iberian peninsula. Begin in the basement, which holds palaeontological material such as skulls, tombs and a mammoth's tusks, still attached to its skull. Some of the most interesting relics are from the area around Madrid itself, such as the many 4,000-year-old neolithic bell-shaped pottery bowls. The first floor holds the museum's most famous possession, the *Dama de Elche*, the stone bust of an Iberian priestess, believed to date from 500BC. In the garden, steps lead underground to a reproduction of the renowned Altamira prehistoric cave paintings in Cantabria.

FREE Museo Casa de la Moneda

C/Dr Esquerdo 36 (91 566 65 44, www.museo casadelamoneda.org). Metro O'Donnell. **Open** 10am-5.30pm Tue-Fri; 10am-2pm Sat, Sun. **Admission** free.

This museum, dedicated to coins and currency, boasts a huge collection, dating from the 18th century, that is among the most important in the world. The history of coins is represented in chronological order, and complemented by various displays of seals, bank notes, engravings, rare books and medals, plus around 10,000 sketches and drawings from Spain, Italy and Flanders, ranging from the 16th to the 18th centuries.

Museo Lázaro Galdiano

C/Serrano 122 (91 561 60 84, www.flg.es). Metro Gregorio Marañón. **Open** 10am-4.30pm Mon, Wed-Sat; 10am-3pm Sun. **Admission** €6;

€3 reductions; free under-12s. Free to all 3.30-4.30pm Mon, Wed-Sat & 2-3pm Sun. **No credit cards. Map** p305 L6.

This unjustifiably little-known museum holds the extraordinarily eclectic collection of 15,000 paintings and objets d'art, covering 24 centuries, that was accumulated over 70 years by the financier and bibliophile José Lázaro Galdiano (1862-1947). Its holdings include paintings by Goya and Bosch, an important collection of work from the Dutch and English schools, and some wonderful Renaissance ornamental metalwork. The four-storey mansion and its gardens are a sight in themselves.

FREE Plaza de Toros de Las Ventas

C/Alcalá 237 (91 356 22 00, museum 91 725 18 57, www.las-ventas.com). Metro Ventas. **Open** *Museum* 9.30am-2.30pm Mon-Fri. **Admission** *Museum* free.

More than 22,000 spectators can catch a bullfight in this, Spain's largest arena, completed in 1929. Like most early 20th-century bullrings, it is in neo-Mudéjar style, with often playful use of ceramic tiling. Around it there is ample open space to accommodate the crowds and food vendors, so it's easy to get a good look at the exterior. It's not necessary to go to a *corrida* to see the ring from within. When the bulls are back on the ranch, concerts are often held here, and alongside the ring there is the small Museo Taurino. The museum holds portraits of famous matadors, as well as *trajes de luces* (suits of lights), including the pink-and-gold outfit worn by the legendary Manolete on the afternoon of his death in the ring in 1947. Among the 18th-century paintings is a portrait of *torero* Joaquín Rodríguez Costillares.

EXPLORE

Beyond the Centre

Cross the city walls to find museums, parks and an Egyptian temple.

EXPLORE

Building restrictions over the centuries have kept even Madrid's more far-flung attractions within reasonably easy reach of the city centre. Many visitors never stray out of the Old City and the triangle defined by the big three art museums. That's all very well – and if this is your first visit it's certainly a reasonable decision – but go further afield and you can take in the Madrid skyline by cable car, visit an authentic Egyptian temple or inspect General Franco's old home. The more distant areas also provide welcome green escapes from the urban density of Madrid's centre, with the woods and hills around El Pardo serving as a refuge for wildlife and humans seeking respite from the summer heat.

But this is Madrid, so there's some magnificent art to see as well, ranging from the frescoes adorning Goya's tomb to the finest collection of pre-Columbian American art to be found in Europe. And away from the attractions there are the quiet pleasures of suburbs such as Vallecas, secure in their own identity.

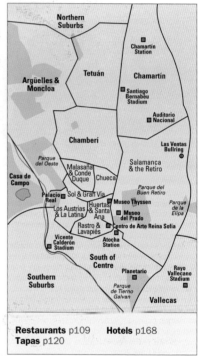

Restaurants p109   **Hotels** p168
Tapas p120

NORTH & WEST

Casa de Campo

Once a royal hunting estate, the verdant, sprawling parkland of the **Casa de Campo**, to the west of the city, was only opened to the public under the Republic in 1931. Five years later, it became a key site for Franco's forces in the Civil War battle for Madrid, its high ground being used to shell the city centre and the university. Remains of trenches still exist.

Today, the Casa is home to the **Parque de Atracciones** funfair and the **Zoo** (for both, *see pp174-178*), as well as **swimming pools** and **tennis courts** (for both, *see pp220-225*), and a large boating lake. The cafés that ring the lake

are good for an outdoor lunch, and cyclists should note that most of the park's roads are closed to cars on Sunday mornings.

Once you stray away from the criss-crossing roads much of the park is surprisingly wild, and it's possible to have a real country walk through its woods and gullies. A favourite way to visit is via the **Teleférico de Madrid** cable car from the **Parque del Oeste**, which runs over the trees almost to the middle of the Casa, where there are viewpoints, an (undistinguished) bar-restaurant and picnic spots.

Couples seeking seclusion favour the Casa de Campo, both by day and by night, and the area by the Teleférico has been a gay cruising spot, although police have been cracking down on this. In contrast, one new feature of the

Teleférico de Madrid.

EXPLORE

modern Casa is that Madrid's city authorities seem near set on turning the roads from Lago metro to the Zoo into a semi-official prostitution zone, with the aim of moving prostitution from the city centre. Consequently, by night, and often by day, there are female and transvestite prostitutes along these roads, displaying their assets pretty outrageously to cruising drivers, and leaving some pretty unpleasant debris behind them. One very Spanish aspect of this is that many of the other users of the park, by day at least, don't let this bother them, but carry on lunching, cycling or whatever, regardless.

Teleférico de Madrid

Paseo del Pintor Rosales (91 541 11 18, www.teleferico.com). Metro Argüelles. **Open** *May-Aug* noon-1.45pm, 3-9pm Mon-Fri; noon-9.30pm Sat, Sun. Opening times for rest of year change on a weekly and monthly basis (see website). **Tickets** (return) €5.75; €5.15 reductions; free under-3s. **Map** p306 B8.
An extraordinary 2.5km (1.5-mile) trip over the Casa de Campo and Parque del Oeste in a cable car. The views of the Palacio Real, Río Manzanares, city sky-line and park are breathtaking. There are even inter-esting close-ups of the park's seedier goings-on. In the winter, the cable cars rarely operate on weekdays.

Argüelles & Moncloa

West of Conde Duque lie the districts known as Argüelles and Moncloa. **Argüelles**, properly speaking, is the grid of streets between Plaza de España, C/Princesa, Plaza de Moncloa and Paseo del Pintor Rosales. The Paseo is known

for its *terrazas* – open-air bars that are ideal for taking the air on summer evenings. The Paseo sits above the **Parque del Oeste**. Designed by Cecilio Rodríguez in the 1900s, it's one of Madrid's most attractive spaces. The park was completely relaid after forming part of the front line in the Civil War. **La Rosaleda**, the rose garden, is beautiful in spring. The Montaña del Príncipe Pío, at its southern end, is one of the city's highest points, with great views of the Palacio Real and the incongruous **Templo de Debod**, an Egyptian temple that was presented to Spain in 1968. This was the site of the Montaña barracks, the Nationalists' main stronghold at the start of the Civil War, before it was demolished and the hill incorporated into the park. Below the Teleférico stop a path leads to the **Ermita de San Antonio de la Florida** with its Goya frescoes, and beyond that, the river. The fountain below the Teleférico used to preside over the roundabout at Príncipe Pío station, but was moved to the park in 1994. In its place by the station there is now the **Puerta de San Vicente** – an entirely new, quite convincing reconstruction of the 18th-century gate that once stood on this side of the city. On Sundays Madrid's Andean community takes over the Parque del Oeste, organising volleyball tournaments and picnics; after dark, the area around the fountain, like the Casa de Campo, becomes a prostitution zone.

In the southern corner of the district, just off Plaza de España, is the **Museo Cerralbo**. In the opposite, northern corner, unmissable at the end of C/Princesa, stands one of the biggest, most significant creations of the Franco regime, the **Ministerio del Aire** or Air Ministry, built in the 1950s, in kitsch Castilian baroque style and popularly known as the 'Monasterio del Aire', because of its resemblance to El Escorial.

Alongside the Ministry is Plaza de Moncloa, Moncloa metro station and the departure points for many bus services to towns north and west of Madrid. There is also Franco's fake Roman triumphal arch, built to commemorate victory in the Civil War. To the north of the *plaza*, in the **Moncloa** district, lies the sprawling campus of the Universidad Complutense, the **Ciudad Universitaria**. Within the university, specific attractions are the **Museo de América** and the **Faro de Moncloa** observation tower, and beyond that, the new **Museo del Traje**.

FREE Ermita de San Antonio de la Florida

Glorieta de San Antonio de la Florida 5 (91 542 07 22). Metro Príncipe Pío. **Open** 9.30am-8pm Tue-Sun. **Admission** free. **Map** p306 B9.

This plain neoclassical chapel was completed by Felipe Fontana for Charles IV in 1798. Quite out of the way, north of Príncipe Pío station on the Paseo de la Florida, it is famous as the burial place of Goya, and for the unique, and recently restored, frescoes of the miracles of St Anthony, incorporating scenes of Madrid life, which he painted here in 1798. In contrast to the staid exterior, the colour and use of light in Goya's images are stunning. Featuring a rare mix of elements, including his unique, simultaneously ethereal and sensual 'angels', they are among his best and most complex works. On the other side of the road into the park is a near-identical second

Ermita de San Antonio de la Florida.

chapel, built in the 1920s to allow the original building to be left as a museum. There are free guided tours of the Ermita, in Spanish and English, at 11am and noon on Saturdays.

Faro de Moncloa

Avda de los Reyes Católicos (www.elfarodemoncloa. com). Metro Moncloa. **Open** Closed until at least late 2013. **Admission** €1; 50¢ reductions.

This former radio and communications tower, 92m (302ft) tall, provides one of the best views of the whole of the city and the *sierras* in the distance. Diagrams along the floor point out highlights of the city. The best bit, though, is the ride up in the glass lift. The tower has been closed for some time while the council attempts to reach an agreement with the nearby university, which owns the land.

Museo de América

Avda de los Reyes Católicos 6 (91 543 94 37, http://museodeamerica.mcu.es). Metro Moncloa. **Open** *May-Oct* 9.30am-8.30pm Tue-Sat; 10am-3pm Sun. *Nov-Apr* 9.30am-6.30pm Tue-Sat; 10am-3pm Sun. **Admission** €3; €1.50 reductions; free under-18s, all Sat pm & Sun. **No credit cards.**

This museum comprises the finest collection of pre-Columbian American art and artefacts in Europe, a combination of articles brought back at the time of the Conquest and during the centuries of Spanish rule over Central and South America, plus later acquisitions generally donated by Latin American governments. The collection includes some near-matchless treasures: there is the *Madrid Codex*, one of only four surviving Mayan illustrated glyph manuscripts in the world; the *Tudela Codex* and illustrated manuscripts from central Mexico, which depict the Spanish Conquest; superb carvings from the Mayan city of Palenque, sent back to Charles III by the first-ever modern survey expedition to a pre-Hispanic American ruin in 1787; and the Gold of the Quimbayas, a series of exquisite gold figures from the Quimbaya culture of Colombia, which were presented to Spain by the Colombian government. All the main pre-Columbian cultures are represented –

Templo de Debod. *See p80.*

further highlights include Aztec obsidian masks from Mexico, Inca stone sculptures and funeral offerings from Peru, and finely modelled, comical and sometimes highly sexual figurines from the Chibcha culture of Colombia. There are also exhibits from the Spanish colonial period, such as the *Entry of the Viceroy Morcillo into Potosí* (1716) by the early Bolivian painter Melchor Pérez Holguín; a series of paintings showing in obsessive detail the range of racial mixes possible in colonial Mexico; and a collection of gold and other objects from the galleons *Atocha* and *Margarita*, sunk off Florida in the 18th century and only recovered in 1988.

The collection is arranged not by countries and cultures, but thematically, so that rooms are dedicated to topics such as 'the family', 'communication' and so on, with artefacts from every period and country alongside each other. Without some knowledge of the many pre-Columbian cultures, this can be confusing and uninformative. Frustrating, then, but it's still a superb, intriguing collection, and temporary shows are usually interesting.

Museo Cerralbo

C/Ventura Rodríguez 17 (91 547 36 46, http:// museocerralbo.mcu.es). Metro Plaza de España. **Open** 9.30am-3pm Tue-Sat; 10am-3pm Sun. **Admission** €3; €1.50 reductions; free under-18s & over-65s. Free to all Thur pm & all day Sun. **No credit cards. Map** p307 E10.

Laid out in a sumptuous 19th-century mansion in Argüelles is the remarkable collection of artworks and artefacts assembled by Enrique de Aguilera y Gamboa, the 17th Marqués de Cerralbo. A man of letters, politician and traveller who collected pieces

everywhere he went, he bequeathed his collection to the state with the stipulation that it should be displayed exactly how he had arranged it himself. Thus the contents are laid out in a crowded manner, with paintings in three levels up the walls, and few items labelled. Among the many paintings, though, there are El Greco's *The Ecstasy of St Francis of Assisi* – the real highlight – and works by Zurbarán, Alonso Cano and other Spanish masters. The upstairs area contains an astonishing collection of European and Japanese armour, weapons, watches, pipes, leatherbound books, clocks and other curiosities. The mansion itself is of interest; it gives a good idea of how the aristocracy lived in the Restoration period.

Museo del Traje (Museum of Clothing)

Avda Juan de Herrera 2 (91 550 47 00, http:// museodeltraje.mcu.es). Metro Moncloa. **Open** 9.30am-7pm Tue-Sat; 10am-3pm Sun. **Admission** €3; free under-18s & over-65s. Free to all 2-7pm Sat & all day Sun. **No credit cards.**

This museum is a must for those interested in any aspect of clothing. The collections comprise around 21,000 garments covering six centuries of Spanish fashion, although there are some much older items, among them fragments of Coptic cloth and Hispano-Muslim pieces. The permanent exhibition shows up to 600 items at any one time, rotating garments frequently both to protect them and to allow returning visitors to appreciate the breadth and diversity of the collection. It is arranged chronologically, in 14 spaces, among which are two outstanding monographic rooms, one covering regional costume, the other containing pieces by Mariano Fortuny y Madrazo, son of the painter, whose creations were

EXPLORE

worn by the likes of Isadora Duncan. Other rooms cover costume from the Enlightenment and the *castizo* (Madrid's working classes), early 19th-century French influences, Romanticism, belle époque, the avant-garde, post-Civil War fashion and the modern era. A room is dedicated to the great couturier Balenciaga and another to Spanish haute couture. Visitors can learn about how clothes are made in 'didactic areas' and a further exhibition space shows temporary displays. Facilities include reading rooms, a bookshop, a café and a restaurant.

FREE **Templo de Debod**
Paseo de Pintor Rosales s/n (91 366 74 15).
Metro Plaza de España or Ventura Rodríguez.
Open *Apr-Sept* 10am-2pm, 6-8pm Tue-Fri;
9.30am-8pm Sat, Sun. *Oct-Mar* 9.45am-1.45pm,
4.15-6.15pm Tue-Fri; 9.30am-8pm Sat, Sun.
Admission free. **Map** p306 D9.

This Egyptian structure, which sits on the outskirts of the Parque del Oeste, dates back 2,200 years and is dedicated to the gods Amun and Isis. It was sent, block by block, by the Egyptian government in 1968 in thanks for Spain's help in preserving monuments threatened by the Aswan Dam. *Photo p79.*

Chamberí

Directly north of Malasaña is the *barrio* of Chamberí, one of the first working-class districts outside the walls to be built up in the second half of the 19th century. Consequently, and generally justifiably, it has become one of the few areas outside the old city considered to have genuine *castizo* character. A pleasant place to while away an evening in this area is the circular **Plaza de Olavide**, ringed with pavement cafés. Just to the east of here is the charming **Museo Sorolla**.

Park Life

Head out to the suburbs to explore an impossibly romantic garden.

Just to the north of the A-2 motorway, now surrounded by Madrid's eastern sprawl, the **Parque El Capricho de la Alameda de Osuna** is a jewel of a romantic fantasy garden, a remarkably preserved monument to 18th-century taste. Within its 14 hectares is an artificial river that meanders between lakes, woods, rose gardens, mock temples and a whole range of cool, surprising corners. The gardens were begun in the 1780s for the Duke and Duchess of Osuna, the most cultivated couple among the Spanish aristocracy, who were enthusiastic promoters of the ideas and enquiring spirit of the Enlightenment and great patrons of the artists, writers and musicians of their day. The Capricho was their country estate and, under the direction of the Duchess, became a special combination of salon and pleasure garden. In the 1790s, an invitation to spend a day there was the hottest ticket in Madrid, for both the aristocracy and the intelligentsia.

The Capricho has been called 'the essence of a feminine garden', and its design closely reflected the Duchess's personal taste. Her main architect was Jean-Baptiste Mulot, a French gardener who had previously worked for Marie Antoinette, although much of the Capricho is in the English style, with simulated natural landscapes between smaller formal gardens. An Italian theatre designer, Angelo Maria Borghini, was brought in to construct

many of the Capricho's fanciful buildings. Wandering visitors were to be surprised and delighted by a succession of different ambiences and experiences: from secluded alcoves to broad vistas; from tranquil boat rides on the lakes out to tiny artificial islands to sampling the simple life at the Casa de la Vieja, a mock peasants' cottage. Also waiting to be discovered were replica Greek and Egyptian temples, a ballroom, an open-air theatre and even an ornate beehive in the shape of a classical temple. Within the Capricho, the Osunas' aristocratic friends, men and women, could mingle with artists and intellectuals and talk freely, whether of gossip or great ideas, in an atmosphere that was very

EXPLORE

On the north side of Chamberí is Madrid's main water supply, the Canal de Isabel II. On C/Santa Engracia, a neo-Mudéjar water tower has been converted into a unique photography gallery, the **Sala del Canal de Isabel II**.

Museo Sorolla

Paseo del General Martínez Campos 37 (91 310 15 84, http://museosorolla.mcu.es). Metro Gregorio Marañón or Iglesia. **Open** 9.30am-8pm Tue, Sat; 10am-3pm Sun. **Admission** €3; €1.50 reductions; free under-65s. Free to all 2-8pm Sat & all day Sun. **No credit cards**. **Map** p305 J6.

Often regarded as a neo-Impressionist, Valencia-born Joaquín Sorolla was really an exponent of 'luminism', the celebration of light. He was renowned for his iridescent, sun-drenched paintings, including portraits and family scenes at the beach and in the

gardens. Sorolla's leisured themes and greetings card-style (and indeed they are often used as such), aesthetic are easy to dismiss, but most find his luminous world at least a little seductive. This delightful little museum, housed in the mansion built for the artist in 1910 to spend his latter years, has been recently restored and boasts 250 works. The works are exhibited on the main floor, in his former studio areas. The salon, dining room and breakfast room are furnished in their original state with the artist's eclectic decorative influence in evidence. The garden, Moorish-inspired but with an Italianate pergola, is a delightful, peaceful oasis of calm, seemingly miles away from the roaring traffic outside.

FREE Sala del Canal de Isabel II

C/Santa Engracia 125 (91 545 10 00, www.madrid. org). Metro Ríos Rosas. **Open** 11am-2pm, 5-8.30pm Tue-Sat; 11am-2pm Sun. **Admission** free.

different from the paralysing etiquette of the royal court. New poems were read, and operas and music performed: Haydn was a favourite composer. This liberal informality encouraged by the Duchess – already deeply suspect for her 'French' ideas – soon led to unstoppable rumours that far more illicit activities were going on among the Capricho's intimate arbours than just chat.

The Duke and Duchess of Osuna were also among the first important patrons of Goya, and their support played a major part in winning him acceptance among high society. Among the several paintings that Goya produced for the Osunas' house at El Capricho were two oddities, the *Aquelarre* (Witches' Sabbath) and *Escena*

de Brujas (Witchcraft Scene) – both now in the Museo Lázaro Galdiano – precursors of his later macabre, sensual paintings, which could indicate a more decadent taste in the Duke and Duchess alongside their more celebrated Enlightenment rationalism. The Capricho is also famous as the place where Goya, then aged 40, met the 23-year-old Duchess of Alba in 1786, and where his obsession with her began. Scandalous and impulsive, known for breaking whichever social conventions suited her, dressing as a Madrid *maja* or street girl and having a string of male escorts from aristocrats to bullfighters, the Duchess of Alba was nevertheless a good friend of the high-minded Duchess of Osuna, and a frequent visitor to El Capricho.

The gardens were badly knocked about by Napoleon's troops – who also shot the head gardener, the French émigré Pierre Prévost – but were later reclaimed by the Duchess of Osuna, who lived on there until her death, aged 82, in 1834. El Capricho then suffered decades of decay and occasional destruction – during the Civil War – before it became the property of the city of Madrid in the 1970s.

Parque El Capricho de la Alameda de Osuna
Paseo de la Alameda de Osuna 25 (91 588 01 14). Metro El Capricho. **Open** Oct-Mar 9am-6.30pm Sat, Sun. *Apr-Sept* 9am-9pm Sat, Sun. **Admission** free.

EXPLORE

This water tower, built in elaborate neo-Mudéjar style between 1907 and 1911, is considered to be a gem of Madrid's industrial architecture. It is now home to a stylish exhibition space that specialises in photography, ranging in quality from good to world-class. Two kilometres north of here, just off the Plaza de Castilla, is the Fundación Canal (www.fundacioncanal.com), another arts and education centre run by the Canal de Isabel II.

Tetuán & Chamartín

North of Chamberí is **Tetuán**, a modern working area centred on C/Bravo Murillo, and, to the east, **Chamartín**, which contains the major business area of modern Madrid. The main point of interest for visitors is the local market, the **Mercado de Maravillas**, at C/Bravo Murillo 122, just north of Cuatro Caminos – it's the largest market in the city. On Sunday mornings, too, a 'Rastro' gets going on C/Marqués de Viana. Also well worth a visit is the **Museo Tiflológico** just north of here. A museum designed especially for blind and partially sighted visitors, it by no means excludes other visitors; in fact, its hands-on approach is particularly suitable for those with children in their group.

Across the Castellana, north-east of Nuevos Ministerios, is **El Viso**, an anomaly in high-rise Madrid. It was developed in the 1920s as a model community on garden-city lines, on the fringes of the city at that time, and some of its individual houses are museum-worthy examples of art deco. Unsurprisingly, the district has retained its desirable (and expensive) status. At the southern tip of this area is the incongruously political cultural centre, the **Residencia de Estudiantes**. Further east again is **La Prosperidad**, also once a model housing development, although most of its early buildings have been replaced by modern blocks. Within it is the **Auditorio Nacional de Música** (*see p210*).

FREE Museo Tiflológico

C/La Coruña 18 (91 589 42 19, http://museo. once.es). Metro Estrecho. **Open** 10am-2pm, 5-8pm Tue-Fri; 10am-2pm Sat. Closed 2wks Aug. **Admission** free.

Owned and run by ONCE, the organisation for blind and partially sighted people, this special museum presents exhibitions of work by visually impaired artists (the name comes from the Greek *tiflos*, sightless). Work here is intended to be touched, and is generally sculptural, three-dimensional, rich in texture and highly tactile. As well as staging temporary shows, the museum holds a large permanent collection of instruments devised over the years to help the blind and a series of scale models of monuments from Spain and around the world.

FREE La Residencia de Estudiantes

C/Pinar 21-23 (91 563 64 11, www.residencia. csic.es). Metro Gregorio Marañón. **Open** (during exhibitions, phone to check) 11am-8pm Mon-Sat; 11am-3pm Sun. **Admission** free.

From its foundation in 1910 until the war in 1936, the Residencia de Estudiantes was the most vibrant cultural centre in Madrid, and a powerful innovative force in the whole country. Although it was a students' residence – García Lorca, Buñuel and Dalí all stayed here in the early days – 'La Resi' also organised visits to Madrid by leading artists and scientists of the day and was active in the propagation of avant-garde ideas from outside Spain. The Civil War and subsequent regime severely stifled intellectual freedom and the Residencia languished until the late 1980s, when it was resurrected as a private foundation sponsored by Spain's official scientific research council. It hosts talks by international figures, conferences and exhibitions, recitals, films and concerts.

The northern suburbs

The northern and western *extrarradio* offers a radical contrast to the south. The thing to do for those with the necessary cash in Madrid has been to adopt the Anglo-Saxon way of life and move out of city flats into house-and-garden districts like **Puerta de Hierro**, north of the Casa de Campo. Named after the 1753 iron gate to the royal hunting reserve of El Pardo, its posh homes are no match for **La Moraleja**, off the Burgos road, an enclave for executives and diplomats.

The growing districts to the east are not nearly so lush. The area along the A-2 towards the airport is intended to be a major commercial development zone, with the Feria de Madrid trade fair complex and the **Parque Juan Carlos I**, which lies between the airport and the Feria de Madrid centre. Oddly enough, the area already contains, swallowed up in the urban spread, one of Spain's most appealing 18th-century gardens, the **Parque El Capricho de la Alameda de Osuna** (*see p80* **Park Life**).

Parque Juan Carlos I

Avda de Logroño & Avda de los Andes. Metro Campo de las Naciones.

This huge park, Madrid's newest green (and brown) space, lies between the airport and the Feria de Madrid trade fair centre. With time it should become one of the city's more attractive spaces, but it has taken a while for the trees to grow to provide shade. That said, the park's current draws include a series of different gardens within a circle of olive trees, an artificial river and other water features.

El Pardo

Around ten miles (15 kilometres) to the north-west of the city lies a vast expanse of verdant and well-tended parkland. This area contains the main residence of the Spanish royal family, the **Palacio de la Zarzuela**, but the reason most people will venture up here is for the peculiar sensation of nosing around in the house where General Franco lived and worked for the 35 years up to his death in 1975, the **Real Palacio de El Pardo**, situated in the peaceful 18th-century town of El Pardo. Today the place serves mainly to host foreign dignitaries and heads of state, most notably in recent years during the 2004 wedding of the heir to the throne, Prince Felipe. The hills and woodlands are also worth a visit, being remarkably unspoilt thanks to those long protected years of dictatorial and regal status. They contain an amazingly rich array of wildlife.

Real Palacio de El Pardo

C/Manuel Alonso (91 376 15 00, www. patrimonionacional.es). Bus 601 from Moncloa. **Open** *Apr-Sept* 10am-7pm daily. *Oct-Mar* 10am-5pm daily. **Admission** €9; €4 reductions; free under-5s. Free to EU citizens Wed & Thur pm. **No credit cards**.

In 1405, Henry III constructed a hunting lodge here, but the first monarch to take a really serious interest in El Pardo's excellent deer and game hunting estate

was Charles I of Spain (Charles V of the Holy Roman Empire), who built a sizeable palace here. His successor, Philip II, added many important works of art but most of these were lost in a fire in 1604, and after various architectural changes the building was finally reconstructed on Charles III's orders by 18th-century architect Francesco Sabatini; superb murals by Bayeu and Maella were added at this time. The current furnishings, paintings and tapestries were added during the 19th and 20th centuries.

In addition to its main role today as a diplomatic rendezvous, the palace is partially open to the public and there are tours of its ornate and gaudy interior with ornamental frescoes, gilt mouldings and some fine tapestries, many of which were woven in the Real Fábrica de Tapices to Goya designs. There's an ornate theatre, built for Charles IV's Italian wife Maria Luisa of Parma, where censorious film fan Franco used to view films with his cronies before deciding on their suitability for the great unwashed, but in truth the only rooms of real fascination are the Generalísimo's bedroom, dressing room and '70s bathroom – decorated to his own specifications.

Outside you can wander in the palace's attractive gardens or picnic in at least part of the magnificent surrounding parkland known as Monte de Pardo – even though much of this is still closed to the public.

EXPLORE

Museo del Ferrocarril. *See p84.*

A Slice of Culture

Madrid's old slaughterhouse has been reinvented as a dynamic arts centre.

In a recession-defying measure, Madrid's city council has launched one of its most dynamic cultural projects ever in the shape of the **Matadero**, an innovative and multidisciplinary arts centre, which the council hopes will be a key socio-cultural symbol for the city.

The vast, ambitious space consists of ten impressive neo-Mudéjar buildings strung along the bank of the Manzanares. These once formed the city's slaughterhouse (*matadero*), and the painted tiles at the entrance to each announce '*deguello de ganado*' (throatcutting of cattle); '*deguello de cerdos*' (throatcutting of pigs), and so on, which can create a slightly melancholy air, though the architecture itself is far too ornate to be gloomy.

Each building is dedicated to a different discipline, with the exception of the offices

Other nearby highlights include the Convento de los Capuchinos del Pardo (Ctra del Cristo, 91 376 08 00, open 8am-1pm, 4.30-8pm daily), famed for Gregorio Fernández's wooden baroque sculpture of Christ; the Quinta del Pardo, a small 18th-century summer house, and the single-storey Casita del Príncipe, built in 1785 by Juan de Villanueva and noted for its lavish lounges, though both have been closed to the public for some years.

SOUTH
South of the centre

The *barrios* of southern **Embajadores** – namely **Delicias**, **Arganzuela** and **Legazpi** – occupy a triangular chunk of land just south of the old city, bordered by the Manzanares river, the M-30 motorway and the rail lines from Atocha. Low rents attract a fair number of resident foreigners. Conventional attractions are few – the **Museo del Ferrocarril** and the **Parque Tierno Galván**, with the **IMAX Madrid** and **Planetario de Madrid** (for both,

see pp174-178) – but the area contains the **Estación Sur** bus station, and two symbols of Madrid, the **Atlético Madrid** stadium and, alongside it, the Mahou brewery. It's also now home to new cultural centre **Matadero Madrid** (*see above* **A Slice of Culture**), in the city's old abattoir (hence the name). Beyond that is the river and the **Puente de Toledo**, which was built by Pedro de Ribera for Philip V in 1718-32.

Just south of the river is the **Parque de San Isidro**, containing a charming 18th-century hermitage dedicated to the city's patron saint. The hermitage is the traditional focus of the Romería (Procession) de San Isidro. The park still fills with life and crowds during the San Isidro *fiestas* every May. At other times it's very tranquil.

Museo del Ferrocarril
Paseo de las Delicias 61 (91 506 83 33, www. museodelferrocarril.org). Metro Delicias. **Open** 10am-3pm Tue-Thur, Sun; 10am-8pm Fri, Sat. **Admission** €5; €3.50 reductions; free under-4s. **No credit cards.**

which shows only documentaries (€3); and the Central de Diseño, which holds design-related workshops, conferences and exhibitions. There are reading rooms with newspapers and Wi-Fi and even a seed bank.

Unusually, the Matadero has been created with Madrid's citizens in mind, rather than its visitors, but there's plenty here to see and be inspired by, all just a short ride south of Atocha station.

Matadero Madrid
Plaza de Legazpi 8 (91 517 73 09, www. mataderomadrid.org). Metro Legazpi. **Open** *Site* 9am-10pm Mon-Fri; 11am-10pm Sat, Sun. *Exhibitions* 4-10pm Tue-Fri; 11am-10pm Sat, Sun. **Admission** free.

and the Cantina, an excellent café-restaurant in the former boilerhouse.

The Nave de la Música contains rehearsal rooms, a recording studio and a performance space, while the Nave del Español is all about theatre, with auditoria and exhibition spaces. The foyer comprises a café with a small stage for theatre groups to showcase work, but the loveliest space is the *plaza*. Mobile platforms carry, variously, speaker stacks or small trees to provide shade for daytime performances.

Other buildings include the Casa del Lector (Reader's House), which has a children's library, literature exhibitions and a Kindle-lending service; the Cineteca,

Housed in the elegant but disused Delicias station, with ironwork by Gustave Eiffel, Madrid's railway museum has an evocative collection of models, old locomotives, railway equipment and memorabilia. There is also a room dedicated to clocks, including the one that marked time when Spain's first ever train chugged from Barcelona to Mataró. You can climb on the trains, have a drink in an old restaurant car or watch film footage of Spanish railways. *Photos p83.*

Vallecas

Vallecas, beyond the M-30 south-east of the city, was already an industrial suburb in the 1930s and remains an area of Madrid with a firm sense of its own identity. The area has its own football team, **Rayo Vallecano**, forever struggling to keep up with its money-laden neighbours. Car stickers proclaim 'Independence for Vallecas' (spelled 'Vallekas' by hipper natives, who have their own punky sense of cool). It also has a pleasant tree-lined main drag, more than enough to mark it out from the other areas around it. There are problem districts not far away, such

as **Entrevías**, which is home to some of Madrid's largest Gypsy communities.

OUTER LIMITS
Southern suburbs

Carabanchel, **Leganés**, **Getafe**, **Móstoles** and **Alcorcón** form the southern industrial belt of Madrid. Areas still within the city, such as **Orcasitas**, blend into the towns of the *extrarradio*, the outskirts, and concrete flyovers and tower blocks make up the urban landscape.

These areas are now better connected thanks to the extension of the metro, and central city dwellers occasionally come down here for entertainment: **Alcorcón** has a flamenco festival, and **Fuenlabrada** has a clutch of teen discos. The popularity of hard rock in these suburbs is also attested to by Calle AC/DC in Leganés, inaugurated by the rock legends themselves in 2000. On the street is a converted bullring that was recently home to music venue **La Cubierta de Leganés** (closed at time of going to press).

Consume

Restaurants

Loosen your belt and tuck into everything from cocido to curry.

Not so long ago dishes from Asturias were thought exotic here in the capital. But today, thanks in no small part to immigration, *madrileños* have become Spain's unlikely flag-bearers for culinary globalisation. Mexican, of course, has always been around, and Asian food now features strongly too. Add in Italian, French, Cuban, Middle Eastern, Thai and Japanese, and you start to wonder about the future of paella. These newcomers bring with them three distinct advantages: style, spice and vegetables. Whereas the dining scene used to be all red-checked tablecloths or old-style elegance,

now those who fancy chic and minimal have a place to go. And if your taste buds are tuned to spice, you can now rest easy in Madrid. Finally, vegetarians can smile too – the options are no longer limited to tortilla or green beans with the ham picked out.

CAPITAL MAINSTAYS

Despite all of the above, this city remains a bastion of unreconstructed Spanish cuisine and what has often been described as 'brown food'. The famous *cocido madrileño* – a stew of various bits of meat, offal and vegetables served up in three courses – is still eaten religiously, particularly at weekends. The down-home *casas de comida* (eating houses) are packed daily with regulars who are perfectly happy with a plain *ensalada mixta* followed by a greasy pork chop and the ubiquitous *flan* for dessert. Even young hipsters are faithful to the less expensive classic *mesones* (old-style taverns), while the most upscale traditional places still require you to join a waiting list.

Gastro bars now alternate with temples to the most traditional *madrileño* cuisine in the area around Los Austrias and La Latina – particularly along C/Cava Baja, leading south

INSIDE TRACK ORDER, ORDER

When the food arrives, if one person hasn't ordered a starter, it's considered polite in some places in Madrid (and in Spain in general) to bring their main course to the table along with the other diners' starters.

from the Plaza Mayor. Chueca is packed with stylish restaurants offering both international and Spanish cuisine (many of which offer great value at lunchtime).

The city's most upmarket restaurants can be found in the Salamanca area, and particularly in the expensive business hotels around the Paseo de la Castellana.

TIMING

Rule number one for visitors to Madrid: don't go out too early. *Madrileños* rarely eat lunch before 2pm, although go after 4pm and you may find people sweeping up around you. Probably due to a combination of substantial lunches and the heat, dinner is usually eaten late as well – around 10pm, and even later in summer. It's advisable to book a table in most places for Friday and Saturday night, and at other times if you're in a big group. Many restaurants close on Sunday evening and all day Monday. August is livelier than it used to be, but most restaurants still close for at least two weeks. Where possible, we've indicated this, but it's best to ring and check.

By law, restaurants are obliged to declare on the menu if VAT (IVA) is included and if there's a cover charge. In practice, however, they almost never do, and there almost always is (strictly speaking cover charges are illegal, but are often disguised as a charge for bread).

CONSUME

❶ Blue numbers given here correspond to the location of each restaurant on the street maps. *See pp305-313*.

LOS AUSTRIAS & LA LATINA

La Botillería de Maxi
C/Cava Alta 4 (91 365 12 49, www.labotilleria demaxi.com). Metro La Latina. **Open** 12.30-4pm, 8.30pm-12.30am Tue-Sat; 12.30-6pm Sun. Closed last 2wks Aug. **Main courses** €7-€10. **Set lunch** €9 Tue-Fri. **No credit cards**. **Map** p311 F13 ❶ Spanish
Fashionably scruffy young waiting staff and blaring flamenco in a no-frills classic setting make for an unpretentious blend of old and new. While the *callos a la madrileña* (tripe in a spicy sauce) are acknowledged as the best in town, there's no shame in going for the *pisto manchego* (aubergine, courgette, pepper and tomato stew) with fried eggs, the partridge pâté or the *mojama* (air-dried tuna).

La Camarilla
C/Cava Baja 21 (91 354 02 07, www.lacamarilla restaurante.com). Metro La Latina. **Open** 1.30-5.30pm, 9pm-midnight Mon, Tue, Thur; 1.30-5.30pm, 9pm-1am Fri; 1pm-1am Sat; 11.30am-midnight Sun. **Main courses** €17-€22. **Set lunch** €15 Mon, Tue, Thur. **Credit** MC, V. **Map** p311 F13 ❷ Spanish
Of the many traditional restaurants on this stretch of road, La Camarilla offers the most innovative versions of Spanish home cooking: gazpacho with mango, *revuelto* (scrambled egg) with mushrooms and parmesan, and tasty cod dishes. The setting is reminiscent of a genteel 1930s hotel, and the staff are incredibly friendly. Creative tapas and a hearty *menú del día* are served in a relaxed front room, along with luxurious gourmet meals in an adjoining formal dining room.

Casa Ciriaco
C/Mayor 84 (91 548 06 20). Metro Ópera or Sol. **Open** 1-4.30pm, 8pm-12.30am Mon, Tue, Thur-Sun. Closed Aug. **Main courses** €12-€35. **Set lunch** €20 Mon, Tue, Thur, Fri. **Credit** DC, MC, V. **Map** p311 E12 ❸ Spanish
Pick your way down the side of the open kitchen to a deep dining room hung with pictures of visiting royals and celebrities, along with rather grimmer photos of the 1906 bombing of the wedding procession for Alfonso XIII and his English wife Victoria Eugenie – which happened right outside the door. Undamaged and still going strong, Casa Ciriaco was a meeting place for the intelligentsia in pre-Civil War days, and although it no longer attracts many thinkers, the Castilian fare is a taste of days gone by. *Gallina en pepitoria* (chicken in an almond and white wine sauce) is the speciality.

★ Casa Lucio
C/Cava Baja 35 (91 365 32 52, www.casalucio.es). Metro La Latina. **Open** 1-4pm, 8.30-11.30pm Mon-Fri, Sun; 9pm-midnight Sat. Closed Aug. **Main courses** €18-€30. **Credit** AmEx, DC, MC, V. **Map** p311 F13 ❹ Spanish
A restaurant unsurpassed by any other in Madrid for its famous patrons: King Juan Carlos, Bill Clinton and Penélope Cruz among them. This is the place of historical rendezvous, where Aznar and Bush's

CONSUME

Casa Lucio.

CONSUME

El Sobrino de Botín.

wives did lunch back when alliances were in the making. It also knows how to cook up one cracking *solomillo* (beef). The key to Lucio's glory is the use of a coal-fired oven and the best olive oil. Another star dish is a starter of lightly fried eggs laid on top of a bed of crisp, thinly cut chips – the King always orders it. Be sure to ask for a table on the first floor.

★ Casa Marta
C/Santa Clara 10 (91 548 28 25, www. restaurantecasamarta.com). Metro Ópera.
Open 9pm-midnight Tue-Sat; 1-4pm Sun. Closed Aug. **Main courses** €13-€17. **Credit** AmEx, DC, MC, V. **Map** p311 F11 ❺ Spanish
Every Saturday, according to the novel, Don Quixote ate *duelos y quebrantes* (scrambled eggs, ham, bacon, chorizo and brains) and you can still try them at Casa Marta – although they usually leave out the brains these days. A quaint old place, it's been a favourite since the beginning of the 20th century, when opera-goers and singers would stop in for a tipple after performances. The satisfying *platos de cuchara* ('spoon food') – warming bowls of *cocido*, beans and lentils – are another star turn that always pulls in the crowds.

Emma y Júlia
C/Cava Baja 19 (91 366 10 23). Metro La Latina.
Open 8pm-midnight Tue; 2-4pm, 8pm-midnight Wed-Thur; 2-4pm, 8pm-1am Fri, Sat; 2-5pm, 9-11.30pm Sun. Closed July. **Main courses** €9.50-€18. **Credit** AmEx, DC, MC, V. **Map** p311 F13 ❻ Italian

Smack in the middle of a street flanked with traditional restaurants and gourmet tapas bars is this popular Italian eaterie – a sound option when a big salad and pizza are in order. The staff are friendly, the environment laid-back and the food solid. The breaded artichokes are divine, and the house red is good and cheap. It's often wise to reserve in advance.

El Estragón
Costanilla de San Andrés 10, Plaza de la Paja (91 365 89 82, www.elestragonvegetariano.com). Metro La Latina. **Open** 1.30-4.30pm, 8pm-midnight Mon-Thur, Sun; 1.30-4.15pm, 8pm-12.45am Fri, Sat. **Main courses** €12-€18. **Set lunch** €23 Mon-Fri. **Credit** AmEx, DC, MC, V. **Map** p311 E13 ❼ Vegetarian
El Estragón's underlying concept appears to be 'vegetarian food for meat-eaters', and thus there is no shortage of soya 'meatballs', 'hamburgers' and so on. Where this place really excels, however, is in its straightforward vegetarian dishes, such as a fabulous towering heap of *risotto verde* containing every green vegetable you can think of, topped with stringy emmental. It's a delightful spot, with terracotta tiles, blue-and-white gingham and views over Plaza de la Paja, where tables are set out in summer.

Julián de Tolosa
C/Cava Baja 18 (91 365 82 10, www.casajulian detolosa.com). Metro La Latina. **Open** 1-4pm, 9-11.30pm Mon-Sat; 1-4pm Sun. **Main courses** €19-€47. **Credit** AmEx, DC, MC, V. **Map** p311 F13 ❽ Spanish

Probably the most modern restaurant in the *barrio*, this upscale Basque establishment is all smooth wood, glass and brick, housed in a 19th-century building. With a very limited, simple menu, the main attraction here is the grilled steak (*chuletón de buey*), a contender for the city's best. Try the smoky idiazábal sheep's cheese, a speciality from the little Basque town of the same name. The maître d' will steer you through an excellent selection of more than 100 wines.

★ Marechiaro

C/Conde de Lemos 3 (91 547 00 42). Metro Ópera. **Open** 9pm-midnight Mon; noon-4.30pm, 9pm-1am Tue-Sat. Closed 2wks Aug. **Main courses** €10-€15. **Set lunch** €12. **Credit** AmEx, DC, MC, V. **Map** p311 F11 **❾** Italian

It's a standard definition of pizza worth, but it still holds up: you know a pizzeria is good when it attracts this many Italians. Two Neapolitans are behind this modest little restaurant that provides some of the best pizzas in the city. Cooked in wood-fired ovens, they have thin, flavourful crusts and fresh ingredients. Pastas are good too, but they definitely play second fiddle. Decor is pungent orange walls sporting a mix of Venetian masks and old photos of Maradona.

La Musa Latina

Costanilla San Andrés 12 (91 354 02 55, www.lamusalatina.com). Metro La Latina. **Open** 12.30pm-midnight Mon-Wed; 12.30pm-12.30am Thur; 9am-2am Fri; 12.30pm-1.30am Sat; 1pm-midnight Sun. **Main courses** €5-€16. **Set lunch** €10 Mon-Fri. **Credit** MC, V. **Map** p311 E13 **❿** Global

A laid-back vibe, tasty tapas and stir-fries, and a great location on Plaza de la Paja all contribute towards making La Musa Latina into a tempting package. Try the fried green tomatoes and the prawn tempura with avocado. There are plenty of indulgent desserts – go for the chocolate brownie or the *dulce de leche* pannacotta. Waiters are super cool but friendly, and the diners well-heeled and hip (note the Junk Club downstairs). There is a sister restaurant in Malasaña, but this one is roomier.
Other location La Musa, C/Manuela Malasaña 18, Malasaña & Conde Duque (91 448 75 58).

★ El Sobrino de Botín

C/Cuchilleros 17 (91 366 42 17, 91 366 30 26, www.botin.es). Metro Sol. **Open** 1-4pm, 8pm-midnight daily. **Main courses** €20-€25. **Set meal** €35. **Credit** AmEx, DC, MC, V. **Map** p311 F12 **⓫** Castilian

Bags packed, milk cancelled, house raised on stilts.

You've packed the suntan lotion, the snorkel set, the stay-pressed shirts. Just one more thing left to do – your bit for climate change. In some of the world's poorest countries, changing weather patterns are destroying lives.

You can help people to deal with the extreme effects of climate change. Raising houses in flood-prone regions is just one life-saving solution.

**Climate change costs lives.
Give £5 and let's sort it *Here & Now***

www.oxfam.org.uk/climate-change

Be Humankind (X) Oxfam

The world's oldest restaurant is still coming up with the goods after nearly 300 years. For all its popularity as a tourist destination, its nooks and crannies add up to an atmospheric – if cramped – dining spot over several floors. Ask for a table in the vaulted cellar for the full effect. Order the suckling pig or the lamb, which are roasted in a huge wood-fired oven. And yes, seeing as you asked, Hemingway did come here.

La Taberna del Alabardero

C/Felipe V 6 (91 547 25 77, www.alabardero.eu). Metro Ópera. **Open** 1-3pm, 9-11pm daily. **Main courses** €18-€50. **Set lunch** €30 daily. **Credit** AmEx, DC, MC, V. **Map** p311 F11 ⑫ **Spanish**
Father Lezama first started up his traditional tavern back in 1974, when he put underprivileged boys to work as waiters in this converted 16th-century townhouse. With a quiet *terraza* on the street that runs along the north side of the Teatro Real, it is still one of the most popular post-theatre dining spots, serving up traditional tapas at the bar and Basque cuisine in the restaurant in the back. Lezama is now a very prosperous restaurateur – he has opened six more restaurants in Spain and one in Washington, DC. Some of those original boys are now shareholders.

Taberna Salamanca

C/Cava Baja 31 (91 366 31 10). Metro La Latina. **Open** 1-4pm, 8.30pm-midnight Tue-Thur; 1-4pm, 8.30pm-1am Fri, Sat; 1-4.30pm Sun. Closed mid July-mid Aug. **Main courses** €7-€15. **Set lunch** €9.50 Tue-Sun. **No credit cards**. **Map** p311 F13 ⑬ **Spanish**
On a street crammed to the hilt with high-priced eateries, this is where the cool, young and more frugal set comes to eat. There are three lunch *menús* to choose from, offering the usual Spanish pickings – the *croquetas*, courgette tortilla and endives with roquefort cheese are all pretty reliable choices. The staff are friendly and young, with a tendency to whack up the stereo.

Vadebaco

C/Campomanes 6 (mobile 680 132 538, www.vadebaco.com). Metro Ópera. **Open** noon-4.30pm, 6pm-midnight Mon-Sat; noon-4.30pm Sun. **Main courses** €9-€18. **Set lunch** €12. **Credit** AmEx, MC, V. **Map** p311 F11 ⑭ **European**
With more than 350 wines on offer – and at least 40 by the glass – you'll probably spend longer choosing what to drink than what to eat at Vadebaco. The wall as you enter is a huge blackboard listing just some of the food and wine on offer, giving you an idea of what to expect in the cool space. Share a few things to get the best experiece: maybe slices of cured beef from León, a really excellent tortilla, lamb meatballs or oyster mushroom ravioli. Stick around after dinner for a cocktail too. The set lunch is great value.

El Viajero.

El Viajero

Plaza de la Cebada 11 (91 366 90 64). Metro La Latina. **Open** 2-4.30pm, 9pm-12.30am Tue-Thur; 2-4.30pm, 9pm-1am Fri, Sat; 2-4.30pm Sun. Closed 3wks Jan & last 2wks Aug. **Main courses** €7-€18. **Set lunch** €12 Tue-Fri. **Credit** AmEx, DC, MC, V. **Map** p311 F13 ⑮ **Mediterranean**
La Latina scenesters in sideburns and retro couture still flock to this three-storey bar/restaurant famous for its rooftop *terraza*. The food, a mixed array of Mediterranean dishes and barbecued meats, is delicious, if a little expensive. The carpaccios are melt-in-the-mouth and the pastas, particularly the *taglioni marinera*, drip with flavour. Discriminating carnivores love El Viajero for the high-quality, hormone-free Argentine meat, while sweet-tooths rejoice over the scrumptious tiramisu.

Viuda de Vacas

C/Águila 2 (91 366 58 47). Metro La Latina. **Open** 1.30-5pm, 9pm-1am Mon-Wed, Fri, Sat; 1.30-4.30pm Sun. Closed July. **Main courses** €9-€16. **Credit** MC, V. **Map** p311 F13 ⑯ **Spanish**
Viuda de Vacas has moved from its location on Cava Alta, where Pedro Almodóvar has filmed on several occasions, but the unpretentious authenticity has survived just about intact at its new home nearby. Classic Castilian home cooking has been in the Canova family for three generations; it was established by the feisty grandmother (the widow of Señor Vacas). Favourite dishes include the stuffed courgettes and the baked hake or sea bream.

Menu Glossary

From almejas to arándanos.

BASICS

Primer plato (entrante) first course; **segundo plato** second or main course; **postre** dessert; **plato combinado** quick, one-course meal, with several ingredients served on the same plate; **aceite y vinagre** oil and vinegar; **agua** water (**con gas/sin gas** fizzy/still); **pan** bread; **vino** wine (**tinto** red, **blanco** white, **rosado** rosé); **cerveza** beer; **la cuenta** the bill; **servicio incluído** service included; **propina** tip.

COOKING STYLES & TECHNIQUES

Adobado marinated; **al ajillo** with olive oil and garlic; **al chilindrón** (usually chicken or lamb) cooked in a spicy tomato, pepper, ham, onion and garlic sauce; **a la marinera** (fish or shellfish) cooked with garlic, onions and white wine; **a la parilla** charcoal-grilled; **al pil-pil** (Basque) flash-fried in sizzling oil and garlic; **a la plancha** grilled directly on a hot metal plate; **al vapor** steamed; **asado** (**al horno de leña**) roast (in a wood oven); **crudo** raw; **en salsa** in a sauce or gravy; **escabechado**, **en escabeche** marinated in vinegar with bay leaves and garlic; **estofado** braised; **frito** fried; **guisado** stewed; **hervido** boiled; **(en) pepitoria** casserole dish, usually of chicken or game, with egg, wine and almonds; **relleno** stuffed.

SOPAS Y POTAJES (SOUPS & STEWS)

Caldo (gallego) broth of pork and greens; **fabada** rich Asturian stew of beans, chorizo and *morcilla* (black blood sausage); **gazpacho** cold soup, usually of tomatoes, red pepper and cucumber; **purrusalda** (Basque) soup of salt cod, leeks and potatoes; **sopa de ajo** garlic soup; **sopa castellana** garlic soup with poached egg and chickpeas; **sopa de fideos** noodle soup.

HUEVOS (EGGS)

Huevos fritos fried eggs (sometimes served with chorizo); **revuelto** scrambled eggs; **tortilla asturiana** omelette with tomato, tuna and onion; **tortilla francesa** plain omelette; **tortilla de patatas** Spanish potato omelette.

PESCADO Y MARISCOS (FISH & SHELLFISH)

Almejas clams; **atún**, **bonito** tuna; **bacalao** salt cod; **besugo** sea bream; **bogavante**

lobster; **caballa** mackerel; **calamares** squid; **camarones** small shrimps; **cangrejo**, **buey de mar** crab; **cangrejo de río** freshwater crayfish; **dorada** gilthead bream; **gambas** prawns; **kokotxas** (Basque) hake cheeks; **langosta** spiny lobster; **langostinos** langoustines; **lubina** sea bass; **mejillones** mussels; **mero** grouper; **merluza** hake; **ostras** oysters; **pescadilla** whiting; **pescaditos** whitebait; **pulpo** octopus; **rape** monkfish; **rodaballo** turbot; **salmonete** red mullet; **sardinas** sardines; **sepia** cuttlefish; **trucha** trout; **ventresca de bonito** tuna fillet; **vieiras** scallops.

CARNE, AVES, CAZA Y EMBUTIDOS (MEAT, POULTRY, GAME & CHARCUTERIE)

Bistec steak; **buey**, **vacuno** (cuts **solomillo**, **entrecot**) beef; **butifarra** Catalan sausage; **callos** tripe; **capón** capon; **cerdo** pork, pig; **chorizo** spicy sausage, served cooked or cold; **choto** kid; **chuletas**, **chuletones**, **chuletillas** chops; **cochinillo** roast suckling pig; **cocido** traditional stew of Madrid; **codillo** knuckle (normally ham); **codornices** quails; **conejo** rabbit; **cordero** lamb; **costillas** ribs; **estofado de ternera** beef stew; **faisán** pheasant; **gallina** chicken; **hígado** liver; **jabalí** wild boar; **jamón ibérico** cured ham from Iberian pigs; **jamón serrano** cured ham; **jamón york** cooked ham; **lacón** gammon ham; **lechazo**, **cordero lechal** milk-fed baby lamb; **liebre** hare; **lomo (de cerdo)** loin of pork; **morcilla** black blood sausage; **pato** duck; **pavo** turkey; **perdiz** partridge; **pollo** chicken; **riñones** kidneys; **salchichas** frying sausages; **sesos** brains; **ternera** veal (in Spain it is slaughtered much later than most veal, so is more accurately young beef).

ARROZ Y LEGUMBRES (RICE & PULSES)

Alubias, **judías** white beans; **arroz a banda** rice cooked in shellfish stock; **arroz negro** black rice cooked in squid ink; **fideuà** seafood dish similar to a paella, but made with noodles instead of rice; **frijoles** red kidney beans; **garbanzos** chickpeas; **judiones** large haricot beans; **lentejas** lentils; **pochas (caparrones)** new-season kidney beans.

VERDURAS (VEGETABLES)

Acelgas Swiss chard; **alcachofas** artichokes; **berenjena** aubergine/eggplant; **calabacines** courgettes/zucchini; **cebolla** onion; **champiñones** mushrooms; **col** cabbage; **ensalada mixta** basic salad of lettuce, tomato and onion; **ensalada verde** green salad, without tomato; **espárragos** asparagus; **espinacas** spinach; **grelos** turnip leaves; **guisantes** peas; **habas** broad beans; **judías verdes** green beans; **lechuga** lettuce; **menestra** braised mixed vegetables; **patatas fritas** chips; **pepino** cucumber; **pimientos** sweet peppers; **pimientos de piquillo** slightly hot red peppers; **pisto** mixture of cooked vegetables, similar to ratatouille; **setas** oyster mushrooms; **tomate** tomato; **zanahoria** carrot.

FRUTA (FRUIT)

Arándanos cranberries, blueberries, redcurrants or blackcurrants; **cerezas** cherries; **ciruelas** plums; **fresas** strawberries; **higos** figs; **macedonia** fruit salad; **manzana** apple; **melocotón** peach; **melón** melon; **moras** blackberries; **naranja** orange; **pera** pear; **piña** pineapple; **plátano** banana; **sandía** watermelon; **uvas** grapes.

POSTRES (DESSERTS)

Arroz con leche rice pudding; **bizcocho** sponge cake; **brazo de gitano** swiss roll; **cuajada** junket (served with honey); **flan** crème caramel; **helado** ice-cream; **leche frita** custard fried in breadcrumbs; **membrillo** quince jelly (often served with cheese); **tarta** cake; **tarta de Santiago** sponge-like almond cake; **torrijas** sweet bread fritters.

QUESOS (CHEESES)

Burgos, **villalón**, **requesón** white, cottage-like cheeses, often eaten as dessert; **cabrales** strong blue Asturian goat's cheese; **idiazábal** Basque sheep's milk cheese; **mahón** cow's milk cheese from Menorca; **manchego (tierno, añejo, semi, seco)** hard sheep's-milk cheese (young, mature, semi-soft, dry); **tetilla** soft cow's milk cheese; **torta del casar** tangy sheep's milk cheese from Extremadura.

CONSUME

Lhardy. *See p99.*

CONSUME

Viva La Vida

Costanilla de San Andrés 16 (91 366 33 49).
Metro La Latina. **Open** noon-midnight Mon-
Wed; 11am-2am Thur-Sun. Closed last 2wks
Aug. **Main courses** €9-€12. **Credit** AmEx,
DC, MC, V. **Map** p311 E13 ⑰ **Vegetarian**
This recently opened vegetarian restaurant has been
a great success. Take a plate (or take-away box) and
make your selection from the buffet, which includes
delicious creative salads, sautéed vegetables, whole-
grains, dips and hot meals such as veggie lasagne.
The staff then weigh the plate to obtain the price.
There's also a good range of juices and sweet things.

Xentes

C/Humilladero 13 (91 366 42 66). Metro La
Latina. **Open** 2-5pm, 9pm-midnight Tue-Sat;
12.30-5pm Sun. Closed Aug. **Main courses**
€6-€25. **Credit** AmEx, DC, MC, V. **Map** p311
F14 ⑱ **Spanish**
With the TV blaring and some half-hearted nautical
decor, this is a rather strange setting for some of the
best seafood in Madrid. But the Galician patrons at
the bar happily gulp down oysters and beer, and the
diners in the back are just as delighted with their
pulpo a gallega (octopus with paprika) and *arroz con*
bogavantes (lobster paella).

SOL & GRAN VÍA

19 Sushi Bar

C/Salud 19 (91 524 05 71, www.19sushibar.
com). Metro Gran Vía. **Open** 1.30-4pm, 8-11.30pm
Mon-Thur; 1.30-4pm, 8.30pm-midnight Fri;

8.30pm-midnight Sat. Closed 2 wks Aug.
Main courses €8-€20. **Credit** DC, MC, V.
Map p307 H11 ⑲ **Japanese**
Going strong since 2005, 19 Sushi Bar is a favourite
among aficionados of Japanese cuisine. The Kobe
beef sashimi, tuna fillet with wasabi and the king
prawn tempura roll are just three of the star dishes.
The decor is typically cool and minimalist, but at
least there's nothing on display to distract you from
the food.

La Bola Taberna

C/Bola 5 (91 547 69 30, www.labola.es). Metro
Ópera or Santo Domingo. **Open** 1-4pm, 8.30-
11pm Mon-Sat; 1-4pm Sun. Closed Aug. **Main**
courses €20-€24. **Set meal** €35. **Credit** MC, V.
Map p307 F11 ⑳ **Spanish**
Holding court on a quiet backstreet, this dignified,
classic Madrid restaurant is considered by many to
be the home of *cocido*, the huge and hearty stew
beloved of *madrileños* and a test for the biggest of
appetites. La Bola Taberna is still run by the same
family that founded it in the 19th century, and the
cocido (which is only served at lunchtime) is still
cooked traditionally in earthenware pots on a wood
fire. Unfortunately, this hugely impressive pedigree
has led to a certain complacency among some of
the waiting staff.

Caripén

Plaza de la Marina Española 4 (91 541 11 77).
Metro Santo Domingo. **Open** 9pm-2am Mon-
Sat. Closed Aug. **Main courses** €12-€35.
Credit DC, MC, V. **Map** p307 E11 ㉑ **French**

Delfos is here to prove that Greek food is not all kebabs and salads. In taverna-style surroundings, with just-on-the-right-side-of-tacky Greek details, friendly waiters serve up an unexpected variety of dishes. A good start is the *pikilia megali*, a platter of garlicky Greek olives, rich fried feta cheese, refreshing tsatsiki, lemony taramasalata, stuffed vine leaves and more. The moussaka and lamb with nuts and honey are also scrumptious.

Don Paco

C/Caballero de Gracia 36 (91 531 44 80). Metro Gran Vía. **Open** 1.30-4pm, 8-11pm Mon-Fri; 1.30-4pm Sat. Closed Aug. **Main courses** €9-€12. **Set lunch** €13 Mon-Sat. **Set dinner** €35 Tue-Fri. **Credit** MC, V. **Map** p308 I11 ㉔ **Spanish**
Don Paco, now in his 80s, is a former bullfighter from Jérez, and the Andalucían matador in him is charmingly apparent in his 45-year-old restaurant. With photos of famous visitors (the King and his parents were regulars) and Andalucían memorabilia covering the walls, it oozes southern style. *Tinto de verano* ('summer wine' cut with lemonade) on tap, ample sherry options... who needs Seville? Don't miss the *tortillitas de camarones* (shrimp fritters).

Gula Gula

Gran Vía 1 (91 522 87 64, www.gulagula.net). Metro Banco de España or Sevilla. **Open** 1-4.30pm, 8.30pm-midnight daily. **Lunch buffet** €9-€12. **Dinner buffet** €25. **Credit** AmEx, DC, MC, V. **Map** p308 I11 ㉕ **International**
Prepare yourself for muscled waiters in scant clothing, singing drag queens and bawdy humour – this is Gula Gula (Greedy Greedy). It's all about the show, darling, less about the food, but even that isn't half

At first glance, this French bistro seems a wee bit run-down, but nonetheless it's all class – in a campy, Broadway kind of way. Behind the dangling blue Christmas tree lights are tables occupied by singing, dancing, canoodling patrons having a very good time, oblivious to the excellent skate in black butter or crêpe with salmon and caviar. The merry atmosphere owes a lot to the staff, particularly Juanjo, who floats through the restaurant spreading his abundant charm.

El Club Allard

C/Ferraz 2 (91 559 09 39, www.elcluballard. com) Metro Plaza de España. **Open** 1.30-5pm, 9-11.30pm Mon-Fri; 9-11.30pm Sat. **Tasting menus** €86-€115. **Credit** AmEx, DC, MC, V. **Map** p306 D10 ㉒ **Modern European**
Club Allard began as a private members club in 1998, only opening its doors to the public in 2007. Its head chef is Diego Guerrero, who earned his second Michelin star in 2011. Things are often not what they seem: fruit and vegetables are reconstructed, mimicked in form and in flavour, to a level that would confound Mother Nature herself, and eating here is an intellectual challenge as much as it is a culinary delight. There is no à la carte, only tasting menus.

Delfos

Cuesta de Santo Domingo 14 (91 548 37 64). Metro Santo Domingo. **Open** 1.30-4.30pm, 8.30pm-midnight Tue-Sat; 1.30-4.30pm Sun. **Main courses** €11.50-€17.50. **Set lunch** €10.95 Tue-Fri. **Credit** AmEx, DC, MC, V. **Map** p307 F11 ㉓ **Greek**

INSIDE TRACK MENU DEL DIA

While the *menú del día* is aimed at workers looking for a cheap three-course lunch, the concept also works well for hungry tourists after a morning's sightseeing. It can be a great way to eat cheaply and well, and all but the swankiest restaurants are obliged to offer one. It usually consists of a starter, main course, dessert, bread and wine. Dishes cost much less than they would do à la carte (although portions tend to be smaller) and the *menú del día* also provides a chance to sample upmarket places on a budget. Standard Spanish restaurants tend to offer typical *comida casera* (home cooking), though, so don't expect fireworks. The *menú del día* should not be confused with the *menú degustación*, a meal featuring tasters of various dishes.

bad. Most people skip the hot dishes (though they have shown some moments of inspiration lately) and stick to the all-you-can-eat salad buffet, which is fair to middling. But what's truly inspiring here are the tiny leather shorts worn by the waiters.

Taj

C/Marqués de Cubas 6 (91 531 50 59, www. restaurantetaj.com). Metro Banco de España. **Open** 1-4pm, 8.30-11.30pm daily. **Main courses** €10.50-€15.50. **Credit** AmEx, DC, MC, V. **Map** p312 I11 ㉖ Indian

Everything about Taj promises serious curry – from the jingly-jangly muzak to the fanned linen napkins and plastic flowers. The menu includes all the usuals, but the *degustación* of samosa, pakora, tandoori chicken, lamb curry, pilau and naan is a good bet. Try to get the curries *picante* (hot), though the waiters may decide that that can't be what you really mean and give you *medio* anyway. Desserts are a bit limited and the decor is slightly naff, which is curiously reassuring.

La Terraza del Casino

C/Alcalá 15 (91 532 12 75, www.casinode madrid.es). Metro Sevilla. **Open** 1.30-4pm, 9-11.45pm Mon-Fri; 9-11.45pm Sat. Closed Aug. **Main courses** €28-€45. **Credit** AmEx, V. **Map** p312 H11 ㉗ Modern European

The sumptuous environs of this gentlemen's club provide the setting for a restaurant inspired and partly overseen by gourmet god Ferran Adrià. Paco Roncero, a former disciple, is at the helm in the kitchen, and has put his own stamp on the cooking, winning two Michelin stars along the way. The menu changes seasonally, but might include such delights as lobster sashimi and crunchy black algae.

HUERTAS & SANTA ANA

Artemisa

C/Ventura de la Vega 4 (91 429 50 92, www. restauranteartesmisa.com). Metro Sevilla. **Open** 1.30-4pm, 9pm-midnight daily. **Main courses** €8.75-€15.65. **Set lunch** €10.45 Mon-Fri. **Credit** AmEx, DC, MC, V. **Map** p312 H/I12 ㉘ Vegetarian

With the nondescript decor so typical of Madrid's vegetarian restaurants, Artemisa might seem no different from the rest. But the salads are bigger and more creative, and the soy burgers have more flavour. The satisfying *menú de degustación* lets you try it all: veggie paella, *croquetas*, aubergine salad and more. They also have a few non-veggie options, such as the (organic) chicken armagnac.
Other location C/Tres Cruces 4, Sol & Gran Vía (91 521 87 21).

★ Come Prima

C/Echegaray 27 (91 420 30 42). Metro Antón Martín. **Open** 9pm-midnight Mon; 1.30-4pm,

9pm-midnight Tue-Sat. Closed 3wks Aug. **Main courses** €15-€40. **Set lunch** €15 Tue-Fri. **Credit** AmEx, DC, MC, V. **Map** p312 H12 ㉙ Italian

The toothsome risottos and own-made pastas here are a godsend for Italian gastronomes. Don't miss the risotto with mushrooms, parmesan and white-truffle oil, or the perfectly executed pasta with lobster. Since it opened a few years ago, Come Prima has brought in a classy crew of Spaniards, who pack the place out every night, even on a Monday. With white curtains and tablecloths, green wood-panelled walls and Italian opera posters, you could almost be in the Tuscan countryside.

Lhardy

Carrera de San Jerónimo 8 (91 521 33 85, www.lhardy.com). Metro Sol. **Open** 1-3.30pm, 8.30-11pm Mon-Sat; 1-3.30pm Sun. Closed Aug. **Main courses** €28-€40.50. **Credit** AmEx, DC, MC, V. **Map** p311 H11 ㉚ Spanish/French

This landmark restaurant, which opened in 1839, is credited with having introduced French haute cuisine into the culinary wilderness of Madrid. Founder Emile Lhardy is said to have been enticed to the city by none other than *Carmen* author Prosper Mérimée, who told him there were no decent restaurants in the Spanish capital. These days, it's rated as much for its belle époque decor as for the food. The menu is as Frenchified as ever, although there's also a very refined *cocido*, good game and *callos* (tripe), in addition to an excellent, if pricey, wine list. *Photos p96.*

★ Le Petit Bistrot

Plaza Matute 5 (91 429 62 65, www.lepetitbistrot. net). Metro Antón Martín. **Open** 1.15-3.45pm, 9.15-11.45pm Tue-Sat; 11.30am-2.30pm Sun. Closed 2wks Aug. **Main courses** €15-€25. **Set lunch** €15 Mon-Fri. **Credit** AmEx, MC, V. **Map** p312 H12/13 ㉛ French

A cosy corner of *la belle France* tucked away in the capital of Spain, with bare-brick walls, yellow paintwork and a roll-call of dishes that verges on the parodic: deep-fried brie; garlicky snails, coquilles St-Jacques, châteaubriand and so on. The Gallic desserts do not disappoint either, and this may be the only place where you can get decent tarte tatin or profiteroles in the city. On Sundays the vibe is a lazy one, with many people settling down to a protracted brunch involving pastries, eggs and a copy of *Le Monde*.

CONSUME

Toilet Training

Learn your chicos from your chicas.

It's a nerve-racking choice. S or C? A-ha, you say, S must be *señor*! The men's room! Well, no. S is, in fact, *señora*, and C is *caballero*, meaning gentleman. But what if you see C and D? Who is the D? That would be *dama*, meaning 'lady'. It's not always so simple. Many bars and restaurants in Madrid seem to have spent hours dreaming up original ways to designate their lavatory doors.

Stromboli (C/Hortaleza 96), for example, has abridged the words *chicos* (boys) and *chicas* (girls), labelling the doors simply 'OS' and 'AS'. That one has even the natives scratching their heads. In cases such as these, it's important to know that words ending in O are male, and words ending in A are female. In **Alqamara** (C/Espíritu Santo), it's useful to know that the bar is run by lesbians, hence the labels *Vosotros* (meaning 'you', masculine plural), and *Nosotras* (meaning 'us', feminine plural).

Then there are those that opt for pictures or symbols. Much simpler, you'd think – well, no. Take **Jellyfish Café** on C/Pelayo. There, a fish tail means men's, a jellyfish means women's. **La Soberbia** on C/Espoz y Mina keeps it nice and Spanish with a small version of roadside Osborne sherry bulls for the men. Easy. The ladies' version is the same as the men's, but painted with a Friesian pattern and with a pink udder attached. Sticking with the trad theme, **Estado Puro** (*see p116*) has a flamenco and matador dolls pinioned behind glass.

Then there's the really obvious. At **Matador** on C/Cruz you will see a graphic pencil drawing of a staggeringly ugly pair of male and female genitals. But however confusing these pictorial or textual signs may be, they're still infinitely preferable to the labelling chosen by **La Huida** (C/Colón 11), where the absence of anything written on either door makes for an entertaining game of toilet roulette.

Other locations C/Ponzano 60, Chamberí (91 399 04 51); C/Príncipe de Vergara 210, Salamanca (91 411 29 21).

Pizzeria Cervantes

C/León 8 (91 420 12 98). Metro Antón Martín. **Open** 9am-1pm Mon, Wed-Sun; 6pm-1am Tue. Closed 2wks July. **Main courses** €8.50-€18. **Set lunch** €10 Mon-Fri. **Credit** AmEx, DC, MC, V. **Map** p312 I12 ㉜ **Italian**
Despite the name, this place exceeds the definition of pizzeria, with a long list of salads, crêpes, risottos and fare such as roast beef and steak. Neighbourhood regulars are fans of the cheap breakfast deal and love to linger over *café con leche* and the papers.

La Vaca Verónica

C/Moratín 38 (91 429 78 27, www.lavaca veronica.es). Metro Antón Martín. **Open** 1-4.30pm, 8.30pm-12.30am Mon-Sat; 1-4.30pm Sun. **Main courses** €10-€35. **Set lunch** €15 Mon-Fri. **Credit** AmEx, DC, MC, V. **Map** p312 J13 ㉝ **Pan-European**
With canary-yellow walls, puffed-up banquettes, bright paintings and a Gallic charm, Veronica the Cow is a whimsical reprieve from the bustling streets of Huertas. Attracting business types and hipsters alike, it's a fine choice for a quality *menú del día*. Pesto pasta, the abundant 'cow's platter' of chorizo, *morcilla* (black blood sausage) and other meats, and various salads are some of the options.

LAVAPIÉS

Baisakhi

C/Lavapiés 42 (91 521 80 31). Metro Lavapiés. **Open** noon-4pm, 8pm-midnight daily. **Main courses** €4.50-€6. **Set lunch** €15. **Credit** MC, V. **Map** p312 H14 ㉞ **Indian**
For good-value Indian food, Baisakhi is probably the best bet along what has become Madrid's answer to London's Brick Lane. The waiters all speak English, and the dishes on the menu include all the old faves. If you like a bit of poke in your curry, then be sure to ask for a spicier version of your chosen dish, as Spaniards don't generally like their food hot. The terrace is preferable to the slightly shabby interior.

★ Casa Lastra

C/Olivar 3 (91 369 08 37, www.casalastra. com). Metro Antón Martín. **Open** 1-4pm, 8pm-midnight Mon, Tue, Thur-Sat; 1.30-4pm Sun. Closed July. **Main courses** €10-€30. **Set lunch** €12 weekdays. **Credit** AmEx, DC, MC, V. **Map** p311 H13 ㉟ **Spanish**
Asturian food is now gaining international acclaim, but the regulars here have known how good it is for a long time. Always packed with happy locals munching *cabrales* (a strong Asturian blue cheese) and *pote asturiano* (a stew with cabbage, haricot beans, black pudding, chorizo and potato) at the bar, or dining on *perdiz* (partridge) at the back, this is the place for good cooking and a glass of still cider.

★ El Económico Soidemersol

*C/Argumosa 9 (91 528 16 55, http://
restauranteeleconomico.es). Metro Atocha
or Lavapiés.* **Open** 9am-2am Tue-Sun. **Main
courses** €8-€17. **Set lunch** €8.95-€9.95 Mon-
Fri; €10.50-€11.50 Sat; €12-€13 Sun. **Credit**
AmEx, DC, MC, V. **Map** p312 H14 ㊱ **Spanish**
Also confusingly known as Los Remedios (turn it
backwards to see why), the Soidemersol is something of an institution. In recent years, the premises
have had a bit of a facelift, but it retains a friendly
neighbourhood feel, along with the wooden furniture
and original tiling. Try the seafood risotto, calf's
liver and onions, or beef ragoût with vegetables.
There are tables outside in summer.

★ Freiduría de Gallinejas

*C/Embajadores 84 (91 517 59 33, www.
mformacion.com/gallinejas). Metro Embajadores.*
Open 11am-11pm Mon-Sat. Closed 3wks Aug.
Main courses €4.50-€8. **No credit cards.**
Map p311 H16 ㊲ **Spanish**
Still going strong after a century, this is the best
place in the city for deep-fried lamb's intestines and
other tasty titbits. Not for weak stomachs, this offal
institution offers superbly prepared testicles, glands
and stomach linings, all accompanied by strong red
wine. Worth checking out just for the lively scene
and a taste of old Madrid's innard circle.

Moharaj

*C/Ave María 26 (91 467 86 02, www.moharaj-
avemaria.es). Metro Lavapiés.* **Open** noon-
5pm, 8pm-midnight daily. **Main courses**
€6.50-€18. **Credit** AmEx, DC, MC, V. **Map**
p312 H14 ㊳ **Indian**
It may not look fancy, but among curry-lovers
Moharaj is widely believed to serve the best Indian
food in Madrid. The secret is that most dishes are
made from scratch when ordered, avoiding that
greasy gloop so prevalent in some establishments.
If there are four of you, order the tasty Moharaj
platter to start, which has samosas, bhajis and more,
then maybe prawns rezala, lamb jalfrezi, beef
madras and matar paneer.

CHUECA

El 26 de Libertad

C/Libertad 26 (91 522 25 22). Metro Chueca.
Open 1-4pm Mon, Sun; 1-4pm, 8-11pm Tue-
Thur; 1-4pm, 9pm-midnight Fri, Sat. **Main
courses** €9.40-€18. **Set lunch** €10.50-€16
Mon-Sat. **Credit** AmEx, DC, MC, V. **Map**
p308 I10 ㊴ **Spanish**
With its deep colours and lavishly set tables, El
26 de Libertad is over-the-top elegance bordering on
the camp. But it's not too fine to be fun, and is a
favourite in the *barrio* – the bar is often brimming
with *caña* drinkers. The food is Spanish, but dishes
such as *morcilla* (black pudding), cannelloni and

anchovies filled with spinach and pine nuts have a
creative edge. At lunchtime only a simple *menú*
is available, so book for dinner to really put them
through their paces.

El Armario

*C/San Bartolomé 7 (91 532 83 77, www.
elarmariorestaurante.com). Metro Chueca or
Gran Vía.* **Open** 1.30-4pm, 9pm-midnight daily.
Closed 3wks July. **Main courses** €10-€20.
Set lunch €10. **Credit** AmEx, DC, MC, V.
Map p308 I10 ㊵ **Mediterranean**
Aptly named the 'Cupboard', this restaurant in the
heart of Chueca makes up for its diminutive size with
generous portions. This is Mediterranean food with
a twist; soups and salads are above the norm. The
menú del día is a find, and might include cream of
spinach soup to start, followed by some oriental
chicken and a pud. It's always packed, so get there
before the crowds, especially for lunch. Charming
service is a real plus when eating at close quarters.

El Bierzo

C/Barbieri 16 (91 531 91 10). Metro Chueca.
Open 1-4pm, 8-11.30pm Mon-Sat. **Main
courses** €9-€18. **Set lunch** €11 Mon-Fri.
Set dinner €15. Closed Aug. **Credit** MC, V.
Map p308 I10 ㊶ **Spanish**
El Bierzo is one of the best of Madrid's long-
established *casas de comida* – honest, dependable
neighbourhood joints where you can get a good
menú del día at a reasonable price. It buzzes, particularly during lunch, with a loyal crowd feasting on
simple dishes: roast chicken, seven types of tortilla
and excellent *setas al ajillo* (wild mushrooms fried
in garlic). It's worth coming here just for a chat with
the friendly owner, Miguel.

El Bogavante del Almirante

*C/Almirante 11 (91 532 18 50, www.bogabar.
com). Metro Banco de España or Chueca.*
Open 1.30-5.30pm, 9pm-12.30am Mon-Sat;
1-4pm Sun. Closed 2wks Aug. **Main courses**
€12-€23. **Credit** AmEx, DC, MC, V. **Map**
p308 J10 ㊷ **Seafood**
Nestled in a cave-like basement, Almirante wins the
award for most fanciful set design. A ponderous lobster claw hangs from the ceiling, while black outlines
of sea creatures swirl across shrimp-pink walls. The
staff, clad in black, add to the scene, which feels more
Manhattan than Madrid. Seafood is the forte. The
fish specials are always excellent, but the *arroz con
bogavante* (lobster paella) takes the prize.

Café Oliver

*C/Almirante 12 (91 521 73 79, http://cafeoliver.
com). Metro Colón.* **Open** 1.30-4pm, 9pm-midnight
Mon-Thur; 1.30-4pm, 9pm-1am Fri, Sat; 11.30am-
4pm Sun. **Main courses** €16.50-€21.50. **Set
lunch** €14. **Credit** AmEx, DC, MC, V. **Map**
p308 J10 ㊸ **European**

CONSUME

Still an 'in' spot for the international crowd, Café Oliver runs the gamut of French, Spanish, Italian and Moroccan without falling into the dreaded (con)fusion trap. Highlights include the *bomba de chocolate*, definitely a candidate for top all-time pudding. The plush red velvet banquettes and large windows looking out on the street make Café Oliver an ideal place for Chueca people-watching. Ideal on a Sunday for American-style brunch. The downstairs cocktail bar is cool and loungy.

★ Casa Manolo
C/Orellana 17 (91 308 73 78, www.comidascasa manolo.es). Metro Alonso Martínez. **Open** 1.30-4.30pm Mon; 1-4.30pm, 9pm-midnight Tue-Sat. Closed Aug. **Main courses** €14-€23. **Set lunch** €15. **Credit** MC, V. **Map** p308 J9 **㊹ Spanish**
One of the best sources of *cocina casera*, or home cooking, in Madrid, Casa Manolo has an endearing, homely atmosphere. But even though it's all about tradition, this place prepares creative mouthwatering salads that put the usual *ensalada mixta* to shame – the aubergine with tomato and goat's cheese, for example, must be one of the best in the city. And then there's lentil soup, *cocido* and other hearty stews, all supremely well prepared.

★ Extremadura
C/Libertad 13 (91 531 82 22, 91 521 03 17, www.restauranteextremadura.com). Metro Chueca. **Open** 1.30-4.30pm Mon; 1.30-4.30pm, 9pm-midnight Tue-Sat. Closed 3wks Aug. **Main courses** €16-€38. **Credit** DC, MC, V. **Map** p308 I11 **㊺ Spanish**
With festive live piano accompaniment, this is the spot to try out specialities from one of Spain's least-known regions, Extremadura. The place is both classy and country – beautifully set tables with enormous glasses (for the excellent wines) combine with painting and pottery from the region. The food is marked by Extremadura's former days of austerity, with game that could be hunted on the dry plains. The trademark dish, *migas*, is a mix of breadcrumbs, chorizo and peppers that shepherds concocted to make use of old bread. Try the *torta del casar*, a soft, pungent regional cheese.

★ Gastromaquia
C/Pelayo 8 (91 522 64 13). Metro Chueca. **Open** 1-4pm, 9-11.30pm Tue-Sat; 1-4pm Sun. **Main courses** €15-€28. **Credit** AmEx, DC, MC, V. **Map** p308 I10 **㊻ Spanish fusion**
Filling the space left by the old Don Pelayo taverna, Gastromaquia has been getting rave reviews since opening a few years ago. The restaurant, located in the heart of Chueca, is run by Catalans Hugo Escolies and Ramon Figuls, and the compact interior is minimalist in style, with a red, white and black colour scheme and bare-brick walls artistically lined with old soda siphons. The Spanish-fusion food is expertly executed and presented: guacamole and

plantain chips, and grilled octopus with potato foam are examples of some of its most celebrated dishes. This is also a popular spot for tapas.

Indochina
C/Barquillo 10 (91 524 03 17). Metro Banco de España. **Open** noon-4pm, 8pm-midnight daily. **Main courses** €9.75-€25. **Set lunch** €20. **Credit** AmEx, DC, MC, V. **Map** p308 J11 **㊼ Asian**
Yes, it's Asian fusion with modern design, but Indochina is more relaxed and less style-conscious than most. It's best for a lunchtime *menú del día*: enjoy piquant sweet and sour soup followed by some decent pad thai and then – the most interesting part – green tea ice-cream with caramelised walnuts on top (trust us, it's good). If you're going à la carte, the Peking duck is a safe bet. Ask for a table in the front, near the tall windows looking out on C/Barquillo; the back rooms are a bit dreary.

Los Jiménez
C/Barbieri 14 (91 521 11 86, http://losjimenez. restaurantesok.com). Metro Chueca. **Open** 12.30-4pm, 9pm-midnight Tue-Sat; 12.30-4pm Sun. Closed Aug. **Main courses** €6.50-€22. **Set lunch** €10. **Credit** MC, V. **Map** p308 I10 **㊽ Spanish**
Refreshingly unpretentious, Los Jiménez was serving no-frills food long before Chueca became the gay capital of Spain. Ghastly fluorescent lights overhead, the smell of frying and a menu board that spans the wall behind the bar – basically, it's a good old-fashioned greasy spoon. Popular with old-time locals and new kids, who come here for all the Andalucian staples: oxtail stew, tripe, *cocido* and generous, if basic, salads.

INSIDE TRACK
EATING ON THE RUN

It's a phenomenon often noted by visitors that Madrid lacks the sandwich bars found on every corner of most European capitals. The Spanish have always been appalled by the idea of lunch as refuelling, let alone – horror of horrors – eating at one's desk. No, lunch here is a leisurely affair. However, if time is short or if you're eating alone and don't fancy a drawn-out affair, then head to Chueca's C/San Marcos for café/takeaway hotspot **Diurno** (No.37) or noodle bar the **Wok** (No.31-33). Another street to note is Malasaña's C/Espíritu Santo, which now has a good Italian café-takeaway in the form of **La Vita é Bella** (No.13), a half-decent crêpe joint, **Crêperie La Rue** (No.18), and the popular **Home** (*see p106*) for gourmet beef in a bun.

Tepic. *See p105.*

La Mordida

C/Belén 13 (91 308 20 89, www.lamordida.com). Metro Chueca. **Open** 1.30-5pm, 8.30pm-1am daily. **Main courses** €10-€10.95. **Credit** AmEx, DC, MC, V. **Map** p308 I9 ㊾ **Mexican**

Joaquín Sabina, the gravelly voiced Madrid musician and legend, does restaurants, too, but who'd have expected it to be Mexican food? And such good authentic Mexican food, too. Usually full to bursting with high-spirited tequila drinkers, this is the place to embrace *mole*, the Mexican chocolate sauce that often scares the uninitiated away.

Other locations throughout the city.

★ La Piazzetta

Plaza Chueca 8 (91 523 83 22). Metro Chueca. **Open** 1.30-4pm, 8pm-12.30am Tue-Sat; 1.30-4pm Sun. **Main courses** €8-€12. **Set lunch** €10-€14 Mon-Thur. **Credit** DC, MC, V. **Map** p308 I10 ㊿ **Italian**

Plaza Chueca has plenty of bars, but only one good restaurant, and this is it. The place is attractively decked out in beige tones, with plenty of natural light. The menu boasts tasty but simple Italian cuisine, with starters such as grilled vegetables or buffalo mozzarella with tomato and aubergine salad, and great pasta mains such as ravioli with pecorino and pear, or tortellini with pumpkin and mushrooms. The tiramisu is a must. Piazzetta is perfect for summer evenings, when you can dine on the terrace.

Other location Boccondivino, C/Castelló 81, Salamanca (91 575 79 47).

El Puchero

C/Larra 13 (91 445 05 77, www.elpuchero. com). Metro Bilbao or Tribunal. **Open** 2-4pm, 9pm-midnight Mon-Sat. Closed Aug. **Main courses** €11-€22. **Credit** AmEx, DC, MC, V. **Map** p308 H8 �51 **Spanish**

Excitingly for El Puchero, red gingham is making a comeback after 30 years in the cold. Here it had never gone away – in tablecloths, cushions, lampshades and curtains. Almost unchanged too is the range of tasty country classics – from *civet de liebre* (hare stew) to *criadillas* (don't ask) – and some excellent seafood. It's a good idea to reserve at lunchtime.

Other location C/Padre Damián 37, Chamberí (91 345 62 98).

★ Ribeira do Miño

C/Santa Brígida 1 (91 521 98 54, www. marisqueriaribeiradomino.com). Metro Tribunal. **Open** 1-4pm, 8-11.30pm Tue-Sun. Closed 2wks Jan & all Aug. **Main courses** €10-€17. **Set lunch** €11. **No credit cards**. **Map** p308 H9 �52 **Seafood**

Gallician in origin, this one's for seafood lovers. Heaped platters of prawns, crab, goose-necked barnacles, lobster and other sea creatures make it the ideal place to roll up your sleeves and get cracking shells. Other typical *gallego* dishes that add a little heat to the fun are pancakes doused in *orujo* (a fiery spirit very similar to grappa) and set aflame, and the *queimada* – a bowl of *orujo* set on fire and then cooled with black coffee. No reservations are allowed, so grab a ticket and wait.

Salvador

C/Barbieri 12 (91 521 45 24). Metro Chueca. **Open** 1.30-4pm, 9-11.30pm Mon-Sat. Closed Aug. **Main courses** €12-€28. **Set lunch** €20 Mon-Fri. **Credit** AmEx, DC, MC, V. **Map** p308 I10 �53 **Spanish**

CONSUME

THE WORLD CAN BE AN UNJUST AND TREACHEROUS PLACE, BUT THERE ARE THOSE WHO STRIVE TO MAKE IT SAFE FOR EVERYONE.

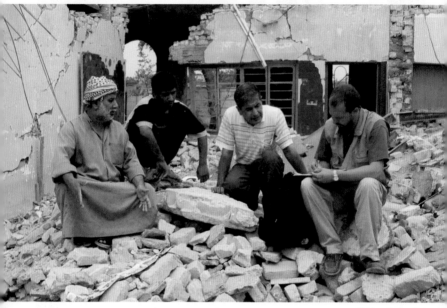

Operating in some of the world's most dangerous and oppressed countries, **Human Rights Watch** conducts rigorous investigations to bring those who have been targets of abuse to the world's attention. We use strategic advocacy to push people in power to end their repressive practices. And we work for as long as it takes to see that oppressors are held accountable for their crimes.

KNOWLEDGE IS POWER. LEARN ABOUT LIFE-CHANGING EVENTS IN YOUR WORLD THAT DON'T ALWAYS MAKE THE HEADLINES AND HOW YOU CAN HELP EFFECT POSITIVE CHANGE.

Stay informed, visit HRW.org

HUMAN
RIGHTS
WATCH

Every inch of this old classic is crammed with bull-fighting memorabilia. You'll find good traditional fare – lentil soup, *revueltos* (concoctions with scrambled egg, often with seafood or asparagus), hake, *solomillo* (sirloin steak) with french fries – but the real treat is the atmosphere.

Tepic
Pelayo 4 (91 522 08 50, www.tepic.es). Metro Chueca. **Open** 1.15-4.30pm, 9pm-midnight Mon-Thur, Sun; 1.15-4.30pm, 9pm-12.30am Fri, Sat. **Main courses** €11-€15. **Credit** AmEx, DC, MC, V. **Map** p308 I10 54 Mexican
The name comes from the capital of Nayarit state in Mexico, and a huge photo of a typical Mexican takes up one wall of this chic restaurant. There is no doubt about what you're going to eat here: quesadillas, guacamole, tacos, enchiladas, enmoladas… all of a much higher standard than at most Mexican joints in Madrid. It's no wonder Tepic is so popular. And the margaritas are so good, there's no way you're going to have just one. *Photo p103.*

Tienda de Vinos (El Comunista)
C/Augusto Figueroa 35 (91 521 70 12). Metro Chueca. **Open** noon-4pm, 8pm-midnight Mon-Sat. Closed mid Aug-mid Sept. **Main courses** €6.50-€12. **No credit cards.** **Map** p308 I10 55 Spanish
This restaurant's popular name comes from its role as a leftie meeting point years ago under Franco (but Tienda de Vinos is all you'll see above the door). It's one of the city's real classics and a visit is essential, but no one makes any grand claims about its unchanging and unchallenging menu. To start, there are soups: gazpacho, lentil or own-made broth, followed by liver and onions, lamb cutlets, kidneys in sherry and plenty of fish. Service is deadpan, but if you're lucky, you'll get one of the two charming great-grandsons of the original owner.

Zara
C/Infantas 5 (91 532 20 74, http://restaurante zara.com). Metro Chueca or Gran Via. **Open** 1-5pm, 8.30-11.30pm Mon-Fri. Closed Aug. **Main courses** €7-€15. **Set menus** €20-€25. **Credit** AmEx, DC, MC, V. **Map** p308 H10/11 56 Cuban
It's easy to walk right past these wooden doors and miss the little Havana with red-chequered tablecloths that lies within. Inés, the owner, left her home city over 30 years ago, but brought the best Cuban recipes with her – try the 'Typically Tropical' dishes such as *ropa vieja* (literally, 'old clothes', but actually shredded beef), black beans and rice with pork, and minced beef with fried bananas. Daiquiris are the drink of the house. Good Cuban food, low prices: you may have to queue as they don't take reservations.

MALASAÑA & CONDE DUQUE

Adrish
C/San Bernardino 1 (91 541 15 41, www. restauranteadrish.com). Metro Noviciado or Plaza de España. **Open** 1-4pm, 8.30pm-midnight Mon-Thur, Sun; 1-4pm, 8.30pm-1am Fri, Sat. **Main courses** €7.60-€28.20. **Set lunch** €9.50. **Credit** AmEx, DC, MC, V. **Map** p307 F9 57 Indian
The looks of the place may be a tad dreary, but you'll forget all about the mauve tablecloths when you taste the tandoori chicken with almonds. Adrish was

Subiendo al Sur. *See p107.*

CONSUME

Taberna Agrado.

one of the first restaurants to appear on the global restaurant street that is C/San Bernardino, and although it rarely seems full, it has survived with dignity. The large tandoori oven and charcoal grill produce some tasty dishes and a variety of naan breads, even if the spiciness has dropped to a level acceptable to local palates.

Bufalino

C/Puebla 9 (91 521 80 31, www.bufalino.es). Metro Gran Vía or Tribunal. **Open** 1-5pm, 8pm-1am Tue-Sat. Closed Aug. **Main courses** €6-€16. **Set lunch** €11.50. **Credit** MC, V. **Map** p307 H10 ❸ **Argentinian/Italian**
Run by an Italian/Argentine couple, Bufalino takes the cuisines of their countries and fuses them, offering a fine selection of fresh pastas made on site, along with panini and polenta. The restaurant gets packed at around 11pm as regulars pop by for a few drinks, and the noise levels in the small space go through the roof. The service always comes with a big smile, and a refurbishment has added sparkle.

Gumbo

C/Pez 15 (91 532 63 61, www.gumbo.es). Metro Noviciado. **Open** 2-4pm, 9pm-midnight Tue-Sat; 2-4pm Sun. Closed 2wks Aug. €8-€18.50. **Set lunch** €10.75. **Credit** DC, MC, V. **Map** p307 G10 ❺ **North American**
Bona fide N'Awlins chef Matthew Scott has some good Creole spices simmering in his gumbo pot. In a simple locale tastefully decorated (with a poster of *Gone with the Wind*), you can sample scrumptious New Orleans classics: fried green tomatoes, seafood gumbo, black steak. For festive group dinners, ask

Matthew to bring out a parade of tapas-like dishes to share. And only a fool would make any attempt to resist the desserts.

Home

C/Espíritu Santo 12 (91 522 97 28, www.home burgerbar.com). Metro Tribunal. **Open** 1.30-4pm, 9pm-midnight Tue-Sat; 1-4pm, 8.30pm-midnight Sun. **Main courses** €8-€15. **Credit** AmEx, MC, V. **Map** p307 H9 ❻ **Burger bar**
If you associate burger bars with junk food, then this restaurant's aim is to make you think again. Home is the brainchild of a French Canadian restaurateur, who has created a carefully thought-out menu using 100% organic produce. The attention to detail is fantastic, from the diner-style decor complete with cheesy table lamps to the menus, which come printed on American supermarket paper bags. There are quite a few vegetarian dishes, and even vegans can enjoy a marinated tofu club sandwich.
Other locations C/San Marcos 26, Chueca (91 521 85 31); C/Silva 25, Sol & Gran Vía (91 115 12 79) and throughout the city.

★ La Isla del Tesoro

C/Manuela Malasaña 3 (91 593 14 40, www. isladeltesoro.net). Metro Bilbao or San Bernardo. **Open** 1.30-4pm, 9pm-midnight daily. **Main courses** €9.50-€12.50. **Set lunch** €9-€11. **Credit** AmEx, DC, MC, V. **Map** p307 H8 ❻ **Vegetarian**
One of Madrid's few vegetarian eateries not stuck in a circa-1978 gastronomic time warp, La Isla del Tesoro (Treasure Island) is often declared hands-down the best vegetarian restaurant in the city.

CONSUME

Matching the international collectibles decor, dishes come from across the globe: try the locally renowned couscous *seitan* or the *buen rollito* (fresh pasta stuffed with spinach, apple, leek, cheese and nuts). The *menú del día* features dishes from a different nation – which can range as far afield as Pakistan and Mexico – each day.
Other location C/Atocha 12, Huertas (91 369 73 73).

Ojalá

C/San Andrés 1 (91 523 27 47, www.grupo lamusa.com/restaurante-ojala). Metro Noviciado or Tribunal. **Open** 9am-midnight Mon-Wed; 9am-1.30am Thur; 9am-2am Fri; 11am-2am Sat; 11am-midnight Sun. **Main courses** €10-€17. **Credit** MC, V. **Map** p307 G9 🇬🇷 **Global**
A shabby-chic restaurant with staff to match. The food is a cosmopolitan hotch-potch of designer salads, hefty meat boards and Middle Eastern treats. Waiters are friendly, the food is well presented and the seating comfortable. Below the main dining room is a bar that resembles a beach cove with an industrial twist: sand coats the floor and harsh craggy bricks are framed by steel pipes on the walls, on to which old black-and-white movies are occasionally projected.

Siam

C/San Bernardino 6 (91 559 83 15). Metro Noviciado or Plaza de España. **Open** noon-4.30pm, 8pm-midnight daily. **Main courses** €8.90-€20. **Set lunch** €15. **Credit** AmEx, DC, MC, V. **Map** p307 F9 🇬🇷 **Thai**

Texan David Haynes has poured his heart and the experience of years spent in Thailand into this restaurant, and the investment has paid off. Authenticity is his thing (please don't ask for bread) and he imports vegetables and spices that he can't get hold of in the city. Try the spicy Thai green curry, or just ask him to recommend a dish. There is also a fabulous range of cocktails and special teas.

★ Subiendo al Sur

C/Ponciano 5 (91 548 11 47, www.subiendo alsur.org). Metro Noviciado or Plaza de España. **Open** *Food served* 2-5pm Mon; 2-5pm, 9pm-midnight Tue-Sat. **Main courses** €11-€13. **No credit cards. Map** p307 F9 🇬🇷 **International**
Easily missed, this co-operative fair trade café-restaurant and shop is a gem. All profits go to good causes, and the charming co-owners take turns in the kitchen, lending ideas from their home country to the daily-changing menu. A wide selection of *empanadas* and pastries sit alongside Zambian *babotie,* Peruvian ceviche, Brazilian *moqueca,* and kebabs. Highly recommended. *Photo p105.*

★ Taberna Agrado

C/Ballesta 1 (91 521 63 46). Metro Gran Vía or Callao. **Open** 2-4pm, 9-11pm Mon-Sat. **Main courses** €14.50-€22. **Set lunch** €12.50. **Credit** MC, V. **Map** p307 H10 🇬🇷 **Global**
Named after a character in Pedro Almodóvar's film *The Flower of My Secret,* Agrado opened in early 2010 and immediately caused a bit of a stir. It's located on an unpromising street just off Gran Vía, but the area is undergoing a bit of a renaissance. The

CONSUME

Bar Tomate. *See p109.*

Restaurants

chef, Byron Canning, is British, with experience in some of London and Madrid's top restaurants. Behind the bar, Hector Monroy shakes up some mean cocktails. The speciality is the melt-in-the-mouth beef and Iberian pork hamburger. There's also octopus carpaccio and, of course, fish and chips.

★ La Tasquita de Enfrente

C/Ballesta 6 (91 532 54 49, www.latasquita deenfrente.com). Metro Gran Vía or Callao. **Open** 1.30-3.30pm, 8.30-11pm Mon-Sat. Closed Aug. **Main courses** €20-€30. **Credit** AmEx, DC, MC, V. **Map** p307 H10 **66** Spanish
One of Madrid's best restaurants, La Tasquita de Enfrente is run by Juanjo López Bedmar, a former executive who chucked it all in to devote himself to cooking. There are only half a dozen tables, so you need to book well ahead. The menu changes according to what is best at any given time, but don't miss the *pochas* (white beans) with clams, if they're avail-

able. Also fabulous are the squid gnocchi, and the slow-cooked acorn-fed Iberian pork cheeks. But the best idea is to go for the special menu of the day.

Toma

C/Conde Duque 14 (91 547 49 96). Metro Noviciado or Plaza de España. **Open** 9pm-12.30am Tue-Fri; 1-4pm, 9pm-12.30am Sat, Sun. Closed 1wk end Dec, 1wk Jan. **Main courses** €16-€20. **Credit** MC, V. **Map** p307 F9 **67** International
A tiny restaurant with cherry-red walls and an informal feel, Toma has quickly become a real favourite of the neighbourhood. Its homely, laid-back atmosphere can make the prices seem rather high, especially if you end up having to sit at the bar. But the food is commensurately good. From duck magret with pak choi to tuna tartare with lemon and soy, or rack of lamb with honey and mustard, the preparation is equally assured. If it's available, be sure to finish with the creamy cappuccino cheesecake.

DiverXO. See p110.

CONSUME

THE RETIRO & SALAMANCA

Casa Portal
C/Doctor Castelo 26 (91 574 20 26, www.casa-portal.com). Metro Goya. **Open** 1.30-4.30pm, 8.30-11pm Mon-Sat. Closed Aug. **Main courses** €12.40-€43.20. **Credit** AmEx, MC, V. **Map** p309 O11 ⑥ **Spanish**
Casa Portal specialises in all things traditional from Asturias, hence the mountain of cheeses in the window and the cider being poured from a great height. Apart from cider, this spot has been serving *fabada* (an Asturian bean stew with chorizo), tortilla, fish and shellfish for more than 50 years. Choose between the bar at the front and the dining room behind.

OTHER DISTRICTS

Asador Donostiarra
C/Infanta Mercedes 79, Tetuán (91 579 08 71, www.asadordonostiarra.com). Metro Tetuán. **Open** 1-4pm, 9pm-midnight Mon-Sat; 1-4pm Sun. **Main courses** €20.50-€39.50. **Credit** AmEx, DC, MC, V. **Steakhouse**
If you love meat and you love Real Madrid, you may want to splurge on a night out at the once-preferred *asador* (steakhouse) of David Beckham and the rest of the team, located near the Bernabéu stadium. The celeb crowd is as legendary as the *solomillo*, and they often give away signed photos and other goodies from the team. Dissenting voices say that all the press has had an adverse effect, and the run-of-the-mill salad, steak and potato offerings are not commensurate with the hefty prices; others still claim it's the best *asador* in Madrid.

Bar Tomate
C/Fernando El Santo 26, Chamberí (91 702 38 70, www.grupotragaluz.com). Metro Colón. **Open** 8.30am-midnight Mon-Wed, Sun; 8.30am-2.30am Thur-Sat. Closed Sun Aug. **Main courses** €8-€10. **Credit** MC, V. **Map** p308 K8 ⑥ **Mediterranean**
Open all day, this establishment is great for breakfast, a snack, lunch or dinner. Part of the wildly successful Tragaluz group, which has several restaurants in Barcelona, Bar Tomate specialises in light and tasty Mediterranean cuisine, such as gorgonzola croquettes, anchovies and red piquillo peppers on toast, asparagus tempura and individual tortillas. There are good deals available at breakfast time, with a selection of little rolls and pastries, and later on you can have cocktails. *Photo p107.*

★ Casa Mingo
Paseo de la Florida 34, Casa de Campo (91 547 79 18, www.casamingo.es). Metro Príncipe Pío. **Open** 11am-midnight daily. **Main courses** €4-€15. **No credit cards**. **Map** p306 B9 ⑦ **Spanish**
A vast and noisy Asturian cider house, open since 1888. This is a great opportunity to rub elbows with *madrileños* really enjoying themselves at one of the

Santceloni. *See p110.*

CONSUME

long wooden tables. The restaurant does only three things: roast chicken, salad and cider. Turn up before the city gets hungry (around 1.30pm) if you want a terrace seat, or take out a chicken and a bottle of cider and head for the River Manzanares for a picnic. At other times, expect to queue.

El Comité

Plaza de San Amaro 8, Chamartín (91 571 87 11). Metro Santiago Bernabéu. **Open** 1.30-4.30pm, 9pm-1am Mon-Fri; 9pm-1am Sat. Closed 1wk Aug. **Main courses** €18-€37. **Credit** AmEx, DC, MC, V. French

Yes, it's out of the way and has the feel of an elite club, but this somehow enhances the appeal. A romantic French restaurant offering exceptionally good food at a price, El Comité also offers the chance to see Madrid's discreetly elegant top people at play. Great starters include Harry's Bar carpaccio and a tempura of langoustines; a main course highlight is the steak tartare, and the snails *bourguignonne* are legendary. A classic.

★ DiverXO

C/Pensamiento 28, Tetuán (91 570 07 66, www.diverxo.com). Metro Tetuán. **Open** 2-4pm, 9-11.30pm Tue-Sat. Closed 3wks Aug. **Tasting menus** €104, €154. **Credit** AmEx, MC, V. Modern Spanish/Asian.

A gastronomic temple in the heart of an unprepossessing residential neighbourhood, DiverXO offers some of the most exciting food in the country at the hands of wunderkind chef David Muñoz. The restaurant's aesthetic is a minimalist one – glass, steel and black paintwork – in contrast to dishes such as yoghurt, strawberry and coffee kimchi with cuttlefish or tortilla 'dim sum'. You'll need to book a few weeks in advance. *Photos p108.*

La Favorita

C/Covarrubias 25, Chamberí (91 448 38 10, www.restaurante-lafavorita.com). Metro Alonso Martínez or Bilbao. **Open** 1.30-4pm, 9pm-midnight Mon, Tue, Thur, Fri; 12.30-4pm, 9pm-midnight Wed; 9pm-midnight Sat. **Main courses** €20-€24. **Set lunch** €15. **Credit** AmEx, DC, MC, V. **Map** p308 I7 ⓩ Spanish

Opera fanatic Javier Otero converted this charming 1920s mansion into a restaurant and filled it with singing waiters – conservatoire students or artists just starting out on their careers. It's a surprisingly fun way to dine. And the food, made using fresh ingredients from Navarra, also hits a high note. Reservations are essential.

El Olivo

C/General Gallegos 1, Chamartín (91 359 15 35/359 03 52). Metro Cuzco. **Open** 1.30-4pm Mon; 1.30-4pm, 9pm-midnight Tue-Sat. Closed last 2wks Aug. **Main courses** €18-€35. **Credit** AmEx, DC, MC, V. Mediterranean

This old-school Mediterranean restaurant still ranks high with more discriminating gastronomes. Olive oil is the keystone: the kindly, very formal waiters wheel a cart of bottles over to the table for you to sample with bread; only the best is used for cooking, and there is even olive oil ice-cream (surprisingly good). Specialities include the lobster and herb salad, the *solomillo* with foie, and a fine tarte tatin.

Santceloni

Hotel Hesperia Madrid, Paseo de la Castellana 57 (91 210 88 40, www.restaurantesantceloni. com). Metro Gregorio Marañón. **Open** 2-4pm, 9-11pm Mon-Fri; 9-11pm Sat. Closed Aug. **Main courses** €37-€65. **Credit** AmEx, DC, MC, V. **Map** p305 K5 ⓯ Spanish

Named after the village where the famed Barcelona restaurateur Santi Santamaria was born, and run by his protégé Oscar Velasco, the Santceloni won its first Michelin star in less than a year. The menu changes frequently to make the most of the best seasonal ingredients, but might include crab in sherry with creamed onion and celery, or one of Santamaria's trademark dishes: ravioli of sliced raw prawn with a filling of ceps. The tasting menu will set you back a pretty penny, but it's a chance to relish the talents of one of Spain's celebrity chefs. *Photos p109.*

Sergi Arola Gastro

C/Zurbano 31, Chamberí (91 310 21 69, www. sergiarola.es). Metro Rubén Dario. **Open** 2-3.30pm, 9-11.30pm Mon-Fri; 9-11.30pm Sat. Closed 3wks Aug, 2wks Dec. **Main courses** €43-€52. **Credit** AmEx, DC, MC, V. **Map** p308 J7 ⓭ Spanish

This is the flagship restaurant of Sergi Arola, one of Spain's top chefs, and has two Michelin stars. There is no menu as such, just a fixed range of courses that changes according to seasonal availability. The art deco dining room makes a change from the bland beigeness of Arola's previous premises at the Hotel Miguel Angel. His wife, Sara, runs the front of house with sommelier Daniel Poveda and barman Diego Cabrera, who mixes fierce cocktails in the downstairs lounge. Together, they make quite a team.

Sudestada

C/Ponzano 85, Chamberí (91 533 41 54). Metro Ríos Rosas or Cuatro Caminos. **Open** 1-4pm, 9.30pm-midnight Mon-Sat. **Main courses** €15-€23.50. **Credit** MC, V. Asian

Run by young Argentines with a passion for Asian food, Sudestada is the new Madrid branch of a Buenos Aires favourite. In its short life it has already received a hugely respected Spanish restaurant award, and it's packed out every night. Given the authentic spiciness of its curries – from all over South-east Asia – this gives the lie to the idea that Spanish diners prefer their food bland. Less *picante* options include Vietnamese rolls and dim sum from Singapore. Reserve ahead, especially at weekends.

Tapas

The world on a plate.

In their more fanciful moments, Spaniards will describe them as 'the world on a plate'. They will tell you that the eating of tapas is proof of the country's gregarious nature, its need to share and the importance it places on spending time in good company. Thanks to the *tapa*, it's possible to spend the whole night in a bar without requiring help to get home. This is the point so often missed by those outside the country, those who reproduce them for dinner parties or nibble them in expensive restaurants in London. For the Spanish, it's not about what you eat, it's about how you eat.

TAPAS TRADITIONS

Tapas vary from region to region, and examples of most can be found in Madrid. Galician bars highlight octopus, prawns and seafood, served in ceramic bowls, traditionally with white Ribeiro wine. In Extremaduran bars you'll find *migas* (crumbs), fried and mixed with chorizo. Asturian bars specialise in cider (*sidra*), theatrically poured from above the head to separate out sediment, accompanied by blood sausage (*morcilla*) or blue cabrales cheese. Andalucían bars offer dry *fino* sherry with *mojama* (dry-cured tuna) or sardines. Madrid's own specialities are *patatas bravas*, offal (particularly *callos*, tripe), and snails in a hot sauce.

Tapas have become more sophisticated and consequently more expensive in recent times, and an evening's *tapeo* can cost more than a full meal in a restaurant.

LOS AUSTRIAS & LA LATINA

El Almendro 13

C/Almendro 13 (91 365 42 52). Metro La Latina. **Open** 1-4pm, 7.30pm-12.30am Mon-Thur; 1-4pm, 7.30pm-1am Fri; 1-5pm, 8pm-1am Sat; 1-5pm, 8pm-12.30am Sun. **No credit cards. Map** p311 F13 ❶
A sleepy, traditional bar during the week, it hots up at weekends, and drinkers often drift on to the pavements. A peculiar speciality is the *rosca*, a sort of oversized, filled bagel. These are invariably accompanied by a glass of the house *manzanilla*.

Bodegas Ricla

C/Cuchilleros 6 (91 365 20 69). Metro Ópera. **Open** 12.30-3.30pm, 7pm-midnight Mon-Thur; 12.30-3.30pm, 7.30pm-1am Fri; 12.30-4pm, 7.30pm-1am Sat; 1-5pm Sun. **No credit cards. Map** p311 F12 ❷
A tiny, bright and friendly mother-and-son operation, Bodegas Ricla does a great line in garlicky *boquerones* and an incongruous one in soft rock. Cheap but good wine and sherry are available by the litre, poured from tall clay urns, or there is vermouth on tap. Also worth trying are the *cecina* (thin slices of cured venison) and cabrales cheese in cider.

La Casa de las Torrijas

C/Paz 4 (91 532 14 73). Metro Sol. **Open** 10am-4pm, 6-10pm Mon-Sat. Closed Aug. **No credit cards. Map** p311 G12 ❸
Formerly known as the As de los Vinos, this is a charmingly unkempt bar, tiled and mirrored, with table-tops constructed from old enamel adverts. Since 1907, it has served little more than *torrijas* – bread soaked in wine and spices, coated in sugar and deep-fried – and house wine. If that doesn't appeal, there are a handful of other, simple tapas, along with a basic set lunch.

★ Juanalaloca

Plaza Puerta de Moros 4 (91 364 05 25). Metro La Latina. **Open** 7pm-midnight Mon; 1-5pm, 7pm-midnight Tue-Thur; 1-5pm, 7pm-1am Fri; 1pm-1am Sat; 1pm-midnight Sun. **No credit cards. Map** p311 E13 ❹

❶ Yellow numbers given in this chapter correspond to the location of each bar as marked on the street maps. *See pp305-313.*

CONSUME

La Torre del Oro.

Where the hip go to *tapear*, this Uruguayan-run tapas bar attracts a stylish mix of Argentinians, Uruguayans, locals and tourists. It's kind of pricey, but offers undeniably creative cooking – such as wild mushroom and truffle croquettes and tuna carpaccio with almond oil and rice. Its tortilla is also renowned.

★ Taberna Matritum

C/Cava Alta 17 (91 365 82 37, www.matritum.es). *Metro La Latina.* **Open** 8.30pm-12.30am Tue; 1-4.30pm, 8.30pm-12.30am Wed-Sun. **Credit** DC, MC, V. **Map** p311 F13 ❺

Its name is Latin for 'Madrid', but Matritum has a great selection of tapas and wine from other regions of Spain, principally Catalonia. Try the *gambas all cremat* (prawns with burnt garlic) or fabulous canapés such as cabrales cheese with apple compôte. The wine list, too, is dominated by Catalan labels, with many notably good bottles from the Penedes.

INSIDE TRACK SUNDAY BEST

In Madrid, Sunday feels like Friday and preparing for Monday isn't given much thought; *madrileños* like to squeeze the most out of their weekends, hence the Sunday post-Rastro drinking tradition in La Latina. On sunny days, the area's squares brim with hedonism. On rainy days, the best bars burst with drinking, talking *madrileños*. The essence of the tradition is vermouth, and the whole ritual, tapas and all, is sometimes known as '*haciendo el vermut*' – 'doing vermouth'.

Taberna Según Emma

C/Conde de Miranda 4 (91 559 08 97, www. emmacocina.com). Metro Ópera. **Open** 1-4.30pm, 8pm-midnight Mon-Thur, Sun; 1-4.30pm, 8pm-12.30am Fri, Sat. **Credit** AmEx, DC, MC, V. **Map** p311 F12 ❻

Step down into this small, lively space with lime-green walls and wooden tables – run by thirtysomethings for thirtysomethings. It used to be an Asturian bar and cheeses from the region along with favourites such as clams with haricot beans remain, alongside newer tapas offerings.

El Tempranillo

C/Cava Baja 38 (91 364 15 32). Metro La Latina. **Open** 8pm-midnight Mon; 1-4pm, 8pm-midnight Tue-Sun. Closed 3wks Aug. **Credit** MC, V. **Map** p311 F13 ❼

Never less than rowdy, decorated in bullring ochre and bare brick, with flamenco on the sound system, El Tempranillo offers an impressive range of labels from nearly every wine-producing region in Spain. The tapas are addictive too: try the wild mushrooms in scrambled egg or the sweetbreads.

La Torre del Oro

Plaza Mayor 26 (91 366 50 16). Metro Sol. **Open** 12.30pm-1am daily. **Credit** AmEx, DC, MC, V. **Map** p311 F12 ❽

It's smack on the Plaza Mayor, so don't expect any bargains, especially if you sit out in the square, but this Andalucian bar is the real deal, with bullfighting memorabilia and incomprehensible waiters. If you can understand and make yourself understood, ask for prawns or whitebait (*pescaítos*), and accompany them with a cold, dry *fino*.

Tapas Glossary

A primer of the classics.

There are three basic sizes of *tapa* portion: a *pincho* (more or less a mouthful), a *tapa* (a saucerful or so) and a *ración* (a small plateful). Some bars offer *media raciones* (a half-*ración*). If there's something you like the look of that isn't identifiable on the menu or the list behind the bar, just point to it. Bread (*pan*) normally comes automatically, but if not, just ask. Most often, you let a tapas bill mount up and pay when you've finished, not when you order; it's usually about 25 per cent more expensive if you sit at a table rather than eat at the bar. For more food terms, *see pp94-95*.

BASICS
Bocadillo sandwich in a roll or part of a French loaf; **cazuelita** small hot casserole; **montados** canapé-style mixed tapas, often a slice of bread with a topping; **pincho/ pinchito** small titbit on a toothpick, or mouthful-sized *tapa*; **pulga/pulguita** small filled roll; **ración** a portion (small plateful); **tabla** platter (of cheese, cold meats); **tosta** slice of toast with topping; **una de gambas, chorizo...** one portion of prawns, chorizo...; **por unidad** per item.

CARNE, AVES Y EMBUTIDOS (MEAT, POULTRY & CHARCUTERIE)
Albóndigas meat balls; **alitas de pollo** chicken wings; **callos** tripe; **cecina** dry-cured beef; **chistorra** Navarrese sausage with paprika; **chorizo** spicy sausage, eaten cooked or cold; **criadillas** bulls' testicles; **flamenquines** ham and pork rolls in breadcrumbs; **longaniza, fuet** mild but chewy, often herby, salami-type sausages; **mollejas** sweetbreads; **morcilla** a black, blood sausage; **oreja (de cerdo)** pig's ear; **pincho moruno** grilled meat brochette; **riñones al Jerez** kidneys cooked in sherry; **salchichón** a large, fatty, soft, salami-type sausage; **San Jacobo** fried ham and cheese escalope; **sobrassada** soft Mallorcan paprika sausage; **torrezno** pork crackling; **zarajo** grilled sheep's intestine on a stick.

PESCADO Y MARISCOS (FISH & SHELLFISH)
Ahumados smoked fish; **almejas** clams; **anchoas** salted conserved anchovies; **anguilas** eels; **angulas** elvers; **berberechos** cockles; **bienmesabe** marinated fried fish; **boquerones en vinagre/fritos** pickled/fried fresh anchovies; **calamares a la romana** squid rings fried in batter; **calamares en su tinta** squid cooked in their ink; **carabineiros** large red ocean prawns; **centollo** spider crab; **chanquetes** tiny fish, served deep-fried; **chipirones en su tinta** small Atlantic squid in their ink; **chopito** small cuttlefish; **cigalas** crayfish; **croqueta de bacalao** salt cod croquette; **fritura de pescado** flash-fried fish; **gambas al ajillo** prawns fried with garlic; **gambas en gabardina** prawns deep-fried in batter; **huevas** fish roe; **mojama** dried and salted tuna fish; **navajas** razor clams; **nécora** swimming crab; **percebes** goose-neck barnacles; **pulpo a feira/a la gallega** octopus with paprika and olive oil; **quisquillas** shrimps; **salpicón** cold chopped salad, often with some shellfish; **sepia** large squid; **soldaditos de pavía** strips of salt cod, fried in light batter; **tigres** mussels cooked with a spicy tomato and béchamel sauce; **zamburiñas** small scallops.

VEGETALES (VEGETABLE TAPAS)
Aceitunas, olivas (adobados, rellenos) olives (pickled, stuffed); **almendras saladas** salted almonds; **pan con tomate** bread rubbed with fresh tomato and olive oil; **patatas bravas** deep-fried potatoes with hot pepper sauce; **perdiz de huerta** lettuce hearts; **pimientos de Padrón** fried, and occasionally hot small green peppers; **queso en aceite** cheese marinated in olive oil; **setas** wild mushrooms.

OTHER TAPAS
Caracoles snails; **croquetas** potato croquettes (which may be made with chicken, ham, tuna, and so on); **empanada** flat pies, usually made with a tuna filling; **empanadilla** small fried pasties, usually with a tomato and tuna filling; **ensaladilla rusa** potato salad with onions, red peppers, usually tuna and other ingredients in mayonnaise, now a completely Spanish dish that's still called a Russian salad; **huevos rellenos** stuffed cold hard-boiled eggs; **migas (con huevo frito)** fried bread-crumbs (with fried egg); **pisto manchego** ratatouille with meat (usually ham) and egg; **revuelto** scrambled eggs.

Txirimiri

C/Humilladero 6 (91 364 11 96, www.txirimiri.es).
Metro La Latina. **Open** noon-12.30am Mon-
Thur, Sun; noon-1am Fri, Sat. **Credit** MC, V.
Map p311 F13 ⑨

The popular Txirimiri specialises in Basque *pintxos*,
and despite its aspirational-sounding tag line of
'haute cuisine in miniature', it's a laid-back, friendly
place, and always rammed on a Sunday. The thirtysomething crowd is drawn by the excellent, well-
priced tapas (don't miss the croquettes and ravioli)
and sociable atmosphere. There's a restaurant area
at the far end.
Other location C/General Diez Porlier 91,
Salamanca (91 401 43 45).

SOL & GRAN VÍA

Casa Labra

C/Tetuán 12 (91 531 00 81). Metro Sol. **Open**
9.30am-3.30pm, 5.30-11pm daily. **Credit** AmEx,
DC, MC, V. **Map** p311 G11 ⑩

Famously the birthplace of the Spanish Socialist
Party back in 1879, this legendary bar, with its brown
1950s paintwork and luggage racks, is worth a visit
for its history alone. Speciality of the house is the cod
croquetas served up by dour white-jacketed waiters.

El Escarpín

*C/Hileras 17 (91 559 99 57, www.sidreriaelescarpin.
com). Metro Ópera or Sol.* **Open** 9am-midnight

Profile Mercado de San Miguel

The recession-defying overhaul of Madrid's most venerable market.

One of Madrid's biggest success
stories of recent times, the
Mercado de San Miguel (www.
mercadodesanmiguel.es) is
the daily food market/tapas
emporium in Plaza de San Miguel,
immediately south-west of the
Plaza Mayor, which reopened its
polished-up glass doors in 2009
after a decade-long restoration.
The 1915 wrought-iron and glass
structure, with boutique-style food
stands inside, has created a new
culinary buzz in the city; the place
is often heaving at lunchtimes
and in the evening, and it
continues in this vein until well
after midnight (when you can
nab bargain tapas). Some say
it's lost some of its original soul
and that it's overpriced, yet the
slick operation – one of the few
covered markets in the city –
is always rammed with smart-
looking *madrileños* and tourists
enjoying *bacalao pinchos* (salt cod
on bruschetta), oysters, tortillas,
wine, sherry, vermouth and, just
as important, conversation.

Have a wander round the
market to check out the different
options before you make your
choices, and then take your
tapas selection to one of the
perches or tables in the centre.
It's difficult to make a bad choice
here with so many delicious
options, but there are some
essential don't-miss highlights.

An excellent starting point is
also one of San Miguel's best-
loved spots: **El Yantar de Ayer**
(www.elyantardeayer.es), a
four-shop affair specialising in
aperitifs – namely vermouth and
sherry – and nibbles with which
to accompany them. With 15
different types of *vermút*, it's an
excellent place to initiate yourself
in the quintessential *madrileño*
tradition. Sherry – known in Spain
simply as *vino de Jerez* – is also
taken seriously here. Whichever
tipple you go for, be sure to
accompany it with some
encurtidos (pickles) to help
lessen the alcoholic punch.

Once you've whet your appetite
here, you'll want to move on
to more solid fodder. Saltcod
specialist **La Casa de Bacalao**,
just along from El Yantar, offers
some of the market's most

Mon-Thur, Sun; 11.30am-1am Fri, Sat. **Credit** (over €10) MC, V. **Map** p311 F11 ⓫

So vast that you'll always find a seat, this Asturian cider bar has the look – bare bricks and long wooden tables – to go with the regional tapas. Natural cider (*sidra*) should be followed by *lacón* (gammon), *fabada asturiana* (bean and pork stew) or chorizo.

HUERTAS & SANTA ANA

Alhambra

C/Victoria 9 (91 521 07 08, http://taberna alhambra.es). Metro Sol. **Open** 11am-1.30am Mon-Wed, Sun; 11am-2am Thur; 11am-2.30am Fri, Sat. **Credit** DC, MC, V. **Map** p311 H12 ⓬

Named after Granada's magical palace and done up in suitably Andaluz-Moorish style, this is a pretty and peaceful spot during the day, serving basic tapas along with oxtail stew and gazpacho, and a simple set lunch. It's a different place at night, though; awash with Spanish pop, techno and hormones.

La Bardemcilla de Santa Ana

C/Núñez de Arce 3 (91 523 11 63, www.la bardemcilla.com). Metro Sol. **Open** 1-5pm, 8pm-2am Tue-Fri; 1-5pm, 8pm-2.30am Sat, Sun. **Credit** AmEx, DC, MC, V. **Map** p312 H12 ⓭

A fun, mellow place, owned by the royal family of Spanish cinema, the Bardems. There are filmic references everywhere, from the cinema posters on the

popular tapas: *pinchos* (small rounds of toast) topped with puréed *bacalao* in a range of different guises, such as with caviar. At €1 per *pincho*, it's tempting to order several, but be sure to save room for the market's other temptations.

Two more stands not to be missed are upmarket **Lhardy**, on the opposite side to La Casa de Bacalao, and, a little way along, the oyster stand. A classic Spanish tortilla from Lhardy will set you back €7, but rest assured it's the real deal. The traditional food store also sells a tempting range of *empanadas*, quiches and meals.

Ostra Sorlut (www.ostrasorlut.com), meanwhile, is a great spot in which to undertake the oyster rite of passage, or, if you're already an aficionado, to enjoy the slippery molluscs (€1.20-€2.50) in suitably salubrious surroundings, knocked back with a cold glass of white wine.

La Alacena de Victor Montes *croquetas* stand is a stall on wheels that's always to be found somewhere in the market – it sells Basque croquettes (filled with salt cod, mushroom, leek and

so on, at €1 each), either ready to eat, or uncooked to take home.

Spanish tapas tend to be fairly heavy, with copious quantities of oil. For a lighter snack, there's **Sushimarket**, next to Lhardy; sushi is becoming more popular in the city as locals have steadily expanded their culinary horizons. Just around the corner from here, there's the equally healthy **Jugosa** juice stall, selling *licuados* (smoothies), *batidos* (milkshakes), lassi and gazpacho. If you want to go in a distinctly unhealthy vein, however, head to the opposite corner. Here you'll find a little block of tempting bakeries, including the **Horno San Onofre**, offering artisanal ice-cream, with original flavours, such as cava and lemon, as well as meringues, sugared almonds and more. Next door, the **Horno La Santiaguesa** is the place for chocolate from Valrhona, and classic *madrileño* churros.

Whichever option you go for, the market is an excellent place to people-watch and marvel at *madrileños* doing what they do best: enjoying food in a civilised fashion, and being social – as if it were a duty, a passion and a performance, all rolled into one.

CONSUME

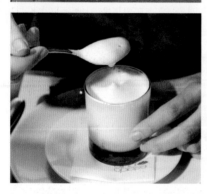

beer head with five founts. Try lambs' trotters, gar-licky prawns, *morcilla* (black pudding) with goat's cheese, or oxtail stew as tapas, or as more substan-tial dishes in the restaurant at the back.

La Casa del Abuelo

C/Victoria 12 (91 121 23 19). Metro Sol. **Open** noon-midnight Mon-Thur, Sun; noon-1am Fri, Sat. **Credit** AmEx, MC, V. **Map** p311 H12
For over a century, the Casa del Abuelo has stuck to one very simple, and winning, formula – prawns and small *chatos* of slightly sweet red wine served in bright, old-school surroundings. The surprisingly drinkable red is for sale by the bottle (€8.90) and when it's over you can even buy the T-shirt.
Other locations C/Goya 57, Salamanca (91 000 01 33); C/Nuñez de Arce 5, Santa Ana (91 000 01 33).

Estado Puro

C/San Sebastian 2 (91 429 98 17, www.tapas enestadopuro.com). Metro Sol. **Open** 1pm-midnight Mon-Thur, Sun; 1pm-2am Fri, Sat. **Credit** AmEx, DC, MC, V. **Map** p312 H12
Chef Paco Roncero mans the kitchen at this NH Hotel initiative , which turns out classic tapas with a mod-ern twist, from fancy takes on *patatas bravas* to deconstructed tortilla. The cool, black interior evokes an upmarket diner while riffing on the trad Spanish theme, with a wave of white mantilla combs arranged artfully overhead and a thousand flamenco dolls in an eruption of kitsch behind the glass of the counter.

La Fábrica

C/Jesús 2 (91 369 06 71). Metro Antón Martin or Sevilla. **Open** 11am-1am Mon-Thur, Sun; 11am-2am Fri, Sat. **No credit cards. Map** p312 I13
There are long, long lists of the canapés on offer, but most are on display. Try the *matrimonio* (preserved and fresh anchovies – the perfect combination) or the *divorcio* (anchovies and mussels – no kind of match), or the *orgia* (all three). Ahem.

★ Los Gatos

C/Jesús 2 (91 429 30 67). Metro Antón Martin or Sevilla. **Open** 11am-1am Mon-Thur, Sun; 11am-2am Fri, Sat. **Credit** AmEx, MC, V. **Map** p312 I13
With their reputation for staying out all night, *madrileños* are popularly known as 'los gatos' (the cats) and there's nowhere better than here to begin a night prowling the tiles. The bar is hung with all manner of paraphernalia from gramophones to choirboy mannequins – here you can get a selection of tasty canapés, and a good frothy beer.

La Platería

C/Moratín 49 (91 429 17 22). Metro Antón Martín. **Open** 7.30am-1am Mon-Fri; 9am-2.30am Sat, Sun. **Credit** MC, V. **Map** p312 J13
Everything from the smoked salmon and red pep-pers to *caldo gallego*, grilled asparagus or baked potatoes with eggs and garlic, is available in half

walls to the names of the tapas. *Jamón, Jamón* is *cro-quetas*; *Victor o Victória* is gazpacho or consommé, depending on the season.

★ Casa Alberto

C/Huertas 18 (91 429 93 56, www.casaalberto.es). Metro Antón Martín. **Open** noon-12.30am Tue-Sat; noon-4pm Sun. Closed Aug & 2wks Xmas. **Credit** AmEx, DC, MC, V. **Map** p312 H12
One of the city's most evocative *tabernas*, hung with oil paintings and presided over by a septuagenarian. It still has its old zinc bar complete with running water trough to keep the wine cool and a draught

An accidental invention, tapas originated in Andalucía and were originally pieces of ham or chorizo that were placed on top of the plate, or slice of bread, used to cover a glass of wine and keep out the dust and flies. The word *tapa*, in fact, means 'lid'. The idea became widely established during the 19th century, with the principal objective of making the customer thirsty in order to sell more drinks. The tapas boom really took off, however, in the 1940s after the Civil War, when many of Madrid's existing bars first appeared.

portions, so this is a perfect place for a quick snack 'twixt two of the big three museums. The bar is rather cramped, but there are tables outside.

Taberna de Conspiradores

C/Moratín 33 (91 369 4741, www.conspiradores. com). Metro Antón Martín. **Open** noon-1am daily. **Credit** AmEx, MC, V. **Map** p312 I13 ⑳
The food, wine and liqueurs on offer here are all from Extremadura, unusually. The speciality is *migas* – fried breadcrumbs baked with sausage, garlic and pancetta – and a dense venison stew. The small space is lined with black-and-white Magnum photographs, and occasionally hosts world music or flamenco gigs.

★ Taberna La Dolores

Plaza de Jesús 4 (91 429 22 43). Metro Antón Martín. **Open** 11am-1am Mon-Thur, Sun; 11am-2am Fri, Sat. **Credit** MC, V. **Map** p312 I12 ㉑
A Madrid classic, with wonderful tiling outside and rows of dusty beer steins inside, La Dolores has been serving ice-cold frothy beer since the 1920s. There's a short list of tapas, which are good if a bit expensive. Specialities are smoked fish, anchovies and *mojama* (wind-dried tuna).

Vinoteca Barbechera

C/Príncipe 27 (91 420 04 78). Metro Antón Martín or Sevilla. **Open** 10am-1am Mon-Thur, Sun; noon-2am Fri, Sat. **Credit** AmEx, MC, V. **Map** p312 H12 ㉒
It looks a lot grander than it is, which is not to say that the tapas aren't good, just that the bill is a pleasant surprise in these rather lofty surroundings. *Pinchos* include smoked salmon with cream cheese, cabrales with quince jelly and goose liver with apple. **Other location** C/Gravina 6, Chueca (91 523 98 16).

RASTRO & LAVAPIÉS

Café Melo's

C/Ave María 44 (91 527 50 54). Metro Lavapiés. **Open** 8pm-1.30am Tue-Sat. Closed Aug. **No credit cards. Map** p312 H14 ㉓
It's got all the aesthetic charm of a kebab shop, but this bright little bar is something of a classic. It's famous for its *zapatillas* – huge, open sandwiches (the word, like ciabatta, means 'slipper') with a

CONSUME

Mercado de San Antón. See p118.

variety of toppings. A big favourite for late-night munchies with the bohemian element of the *barrio*.

Casa Amadeo Los Caracoles

Plaza de Cascorro 18 (91 365 94 39). Metro La Latina. **Open** 11am-4pm, 7-10pm Tue-Sat; 10am-4.30pm Sun. **No credit cards. Map** p311 F14 ㉔
Again, this is no looker, but it's a popular post-Rastro stop. Its specialities include the eponymous snails in spicy sauce, knuckle of ham, and *zarajo*, the lamb's intestines wrapped round sticks, without which your Madrid trip would not be complete.

Casa de Granada

C/Doctor Cortezo 17 (91 420 08 25). Metro Tirso de Molina. **Open** noon-midnight daily. **Credit** AmEx, DC, MC, V. **Map** p311 G/H13 ㉕
A very ordinary bar serving very ordinary food, which has an extraordinary view. To get in, ring the buzzer on street level, and then ride the lift all the way up to the sixth floor – in summer you'll have to fight tooth and nail for a seat on the terrace.

La Casa de las Tostas

C/Argumosa 29 (91 527 08 42). Metro Lavapiés. **Open** noon-midnight daily. **Credit** MC, V. **Map** p312 I15 ㉖
Welcome to the House of Toast. Toast with scrambled eggs, prawns and wild mushrooms; toast with salmon in white vermouth; toast with gammon and melted cheese; toast with anchovies and roquefort; toast with cod pâté. And most importantly, toast with wine, many available by the glass.

Los Hermanos

C/Rodas 28 (91 468 33 13). Metro Tirso de Molina. **Open** 6am-11pm Mon-Sat; 6am-5pm Sun. Closed Aug. **Credit** V. **Map** p311 G14 ㉗
Just off the main drag of the Rastro, this bar has a strong neighbourhood feel, generous complimentary tapas, a huge range of *raciones* and a great range of *bocadillos*, including a hangover-busting bacon and egg. On Sundays, there's a well-priced *menú del día* for the market crowd, available in a quieter side room.

La Musa de Espronceda

C/Santa Isabel 17 (91 539 12 84). Metro Antón Martín. **Open** 11am-4pm, 7pm-1am Tue-Sat; noon-4pm Sun. **Credit** DC, MC, V. **Map** p312 I14 ㉘
La Musa is known for its *pinchos* – don't miss the butternut squash, goat's cheese and caramelised onion, or the brie wrapped in bacon. The tortilla is also excellent, while the mojitos are well made and priced. Blackboards, literary posters and globe lights around a central bar lend the place an arty vibe.

★ La Taberna de Antonio Sánchez

C/Mesón de Paredes 13 (91 539 78 26). Metro Tirso de Molina. **Open** noon-4pm, 8pm-midnight Mon-Sat; noon-5pm Sun. **Credit** MC, V. **Map** p311 G13 ㉙

Little changes at this historic bar, from the zinc bar to the bull's head hanging on the wall. Its various owners have all been involved in bullfighting, and *tertulias* of critics, *toreros* and aficionados are still held here. It's local and friendly, with superior tapas (the best bet is the scrumptious salad you get free with a drink).

Taberna El Sur

C/Torrecilla del Leal 12 (91 527 83 40). Metro Antón Martín. **Open** 8pm-midnight Tue-Thur; 1-5pm, 8pm-1am Fri-Sat; 1.30-5pm Sun. **Credit** AmEx, MC, V. **Map** p312 H13 ㉚
Taberna El Sur is named after Victor Erice's seminal film, decorated with cinematic posters and popular with long-haired soulful types returning from the nearby Filmoteca (*see p183*). Juan, the friendly owner, offers an interesting selection of *raciones*: try *ropa vieja* (shredded beef, Cuban style) with fried potatoes or 'Arabian' lentils.

CHUECA

El Bocaíto

C/Libertad 4-6 (91 532 12 19, www.bocaito.com). Metro Chueca. **Open** 1-4pm, 8.30pm-midnight Mon-Fri; 8.30pm-midnight Sat. Closed Aug. **Credit** DC, MC, V. **Map** p308 I11 ㉛
El Bocaíto is film-set traditional, from the bullfight posters and Andalucian ceramics to the old-school tapas and unsmiling, white-jacketed waiters. If you're famous, though, they'll grin for the camera, just as they did with Pedro, Hugh and, goddammit, Mark Knopfler.

★ Mercado de San Antón

C/Augusto Figueroa 24 (91 330 07 30, www.mercadosananton.com). Metro Chueca. **Open** Shops 10am-10pm Mon-Sat. Bars 10am-midnight daily. **Credit** varies. **Map** p308 I10 ㉜
Part gastro market, part tapas village, the covered Mercado de San Antón opened in 2011 and has been rammed with appreciative customers ever since. Stalls selling immaculate produce are on the ground floor, tapas bars specialising in all manner of things, from topped blinis to sushi. are on the next floor, and at the top is a bar-restaurant with a great view over the rooftops. *Photo p117.*

El Tigre

C/Infantas 30 (91 532 00 72). Metro Banco de España or Chueca. **Open** 11am-1am Mon-Thur, Sun; noon-2am Fri, Sat. **Credit** MC, V. **Map** p308 I11 ㉝
If you can actually make it through the door, order a beer or cider and marvel at the hefty tapas that come with it – patatas bravas, *jamón serrano*, tortilla… it's all free, and each plate varies with each round. The bar itself is noisy, smoky and always rammed. **Other locations** C/Infantas 23, Chueca (91 532 02 59); C/Hortaleza 23, Chueca (91 523 13 28).

Casa do Compañeiro.

MALASAÑA & CONDE DUQUE

Albur

C/Manuela Malasaña 15 (91 594 27 33, www. restaurantealbur.com). Metro Bilbao. **Open** 12.30pm-1am Mon-Thur, Sun; noon-2am Fri, Sat. **Credit** MC, V. **Map** p307 H8 ㉞

The speciality is *revueltos* (scrambled egg) with prawns, wild mushrooms and so on, but there's also good ham, chorizo and black pudding, and a variety of decent wines to accompany them. Generally a quiet place, with soothing buttercup-yellow walls, it gets quite lively later on in the evening with a young Malasaña crowd.

★ Casa do Compañeiro

C/San Vicente Ferrer 44 (91 521 57 02). Metro Noviciado. **Open** 1.30pm-2am Mon-Sat. **No credit cards**. **Map** p307 G9 ㉟

A tiny jewel among tapas bars, with wonderful tiling. The tapas are mainly from Galicia, with lots of octopus, gammon, pig's ear and, of course, *caldo gallego*, a broth made with cabbage and pork. A glass of crisp, dry *fino* makes the perfect accompaniment.

La Casta

C/Cristo 1 (91 547 77 40). Metro Noviciado. **Open** 1-4pm, 7pm-1am daily. **No credit cards**. **Map** p307 F8 ㊱

A cool and relaxing tapas bar with gently revolving ceiling fans and terracotta floors. Tapas include smoked cod, trout and salmon, or there are wooden *tablas* spread with cheese or ham. More unusually for Madrid, there is Leffe and Guinness on tap. C/Cristo is pedestrianised and there are some tables outside, but be prepared to be assailed by a mixed bag of buskers.

Conache

C/Santa Barbara 11 (91 522 95 00). Metro Tribunal. **Open** 10am-1am Mon-Thur; 10am-2am Sat; noon-8pm Sun. **Credit** (min €6) AmEx, MC, V. **Map** p307 H9 ㊲

The Conache look is casually hip, even though the bright lighting and fruit machines keep scenesters at bay. The food, however, is absolutely where it's at. Try stir-fried vegetables with prawns, little rolls of venison and apple, or spinach and brie with figs, and be sure to finish with the cheese mousse with fruits of the forest.

INSIDE TRACK FINGER FOOD

Don't be afraid to dispose of the debris (olive stones, prawn shells and screwed-up napkins) by dropping them on the floor, except in the more upmarket places, where you should copy what the locals are doing; and remember that a lot of tapas are designed to be eaten with your fingers.

INSIDE TRACK
PLAZA DE OLAVIDE

Chamberí's Plaza de Olavide is something of a neighbourhood hub, and makes a great place to enjoy tapas alfresco. On summer evenings, the place buzzes with relaxed conversation. Try **Arco Iris** (No.2), renowned for its excellent *tortilla de patata*.

★ El Maño

C/Palma 64 (91 521 50 57). Metro Noviciado. **Open** 7.30pm-12.30am Mon-Thur; 12.30-4.30pm, 7.30pm-1.30am Fri, Sat. **Credit** MC, V. **Map** p307 F8 ⑲

A relaxed place, with french windows opening on to the street in summer, marble-topped tables and bar, faded yellow paintwork and art deco touches. A good selection of wine is chalked up on the walls, some of it poured from ancient barrels, and there are tortillas served with *pisto*, ragu or squid, brochettes of chicken and lamb and a small selection of canapés.

Pez Gordo

C/Pez 6 (91 522 32 08). Metro Noviciado. **Open** 6.30pm-2am daily. **Credit** MC, V. **Map** p307 G10 ⑲

Popular with audiences and actors from the nearby Teatro Alfil, the Fat Fish (the Spanish equivalent to 'Big Cheese') buzzes at night and is fabulously mellow earlier in the evening. The main attraction (aside from the photos of the owner's hideous bulldog) comes in the shape of the creative tapas. Try fried plantain with guacamole, goose confit with red fruit compôte, or the *patatas* Pez Gordo, with alioli, anchovies and hot peppers.

La Taberna del Corps

Plaza Guardia de Corps 1 (mobile 690 177 301). Metro Ventura Rodríguez. **Open** 1pm-midnight Mon-Thur, Sun; 1pm-1.30am Fri, Sat. **No credit cards. Map** p307 F8 ⑳

The *surtido* (mixed plate) of canapés and excellent selection of wines aside, the main attraction here is the location on a quiet leafy plaza. Grab a Rioja or a draught *vermut* and settle down with the papers.

La Tabernilla del Gato Amadeus

C/Cristo 2 (91 541 41 12). Metro Noviciado. **Open** 1pm-1am daily. **Credit** MC, V. **Map** p307 F8 ㉑

Named after a late, great, Persian cat, this is a tiny, welcoming bar, whose *croquetas* are the stuff of legend. The other favourite is the *patatas con mojo picón* (baked new potatoes with a spicy sauce). Although there's not much seating inside the premises (the sister bar nearby is bigger), in summer there are tables outside.

Other location C/Limón 32, Malasaña & Conde Duque (91 542 54 23).

THE RETIRO & SALAMANCA

Cervecería Santa Bárbara

C/Goya 70 (91 575 00 52, www.cerveceriasanta barbara.com). Metro Goya. **Open** 8am-midnight daily. **Credit** AmEx, MC, V. **Map** p309 O9 ㊷

The prawns are the thing here, consumed in rosy platefuls by the uptown shoppers crowded round the horseshoe-shaped bar. Always full, with a loyal clientele, it is one of the city's meeting places, with a good selection of beers, and tables outside.

Other locations Plaza de Santa Bárbara 8 (91 319 04 49); C/José Castán Tobeñas 1 (91 570 09 71).

Estay

C/Hermosilla 46 (91 578 04 70, www.estay restaurante.com). Metro Velázquez. **Open** 8am-1am Mon-Thur; 8am-2am Fri, Sat. **Credit** AmEx, DC, MC, V. **Map** p309 M9 ㊸

The bright, air-conditioned interior, usually filled with baying young mothers heavily laden with shopping bags, does not immediately suggest gastronomic promise. Stick with the place, however, and you'll enjoy scrumptious and sophisticated tapas and cheap wines by the glass.

Hevia

C/Serrano 118 (91 561 46 87, www.hevia madrid.com). Metro Gregorio Marañón. **Open** Sept-July 9am-1am Mon-Sat. Closed 1wk Aug. **Credit** AmEx, DC, MC, V. **Map** 305 L6 ㊹

A quiet, well-heeled crowd frequents this smart bar. Tapas are correspondingly sophisticated – foie gras, caviar, crab and duck liver pâté – and pricey. In summer, the tables outside can prove irresistible.

José Luis

C/Serrano 89 (91 563 09 58, www.joseluis.es). Metro Núñez de Balboa. **Open** 9am-1am Mon-Sat; noon-1am Sun. **Credit** AmEx, DC, MC, V. **Map** 305 L6 ㊺

Probably one of Madrid's most famous tapas bars and name-checked in a song by the Catalan folk singer Serrat, the food here is little changed since the 1950s and of a high standard. If your appetite is up to it, try the *brascada* (sirloin with ham and onions).

Other locations throughout the city.

NORTH & WEST
Chamberí

Bodegas la Ardosa

C/Santa Engracia 70 (91 446 58 94). Metro Iglesia. **Open** 10am-3pm, 7-11pm Mon, Tue, Thur-Sun. Closed mid July-mid Aug. **No credit cards.**

A tiny bar with a lovely old tiled exterior (confusingly marked No.58) and walls lined with bottles. There are especially good *patatas bravas* and fried pigs' ears, as well as sardines and beer. Not to be confused with the Malasaña bar of the same name (*see p128*).

CONSUME

Cafés & Bars

Capital drinking

The outrageous claims abound: Madrid has more than 100,000 bars (about one per 100 residents); the Calle Alcalá has more bars than Belgium; the city has more bars per square metre than anywhere else in Europe. The amazing thing is that they're probably all true. *Madrileños*, even by normal Spanish standards, are a very sociable bunch who place a lot of importance on eating and drinking in company. Consequently the first coffee of the day tends to be drunk in a bar on the way to work, and the second (sometimes accompanied by a glass of wine) will be had at around 10.30am or so when groups of office workers head out for breakfast.

COFFEE AND TEA

A *café con leche* is a largish milky coffee, which can also be served in a glass (*vaso*); ask for a *taza grande* if you want it even bigger. An espresso is a *café solo*; the same with a dash of milk is *un cortado*, while *un americano* is diluted with twice the normal amount of water. With a shot of alcohol, a *solo* becomes a *carajillo*. A true *carajillo* is made with coffee, sugar, some coffee beans and brandy, and is then set alight on top so that the mixture gets mulled a little; a *carajillo* can also be just a *solo* with a shot of *coñac*, and you can equally ask for a *carajillo de whisky*, *de ron* (rum), *de Bailey's* (pronounced ëbye-leesi), *de anís* or anything else you fancy. Decaffeinated coffee is *descafeinado*, and you will normally be asked if you want it from a sachet (*de sobre*) or the machine (*de máquina*). In summer, a great alternative is *café con hielo* – iced coffee.

Tea in bars is usually awful, and, unless you specifically request otherwise will often come as a glass of hot milk with a teabag on the side. Very popular, however, are herbal teas (*infusiones*), such as *menta* (mint) or *manzanilla* (camomile). And nowadays, if the cloud of globalisation has a silver lining, it is that there are a few more cafés around that have some awareness of what decent tea might be.

BEER

Draught beer (*de barril*) is served in *cañas*, a small measure that varies but is less than half a pint, as *tubos* in a tall thin glass, or as *dobles* (a little bigger). Some places even serve *pintas* (pints), often in a *jarra*, a large, heavy glass with

a handle. Bottled beer usually comes in *tercios*, a third of a litre, or in *botellines*, a quarter of a litre. Spain produces some good-quality beers. In Madrid, the favourite is the local Mahou, with two basic varieties – green label Mahou Clásica and stronger red label Cinco Estrellas. San Miguel is less common, while Andalucían favourite Cruzcampo is growing in popularity. A darker Mahou beer (*negra*) is also available. Shandy is *clara*, and is made with bitter lemon. Imported beers are now common, too, but nearly always cost more.

WINES, SPIRITS AND OTHER DRINKS

All bars have a sturdy, cheap red wine (*tinto*) on offer, and usually there's a white (*blanco*) and a rosé as well (*rosado*). Madrid's traditional summer drink is *tinto de verano* (red in a tall glass over ice, with a slice of lemon and topped up with lemonade). Most bars listed here will have at least one decent Rioja and probably a

---

INSIDE TRACK HIGH SPIRITS

Be warned: spirit measures in Madrid are much more generous than they are in the UK. When ordering a gin and tonic (or vodka equivalent), it's customary for the barman to keep pouring the gin into the glass until the customer tells him or her to stop, meaning that you'll often end up with half gin, half tonic.

CONSUME

Café de Oriente.

cava, but truly good wines are normally only found in the new-style *tabernas* that take real pride in their lists.

Sherry is *jerez*. The type virtually always drunk in Spain is dry *fino*, served very cold. A good fuller-bodied variety is *palo cortado*. Sweet sherries have traditionally been for export only. Red vermouth (*vermut*) with soda is another Madrid tradition, usually as an aperitif, and has recently come back into fashion a little. For a powerful after-dinner drink, try Galician *orujo*, a fiery spirit similar to grappa that normally comes plain (*blanco*) or *con hierbas*, in a luminous green colour. Other *digestivos* include *patxarán*, a fruity aniseed-flavoured liqueur from Navarra, and the more Castilian *anís*, the best of which hails from Chinchón and is available dry (*seco*) or sweet (*dulce*).

NON-ALCOHOLIC DRINKS

Low- and alcohol-free beers (Laiker, Buckler, Kaliber) have an important niche in the market; other favourites for non-alcohol drinkers are the Campari-like but booze-free Bitter Kas, and plain tonic (*una tónica*) with ice and lemon. Fresh orange juice, *zumo de naranja*, is often available. Trinaranjus is the best-known bottled juice brand; favourite flavours are orange (*naranja*), pineapple (*piña*) and peach (*melocotón*). *Mosto* is grape juice, served in small glasses, sometimes

❶ Green numbers given in this chapter correspond to the location of each bar as marked on the maps. *See pp305-313.*

with ice and a slice. A great and unappreciated Spanish speciality, though, are its traditional summer refreshers: most unusual is *horchata*, a milky drink made with tiger nuts. It has to be drunk fresh, from a specialised shop, as it curdles once made. The same places also offer *granizados* – crushed ice with fresh lemon, orange or coffee. Mineral water (*agua mineral*) can be ordered anywhere, either sparkling (*con gas*) or still (*sin gas*).

Many entries in the **Nightlife** and **Tapas** chapters are also good all-rounders, acting as cafés or bars for at least part of the day.

LOS AUSTRIAS & LA LATINA

Almacén de Vinos (Casa Gerardo)

C/Calatrava 21 (91 221 96 60, www.almacen devinos.es). Metro Puerta de Toledo. **Open** 1-4pm, 7.30pm-12.30am Mon-Fri; 1-5pm, 8.30pm-12.30am Sat, Sun. **No credit cards. Map** p311 E14 ❶
A lively and unpretentious wine bar, Gerardo is an essential part of the neighbourhood, offering excellent sausage, ham and seafood tapas, as well as a particularly good selection of cheeses.

El Anciano Rey de los Vinos

C/Bailén 19 (91 559 53 32, www.elancianoreydelos vinos.es). Metro Ópera. **Open** 9am-2.30am Mon, Wed-Sun. **Credit** MC, V (table only). **Map** p311 E12 ❷
Kept much as it has been for the last century – very simple, but spacious and light inside with a wide counter and mirrored walls – the King of Wines serves good canapés, and is a great place for a drink after visiting the cathedral. Prices are quite high, especially if you sit outdoors.

La Cabra en el Tejado

*C/Santa Ana 29 (91 142 46 43, www.lacabra
eneltejado.com). Metro La Latina.* **Open** 6pm-3am
Mon-Thur; 4pm-3am Fri; 1pm-3am Sat; 11am-3am
Sun. **Credit** AmEx, MC, V. **Map** p311 F14 ❸

A clear fave among creative types, the 'Goat on the
Rooftop' is a little hidden away, but worth seeking
out for its selection of good, cheap and unusual tapas
– including quiches, crêpes, *tostas*, salads, and sweet
options such as brownies. The space is nicely decorated, with a huge mural on one wall and a retro feel.

Café del Nuncio

*C/Nuncio 12 & C/Segovia 9 (91 366 08 53). Metro
La Latina.* **Open** 1pm-2am Mon-Thur; 1pm-2.30am
Fri-Sun. **Credit** MC, V. **Map** p311 F13 ❹

Split into two halves at either end of the narrow
Escalinata del Nuncio, the Café del Nuncio has
delightfully cool, dark interiors with gently rotating
ceiling fans and soft classical music. The real charm
of the place, however, lies in the terrace outside on
the stepped slope dividing the two spaces; this is one
of the most picturesque streets in the old city.

Café de Oriente

*Plaza de Oriente 2 (91 541 39 74. www.grupo
lezano.es). Metro Ópera.* **Open** 8.30am-1.30am
Mon-Sat; 9am-1.30am Sun. **Credit** AmEx, DC,
MC, V. **Map** p311 E11 ❺

The belle époque interior is entirely fake yet entirely
convincing, making this one of the most peaceful
and elegant spots to flick through the newspapers
or recover from the exertions of the Palacio Real
opposite. Despite its location, with tables outside on
the stunning Plaza de Oriente, the café seems to be
more popular with locals than tourists, who are perhaps put off by its air of grandeur.

Café del Real

Plaza de Isabel II 2 (91 547 21 24). Metro Ópera.
Open 9am-midnight Mon-Thur; 9am-2am Fri;
10am-2am Sat; 10am-11pm Sun. **No credit cards**.
Map p311 F11 ❻

This likeable, cramped café with a lovely façade is a
good place for coffee and cake (chocolate or carrot),
though prices are a tad on the high side. Head
upstairs to a low-beamed room with red leather
chairs and old opera posters, overlooking the *plaza*.
The café was a favourite haunt of intellectuals, artists
and actors in the 1980s, but it's popular with a wider
crowd these days.

★ Chocolatería San Ginés

*Pasadizo de San Ginés 5 (91 365 65 46). Metro
Ópera or Sol.* **Open** 24hrs daily. **Credit** (min €12)
AmEx, DC, MC, V. **Map** p311 G11 ❼

Serving chocolate and *churros* (deep-fried batter
sticks) to the city night and day since 1894, this veritable institution has had to introduce a ticketing
system – pay before you order – to deal with the 5am
queues of exhausted clubbers and chipper old ladies.
The lighting is a bit much if you fall into the former
category, but at least there are tables outside.

Delic

*Costanilla de San Andrés 14, Plaza de la Paja (91
364 54 50, www.delic.es). Metro La Latina.* **Open**
7pm-2am Mon; 11am-2am Tue-Thur, Sun; 11am-
2.30am Fri, Sat. **No credit cards**. **Map** p311 E13 ❽

A perennial favourite with seemingly everybody,
from those looking for a morning coffee on the leafy
Plaza de la Paja to those meeting up for a few bol-
stering cocktails before a big night out. In fact, it gets
so busy at certain times that they've employed a
bouncer and a one-in/one-out policy. A globetrotting

CONSUME

Delic.

menu includes tabouleh, Japanese dumplings and filled ciabattas, and the Chilean chocolate cake is utterly irresistible.

La Fontanilla
Plaza Puerta Cerrada 13 (91 365 22 91). Metro La Latina. **Open** 11am-2am daily. **Credit** DC, MC, V. **Map** p311 F12 ❾
La Fontanilla claims to be not the biggest or the best or the oldest, but the smallest Irish pub in Madrid. There's no disputing this singular claim, but the place does manage to cram in a couple of wooden tables alongside wide hatches opening on to the street. The myriad beers racked up on the walls are sadly not for sale, but there is Murphy's and Guinness.

El Ventorillo
C/Bailén 14 (91 366 35 78). Metro Ópera. **Open** 11am-1am Mon-Fri, Sun; 11am-2am Sat. **Credit** AmEx, MC, V. **Map** p311 E13 ❿
Just down from the Palacio Real, this *terraza* offers the finest sunsets in Madrid, looking out over the Casa del Campo and all the way to the Guadarrama.

SOL & GRAN VÍA

Café del Círculo de Bellas Artes
C/Alcalá 42 (91 360 54 00). Metro Banco de España. **Open** 9am-1am Mon-Thur; 9am-3am Fri, Sat; 8am-midnight Sun. **Admission** €1; free 2-4pm daily. **Credit** MC, V. **Map** p312 I11 ⓫
A quintessential point of reference in the city's café society, the Bellas Artes is utterly elegant. Under new ownership, it's now free to enter at lunchtime for the *menú del día*. Otherwise take a seat amid the columns and female nudes and frown over *El País* with coffee and a croissant to fit right in.

★ La Mallorquina
Puerta del Sol 8 (91 521 12 01). Metro Sol. **Open** 9am-9.15pm daily. Closed mid July-Aug. **No credit cards. Map** p311 G11 ⓬
While the atmospheric bakery downstairs supplies box after ribbon-tied box of flaky pastries, croissants and *napolitanas* to what seems like half of Madrid, the upstairs *salón* crackles with the animated chat of *madrileña* blue-rinses and savvier tourists.

Grape Expectations
Spanish wines are not to be sniffed at.

CONSUME

Madrid is an oenophile's playground, with none of the solemnity and hefty price tags attached to wine-drinking elsewhere. Everyone drinks it here, from builders to nuns. It so pervades daily life, in fact, that the Spanish Ministry of Agriculture categorises wine as food rather than an alcoholic beverage.

Wine-lovers around the globe have now caught on to the fact that Spanish labels are the best value for your euro. US wine tsar Robert Parker claims Spain is one of the hottest regions in Europe. The sad fact remains, however, that a lot of bars serve plonk. To taste the good stuff, get to a wine bar. Madrid has a number of cosy little *enotecas* where you can settle in at the bar and try different wines by the glass. **La Cruzada** (C/Amnistía 8, 91 548 01 31), for example, offers a delectable selection of reasonably priced *vinos*. King Alfonso XII reportedly used to frequent this bar when he needed to escape the nearby royal palace for a tipple. Check out the lovely carvings of bare-breasted women on the bar, dating back to 1827.

Other spots for quality wines include **González** (C/León 12, 91 429 56 18) and **Entrevinos** (C/Ferraz 36, 91 548 31 14).
An entertaining way to dive into Spanish wine is to attend one of Madrid's wine-tasting classes, known as *cursos de cata*, which get you swirling, sniffing and sipping good wine. **Lavinia** (C/José Ortega y Gasset 16, 91 426 06 04, www.lavinia.es) is a good bet, and has an impressive collection. **AtSpain** (91 547 50 91, www.atspain.com), an online shop for gifts and gourmet products, also arranges fun English-language wine and tapas classes with sommeliers from Madrid's best wine stores. You might also visit Torres Bodega's **Centro Cultural del Vino** (C/Martires Concepcionistas 19, 91 401 77 62, www.torres.es) for professional classes covering everything from soil types to food pairing. Many of the city's best wine shops, such as **Reserva y Cata** (C/Conde de Xiquena 13, 91 319 04 01) and **Bodegas Santa Cecilia** (C/Blasco de Garay 72-74, 91 445 52 83), also offer regular *cursos de cata* in Spanish.

Windows overlooking the Puerta del Sol make this an unbeatable central spot for breakfast. The coffee is cheap and very good.

★ Museo Chicote

Gran Vía 12 (91 532 67 37, www.museo-chicote. com). Metro Gran Vía. **Open** 5pm-3am Mon-Sat. Closed Aug. **Credit** MC, V. **Map** p308 I11 ⑬

Its art deco interior is starting to look a bit shabby around the edges, but Chicote is still the doyen of Madrid cocktail bars. This was famously where Hemingway and other international press hacks would spend their days sheltering from the artillery shells flying down the Gran Vía during the Civil War. Grace Kelly and Ava Gardner, along with just about every Spanish writer, actor or artist of the last 60 years, have passed through too. These days, the place is run by Trip Family, one of the biggest promoters on the Madrid nightlife scene. There are various resident DJs, but if you're lucky you might catch Spain's answer to Gilles Peterson, DJ Sandro Bianchi, playing electro-soul, funk, hip hop and anything with a groove.

HUERTAS & SANTA ANA

Casa Pueblo

C/León 3 (91 420 20 38). Metro Antón Martín. **Open** 6pm-2am Mon-Thur; 3pm-3am Fri-Sun. Closed Aug. **Credit** AmEx, MC, V. **Map** p312 I12 ⑭

A handsome, old-fashioned jazz bar hung with antique clocks and black and white photos, Casa Pueblo is popular with a slightly older crowd that knows its whisky. Occasional live music includes jazz and tango (on a Wednesday).

Cervecería Alemana

Plaza Santa Ana 6 (91 429 70 33). Metro Sol. **Open** 11am-midnight Mon-Thur, Sun; 11am-2am Fri, Sat. **Credit** DC, MC, V. **Map** p312 H12 ⑮

Famous for being Ernest Hemingway's daily haunt (his table, should you be wondering, was the one in the near right-hand corner). The decor is fin de siècle German bierkeller, with dusty old paintings and dark wood. The tapas can be uninspired and the waiters are unfailingly gruff, but for many this will be an essential stop.

Cervecería Santa Ana

Plaza Santa Ana 10 (91 429 36 35, www.cerveceria santaana.es). Metro Antón Martín or Sol. **Open** 11am-1.30am Mon-Thur, Sun; 11am-2.30am Fri, Sat. **Credit** MC, V. **Map** p312 H12 ⑯

Another on this strip of beerhouses (the most exotic brew on offer here is Guinness), this one was never frequented by Hemingway and is consequently cheaper. Two entrances lead into two different spaces – one with seating and one without – and there are tables outside. Good for a light lunch, with decent salads and a range of *pulgas* (small rolls).

Dos Gardenias

C/Santa María 13 (mobile 627 003 571). Metro Antón Martín. **Open** 9.30am-2.30am Tue-Sun. **No credit cards. Map** p312 I13 ⑰

There's no sign on the door – just look out for this mellow little space painted in warm yellow, orange and blue, and the emanating chilled-out vibes, soft flamenco and Brazilian jazz. Kick back on a velvet sofa with the house speciality: a mojito made with brown sugar and Angostura bitters.

Naturbier

Plaza Santa Ana 9 (91 429 39 18, www.naturbier. com). Metro Antón Martín or Sol. **Open** noon-12.30am Mon-Thur, Sun; noon-1.30am Fri, Sat. **Credit** MC, V. **Map** p312 H12 ⑱

The least exciting-looking of all the beer cellars lining this side of the Plaza Santa Ana, Naturbier's big draw is its own-made organic beer – in fact, it's the only place in Madrid to brew its own. The tapas are also worth checking out despite the pricing, which is somewhat creative.

Sol y Sombra

C/Echegaray 18 (91 542 81 93, www.solysombra. name). Metro Sevilla or Sol. **Open** 10pm-3.30am Tue-Sat. **Credit** V. **Map** p312 H12 ⑲

A curious fusion of neon lighting and taurine decor (the name refers to the seats at a bullfight), which just about works. It's certainly very popular with the mix of thirtysomething minor celebs and their well-heeled friends. Live acts feature every night from Wednesday to Saturday, with a mix of Spanish cheese, flamenco-chill and lounge on offer. A sniffy door policy discourages scruffy trainers.

★ La Venencia

C/Echegaray 7 (91 429 73 13). Metro Sevilla or Sol. **Open** 3.30-10.30pm daily. **No credit cards. Map** p312 H12 ⑳

Totally unreconstructed, La Venencia is gloriously shabby, with old, peeling sherry posters, barrels behind the bar and walls burnished gold by decades of tobacco smoke. It serves only sherry (locals will order a crisp, dry *fino* or *manzanilla*, leaving the sweet stuff to the occasional tourist who stumbles in here), along with manchego cheese, *cecina* (air-dried beef) and chorizo by way of tapas. Orders are still chalked up on the bar, and an enamel sign asks customers not to spit on the floor.

RASTRO & LAVAPIÉS

★ Los Chuchis

C/Amparo 82 (91 127 66 06). Metro Lavapiés. **Open** 11am-midnight Tue-Fri; noon-12.30am Sat, Sun. Closed 2wks Aug. **Credit** DC, MC, V. **Map** p312 H15 ㉑

A warm and welcoming little café, with perky teal paintwork and chequerboard floor, just off the main Rastro drag. The British influence in the team behind

CONSUME

it is evident everywhere, from the collection of teapots to the bowler hat on a rack, the Penguin Classics and the complete works of British chefdom – Jamie, Delia, Nigella et al – that influences the kitchen.

Gau Café

C/Tribulete 14 (91 528 25 94, www.gaucafe.com). *Metro Lavapiés.* **Open** 11am-midnight Mon-Fri; 1.30pm-midnight Sat. **No credit cards.** **Map** p311 H15 ㉒

Gau (formerly known as Gaudeamos) has attracted cultured types in their droves since it first opened in 2007. They come for the large roof terrace, with spectacular views of the *barrio*'s rooftops, and the 'in-the-know' vibe (the place isn't visible from the outside – you have to walk through the university building to reach the lift that takes you up to the café). The restaurant has two seatings: at 8.30pm and 10.15pm. *Photo p128.*

La Heladería

C/Argumosa 7 (91 528 80 09). Metro Lavapiés. **Open** 10am-midnight Mon-Thur, Sun; 10am-1am Fri, Sat. Closed Nov-Mar. **No credit cards.** **Map** p312 H14 ㉓

Peruvian owner Yoli is unfailingly charming, and happy to let you try her excellent ice-creams before you buy – blackberry (*mora*) and lemon come recommended. Try the *blanco y negro*, a delicious café-frappé with ice-cream, or one of her milkshakes.

Nuevo Café Barbieri

C/Ave María 45 (91 527 36 58). Metro Lavapiés. **Open** 4pm-12.30am Tue, Wed; 4pm-1.30am Thur; 4pm-2.30am Fri, Sat; 4-11.30pm Sun. Closed 2wks Aug. **Credit** (min €5) MC, V. **Map** p312 H14 ㉔

An airy and peaceful space with high ceilings and a dusty elegance, its marble-topped tables slightly chipped and its red-velvet banquettes a little worn. A favourite haunt of journos and wannabe travel writers, Barbieri has plenty of newspapers and magazines, but its ordinary coffee comes at a premium.

★ Oliveros

C/San Millán 4 (91 354 62 52). Metro La Latina. **Open** 1.30pm-midnight Tue-Sun. Closed Aug. **Credit** AmEx, MC, V. **Map** p311 F13 ㉕

Oliveros is the genuine article, and although it was closed for years, it has been miraculously preserved in its original mid 19th-century bare-bricked state, complete with tiles and zinc bar. However, it might be worth ringing before going there, as opening hours can be somewhat erratic.

Taberna de Tirso de Molina

Plaza de Tirso de Molina 9 (91 429 17 56). *Metro Tirso de Molina.* **Open** 8am-2am daily. **Credit** AmEx, MC, V. **Map** p311 G13 ㉖

It has a good stab at looking traditional with tiles, nautically uniformed waiters and exposed brickwork, but this *taberna* is, in fact, relatively new.

There are plenty of tables where you can eat a decent breakfast on the way to the Rastro, or a very generous set lunch for €11.50. Tapas are available all day, along with heftier dishes such as the towering *parrillada de marisco* (seafood platter).

Vinícola Mentridana

C/San Eugenio 9 (91 527 87 60). Metro Antón Martín. **Open** 1pm-1am Mon-Thur, Sun; 1pm-2am Fri, Sat. Closed 3wks Aug. **Credit** AmEx, MC, V. **Map** p312 I14 ㉗

Frequented by the hip element of Lavapiés, this cool wine bar with tall windows opening on to the street is gently evocative of the old *bodega* it used to be. An impressive list of well-priced wines by the glass is complemented by tasty canapés, along with mulled wine and *caldo* (broth) in winter, or gazpacho and *granizado* in the summer months.

CHUECA

Ángel Sierra

C/Gravina 11 (91 531 01 26). Metro Chueca. **Open** noon-2am Mon-Thur, Sun; noon-2am Fri, Sat. **Credit** MC, V. **Map** p308 I10 ㉘

This battered old bar with its tiled bar, zinc bar top, overflowing sink and glasses stacked on wooden slats has become the Chueca meeting place par excellence, thanks to its position overlooking the main square. A newer room to the back of the bar, however, has a faux pub look enhanced with amplified MOR radio and a rule that only doubles and pints are served after midnight.

Bar Cock

C/Reina 16 (91 532 28 26, www.barcock.com). *Metro Gran Vía.* **Open** *Sept-May* 8pm-3am daily. *June-Aug* 8pm-3am Mon-Sat. **Credit** AmEx, MC, V. **Map** p308 I11 ㉙

A former brothel, Bar Cock is pricey and very stagey, furnished in what Spaniards think to be the style of an English pub (red velvet curtains, embossed leather armchairs and a fake half-timbered effect). It still continues to attract those who like to think of themselves as being in the know, and it can get extremely crowded as a result.

★ Le Cabrera

C/Bárbara de Braganza 2 (91 319 94 57, www. lecabrera.com). Metro Colón. **Open** *Cocktail bar* 4pm-2am Mon-Thur; 4pm-2.30am Fri, Sat. *Tapas bar* 1.30-4pm, 8.30pm-midnight Mon-Thur, Sun; 1.30-4pm, 8.30pm-2am Fri, Sat. **Credit** AmEx, MC, V. **Map** p308 J10 ㉚

This excellent two-storey cocktail bar opened in 2010, with the aim of revolutionising Madrid's cocktail scene through the heady talents of barman and namesake Diego Cabrera. The ground-floor bar serves wine and quality tapas, while the basement area has a hidden, intimate feel and is the place to sample the bar's long list of both classic and innovative cocktails. *Photo p129.*

Del Diego

C/Reina 12 (91 523 31 06). Metro Gran Vía. **Open** 7pm-3am daily. Closed 3wks Aug. **Credit** MC, V. **Map** p308 H11 ㉛

Not to all tastes, with an unchanging, late 1980s, steel-and-blond-wood *Wall Street* vibe, Del Diego is nevertheless deservedly renowned for its consummately smooth barmen and superb cocktails. Pull up a stool and try a zingy mint julep del Diego to kickstart a night's wheeling and dealing.

Finnegan's

Plaza de las Salesas 9 (91 310 05 21). Metro Alonso Martínez. **Open** 9am-2am Mon-Thur; 9am-2.30am Fri; 1pm-2am Sat, Sun. **Credit** (min €7) AmEx, MC, V. **Map** p308 J9/10 ㉜

One for rugby fans, Finnegan's has its own team, the Madrid Lions, and a talent for sniffing out every conceivable match to show on its large screens. In lean sporting times, the void is filled with pub quizzes and DJs (mostly rock) at weekends. Pints of Beamish, Newky Brown and John Smith's complement burgers and other pub grub.

Los Chuchis. *See p125.*

CONSUME

CONSUME

Gau Café. See p126.

Isolée

C/Infantas 19 (902 876 136, www.isolee.com). Metro Banco de España. **Open** 11am-9pm Mon-Sat. **Credit** MC, V. **Map** p308 I11 ③③
The tendrils of cool emanating from Chueca are creeping ever further afield, as evinced by Isolée, a multifaceted café, CD, clothes and kitchenware shop. The café is a little on the pricey side, but it does serve decent sushi and bagels. Mostly, though, it's a place to sip espressos and make use of the Wi-Fi.

Olivera

C/Santo Tomé 8 (mobile 697 198 543). Metro Chueca. **Open** 6pm-2am Mon-Thur, Sun; 6pm-2.30am Fri, Sat. **Credit** MC, V. **Map** p308 J10 ③④
A relaxed lounge bar, presided over by a portrait of the owner's mother, Yugoslav film star Olivera Markovic. The musical mood is nu jazz and funk, and the mismatched armchairs and sofas make it easy to end up staying all night.

★ Stop Madrid

C/Hortaleza 11 (91 521 88 87, www.stopmadrid.es). Metro Chueca or Gran Vía. **Open** noon-1am Mon-Wed; noon-2am Thur; noon-2.30am Fri, Sat; noon-12.30am Sun. **Credit** MC, V. **Map** p308 H11 ③⑤
When it opened in 1929, this was the first ham and charcuterie shop in Madrid. It's undergone a few changes since then, but many of the original fittings have been retained, and great pride is taken in sourcing the best ingredients for tapas. Of the 50-strong wine list, all are available by the glass.

Zanzíbar

C/Regueros 9 (91 319 90 64, www.zanzibar madrid.es). Metro Alonso Martínez. **Open**
Sept-July 8pm-3am Mon-Thur, Sun; 8pm-3.30am Fri, Sat. Aug 8pm-2am Thur; 8pm-3.30am Fri, Sat. **No credit cards. Map** p308 I9 ③⑥
Good causes and ethnic chic combine to create a cute and colourful hangout for right-on revellers. On a small stage at the back there are frequent appearances by bossa nova bands, singer-songwriters and storytellers; at other times soft flamenco and reggae tickle the speakers. A few bar snacks are available, along with fair-trade coffee.

MALASAÑA & CONDE DUQUE

★ La Ardosa

C/Colón 13 (91 521 49 79, www.laardosa.com). Metro Tribunal. **Open** 8.30am-2am Mon-Thur; noon-2.30am Fri, Sat; noon-2am Sun. **No credit cards. Map** p307 H9/10 ③⑦
Having an affair? Then simply duck under the counter to find the most intimate bar room you could wish for. Out front, meanwhile, this is a lovely old tiled taberna lined with dusty bottles, old black-and-white lithographs and beer posters. A range of canapés has just been added, and the speciality of the house is its draught beer – Bombardier, Budvar and, especially, Guinness.

★ Bar El 2D

C/Velarde 24 (91 448 64 72). Metro Tribunal. **Open** noon-2am Mon-Thur, Sun; noon-2.30am Fri, Sat. **Credit** (min €12) MC, V. **Map** p307 H8 ③⑧
The emblematic Malasaña hangout, packed at weekends and drowsily mellow in the afternoons, with a tiled bar and engraved mirrors, nicotine-stained walls and lazily circling ceiling fans. To drink, there's vermouth, lager and Beamish on tap, plus

plenty of bottled beers and a small selection of wines, served (if you dare) in *porrones*, which are long-spouted drinking jars.

Bar El Palentino

C/Pez 12 (91 532 30 58, www.myspace.com/bar palentino). Metro Callao or Noviciado. **Open** 8.30am-2am Mon-Sat. **No credit cards. Map** p307 G10 ❸
Something of a Madrid institution, this old-school neighbourhood bar is popular with seemingly everyone – the place is always packed in the evenings. Wooden panelling, fluorescent strip ceiling lamps, a much-loved owner and notoriously cheap (but good) drinks attract punters of all ages, creating a buzzing, sociable and quintessentially *madrileño* vibe. Sandwiches help to soak up the *cañas*.

★ Café Comercial

Glorieta de Bilbao 7 (91 521 56 55). Metro Bilbao. **Open** 7.30am-midnight Mon-Thur, Sun; 7.30am-2am Fri, Sat. **Credit** (min €10) AmEx, MC, V. **Map** p307 H8 ❹
Still the classic Madrid bar, with its original battered brown leather seats, revolving doors and marbled walls. A cursory nod to the modern age comes in the shape of the internet terminals upstairs, where American gap-year students write home about the old men playing chess alongside them.

Café Isadora

C/Divino Pastor 14 (91 445 71 54). Metro Bilbao. **Open** 4pm-2.30am daily. **Credit** MC, V. **Map** p307 G8 ❹
An elegant shrine to Isadora Duncan, with a chequered floor, marble-topped tables and an eerie collection of prints of *that* scarf, alongside frequently

changing exhibitions. Along with a decent range of *patxaráns* (sloe-flavoured liqueurs, many of them own-made), is a list of *ëaguasi* (cocktails made with cava). *Agua de Valencia* is the original and best, featuring orange juice, gin, Cointreau and vodka.

Café Manuela

C/San Vicente Ferrer 29 (91 531 70 37). Metro Tribunal. **Open** 4pm-2am Mon-Thur, Sun; 4pm-2.30am Fri, Sat. **Credit** (min €10) MC, V. **Map** p307 H9 ❹
Stacked to the rafters with board games, Café Manuela has been a hive of activity since the Movida days. Its handsome art nouveau decor and conveniently nicotine-coloured walls are still the backdrop to occasional live music and other performances, but otherwise it's a great place to reacquaint yourself with Cluedo and Mastermind.

Café El Moderno

Plaza de las Comendadoras 1 (mobile 669 452 278, www.cafemodernomadrid). Metro Noviciado. **Open** noon-1.30am Mon-Thur, Sun; noon-2.30am Fri, Sat. **Credit** DC, MC, V. **Map** p307 F8 ❹

Le Cabrera. *See p127.*

CONSUME

El Moderno's art deco look is entirely fake, but none the worse for it, and, along with its large terrace, attracts a mixture of local characters and curious tourists. The specialities are teas, milkshakes and hot chocolates, with an impressive 30 varieties of each. Fans of *Sex and Lucia* will recognise the building as Lorenzo's apartment block.

Café de Ruiz

C/Ruiz 11 (91 446 12 32). Metro Bilbao. **Open** 3.30-11.30pm Mon-Thur; 3.30pm-3.30am Fri, Sat; 3-11pm Sun. **Credit** MC, V. **Map** p307 G8 ㊹
A quiet favourite with the smarter denizens of the neighbourhood, Café de Ruiz is an elegant place, with comfortable sofas and dramatic flower arrangements. A big draw is its own-made ice-cream and other tempting sweet treats, such as milkshakes and home-made cakes.

Café Rustika

C/Limón 11 (91 542 15 67, www.rustikacafe.net). Metro Noviciado. **Open** 7pm-1.30am Tue-Thur; 7pm-2.30am Fri, Sat; 1pm-1am Sun. **Credit** MC, V. **Map** p307 F9 ㊺
Whimsical interiors, funky lo-fi music and lots of hanging lanterns make this one of the most relaxing cafés in a neighbourhood full of them. New ownership brings a randomly international menu, with dishes from couscous to chop suey to chocolate cake and a wide selection of teas.

Casa Camacho

C/San Andrés 4 (91 531 35 98). Metro Tribunal. **Open** noon-1.30am Mon-Sat. Closed Aug. **No credit cards. Map** p307 G/H9 ㊻
A rough diamond, the diminutive Casa Camacho has changed little since it opened in 1928, except for the addition of a fruit machine and a TV – both in constant use. Pre-war dust coats the bottles and plastic flowers on display and the floor is a sea of toothpicks and cigarette ends, but for a slice of real neighbourhood life it can't be beat.

★ La Huida

C/Colón 11 (mobile 600 870 509). Metro Tribunal. **Open** 1pm-2am daily. **No credit cards. Map** p307 H9/10 ㊼
La Movida meets *Friends* in this cramped but jolly little café, where everybody knows everybody else. This is where the painfully cool neo-punks from the nearby Mercado Fuencarral come to let their guard down, tucking into leek and mushroom quiche at the scrubbed pine tables. Sundays are especially mellow: the perfect set for the The One Where They All Got Tattoos.

★ El Jardín Secreto

C/Conde Duque 2 (91 541 80 23). Metro Plaza de España or Ventura Rodríguez. **Open** 5.30pm-1.30am Mon-Thur; 6.30pm-2.30am Fri, Sat; 5.30pm-2.30am Sun. **Credit** MC, V. **Map** p307 E9 ㊽

Although it also functions as a restaurant, El Jardín Secreto – decked out with mismatched furniture and arty knick-knacks – is most popular as a *merienda* (afternoon tea) spot. The crowds tend to show up when the place opens. Its cakes and desserts – in particular the chocolate orgasm – are much talked about, and there's a large selection of chocolate drinks, teas and coffees on the menu. Open late, it's also popular as a cocktail spot.

Laydown

Plaza Mostenses 9 (91 548 79 37, www.laydown.es). Metro Plaza de España. **Open** 8pm-2.30am Wed-Sat; 1pm-1am Sun. **Credit** AmEx, MC, V. **Map** p307 F10 ㊾
This flashy, minimalist bar, restaurant and club – which also has branches in Barcelona and Valencia – is known for its chic lounge chairs with comfy mattresses (the clue is in the name). Dinner is a set meal and there is live music or theatre performances most nights. Once dinner is over, it's DJ time, as everyone clambers out of bed to bust a few grooves. The Sunday brunch is very popular. *Photo p132.*

Lola Loba

C/Palma 38 (mobile 630 839 816). Metro Noviciado. **Open** *Winter* 5pm-2am Mon-Thur; 5pm-2.30am Fri, Sat. *Summer* 3.30pm-2am Mon-Thur; 1.30pm-2am Sat, Sun. **No credit cards. Map** p307 G8/9 ㊿
Lola Loba is named after a *copla* singer who ran away from her abusive American millionaire husband and opened this bar. In 1872 he found her and murdered her, and it's said her ghost still prowls within the red-brick walls. What is not known is whether she approves of the jazz, funk and house, or the fab *tostas*, slathered in mozzarella, tomato and basil, caramelised onion with brie, or smoked salmon with camembert.

★ Lolina Vintage Café

C/Espíritu Santo 9 (91 523 58 59, www.lolinacafe.com). Metro Tribunal. **Open** 10am-1am Mon-Thur, Sun; 10am-3am Fri, Sat. **Credit** MC, V. **Map** p307 H9 �51
Now a few years old, Lolina was among the new wave of openings on Calle Espíritu Santo. The cute, retro space – with its 1970s wallpaper and vintage floor lamps – is a popular hangout for arty types and young expats, drawn by its pan-European vibe, brunch-style menu and large selection of teas, coffees and juices. The good-value breakfasts start from €2.50; and if you visit in the evening, be sure to order a mojito or caipirinha – the house specialities.

Naif

C/San Joaquín 16 (91 007 20 71, www.naif madrid.es). Metro Tribunal. **Open** 11am-1am daily. **Credit** AmEx, MC, V. **Map** p307 H9 �52
Naif is very much of its time; a high-ceilinged post-industrial space with Banksy-inspired murals, exposed ventilation ducts, recycled furniture and a

In the Frame Tertulias

The favoured forum of the literati.

The intellectual life of Spain once revolved around the ephemeral institution known as the *tertulia*. Originating in the humanist salons of 16th-century Seville, the *tertulia* is a gathering of people united by a common interest, which can range from mathematics to gastronomy, but has traditionally been literature. And Spain being a country where people tend to go out rather than meet in each other's houses, these gatherings have invariably been held in bars and cafés.

The rise of the *tertulia* in Madrid, as depicted in many paintings of the time, coincided with the city's emergence in the early 19th century as the centre of a café life rivalling that of Paris and Vienna. Café life has always flourished at times of great political repression, the café being a place whose proverbial smoky gloom has provided a suitably furtive retreat for dissidents. During the grey, autocratic rule of Spain's Ferdinand VII, the *tertulia* became an expression of political and cultural freedom.

Tertulias took place in many of the cafés that by the 1830s had almost entirely encircled the Puerta del Sol. But the most influential of these gatherings was the one associated with a tiny, rat-infested basement café next to the neo-classical Teatro Español (the present bland reconstruction bears little resemblance to the original establishment). The place was officially called the Café del Príncipe, but everyone came to know it as the 'Parnasillo' or 'Little Parnassus', on account of its attracting all the fashionable writers of the day. Among these were the much revered satirical essayist Mariano José de Larra and

the writer Ramón de Mesonero Romanos, who famously wrote that in 'this miserable little room' they succeeded in shaking the very foundations of Spanish life and culture.

With the evolution towards the end of the 19th century of Madrid's idiosyncratically late eating and drinking hours, *tertulias* proliferated as never before, reaching their apogee in the 1920s under the guidance of a writer sometimes referred to as the 'second of the Ramones', Ramón Gómez de la Serna. Every Saturday night, from around 10pm until dawn, a *tertulia*, presided over by Gómez de la Serna, was held in what was soon dubbed the 'Sacred Crypt of the Pombo', a now vanished café off the Puerta del Sol. The solemnity of these celebrated meetings was captured in a sombre painting by José Gutiérrez Solana (*pictured*). La Serna is seen standing in the centre. These gatherings were also slightly ridiculed by filmmaker Luis Buñuel, who described how 'we used to arrive, greet each other and order a drink – usually coffee, and a lot of water – until a meandering conversation began about the latest literary publications or political upheavals.'

Most liberal and avant-garde associates of the Pombo went into exile after the Civil War, thus radically diminishing the cultural life of the capital. Subsequently, many of the cafés in the centre of Madrid were succeeded by the HQs of large banks, and many more suffered the humiliation of being transformed into Formica-lined, American-style cafeterias.
La Tertulia del Café Pombo is on display at the Reina Sofía (see p52).

(see p52)

CONSUME

bit of attitude behind the bar. It's sympathetically lit, though, does a great burger and is one of very few places to serve BLTs or pastrami with mustard.

La Palmera

C/Palma 67 (mobile 630 884 470). Metro Noviciado. **Open** 8pm-2am Mon-Thur; 8pm-2.30am Fri, Sat. **No credit cards. Map** p307 F8 ⑤

The tiles in this tiny, crowded bar date back to its opening at the beginning of the last century, and have featured in various magazines. For years it lay in terminal decline, until it was bought in the late 1990s by a long-term regular. It almost exclusively serves vermouth and beer to a loyal crowd.

El Parnasillo

C/San Andrés 33 (91 447 00 79). Metro Bilbao. **Open** 2.30-11pm Mon-Thur, Sun; 2.30pm-3.30am Fri, Sat. **No credit cards. Map** p307 H8 ⑤

Long frequented by writers, artists, journalists and intellectuals, the art nouveau El Parnasillo was very much at the centre of Madrid's cultural renewal in the 1970s and '80s, to the extent that it was bombed by a far-right group. It's unlikely to excite the same emotions these days, but it's still an evocative place for a cocktail or *pa tumaca* (bread rubbed with tomato) topped with cheese, ham or smoked salmon.

★ Passenger

C/Pez 16 (91 169 49 76). Metro Noviciado. **Open** 5pm-1am Mon-Thur; 3pm-3am Fri-Sun. Closed Aug. **Credit** MC, V. **Map** p307 G9 ⑤

Party like it's 1939 in this supremely elegant Orient Express lookalike bar. Long and narrow, with wood panelling, an art deco bar, leather banquettes and screens showing footage of scenery in mocked-up

windows – sure, it's a gimmick, but it's one hell of a gimmick. Cocktails are the speciality and there's a long list of tequilas and organic whiskies, then there's great coffee and brunch on a Sunday with live jazz.

★ Pepe Botella

C/San Andrés 12 (91 522 43 09, www.pepebotella. com). Metro Tribunal. **Open** 10am-2.30am daily. **Credit** MC, V. **Map** p307 H8 ⑤

A cineaste's delight, the colourful Pepe Botella is frequented by the likes of director Alejandro Amenábar and actor Eduardo Noriega. For all that, it's wonderfully unpretentious, and attracts an intelligent bunch of mainly thirty- and fortysomethings, engaged in lively debate. The place has free Wi-Fi.

El Rincón

C/Espíritu Santo 26 (91 522 19 86). Metro Tribunal. **Open** 10am-2am daily. **Credit** MC, V. **Map** p307 H9 ⑤

Popular with both locals and expats, laid-back El Rincón has a new-wave Malasaña feel, with chequered floors, powder blue walls, black-and-white photos on the walls, mismatched wooden tables and a boho vibe (a sign outside reads 'Don't smoke joints on the terrace'). For a bite to eat, try the house gazpacho (€3.50) or the excellent sandwiches and cakes. There's also good coffee and a range of teas.

THE RETIRO & SALAMANCA

El Botánico

C/Ruiz de Alarcón 27 (91 420 23 42). Metro Banco de España. **Open** 8am-midnight Mon-Fri; 9am-1am Sat, Sun. **Credit** AmEx, DC, MC, V. **Map** p312 K13 ⑤

Laydown. *See p130.*

Passenger.

Confusingly, this quiet bar-restaurant actually sits on C/Espalter, overlooking the botanical gardens. Tucked away from the tourist drag, it's very quiet considering its proximity to the Prado, and has a peaceful, shaded terrace. It's a good spot for breakfast, and there are tapas later in the day.

★ Café Gijón

Paseo de Recoletos 21 (91 521 54 25, www.cafe gijon.com). Metro Banco de España or Colón. **Open** 8am-midnight daily. **Credit** AmEx, MC, V. **Map** p308 J10 ❺❾
Still charming after all these years, this is Madrid's definitive literary café, open since 1888. It still holds poetry *tertulias* on Monday nights, and publishes a magazine filled with doodles and thoughts from visiting writers. A pianist tinkles the ivories to a packed terrace in summer.

Castellana 8

Paseo de la Castellana 8 (91 578 34 87, www. castellana8.es). Metro Colón. **Open** 12.30pm-2.30am Mon-Fri; 5pm-3.30am Sat, Sun. **Credit** AmEx, MC, V. **Map** p308 K8 ❻⓪
Castellana 8 is a supremely smooth bar-restaurant-club, its black walls softened by clever uplighting, orange velvet cushions and a mellow soundtrack of jazz and blues. Brunch on Sundays is dished up with cocktails and live music, though not, sadly, on the terrace outside, which is limited to drinking only.

James Joyce

C/Alcalá 59 (91 575 49 01, www.jamesjoycemadrid. com). Metro Banco de España. **Open** 9am-2am Mon-Thur; 11am-2.30am Fri, Sat; 11am-2am Sun. **Credit** AmEx, DC, MC, V. **Map** p308 K11 ❻❶

Previously known as Kitty O'Shea's, this is the Madrid outpost of what is now a global chain of Oirish theme pubs. With both Guinness and Murphy's on tap, pub grub, chatty staff and plenty of rugby and Premier League matches showing on two big screens and three TVs, it's all much as you'd expect. Of more interest, perhaps, is the fact that the pub sits on the site of the historic Café Lion, a haunt of post-Civil War literati.

El Pavellón del Espejo

Paseo de Recoletos 31 (91 319 11 22, www. restauranteelespejo.com). Metro Colón. **Open** 8am-midnight Mon-Fri; 10am-midnight Sat, Sun. **Credit** AmEx, MC, V. **Map** p308 K9/10 ❻❷
Not nearly as historic as the neighbouring Gijón, although it may look it: when it opened in 1978, 'The Mirror' set out to be the art nouveau bar Madrid never had, with positively Parisian 1900s decor. Its terrace bar out on the Paseo de Recoletas occupies a splendid glass pavilion reminiscent of a giant Tiffany lamp. Fashionable and comfortable, it has excellent tapas at reasonable prices.

INSIDE TRACK
ALFONSO OF CAFE GIJON

Alfonso, who sold cigarettes, matches and lottery tickets just inside the entrance of Café Gijón (*see left*) for more than 30 years, sadly died in 2006; a portrait and plaque – above the cigarette machine that replaced him – commemorate his life and long contribution to the café.

Shops & Services

High-street giants and hipster boutiques.

The high streets of Madrid have undeniably taken on the identikit look of most European capitals, albeit with Spanish chains – Zara, Mango, System Action – proliferating; but get off those main thoroughfares and what strikes you is the curious mix of the traditional and the new. Here the chains and international franchises rub shoulders with museum-piece, family-run businesses and ancient shops dedicated to just one product – espadrilles, maybe, or Spanish ceramics.

Visitors from cities with cutting-edge fashion scenes, such as London, New York and Berlin, are sometimes disappointed by Madrid's clothes shops; however, the scattering of hip new openings around Malasaña, Conde Duque and Alonso Martínez is starting to raise consumer expectations.

WHERE TO SHOP

Madrid isn't a large city, and its main shopping areas break down into several distinctive zones, all conveniently within walking distance – or a short metro ride – of one another. Between Sol and Gran Vía are **C/Preciados** and **C/Carmen**, always bustling with shoppers, and boasting a mix of chains and smaller stores selling cheap and mid price clothes, shoes and accessories. Several branches of El Corte Inglés are to be found in this area. **Gran Vía** itself is given over to the flagship stores of many a household name – H&M, Zara and the Nike Store, to name but three. After battling through the crowds of dawdling shoppers, the tranquil area of **Los Austrias** comes as a welcome respite, with its musical instrument stores, bohemian gift shops and treasure troves of decorative items.

If you're all about labels, then **Salamanca** is the place to be, in particular C/Serrano, where on the same block you will find Loewe, Yves St Laurent and La Perla, as well as smaller designer boutiques throughout the area. **Chueca** houses a host of hip independents, such as Bunkha (*see p140*), vintage store Lotta (*see p140*) and bookshop Panta Rhei (*see p137*), as well as the youth-orientated brands of **C/Fuencarral** (home to MAC, Diesel, Puma, Fornarina, as well as Spanish brands Hoss Intropia and Hakei). Here you'll also find the shopping mall **El Mercado de Fuencarral**, a popular hangout for fashion-conscious teens

and twentysomethings, hosting streetwear shops with names like Fuck, Alter-nativa and Cannibal, as well as tattoo parlours and trendy hairdressers. For shoes, head down C/Augusto Figueroa, and then continue north up C/Barquillo for the more refined fashion boutiques, most of which are squeezed into the area between C/Argensola and Plaza Santa Barbara. West of here, the trendy triangle recently named **triBall**, just west of where C/Fuencarral meets Gran Vía, and the area around **C/Conde Duque** are now home to some of the city's most interesting boutiques.

The city's flea market, the **Rastro** (*see p149*) is an obligatory visit, but more for the atmosphere than the goods – you will almost certainly walk away empty-handed.

OPENING HOURS

Opening times are changing, as is the traditional August break. While smaller stores will still close for two or three hours at lunch and stay shut on Saturday afternoons, some mid-size and nearly all large outlets will remain open all day. If you have yet to get used to a 2pm lunch and can face the heat in the summer, head to the bigger stores in the early afternoon and you will miss the crowds. Pressure from large retailers brought about a relaxation of the laws on Sunday opening too, all amid much grumbling from small businesses, who find it very hard to compete with such timetables.

CONSUME

As a result, large retailers can – and do – open every first Sunday of the month. As revenue from tourists becomes more vital to the shopkeepers of Madrid, August is no longer a month when the city closes down.

ONE-STOP SHOPS

El Corte Inglés

C/Preciados 1-3 & 9, Sol & Gran Vía (all branches 91 379 80 00/Tel-entradas ticket phoneline 902 400 222, www.elcorteingles.es). Metro Sol. **Open** 10am-10pm Mon-Sat; 11am-9pm Sun. **Credit** AmEx, MC, V. **Map** p307 G11.

Spain's biggest retail concern has blown all the rest of the competition out of the water. El Corte Inglés is the solution when all else fails for some, but the first choice for many. You can get practically everything you need, be it clothes, household goods, books or multimedia products, and the store also offers a range of services from cutting keys to booking tickets. Most outlets also have well-stocked, if expensive, supermarkets. Information points staffed by multilingual employees are a plus. The branches on C/Preciados specialise in film, music, electronics, books, fashion and sports. This branch on the Plaza de Callao has homewares, toys and electronics. **Other locations** throughout the city.

FNAC

C/Preciados 28, Sol & Gran Vía (902 100 632, www.fnac.es). Metro Callao. **Open** 10am-9.30pm daily. **Credit** AmEx, MC, V. **Map** p307 G11.

The French giant offers a huge range of CDs, DVDs, videos and books, plus computer hardware and software, all at competitive prices and under one roof. Among the CDs there are good world music and flamenco sections, and the helpful staff can look up titles on the database. There is a reasonable English-language book section, with recent paperbacks as well as classics. On the second floor is a room where you can sit and read while listening to music. Downstairs there's a ticket booking service, a café and paper shop with a good range of foreign press and magazines, and the FNAC Forum, which hosts readings and film and record launches.

After-hours

OpenCor

C/Fuencarral 118, Chamberí (91 591 38 96). Metro Bilbao. **Open** 8am-2am daily. **Credit** AmEx, DC, MC, V. **Map** p307 H7.

Stocks supermarket products, fresh food, CDs, DVDs, books and gifts. **Other locations** throughout the city.

Sprint

C/Arenal 28, Los Austrias (no phone). Metro Ópera. **Open** 24hrs daily. **No credit cards.** **Map** p311 F11.

Sprint is 7/11 rebranded and sells prepared food, hot and cold drinks, newspapers and magazines. **Other locations** throughout the city.

Vip's

Gran Vía 43, Sol & Gran Vía (91 275 20 93, www.vips.es). Metro Callao or Santo Domingo. **Open** 8am-3am Mon-Fri; 9am-3am Sat, Sun. **Credit** AmEx, DC, MC, V. **Map** p307 G11.

Vip's has branches all over town and stocks much the same as Sprint and OpenCor, along with Spanish and English-language press. **Other locations** throughout the city.

SHOPPING CENTRES

ABC Serrano

C/Serrano 61 & Paseo de la Castellana 34, Salamanca (91 577 50 31, www.abcserrano.com). Metro Rubén Darío. **Open** 10am-9pm Mon-Sat; noon-8pm 1st Sun of mth. **Map** p309 L6/7.

Occupying the building that once housed the ABC newspaper, this upmarket and perfectly located shopping mall has eight floors. Four of them are dedicated to fashion, designer and high street, sportswear, jewellery, crafts and hi-fi. There are three restaurants on the upper floors, a café on the ground floor and a lively summer *terraza* on the fourth, plus a gym at the top.

Centro Comercial La Vaguada

Avda Monforte de Lemos 36, Barrio del Pilar (information 91 730 10 00, www.enlavaguada. com). Metro Barrio del Pilar. **Open** 10am-10pm Mon-Sat; 11am-9pm Sun.

Madrid's first giant mall, and still the largest in the city, La Vaguada has around 350 outlets. There's a branch of El Corte Inglés (*see left*), and the upper floor is given over to leisure, with cinemas and a bowling alley. It's a bit of a trek to get here, but the metro line is fast.

Centro Comercial Príncipe Pío

Paseo de la Florida s/n, Moncloa (91 758 00 40, www.principepio.es). Metro Príncipe Pío. **Open** 10am-10pm Mon-Sat; 11am-10pm Sun. **Map** p306 C11.

CONSUME

CONSUME

Tiempos Modernos.

A welcome addition to one of the city's main transport hubs. Built into the shell of the old train station, the mall manages to pack in a deceptively large number of shops and eateries, ranging from the Body Shop and H&M to a Vip's restaurant and the obligatory Starbucks.

El Jardín de Serrano

C/Goya 6-8, Salamanca (91 577 00 12, www.jardindeserrano.es). Metro Serrano. **Open** 9.30am-9.30pm Mon-Sat. **Map** p309 L9.
This Salamanca mall may be small but it's a retail gem, with designer boutiques, expensive shoe shops and a classy café.

ANTIQUES

If you want antiques, head to the **Rastro** (*see p145*). On the main drag, C/Ribera de Curtidores, are several arcades where you'll find everything from old junk to authentic antiques. The adjoining streets, such as C/Mira el Río Alta and C/Carnero, are more downmarket and can yield real bargains. Elsewhere, there are a handful of antique shops in the C/Prado and, over in Salamanca, on and around C/Claudio Coello, are lots of upmarket, specialist dealers.

Centro de Anticuarios Lagasca

C/Lagasca 36, Salamanca (91 577 37 52). Metro Serrano. **Open** 11am-2pm, 5-8.30pm Mon-Fri; 11am-2pm Sat. Closed Aug. **Credit** varies. **Map** p309 L9.
An upmarket antiques arcade selling furniture, art and ornaments of every stripe.

Galerías Piquer

C/Ribera de Curtidores 29, Rastro & Lavapiés (no phone, www.dai.es/piquer). Metro Puerta de Toledo. **Open** 10.30am-2pm, 5-8pm Mon-Fri; 10.30am-2pm Sat, Sun. **Credit** varies. **Map** p311 G15.
The antiques shops in this Rastro arcade stock pieces for punters who don't want to have to brush the dust off their purchases. Opening times may vary.

Tiempos Modernos

C/Arrieta 17, Los Austrias & La Latina (91 542 85 94, www.tiempos-modernos.com). Metro Ópera. **Open** 11am-8pm Mon-Fri; 11am-2pm Sat. Closed 3wks Aug. **Credit** AmEx, MC, V. **Map** p307 E11.
Tiempos Modernos deals in modern Spanish painting, and hosts temporary shows and exhibitions of photography and artwork. The main line of business, though, is the great range of 1940s, '50s and '60s furniture.

El Transformista

C/Mirá el Río Baja 18, Rastro & Lavapiés (91 539 88 33). Metro Puerta de Toledo. **Open** 11am-2pm daily. **Credit** MC, V. **Map** p311 F15.
Original '50s and '60s furniture and collectibles are up for grabs at this shop. Almodóvar is rumoured to source items for his movies here.

BOOKS

FNAC (*see p135*) has an excellent general selection. A traditional centre of the book trade is **Calle de los Libreros** ('Booksellers' Street') off Gran Vía, with many specialist bookshops.

★ La Casa del Libro

Gran Vía 29 (902 026 402, www.casadellibro.
com). Metro Gran Vía. **Open** 9.30am-9.30pm
Mon-Sat; 11am-9pm Sun. **Credit** AmEx, DC,
MC, V. **Map** p307 H11.
La Casa del Libro covers just about every subject
imaginable in Spanish, but also has good sections of
literature, reference and teaching material in English
and other languages.

Librería de Mujeres

C/San Cristóbal 17, Los Austrias (91 521 70
43). Metro Sol. **Open** *Oct-May* 10am-2pm,
5-8pm Mon-Fri; 10am-2pm Sat. *June-Sept* 10am-
2pm, 5-8pm Mon-Fri. **Credit** AmEx, MC, V.
Map p311 G12.
Madrid's best women's bookshop goes by the motto
'*Los libros no muerden, tampoco el feminismo*' –
'Books don't bite, neither does feminism'.

★ Ocho y Medio

C/Martín de los Heros 11, Argüelles (91 559
06 28, www.ochoymedio.com). Metro Plaza
de España. **Open** 10am-9pm Mon-Sat. **Credit**
MC, V. **Map** p307 E9.
This superb cinema bookshop is a treat for film
buffs, with plenty of works in English and other languages, plus DVDs and film paraphernalia.

★ Panta Rhei

C/Hernán Cortés 7, Chueca (91 319 89 02,
www.panta-rhei.es). Metro Chueca. **Open**
10.30am-8.30pm Mon-Fri; 11am-8.30pm Sat.
Credit MC, V. **Map** p308 H10.
This friendly Chueca bookshop sells an excellent
range of illustrated and photography books. Plenty
of them are in English and many have a humorous
bent. The shop's stylish cotton totes make nice,
cheap souvenirs too.

Children

Mar de Letras

C/Santiago 18, Los Austrias (91 541 71 09,
www.lamardeletras.com). Metro Ópera. **Open**
10.30am-2pm, 5-8.30pm Mon-Fri; 10.30am-2.30pm,
5-8.30pm Sat. Closed 2wks Aug. **Credit** MC, V.
Map p311 F11/12.
Mar de Letras is a well-stocked bookshop specialising in kids' editions. Look out, too, for the English-
language titles and educational toys.

English-language specialists

Panta Rhei and **Ocho y Medio** (for both,
see left) stock lots of English-language books;
the former specialises in art and design, the
latter in film.

Booksellers

C/Fernández de la Hoz 40, Chamberí (91 442 79
59, www.booksellers.es). Metro Iglesia. **Open**
9.30am-2pm, 5-8pm Mon-Fri; 10am-2pm Sat.
Credit AmEx, DC, MC, V. **Map** p308 J6.

CONSUME

Cuesta de Moyano. *See p138.*

Madrid's best English-language bookshop sells a wide selection of literature, videos and DVDs, as well as materials for TEFLers. The branch below also has a children's book section.
Other location C/Santa Engracia 115, Chamberí (91 702 79 44).

J&J Books & Coffee

C/Espíritu Santo 47, Malasaña (91 521 85 76, www.jandjbooksandcoffee.com). Metro Noviciado. **Open** noon-midnight Mon-Thur, Sat; noon-2am Fri; 4-10pm Sun. **Credit** MC, V. **Map** p307 G9.
J&J is at once a relaxing little café (at ground-floor level) and a well-stocked second-hand bookshop (in the basement). Activities include open-mic sessions, language exchanges (Wednesdays, Thursdays and Saturdays from 8pm) and quizzes (Fridays from 11pm). Staff can source books that aren't in stock. The 'happy hour' is 4-7pm Monday to Friday.

Pasajes

C/Génova 3, Chueca (91 310 12 45, www.pasajes libros.com). Metro Alonso Martínez. **Open** 9.30am-9.30pm Mon-Sat. **Credit** MC, V. **Map** p308 J8.
This linguists' treasure trove sells a great range of fiction and non-fiction, language-learning materials, maps, audio books and videos. Most things are in English, French, German and Spanish.

Petra's International Bookshop

C/Campomanes 13, Sol & Gran Vía (91 541 72 91, www.petrasbookshop.com). Metro Ópera or Santo Domingo. **Open** 11am-9pm Mon-Sat. **Credit** MC, V. **Map** p311 F11.

A great range of second-hand books in English and other languages is on offer in this laid-back little shop. Here you can offload excess books or trade them for others. Sadly, Petra the cat, who gave the shop its name, has now passed on.

Second-hand & rare

Most bookshops dealing in rare and antique books are around pedestrianised **C/Huertas**. A great place for cheap second-hand books is the **Cuesta de Moyano**, on C/Claudio Moyano, by the Jardín Botánico (*photo p137*). It has a line of kiosks selling second-hand books, from rare editions to remainders. Some are open all week, but Sunday mornings are busiest.

Librería San Ginés

Pasadizo de San Ginés 2, Sol (91 366 46 86). Metro Ópera or Sol. **Open** 10am-8pm daily. **Credit** MC, V. **Map** p311 G11.
This Old Curiosity Shop-style place, in an atmospheric passageway, sells everything from scruffy English paperbacks to antique editions.

Travel & maps

Libreria Desnivel

Plaza Matute 6, Santa Ana (91 369 42 90, www.libreriadesnivel.com). Metro Antón Martín. **Open** 10am-2pm, 4.30-8.30pm Mon-Sat. **Credit** AmEx, MC, V. **Map** p312 H13.
This excellent travel and adventure bookshop sells a wide range of maps and books covering Spain and

Madrid al Cubo.

other countries. Desnivel's own publications include walking and climbing guides, and the shop also has information on organised walks, hikes and so on.

La Tienda Verde

C/Maudes 23 & 38, Chamberí (91 534 32 57, www.tiendaverde.es). Metro Cuatro Caminos. **Open** 10am-2.30pm, 4-8.30pm Mon-Fri; 10am-2pm Sat. **Credit** AmEx, DC, MC, V.
Madrid's original and best shop for travel books and maps, the 'Green Shop' now occupies two premises on the same street. At No.23 you will find tourist and nature guides, while No.38 sells maps and specialised mountaineering books.

CHILDREN
Clothes

DPAM

Plaza Puerta del Sol 6, Sol (91 523 16 14, www. dpam.es). Metro Sol. **Open** 10am-9pm Mon-Sat. **Credit** AmEx, MC, V. **Map** p311 H11.
DPAM (Du Pareil au Même) is a French chain specialising in original, colourful clothes for kids up to age 12. Its clothes for babies and toddlers are especially funky and make great presents.

Max Kinder

C/Carretas 8, Los Austrias (91 521 69 47, www.maxkinder.es). Metro Sol. **Open** 10am-9pm Mon-Sat. **Credit** MC, V. **Map** p311 H11.
This shop is the junior version of Max Moda, across the street, and does a reasonable range of basic clothes for children from three months to 16 years.

Toys

Don Juego

C/Alcalá 113, Salamanca (91 435 37 24, www. donjuego.es). Metro Príncipe de Vergara. **Open** 10am-9pm Mon-Sat; 11am-3pm Sun. **Credit** DC, MC, V. **Map** p313 M10.
This shop specialises in board games for both kids and adults – as well as mah-jong, solitaire, Chinese chequers and chess, it stocks Go.

Sanatorio de Muñecos

C/Preciados 19 1ª, Sol (91 521 04 47). Metro Sol. **Open** 10am-2pm, 5-8pm Mon-Fri. **Credit** MC, V. **Map** p307 G11.
The 'dolls' hospital' does indeed mend dolls, but also functions as the oldest toy shop in Madrid, full of parents gazing nostalgically at the old-school model cars, teddy bears and so on.

CLEANING & LAUNDRY

Self-service *lavanderías* (launderettes) are rather thin on the ground in Madrid: in most there will be an attendant on duty.

Lavandería Donoso Cortés

C/Donoso Cortés 17, Chamberí (91 446 96 90). Metro Quevedo or Canal. **Open** *Sept-July* 9am-2pm, 3.30-8pm Mon-Sat. *Aug* 9am-2.30pm Mon-Sat. **No credit cards**.

CRAFTS & GIFTS

★ Antigua Casa Talavera

C/Isabel la Católica 2, Sol & Gran Vía (91 547 34 17). Metro Santo Domingo. **Open** 10am-1.30pm, 5-8pm Mon-Fri; 10am-1.30pm Sat. **Credit** AmEx, MC, V. **Map** p307 F11.
This long-standing family business specialises in traditional blue and white Spanish ceramics. Every available space is crammed with hand-painted designs, all sourced from small Spanish producers. The charming owner speaks good English.

Madrid al Cubo

C/Cruz 35, Sol & Gran Vía (mobile 627 45 20 53, www.madridalcubo.com). Metro Tirso de Molina. **Open** *Jan, Feb* 10.30am-2.30pm, 5-9pm Mon-Thur; 10.30am-2.30pm, 5-11pm Fri, Sat. *Mar-Dec* 10.30am-2.30pm, 5-9pm Mon-Thur; 10.30am-2.30pm, 5-11pm Fri, Sat; 11am-3pm Sun. **Credit** AmEx, DC, MC, V. **Map** p311 H12.
Tourist shop Madrid al Cubo sells a decent range of cool alternative souvenirs, including graphics-based prints, T-shirts and mugs, coffee-table books, tote bags and original postcards.

Piedra de Luna

C/Príncipe 14, Santa Ana (91 521 63 73). Metro Sevilla. **Open** 10.30am-2.30pm, 4.30-9.30pm Mon-Sat; 4.30-9.30pm Sun. **Credit** AmEx, DC, MC, V. **Map** p312 H12.
A selection of good-quality craftwork from around the world. Tuareg kilims, Moroccan ceramics and Indian silver jewellery and painted wooden furniture all feature on the shelves.

Popland

C/Manuela Malasaña 24, Malasaña (91 591 21 20, www.popland.es). Metro Bilbao. **Open** 11am-9pm Mon-Sat. **Credit** MC, V. **Map** p307 G8.

CONSUME

For times when only a Jesus action figure will do, Popland saves the day. The shop is packed with all things pop-culture and plastic, but also film posters, shower curtains and T-shirts. There's also a good range of greetings cards – quite a rarity in Madrid.

La Vida es Sueño
C/Mayor 59, Sol & Gran Via (91 364 16 82, www.lavidaessueno.es). Metro Sol. **Open** 11am-3pm, 5-8pm Mon, Tue, Thur-Sun. **Credit** DC, MC, V. **Map** p311 F12.
Souvenirs with a difference, with traditional toys and classy Madrid-themed knick-knacks of the type you'd normally only find in museum gift shops.

DESIGN & HOUSEHOLD

BD Madrid
C/Villanueva 5, Salamanca (91 435 06 27, www.bdmadrid.com). Metro Serrano. **Open** 9.30am-1.30pm, 4.30-8pm Mon-Fri; 10am-2pm Sat. Closed Aug. **Credit** AmEx, MC, V. **Map** p309 L10.
BD carries a stunning selection of contemporary furniture designs from Spanish and international names, many with a retro feel. The company is now producing its own pieces, including a kitchen range. Hefty price tags, but worth a visit if only to peruse.

Expresión Negra
C/Piamonte 15, Chueca (91 319 95 27, www.expresionnegra.org). Metro Chueca. **Open** 11am-2.30pm, 5-8.30pm Mon-Sat. **Credit** AmEx, DC, MC, V. **Map** p308 J10.
Expresión Negra is a great place to indulge in a spot of retail therapy and help the environment at the same time. As well as breathing new life into recycled objects – briefcases, lamps and other objects made out of used Coke cans, sardine tins and so on – the shop also puts a different spin on African handicrafts, with brightly coloured throws, textiles and some unusual metalwork.

PlazAAarte
Costanilla de los Capuchinos 5, Chueca (91 522 85 93, www.plazaarte.com). Metro Chueca. **Open** 11.30am-2pm, 5.30-9pm Mon-Sat. Closed 1wk Aug. **Credit** MC, V. **Map** p308 H10.
This is a trendy, Swedish-owned shop/gallery that specialises in contemporary items for the home by up-and-coming national and international designers.

Víctimas del Celuloide
C/Santiago 8, Los Austrias (91 547 61 35, www.victimasdelceluloide.com). Metro Ópera. **Open** 7.30-10pm Mon; noon-2pm, 7-10pm Tue-Fri; noon-3pm Sat. **Credit** MC, V. **Map** p311 F12.
'Because we are all victims of celluloid,' says the proprietor of this shop selling interior design pieces with a twist, mainly from Nordic suppliers. A pop art influence is noticeable in the selection.

FASHION
Boutiques & designer

Agatha Ruiz de la Prada
C/Serrano 27, Salamanca (91 319 05 01, www.agatharuizdelaprada.com). Metro Serrano. **Open** *Sept-June* 10am-8.30pm Mon-Sat. *July, Aug* 10am-2pm, 5-8pm Mon-Sat. **Credit** AmEx, DC, MC, V. **Map** p309 L8.
Loud, colourful patterns characterise this designer's work, many emblazoned with her trademark hearts and flowers. The childrenswear range is hugely popular, as are the homewares.

★ Bunkha
C/Santa Bárbara 6, Malasaña (91 522 09 50, www.bunkha.com). Metro Tribunal or Gran Vía. **Open** 11am-3pm, 5-9pm Mon-Sat. **Credit** MC, V. **Map** p307 H9.
The stylish boutique stocks a host of upmarket yet hip labels, such as Swedish brand Uniforms for the Dedicated, Spanish brand Broken Porcelain and Italian label Camo. Menswear is in the front space, while womenswear is in the mezzanine area.

Jocomomola
C/Colón 4, Malasaña (91 575 00 05, www.jocomomola.com). Metro Tribunal. **Open** 11am-9pm Mon-Sat; noon-8pm Sun. Closed 2wks Aug. **Credit** AmEx, MC, V. **Map** p308 H10.
Top-flight designer Sybilla has suffered in the economic crisis, but Jocomomola, her playful, colourful range aimed at a younger crowd, continues to thrive.

★ Lotta
C/Hernán Cortés 9, Chueca (91 523 25 05, www.lottavintage.com). Metro Chueca or Tribunal. **Open** noon-2.30pm, 5-8.30pm Mon-Sat. **Credit** MC, V. **Map** p308 H10.
The Swedish proprietor of Lotta set up her first vintage clothing store in the Rastro in 1992. The shop carries vintage clothing from the '50s to the '80s and also stocks colourful dresses by the owner herself.

Chains & high street

For famous Spanish leather specialist **Loewe**, *see p145*. International high-street chains are to be found on Gran Via (with H&M at no.32) and C/Fuencarral. Global Spanish chains **Mango** (C/Fuencarral 70) and **Zara** (C/Fuencarral 126-128 and Gran Via 34) are slightly cheaper here than in shops outside Spain. There's a branch of **Topshop** at Puerta del Sol 6.

Adolfo Domínguez
C/Ortega y Gasset 4, Salamanca (91 576 00 84, www.adolfodominguez.es). Metro Rubén Darío. **Open** 10am-8.30pm Mon-Sat. **Credit** AmEx, DC, MC, V. **Map** p309 L7.

CONSUME

Street Style

The lowdown on Madrid's fashion clans.

Heavies

Pronounced with a guttural, Scottish 'ch' at the beginning, these are the rockers that time forgot. Look for leather and studs, heavy metal T-shirts and boots.
Where to find them: In a *plaza* engaging in a *botellón* (piss-up), and in the suburbs. The famous 'heavies of Gran Vía' twins always stand outside the former Madrid Rock shop – now a branch of Bershka.
Essential accessories: Bottle of Mahou beer, cigarettes and unruly facial hair.
Seen at: the Rastro *(see p149)* for Metallica T-shirts, Sprint *(see p135)* for beer and baccy.

Muscu-locos

The Muscle-Boys. A play on words – a mix of 'muscular' and 'crazy about muscles'. Tight tops and vests for this lot; biceps as big as your head warrant showing off. These boys are mad about their image and cultivate it in the gym and Chueca's boutiques.
Where to find them: Chueca is the place to marvel at their chiselled features and sculpted torsos. Here they shop, bar-hop and admire one another from afar... and sometimes not so afar.

Essential accessories: Very short shorts, Speedos for the pool, and a roving eye.
Seen at: Amantis for toys, Berkana for books and SR for leather goods (for all, *see p188*).

Fiesteros

The party people. Pierced and tattooed to the hilt, this polysexual crew are the hippest of the hip kids.
Where to find them: Their natural habitat is Malasaña and the Fuencarral market, where they shop, chat and get more piercings.
Essential accessories: VIP passes for the next big party, fashionable mullet haircuts from Juan ¡por Diós! *(see p151)*, and sunglasses.
Seen at: The Malasaña boutiques on Calle del Pez and Corredora Baja de San Pablo.

Pijos & pijas

The posh kids. Big, floppy '80s-style barnets – and that's just the boys. Lacoste polo shirts, a jumper tied around the shoulders, white jeans and espadrilles top off the look.
Where to find them: Branches of El Corte Inglés in the designer sections, Calle Serrano and any bar or club that was cool with the *fiesteros* two months previously.
Essential accessories: Daddy's credit card, a Mini Cooper and a comb to keep that floppy hair in check.
Seen at: ABC Serrano *(see p135)* shopping centre, Adolfo Domínguez *(see p140)* for sporty sweaters and Sana Sana *(see p151)* for a post-shopping massage.

Señores y señoras

The mature couple. For *él*, distinguished grey hair will be slicked back and the obligatory moustache neatly trimmed. For *ella*, an immaculately coiffed 'do is a must, with the make-up erring on the heavy side. A camel-hair jacket for him, a fur coat for the lady. Cigars and cigarettes respectively.
Where to find them: Salamanca, where they'll double-park for an hour while *la señora* gets a new bag.
Essential accessories: A small yappy dog, a Mercedes and plenty of bling.
Seen at: Purificación García *(see p142)* for something smart, Mantequerías Bravo *(see p148)* for posh nosh, and Loewe *(see p145)* for indulgent leather accessories.

CONSUME

INSIDE TRACK
BOUTIQUE BROWSING

The best spots for browsing independent boutiques are Conde Duque, around Plaza Guardias de Corps; the Alonso Martínez part of Chueca, between C/Argensola, C/Genova, Plaza Santa Bárbara and C/Fernando VI; and the trendy triangle now known as triBall (meaning 'triangle of Ballesta', after one of the area's best streets), formed by C/Corredera Baja de San Pablo, C/Valverde and C/Desengaño.

Simple, classic pieces from the well-known Galician designer. The suits are well cut and long-lasting, while the accessories and shoes are also some of the brand's strong points.
Other locations throughout the city.

Custo

C/Fuencarral 29, Chueca (91 360 46 36, www. custo-barcelona.com). Metro Gran Vía or Chueca. **Open** 10am-9pm Mon-Sat; 11.30am-8.30pm Sun. **Credit** AmEx, DC, MC, V. **Map** p308 H10.
This Catalan designer is famous for his funky patterned T-shirts, but has expanded the range to include creative and flattering dresses, skirts and coats. Custo sells in boutiques around the world, but is also rapidly expanding its own network of shops, with a new branch on C/Mayor.
Other locations throughout the city.

Hakei

C/Fuencarral 35, Chueca (91 522 09 34, www. hakei.com). Metro Chueca. **Open** 11am-9pm Mon-Sat; noon-8pm Sun. **Credit** DC, MC, V. **Map** p308 H10.
This nationwide womenswear chain – which is pretty similar in style to the UK brand Jigsaw – has yet to venture beyond the Spanish borders. Clothes, shoes and accessories are stylish, feminine and well-priced, with the large range of leather bags especially covetable.
Other locations C/Arenal 8, Sol & Gran Vía (91 521 47 26); C/Ayala 34, Salamanca (91 575 45 75); C/Goya 41, Salamanca (91 575 05 11).

Purificación García

C/Serrano 28, Salamanca (91 435 80 13, www.purificaciongarcia.es). Metro Serrano. **Open** 10am-8.30pm Mon-Sat; noon-8.30pm Sun. **Credit** AmEx, MC, V. **Map** p309 L9.
Purificación García is where the capital's older but elegant woman heads when she wants something smart for the office. Well cut and using natural materials, the clothes are very well priced for the quality of the fabrics.
Other locations throughout the city.

Peseta. *See p144*.

Street, casual & clubwear

The shopping mall **El Mercado de Fuencarral** (*see p134*) is home to a large number of the city's indie streetwear brands.

Desigual

C/Fuencarral 36-38, Chueca (91 521 49 07, www.desigual.com). Metro Tribunal or Gran Via. **Open** 10am-9pm Mon-Sat. **Credit** AmEx, MC, V. **Map** p307 H10.

Desigual has become a real hit with the club-kids, and it's easy to see why: gorgeous shop assistants, pumping house music and affordable, quality club and streetwear for men, women and children.

Flip

C/Mayor 17, Los Austrias (91 364 16 87, www.flipmadrid.com). Metro Sol. **Open** 10.30am-9pm Mon-Sat; noon-8pm Sun. **Credit** AmEx, MC, V. **Map** p311 G11/12.

Well-chosen range of labels from the likes of Carhartt, Diesel, Energie, G-Star Raw and Scotch&Soda, all presided over by über-hip and highly pierced, highly tattooed staff.

Lanikai

C/Alberto Aguilera 1, Malasaña (91 591 34 13, www.lanikai.es). Metro San Bernardo. **Open** 10.30am-9pm Mon-Sat. **Credit** AmEx, MC, V. **Map** p307 G7.

This three-storey emporium has all the essentials for the keen snowboarder, surfer and skateboarder, or anyone looking for streetwear by the likes of Etnies, Carhartt, Diesel and Stylelab.

★ Nonstop Sneakers

C/Pez 14, Malasaña (91 523 26 46). Metro Callao or Noviciado. **Open** 11am-2.30pm, 5-8.45pm Mon-Sat. **Credit** MC, V. **Map** p307 G10.

Madrid's best trainers shop sells a good range of New Balance and Nike, with plenty of rare editions and exclusive models. Be prepared for a bit of attitude from the staff, though.

Pepita is Dead

C/Doctor Fourquet 10, Lavapiés (91 528 87 88, www.pepitaisdead.es). Metro Atocha. **Open** 11am-2.30pm, 5-8.30pm Mon-Sat. Closed 3wks Aug. **Credit** MC, V. **Map** p312 I14.

Pepita is Dead specialises in vintage clothing. These items – mens-, womens- and childrenswear, plus accessories – are all unworn originals, carefully chosen from the '60s to the '80s.

Snapo

C/Espíritu Santo 5, Malasaña (91 532 12 23, www.snaposhop.com). Metro Noviciado or Tribunal. **Open** 11am-2pm, 5-8.30pm Mon-Sat. **Credit** AmEx, DC, MC, V. **Map** p307 H9.

Snapo stocks streetwear with attitude. Designs are funny and cheeky. The collection is mainly T-shirts, plus some bags, caps and womenswear.

★ Sportivo

C/Conde Duque 20, Malasaña (91 542 56 61, www.gruposportivo.com). Metro San Bernardo. **Open** 10am-9pm Mon-Sat. **Credit** AmEx, MC, V. **Map** p307 F8.

With a great range of menswear labels, including Cantskate, Burro, Levi's Red and Vintage, New York Industries, YMC and Duffer of St George, Sportivo is an unmissable stop. The staff are extremely helpful.

Lingerie & underwear

¡Oh, qué luna!

C/Ayala 32, Salamanca (91 431 37 25, www.ohqueluna.com). Metro Serrano. **Open** 10am-8.30pm Mon-Fri; 11am-2pm, 5-8.30pm Sat. **Credit** AmEx, MC, V. **Map** p309 L8.

Glam, sexy lingerie, negligées and dressing gowns. It also does a line in bedlinen and swimwear.

FASHION ACCESSORIES

Jewellery & accessories

Concha García

C/Goya 38, Salamanca (91 435 49 36, www.concha-garcia.com). Metro Goya. **Open** 10.30am-

CONSUME

Antigua Casa Crespo.

8.30pm Mon-Fri; 10.30am-2.30pm, 5-8.30pm Sat.
Credit DC, MC, V. **Map** p309 N9.
Concha García's two shops-cum-galleries are important showcases for contemporary and ethnic jewellery design, both national and international.

Joaquín Berao

*C/Lagasca 44, Salamanca (91 577 28 28,
www.joaquinberao.com). Metro Serrano.* **Open**
Sept-July 10am-2pm, 5-8.30pm Mon-Fri; 10.30am-
2.30pm, 5-8.30pm Sat. *Aug* 10am-2pm, 5-8.30pm
Mon-Fri; 10am-2pm Sat. **Credit** AmEx, DC,
MC, V. **Map** p309 L9.
Chunky, twisted and contorted, but also fluidly
elegant, Joaquín Berao's solid silver bracelets,
necklaces, earrings and chokers are increasingly the
choice of those in the know.

★ Peseta

*C/Noviciado 9, Conde Duque (91 521 14 04,
www.peseta.org). Metro Noviciado or Plaza de
España.* **Open** 5.30-8.30pm Mon-Fri; 10.30am-
3.30pm Sat. **Credit** AmEx, DC, MC, V. **Map**
p307 F9.
This cute shop-atelier in a creative quarter of Conde
Duque sells artisan bags, purses, laptop and passport cases, bicycle caps, handkerchiefs, keyrings and
badges from the Peseta range, all made using vintage-
style fabrics. It also sells Harinezumi 2 Japanese
digital cameras. The shop itself is lovingly kitted
out with retro furniture, and its owners, Laura and
Jaime, are often at work in the attached atelier (you
may need to ring the bell at such times). *Photos p142.*

Scooter Hombre

*C/Jorge Juan 14, Salamanca (91 576 47 49,
www.scooterhombre.com). Metro Serrano.*
Open 10.30am-8.30pm Mon-Sat. **Credit** AmEx,
MC, V. **Map** p309 L10.
Accessories are the main focus of this French store,
with funky, chunky jewellery, Anya Hindmarch
bags and gorgeous flip flops by Dorotea. The clothes
– a mix of funky and ethnic – are definitely worth
a look too.

Shoes, bags & leather products

Spain is a major producer of footwear, with
the Valencia and Alicante areas dominated
by shoe factories. As a result, Madrid is a
haven for the confirmed shoe addict. Head for
Augusto Figueroa, in the heart of Chueca.
Here you'll find a street packed with factory
'muestrarios' (selling samples) such as Vime
or Caligae.

Artisan shop **Peseta** (*see left*) sells a
beautiful range of fabric bags.

★ Antigua Casa Crespo

*C/Divino Pastor 29, Malasaña & Conde Duque
(91 521 56 54, www.alpargateriacrespo.com).
Metro Bilbao.* **Open** 10am-1.30pm, 5-8.15pm
Mon-Sat. Closed last 2wks Aug. **No credit
cards. Map** p307 G8.
This perfectly preserved old-fashioned, family-run
store, founded in 1863, is dedicated to espadrilles
of all sizes and colours.

Camper

*C/Serrano 24, Salamanca (91 578 25 60, www.
camper.com). Metro Serrano.* **Open** 10am-9pm
Mon-Sat; noon-8pm Sun. **Credit** AmEx, DC,
MC, V. **Map** p309 L10.
Branches of the Mallorcan family firm continue to
spring up all over the city (and all over the world).
At this one, two large plinths display the entire
men's and women's collection – brightly coloured,
fun shoes and sandals.
Other locations throughout the city.

Loewe

*C/Serrano 26 & 34, Salamanca (91 577 60 56,
www.loewe.com). Metro Serrano.* **Open** 10am-
8.30pm Mon-Sat; 11am-8pm Sun. **Credit** AmEx,
DC, MC, V. **Map** p309 L8/9.
The world-famous, elite Spanish leather goods
company, selling bags, shoes, cases and a small
range of clothes. Womenswear is located at no.26
and menswear at no.34.
Other locations throughout the city.

Piamonte

*C/Marqués de Monasterio 5, Chueca (91 702 55
61, www.piamontemadrid.com). Metro Chueca.*
Open 11am-8.30pm Mon-Fri; 11am-2.30pm,
5-8.30pm Sat. **Credit** AmEx, DC, MC, V.
Map p308 J10.
Desirable bags in all shapes, sizes and fabrics, from
denim to super-soft leather.

Other locations C/Lagasca 28, Salamanca
(91 575 55 20); C/Villanueva 16, Salamanca
(91 435 37 47).

★ Taller Puntera

*Plaza Conde de Barajas 4, Los Austrias (91
364 29 26, www.puntera.com). Metro Ópera,
La Latina or Tirso de Molina.* **Open** 10am-2pm,
5-9pm Mon-Sat; 10am-2pm Sun. **Credit** DC,
MC, V. **Map** p311 F12.
This lovely leather accessories shop/workshop
opened on Plaza Conde de Barajas in 2009, but its
sister shop in Malasaña was established over a
decade ago. Simple but stylish bags, satchels, ruck-
sacks, wallets, notebooks and more, all in top-quality
leather, are for sale in a range of tasteful colours. Each
'piece' has a story behind it, and you can personalise
it by getting your name engraved for free. What's
more, the staff are genuinely friendly and the prices
excellent for this level of workmanship. A gem.
Other location C/Cristo 3, Malasaña (91 541 33 60).

★ Vialis

*C/Jorge Juan 9, Salamanca (91 575 99 33, www.
vialis.es). Metro Retiro.* **Open** 10.30am-8.30pm
Mon-Sat. **Credit** AmEx, MC, V. **Map** p308 H10.
Madrid's only branch of the stylish Spanish
footwear brand is located just off the Fuencarral, on
the edges of Malasaña. Expect chunky but hip shoes
and boots, and a small selection of high-quality
leather bags.

Taller Puntera

CONSUME

CONSUME

Retail Groups

Many of the capital's shopping streets have their own particular speciality.

Up until Madrid's promotion to capital status in 1561, and the construction of the Plaza Mayor, guilds of tradespeople and artisans tended to cluster together in certain streets or quarters. A brief glance at a map of the higgledy-piggledy street layout in the environs of the Plaza Mayor shows this clearly: many streets are named after the guilds, *gremios*, that were concentrated in the immediate vicinity.

A little north of the Plaza Mayor, just across the Calle Mayor, is the Plaza de Herredores, 'Blacksmiths' Square', and running from there to Calle Arenal is the Calle de las Hileras, or 'Spinners' Street'. Parallel to this is Calle Bordadores, 'Embroiderers' Street', whose artisans presumably bought their supplies of *hilo*, thread, one street over. Also serving the textile trade were the *coloreros*, purveyors of dyes, who were established in the tiny street of the same name just a few yards away. To the west of Plaza Mayor is the Calle Sal, thus named because salt was sold from the royal deposits there. A few yards away is the minuscule Calle Botoneras, where buttons were sold, and close by is the Calle de los Esparteros, where mats were manufactured from esparto grass, still used nowadays to

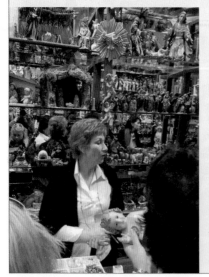

make espadrilles. To the south of the square is the Calle Latoneros, where the brassmongers traded. This street feeds into the Calle de los Cuchilleros, 'Knifemakers' Street', where Plaza Mayor butchers bought their cleavers. A little further south, what is nowadays the main drag of the Rastro, the Ribera de Curtidores, 'Tanners' Alley', was close to the city's slaughterhouse. The name 'Rastro' very possibly has its origin in the blood-stained trail, or *rastro*, left by the slaughtered animals.

As the centuries went by and Madrid expanded, these trades slowly disappeared or moved out and other commercial establishments sprang up. During the 19th and 20th centuries other shopping thoroughfares became associated with vendors of certain types of product, even though the street names now had nothing to do with the wares on sale. Right up until the advent of the PC, if you wanted to buy a typewriter you headed for Hortaleza and Hernán Cortés streets (a couple of shops selling Remington portables are still on the latter). If you needed anything orthopaedic you went to the Carretas street, where there are still a couple of establishments selling these items. Books – both new and second-hand – you found in the Calle de los Libreros and the Cuesta de Moyano, as you still do today. The Calles de la Paz and Postas have long had a tradition of shops dealing in religious artefacts, and the Plaza de Pontejos still has several haberdashers and remnants shops.

More recently, specialised streets have started to deal in modern goods. Walk along the Calle Barquillo in Chueca, and you'll notice an abundance of shops selling hi-fi equipment, hence the nickname Calle del Sonido ('Sound Street'). From here runs the Calle Almirante, which since the '80s has been colonised by a number of designer fashion shops, earning it the moniker 'Calle de la Moda', a title for which C/Claudio Coello in the Salamanca neighbourhood would now contend. More fashion, of the street- and clubwear variety, is concentrated along the C/Fuencarral, riding the Mercado de Fuencarral wave of the last few years. They may not be tinsmiths or button sellers any more, but many of Madrid's retailers still seem happier having their direct competitors just across the street.

FOOD & DRINK
Chocolates, cakes & sweets

★ Cacao Sampaka
C/Orellana 4, Huertas (91 319 58 40, www.cacaosampaka.com). Metro Alonso Martínez.
Open *Shop* 10am-9.30pm daily. *Café* 10am-9pm Mon-Sat. **Credit** AmEx, MC, V. **Map** p308 J9.
Handmade choccies arrayed in dazzling displays and for sale singly or in themed boxes, such as 'Spices of the Americas' or 'Flowers and herbs'. There are also chocolate jams, chocolate sauces and chocolate ice-creams, and a café on hand to sample its delights over a cup of coffee.

★ La Duquesita
C/Fernando VI 2, Chueca (91 308 02 31). Metro Alonso Martínez. **Open** 9.30am-2.30pm, 5-9pm Tue-Sun. Closed Aug. **Credit** MC, V. **Map** p308 I9.
This traditional *pastelería*, dating from 1914, has featured in lots of period-piece movies. Gorgeous chocolates and cakes are offered, along with *turrón* in the run-up to Christmas.

Happy Day
C/Espíritu Santo 11, Malasaña (91 522 91 33). Metro Tribunal. **Open** 10.30am-10pm Mon-Thur, Sun; 10.30am-midnight Fri, Sat. **Credit** MC, V. **Map** p307 H9.
The cupcake phenomenon is now huge in Madrid, and Happy Day was one of the pioneers. The 1950s-style *pastelería* is kitted out in pastel shades, and has a café table if you want to indulge your sweet tooth in-store.
Other location C/Cuchilleros 14, Los Austrias (same phone as above).

★ La Mallorquina
Puerta del Sol 8, Sol & Gran Vía (91 521 12 01). Metro Sol. **Open** 9am-9.15pm daily. Closed mid July-Aug. **No credit cards. Map** p311 G11.
Always bustling with locals, La Mallorquina occupies a prime location right on the Puerta del Sol. Downstairs, the pastry shop sells great cakes and savouries, all baked on the premises. The upstairs café has a pre-war feel and a team of old-school waiters in attendance.
▶ *For the review of the café, see p124.*

El Riojano
C/Mayor 10, Los Austrias (91 366 44 82, www.confiteriaelriojano.com). Metro Sol. **Open** 10am-2pm, 5-9pm daily. **Credit** AmEx, MC, V. **Map** p311 G11.
El Riojano has been in business since 1885, selling irresistible cakes, pastries, meringues and seasonal goodies. All are made in the traditional way, with meringues a particular speciality. Enjoy one with a coffee in the café out back.

Cacao Sampaka.

CONSUME

INSIDE TRACK 'BLANKET-TOPS'

A common sight in Madrid is people running with sheets in their hands, especially around the areas of Sol, Atocha and Bravo Murillo. They're not taking part in the capital's version of the running of the bulls, but rather they are '*los top manta*' ('the blanket-tops'), who sell their pirated CDs and DVDs laid out on squares of material. Once a policeman is spotted, strings tied to the corners of the material are hastily pulled and off they sprint.

Delicacies

Magerit, stand No.20/21 in La Cebada market (*see p149*), is an excellent place to buy cheese. For olives of all varieties, **F Illanas**, stalls 33-44 in the Mercado de Chamberí, C/Alonso Cano 10 (91 446 95 89), is a good bet. Several branches of **El Corte Inglés** (*see p135*) and most **OpenCor** outlets (*see p135*) have luxury food sections called El Club del Gourmet. But for the most atmospheric experience, head along to sample the goods from the gourmet-food specialists at **El Mercado de San Miguel** (*see p149* and *pp114-115* **Profile**).

La Boulette

Stands 63-68, Mercado de La Paz, C/Ayala 28, Salamanca (91 431 77 25, www.laboulette.com). Metro Serrano. **Open** 9am-8pm Mon-Fri; 9am-2.30pm Sat. **Credit** MC, V. **Map** p309 L8.
La Boulette probably has the largest selection of cheeses in Madrid and possibly the country, with over 400 varieties, both Spanish and imported, on sale. The range of goods in the charcuterie section is similarly impressive.

González

C/León 12, Huertas & Santa Ana (91 429 56 18). Metro Antón Martín. **Open** *Sept-June* 9am-midnight Mon-Thur; 9.30am-1am Fri, Sat; 11am-6pm Sun. *July, Aug* 6pm-midnight Mon-Sat. **Credit** AmEx, DC, MC, V. **Map** p312 I12.
Once a local grocer's, González is now a smart delicatessen with a fine range of cheeses, charcuterie, preserves, fruit and nuts, olive oils and plenty more besides. The back room houses a pleasant, well-stocked wine bar.

Mantequerías Bravo

C/Ayala 24, Salamanca (91 576 02 93). Metro Serrano. **Open** 9.30am-2.30pm, 5.30-8.30pm Mon-Fri; 9.30am-2.30pm Sat. Closed Aug. **Credit** AmEx, DC, MC, V. **Map** p309 L8.
A marvellous selection of foodstuffs is on sale in this Salamanca shop, including meats and cheeses, wines and spirits, and coffees and teas. Homesick Brits will be pleased with imports such as English mustard and cream crackers.

Museo del Jamón

Carrera de San Jerónimo 6, Huertas & Santa Ana (91 521 03 46, www.museodeljamon.es). Metro Sol. **Open** 9am-12.30am Mon-Thur; 9am-1am Fri, Sat; 10am-12.30am Sun. **Credit** MC, V. **Map** p311 H11.
Dotted around town, the various branches of the 'Ham Museum' are a sight to behold, with dozens of hams dangling from the ceiling. Sample their wares at the bar or in their restaurants.
Other locations throughout the city.

Patrimonio Comunal Olivarero

C/Mejía Lequerica 1, Chueca (91 308 05 05, www.pco.es). Metro Alonso Martínez. **Open** 10am-2pm, 5-8pm Mon-Fri; 10am-2pm Sat. Closed Aug. **Credit** MC, V. **Map** p308 I9.
Olive oil from every region of Spain that produces the stuff is on sale at Patrimonio Comunal Olivarero. Quantities go from two-litre bottles to five-litre cans, and some make lovely gifts.

Health & herbs

NaturaSí

C/Doctor Fleming 1, Chamartín (91 458 32 54, www.naturasi.eu). Metro Santiago Bernabéu. **Open** 10am-9pm Mon-Sat. **Credit** AmEx, DC, MC, V.
This 'natural' supermarket sells a huge range of ecological and natural foodstuffs, among them fresh fruit and veg, cheese and herbal products.

Salud Mediterranea

Paseo Santa María de la Cabeza 3, Atocha (91 527 89 29, www.saludmediterranea.com). Metro Atocha. **Open** 10am-8pm Mon-Fri; 10am-2pm Sat. **Credit** MC, V. **Map** p312 J15.
The huge selection of organic and macrobiotic products at this shop includes hard-to-find Japanese items and pollen from the bees in the Sierra de Madrid. **Other location** C/Ortega y Gasset 77, Salamanca (91 309 53 90).

Markets

Madrid's markets are a noisy, colourful way to get close to the locals – and to stock up on cheap food. They offer a vast range of fruit and veg, meat, wet fish, cheese, charcuterie and offal. All the following markets are open from around 9am-2pm and 5-8pm (15 May-15 Sept until 8.30pm) during the week, and 9am-2pm on Saturdays, unless otherwise stated.

Mercado de Anton Martín

C/Santa Isabel 5, Lavapiés (91 369 06 20). Metro Antón Martín. **Map** p312 I13.

Mercado de La Cebada
Plaza de la Cebada s/n, La Latina (91 365 91 76).
Metro La Latina. **Map** p311 F13.

Mercado de Chamartín
C/Bolivia 9, Chamartín (91 457 53 50,
http://mercadodechamartin.com). Metro Colombia.
In an upmarket neighbourhood with many affluent
foreign residents, and produce to match.

Mercado de Chamberí
C/Alonso Cano, 10, Chamberí (no phone).
Metro Iglesia.
Big, with lots of variety. The fruit and veg stalls in
the middle are among the best in town.

Mercado de Maravillas
C/Bravo Murillo 122, Tetuán (no phone).
Metro Alvarado.
Madrid's biggest market, and the best for fish.

★ Mercado de la Paz
C/Ayala 28, Salamanca (91 435 07 43, http://
mercadodelapaz.blogspot.com). Metro Serrano.
Map p309 L8.
A high-end market, with a dazzling range of products. Don't miss gourmet cheese stall La Boulette
(*see p148*).

Mercado de San Anton
C/ Augusto Figueroa 24, Chueca (91 330 07 30,
www.mercadosananton.com). Metro Chueca.
Open 10am-10pm Mon-Sat. **Map** p308 I10.
A high-end market, with a great range of products
and eateries to match. *Photos p150.*

★ Mercado de San Miguel
Plaza de San Miguel, Los Austrias (91 548 12
14). Metro Sol. **Map** p311 F12.
This elegant market, with a restored 19th-century
wrought-iron façade, has been a huge success story
since reopening in 2009. There's a good selection of
quality produce, but the market is designed more as
a spot for tapas munching than as a place to stock
up on essentials. For details of the market's outlets,
see pp114-115 **Profile.**

Los Mostenses
Plaza de Los Mostenses, Malasaña (no phone).
Metro Plaza de España. **Map** p307 F10.
A huge market in Malasaña with an international
atmosphere: Chinese and Mexican products are
much in evidence.

El Rastro
C/Ribera de Curtidores, between Plaza de Cascorro
& Ronda de Toledo (no phone, www.elrastro.org).
Metro La Latina. **Open** 9am-approx 2pm Sun.
Map p311 G14.
The city's most famous flea market dates back
nearly five centuries. Stalls start setting up from
around 8am, with the hardcore bargain-hunters
arriving soon afterwards, though trading officially
begins at 9am. In truth, there are few real deals
to be had these days, but in among the tat are
Moroccan stalls selling lovely leather bags (though
be sure to haggle hard), and antiques stalls and
shops that are worth a trawl. In any case, it's still a
quintessential stop on the tourist map – especially
as a pre-La Latina tapas bars jaunt. Do keep an eye
on your bag, though. *Photo p152.*

CONSUME

Mercado de Maravillas.

Mercado de San Antón

Supermarkets

Hypermarkets are mostly to be found on the main roads around the edge of the city, and are mainly accessible only by car. If you're mobile and need to stock up, look for ads for Alcampo, Continente or Pryca. Many branches of **El Corte Inglés** (*see p135*) also have (pricey) supermarkets. For information on Sunday opening, *see p134*. In town, keep your eye out for branches of **Caprabo** (www.caprabo.es), **Carrefour Express** (www.carrefour.es), **Sabeco** (www.simply.es) and **Lidl** (www.lidl.es).

Wine & drink

Bodegas Santa Cecilia
C/Blasco de Garay 72-74, Chamberí (91 445 52 83, www.santacecilia.es). Metro Islas Filipinas. **Open** 10am-9pm Mon-Sat. **Credit** AmEx, DC, MC, V. **Map** p307 E6.
This *bodega*, occupying two almost-adjacent locales, stocks a vast array of wines, beers and spirits – over 4,000 in total. Wines are mainly Spanish, while beers and spirits come from all over. The gourmet shop, No.72, hosts frequent tasting sessions.

INSIDE TRACK DOWN AT HEEL

All markets and most streets have a shoe repairer – look out for *rápido* or *reparación de calzados* signs.

Other location C/Bravo Murillo 50, Cuatro Caminos (91 442 35 32).

★ Lavinia
C/José Ortega y Gasset 16, Salamanca (91 426 06 04, www.lavinia.es). Metro Nuñez de Balboa. **Open** 10am-9pm Mon-Sat. **Credit** AmEx, DC, MC, V. **Map** p309 M7.
No oenophile should miss visiting Lavinia, which claims to be Europe's largest wine shop. In stark contrast to many of Madrid's dusty old *bodegas*, it's bright, airy and spacious, and staff are knowledge-able and helpful.

Mariano Madrueño
C/Postigo de San Martín 3, Sol & Gran Vía (91 521 19 55, www.marianomadrueno.es). Metro Callao. **Open** 10am-2pm, 5.30-8.30pm Mon-Sat. Closed 2wks Aug. **Credit** MC, V. **Map** p311 G11.
This classic old *bodega*, dating back to 1895, has a charming interior, complete with wrought-iron columns and carved wooden shelves. As for the booze on sale, the selection is enormous, with wines and spirits, plus the *bodega*'s own (lethal) coffee and orange liqueurs.

Reserva y Cata
C/Conde de Xiquena 13, Chueca (91 319 04 01, www.reservaycata.com). Metro Chueca. **Open** 11am-2.30pm, 5-9pm Mon-Fri; 11am-2.30pm Sat. **Credit** AmEx, MC, V. **Map** p308 J10.
This shop is crammed full of wines from Spain and abroad, all displayed with helpful information and often at prices lower than in the supermarkets. Tasting sessions and courses are also offered.

HAIR & BEAUTY

Cosmetics & perfumes

Branches of upmarket international cosmetics and skincare brands, such as **MAC**, **Kiehls** and **Korres**, can be found on C/Fuencarral. There are branches of the Parisian cosmetics and perfume shop **Sephora** in Conde Duque (C/Alberto Aguilera 62, 91 550 20 50) and on the Puerta del Sol (No.3, 91 523 71 71).

Hairdressers

Jofer
C/Galileo 56, Chamberí (91 447 51 60, www.jofer. com). Metro Quevedo. **Open** 8am-10pm Mon-Sat. **Credit** MC, V. **Map** p307 F6.
A good bet if you just want to get a quick trim or a blow-dry. Prices vary but are generally pretty reasonable, and at most branches you don't need an appointment. Waxing, tanning and other beauty services are also on offer, and you can even arrange for a home visit.
Other locations throughout the city.

Juan, ¡por Diós!
C/Pérez Galdós 3, Chueca (91 523 36 49, www.juanpordios.com). Metro Chueca or Gran Vía. **Open** 10am-9pm Mon-Sat. **Credit** AmEx, DC, MC, V. **Map** p308 H10.
Currently the place to get your hair cut in Madrid's trendiest quarter, this innovative salon also stocks international style magazines and CDs, and even has a Wi-Fi connection.

Spas & massages

See also p225 **Bath Time**.

Chi Spa
C/Conde de Aranda 6, Salamanca (91 578 13 40, www.thechispa.com). Metro Retiro. **Open** 10am-9pm Mon-Fri; 10am-6pm Sat. **Credit** AmEx, DC, MC, V. **Map** p309 L10.
A sleek, sophisticated space that has separate areas for men and women offering specialised body and relaxation treatments, massages with essential oils and spices, hydrotherapy and aromatherapy.

Sana Sana
C/Zurbano 51, Chamberí (91 310 54 24, www.sanasaludsana.es). Metro Rubén Darío. **Open** 11am-9pm Mon-Fri; 11am-3pm Sat. **Credit** MC, V. **Map** p308 J6.
An instant massage chain that offers a ten-minute workover for the harassed exec using specially designed chairs. It also offers shiatsu, sports and anti-stress massage, and beauty treatments. No booking is necessary for the short massage.

Tattoos & body piercing

Factory Tattoo
C/Montera 24, Sol & Gran Vía (91 521 44 69). Metro Gran Vía or Sol. **Open** 10am-10pm Mon-Sat; 5-10pm Sun. **Credit** MC, V. **Map** p311 H11.
Factory is the most popular of the city's tattoo parlours, its seedy location no doubt adding to its allure. If your pain threshold is low, it's worth a visit just to see – and wince at – photos of piercings past.

CONSUME

MUSIC

For wannabe DJs, **C/La Palma** and the surrounding streets are the places to be, with all genres of dance and rock music covered in a plethora of record shops. Head to **FNAC** (*see p135*) for the best selection of DVDs and music CDs; El Corte Inglés has an ineffective classification system and a sprawling layout.

El Flamenco Vive

C/Conde de Lemos 7, Los Austrias (91 547 39 17, www.elflamencovive.es). Metro Ópera. **Open** 10am-2pm, 5-9pm Mon-Sat. **Credit** AmEx, MC, V. **Map** p311 F11.
Even if you harbour only a passing interest in flamenco, the brilliant range of CDs, guitars, books and other paraphernalia at this shop will lure you in.

★ Radio City

C/Conde Duque 14, Conde Duque (91 547 77 67, www.radiocitydiscos.com). Metro Noviciado, Plaza de España or Ventura Rodríguez. **Open** 11am-2pm, 5-8.30pm Mon-Sat. **Credit** MC, V. **Map** p307 F8.
One of the city's best record shops, with a host of independent labels covering everything from indie folk to rare soul and R&B via Latin beats, on vinyl and CD. A selection of vintage LPs is also stocked.

Up Beat Discos

C/Espíritu Santo 6, Malasaña (91 522 76 60, www.upbeat.es). Metro Noviciado or Tribunal. **Open** 11am-2pm, 5-8.30pm Mon-Sat. **Credit** MC, V. **Map** p307 G9.

Soul, jazz and reggae dominate the shelves here, with a hand-picked collection of CDs and vinyl, along with a sideline in donkey jackets, parkas, Dr Martens, and so on. The shop has a fab '60s feel, with a space dedicated to scooter parts. Staff can track down rareties.

OPTICIANS

+ Visión

Puerta del Sol 14, Sol (91 701 49 80, www.masvision.es). Metro Sol. **Open** 10am-9pm Mon-Sat; 11am-3pm, 4-8pm Sun. **Credit** AmEx, DC, MC, V. **Map** p311 H11.
This high-street optician is part of the same group as the UK's Vision Express. There's a wide range of frames and contacts. Prescription glasses or sunglasses take an hour to make up.
Other locations throughout the city.

PHARMACIES

For general information on pharmacies, *see* **Resources A-Z**.

Farmacia Central

Paseo de Santa María de la Cabeza 64, Embajadores (91 473 06 72). Metro Embajadores. **Open** 24hrs daily. **Credit** MC, V.

Farmacia Lastra

C/Conde de Peñalver 27, Salamanca (91 402 43 01). Metro Goya. **Open** 8am-11pm daily. **Credit** AmEx, DC, MC, V. **Map** p309 O9.

El Rastro. *See p149.*

PHOTOGRAPHIC

FNAC (*see p135*) has a good photography department, with helpful staff.

Fotocasión

C/Ribera de Curtidores 22, Rastro (91 467 64 91, www.fotocasion.es). Metro Puerta de Toledo. **Open** 10am-2pm, 4.30-8.30pm Mon-Fri; 10am-2pm Sat, Sun. **Credit** MC, V. **Map** p311 F/G15.
A treasure trove for photographers and camera collectors. Owner José Luis Mur has great offers on spare parts and new and second-hand cameras.

SPECIALITY SHOPS

Almirante 23

C/Almirante 23, Chueca (91 308 12 02, www.almirante23.net). Metro Chueca. **Open** 11am-1.30pm, 5-7.30pm Mon-Fri; 11am-1.30pm Sat. **Credit** MC, V. **Map** p308 J10.
This curiosity shop is packed full with all manner of old stuff, including toys, tacky postcards, prints, cameras, watches, bullfighting programmes and more. Brilliant for browsing – and buying gifts.

Belloso

C/Mayor 23, Los Austrias (91 366 42 58, www.belloso.es). Metro Sol. **Open** 9.45am-2pm, 4.45-8pm Mon-Fri; 9.45am-2pm Sat. **Credit** AmEx, DC, MC, V. **Map** p311 G11.
This neighbourhood has an abundance of shops selling Catholic paraphernalia, but Belloso is one of the best. The gear on offer covers a huge range, including rosaries, crucifixes and statues of the Virgin.

La Casa de los Chales

C/Duque de Sesto 54, Salamanca (91 574 25 73, http://lacasadeloschales.com). Metro Goya or O'Donnell. **Open** 8am-1.30pm, 5-9pm Mon-Sat. **Credit** AmEx, MC, V. **Map** p309 O10.
The 'House of Shawls' has a huge range of *mantones de Manila*, beautifully made fringed and embroidered shawls. Capes, handbags and feather boas complete the stock.

Casa de Diego

Puerta del Sol 12, Sol (91 522 66 43, www.casadediego.com). Metro Sol. **Open** 9.30am-8pm Mon-Sat. **Credit** AmEx, DC, MC. **Map** p311 H11.
This much-loved shop specialises in hand-painted fans, umbrellas and classy walking sticks.

Guantes Luque

C/Espoz y Mina 3, Santa Ana (91 522 32 87). Metro Sol. **Open** 10am-1.30pm, 5-8pm Mon-Fri; 10.30am-1.30pm Sat. Closed Aug. **Credit** DC, MC, V. **Map** p311 H12.
This old-fashioned glove shop in Santa Ana has been open for more than 125 years. Luque sells gloves in all sizes, colours and materials, covering all types of wool, silk and leather. If you can't find them here you won't find them anywhere. Prices range from €20 to €300.

Objetos de Arte Toledano

Paseo del Prado 10, Huertas (91 429 50 00, www.armasmedievales.com). Metro Banco de España. **Open** 10am-8.15pm Mon-Sat. **Credit** AmEx, DC, MC, V. **Map** p312 J12.
Located across from the Prado, this souvenir shop par excellence sells traditional *españoladas* such as fans and flamenco and bullfighting dolls. A great place to find that gift for your kitsch-loving friends.

SPORT

For trainers, *see also p143* **Nonstop Sneakers**.

Área Real Madrid

C/Carmen 3, Sol (91 521 79 50). Metro Sol. **Open** 10am-9pm Mon-Sat; 11am-8pm Sun. **Credit** AmEx, MC, V. **Map** p311 G/H11.
A true emporium for the Real Madrid-inclined. On sale are, naturally, replica shirts and all manner of other stuff bearing the club's logo, from ashtrays to mouse mats, bath towels to undies.

Supporters Shop

C/Goya 50, Salamanca (91 575 88 68). Metro Goya. **Open** 10.15am-2pm, 5-8.30pm Mon-Sat. Closed Aug. **Credit** AmEx, DC, MC, V. **Map** p309 N9.
Selling shirts and other memorabilia from over 500 clubs worldwide, Supporters Shop can usually kit out fans of even the most obscure teams.

Tornal Moya Deportes

Ronda de Valencia 8, Lavapiés (91 527 54 40, www.tornalmoya.com). Metro Embajadores. **Open** 10am-2pm, 5-9pm Mon-Sat. **Credit** MC, V. **Map** p312 H15.
This big, well-laid-out shop stocks the lot: top-name sportswear, trainers, walking boots, swimwear, tennis rackets, replica football shirts and bags.

STAMPS & COINS

Stamp & Coin Market

Plaza Mayor, Los Austrias. Metro Sol. **Open** *approx* 9am-2pm Sun. **Map** p311 G12.
On Sunday mornings, an avid mass of stamp and coin collectors swarm over the Plaza Mayor, buying, selling and eyeing up one another's wares. Other

traders sell old magazines, second-hand books, post-cards, badges and ex-Soviet bloc military regalia. You can even get phonecards nowadays, along with just about anything else that someone, somewhere, considers collectable.

TICKET AGENTS

There are all manner of ways to buy tickets (*entradas*) for shows and gigs these days, among them telesales, online purchase and cashpoints. Some of the biggest players in this game are savings banks (*cajas de ahorro*), who do advance sales by phone, as does the all-embracing Corte Inglés. **FNAC** (*see p135*) is a useful place to pick up concert tickets.

El Corte Inglés

www.elcorteingles.es. **Credit** AmEx, DC, MC, V.
El Corte Inglés sells tickets for a huge range of shows and events, either online or at any of its stores.

Entradas.com

www.entradas.com. **Credit** AmEx (some venues), DC, MC, V.
Tickets can be collected at the event box office.

Telentrada/Caixa de Catalunya

www.telentrada.com. **Credit** MC, V.
Through the Caixa de Catalunya you can book tick-ets for theatres, venues and concerts, pay by credit card and pick them up either at a branch of the bank or from the venue's box office itself (depend-ing on the show and the venue).

Ticketmaster/La Caixa

www.ticketmaster.es. **Credit** AmEx, DC, MC, V.
Ticketmaster sells tickets for a vast range of shows and events.

TOBACCO & SMOKING

The easily spotted maroon-and-yellow *Estancos* (tobacco shops) can be found all over town.

La Cava de Magallanes

C/Magallanes 16, Chamberí (91 446 28 17).
Metro Quevedo. **Open** *Sept-June* 8.30am-2.30pm, 4.30-8.30pm Mon-Fri; 9am-2pm Sat. *July, Aug* 8.30am-2pm, 5-8.30pm Mon-Fri; 9am-2pm Sat. **Credit** (over €30) MC, V. **Map** p307 G6.
A temple to tobacco, La Cava de Magallanes stocks over 350 different types of cigar, all maintained at optimum temperature in a special humidified room. The knowledgeable owner speaks a little English. There is a good range of accessories too.

TRAVEL SERVICES

Forocio

C/Mayor 4, 5ª (91 522 56 77, www.forocio.com).
Metro Sol. **Open** *Sept-July* 10am-2pm, 3-7pm Mon-Fri. *Aug* 10am-5pm Mon-Fri. Closed 1 wk in Aug. **Credit** DC, MC, V. **Map** p312 H11.
This multi-purpose agency offers services for young foreigners, such as hosting 'International Parties' and providing Interrail and student cards, setting up language exchanges, and organising budget flights, day trips and weekend tours. The 'Tarjeta Forocio' gives a 10% discount on trips.

Viajes Zeppelin

Plaza de Santo Domingo 2, Sol & Gran Vía (91 758 10 40, www.iaviajes.com). Metro Santo Domingo. **Open** 9am-7.30pm Mon-Fri. **Credit** AmEx, DC, MC, V. **Map** p311 F11.
This well-established agency with friendly service specialises in cheap European charter flights and long-haul youth fares. You can also book online.

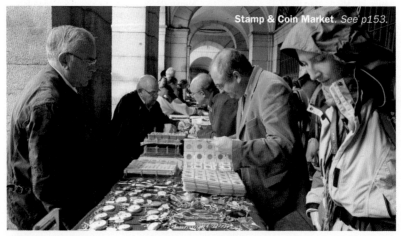

Stamp & Coin Market. *See p153.*

CONSUME

Hotels

Luscious lodgings.

For a compact city, Madrid has an unusually large number of hotels. In fact, so many new properties have opened in the past few years that some locals believe there are too many, in the centre at least. For visitors, of course, this can only be a good thing. Intense competition means higher standards of accommodation and service, even in the lower-priced places. In particular, the difference between budget and mid-range hotels is becoming increasingly marginal, with the newer *hostales* now offering en suite bathrooms in most rooms. And, across all price brackets, staff are friendlier and keener to help than ever before. Fans of boutique hotels, meanwhile, will be pleased to hear that the concept has finally made it to Madrid.

STARS, PRICES AND DISCOUNTS
Star ratings are somewhat arbitrary in Spain, and the difference between four- and five-star hotels can be hard to spot. Mid-range hotels have not been the city's strong point, but this is beginning to change thanks to chains such as **Room Mate** and **High Tech Hotels**.

In this chapter we have arranged hotels and *hostales* by area and price category, according to the cost of a standard double room. Hotels charging over €250 per night are categorised as 'luxury'; those costing between €170 and €250 are classed as 'expensive'; 'mid-range' is between €70 and €170; 'budget' is less than €70. Breakfast is not included unless stated. All prices shown are for online advance bookings. Where a price range is shown, this represents the cheapest available double room in the low and high season. Prices tend to be highest in January (somewhat surprisingly), when some hotels require a minimum of two to three nights. Also note that the cheapest online rate is often non-refundable.

LOS AUSTRIAS & LA LATINA

Mid-range

chic&basic Mayerling
C/Conde de Romanones 6 (91 420 15 80, www.chicandbasic.com). Metro Tirso de Molina. **Rates** (incl breakfast) €75-€130. **Map** p311 G12 ❶

This former textiles warehouse, on the border of Lavapiés, houses one of three Madrid hotels from the chic&basic mini chain. Chic&basic Mayerling opened in 2009, and offers 22 simple but stylish lodgings (with an abundance of white, plus glass-walled bathrooms with power showers) in M, L and XL. Complimentary continental breakfast, tea- and coffee-making facilities and a great sun terrace with loungers add to the appeal. *Photo p156.*
Disabled-adapted room. Internet (free wireless). TV.
Other locations C/Atocha 113, Huertas & Santa Ana (91 369 28 95); chic&basic Colors, C/Huertas 14, Huertas & Santa Ana (91 429 69 35).

Hostal Gala
C/Costanilla de los Ángeles 15 (91 541 96 92, www.hostalgala.com). Metro Santo Domingo. **Rates** €60-€85 double. **Credit** MC, V.
Map p311 F11 ❷

This well-located boutique *hostal* on a quiet but central street is run by a very friendly couple. The 22 rooms are comfortable and tasteful, with wooden floors, air-conditioning, retro-modern wallpaper and spacious bathrooms with power showers. Some rooms have balconies, while the superior double has a lounge area. An excellent option.
Internet (free wireless). TV.

> ❶ Red numbers given in this chapter correspond to the location of each hotel on the street maps. *See pp305-313.*

CONSUME

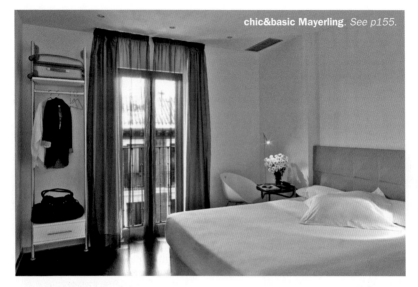

chic&basic **Mayerling**. *See p155.*

Hotel Palacio San Martín

Plaza de San Martín 5 (91 701 50 00, www. intur.com). Metro Ópera or Sol. **Rates** €86-€116 double. **Credit** AmEx, DC, MC, V. **Map** p311 G11 ❸

The Hotel Palacio San Martín is housed in a 19th-century former palace. On a tranquil, central square, it has maintained much of the glory of its previous incarnation, with period façade, high stucco ceilings, wood panelling and an attractive central courtyard. A lovely rooftop terrace restaurant looks out over the surrounding area, while a huge presidential suite, also on the rooftop, comes complete with jacuzzi – and more of those striking views.
Business centre. Gym. Internet (wireless). Restaurant. Room service. TV (pay movies).

Petit Palace Arenal

C/Arenal 16 (91 564 43 55, www.hthoteles.com). Metro Sol. **Rates** €70-€131 double. **Credit** AmEx, DC, MC, V. **Map** p311 F11 ❹

Fans of chintz should steer well clear, but the good-value High Tech chain of hotels is perfect for techno fiends on a budget. The Arenal's compact but sleekly designed rooms have flatscreen TVs and free ADSL connection, and more expensive rooms come equipped with a PC (also with free net access) and an exercise bike. Some of the superior rooms have showers fitted with solariums, saunas and radios.
Business centre. Disabled-adapted room. Internet (high-speed). TV.
Other locations Posada del Peine, C/Postas 17, Sol & Gran Via (91 523 81 51); Tres Cruces, C/Tres Cruces 6, Sol & Gran Via (91 522 33 27); Puerta del Sol, C/Arenal 4, Sol & Gran Via (91 521 05 42).

Posada del León de Oro

C/Cava Baja 12 (91 119 14 94, www.posada delleondeoro.com). Metro La Latina. **Rates** €69-€243 double. **Credit** DC, MC, V. **Map** p311 F13 ❺

A converted 19th-century coaching inn, the León de Oro has a somewhat stark approach to modern design, but is comfortable and friendly, with decent-sized beds and underfloor heating. Its 17 rooms sit around a central atrium, their minimal lines softened by wooden beams and bold splashes of colour.
Bar. Internet (free wireless). Restaurant. TV.

Budget

★ Hostal Oriente

C/Arenal 23 (91 548 03 14, www.hostal oriente.es). Metro Ópera. **Rates** €50-€68 double. **Credit** DC, MC, V. **Map** p311 F11 ❼

Right on the doorstep of the opera house, and just a short walk from Sol, the comfortable Oriente is in an excellent location. All 34 rooms, decorated with old-school flowered bedspreads and swagged curtains, have compact bathrooms and TVs, and Wi-Fi and the friendly staff are a further draw.
Internet (free wireless). TV.

Hostal Riesco

C/Correo 2, 3ª (91 522 26 92, www.hostal riesco.es). Metro Sol. **Rates** €55 double. **No credit cards. Map** p311 G11 ❻

The Riesco is a *hostal* that feels more like a hotel, what with its dark wood lobby, stucco ceilings and chintzy curtains. All rooms come with en suite bathrooms, and several have balconies bedecked

with flowers. The location is hard to beat – it's rare to find such good-value accommodation so close to Sol and the Plaza Mayor.
TV.

SOL & GRAN VÍA

Expensive

Tryp Ambassador
Cuesta de Santo Domingo 5-7 (91 541 67 00, www.melia.com). Metro Santo Domingo. **Rates** €92-€210 double. **Credit** AmEx, DC, MC, V. **Map** p307 F11 ❽
Located in a former palace, the Ambassador manages to retain a vaguely baronial air despite being part of a chain. Suits of armour stand guard in the corridors, while plush upholstery adorns the public spaces and the large, light-filled atrium. Breakfast is expensive (€26) but abundant and good.
Bar. Business centre. Internet (free wireless). Restaurant. Room service. TV (satellite).

Mid-range

Hotel Arosa
C/Salud 21 (91 532 16 00, www.bestwesternarosa. com). Metro Gran Via. **Rates** €64-€148 double. **Credit** AmEx, DC, MC, V. **Map** p307 H11 ❾
This friendly, well-equipped and good-value 134-room hotel is situated right in the heart of the action. The spacious, air-conditioned rooms all come with clean, modern wooden furnishings and bright marble bathrooms, and some of the more expensive

doubles have a private seating area looking out on to the busy Gran Via. The public areas include a kitschy fake leopard-skin reception, and a restaurant and bar that Almodóvar would be proud of.
Bar. Internet (free wireless). Parking (€27 per day). Restaurant. Room service. TV (satellite, pay movies).

Hotel Carlos V
C/Maestro Victoria 5 (91 531 41 00, www. bestwesternhotelcarlosv.com). Metro Sol. **Rates** €70-€159 double. **Credit** AmEx, DC, MC, V. **Map** p307 G11 ❿
The corporate feel is avoided in this Best Western hotel with homely touches, from the motley but charming crew running reception and the trompe l'oeil lift door, to the tapestries in the corridors and the botanical prints in the colourful and elegant breakfast room. The rooms on the top floor are the nicest, and some have their own large, Astroturfed terraces (though you pay a bit extra for this).
Bar. Internet (free wireless). Room service. TV (satellite).

Hotel Emperador
Gran Via 53 (91 547 28 00, www.emperador hotel.com). Metro Santo Domingo. **Rates** €72-€120 double. **Credit** AmEx, DC, MC, V. **Map** p307 F10 ⓫
While the traffic speeds by on the Gran Via outside, the Emperador has to deal with a flow of student groups and tourists that is almost as unrelenting. It's little surprise that it's so booked up, since the hotel is well situated for visiting the city's major

Hostal Oriente

CONSUME

What's Where

A short guide to the barrios of Madrid.

Although Madrid is pretty small for a capital city, its accommodation is spread over a wide area, so it's good to have an idea of what you want before you book.

Sol and **Gran Vía** are the best areas for mid-range accommodation right in the thick of things, and, though pretty touristy, are home to a clutch of decent bars and restaurants. Heading north from here, **Malasaña** has a choice of good budget *pensiones*, particularly along C/Palma. Bordering Malasaña to the east, **Chueca** is home to some great one-off properties. Both areas, especially Malasaña, boast a real neighbourhood vibe.

South of Chueca, lively **Huertas** and **Santa Ana** are both great areas for cheap *pensiones* and, increasingly, boutique hotels. On the edge of here, the Paseo del Prado provides a variety of budget accommodation right on the doorstep of the big three art museums. Upmarket areas include **Retiro** and **Los Austrias**. Although located across town from each other (Retiro is between the Prado and the Retiro park in the east, Los Austrias is adjacent to the Royal Palace to the west), both are home to Madrid's old money, and both are peaceful – though bars and restaurants can be expensive.

Just north of the Parque del Retiro, around the chic shopping street C/Serrano, is **Salamanca**. If you feel at home among the smart, wealthy set, you'll blend in well here. Business travellers should head for **Chamberí**, to the north of the centre, and, further north, to **Chamartín**, both of which are convenient for the airport.

---

sights and has a wonderful rooftop swimming pool (which is also open to non-residents for a fee). Rooms are conservatively decorated; the renovated bathrooms are a huge improvement on the old brown 1970s-style suites.

Bar. Business centre. Disabled-adapted rooms (9). Gym. Internet (wireless). Parking (€22.47 per day). Room service. Pool (outdoor). TV (satellite).

★ Hotel de las Letras

Gran Vía 11 (91 523 79 80, www.hoteldelasletras. com). Metro Gran Vía. **Rates** €85-€167 double. **Credit** AmEx, DC, MC, V. **Map** p308 H11 ⑫

The Hotel de las Letras laughs in the face of the current hotel vogue for teak and slate, and plumps instead for bold paintwork in red, orange and purple, with literary quotations strewn across its walls. It does this with remarkable aplomb, thanks to stylish furniture and well-designed rooms. Bathrooms are huge, and even standard rooms come with balconies. Downstairs is a comfortable spa and gym, along with a small library with free internet access. The ground-floor bar hums with bright young things day and night. A gem. *Photos p160.*

Bars (2). Disabled-adapted room. Internet (wireless). Restaurant. Room service. Spa. TV (satellite).

★ Hotel Mercure Santo Domingo

C/San Bernardo 1 (91 547 98 00, www.hotel santodomingo.es). Metro Santo Domingo. **Rates** €80-€167 double. **Credit** AmEx, DC, MC, V. **Map** p307 F11 ⑬

Courteous staff welcome guests to this well-located, slick hotel, which is part of the Mercure chain. The hotel features a small(ish) but appealing rooftop pool

and 200 individually decorated rooms. The huge white lobby hints at the design focus found within, yet the modern feel is tempered with displays of classical 19th-century paintings belonging to the hotel's owner. Huge walk-in showers are a bonus.

Bar. Disabled-adapted room. Internet (free wireless). Parking (€27 per day). Pool (outdoor). Restaurant. Room service. TV (satellite).

Budget

Hostal Andorra

Gran Vía 33, 7ª (91 532 31 16, www.hostal andorra.com). Metro Gran Vía. **Rates** €63 double. **Credit** AmEx, DC, MC, V. **Map** p307 G11 ⑭

Brightly painted rooms, floral bedspreads and comfortable leather recliners confirm the homely atmosphere of this centrally located *hostal*. While the roar of the Gran Vía's traffic is unforgiving, the interior is calm, with cleanliness and facilities that belie the rates. Every room has satellite TV, and the bathrooms, while compact, are clean and modern.

Bar. Internet (wireless). TV room.

Hostal Triana

1st floor, C/Salud 13 (91 532 68 12, www.hostal triana.com). Metro Gran Vía. **Rates** €55 double. **Credit** MC, V. **Map** p307 H11 ⑮

A popular and efficiently run business, this traditional, good-value 40-room *hostal* has been open for more than four decades, and attracts guests of all ages. Rooms are sparklingly clean with modern en suite bathrooms. It's worth booking early.

Disabled-adapted room. Internet (wireless). TV.

CONSUME

HUERTAS & SANTA ANA

Luxury

Westin Palace

*Plaza de las Cortes 7 (91 360 80 00, www.westin
palacemadrid.com). Metro Banco de España.*
Rates €225-€360. **Credit** AmEx, DC, MC, V.
Map p312 I12 ⑯

One of the most famous hotels in Madrid, the Palace
successfully mixes old-world elegance with cutting-
edge facilities. The lounge areas and atrium are
sumptuous, and the latter features opera performances once a month. The hotel's reasonably priced,
comfortable bars and restaurants are popular with
visiting celebs and politicians. The hotel is brought
into the 21st century with a fully equipped fitness
centre, sauna and solarium.

*Bar. Business centre. Disabled-adapted room.
Gym. Internet (high speed, wireless). Parking
(€34.15 per day). Restaurants (2). Room service.
TV (satellite, pay movies).*

Expensive

Hotel Urban

*Carrera de San Jeronimo 34 (91 787 77 70,
www.derbyhotels.com). Metro Sevilla or Sol.*
Rates €160-€225 double. **Credit** AmEx, DC,
MC, V. **Map** p312 I11 ⑰

The Derby chain (of which the Hotel Villa Real is
also part; *see p161*) is owned by Catalan archaeolo-
gist Jordi Clos, and ancient figurines and artworks
are found throughout the rooms, common areas and
in the Egyptian museum in the basement. This cultural treasure trove is a perfect counterpoint to the
painfully hip surroundings – a glass and steel
atrium, rooms sexily designed with teak and leather,
and what must be the coolest doormen in the city.
Other pluses include extremely friendly staff and a
much needed plunge pool on the roof. Note that some
of the rooms are very small.

*Bar. Business centre. Gym. Internet (pre-pay
wireless). Parking. Pool (outdoor). Restaurant.
Room service. TV (satellite).*

Hotel de las Letras. *See p159.*

CONSUME

Hotel Villa Real

Plaza de las Cortes 10 (91 420 37 67, www. derbyhotels.com). Metro Banco de España. **Rates** €130-€210 double. **Credit** AmEx, DC, MC, V. **Map** p312 I12 ⓲

The Villa Real – as the name suggests – reflects owner Jordi Clos's interest in Roman archaeology. The guest rooms are elegant, with marble bathrooms boasting large picture windows, and many have panels of Roman mosaics. Most double rooms have split-level sitting areas, some duplex suites come with their own jacuzzi, and the luxury suites have private terraces.

Bar. Business centre. Internet (wireless). Parking (€27 per day). Restaurant. Room service. TV (satellite).

ME Madrid

Plaza Santa Ana 14 (91 701 60 00, www. memadrid.com). Metro Sevilla or Sol. **Rates** €175-€255 double. **Credit** AmEx, DC, MC, V. **Map** p312 H12 ⓳

Although plans to turn this into Europe's first Hard Rock hotel didn't quite come off, the Melia chain appropriated the lovely old Hotel Reina Victoria to showcase its ME brand. Rooms are small but comfortable, with luxury bedlinen, Aveda toiletries and lots to keep gadget-fiends happy, with plasma screens, CD and DVD players, iPod adapters, Nintendo Wiis and Nespresso machines. The rooftop bar has amazing views of the city.

Bar. Business centre. Disabled-adapted rooms (4). Gym. No-smoking floors (5). Internet (high speed, wireless). Parking (€30 per day). Restaurant. Room service. TV (pay movies, satellite).

★ Palacio de Tepa

C/San Sebastian 2 (91 389 64 90, www. nh-hotels.com). Metro Sol. **Rates** €176-€440. **Credit** AmEx, DC, MC, V. **Map** p312 H12 ⓴

The NH group prides itself on comfort and customer service, and the five-star Palacio de Tepa is no exception. A sombre palette of creams and browns guides the modern decor, and won't frighten the horses, but it's the little touches that make the place, such as the ground-floor sitting room with complimentary tea, coffee, mineral water and newspapers. Original features of the 1808 building, with façade by Juan de Villanueva, have been respected, and superior rooms are under the eaves, with wooden ceilings. Like the suites, these have Nespresso machines, iPod docking systems and a 'pampering' menu. *Photos p164.*

Bar/restaurant. Business centre. Disabled-adapted rooms (2). Gym. Internet (free wireless). Room service. TV.

Mid-range

Hotel Lope de Vega

C/Lope de Vega 40 (91 360 00 11, www.hotel lopedevega.com). Metro Antón Martín. **Rates**

€60-€127 double. **Credit** AmEx, DC, MC, V. **Map** p312 J12/13 ㉑

A stone's throw from the Prado, this anonymous-looking hotel's rooms are done up in standard-issue mid-range decor, but are a good size and comfortable, and many have large balconies. Posted outside each one is information about playwright Lope de Vega, and the corridors are lined with pictures of his productions. Other nice touches on the landings include books about the great man himself.

Bar. Internet (wireless). Parking (€24.84 per day). Room service. TV (satellite).

Hotel El Prado

C/Prado 11 (91 369 02 34, www.pradohotel.com). Metro Antón Martín. **Rates** €72-140 double. **Credit** AmEx, DC, MC, V. **Map** p312 H/I12 ㉒

The sister hotel to the Lope de Vega (*see above*), the Prado also has an anonymous look from the outside, but the rooms are prettily furnished, this time with a wine theme. Curtains and upholstery are adorned with vine patterns and the downstairs lounge is filled with books, videos and magazines about viticulture. There are bowls of fruit to munch on in the public areas and free internet access in the lounge. *Internet (free wireless). TV (satellite).*

★ Room Mate Alicia

C/Prado 2 (91 389 60 95,www.room-matehotels. com) Metro Antón Martín. **Rates** €89-€175 double. **Credit** AmEx MC, V. **Map** p312 H12 ㉓

Another hit from this classy but reasonably priced chain; *see also p165* Room Mate Oscar. Like its stablemate, the Alicia embraces a retro chic aesthetic in its common areas, and its bedrooms are livened up with splashes of colour on the bedspreads and cushions, and adorned with Roy Lichtenstein prints. It's worth shelling out an extra €10 to get your hands on an executive room – no bigger than a standard, but with a private terrace. *Photos p166.*

Internet (free wireless). TV (satellite).

Budget

Hostal Alaska

C/Espoz y Mina 7, 4ª (91 521 18 45, www. hostalalaska.es). Metro Sol. **Rates** €30-€100 double. **Credit** MC, V. **Map** p311 H12 ㉔

Exceptionally large rooms for this price range, decorated with splashes of bright blue, give this comfortable, colourful *hostal* a bit of a beachside feel. The atmosphere is homely, and guests have use of a fridge and washing machine. The five doubles and one single all come with bathrooms, and many have balconies. It's on the fourth floor but there's a lift. *Internet (wireless). TV.*

Hostal Armesto

C/San Agustín 6, 1ª (91 429 90 31, www.hostal armesto.com). Metro Antón Martín. **Rates** €32-€36 double. **Credit** MC, V. **Map** p312 I12 ㉕

CONSUME

This great-value six-room *hostal* in the centre of Huertas is run by a friendly husband and wife team. Rooms are spotless and all of them have their own small bathroom with shower; some have views over the garden of the San Agustín palace next door. The Armesto is a good choice for art lovers on a budget, being well situated for the art museum triumvirate. *Internet (free wireless). TV.*

Hostal Astoria
Carrera de San Jerónimo 30-32, 2ª (91 429 11 88, www.hostal-astoria.com). Metro Sevilla or Sol. **Rates** €40-€70 double. **Credit** DC, MC, V. **Map** p312 H11 ❷⑥
Managed by (mostly) friendly staff, the Astoria is a good choice if you want to be centrally located, with access to basic facilities at a very good price. All 26 rooms are relatively spacious and have en suite bathrooms, but try to get the biggest available, and preferably one facing away from the street. *Business centre. Internet (free wireless). TV.*

Hostal Casanova
C/Lope de Vega 8, 1ª (91 429 56 91, www.hostalcasanova.es). Metro Antón Martín. **Rates** €45 double. **Credit** MC, V. **Map** p312 I12 ❷⑦
Run by a friendly family and in a quiet street, this *hostal* is especially good value for those travelling in threes. Rooms are basic but bright, some with bathrooms, and all with air-conditioning. *TV.*

Hostal Delvi
Plaza Santa Ana 15, 3ª (91 522 59 98, www.hostaldelvi.com). Metro Sevilla or Sol. **Rates** €45 double. **Credit** MC, V. **Map** p312 H12 ❷⑧
Located on lively Plaza Santa Ana and in a delightfully eccentric building, the Casa de Guadalajara, the Delvi is ideal for backpackers. An entrance hall decorated with ceramics of winged cherubs leads you past the Guadalajara Club, then up to the third floor (there's no lift) where an elderly couple run this good-value *hostal*. Rooms are basic, but some have a shower and toilet, and others have views of the square.

★ Hostal Horizonte
C/Atocha 28, 2ª (91 369 09 96, www.hostalhorizonte.com). Metro Antón Martín. **Rates** €38-€72 double. **Credit** MC, V. **Map** p311 H13 ❷⑨
One of the oldest *pensiones* in Madrid, the Horizonte has stayed in the same friendly family throughout its 65-year history. The manager is the young and helpful Julio César, a font of knowledge about the city. Rooms are colourfully decorated, clean and comfy, and the welcoming atmosphere is unbeatable. *Internet (free wireless).*

Hostal Martín
C/Atocha 43, 1ª (91 429 95 79, www.hostalmartin.com). Metro Antón Martín. **Rates** €35-€66 double. **Credit** MC, V. **Map** p311 H13 ❸⓪

This very friendly, first-floor *hostal* has a pleasantly rough-and-tumble family feel about it. The 20 high-ceilinged, air-conditioned rooms all come with an en suite bathroom and decent shower. The helpful couple who run it speak various languages between them and can book you into other hotels if you're moving on to other parts of the country. The hearty breakfast includes plenty of fresh fruit and very good coffee. *Internet (free wireless). Parking. TV (satellite).*

Hostal Persal
Plaza del Ángel 12 (91 369 46 43, www.hostalpersal.com). Metro Sol or Antón Martín. **Rates** €55 double. **Credit** AmEx, MC, V. **Map** p312 H12 ❸①
The Persal's rooms don't quite live up to the first impressions given by the glass front and swish lobby, but thankfully they're modern, spotlessly clean and more than functional (it's well worth asking for a nicer one on the upper floors). If you're travelling as a family or a group, the hard-working staff are especially welcoming and helpful. *Bar. Internet (wireless). TV (satellite).*

Hostal San Antonio
C/León 13, 2º (91 429 51 37, www.hostalsanantonio.es). Metro Antón Martín. **Rates** €50 double. **Credit** MC, V. **Map** p312 I12 ❸②
A clean, quiet and cool modern *hostal,* tranquil by day, buzzing on weekend nights. Rooms are comfortable and generously sized for the price, and all come with air-conditioning, and en suite toilet and shower room. Most look out on to a busy street, so it can get quite noisy at night. *Internet (free wireless). TV.*

★ Hostal Sud-Americana
Paseo del Prado 12 (91 429 25 64, www.hostalsudamericana.com). Metro Banco de España. **Rates** €24-€40 double. **Credit** MC, V. **Map** p312 J12 ❸③

This place has a real feel of Old Madrid, with mini Goya reproductions lining the creaky, wooden-floored hallway. Whitewashed walls, high ceilings and wooden furniture give the rooms a centuries-old atmosphere, and some have lovely views over the treetops of the Paseo del Prado. One bathroom is shared between eight rooms, but all have their own washbasin. You'll find it very difficult to find this sort of old-world elegance elsewhere at such a cheap price, particularly if you're after a single.

Hotel Asturias
C/Sevilla 2 (91 429 66 76, www.hotel-asturias. com). Metro Sevilla. **Rates** €34-€94 double. **Credit** MC, V. **Map** p312 H11 ❹
Located within spitting distance of Sol, this bustling hotel in a 19th-century building is nothing to write home about from the outside. Inside, though, the 170 rooms are bright and spacious, decorated in simple whites and creams, with carpets and furnishings that blend well with the wooden floors and fittings. Some have views over the gorgeous Teatro Reina Victoria, but ask for an interior room if noise bothers you.
Bar. Restaurant. TV (satellite).

Hotel Mora
Paseo del Prado 32 (91 420 15 69, www.hotel mora.com). Metro Atocha. **Rates** €60-€86 double. **Credit** AmEx, DC, MC, V. **Map** p312 J13 ❺
If you like marble, you'll love the Mora's foyer, with its caramel-coloured columns and chandeliers. The rooms are functional but comfortable, and some have views over the tree-lined Paseo del Prado. Not surprisingly, given the location and price, it can be hard to get a room, so try to book early.
Bar. Internet (wireless). TV.

Hotel Santander
C/Echegaray 1 (91 429 95 51, www.hotel santandermadrid.com). Metro Sevilla or Sol. **Rates** €38-€86 double. **Credit** MC, V. **Map** p312 H11 ❻
The Santander's glamorous, gilded entrance makes for a foyer with character, and if you can get over

Palacio de Tepa. *See p161.*

the rather off-putting list of house rules (no visitors after midnight, no noise after 11pm) you'll enjoy your stay. Rooms are elegant, kitted out with decent furniture and wooden floors. Some are more like suites, with small seating areas for breakfast.
TV.

★ Lapepa Chic B&B
Plaza de las Cortes 4, 7ª (mobile 648 474 742, www.lapepa-bnb.com). Metro Banco de España. **Rates** (incl breakfast) €53-€90 double. **Credit** MC, V. **Map** p312 I12 ❼
A new and cheerful B&B with an unbeatable location between the major art museums and the bars of Santa Ana. All 14 rooms are pristine, en suite, and decorated in red and white. Breakfast is included and available until noon.
Internet (free wireless). TV.

CHUECA
Mid-range

Petit Palace Ducal
C/Hortaleza 3 (91 521 10 43, www.hthoteles.com). Metro Gran Vía. **Rates** €63-€118 double. **Credit** AmEx, DC, MC, V. **Map** p308 H11 ❽
The Petit Palace Ducal blends seamlessly into its cool Chueca surroundings. Staff are young and friendly, and the striking red and black design is eye-catching. So-called High Tech rooms come with flatscreen

---

INSIDE TRACK TAKE A PLUNGE

Considering how hot Madrid gets in the summer months, it's disappointing that there are relatively few hotels in the city with outdoor swimming pools. If you're visiting between May and September, and a pool and lounge terrace are a priority, then check in to the **Hotel Emperador** (*see p157*; the pool is also open to non-guests for a fee), **Hotel Mercure Santo Domingo** (*see p159*), **Hotel Wellington** (*see p167*) or **Room Mate Oscar** (*see right*).

CONSUME

PCs, exercise bikes and sauna or hydromassage showers. The Ducal is also practical in its provision of family rooms. Given all this, the prices are reasonable, and it's definitely worth spending extra for a sixth-floor room with small terrace. The High Tech chain manages other hotels around the city; see the website for details.

Bar. Business centre. No-smoking floors (5). Internet (free high speed, wireless). Restaurant. TV (satellite).

★ Room Mate Oscar

Plaza Vázquez de Mella 12 (91 701 11 73, www.room-matehotels.com). Metro Chueca or Gran Vía. **Rates** (incl breakfast) €78-€143 double. **Map** p308 H11 ❻

The latest in a chain of stylish, mid-range hotels, especially popular among a design-appreciative public (for which, often, read 'gay'). Room Mate Oscar oozes affordable chic, from the ergonomic white plastic chairs to the smart chequered grey and white bathrooms. The staff (all black-shirted, naturally) are as welcoming and easy on the eye as the spacious rooms, and the location in one of Chueca's main squares is unbeatable. The huge roof terrace – which comes complete with a bar and swimming pool – is a big plus, and a prime hangout on the city's gay scene.

Bars (2). Business centre. Disabled-adapted room. Internet (free wireless, free shared terminal). Restaurant. TV.

Other locations Room Mate Alicia (see p161); Room Mate Laura, Travesía de Trujillos 3, Sol & Gran Vía (91 701 16 70); Room Mate Mario, C/Campomanes 4 (91 548 85 48).

Budget

Hostal Benamar

C/San Mateo 20, 2ª (91 308 00 92, www.hostalbenamar.es). Metro Alonso Martínez or Tribunal. **Rates** €49.90 double. **Credit** MC, V. **Map** p308 I9 ❼

Well situated between Chueca and Alonso Martínez, this *hostal* can be divided into two different parts. The friendly owners promote the recently renovated section, which has marble floors, modern en suite bathrooms and computers in every room. The other section is older but clean, with shared bathrooms. *Internet (high-speed). TV.*

Hostal Santa Bárbara

Plaza de Santa Bárbara 4, 3º (91 446 93 08, www.hostalsantabarbaramadrid.com). Metro Alonso Martínez. **Rates** €34-€40 double. **Credit** MC, V. **Map** p308 I8 ❽

This *hostal* provides friendly service in a secure building. The rooms are pretty basic but they are also clean, and each one features walk-in shower facilities. The staff all speak good English. *TV.*

CONSUME

MALASAÑA & CONDE DUQUE
Mid-range

Hotel Abalu
C/Pez 19 (91 531 47 44, www.hotelabalu.com).
Metro Noviciado. **Rates** €75-€119 double.
Credit AmEx, DC, MC, V. **Map** p307 G9 ❷
The Abalu is near the Gran Vía and metro, but its
extravagant interior design pulls in as many visitors
as its location does. Rooms range from restrained to
gloriously over the top; the staff are generally
friendly although sometimes hard to pin down.
Internet (wireless). Restaurant. TV.

Budget

Hostal Sil & Serranos
C/Fuencarral 95 (91 448 89 72, www.silserranos.
com). Metro Bilbao. **Rates** €54 double. **Credit**
MC, V. **Map** p307 H8 ❸
Clean and smartly decorated, these *hostales* are well
located for night-time revelling – indeed, rooms looking out on to C/Fuencarral will bear witness to the
madrileño enthusiasm for partying. Although interior rooms are a little darker, the noise is minimal
and the price slightly lower. All rooms have air-con,
small bathrooms and digital TV, and the properties
are run by a fun couple.
Internet (high-speed). TV (satellite).

THE RETIRO & SALAMANCA
Luxury

Hotel Ritz
Plaza de la Lealtad 5 (91 701 67 67, www.ritz
madrid.com). Metro Banco de España. **Rates**
€260-€390 double. **Credit** AmEx, DC, MC, V.
Map p312 J12 ❹
Madrid's Ritz was built in 1910, thanks to a personal
intervention by King Alfonso XIII, who had been
embarrassed at the time of his wedding to Princess
Victoria four years earlier because his guests could
not find a hotel that was up to scratch. When the
hotel first opened, the handful of bathrooms, one
telephone per floor and lift were considered the
height of luxury, and it soon attracted politicians,
royalty and writers. Today, the 167 rooms maintain
some of the original belle époque style, though the
swirly carpets and occasionally shabby fittings
are incongruous in such a setting. And, for the price,
it has fairly minimal fitness facilities (and no swim-
ing pool). The Ritz has shaken off its slightly stuffy
image and now welcomes celebs it once shunned;
however, guests must abide by a strict dress code
in the restaurant.
Bars (2). Business centre. Disabled-adapted room.
Gym. Internet (free high-speed, wireless). No-
smoking floors (2). Restaurant. Room service.
TV (satellite).

Room Mate Alicia. *See p161.*

Palacio del Retiro

C/Alfonso XII 14 (91 523 74 60, www.ac-hotels. com). Metro Banco de España or Retiro. **Rates** €250-€325 double. **Credit** AmEx, DC, MC, V. **Map** p312 K11

With their palette of greys and browns, the rooms can seem a little dour and masculine after the frothy extravagances of the belle époque building in which they are housed. The hotel is beautifully located near the park and Prado, however, and the staff members are eager to please. Amenities are good – rooms feature plasma-screen TVs and CD players – as is breakfast (as one would expect for €29).
Bars (2). Business centre. Disabled-adapted rooms (2). Internet (free wireless). No-smoking floors (3). Restaurant. Room service. Spa. TV (satellite).

Villa Magna

Paseo de la Castellana 22 (91 587 12 34, www.villamagna.es). Metro Rubén Darío. **Rates** €248-€416 double. **Credit** AmEx, DC, MC, V. **Map** p308 K7/8

Although it's a modern, rather nondescript building from the outside, the lavishly entitled Villa Magna, a Park Hyatt hotel, more than lives up to its reputation – and tariffs – on the inside. The huge lobby, full of jewellery displays, international businessmen and polite staff, leads to two excellent restaurants and a champagne bar, whose lunch menu is surprisingly reasonably priced. The 150 rooms and suites,

looking out over the busy Paseo de la Castellana or the exclusive C/Serrano, have good facilities and, like the rest of the hotel, are spacious and elegantly decorated. There's also a top-notch gym.
Bars (2). Business centre. Disabled-adapted rooms (10). Gym. Internet (free high-speed, wireless). No-smoking floors (7). Parking. Restaurants (2). Room service. Spa. TV (DVD, satellite).

Expensive

★ Hotel Único

C/Claudio Coello 67 (91 781 01 73, www.unico hotelmadrid.com). Metro Serrano. **Rates** €185-€235. **Credit** AmEx, DC, MC, V. **Map** p309 L8

Formerly known as the Selenza, the Hotel Único achieves the perfect blend of modern and classic. It's housed in a graceful 19th-century Salamanca building with slick black-and-white chequered tiles and upholstered chairs in the public areas, impressive staircases that are perfect for making a grand entrance, and mod cons throughout. The 44 spacious rooms and suites are comfortable and well-designed, with huge comfy beds, wooden floors, muted tones and patterns, slick bathrooms and Molton Brown toiletries. The Michelin-starred restaurant is another plus.
Bar. Business centre. Disabled-adapted rooms. Internet (free high-speed, wireless). Parking. Restaurant. Room service. TV (DVD, satellite).

Hotel Wellington

C/Velázquez 8 (91 575 44 00, www.hotel-wellington.com). Metro Retiro. **Rates** €170-€232 double. **Credit** AmEx, DC, MC, V. **Map** p309 M10

More than half a century after it opened, the Wellington remains an extremely graceful place in which to stay, with chandeliers, marble and murals, and groups of guests in formal eveningwear milling around in the lobby. The hotel is just a stone's throw from the city's most expensive shopping area, Salamanca, and has a summer pool with terrace – an ideal location for relaxing after all that retail therapy. Rooms vary in size and are decorated in a conservative but classic style.
Bar (3). Business centre. Internet (free high-speed, wireless). No-smoking floors (4). Parking (€20 per day). Pool (outdoor). Restaurants (2). Room service. Spa. TV (satellite).

Mid-range

Hotel Alcalá

C/Alcalá 66 (91 435 10 60, www.nh-hoteles. com). Metro Príncipe de Vergara. **Rates** €55-€133 double. **Credit** AmEx, MC, V. **Map** p309 M/N10

Even though the chain status of this hotel gives it uniformity and a certain anonymity, the Hotel Alcalá provides visitors with modern accommodation,

supplemented by good facilities and professional staff. Not surprisingly, its location (near the Retiro) and style (rooms with contemporary decor and good sound-proofing) make it a popular choice.
Bars (2). Internet (free wireless). Parking (€22 per day). Restaurant. Room service. TV (pay movies, satellite).

Hotel Meliá Galgos

C/Claudio Coello 139 (91 562 66 00, www.melia galgos.com). Metro Rubén Darío. **Rates** €92-€162 double. **Credit** AmEx, DC, MC, V. **Map** p309 L6 ⑤⓪
This large, glitzy and bustling hotel is part of the Sol Meliá group. It's located in the heart of the business district, so it comes as no surprise that there are ten conference rooms – but it is also popular with the well-heeled leisure set. The 'Servicio Real' floor offers a separate reception, a free bar, yet more mod cons in the rooms and secretaries for hire, and even the standard rooms are large and comfortable – if somewhat dated in decor. The gym comes complete with sauna and whirlpools, while the breakfast spread is spectacular.
Bar. Business centre. Gym. Internet access (high-speed, wireless). Parking. Restaurants (2). Room service. TV (pay movies, satellite).

Radisson Blu Madrid Prado

C/Moratín 52 (91 524 26 26, www.radissonblu. com/pradohotel-madrid). Metro Antón Martín. **Rates** €120-€170 double. **Credit** AmEx, DC, MC, V. **Map** p312 J13 ⑤①
In prime tourist territory, on the corner of the Paseo del Prado, the Radisson Blu is a useful new addition to the city's hotel offerings, with a slick interior, modern artwork and comfortable rooms (54 bedrooms and six suites), equipped with all mod cons, black-slate bathrooms and great views. The hotel also offers what it calls economy rooms: smaller and cheaper, but equipped with all the same features as the larger standard doubles.
Bar. Business centre. Disabled-adapted rooms. Gym. Internet (free high-speed, wireless). Pool (indoor). Restaurant. Room service. Spa. TV (pay movies, satellite).

Budget

Hostal Arco Iris

C/O'Donnell 27, 6ª 6º (mobile 620 936 277, www.hostalarcoiris.com). Metro O'Donnell. **Rates** €61-€83 double. **Credit** MC, V. **Map** p309 O10 ⑥②
Although it's a little more expensive than most *hostales*, the Rainbow's colour schemes make a refreshing change when compared with the dark corridors of the other budget accommodation in the city centre. Rooms are modern and bright, with clean bathrooms, and the friendly staff members are happy to add extra beds to make triples or twins. Stays of two nights or more receive a discount.
Internet (free wireless). TV.

Hostal-Residencia Don Diego

C/Velázquez 45 (91 435 07 60, www.hostal dondiego.com). Metro Velázquez. **Rates** €55-€93 double. **Credit** AmEx, MC, V. **Map** p309 M8 ⑤③
The Hostal-Residencia Don Diego lies above a row of upmarket private apartments on one of Madrid's most exclusive streets. Rooms are plain but clean and good value, and, because of the location, the *hostal* is popular with the business crowd and those attending trade shows at the IFEMA.
Internet (free wireless in hotel lounge). Parking. TV (satellite).

ARGÜELLES

Expensive

Hotel Husa Princesa

C/Princesa 40 (91 542 21 00, www.hotelhusa princesa.com). Metro Ventura Rodríguez. **Rates** €90-€300. **Credit** AmEx, DC, MC, V. **Map** p306 D8 ⑤④
Beyond the Plaza de España and the hustle and bustle of Gran Vía lies the Husa Princesa, decorated with large reproductions of Goya and Velázquez classics in each room. Two floors are known as 'club class', providing extra amenities such as a pillow menu, butler service and mid-morning snacks. The hotel's gym and large sports complex are impressive, incorporating an indoor pool, saunas, steam baths and 150 exercise machines, plus a beauty treatment area. The hotel is a favourite of airline staff, who can often be seen sunning themselves on the outdoor terrace.
Bar. Business centre. Disabled-adapted rooms. Gym. Internet. Parking. Pool (indoor). Restaurant. Room service. TV (pay movies, satellite).

Mid-range

Hotel Tirol

C/Marqués de Urquijo 4 (91 548 19 00, www. t3tirol.com). Metro Argüelles. **Rates** €60-€100 double. **Credit** AmEx, MC, V. **Map** p306 D7 ⑤⑤
The most child-friendly hotel in the city features family rooms with separate spaces for kids, a play area and discounts for family stays. Situated within easy reach of the Parque del Oeste, the Tirol is also well located for those wishing to discover the greener side of Madrid. The hotel is now part of the T3 chain.
Business centre. Gym. Internet (high-speed, wireless). Parking (€22 per hour). TV (satellite).

CHAMBERÍ

Luxury

Hotel Orfila

C/Orfila 6 (91 702 77 70, www.hotelorfila.com). Metro Alonso Martínez or Colón. **Rates** €200-€437 double. **Credit** AmEx, DC, MC, V. **Map** p308 J8 ⑤⑥

CONSUME

Going Flat Out

How to rent a home away from home.

APARTMENT RENTALS

An increasing number of properties in Madrid – most equipped with fully-fitted kitchens, balconies or terraces, and all mod cons – are now available for tourists to rent on a daily, weekly or monthly basis as an alternative to hotels. If you're in town for a week or more, this can work out as a more economical way to lodge in the city than staying in hotels; even with luxurious apartments, the rates can work out the same as many mid-range hotels if you stay for a week or more. They're also a godsend for those who like to actually get a sense of what it's like to live in the city they're visiting – or who simply want a sense of independence or privacy. What's more, you'll save money on food if you cook on some nights.

Apartment rental agencies save you the hassle of contractual negotiations or guarantees that you'd encounter if you were to rent an apartment independently, and include a cleaning service, 24-hour assistance and free Wi-Fi. For short-term rentals all over town, the best agency to try is **Spain Select** (91 523 74 51, www.spain-select.com), which offers a host of hand-picked, high-quality and centrally located properties. Most of the properties sleep between two and six people. If you want to stay in the heart of the action, in luxurious surroundings, then opt for the Plaza Mayor apartment (€1,190-€1,260 per week, based on two people sharing) housed in an 18th-century building and with a balcony overlooking the square. An equally attractive apartment in the characterful Plaza de la Paja, in the heart of the city's tapas scene, costs between €875 and €945 for two people. There are hundreds more options all over town, with a decent number in the traditional *barrio* of Salamanca.

Another agency with plenty of apartments on its books is **Friendly Rentals** (93 268 80 51, www.friendlyrentals.com). Less focused on luxury and personal service than Spain Select, it's nevertheless a good option for those looking for a nicely decorated home from home in a central Madrid location.

APARTHOTELS

Aparthotels are generally made up of self-catering suites or small apartments, usually with kitchen facilities (sometimes basic), as well as standard hotel services, such as a reception, maid service, concierge and room service. They're normally available on weekly, monthly or longer-term rates, so are handy if you're staying in town for a while.

Halfway between a conventional hotel and apartment, the **Aparto-Hotel Rosales** (C/Marqués de Urquijo 23, Argüelles, 91 542 03 51, www.apartohotel-rosales.com) provides accommodation ranging from spacious and comfortably furnished bedsits to suites. All boast kitchens and marble-clad bathrooms, and larger rooms also have a lounge. Other facilities include a coffee shop and a decent restaurant. Double studios cost between €85 and €175 per night, while double apartments are between €124 and €235.

A more centrally located option is the **Apartamentos Príncipe 11** (C/ Príncipe 11, Santa Ana, 91 429 44 70, www.atprincipe 11.com), on a pleasant street not far from Plaza Santa Ana. The 36 apartment rooms have a kitchen area (with hob, microwave, fridge and basic utensils), while rates for double rooms vary from €48 to €87 per night. There are also larger family rooms.

Spain Select apartment.

This small mansion in a tranquil residential area has been transformed into an elegant five-star hotel. Built in the 1880s as a private home for an artistic family, the Orfila also contained a theatre and a literary salon during the 1920s. Thankfully, the hotel has held on to its 19th-century decor, not to mention its façade, carriage entrance and dramatic main stairway. Bedrooms are wonderfully quiet. The elegant restaurant looks on to the lovely garden patio, and guests take tea in the lobby in the afternoon. *Bar. Internet access (wireless). Parking (€25 per day). Restaurant. Room service. TV (pay movies, satellite).*

★ Hotel Santo Mauro

C/Zurbano 36 (91 319 69 00, www.hotelacsanto mauro.com). Metro Rubén Darío. **Rates** €297-€350 double. **Credit** AmEx, DC, MC, V. **Map** p308 J7 ⑰

Famous in recent times as the Beckhams' first residence in Madrid, this exquisite hotel is discreetly hidden away in the embassy-lined streets that separate the Castellana from busy C/Santa Engracia. The elegant and peaceful entrance prepares guests for the experience to come. The 51 rooms, housed in two parts of what was the residence of the Duke of Santo Mauro, are luxuriously decorated, and boast king-size beds and floor-to-ceiling picture windows hung with opulent silk drapes. The old palace library has been converted into a high-class restaurant and former ballrooms are now conference rooms opening on to an immaculately kept garden. *Bar. Business centre. Disabled-adapted room. Gym. Internet (wireless). Parking. Pool (indoor). Restaurant. Room service. TV (satellite).*

Expensive

Gran Hotel Conde Duque

Plaza Conde del Valle Suchil 5 (91 447 70 00, www.hotelcondeduque.es). Metro San Bernardo. **Rates** €77-€190 double. **Credit** AmEx, DC, MC, V. **Map** p307 F7 ⑱

A quiet, out-of-the-way hotel with front rooms facing a pretty, leafy *plaza*. Rooms are tastefully kitted out with yellow and green upholstery, while the belle époque salon downstairs serves afternoon tea. Beds are king-size and one room, 315, has a waterbed. Previous guests have included Celia Cruz and Marcel Marceau, and Pedro Almodóvar has been spotted in the bar. Guests can use the gym on the other side of the square. *Bar. Business centre. Gym. Internet access (high-speed, web TV). Parking. Restaurant. Room service. TV (pay movies, satellite).*

InterContinental Madrid

Paseo de la Castellana 49 (91 700 73 00, www.madrid.intercontinental.com). Metro Gregorio Marañón. **Rates** €120-€184 double. **Credit** AmEx, DC, MC, V. **Map** p307 K6 ⑲

The InterContinental is a long-standing Madrid favourite. The elegant decor in the lobby extends to the rooms, most of which overlook the Paseo de la Castellana. The hotel appeals to a wide-ranging clientele, being well located for the business districts but also offering special packages for fans visiting the Bernabéu football stadium. In terms of eating and drinking options, the modern Bar 49 is perfect for a cocktail or two before dinner, the El Jardin restaurant serves French cuisine outdoors during the summer months, and the café serves light meals overlooking the lovely garden. *Bar. Business centre. Disabled-adapted rooms (4). Gym. Internet (high-speed, wireless). No-smoking floors (5). Parking (€30 per day). Restaurants (2). Room service. TV (pay movies, satellite).*

Mid-range

Hotel Zurbano

C/Zurbano 79-81 (91 441 45 00, www.nh-hoteles. com). Metro Gregorio Marañón. **Rates** €49-€120. **Credit** AmEx, DC, MC, V. **Map** p305 J5 ⑳

Part of the NH chain, the Zurbano is split between two buildings. Rooms are immaculate (if a little bland) and incredibly well soundproofed, given the location right near the chaotic C/José Abascal and its never-ending traffic jams. The size of the rooms varies according to the building (the one furthest up the street tends to have the biggest bedrooms). For travellers needing to be near the northern business district or within easy reach of Barajas airport, the location couldn't be better. *Bar. Business centre. Disabled-adapted room. Internet access (wireless). No-smoking floor. Parking. Restaurant. Room service. TV (pay movies, satellite).*

OTHER AREAS

Expensive

★ Hotel Puerta América

Avda America 41, East of centre (91 744 54 00, www.hoteles-silken.com) Metro Cartagena. **Rates** €91-€201 double. **Credit** AmEx, DC, MC, V.

The Puerta América will not be to all tastes, least of all, probably, those business travellers attracted by its proximity to the airport, but it is a wonderland for design buffs. Each of its 12 floors and public spaces is designed by an all-star cast of architects, including Norman Foster, Richard Gluckman, Marc Jewson and Ron Arad. Guests can select the floor of their choice on arrival, but most popular tend to be Zaha Hadid's rooms (which appear to be sculpted from snowdrifts) or Arata Isozaki's studies in Japanese minimalism. The building itself (along with the pool and gym) was designed by Jean Nouvel. *Bars (2). Disabled-adapted rooms (8). Gym. Internet (wireless). No-smoking floors (2). Pool (indoor). Restaurants (3). Room service. Spa. TV (satellite).*

CONSUME

Mid-range

Hotel Don Pío

Avda Pío XII 25, Chamartín (91 353 07 80, www.hoteldonpio.com). Metro Pío XII. **Rates** €100-€160 double. **Credit** MC, V.
Just 15 minutes from the airport, this hotel offers good facilities for the price. The lobby is decorated with dark wooden panelling and antique furniture, while the 41 spacious rooms, arranged round a glass-roofed atrium, are clean, bright and spacious.
Bar. Business centre. Disabled-adapted room. Gym. Internet (free wireless). No-smoking floors (2). Parking. Restaurant. Room service. TV (satellite).

Hotel Eurobuilding

C/Padre Damián 23, Chamartín (91 353 73 00, www.nh-hoteles.com). Metro Cuzco. **Rates** €55-€134 double. **Credit** AmEx, DC, MC, V.
The very name conjures up images of blandness, but this hotel is set in an appealing residential area. Yes, it's a twin-tower giant, with 440 rooms, but for sports fans and business travellers the location is hard to beat, near the Palacio de Congresos and Real Madrid's Estadio Bernabéu. The hotel offers a range of services, including a spa and beauty salon. Apartment-size suites are available for long stays.
Bar. Business services. Disabled-adapted rooms. Gym. Internet (free wireless). Restaurant (3). Room service. Spa. TV (satellite).

YOUTH HOSTELS

Much of Madrid's youth hostel accommodation is situated outside the city centre, within easy reach of the mountains.

Albergue Juvenil Municipal

C/Mejia Lequerica 21, Chamberí (91 593 96 88, www.ajmadrid.es). Metro Bilbao or Alonso Martínez. **Rates** (incl breakfast) €20 per person under-26s; €22.50 over-26s. *Towel* €3. **Credit** AmEx, DC, MC, V. **Map** p308 H8 ⑤
Open since 2007, this is the only council-run hostel in the city centre. Conditions are well above average, and communal areas include a multimedia room with free internet access, a room full of exercise bikes, a games and TV room, and a diner.

INSIDE TRACK
CALL THE COUNCIL

A list of council-owned youth hostels in and around the city can be found on the website www.esmadrid.com (go to 'Services' then 'Hotels', then select 'Youth Hostels' in the 'Accommodation Guide' box). The site also has an extensive list of hotels.

Albergue Juvenil San Fermín

Avda de los Fueros 36, South of centre (91 792 08 97, www.san-fermin.org). Metro San Fermín/ bus 23 from Plaza Mayor. **Rates** (incl breakfast) €19.80 over-30s; €15.40 per person 25-30; €14 under-25s. €40 double. *Locker* €3. *Towel* €3. **Credit** AmEx, DC, MC, V.
This great-value hostel is aimed specifically at young people and is part of a local regeneration project for the San Fermín area, which lies to the south of the city. The modern building houses clean and bright dorms as well as computer facilities, a TV room, gardens and a hall for cultural events. It is non-smoking throughout.

Barbieri International Hostel

2nd floor, C/Barbieri 15, Chueca (91 531 02 58, www.barbierihostel.com). Metro Chueca or Gran Vía. **Rates** (incl breakfast) €18 per person. *Daytime use incl storage & facilities* €5. *Locker* €1. **Credit** MC, V. **Map** p308 I10 ⑫
Right in the middle of Chueca, this hostel is popular with budget travellers of all nationalities. The double rooms and dorms for three or seven people are basic but clean, and there are kitchen facilities, a TV room with DVD player and a book exchange service. Staff members are very friendly, the atmosphere is relaxed and there's no curfew.

CAMPSITES

There's a fair sprinkling of campsites around Madrid and towards the Guadarrama and Gredos mountains. Most are open year-round. A full list is available from tourist offices.

Camping El Escorial

Ctra de Guadarrama a El Escorial, km 3.5 (91 890 24 12, www.campingelescorial.com). Bus 664 from Moncloa. **Rates** €6.10-€7.25 per person, per car, per tent. *Electricity* €4.50. *Plots* (incl tent, car and electricity) €18.50-€29. **No credit cards**.
This luxury campsite, in the foothills of the Sierra de Guadarrama around 45 minutes from Madrid, is set in 40 hectares (99 acres) of grounds. There are wooden chalets (€70-€143) that accommodate five people and have heating for winter stays, as well as pitches for caravans, tents and motorhomes. Facilities are ample: four swimming pools, various sports courts, two discos, a restaurant, café-bar, launderette and supermarket, plus activities for kids.

Camping Osuna

Avda de Logroño s/n, Northern suburbs (91 741 05 10). Metro Canillejas. **Rates** €6.90 per person, tent, car or caravan; €6 bike. *Electricity* €5.70. **No credit cards**.
This is the closest campsite to central Madrid, and the only one within reasonable distance of a metro station. Services include a supermarket, laundry, restaurant and bar with summer terrace.

...Arts & Entertainment

Children

Kids rule in the Spanish capital.

This is a city where children are welcome almost everywhere. *Madrileños* are, in general, a friendly bunch and if you have kids in tow their amiability is sure to be turned up a notch or two. The care of children is considered everybody's business. Waitresses will scoop your baby up to show off to the kitchen staff and old ladies will happily advise you that your child is wearing too few/too many clothes for the season.

Taking children to restaurants or pavement cafés is considered the norm, but be prepared to adapt to Spanish meal times; lunch is normally eaten around 2pm, and dinner is from 10pm. If your kids really can't wait, then the numerous fast-food or pasta and pizza places are your best hope, and high chairs and children's menus can usually be found in these joints.

MANAGING THE DAY

In summer, afternoon temperatures can hover around a very uncomfortable 40ºC, so outdoor activities are best done in the morning. After a late lunch, a siesta is the best option before venturing out into the relatively cool evening air. The city comes alive again in the hour or two before dusk when families come out to stroll, eat ice-cream and watch the world go by.

Be warned that few metro stations have lifts (they are listed at www.metromadrid.es under 'Accesibility'), and buses will only admit pushchairs if they are folded. Baby-changing facilities are limited to major shopping centres, the department store El Corte Inglés (*see p135*), and the airport.

Note that prices for Madrid's theme parks and similar attractions are often ten per cent cheaper if you can organise buying tickets online before your visit.

ATTRACTIONS

Kids also enjoy the **Teleférico** cable-car (*see p77*) that runs from the Parque del Oeste deep into the Casa de Campo.

Faunia

Avda de las Comunidades 28, Eastern suburbs (91 301 62 10, www.faunia.es). Metro Valdebernardo. **Open** times vary, check website or call for details. **Admission** €25.95 over-8s; €19.95 3-7s, over-65s;

free under-3s. Discounts for tickets purchased through website. **Credit** AmEx, MC, V.

Part zoo, part theme park, Faunia recreates the world's different ecosystems in a series of domes. Best of the bunch is the Amazon jungle house, which echoes with the screech of exotic birds; an intense tropical storm is simulated every half hour. In summer, Penguin World – an impressive reconstruction of a polar zone, where you can see the little fellas nipping about – is wildly popular. Faunia is not a cheap day out, and queues can be long.

IMAX Madrid

C/Meneses s/n, Parque Tierno Galván, Legazpi, South of centre (91 467 48 00, www.imaxmadrid.com). Metro Méndez Alvaro. **Admission** €8.55-€9.95. **Credit** AmEx, MC, V.

The wildlife and scientific shows (usually one or two shows a day during the week, four or five at weekends) are in Spanish only, but the 3D and Omnimax presentations are impressive enough to be enjoyed by all children.

Palacio de Hielo

C/Silvano 77, Eastern suburbs (ice rink 91 716 01 59, www.sporthielo.com, www.palaciodehielo.com). Metro Canillas. **Open** *Ice rink* Sept-May 8.45-10.15pm Wed, Thur; 5.30pm-midnight Fri; 12.30-3pm, 5.30pm-midnight Sat; 12.30-3pm, 5.30-10.30pm Sun. Closed June-mid Sept. *Bowling alley* 3-11pm Mon-Thur; 11am-2am Fri, Sat; 11am-11pm Sun. **Admission** *Ice rink* €6-€12.50. *Bowling alley* €3-€6. **No credit cards.**

The Ice Palace is a huge leisure complex dominated by an 1,800sq m ice rink. With a curling and skating school, 24-lane bowling alley and 15-screen cinema, it's a good option for a rainy day. The site, out towards Barajas Airport, is also home to a shopping centre (10am-10pm daily), numerous cafés and restaurants, and a nursery for kids aged three to 11.

Parque de Atracciones

Casa de Campo (902 345 009, 91 526 80 30, www.parquedeatracciones.es). Metro Batán. **Open** times vary (see website for details). **Admission** €29.90 over 120cm; €23.90 90cm-120cm; €16 over-65s. **Credit** MC, V.
A funfair with something for everyone. The wildest ride is El Abismo (The Abyss), which is a 49m high-roller that follows a route of scary drops at 100km/h. There is now a children's version, too, so nobody has to miss the terror. Other new features include indoor paintball and a 4D cinema. There are long queues for some rides.

Planetario de Madrid

Avenida del Planetario 16, Parque Tierno Galván, Legazpi, South of centre (91 467 34 61, www.planetmad.es). Metro Arganzuela-Planetario. **Shows** vary; phone to check, or see website. Closed Mon & 1st 2wks Jan. **Admission** €3.65; €1.65 2-14s, over-65s. **No credit cards.**
Close to the IMAX (*see p174*), the Planetarium has seasonal exhibitions on the solar system as well as

Zoo Aquarium Madrid.

INSIDE TRACK ROYAL TREAT

At 11am every Wednesday, from October to July, you can watch the Changing of the Guard in front of the baroque magnificence of the Palacio Real (*see p38*).

45-minute shows. Like the IMAX, the narration here is only in Spanish and may test your kids' interest in the heavens if they are non-Spanish speakers.

Zoo Aquarium Madrid

Casa de Campo (91 512 37 70, www.zoomadrid. com). Metro Batán. **Open** times vary (check the website or call for details). **Admission** €22.90 over-8s; €18.55 3-7s, over-65s; free under-3s. Discounts for tickets purchased through website. **Credit** MC, V.
This attractively landscaped zoo is located slap bang in the heart of the Casa de Campo. The animals look as happy as can be expected of beasts held in captivity, although the big cats could really do with a bit more leg-room. At the Tierra de Gorilas ('Land of Gorillas'), a sheet of reassuringly thick glass separates you from the massive, glowering silverbacks prowling about. Children will enjoy walking through the shark tank and dolphinarium. There's also a petting zoo and a train ride.

BABYSITTING & CHILDCARE

English-speaking babysitters can be found through local English-language publications; for a list of magazines and newspapers in English published in Madrid, *see p287*. Alternatively, parents can leave children aged four to 12 for short periods at any of the following *ludotecas* (play centres) around town.

Centro de Recreo Infantil Dinopeppino

C/Mártires de Alcalá 4, Malasaña & Conde Duque (91 559 22 04, 91 559 61 21, www. dinopeppino.com). Metro Ventura Rodríguez. **Open** 4.30-8.30pm Mon-Fri; 11.30am-2pm, 4.30-8.30pm Sat, Sun. **Admission** (per hr) €6.80; €55 10hr multi-entry. **No credit cards**. **Map** p307 E8.
A well-equipped and spacious play centre.

Al Trote

C/Bolivia 40, Chamartín (91 345 02 93, www. altrote.net). Metro Colombia. **Open** 4.30-8.30pm Mon-Fri; noon-2pm, 5-9pm Sat, Sun. **Admission** (per hr) €6.50 per hr weekdays, €7 per hr weekends. **Credit** MC, V.
A popular play centre, with everything from slides and ball pools to a Wii area. It also offers themed birthday parties.

ARTS & ENTERTAINMENT

CosmoCaixa.

ENTERTAINMENT

Events aimed at children are dotted throughout the year, starting in January with a parade on 5 January – the eve of **Reyes**, when Spanish children traditionally receive their Christmas presents. The parade features floats from which the Three Kings throw sweets to children along the route. During **Carnaval** (*see p39*), kids' activities are organised, and there are also children's events during **San Isidro** (*see p25*) and **Veranos de la Villa** (*see p28*). In April, festivities for **El Día del Niño** (Day of the Child) are held in C/Bravo Murillo in Tetuán. The street is taken over by bouncy castles, puppet shows, foam-spraying firemen and candy floss stalls.

Look out, too, for children's theatre. **Teatro San Pol** in the Casa de Campo (C/San Pol de Mar 1, 91 541 90 89, www.teatrosanpol.com, closed July & Aug) puts on occasional shows in English. The **Madrid Players**, an English-language theatre group (91 326 24 39, www.madridplayers.org), puts on a pantomime at Christmas and hosts occasional theatre workshops for kids (check website for details).

In the Retiro park, the permanent **Teatro Municipal de Títeres** (91 792 41 12, mobile 670 72 33 60, www.titirilandia.org), near the boating lake, has free puppet shows most weekends, albeit in Spanish. **La Casa Encendida** (*see p52*) runs children's

workshops on diverse subjects; storytelling sessions are on Fridays, and at weekends there are concerts and shows.

MUSEUMS

The **Museo del Ferrocarril** (*see p84*) houses steam, diesel and electric locomotives. Children's activities include theatre at weekends, a mini-train on Saturdays and a monthly market for model train enthusiasts.

CosmoCaixa
C/Pintor Velázquez s/n, Alcobendas (91 484 52 00, www.fundacio.lacaixa.es). Bus 157 from Plaza Castilla. **Open** 10am-8pm Tue-Sun. **Admission** €3; €2 reductions; free under-8s. **Credit** MC, V. Kids and adults uncover the mysteries of science via hands-on interactive exhibits. The *Clik de los Niños* (3-8yrs), where processes can be tried out, is popular, while the *Toca, Toca* (touch, touch) area for small children features animals to stroke. CosmoCaixa's future is uncertain, and it may be forced to close at the end of 2013 unless funding is found.

Museo de Cera (Wax Museum)
Paseo de Recoletos 41, Salamanca (91 319 26 49, www.museoceramadrid.com). Metro Colón. **Open** 10am-2.30pm, 4.30-8.30pm Mon-Fri; 10am-8.30pm Sat, Sun. **Admission** €12-€17. **No credit cards**. **Map** p308 K9.
Madame Tussauds it isn't (there's no queueing for starters), yet this waxwork museum still has a certain tacky charm. Along with the usual rogues, celebrities and politicians – among them the Beatles, Clark Gable and George W Bush – there's a Tren de Terror (ghost train).

PARKS & PLAYGROUNDS

Small neighbourhood parks are not Madrid's strong point; play areas have improved in recent years but are still a little tame. One of the better play areas is in the **Plaza de Oriente**, next to the Palacio Real. The **Paseo del Prado** central boulevard has safe wooden climbing frames and slides, and **Dos de Mayo** in Malasaña has play areas for toddlers and *terrazas* for adults, as does the nearby **Plaza de las Comendadoras**. C/**Fuencarral** was done up a few years ago, with widened pavements, and now boasts six small play areas. There are a couple of play areas in the Plaza Santa Ana, especially popular with parents because of its numerous pavement cafés.

The **Retiro** (*see p65*) has a boating lake, cafés around the edge, buskers, artists, puppet shows, sports facilities and a good play area by the Puerta de Alcalá entrance. To the west is the Parque del Oeste, which has great views, decent play areas, ice-cream parlours and the

Teleférico. The huge **Casa de Campo** (*see p76*) has the Zoo, the Parque de Atracciones funfair, an even bigger boating lake and the best outdoor pools in Madrid (*see p224*), with a shaded and shallow kids' pool.

In summer, Madrid gets its own urban beach, which spreads out along the banks of the River Manzanares in the modern Parque de la Arganzuela. There's no swimming, but you can rent deckchairs for a couple of euros and watch as kids shriek delightedly as they run through the fountains, which jet up at different speeds. Other attractions in the park include several play areas and cafés.

OUT OF TOWN

Most rides in the waterparks around town are suited to older kids, but there are usually areas for small children. For general pools, *see p224*.

Aquópolis de San Fernando de Henares
Crta de Barcelona (A-2), km 15.5, San Fernando de Henares (902 345 022, www.aquopolis.es). Bus (Continental) to Alcalá de Henares or Torrejón from Avda de América/by car A-2. **Open** *Last 2wks June* 12.30-7pm Mon-Fri; noon-7pm Sat, Sun. *July, Aug* 12.30-8pm Mon-Fri; noon-8pm Sat, Sun. Closed Sept-mid June. **Admission** €15.50-€20.50. Discounts for tickets bought on website. **Credit** MC, V.
Madrid's first waterpark, with giant water slides, pools for smaller and larger kids, wave pools and wilder attractions for reckless youths.

Aquópolis de Villanueva de la Cañada
Avda de la Dehesa, Villanueva de la Cañada (902 345 006, www.aquopolis.es). Bus 627 or 581 from Moncloa/by car Ctra de La Coruña (A-6), exit 41, then M503. **Open** *Last 2wks June & 1st wk Sept* noon-7pm daily; *July, Aug* noon-7pm Mon-Fri; noon-8pm Sat, Sun. Closed early Sept-mid June. **Admission** €23.95 adults taller than 1.4m; €19.90 over-65s, children between 0.9m and 1.4m. Discounts for tickets bought on website. **Credit** AmEx, MC, V.
One of the largest waterparks in Europe, run by the same company as the Aquópolis de San Fernando and with similar attractions.

De Pino a Pino
Área Recreativa del Chorro, Navafría (mobile 659 45 45 68, www.depinoapino.com). By car A-6/ AP-61 to Segovia (100km), then N110 to Navafría (20km). **Open** *Feb* (prior bookings only) 11am-7pm daily. *Mar* 11am-7pm daily. *Apr, May, Oct* 11am-7.30pm daily. *June, Sept* 11am-8pm daily. *July, Aug* 11am-3pm, 4.30-8pm Mon-Fri; 11am-8pm Sat, Sun. *Nov* 11am-6.30pm daily. *Dec* 11am-6pm daily. Closed Jan. Last entry 2hrs before closing. **Admission** (for free access to all circuits) €25; €23 5-18s. Individual activities €13-€18. **No credit cards**.
A trek from Madrid but well worth the effort, 'From Pine to Pine' is a forest-based adventure park where logs, hanging bridges and tree platforms are incorporated into routes that criss-cross the pine forests. Courses are designed with varying levels of difficulty according to kids' ages and each takes an hour.

ARTS & ENTERTAINMENT

The Retiro.

Madrid Xanadú

Autovía A-5, km 23.5, Arroyomolines (902 263 026, www.madridxanadu.com). Bus 528, 534 or 539 from Príncipe Pío, or 498A, 524 or 529H from Móstoles. **Open** 10am-10pm Mon-Thur; 10am-2am Fri-Sun. **Admission** (excl equipment hire) *1hr* €22; €19 under-13s. *4hrs* €30; €27 under-13s. **Credit** AmEx, DC, MC, V.

Madrid Xanadú is home to the Madrid SnowZone (902 361 309, www.madridsnowzone.com), which boasts 24,000sq m of indoor ski slopes. All the equipment can be hired. There are also go-karts, a 15-screen cinema, 200 shops and around 30 restaurants.

Parque Warner Madrid

San Martín de la Vega (91 821 12 34, 902 024 100, www.parquewarner.com). By car A-4 to km 22, then M-506 to San Martín de la Vega/by train C-3 from Atocha to Parque de Ocio. **Open** times vary (see website for details). **Admission** €39 adults, children over 140cm; €35 children 100cm-140cm, over-60s. Free for children shorter than 100cm. **Credit** AmEx, DC, MC, V.

The park has five themed areas with rides to match: Hollywood Boulevard, Cartoon Village, Old West Territory, DC Super Heroes and Warner Brothers Studios. Tickets are valid for two days, but you must validate your entrance bracelet for a second day before you leave the park on your first day.

Safari de Madrid

Aldea del Fresno, Ctra de Extremadura (A-5), km 32 (91 862 23 14, www.safarimadrid.com). By car A-5 to Navalcarnero, then M-507 to Aldea del Fresno. **Open** 10.30am-7pm daily. **Admission** €16; €12 3-10s. **Credit** AmEx, DC, MC, V.

A drive-through safari park where giraffes, elephants, big cats and monkeys roam free. In summer there's a swimming pool, a lake with pedalos, a go-kart track, mini-motorbikes and a giant slide.

Tren de la Fresa (Strawberry Train)

Paseo de las Delicias 61 (902 22 88 22, www.renfe.com). Metro Delicias. **Open** 10am Sat, Sun (return from Aranjuez 6.25pm). Closed mid Oct-late Apr, mid July-mid Sept. **Tickets** €12; under-6s free (as long as they don't occupy a separate seat). **Credit** MC, V. **Map** p313 L15/16.

A relaxing steam train ride to Aranjuez. The 1920s 'strawberry' train departs from the Museo del Ferrocarril (*see p84*), and the ticket price includes a guided tour of the town and the palace gardens.

Tail of Madrid

There's a mouse about the house.

Ask any Spanish child to name the most famous mouse in the world and few of them will come up with Mickey. By far the most celebrated rodent in Spain and much of South America is **Ratoncito Pérez**, the mythical mouse who sneaks into children's rooms at night to slip money under the pillow when a tooth falls out. What few people know is that Pérez is actually a *madrileño*.

Stroll half a minute from the Puerta del Sol and you can see a plaque marking the house where Pérez lived in a biscuit tin in the basement of a pastry shop. The ground floor of C/Arenal 8 is now a small museum (www.casamuseoratonperez.es, admission €2.50) and shop. Inside, you'll find a mouse-sized statue (well, hamster-sized, perhaps), and the biscuit-tin home of Ratoncito Pérez – although it's unlikely you'll catch him at home, given how many children's teeth he needs to collect.

There are also illustrated panels telling the story of the mouse and his creator, a Jesuit priest, Father Coloma. Juan Coloma, who found God after nearly killing himself while cleaning his revolver as a young man, first published the story of *Ratoncito Pérez* in 1902. He dedicated the book to the young King Alfonso XIII, to whom he had told the story while the monarch was a sickly child. According to the story, the mouse would frequently escape from the basement by means of the sewers. From this labyrinth he could then find his way into the bedroom of any child, from the boy-king to the poorest *niño* in the land, exchanging a lost tooth for money or a small gift. The story sparked the tradition that continues to this day.

In 2003, the mayor of Madrid unveiled the plaque to Ratoncito Pérez, announcing rather grandly that, just as the Americans have Mickey, Pérez 'deserves recognition as a symbol of the hopes and dreams of all children, and because he is *our* mouse'.

Film

The recession-hit movie scene still has plenty to offer.

Madrileños and movies go together like chocolate and *churros*. Indeed, this happy foursome is all that's needed for a perfect night out. Ticket prices have risen, but are still affordable, and the range of film fare is easily a match for Paris or London.

Spanish film goes from strength to strength, but it's been a mixed few years for Madrid's cinephiles, with several of the city's much-loved movie-houses, such as La Enana Marrón, closing down. However, the opening of Sala Berlanga, in the refurbished California cinema in the district of Argüelles, has been something of a silver lining. The cinema offers Spanish, Iberoamerican and European films in their original (undubbed) versions, and it joins a decent list of arthouse cinemas in the city – including the excellent Cine Doré Filmoteca (the national film theatre) in Lavapiés, showing old films in VO (*versión original*) – as well as a host of multiplexes.

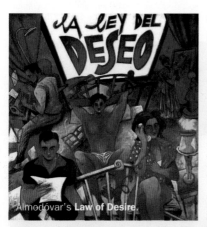

Almodóvar's **Law of Desire**.

INSIDE TRACK
ALBERTO IGLESIAS

What the films of directors Pedro Almodóvar and Julio Médem have in common is the composer Alberto Iglesias, whose exquisite soundtracks are a prime contributing factor to their pleasure and popularity.

SPANISH CINEMA

Spain has no film censorship and its movie aficionados have long indulged their considered taste for avant-garde cinema, which, in turn, has inspired the works of home-grown masters such as Pedro Almodóvar and Julio Médem. Once the enfant terrible of Spanish cinema, the deservedly garlanded Almodóvar now makes mature and richly textured films that are both emotionally and stylistically audacious. The metaphysical Médem, whose thrilling documentary on the Basque conflict, *Basque Ball*, made him a controversial figure in Spain, continues to court attention, as with his 2010 erotic lesbian drama *Room in Rome*.

Other names to keep an eye out for are the social realists Iciar Bollaín and Fernando León de Aranoa; Catalan director Isabel Coixet; the satirist Álex de la Iglesia; and the precocious maestro that is Alejandro Amenábar, who directed Nicole Kidman in *The Others*. Added to this roster are veterans such as Carlos Saura, who is still going strong.

Due to complex funding and distribution policies, an enormous number of films are made in Spain when compared with how many eventually make it into mainstream cinemas. However, a plethora of film festivals of every persuasion provide a springboard for new filmmakers and the production of short films is booming, with

INSIDE TRACK
SCREENING TIMES

Screenings tend to start promptly with few trailers or ads, though a brisk turnover means that credits are curtailed and latecomers are a constant hazard.

arthouse cinemas programming some of the best before their main features. For more on Spanish film, *see pp21-23* **Movida Movies**.

VENUES

There is no shortage of multiplexes throughout the city showing Hollywood fodder dubbed into Spanish. However, if you're after a more refined experience, try the commercially viable arthouse cinemas showing Spanish auteurs, documentaries, foreign films in VO (*versión original* – undubbed and with subtitles), and an exhilarating variety of quirky, classic and controversial features. For film seasons and older films, both in Spanish and VO, head for the grand Filmoteca.

Tickets & times

Daily newspapers, the weekly *Guia del Ocio* and the http://madrid.lanetro.com website have film reviews and full listings. Screenings (*pases*) usually start at around 4pm. The 8pm screening is the most popular, though the late screenings (*sesiones de madrugada*) at midnight and 1am can be surprisingly packed if they're showing cult films or current favourites. Read the newspapers for VO listings, and once there check whether your seating is allocated (*numerada*) before paying. Be warned of the rarity of adequately tiered seating – Spaniards are getting taller but the screens are yet to be put any higher. Monday and Wednesday are often *días del espectador* ('spectator days'), offering special discounts, though every cinema has its own policy on price reductions. Internet reservations are available through www.entradas.com, and many cinemas will take advance bookings for busy times and popular films.

VO CINEMAS

Cine Estudio de Bellas Artes
C/Alcalá 42, Huertas & Santa Ana (91 389 25 00, www.circulobellasartes.com). Metro Banco de España. **Tickets** €5.50; €4 members & reductions. **No credit cards. Map** p312 I11. Originally a theatre, this repertory cinema is part of the grand Círculo de Bellas Artes building. The sound system is excellent, and the programme of themed film seasons goes down well with the trendy audience.

Sala Berlanga. *See p182*.

Essential Madrid Films

Celluloid city.

Volver.

DÍA DE LA BESTIA (THE DAY OF THE BEAST) ALEX DE LA IGLESIA (1995)

A devilishly funny horror-comedy in which a priest becomes convinced that the Antichrist will be born in Madrid on Christmas Day. Immersing himself in evil, he searches for clues among the city's human detritus and in the lyrics of death metal songs, before kidnapping, with the help of a gonzoid record-shop assistant, a famous TV para-psychologist.

ABRE LOS OJOS (OPEN YOUR EYES) ALEJANDRO AMENÁBAR (1997)

A dazzling thriller that toys with our perceptions to exquisite effect. Playboy César seems to have it all – until his obsessive ex-girlfriend tries to kill him, leaving him so disfigured that he needs a prosthetic mask. But his problems are just beginning as the film lurches from noir-ish poser to latter-day *Beauty and the Beast*, and eventually to head-spinning sci-fi mode.

LOVERS OF THE ARCTIC CIRCLE JULIO MEDEM (1999)

A love story that burns like ice. Otto is just eight years old when he falls in love with Ana. The first time she lays eyes on him, she sees her dead father looking back at her. And Otto's father, Alvaro, also falls in love, with Ana's mother Olga. They make a family with a faultline running through its heart. Teasing, allusive and elusive, this is also Medem's most deeply felt movie to date.

EL MÉTODO (THE METHOD) MARCEL PIÑEYRO (2005)

Competing for a post at a Madrid corporation, seven candidates are exposted to the sadistic 'Grönholm Method' that forces them to identify a mole in their midst, eliminate others and plead to stay on. The anti-capitalist argument is hammered home (as the candidates clash, anti-globalisation protestors rip up the city), but the strong cast maintains the intensity and malicious humour.

VOLVER PEDRO ALMODÓVAR (2006)

Penélope Cruz stars as a working-class housewife in this fable of long-suffering drudgery overcome by domestic homicide and the whiff of quotidian magic (and bodily odours). The story is at once hysterical and mundane, founded in abuse, rape, murder and corpse disposal, yet ultimately about none of these so much as the endurance of the characters involved.

THE BOURNE ULTIMATUM PAUL GREENGRASS (2007)

Madrid plays itself and also stands in for Turin in this, the third part of the most satisfying action franchise of the decade. Bourne (Matt Damon) is still on the run, gradually remembering how US security forces reshaped him as a super-assassin while trying to avoid their determined efforts to neutralise him. A UK newspaper exposé makes his position all the more dangerous.

EDICIÓN ESPECIAL COLECCIONIST

abre los ojo

una película de Alejandro Amenábar t

INSIDE TRACK
ALEJANDRO AMENÁBAR

Alejandro Amenábar, who was born in 1972, is one of the city's most precocious directors. He studied cinema at Madrid's Universidad Complutense, and despite not completing the course has gone on to direct such celebrated films as Academy Award-winning *Mar Adrento* (*The Sea Inside*), *Abre los Ojos* (*Open Your Eyes*) and, most recently, *Agora*, starring Rachel Weisz. In addition to writing and directing his own films, Amenábar has composed several film scores, such as for José Luis Cuerda's *La Lengua de las Mariposas*. Widely regarded as one of the film world's most sincere and modest hot shots, he came out to the media in 2004, and is often spotted in bars around town.

Golem

C/Martín de los Heros 14, Argüelles (information 91 559 38 36, www.golem.es). Metro Plaza de España. **Tickets** €6.30 Mon & 1st session daily; €8.40 Tue-Fri; €8.90 Sat, Sun. **Credit** MC, V. **Map** p307 E9.

This legendary four-screener, until recently known as the Alphaville, was the first of Madrid's arthouse cinemas and played a crucial role in the Movida during the 1980s. The screens and sound systems are showing their age and tiering is inadequate, but the basement café is still a fashionable meeting place with a bohemian atmosphere.

Ideal Yelmo Cineplex

C/Doctor Cortezo 6, Lavapiés (information 91 369 25 18, box office 902 22 09 22, www.yelmocineplex.es). Metro Tirso de Molina. **Tickets** €9.20; €7.30-€7.90 Mon & Wed. **Credit** MC, V. **Map** p311 H13.

This hugely popular nine-screen multiplex is an efficient if somewhat characterless venue for international mainstream films in *versión original.*

Pequeño Cine Estudio

C/Magallanes 1, Chamberí (91 447 29 20, www.pcineestudio.es). Metro Quevedo. **Tickets** €8.50; €6.50 Mon & reductions; *six films* €30. **No credit cards.** Map p307 G6.

It's always worth keeping an eye on this peculiar little VO cinema because its rapid turnover means that rarely viewed classics from Hollywood and world cinema often make it on to the programme.

Renoir Plaza de España

C/Martín de los Heros 12, Argüelles (information 91 541 41 00, box office 902 22 91 22, www.cinesrenoir.com). Metro Plaza de España.

Tickets €6 Mon; €7.50 Tue-Fri; €9 Sat, Sun. **Credit** MC, V. **Map** p307 E9.

This is the flagship cinema of the enterprising Renoir chain. Screens are on the small side and the queuing system in the cramped foyer is somewhat haphazard, but good sound systems and a keen crowd of film fans ensure enjoyable viewing. The Cuatro Caminos branch is also worth a mention for its larger screens, decent bar and intelligent balance of Spanish and world cinema, while the Princesa features an eclectic mix of Spanish, European and independent American cinema.

Other locations (phone numbers for all as above) Renoir Cuatro Caminos, C/Raimundo Fernández Villaverde 10, Chamberí; Cines Princesa, C/Princesa 3, Moncloa; Renoir Retiro, C/Narváez 42.

★ Sala Berlanga

C/Andrés Mellado 53, Argüelles (91 455 08 77, www.salaberlanga.com). Metro Argüelles, Islas Filipinas or Moncloa. **Tickets** €2-€3. **No credit cards.** Map p307 E6.

The old California cinema, refurbished to the tune of €2 million by SGAE, reopened as Sala Berlanga in 2010 – much to the delight of local cinephiles. Named after Spanish film director Luis García Berlanga, the 250-seat VO-only cinema is one of the city's most

ARTS & ENTERTAINMENT

technologically advanced. It runs special seasons and festivals, with a strong focus on documentaries, shorts and underground films. *Photo p180.*

Verdi

C/Bravo Murillo 28, Chamberí (information 91 447 39 30, www.cines-verdi.com/madrid). Metro Canal or Quevedo. **Tickets** €6 Mon; €8 Tue-Thur; €9 Fri-Sun; €7 reductions. **No credit cards**.
This relative newcomer to the ranks of VO cinemas has five screens showing a lively mix of arthouse, Spanish, independent and mainstream foreign films.

THE FILMOTECA

★ Cine Doré (Filmoteca Española)

C/Santa Isabel 3, Lavapiés (box office 91 369 11 25, information 91 369 21 18, bookshop 91 369 46 73, www.mcu.es/cine). Metro Antón Martín. **Open** *Bar-cafés* 5pm-12.45am Tue-Sun. *Bookshop* 5.30-10pm Tue-Sun. **Tickets** €2.50; €2 reductions. *Ten films* €20; €15 reductions. **No credit cards**. **Map** p312 I13.
Known affectionately as *la filmo* and featured in films by Almodóvar, this chic art nouveau national film theatre was founded more than 50 years ago. The neon-lit foyer/café is a lively meeting place and the tiny bookshop is always full of browsers. A free, expansive, fold-out monthly programme guide features details of its eclectic seasons of films from the Spanish National Archive and world cinema. The grand auditorium is an especially marvellous place to see silent movies, sometimes accompanied by live music. The outdoor rooftop cinema and bar are open – and unsurprisingly very popular – during the summer months. Note that the box office opens at 5.15pm and stays open until 15 minutes after the start of the last performance of the night. Advance tickets can only be bought for the following day's performance and then only until a third of the capacity has been booked. Note also that you can only buy three tickets per person for each performance.

OPEN-AIR CINEMA

Fescinal (Cine de Verano)

Parque de la Bombilla, Avda de Valladolid, La Florida (91 541 37 21, www.fescinal.es). Metro Príncipe Pío. **Tickets** €5.50; €4.50 reductions; free under-5s. **No credit cards**.
This open-air night-time venue in Parque de la Bombilla shows double bills of mainstream films during the Veranos de la Villa festival, which takes place between July and September. As well as the massive screen (with wayward sound), Fescinal also offers a smaller one for kids, plus the opportunity to munch on *bocadillos* washed down with *cerveza*. Some of the films are dubbed – check out the website for details.

ARTS & ENTERTAINMENT

Cine Doré.

Gay & Lesbian

Out and about in one of Europe's most exciting gay hubs.

The transformation of Chueca from a haven for winos and junkies into a vibrant gay quarter has let Madrid establish itself as one of the world's most gay-friendly cities. What's more, former prime minister José Luis Rodríguez Zapatero came good on his first pre-election promise to legalise same-sex marriage, making Spain the third country to do so, after Belgium and Holland. Further positive legislative changes have included the Law of Gender Identity, which gives transsexuals the right to have their change of sex reflected on their ID cards and passports.

THE SCENE

The throbbing heart of the scene (*el ambiente*) is the Plaza de Chueca. Tightly packed around what is an otherwise nondescript square in the centre of town, it's home to a dazzling array of bars and services aimed almost exclusively at one of Madrid's most vociferous and dynamic communities. With bars, cafés, hotels, saunas, travel agencies and bookshops, the formerly run-down neighbourhood has emerged as one of the city's liveliest and trendiest areas. But Chueca has become, perhaps, a victim of its own success, its hip hangouts attracting a non-gay crowd in recent years. Now, many want their ghetto back, at least for cruising, and plenty of shag-and-go

male-only bars have popped up all over the place. Special events aimed at specific subcultures are a growth industry too: there are camping weekends for bears in the nearby mountains, an action-packed 'Sleazy Madrid' long weekend every spring, plus lesbian raves with dykey darkrooms, body-shaving bashes and sloppy mud parties.

CAFES & RESTAURANTS

As well as the places listed below (all of which are in Chueca), other restaurants that are noticeably popular among the gay community include **El Armario** (*see p101*), **Gula Gula** (*see p97*) and **El 26 de Libertad** (*see p101*).

Café Acuarela.

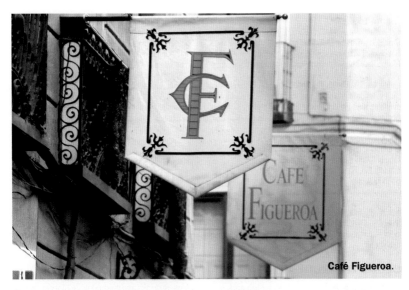

Café Figueroa.

Ángel Sierra (*see p126*), while not a gay bar per se, is smack on the Plaza de Chueca and therefore an ideal place to start the evening.

Café Acuarela

C/Gravina 10 (91 522 21 43). Metro Chueca.
Open 2pm-2.30am daily. **Credit** MC, V.
Map p308 I10.
By day a quiet, mixed haven to duck into and catch your breath: curl up with a book and sample one of the teas. After sundown, sip a cocktail, sink into a deep sofa and admire the decor – a mix of kitsch, retro glamour and exuberant baroque.

★ Café Figueroa

C/Augusto Figueroa 17 (mobile 677 541 716). Metro Chueca. **Open** *Oct-May* noon-1am Mon-Thur; noon-2.30am Fri, Sat; 4pm-1am Sun. *June-Sept* 4.30-11.30pm daily. **No credit cards.**
Map p308 H10.
Madrid's original gay café is a sedate place where the lace curtains, 19th-century chandeliers and winding wooden staircase lend themselves nicely to a cosy destination for those who want gay in an old Spain way. There's a pool table upstairs.

Café La Troje

C/Pelayo 26 (91 531 05 35). Metro Chueca.
Open 5pm-2am Mon-Thur, Sun; 5pm-2.30am Fri, Sat. **No credit cards. Map** p308 I10.
A romantic and popular stop, with friendly service and big screens playing chill-out videos. It gets chock-a-block at weekends with an amiable and mixed crowd, who are generally stopping in on their way somewhere else.

Colby Urban

C/Fuencarral 52 (91 521 25 54, www.restaurante colby.com). Metro Chueca. **Open** 9.30am-1.30am Mon-Thur; 9.30am-2.30am Fri, Sat; 11.30am-1am Sun. **Credit** AmEx, DC, MC, V. **Map** p308 H10.
It's red, it's urban, it's aspirational. Colby Urban is the flagship of a string of cool eateries and chilled-out cafés with a concept. We're not sure what the concept is, but the location is handy, the custom is pretty and the diner-style food hits the spot.

D'Mystic

C/Gravina 5 (91 308 24 60). Metro Chueca.
Open 9am-2am Mon-Fri; 9.30am-2.30am Sat, Sun. **Credit** DC, MC, V. **Map** p308 I10.
This den of cool is located at a strategic crosssroads, and its bigger-than-average cocktails make up for the aloof staff. Watch the real world stroll by outside or gaze at the natural world on the New Agey videos on the screens inside. Relax, listen to the whale songs and the waterfalls. Then get out and head for Leather Club (*see p187*).

★ Diurno

C/San Marcos 37 (91 522 00 09, www.diurno. com). Metro Chueca. **Open** 10am-midnight Mon-Thur; 10am-1am Fri; 11am-1am Sat; 11am-midnight Sun. **Credit** AmEx, DC, MC, V. **Map** p308 I10.
A minimalist and sexy film-rental café spinning all-day chill-out sounds (and occasional techno). As well as offering a fabulous selection of movies, there are delicious sandwiches, salads, pasta dishes and cakes. A peaceful place to start the day, upbeat and lively at night.

Mama Inés

C/Hortaleza 22 (91 523 23 33). Metro Gran Vía.
Open 10am-2am Mon-Thur, Sun; 10am-3am Fri,
Sat. **No credit cards. Map** p308 H10.
Mama Inés successfully combines a decent breakfast
with plenty of eye candy. Chill-out and nu flamenco
tunes waft through this modern but surprisingly
intimate café during the daytime; then, in the
evening, house music takes over and the T-shirts get
progressively tighter and tighter.

XXX Café

C/Clavel 2 (91 522 37 77). Metro Gran Vía.
Open 3.30pm-2am Mon-Thur, Sun; 3.30pm-
2.30am Fri, Sat. **No credit cards. Map**
p308 I11.
Quiet until the pre-dinner crowd arrives to shake the
place up, this is a small and popular meeting point
where the staff are gorgeous and the regulars are
friendly. Park yourself by the window for the best
view – with any luck, you'll be snapped up in no
time at all.

CLUBS & DISCOBARES

A *discobar* treads the line between club and
regular drinking den. Admission is generally
free (exceptions are noted below), and there
is normally a diminutive dancefloor to justify
the pricier-than-average drinks.

As well as the venues we've listed below,
clubs **Ohm** (*see p193*) and **Weekend** (*see
p194*) also have a big gay following. Unless
otherwise stated, all of the following are
located in Chueca.

Black & White

*C/Libertad 34 (91 531 11 41, www.discoblack-
white.net). Metro Chueca.* **Open** 10pm-5.30am
Mon-Thur, Sun; 10pm-6am Fri, Sat. **No credit
cards. Map** p308 I10.
The grubby upstairs bar is a hit with cocky *latino*
rent boys and their older prospective patrons, and
plays host to some of the best cabaret shows in town.
Downstairs things really liven up in the heaving *discobar* that is popular with revellers of all ages and
orientations. A classic.

★ Liquid

*C/Barbieri 7 (91 523 28 08, www.liquid.es). Metro
Chueca.* **Open** 9pm-3am Mon-Thur; 9pm-3.30am
Fri, Sat. **Credit** AmEx, DC, MC, V. **Map** p308 I11.
A cool, happening place in which to see and be seen,
with a contemporary, minimalist interior, lit up with
mega-screens showing dance music videos. It might
be a bit tame for some, but it's a friendly crowd.

Rick's

C/Clavel 8 (91 531 91 86). Metro Gran Vía.
Open 11.30pm-5.30am daily. **Admission** (incl
1 drink) €8. **No credit cards. Map** p308 I11.
Expensive drinks and an expensive, older crowd are
the hallmarks of this friendly late-night alternative
to the discos. With hi-NRG beats and camp Spanish
hits, it's standing-room only at weekends.

Teatro Kapital

*C/Atocha 125, Huertas & Santa Ana (91 420
29 06, www.grupo-kapital.com). Metro Atocha.*
Open midnight-6am Wed-Sat. **Admission**
varies. **Credit** AmEx, DC, MC, V. **Map** p312 J14.

Teatro Kapital.

Another place to brighten up a dull Sunday. Keep your bearings as you make your way through the main dancefloor area and assorted bars of Madrid's seven-storey mega-club, and head for the gay corner of this vast empire of decadence and dance. There's a karaoke studio on the second floor and a rooftop terrace too.

EXCLUSIVELY MALE/HARDCORE

Copper

C/San Vicente Ferrer 34, Malasaña (no phone, www.copperbar.net). Metro Tribunal. **Open** 2pm-3am Mon-Thur, Sun; 2pm-3.30am Fri, Sat. **Admission** (incl 1 drink) €10; €5 under-25s. **No credit cards. Map** p307 G9.

The friendly guys at this sloppy and sweaty club got tired of trying to enforce the dress code, with underwear, jockstraps and fetish gear now allowed every day. The place can get pretty hardcore, but there's always a chatty crowd out front and a popular large backroom.

Cruising

C/Pérez Galdós 5, Chueca (91 521 51 43). Metro Chueca. **Open** 8pm-3.30am Mon-Fri; 8pm-4.30am Sat, Sun. **No credit cards. Map** p308 H10.

A fun, sleazy cruising club that puts the 'laid' into 'laid-back'. Upstairs there's a quieter pub-like area, and a diminutive porn cinema; downstairs there's a dancefloor and a spacious public loo-like darkroom. The place could do with a lick of paint, but its faded glory is part of its enduring charm.

Hot

C/Infantas 9, Chueca (91 522 84 48, www.bar hot.com). Metro Chueca. **Open** 6pm-3am Mon-Thur, Sun; 6pm-3.30am Fri, Sat. **Admission** free. **No credit cards. Map** p308 H11.

Hot, hairy, homo heaven at this fun bear den for hirsute late thirty- and fortysomethings. Things get even hotter downstairs in the darkroom. Two drinks for the price of one, every day until midnight.

Leather Club

C/Pelayo 42, Chueca (91 308 14 62). Metro Chueca. **Open** 8pm-3am daily. **Admission** free. **No credit cards. Map** p308 I10.

The name of this big, two-floor hangout is a bit misleading as little leather is in evidence, but the crowd is raunchy and can be found in the large darkroom or lurking in anticipation in the cabins. Check out the individual movie screens over the urinals.

Odarko

C/Loreto Chicote 7, Malasaña (no phone, www. odarko.com). Metro Callao. **Open** 10pm-4am Mon-Fri; 10pm-very late Sat; 6-11pm Sun. **Admission** (incl 1 drink) €8 10pm-midnight; €10 midnight-close. **Credit** DC, MC, V. **Map** p307 G10.

The seedy backstreets off Gran Vía make the perfect approach to this lively sex club, where chains chink, bars rattle and boots scuff the soiled floor. Dress code is strictly enforced on weekends and some of the nights are pretty full-on. Check the website in advance, lest you turn up in a crisp Fred Perry top to find it's the Wild & Wet Piss session. Improbably, the owners run a little B&B upstairs.

ARTS & ENTERTAINMENT

Madness

*C/Tres Peces 30, Lavapiés (no phone, www.
madness.es). Metro Antón Martín.* **Open**
4pm-midnight Mon-Thur, Sun; 6pm-2am Fri,
Sat. **Admission** varies. **No credit cards**.
Map p312 H14.
Hardcore bar on two levels with maze and darkroom.
Thursdays are 'Workers' Night' (come in uniform),
while Friday is Piss & Feet and Saturday is Fist &
Spank. Not for the fainthearted.

Paw

*C/Calatrava 29, La Latina (91 366 60 93,
www.thepawmadrid.com). Metro Puerta de
Toledo.* **Open** 8pm-6am Mon-Sat; 5pm-4am
Sun. **Admission** (incl 1 or 2 drinks) €10-€12.
No credit cards. Map p311 E14.
Formerly known as Into the Tank, this louche little
joint is off the beaten track but well worth the effort
for dress code and fetish fans. If you forgot to pack
your cop uniform, don't worry, you can go naked
every night. Check out the hot underwear parties:
log on to the website for all the lurid details.

Strong Center

*C/Trujillos 7, Sol & Gran Vía (91 541 54 15,
www.strong-center.com). Metro Ópera.* **Open**
midnight-6am daily. **Admission** (incl 1 or 2
drinks) €12 midnight-2am; €11 2am-close Mon-
Thur, Sun; €13 Fri; €15 Sat. **No credit cards**.
Map p311 G11.
The dancefloor here is a forlorn, empty place. Don't
be dismayed, however, as no one comes for the
music, and you're just about to discover Spain's
biggest and most labyrinthine darkroom, where you
can lose yourself among hundreds of hot, horny men.

Saunas

Balneario Paraíso

*C/Norte 15, Conde Duque (91 522 58 99, www.
mundoplacer.com). Metro Noviciado.* **Open** noon-
midnight Mon-Thur; 24hrs Fri-Sun. **Admission**
€7.50-€15. **No credit cards. Map** p307 F9.
Located in what used to be a popular flamenco club,
this extensive, spotlessly clean sauna has maintained its original evocative mosaics. The young,
hunky clients often seem more interested in their
own well-toned pecs than in you, but there is a small
pool, porn cinema, bar, darkroom and cabins as consolation. Massage and sunbeds are also available.

Men

*C/Pelayo 25, Chueca (91 531 25 83). Metro
Chueca.* **Open** 3.30pm-midnight Mon-Wed, Sun;
3.30pm-7am Thur, Fri; 4pm-9am Sat. **Admission**
€10; €5 18-25s. €5 for 2 people Tue; €8 for 2 people
Wed, Thur. **No credit cards. Map** p308 I10.
A small, dowdy sauna with a perplexing door policy
(though cute young guys are usually safe). Located
right at the heart of the gay scene, Men is always

rammed with a cross-section of gay Madrid. There's
a bar, darkroom and a few cabins in which to spend
a steamy hour or two.

Sauna Príncipe

*Travesia de las Beatas 3, Malasaña (91 559
02 59, www.mundoplacer.com). Metro Plaza de
España.* **Open** noon-midnight daily. **Admission**
€13. **No credit cards. Map** p307 F10.
This sauna is better equipped than its rivals and
caters for a varied crowd, though it's particularly
popular with bears, not to mention tourists.

GAY & LESBIAN SHOPS

Amantis

*C/Pelayo 46, Chueca (91 702 05 10, www.
amantis.net). Metro Chueca.* **Open** 10am-10pm
Mon-Sat; 4.30-9pm Sun. **Credit** AmEx, DC,
MC, V. **Map** p308 I10.
The most discreet of the city's sex shops in terms of
location, Amantis has a sunny feel and seems rather
like a small-town shop. Albeit a small-town shop
filled with condoms, lube, improbable dildos, porn
mags, videos and DVDs.

Berkana

*C/Hortaleza 64, Chueca (91 532 55 99, www.
libreriaberkana.com). Metro Chueca.* **Open**
10.30am-9pm Mon-Fri; 11.30am-9pm Sat; noon-
2pm, 5-8pm Sun. **Credit** AmEx, DC, MC, V.
Map p308 H10.
There are books and videos in English here, and
members of staff are friendly and helpful. Browsing
is encouraged, and you can linger over some of the
erotica at the in-store café.

City Sex Store

*C/Hortaleza 18, Chueca (91 181 27 23). Metro
Chueca.* **Open** 11am-10pm Mon-Fri; 11am-11pm
Sat; 12.30-9.30pm Sun. **Credit** AmEx, DC, MC, V.
Map p308 H10.
Bright, shiny and well organised, City Sex Store is
a veritable supermarket of porn, with merchandise
spread out over two floors.

Different Life

*C/Pelayo 30, Chueca (91 532 96 52, www.
differentlife.es). Metro Chueca.* **Open** 10.30am-
9.30pm daily. **Credit** AmEx, DC, MC, V.
Map p308 I10.
A well-stocked bookshop, with some titles in
English, plus magazines and a range of cheesy gay
gifts. Downstairs you'll find an eye-popping range
of porn videos, which can be bought or rented.

SR

*C/Pelayo 7, Chueca (91 523 19 64, www.sr-
shop.es). Metro Chueca.* **Open** 5.30-9pm Mon;
11am-2pm, 5-9pm Tue-Sat. **Credit** AmEx, DC,
MC, V. **Map** p308 I10.

Pride Without Prejudice

LGBT Madrid marches on.

On taking power in 2004, Spain's Socialist government wasted no time in addressing gay rights, legalising gay marriage and allowing transsexuals to choose whichever gender they wished on their identity cards. Milestone achievements that were celebrated with leather, rubber, bears, tanned toned flesh and non-stop hedonism in the Gay Pride (Orgullo Gay) parade. In recognition of his efforts for equality, Zapatero was awarded the Civic Courage Prize from Berlin-based gay-rights association Christopher Street Day.

Orgullo Gay (www.orgullogaymadrid.com), organised by COGAM and FELGBT, has continued to grow since then, despite continued threats to the event by some Chueca residents, who want the week-long June party to be moved to the outskirts of the city. The parade runs from the Puerta de Alcalá to Plaza España, and attracts some 1.5 million people. For an entire week, the city is invaded by visitors from all over the world, partying hard at night and sporting an array of ludicrously coloured banana hammocks at the swimming pools by day, with the rooftop terrace of the Room Mate Oscar hotel (*see p164*) a big hotspot.

As well as the parties and the parades, the week boasts some 300 cultural, artistic and sporting events – kicking off with the Carrera en Tacones (a running race where contestants run in stilettos) – as well as off-site parties at the end of the week.

Despite such leaps, bounds and high-heeled trotting towards an equal Spain, there is much still to be done, according to Madrid's numerous gay rights associations. In March 2013, Interior Minister Jorge Fernández Díaz said that 'the survival of the species' was not guaranteed as a result of same-sex marriages. Madrid may be one of the most tolerant cities in the world, but there is still plenty to march for.

ARTS & ENTERTAINMENT

Everything for the discerning leather and fetish fan. Leatherwear, uniforms, rubber and SM gear, plus indispensable accessories – masks, slings, chains and handcuffs to help you turn that unused boxroom into your very own dungeon. And no, we don't know what the live crocodiles are for, either.

LESBIAN MADRID

All those places for the boys, and barely enough bars to make a decent pub crawl for lesbians – what's a girl to do? Keep her eyes peeled, that's what. Madrid's lesbian scene is growing, but it still has a long way to go before catching up with the gay male *ambiente*. There are lots of one-nighters throughout the year, one organised by the Supernenas and another by Diversité – look for flyers in the venues on and near Plaza de Chueca. The square is where you should start off, in any case: every bar here seems to be owned by lesbians, even though the clientele is mixed.

Cafés, bars & clubs

As well as the following, another venue popular with lesbians is **Café Acuarela** (*see p185*).

Escape

C/Gravina 13, Chueca (91 532 52 06, www. escapechueca.com). Metro Chueca. **Open** midnight-5.30am Mon-Thur, Sun; midnight-6am Fri, Sat. **Admission** (incl 1 drink) €8-€10. **Credit** MC, V. **Map** p308 I10.
This cavernous dancehall draped in bullfighter red is one of the most popular destinations for women

and is filled to the brim with the sexiest *chicas* in the city at weekends. In fact, its popularity has spiralled to the extent that it's now one of the more boisterous clubs around Plaza de Chueca.

Medea

C/Cabeza 33, Lavapiés (91 369 33 02). Metro Antón Martín or Tirso de Molina. **Open** 11pm-7am Tue-Sun. **Admission** €10 (incl 1 drink) or €12 (incl 2 drinks). **Credit** AmEx, DC, MC, V. **Map** p311 H13.
Decorated in muted rainbow colours, this welcoming women's disco is one of the clear favourites on the lesbian scene. Men are admitted only in the company of Sapphic sisters.

★ El Mojito

C/Olmo 6, Lavapiés (no phone). Metro Tirso de Molina or Antón Martín. **Open** 9pm-2.30am daily. **Admission** free. **No credit cards.** **Map** p312 H13.
This cute Lavapiés locale has a retro vibe (Barbie dolls in compromising positions are part of the decor) and excellent cocktails. It attracts a friendly, mixed crowd of both gays and metrosexuals.

Truco

C/Gravina 10, Chueca (91 532 89 21). Metro Chueca. **Open** 5pm-3am Mon-Thur; noon-3am Fri, Sat. **Credit** V. **Map** p308 I10.
Truco is often very crowded and usually with a very young and loud crowd. No matter: this high-octane corner joint remains *the* place for gals who are looking for gals in the earlier part of the evening. It is also a stone's throw from Escape (*see left*).

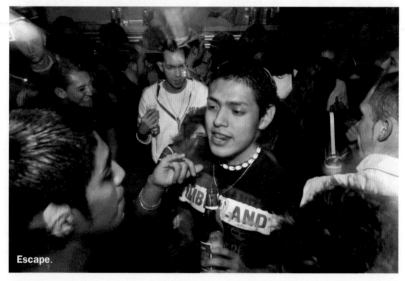

Escape.

Nightlife

From funk to flamenco, the capital shines brightly after dark.

While the pace of Madrid's nightlife scene may have slowed down somewhat from its early noughties heyday, *madrileños* still party harder – and later – than most. And they do so in spite of interference from the local council, which fails to see the value of the capital's after-dark antics. But that gives the whole scene an underground feel and promoters are constantly coming up with new nights, meaning that what's on offer is varied and ever-changing. One thing's for sure, though – wherever you're going, don't head out until after 10pm or you'll find yourself dancing alone.

Many Madrid clubs double up as gig venues too, giving much-needed space to the city's up-and-coming bands. The best way to see flamenco is to bar-hop in the streets that live and breathe it, such as C/Echegaray. Rule of thumb: the more the punters look like the performers, the more chance there is that you've found the right place.

Clubs

Nightlife here has distinct stages. In the early evening, from 6pm until midnight, teenagers take to the streets. Most of them congregate in parks and squares, and engage in what is known as the *botellón*.

At around 11pm, a more mature crowd starts to spill out of the restaurants and hits the bars. Generally, bars break down into a few distinct categories. *Bares de copas* sell spirit-based drinks with or without a DJ in the corner. Next come the *discobares,* which may require a cover charge and bang out international and Spanish pop, perfect for their alcohol-fuelled clientele. Then there are the funkier pre-club bars, often with a house DJ warming you up for a night on the town. City legislation says that bars must close at around 3am: precisely the moment when the clubs or *discotecas* start to fill up. (*Discoteca* carries no cheesy connotations in Spanish; in fact, be careful what you ask for when talking to locals – *club* in Spanish usually means brothel.)

A lot of nightclubs will let you in free before 1am. Any later and there'll be a cover charge of €10-€15, but that will normally include one or even two drinks at the bar.

The late-night clubs start closing their doors at around 6am, but the night's still not over.

Plenty of clubbers spill out into what are commonly referred to as 'old man's bars' for a few early-morning beers, before finally staggering home. But those with energy to burn seek out the after-hours bars (*los afters*). There aren't as many as there used to be, but they are out there; you just need to ask around.

LOS AUSTRIAS & LA LATINA

Kathmandú

C/Señores de Luzón 3 (no phone, http:// kathmanduclub.com). Metro Ópera or Sol. **Open** midnight-5am Thur; midnight-6am Fri-Sun. **Admission** €9 (incl 1 drink) Fri-Sun; free Thur & before 2am. **No credit cards. Map** p311 F12. This basement club, which has recently been refurbished, is cosy, friendly and nicely chilled. The DJs

> **INSIDE TRACK**
> **SWEET ENDINGS**
>
> The *madrileño* chocolate and *churros* tradition truly comes into its own in the *madrugada* (pre-dawn hours). Old-school fave **Chocolatería San Ginés** (*see p123*) is open until 7am daily, and is a hive of activity once the bars and clubs shut.

spin a delicious mix of funk, soul, jazz and hip hop, luring the friendly clientele on to the dancefloor by about 3am. Non-dancers slouch on the ample seating in the cave-like venue and nod along.

Marula

C/Caños Viejos 3 (91 366 15 96, www.marula cafe.com). Metro La Latina. **Open** 11pm-6am daily. **Admission** varies. **No credit cards**. **Map** p311 E13.

This small venue serves as bar, club and live music venue. Tuesday nights are for gigs, and there are late-night jams on Mondays and Wednesdays. But the place really hots up at weekends, attracting DJ sessions from local talent such as Antonio Requena, Casbah 73 and Kwenya Carreira. The summertime terrace is a big pull, filling up by midnight and staying that way.

FREE El Nuevo Barbú

C/Santiago 3 (91 542 56 98, www.elbarbuclub. com). Metro Ópera or Sol. **Open** 7pm-3.30am Tue-Fri; 5pm-4am Sat. **Admission** free. **Credit** V. **Map** p311 F12.

The slightly intimidating steel door, guarded by a bouncer, and velvet-covered windows give the impression that you're slipping into some kind of speakeasy. Waitresses serve bottled beers and cocktails to a grown-up crowd in the early evening, before the funk, soul, pop and ska tempts the punters on to the dancefloor in the backroom. This is more the kind of place to give you a warm glow than to really light your fire.

Painting the Monkey

Paseo de los Olmos 13 (91 365 22 22, mobile 608 483 424, www.themonkey.es). Metro Puerta de Toledo or Pirámides. **Open** 10pm-6am Fri, Sat. **Admission** €10 (incl 1 drink). **Credit** AmEx, MC, V. **Map** p311 E16.

The fact that this indie club is a little off the beaten track only adds to its appeal, as the clientele know exactly what they came here for. Pop, rock, nu jazz

INSIDE TRACK
PRICE TO PARTY

The ticket you're given on the door of a club is almost always valid for a drink, so don't toss it away. Spain has recently seen a hike in prices across the board and some of the swankier clubs will charge you as much as €12 for a long drink, and €10 for a beer. Remember, though, measures for long drinks are huge, so if you're on a tight budget stick to the rum and Coke. Before you head out, it's also worth checking club websites for printable flyers that'll get you in for a discount.

and funk all get an outing, while the friendly crowd is lubricated by well-mixed – and very strong – cocktails and long drinks. Get there early to check out a mix of local cabaret acts, stand-up and bands.

Reverse Club

La Riviera, Paseo Bajo la Virgen del Puerto s/n (mobile 627 428 549, www.reverseclub.es). Metro Príncipe Pío. **Open** midnight-6am Fri. **Admission** €15-€18. **Credit** MC, V. **Map** p310 B/C12.

La Riviera doubles as a mid-sized concert venue, but after midnight it's home to a seething mass of party energy, thanks to the big names that the Reverse Club pulls in. Recent titans of the dance music scene to swing by include Miss Kittin, Derrick May and 2ManyDJs.

Shôko Restaurant & Lounge Club

C/Toledo 86 (91 354 16 80, www.shokomadrid. com). Metro Puerta de Toledo or La Latina. **Open** 11.30pm-6am Fri, Sat. **Admission** varies. **Credit** MC, V. **Map** p311 F14.

This popular space houses an Oriental restaurant (at the top), and a slick lounge-club with high ceilings and minimalist decor made up of bamboo, water features, Japanese panels and contemporary furniture. Its non-fussy music policy – commercial dance and Latin – attracts a fun-seeking crowd in their twenties and early thirties, who get dressed up for the occasion and are mostly on the pull.

FREE Terraza Atenas

C/Segovia & C/Cuesta de la Vega (mobile 608 153 298, www.terrazadeatenas.com). Metro Ópera or Puerta del Ángel. **Open** noon-3am daily. Closed Nov-Mar. **Admission** free. **No credit cards**. **Map** p310 D12.

A super-cool *terraza* that's set in its own small park. The plentiful tables in the front bar are filled by midnight and the overflow swells on to the surrounding gentle grass slope. With no neighbours to worry about, the crowd can enjoy the easy sounds of soul, funk and lounge long after other *terrazas* have called it a night.

SOL & GRAN VÍA

For the much-loved cocktail/DJ bar **Museo Chicote**, *see p125*.

Bash Line

Sala Bash, Plaza Callao 4 (no phone). Metro Callao. **Open** midnight-5.30am Wed. **Admission** (incl 1 drink) €10. **Credit** MC, V. **Map** p307 G11.

Wednesday is firmly established as hip hop night in Madrid. Bash doesn't really get going until after 1am, but once it does there's no room to move. Resident DJs specialise in the latest R&B and rap, attracting a mixed crowd of Spaniards, Latin Americans and foreign students.

Club Classic

Deep has come to define the capital's nightlife scene.

Club nights come and go with alarming regularity in Madrid. This is partly becuase of interference from the city council, which likes to do its best to quash the capital's nocturnal high jinks, and partly due to the recession. But there are a few names that have managed to stick it out over the years, and define the nightlife scene in the Spanish capital.

Deep is the granddaddy of them all, and the man behind the legendary name is founding promoter and star DJ, JL Magoya. Originally from Argentina, Magoya began Deep in Marbella back in 1996, seeking to recreate the burgeoning Ibiza club scene. After the success of the night down south, he and his team brought the party to Madrid in 1998. 'We wanted to do what we saw happening all over Europe and bring in guest DJs,' explains Magoya. 'Madrid had a culture of local resident DJs, and the public wasn't that open to new things at the time.'

The night started in the Maxime nightclub in Puerta de Toledo, but has popped up all over the city since –

from all-day Sunday sessions in the now-demolished Aqualung to Friday nights in Sala Wind. Magoya also turned his hand to a few of the city's first – and still-legendary – after-hours clubs, including Bocaccio and MidDay. But the objective was always the same: bring the best house music and DJs to the *madrileño* public. Laurent Garnier, Carl Cox and François Kevorkian are just a few of the big names to have come to the city for the first time courtesy of Deep.

While Deep is without a permanent home right now, Magoya is still working his magic, bringing in rising international stars for special parties on nights before public holidays at **Cocó** (*see below*) and a monthly session on a Thursday at the sublime **Mondo** (*see p195*). And in this famously fickle scene, the key to Deep's longevity is clear for the DJ and promoter: 'The secret is to bring artists to the public at the time that they're on the up. People understand that Deep is synonymous with quality electronic music or house; a lot of people trust that brand.'

Charada

C/Bola 13 (no phone, www.charada.es). Metro Santo Domingo. **Open** midnight-5.30am Wed, Thur; 12.30am-6am Fri, Sat; 8pm-2am Sun. **Admission** €15 (incl 1 drink). **Credit** MC, V. **Map** p307 F11.

Yet another club to have suffered enforced closure, Charada has managed to bounce back with verve and reoccupy its spot as a temple for cutting-edge electronica. A split-level venue means two different styles are on offer every night, with crowd-pleasing tunes on the ground floor and an eclectic edge down in the basement. Highlights include Fridays, when Silvia Superstar from El Fabuloso (*see p199*) comes to call, and the Kill sessions on Saturdays.

Cocó

C/Alcalá 20 (no phone, www.cocomadrid.com). Metro Sevilla. **Open** 12.30am-6am Wed-Sun. **Admission** varies. **Credit** V. **Map** p312 I11.

Cocó is located on the site of the former Alcalá 20 club, where 81 people lost their lives in a fire in 1983. The site lay empty until 2010, when a huge and impressive renovation project was completed – think glitter balls and laser lighting. DJs spin R&B, funk, house and hip hop on Fridays and Saturdays, plus electronica on Thursdays. Look out for the Deep sessions (*see above* **Club Classic**), which usually feature an up-and-coming international guest DJ.

Ohm

Sala Bash, Plaza Callao 4 (91 541 35 00, www.tripfamily.com). Metro Callao. **Open** midnight-6am Fri. **Admission** with flyer €15 (incl 2 drinks). **Credit** MC, V. **Map** p307 G11.

While some nights come and go with alarming speed, Trip Family's Ohm is one that's here for the duration. Strictly speaking it's a gay night, but it's too much fun (and too central) for the straight crowd to resist. The result is a friendly party atmosphere with soulful, vocal-driven house tracks mixed to perfection by residents Kike Boy and Arnaitz.

Sala Wind

Plaza del Carmen s/n (no phone, www.salawind. com). Metro Gran Vía or Sol. **Open** midnight-6am Fri, Sat. **Admission** varies. **No credit cards**. **Map** p311 H11.

This smart, mid-sized basement club is located just a stone's throw from the Gran Vía. Friday nights are for the electronic music crowd, while Saturdays are usually gay night, complete with hunky semi-naked waiters.

★ El Sol

C/Jardines 3 (91 532 64 90, www.elsolmad.com). Metro Gran Vía or Sol. **Open** midnight-5.30am Tue-Sat. **Concerts** vary. **Admission** (incl 1 drink) €10. **Credit** MC, V. **Map** p312 H11.

ARTS & ENTERTAINMENT

ARTS & ENTERTAINMENT

To call this music joint and club 'no-frills' is an understatement – as its faded yellow walls and middle-aged bar staff attest. However, as everyone knows, it's the music and crowd that make a night, and that's where El Sol is a winner. The DJ serves up an eclectic selection of unmixed rock, soul, funk and R&B. Before long you're lured on to the floor and there you'll stay, getting down with a varied crowd of twenty- and thirtysomethings. The venue is the city's classic climax to a big night out.

Weekend

Sala Bash, Plaza Callao 4 (91 541 35 00, www.tripfamily.com). Metro Callao. **Open** midnight-6am Sat. **Admission** with flyer €15 (incl 2 drinks). **Credit** MC, V. **Map** p307 G11.

One of the longest-standing and most successful club nights in Madrid. In 2013 it made the move from Sunday to Saturday, adding to its mass appeal. The music has a cool electro vibe, thanks mostly to the sublime skills of DJ Sandro Bianchi (Spain's answer to Gilles Peterson), while the gay-friendly crowd are some of the hardest partiers in the city. Look out for monthly Sunday night sessions, when the Goa after-party Weekend Disko takes place.

Ya'sta

C/Valverde 10 (no phone, www.facebook.com/yasta.madrid). Metro Gran Vía. **Open** midnight-5.30am Wed; midnight-6am Thur-Sat. **Admission** with flyer €15 (incl 2 drinks). **No credit cards**. **Map** p307 H10.

There's perhaps only one place in Madrid where you'll find funk, breaks, reggae, techno, dubstep, salsa, swing, country and boogie all under one roof – and Ya'sta is it. The club itself is industrial-style,

with psychedelic projections on the walls and graffiti in the corridors. Depending on the night, the venue attracts anyone from young techno-heads and break-dancers to a more grown-up rock crowd.

HUERTAS & SANTA ANA

La Boca del Lobo

C/Echegaray 11 (91 429 70 13, www.labocadellobo.com). Metro Sevilla. **Open** 9.30pm-3am Wed, Thur; 9.30pm-3.30am Fri, Sat. **Admission** *Club* free. *Gigs* €5-€10. **Credit** AmEx, V. **Map** p312 H12.

Unselfconsciously hip and unremittingly friendly, La Boca del Lobo combines live music with a heady mix of rock, indie, funk and reggae. There are jam sessions on Wednesday and Thursday nights, and visiting bands on Fridays and Saturdays. If you like your clubs dark, packed and intimate, this is for you.

FREE El Burladero

C/Echegaray 19 (mobile 620 370 662, www.elburladerocopas.com). Metro Sevilla or Sol. **Open** 9pm-4am daily. **Admission** free. **Credit** AmEx, MC, V. **Map** p312 H12.

A cosmopolitan crowd, buzzing to the sound of flamenco and rumba, throngs the Moorish arches amid Andalucian tiles and a rogues' gallery of bullfighters. Upstairs the rumba rumbles but doesn't dominate. Head up here for respite and a chat with the languid barman, but the frenzied guitar and pistol-shot hand-clapping will eventually lure you back.

FREE La Comedia

C/Principe 16 (91 521 51 64). Metro Sevilla or Sol. **Open** 10pm-3.30am Wed-Sun. **Admission** free. **Credit** MC, V. **Map** p312 H12.

Teatro Kapital. *See p197*.

There's nothing funny about Bar de la Comedia. Instead expect a welcome change of pace on this frenzied strip. An international crowd do their thing to a steady soundtrack of hip hop, R&B and dancehall grinders. The door staff are somewhat capricious in their admissions policy, and may make you pay for drinks upfront on the door.

★ FREE Las Cuevas de Sésamo

C/Príncipe 7 (91 429 65 24). Metro Sevilla or Sol. **Open** 6pm-2am daily. **Admission** free. **No credit cards**. **Map** p312 H12.

If you want proof that partying Spaniards are among the noisiest, most raucous people on the planet, then Sésamo is the ideal place to put that to the test. You'll be attended to by smartly dressed waiters, who will accommodate you at a table no matter how big your group. A piano player does his best to make himself heard above the cacophony that reigns between 9pm and 1am, as a young crowd that's mostly composed of students enjoys the cheap beers and jug after jug of the famous sangría. A good choice to start the night rather than a final destination.

FREE La Fontana de Oro

C/Victoria 1 (91 531 04 20, www.fontanadeoro. com). Metro Sol. **Open** 4pm-5.30am Mon-Thur, Sun; 4pm-6am Fri, Sat. **Admission** €8 Fri, Sat after 2am (incl 1 drink); free Mon-Thur & before 2am. **Credit** AmEx, DC, MC, V. **Map** p311 H12.

With the kudos of being Madrid's oldest bar, this place used to be a real institution. These days, though, it's an Irish theme pub. It's run of the mill by day, but everything changes when night falls. Then the crowd packs in, fuelling up for the night

ahead and losing themselves to a mix of classic beer anthems and a variety of live music.

★ Mondo

C/Arlabán 7 (91 523 86 54/91 522 88 26, www.web-mondo.com). Metro Sevilla. **Open** 12.30am-6am Thur, Sat. **Admission** (incl 1 drink) €13 (€11 before 2.30am) Thur; €14 (€12 before 2.30am) Sat. **Credit** AmEx, DC, MC, V. **Map** p312 I11.

If you go to only one club in Madrid, make sure it's this one. Launched in 2000, Mondo has become one of the most lauded spots in the city for enjoying electronica and techno, but you can also expect to hear funk, house and disco on any given night. A regular stable of high-profile guest DJs play here, with previous visitors including John Digweed, Josh Wink and Andy Weatherall.

The Roof

Hotel ME Madrid Reina Victoria, Plaza Santa Ana 14 (91 701 60 20, http://es.melia.com). Metro Sol or Antón Martín. **Open** *Winter* 9pm-2am Wed, Thur; 9pm-3am Fri, Sat. *Summer* 9pm-3am daily. **Admission** summer €15 (incl 1 drink). **Credit** AmEx, DC, MC, V. **Map** p312 H12.

If you're looking to impress on a date and feel like splashing some cash then head to the side door of the ME Madrid hotel, which is guarded by a couple of menacing-looking bouncers. If your attire passes muster they'll usher you into an express lift, which will take you up to one of the swishest terraces in town, with amazing views of the city in all its neon glory. Drinks are pricey, but the loungers, bed-like chill-out booths and carefully crafted soundtrack make it worth a visit.

Teatro Kapital
C/Atocha 125 (91 420 29 06, www.grupo-kapital. com). Metro Atocha. **Open** midnight-4am Wed; midnight-5.30am Thur; midnight-6am Fri, Sat. **Admission** €10-€30. **Credit** AmEx, DC, MC, V. **Map** p312 J14.
This giant among Madrid clubs offers splendid views of the main dancefloor from many of the upper balconies. Each of the seven levels has something different to offer: the main dancefloor and bars are at ground level; the first floor has karaoke; the second R&B and hip hop; the third a cosy cocktail bar; the fourth is the so-called 'Party Zone'; the fifth is all about mojitos; and at the top is a terrace with a retractable roof and smoking area. Smart casual is the order of the day. *Photos pp194-195.*

Torero
C/Cruz 26 (91 523 11 29). Metro Sol. **Open** 10pm-4.30am Mon-Wed, Sun; 10pm-6am Thur-Sat. **Admission** €10 (incl 1 drink) Thur-Sat; free Mon-Wed, Sun. **Credit** MC, V. **Map** p311 H12.
Don't be put off by the forbidding exterior, the only thing not dancing inside Torero is a wall-mounted bull's head that stares down impassively at the mostly local crowd. The ground-floor bar is open midweek, but on weekends the basement hots up as a mixed crowd of Spaniards and tourists gyrates to Spanish and Latin beats, commercial dance and house.

RASTRO & LAVAPIÉS

If you're interested in some impromptu late-night flamenco, try **Candela** (*see p207*).

★ El Juglar
C/Lavapiés 37 (91 528 43 81, www.salajuglar. com). Metro Lavapiés. **Open** 9.30pm-3am Tue-Thur, Sun; 9.30pm-3.30am Fri, Sat. *Concerts* usually start at 10pm or 10.30pm. **Admission** €5-€10. **Credit** MC, V. **Map** p311 H14.
Epitomising Lavapiés, El Juglar is a laid-back hangout for those who like the tempo of their evening to be energetic but not too frenetic. The bare red brick and chrome front bar provides a chilled background for the broad-based crowd to enjoy a soundtrack of jazz and soul. After midnight the rhythm speeds up in the back as the resident DJs play a mix of souped-up soul, Latin and funk. Sunday nights are the real highlight, with a tourist-free, bohemian night of flamenco dancing at 10pm.

FREE La Ventura
C/Olmo 31 (no phone, http://clubventura.net). Metro Antón Martín. **Open** 9pm-2.30am Thur-Sat. **Admission** free. **No credit cards**. **Map** p312 H13.
Tucked away behind a distinctive green metal door, La Ventura is a stalwart of the Madrid night

INSIDE TRACK SURVIVAL TIPS

Having changed your body clock to suit your schedule in Madrid, there are just a few more things you need to bear in mind before you go out seeking *la marcha*, or a good time. Firstly, don't get too dolled up; with some exceptions, Madrid is not a town where people dress to impress. Creativity is more important than couture. Secondly, be careful with the drinks; measures poured here are such that you may, for once, ask the bartender to put a little less in. And lastly, be aware that there's a specific window of time for every venue in Madrid – if you turn up to a club or bar and it's empty, you might just have arrived at the wrong hour.

scene. It's more chilled out at weekends than it used to be – perhaps becuase of its dual role as a 'members-only' after-hours, running from 6am to 1pm on Saturdays and Sundays. At night, though, it's still a good place for a warm-up beer if you're out and about in the neighbourhood. Breakbeat, electronica and house are the sounds you'll hear from the DJ booth.

CHUECA

For gay clubs in Chueca (and elsewhere), *see pp186-188.*

FREE Areia
C/Hortaleza 92 (91 310 03 07, www.areiachill out.com). Metro Chueca. **Open** 12.30pm-3am daily. **Admission** free. **Credit** AmEx, DC, MC, V. **Map** p308 I9.
Once an Irish bar, Areia has been transformed beyond recognition into a chill-out space that has all the angles covered: by day it's somewhere to get lunch or a snack, in the afternoon it becomes a place to chill, and by the evening the vibe has hotted up enough for a cool crowd that passes through on their nightly tour of the city. The seductive eastern decor, along with sofas and cushions on which to lounge, can make it difficult to leave.

Ocho y Medio
Sala But, C/Barceló 11 (no phone, www.ocho ymedioclub.com). Metro Tribunal. **Open** midnight-6am Fri, Sat. **Admission** €15 with flyer (incl 1 drink). **Credit** MC, V. **Map** p308 H8.
This popular club night has been running since the late 1990s, and relies on an alcohol-fuelled mass of party energy that's driven by the eclectic mix of indie, electro-clash, electro-pop, new wave and New York rock spun by the resident DJs. Located practically in the basement of Teatro Barceló (*see p198*),

ARTS & ENTERTAINMENT

Closing Time

Promoters and city authorities can't see eye to eye after dark.

Speak to any club or music promoter in Madrid and they'll tell you the same story: the council sees things that take place after dark as low culture. It's notoriously difficult for venues to get their licence and papers in order, meaning that the council can shut them down at a moment's notice – whether it's to do with noise pollution or failing to observe the city's strictly defined opening hours.

What's more, whenever there's any kind of serious incident, the council comes down hard and ensures the temporary closure of the venue involved, but often fails to address the underlying issues that caused the problems in the first place.

The biggest such incident to cause a massive backlash was the Madrid Arena tragedy of 2012, when five young girls were killed in a crush at a Halloween party at the council-owned and run venue. The party was promoted by the FSM group, which for years has been behind some of the biggest *fiestas* in the city, including

the legendary Sunday session Space of Sound and the Klubbers Day festival.

In the aftermath of the tragedy, the council blamed the promoter for overselling tickets for the event. The press, meanwhile, seized on the fact that the Madrid Arena was woefully inadequate for such a party, given that it was designed mostly for sports events such as tennis rather than a 15,000-strong rave.

The reaction from the council was swift and decisive. The mayor decreed an end to such events in council-owned venues and FSM promptly packed up its offices, closing the doors of its many clubs – including Space – and leaving a gaping hole in the nightlife calendar.

However, as many have since pointed out, perhaps the key to these issues is not to ban any more big parties, but simply to make sure they're done right in the first place. Until the council comes round to that way of thinking, though, the battle between the promoters and the city administration shows no signs of abating.

this is the place to head to if the glammed-up crowds jostling to get in via the VIP queue of that club fill you with dread.

Teatro Barceló

C/Barceló 11 (91 447 01 28). Metro Tribunal. **Open** midnight-5.30am Thur; midnight-6am Fri, Sat. **Admission** €16 (incl 1 drink). **Credit** AmEx, DC, MC, V. **Map** p308 H8.

Until 2013 this was the Madrid branch of Ibiza superclub Pachá, but the team behind this glitzy nightspot have ditched the brand to go it alone, taking the new name from Teatro's home street. Everything else remains the same, with the clientele mostly rich kids and poseurs. Dress up to get in, and expect glamorous go-gos, on-stage dance routines and themed parties, enacted to a soundtrack of soulful and commercial house.

MALASAÑA & CONDE DUQUE

BarCo

C/Barco 34 (no phone, www.barcobar.com). Metro Tribunal. **Open** 10pm-5.30am Mon-Thur, Sun; 10pm-6am Fri, Sat. **Admission** *Concerts* €9 (incl. 1 drink). *Club* €8 (incl 1 drink). **No credit cards.** Map p307 H10.

The lines snaking up Calle del Barco will give away the location of this excellent venue, which hosts

concerts in the early evening and then DJs till the wee small hours. Everything from funk and soul to rap-metal goes on the turntables, letting the crowd go wild in the near pitch-black ground floor and basement areas. A relative newcomer, but already a classic in the 'hood.

★ FREE Démodé

C/Ballesta 7 (mobile 680 202 576). Metro Gran Vía. **Open** 11pm-3am Thur; 11pm-3.30am Fri, Sat. **Admission** free. **Credit** AmEx, MC, V. **Map** p307 H10.

The flyers let you know what you're in for at Démodé – an elegant figure reclines against a backdrop of flock wallpaper in a juxtaposition of the über-trendy and the super-cheesy. This hugely popular pre-club joint is housed in an old brothel. Faux oil paintings still adorn the walls, but red lighting, sofas and an ample sound system have transformed it into one of the coolest nightspots in town. DJs spin everything from nu disco and tech-house to deep house and disco for an appreciative mixed gay/straight crowd.

FREE Evaristo Club

C/Marqués de Santa Ana 11 (mobile 661 694 706, www.evaristoclub.com). Metro Noviciado. **Open** 10.30pm-3.30am Thur-Sat. **Admission** free. **Credit** MC, V. **Map** p307 G9.

You'll never have to worry about being the first to stray into the centre of the dancefloor at Evaristo, given that the venue is a rectangle of corridors. Get comfy on the ample sofas and chairs before throwing some shapes to the house, electro-house and lounge played by local names such as Álvaro Cabana and Sandro Bianchi. With 26 types of gin on offer and a free cloakroom, this is a perfect warm-up venue.

FREE El Fabuloso

C/Estrella 3 (mobile 651 829 373). Metro Noviciado or Callao. **Open** 8pm-3am Mon-Thur, Sun; 8.30pm-3.30am Fri, Sat. **Admission** free. **Credit** AmEx, MC, V. **Map** p307 G10.
The glamorous Silvia Superstar is behind this neighbourhood favourite, which is tucked away in a corner off one of the seedier squares in the capital. The former frontwoman of the splendidly monikered Killer Barbies rock group, Silvia is often to be found behind the decks, either in the kitsch upstairs lounge or on the heaving basement dancefloor. Along with the other Fabuloso DJs, she plays a heady mix of northern soul, swing, rock 'n' roll and 1960s and '70s classics. A magnet for gorgeous Malasaña hipsters.

Nasti

C/San Vicente Ferrer 33 (91 521 76 05, http://nasti.es). Metro Tribunal. **Open** 1am-5.30am Thur-Sat. **Admission** varies. **No credit cards.** **Map** p307 G9.
The remit at Nasti is simple – pack out a small and grimy *sala* with fiercely loyal punters, and play anything from the Sex Pistols to Joy Division to make them dance. A riotous, grungy and alternative crowd find their home here, enjoying the DJ sets and live acts such as Chain & the Gang, Dead Skeletons and Tweak Bird.

★ El Perro de la Parte Atrás del Coche

C/Puebla 15 (mobile 618 783 054, www.myspace.com/elperroclub). Metro Gran Vía. **Open** 8pm-3am Tue; 10pm-3.30am Thur-Sat. **Admission** €10 (incl 1 drink) Fri, Sat; free Tue, Thur & before 1am. *Concerts* €3-€10. **No credit cards.** **Map** p307 G10.
You're guaranteed a top night at El Perro, a quirky basement club with a vaulted ceiling whose full name translates as 'the nodding dog'. After the early live gigs, resident DJ and owner Jamie Steel mixes up everything from pop and rock to early electro on Friday and Saturday nights, while there are all kinds of weird and wonderful live acts on Thursdays, followed by a session from DJ Psychocandy. For something different, head down on Tuesdays for the free swing night, with dance classes for the uninitiated.

Siroco

C/San Dimas 3 (91 532 13 57, www.siroco.es). Metro Noviciado. **Open** 9pm-5am Tue-Thur; 9pm-6am Fri, Sat. **Admission** varies. **Credit** MC, V. **Map** p307 F8.

A wonderfully creative crew run Siroco, something that is abundantly clear from the flyers, the programme and the visuals of the club itself. Doubling as a live music venue, it starts to hot up after concerts finish at around 2am, when a crowd composed mainly of wannabe b-boys, club kids and beardy young students get down to the soul, funk and rare groove seven-inchers deftly woven together by the resident DJs.

Tempo

C/Duque de Osuna 8 (91 547 75 18, www.tempoclub.net). Metro Plaza España. **Open** *Café* 6pm-3am Mon-Thur, Sun; 4pm-3.30am Fri, Sat. *Club & concerts* 11pm-5.30am Thur-Sat. Closed Aug. **Admission** *Café* free. *Club & concerts* varies. **Credit** MC, V. **Map** p307 E9.
A very cosy little venue that doubles as a daytime café and a nighttime venue for live acts and DJs. You can sit and have a bite or an early cocktail in the pleasant upstairs lounge, before heading downstairs to the dancefloor to enjoy the funk, afrobeat and soul tunes from the DJs or local bands.

★ FREE Tupperware

C/Corredera Alta de San Pablo 26 (91 446 42 04, www.facebook.com/tupperwarebar). Metro Tribunal. **Open** 9pm-3am Mon-Wed, Sun; 9pm-3.30am Thur-Sat. **Admission** free. **No credit cards.** **Map** p307 H9.
Truly postmodern, this popular bar is outrageously kitsch but with a pop art sensibility that saves it from crossing over too far into tackiness. The fake fur, *Star Wars* pictures, 1970s toys and faux-cool psychedelia hang together surprisingly well, and there's a pleasant anything-goes music policy that brings all kinds of sounds, from rock and indie to funk and soul, to a sociable, slightly older crowd. Something of a neighbourhood nightlife institution.

SALAMANCA & THE RETIRO

FREE Almonte

C/Juan Bravo 35, Salamanca (91 563 54 70, www.almontesalarociera.com). Metro Diego de León. **Open** 9pm-5am Mon-Thur, Sun; 9pm-6am Fri, Sat. **Admission** free. **Credit** AmEx, MC, V. **Map** p309 N6.
This 'flamenco disco' attracts a youthful crowd. The beautiful patrons flaunt it freestyle before *sevillanas* prompt a free-for-all. Try to work your way downstairs, where the most attention-grabbing moves can be admired and – go on – attempted.

NORTH & WEST

Argüelles

Diamante Club

Sala Pirandello 2, C/Ventura Rodríguez 7 (no phone, www.facebook.com/diamanteclubfanpage).

ARTS & ENTERTAINMENT

Metro Plaza de España. **Open** midnight-6am Fri, Sat. **Admission** €8 (incl 1 drink) before 1am; €15 (incl 1 drink) after 1am. **Credit** AmEx, MC, V. **Map** p307 E9.

Sala Pirandello 2 is one of three venues run by the same team and all practically connected in the same block – the others are Sala Marco Aldany and Sala Pirandello I. This is the baby sister of the trio and suits more eclectic tastes than its siblings. Expect drag queens, outrageous costumes and a mixed gay/straight crowd. With nights with names such as Fiesta Tetas (Tits Party) you know you're in for something out of the ordinary here.

Sala Pirandello 1

C/Martín de los Heros 14 (no phone, www. salarena.es). Metro Plaza de España. **Open** midnight-6am Thur-Sat. **Admission** free; €12 (incl 1 drink) after 2.30am. **Credit** AmEx, MC, V. **Map** p307 E9.

Fridays are a night for younger clubbers at Sala Pirandello, who go wild for electro house, dubstep, drum'n'bass, rock and rap. Up on Saturdays attracts a more mature crowd, who go in search of techno and house from the likes of guest DJs Nina Kravitz and Felix Kröcher.

Twist

Sala Marco Aldany, C/Princesa 1 (moobile 651 743 242, www.facebook.com/twistmadrid). Metro Plaza de España. **Open** midnight-5.30am Thur. **Admission** free; €12 (incl 1 drink) after 2.30am. **Credit** AmEx MC, V. **Map** p307 E9.

This long-running and popular drum 'n' bass night brings in a regular crowd of dreadlocked, pierced

and tattooed clubbers, who come to hear breakbeats from local stars such as XOL and Vikbass, plus Spanish and international guest DJs. As well as the regular nights at Sala Marco Aldany, Twist often appears in Sala Pirandello, so check online for the latest events.

Zombie Club

Sala Marco Aldany, C/Princesa 1 (no phone, www.zombiestudio.es). Metro Plaza de España. **Open** midnight-6am Fri. **Admission** €10 (incl 1 drink). **Credit** AmEx, MC, V. **Map** p307 E9.

The team behind Zombie Club has managed to establish one of the most fashionable hipster brands in the city, not just focusing on club nights but also on its Malasaña café, clothing line and online arts guide. The Zombie Club night was so popular in its midweek Wednesday slot that it soon got moved to Fridays, and now a hugely excitable crowd goes crazy to the indie, disco, electro-rock, nu disco and electro-hop played by the resident and guest DJs. Saturday nights at the same venue play host to Zoológico, with DJs playing jump up rock and rave.

Chamberí

Moma 56

C/José Abascal 56 (91 399 09 00, www.moma56. com). Metro Alonso Cano or Gregorio Marañón. **Open** midnight-6am Wed-Sat. **Admission** €12 (incl 1 drink). **Credit** AmEx , DC, MC, V. **Map** p305 J5.

If it's a touch of glamour you're after and you feel up to the challenge of getting past the door, then you should check out Moma 56. The multi-functional

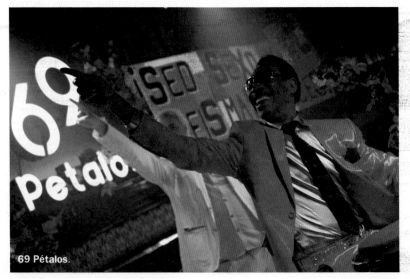

69 Pétalos.

New York-style venue is a mixture of restaurant, bar and nightclub, with stylish decor and a semi-celebrity crowd.

Chamartín

Club Musée

C/Alberto Alcocer 33 (mobile 620 642 539, www.musee.es). Metro Colombia or Cuzco. **Open** midnight-5.30am Thur; midnight-6am Fri, Sat. **Admission** €12 Thur; €15 Fri, Sat. **Credit** AmEx, MC, V.

As the name suggests, an art theme pervades this classy spot, with the walls of the design-conscious venue adorned with all manner of high-impact photos. Thursday nights are aimed at a younger crowd in their early twenties, while Fridays and Saturdays are given over to a more glamorous, mature crew. Expect commercial house, electronica and rock on the turntables, and dress to impress if you want a chance of getting into the VIP lounge.

69 Pétalos

C/Alberto Alcocer 32 (91 156 94 44, www.grupo 69petalos.com). Metro Colombia or Cuzco. **Open** midnight-6am Thur-Sat. **Admission** (incl 1 drink) €16. **Credit** V, MC.

With its tongue firmly in its cheek, 69 Pétalos bills itself as 'the best club on Planet Earth'. That claim might be somewhat outlandish, but equally so are the burlesque-style shows that feature nightly at this kooky venue. The DJs play everything from rock and rap to 1980s classics, while go-gos, actors and musicians dress in outrageous costumes and take to the stage to play instruments, interact with the crowd and ensure the night goes with a bang. It attracts a mature, moneyed and glamorous crew, but one that doesn't take itself too seriously. A must-visit club if you're in the neighbourhood.

SOUTH OF CENTRE

Fabrik

Avda de la Industria 82, Ctra Fuenlabrada-Moralejos de Enmedio (mobile 902 930 322, www.grupo-kapital.com/fabrik). Metro Fuenlabrada then bus 496, 497. **Open** 11.30pm-6am Sat; 3pm-3am occasional Sun. **Admission** varies. **Credit** MC, V.

Fabrik is a converted warehouse that's kitted out with a dazzling array of disco surprises: there's a huge outdoor terrace complete with a fake river and two covered dancefloors; and, in the main arena, a vertical and horizontal megatron to shoot freezing bursts of nitrogen gas into the crowd. The nighttime sessions attract a young, up-for-it crowd seeking hard techno or electronica, but the monthly all-day Sunday Goa party is the highlight (see www.tripfamily.com for more information). It's a bit of a trek to get here, but buses are usually laid on from the centre.

Music

Spare a thought for music promoters in Madrid – they don't have an easy time of it. On the one hand there's the council, which seems hell bent on making life as difficult as possible for those who promote what it obviously deems to be low culture. Then there are the regulations, such as the ban on under-18s at gigs (an attempt to deal with underage drinking). Throw in greedy landlords – one of whom sounded the death knell for classic venue Ritmo y Compás in early 2013 – and you're looking at an uphill struggle.

But despite such fervent opposition, the music scene continues to thrive against all the odds, with the city's jazz bars in particular the envy of other capitals. Just don't expect to see the mayor nodding her head along to a sax solo in Café Central any time soon.

VENUES

Apart from the Palacio de Deportes, concert venues are mostly small, intimate affairs in the centre of the city, with bigger acts usually requiring a trip out to the suburbs. The bullring at Las Ventas (*see p19* **Ringside Seats**) sometimes hosts gigs, as does the home ground of Atlético de Madrid, on the banks of the Manzanares river. Venues listed don't charge admission unless otherwise stated. These days, smaller bands usually pay to play in venues, with the take on the door going directly to them – along with a cut of the bar take too, if they're lucky. Few venues accept credit cards on the door, although many will at the bar. To make licensing issues easier, a lot of listed venues stay open as nightclubs after the concerts.

Rock, pop & world

BarCo

C/Barco 34, Malasaña & Conde Duque (no phone, www.barcobar.com). Metro Tribunal. **Open** 10pm-5.30am Mon-Thur, Sun; 10pm-6am Fri, Sat. **Concerts** times vary. **Admission** *Concerts* €9 (incl 1 drink). *Club* €8 (incl 1 drink). **No credit cards. Map** p307 H10.

Local covers bands, rock groups and Brazilian outfits mostly make up the bill at BarCo, which promotes young up-and-comers on the Madrid scene. A crisp sound system and friendly crowd mean that there's always a good night to be had here. After the gigs the resident DJs take over, banging out tunes until dawn. It's packed at the weekends and a good option for a late-night session midweek.

Boîte

C/Tetuán 27, Sol & Gran Vía (no phone, www.boite live.es). Metro Gran Vía. **Open** 9.30pm-midnight

Mon-Fri, Sun. Closed Aug. *Concerts* times vary. **Admission** varies. **Credit** MC, V. **Map** p311 H11.

With a basement location, warm lighting, chandeliers and shiny wood floor, Boîte looks like it was once a venue for clandestine dance parties. But instead it's now home to regular concerts, mixing up everything from rock and metal to hip hop and blues. It also doubles as a club come the weekend.

Búho Real

C/Regueros 5, Chueca (91 308 48 51, www.buho real.com). Metro Alonso Martínez or Chueca. **Open** from 8pm daily. *Concerts* 9.30pm. **Admission** varies. **No credit cards. Map** p308 I9.

The lights go down very low in the Búho Real, and the spots come up on a tiny stage. The size limitations here dictate the acts – expect local jazz or acoustic groups, most of them just two- or three-piece bands. The name means the 'Royal Owl', which goes some way towards explaining the large collection of miniature owls on display.

Café la Palma

C/la Palma 62, Malasaña (91 522 50 31, www. cafelapalma.com). Metro Noviciado. **Open** 5pm-3am Mon-Thur, Sun; 5pm-3.30am Fri, Sat. *Concerts* 10pm; *DJs* from midnight. **Admission** *Concerts* €5-€10 (incl 1 drink); *DJ sets* free. **Credit** MC, V. **Map** p307 F8.

This is a longstanding favourite with the Malasaña crowd and has been going for 18 years. Choose from an area with tables; a chill-out zone where everyone lazes around on cushions on the floor; or the main room, where you can catch concerts from big local names such as Betamotion or Cosmonauta from Thursday to Saturday. *Photo p204.*

Contraclub

C/Bailén 16, Los Austrias (91 365 55 45, office 91 523 15 11, www.contraclub.es). Metro La Latina. **Open** 10pm-6am Thur-Sat (11pm-6am non-concert nights). **Admission** free; €10 (incl 1 drink) after 2am. *Concerts* prices vary. **Credit** AmEx, DC, MC, V. **Map** p311 E13.

A dark and rather labyrinthine venue, Contraclub is a favourite with the acting set – not long ago local lush Javier Bardem was in attendance, accompanied by Woody Harrelson. The groups appearing here tend to be Spanish acts, and range from singer-songwriters and jazz groups to fusion outfits. DJs take over after the gigs are done.

La Coquette

C/Hileras 14, Los Austrias (no phone). Metro Ópera or Sol. **Open** *Sept-Apr* 8pm-3am Tue-Sun; *May-Aug* 9pm-3am Tue-Sun. **Admission** free. **No credit cards. Map** p311 F11.

This basement bar, which has been going for some 30 years now, was Madrid's first venue dedicated exclusively to blues. It's run by a Swiss-Spanish guy called Albert, who has a large collection of old records that won't disappoint, and there are live acts featuring local bluesers from Tuesday to Thursday.

Costello Club

C/Caballero de Gracia 10, Sol & Gran Via (91 522 18 15, www.costelloclub.com). Metro Sol or Gran Via. **Open** 9pm-2.30am Mon; 8pm-3am Tue-Thur; 8pm-3.30am Fri, Sat; 4.30pm-1am Sun. **Admission** €5-€10. **Credit** MC, V. **Map** p308 H11.

Don't be put off by the seedy street – Costello Club is a centrally located, popular live music venue, with two distinct areas. Head to the comfy ground floor space to enjoy an expertly mixed gin and tonic, before heading downstairs to the cave-like basement to catch a live gig. The schedule takes in everything from pop and rock to indie and folk, and there are also theatre productions, stand-up comedy and even magic shows.

Garibaldi Café

C/San Felipe Neri 4, Los Austrias (mobile 606 643 597, www.salagaribaldi.com). Metro Ópera. **Open** 11pm-6am Fri, Sat. **Admission** varies. **No credit cards. Map** p311 F12.

A roomy venue with a good sound system and varied programme. Staple fare is up-and-coming local bands, but there are also late-night DJ sessions and stand-up comedy.

Gruta 77

C/Cuchillo 6, Southern suburbs (91 471 23 70, www.gruta77.com). Metro Oporto. **Open** 9pm-4am midweek concert nights; 11pm-6am Fri, Sat. **Admission** varies. **No credit cards.**

A mix of local unsigned groups and touring bands from the US, Australia and Japan pass through this 300-seater *sala*, on the corner of Cuchillo and Nicolás Morales. Punk, rock, ska and *mestizaje* tastes are catered for. An excellent sound system makes it worth the trip out to the suburbs.

Honky Tonk

C/Covarrubias 24, Chamberí (91 445 61 91, www.clubhonky.com). Metro Bilbao. **Open** 9.30pm-5am Mon-Thur, Sun; 9.30pm-6am Fri, Sat. *Concerts* 12.30am. Closed Sun during Aug. **Admission** free Mon-Thur, Sun; €10 (incl 1 drink) Fri, Sat. **Credit** MC, V. **Map** p308 I7.

Honky Tonk hosts local pop and rock acts nightly, and also offers an open mic night on Mondays, should you fancy stepping up and belting out a few tunes yourself. Get here early, as the large pillars that hold up the building tend to restrict your view if you're not up the front.

El Intruso

C/Augusto Figueroa 3, Chueca (91 531 89 96, www.intrusobar.com). Metro Chueca. **Open** 9pm-5.30am Mon-Thur, Sun; 9pm-6am Fri, Sat. **Admission** varies. **Credit** MC, V. **Map** p308 H10.

Essential Madrid Albums

Sounds of the city.

DE ALASKA A FANGORIA ALASKA (2005)
Alaska – a feisty flame-haired darling of the Movida cultural explosion of the late 1970s and '80s, is Mexican-born but viewed as the quintessential *madrileña*. As a performer, she's still going strong as part of electro pop duo Fangoria, but this album chronicles her various incarnations.

CONCIERTO DE ARANJUEZ JOAQUÍN RODRIGO (1939)
The best-known piece of Spanish classical music in the world, the *Concierto de Aranjuez* was inspired by the gardens of the royal palace at Aranjuez, just 40 minutes from Atocha station. Composer Joaquín Rodrigo was a pianist, but wrote the piece for classical guitar and orchestra.

MALAS COMPAÑÍAS JOAQUÍN SABINA (1980)
After a period of exile in London in the '70s, Sabina moved to Madrid following Franco's death and had his musical breakthrough when he was signed by Sony and produced *Malas Compañías* (Bad Company). This yielded his best-loved hit, 'Pongamos que hablo de Madrid' (Let's say I'm talking about Madrid').

SONGHAI KETAMA (1988)
Leading proponents of the New Flamenco movement, this trio opened up musical horizons when they adopted rhythms from around the world – rumba, reggae, salsa and funk among them – and created a whole new sound. While *Songhai* isn't their most typically Spanish album, it's probably their best.

DESCANSO DOMINICAL MECANO (1988)
Unabashedly poppy trio Mecano have sold over 25 million albums in their time, and had more international success than any other Spanish group. *Descanso Dominical* contains perhaps their two most popular hits – 'Mujer contra mujer' (radical for its time in that it deals with lesbianism), and 'La fuerza del destino'.

FUERTEVENTURA RUSSIAN RED (2011)
Young singer-songwriter Lourdes Hernández, known as Russian Red, is inspired by artists such as Joanna Newsom and Feist, which comes through in her own brand of fey nu folk. She sings in English and, on this Glasgow-produced album, collaborated with Belle & Sebastian, with whom she has also toured.

ARTS & ENTERTAINMENT

The name means 'the intruder', and that's what you may feel like as you slip into this new venue, which is housed in what looks like an office block and lies behind a large, intimidating wood-panelled door. But you're on safe ground once inside, where you can get comfy at the tables or perch on the diner-style bar stools. The small stage plays host to a variety of local acts, including bigger names such as Gecko Turner, as well as international visitors such as Bob Stroger. Late opening makes it perfect if you're on a midweek bender.

Moby Dick

Avda del Brasil 5, Tetúan (91 555 76 71, www.mobydickclub.com). Metro Cuzco or Santiago Bernabéu. **Open** 10pm-3am Mon-Thur; 10pm-5am Fri, Sat. **Admission** €5-€15. **Credit** MC, V.

With music on two different levels, Moby Dick caters for a range of tastes. It's mainly a venue for local groups and touring Spanish bands, but it can still pull a few surprises – the Long Blondes, the Libertines and Micah P Hinson have all played here. Start the evening off with a pint of Guinness in its sister bar, the Irish Rover, next door.

Palacio de Deportes

Av. Felipe II s/n, Salamanca (91 444 99 49, www.palaciodedeportes.com). Metro Goya. **Open** times vary. **Admission** varies. **Map** p309 O9.

Doubling as a sports stadium, this excellent venue has played host to big-hitters such as Coldplay, Muse, Foo Fighters and Bruce Springsteen. There's room for 18,000 people between the pitch and the stands – although tickets are not always for a specific area, so check carefully and get there early if you want access to the mosh pit. Look out for the little red lights in the crowd – they're attached to backpacks full of beer for those who don't want to make a bar run.

Palacio Vistalegre

C/Utebo 1, Southern suburbs (91 422 07 81, www.palaciovistalegre.com). Metro Oporto or Vista Alegre. **Open** times vary. **Admission** varies.

This venue is what the Spanish call *multiusos*, so it serves as a basketball stadium and conference hall, as well as a concert venue. Visiting bands have included Kings of Leon, Red Hot Chili Peppers and Marilyn Manson. For smaller gigs, a stage is erected underneath the stands – sounds odd, but it works well.

La Riviera

Paseo Bajo de la Virgen del Puerto s/n, Los Austrias (91 365 24 15, www.salariviera.com). Metro Puerto del Ángel. **Open** *Concerts* times vary. *Club* midnight-6am Fri, Sat. **Admission** varies. **Credit** MC, V. **Map** p310 B12/C12.

This club on the banks of the Manzanares river is a major player on the Madrid music scene and ranked by many as the city's best medium-sized venue. It's

Café la Palma. *See p202.*

certainly popular, and comes equipped with an excellent sound system. All sorts of acts have passed through in recent times, among them Lana del Rey, Eels and Yann Tiersen.

La Sala

Avda Nuestra Señora de Fátima 42, Carabanchel (91 525 54 44, www.lasala.biz). Metro Carabanchel. **Open** 8pm-5.30am Wed-Sun. **Admission** varies. **Credit** V.

With neon and neoclassical columns in the entrance, and torch lighting inside, La Sala feels a bit like a strip joint. But don't let that, or the suburban location, put you off. With a concert space for 700 people, La Sala's mixed bag of gigs mainly features Spanish pop, but there have also been performances from the likes of Deacon Blue and Ron Wood.

Sala Caracol

C/Bernardino Obregón 18, Embajadores (91 527 35 94, www.salacaracol.com). Metro Embajadores. **Open** times vary. **Admission** varies. **No credit cards. Map** p311 H16.

The much-cherished Caracol may be a cosy venue, but it has still hosted the likes of Queens of the Stone Age, Papa Roach, Placebo and Editors since it opened more than 20 years ago. Once known for flamenco and world music, it's now more likely to feature rock and has its own competition for up-and-coming bands. At the time of writing, its (hopefully temporary) closure by the council had raised many hackles among Madrid's night owls.

ARTS & ENTERTAINMENT

Sala Marco Aldany

C/Princesa 1, Argüelles (91 547 57 11, www. salarena.com). Metro Plaza de España. **Open** times vary. **Admission** varies. **Credit** AmEx, MC, V. **Map** p307 E9.

It was once Sala Arena, then Sala Heineken, and now it's Sala Marco Aldany, taking its name from its sponsor, a chain of hairdressers. The intimate space plays host to several club nights, but is also a pretty decent live music venue. The Kaiser Chiefs and the Raveonettes have both played here.

Siroco

C/San Dimas 3, Malasaña (91 532 13 57, www.siroco.es). Metro Noviciado or San Bernardo. **Open** 9pm-5am Tue-Thur; 9pm-6am Fri, Sat. **Admission** varies. **Credit** MC, V. **Map** p307 F8.

Regulars at this long-established joint know just what they want, and the owners are more than happy to provide it, putting on a steady schedule of well-established local rock, indie, pop and funk outfits, as well as providing a stage for young hopefuls. In addition, there are late-night DJ sessions covering a broad range of tastes. The venue has just had a total refurbishment, complete with a new sound system.

El Sol

C/Jardines 3, Sol & Gran Vía (91 532 64 90, www. elsolmad.com). Metro Gran Vía. **Open** midnight-5.30am Tue-Sat. *Concerts* 10pm unless otherwise advertised. **Admission** varies. **Credit** MC, V. **Map** p311 H11.

A steady flow of top live acts pass through El Sol, a remnant of the Movida. The decor isn't up to much, but the vibe and programming make up for that – a mixture of rock, rhythm and blues, punk, soul and hip hop from Spanish outfits, plus occasional gigs from international acts such as the Bellrays and Gigolo Aunts. Keep an eye out for the outrageous Anti-Karaoke night, run by US comic Rachel Arieff.

Jazz

Other venues with occasional live jazz acts include **Marula** (*see p192*) and the otherwise sleepy **Café El Despertar** (C/Torrecilla del Leal 18, 91 530 80 95, www.cafeeldespertar.com) in Lavapiés. Fairtrade café **Zanzíbar** (*see p128*) in Chueca has a varied programme of jazz, blues and bossa nova.

Bogui Jazz

C/Barquillo 29, Chueca (91 521 15 68, www. boguijazz.com). Metro Chueca. **Open** 10pm-1.30am Wed, Thur; 10pm-6am Fri, Sat; 6.30-9.30pm every other Sun. *Concerts* 10.30pm, 11.30pm. **Admission** varies. **Credit** AmEx, MC, V. **Map** p308 I10.

The pet project of an American who has lived in Madrid for more than 40 years, Bogui is now a reference point for local and visiting jazz musicians alike. But this relative newcomer faced troubling times in

2008, when the council forced it to shut down for two-and-a-half years – it seems Bogui was getting up the noses of a few local residents. Fortunately it's back, with an intimate 50-seat concert space and a basement bar with TVs screening the show. Once the live stuff is over, DJs take over. Wednesday is blues night.

Café Berlin

C/Jacometrezo 4, Sol & Gran Vía (91 521 57 52, www.cafeberlin.es). Metro Callao or Santo Domingo. **Open** 10pm-5.30am Tue-Sat; 9pm-3am Sun. **Admission** varies. **Credit** MC, V. **Map** p307 G11.

A stalwart on the Madrid scene, Café Berlin has been given a new lease of life lately with a wider music choice and late-night DJ sessions. Gigs usually get going at 10pm, while on Tuesdays and Thursdays there's a jam session from 2am to 5am. The premises also hosts basement club Oba-Oba, which serves up Brazilian beats and the best caipirinhas in the city.

Café Central

Plaza del Ángel 10, Huertas & Santa Ana (91 369 41 43, www.cafecentralmadrid.com). Metro Antón Martín or Sol. **Open** noon-2.30am Mon-Thur, Sun; noon-3.30am Fri, Sat. *Concerts* 9-11pm. **Admission** *Concerts* €10-€15. **Credit** MC, V. **Map** p311 H12.

For many years now, this beautiful space, with high ceilings and elegant decor, has been *the* place to get your jazz fix in Madrid. The artists it attracts place it among Europe's best jazz venues. George Adams, Don Pullen, Ben Sidran and Bob Sands have all graced the stage, along with non-jazz artists such as Javier Krahe, Lucrecia and Ara Malikian.

Café Populart

C/Huertas 22, Huertas (91 429 84 07, www. populart.es). Metro Antón Martín. **Open** 6pm-2.30am Mon-Thur, Sun; 6pm-3.30am Fri, Sat. *Concerts* 10.45pm, midnight. **Admission** free. **No credit cards. Map** p312 I12.

Escape from the beer-crawl route on Huertas by slipping into this superb jazz club. There's no cover

INSIDE TRACK GIG GUIDES

Listings mags *Guía del Ocio* and *Salir Salir* and the Friday supplements of many Spanish newspapers have details of forthcoming gigs. Otherwise, information comes via posters, flyers and in free magazines found in bars and music and fashion shops. Magazines to look out for include *MondoSonoro, Punto H, Rockdelux, GO* and the irregular *Undersounds*. Concert information is also available (if you speak Spanish) at www.lanetro.com, www.madridmusic.com and www.mondosonoro.com.

ARTS & ENTERTAINMENT

charge, but the drinks are a bit pricey. A strong backer of Spanish jazz and host to many an international artist, Populart features jazz and blues every night with two shows, one at 10.45pm and the other at midnight.

Clamores

C/Alburquerque 14, Chamberí (91 445 79 38 /91 445 54 80, www.salaclamores.com). Metro Bilbao. **Open** 6pm-2am Mon-Thur, Sun; 6pm-6am Fri, Sat. **Admission** varies. **Credit** DC, MC, V. **Map** p307 H7.

This legendary jazz club opened in 1979, and for eight years served as the set for TV show *Jazz Entre Amigos*. It has a hugely varied programme these days, with tango, pop, rock, bossa, samba and folk all on the bill, as well as the jazz that made its name.

All That Jazz

Madrid's jumping joints.

Madrid is a city lacking a long history of jazz culture, but things are changing. Practically every night of the week there's a jazz jam in some corner of the capital, often featuring foreign musicians living in Madrid. But there are also more and more local jazz talents – many of whom have spent time living and playing in other cities around the world.

Founded in 1982, **Café Central** (*see p205*) is the classic venue on the scene, often booking invited artists for a whole week, thus allowing performances to evolve. On Mondays, you can choose between the jazz jam at **Soul Station** (C/Cuesta de Santo Domingo 22, no phone), or the one at **Marula** (*see p192*), which is the choice of many of the local La Latina bar staff on their night off.

If it's the quality of the sound that really matters, then the best blue notes in the city are to be heard at **Bogui Jazz** (*see p205*), with blues on Wednesdays and jazz from Thursday to Saturday. Not so long ago, stalwart venue **Café Berlin** (*see p205*) looked like it was unlikely to survive, but thanks to new owners it has a new lease of life, with very late-night jams on Tuesdays and Thursdays. **BarCo** (*see p198*) is a relative newcomer that attracts interesting performers from the School of Creative Music. But the granddaddy of them all is still **Clamores** (*see above*), which first opened its doors in 1979 and offers jam sessions on Fridays and Saturdays.

The live acts sprawl into late-night jam sessions on Friday and Saturday nights, helped along by one of the city's widest range of cavas and champagnes.

El Johnny

Auditorio Jesús Cobeta, Colegio Mayor Universitario San Juan Evangelista, Avenida Gregorio del Amo 4, Moncloa (91 534 24 00, http://cmusanjuan.com). Metro Metropolitano. **Open** times vary. **Admission** varies. **No credit cards**.

This auditorium, located in a student residence, is much more prestigious than you might think. Contrary to appearances, it's one of the city's most discerning jazz clubs – hundreds of great names have passed through the doors during its 30-plus years. Along with regular jazz and flamenco performances, it also stages theatre and dance shows.

★ El Junco

Plaza Santa Bárbara 10, Chueca (91 319 20 81, www.eljunco.com). Metro Alonso Martínez. **Open** 11pm-5.30am Tue-Thur, Sun; 11pm-6am Fri, Sat. **Admission** €5 (incl 1 drink); €8 (incl 1 drink) Fri, Sat. **Credit** AmEx, V. **Map** p308 I8.

This is the ultimate late-night jazz spot in the city, boasting jam sessions and gigs nearly every night of the week. When there aren't live musicians for your listening pleasure, DJs spin vinyl with just the right amount of off-beats.

Segundo Jazz

C/Comandante Zorita 8, Cuatro Caminos, Tetúan (91 554 94 37, www.segundojazz.es). Metro Cuatro Caminos or Nuevos Ministerios. **Open** 7pm-3.30am daily. **Admission** free. **Credit** AmEx, DC, MC, V.

Founded many years ago by the owner of the legendary Whisky Jazz Club, this is Madrid's longest-standing jazz joint. Nowadays, as well as jazz, the gig calendar features Brazilian groups, singer-songwriters and 1960s covers bands banging out Beatles and Rolling Stones songs. A great atmosphere and friendly staff make it an essential stop, with sets at around 9pm or towards midnight.

Latin

Galileo Galilei

C/Galileo 100, Chamberí (91 534 75 57, www. salagalileogalilei.com). Metro Islas Filipinas or Quevedo. **Open** 5pm-2am Mon-Wed; 5pm-5.30am Thur-Sun. **Admission** varies. **No credit cards**. **Map** p307 F7.

Galileo Galilei presents possibly the widest range of artists in Madrid. Whatever kind of music you like, you'll probably find it here. There's Latin jazz, flamenco, salsa, singer-songwriters and myriad types of fusion. There are also occasional comedy nights. It's a former cinema, and as such is very spacious, though the mock-Hellenic decor can be a bit over the top.

ARTS & ENTERTAINMENT

El Junco.

Oba-Oba

C/Jacometrezo 4, Sol & Gran Vía (no phone, www.obaobabardiscoteca.es). Metro Callao. **Open** 11pm-6am Wed-Sun. **Admission** free; €10 (incl 1 drink) after 1am Fri, Sat. **Credit** MC, V. **Map** p307 G11.

An old favourite, the larger-than-life Oba-Oba has been serving up fabulous samba for more than 30 years to its good-time clientele. There are live acts from Wednesday to Sunday, almost all of them Brazilian. The founder of Oba-Oba lays claim to having introduced caipirinhas to Madrid – and it still serves the city's finest.

Flamenco

The most authentic flamenco inhabits a closed world and is proud of it; but if you know where to go and are lucky on the night, you might be granted a peek. Where people are most likely to see flamenco, though, is at a *tablao,* of which there are several in Madrid; below is a selection of those with more genuine performances. As well as the show, you can dine or just drink; both are appallingly expensive, but if you stay till closing you may get your money's worth. The fun really starts around midnight, when most tourists go off to bed and the major artists appear; until then you may just get the kitsch jollity of the *cuadro de la casa* (the house musicians and dancers). Flamenco purists are notoriously snobbish about what's on offer in Madrid, but even they are thrilled by the performances at **Casa Patas**, where guitarists are skilled, dancers ooze power and grace, and singers are as they should be – bloody terrifying.

FESTIVALS

A great way to experience flamenco is as part of the city festivals in honour of **San Isidro** and the summer's **Veranos de la Villa**, while the **Festival Flamenco Cajamadrid** is held in February and March in the Teatro Albéniz (C/Príncipe 25, Huertas & Santa Ana, 91 360 14 80). The biggest flamenco festival, though, is the month-long **Suma Flamenca**. For details of these festivals and others, *see pp24-29.*

VENUES

Café de Chinitas

C/Torija 7, Sol & Gran Vía (91 559 51 35/91 547 15 02, www.chinitas.com). Metro Santo Domingo. **Open** 8pm-1.30am Mon-Sat. *Performances* 8.30pm, 10.15pm Mon-Sat. **Admission** €28. **Credit** AmEx, DC, MC, V. **Map** p311 F11.

An indulgent evening's entertainment for those who like to play at being 19th-century aristocrats – and don't mind paying 21st-century prices. At least this self-styled 'Cathedral of Flamenco' makes an effort, with sumptuous decor that contributes to the experience. The food and floorshow are expensive, yes, but at least it means the owners can afford to pay top euro for flamenco stars, who will send you reeling into the night.

★ Candela

C/Olmo 2, Lavapiés (91 467 33 82). Metro Antón Martín. **Open** 10.30pm-6am daily. *Performance* 10.30pm Thur. **Admission** *Show* €10. *Bar* free. **No credit cards. Map** p312 H13.

An ideal place to soak up some atmosphere, though performances are impromptu (except for the regular Thursday slot) and only take place downstairs and after hours. Still, this in-the-know watering hole for professional musicians and amateurs is welcoming to knowledgeable and respectful aficionados.

Las Carboneras

Plaza del Conde de Miranda 1, Los Austrias (91 542 86 77, www.tablaolascarboneras.com). Metro Sol. **Open** 7.30pm-midnight Mon-Sat. *Performances* 8.30pm, 10.30pm Mon-Sat. **Admission** (incl 1 drink) €33.40. **Credit** AmEx, DC, MC, V. **Map** p311 F12.
Packed with tourists, this bar-restaurant still offers good value for money, with an energetic, passionate show. The set menus comprise typical fare, and diners are exempt from the admission charge. Highly polished flamenco guarantees an inauthentic but unashamedly fun night out.

Cardamomo

C/Echegaray 15, Santa Ana (91 429 98 75, www.cardamomo.es). Metro Sevilla. **Open** 6pm-4am daily. *Performance* 10pm daily. **Admission** (incl 1 drink) €39, (incl dinner) €72. **Credit** AmEx, DC, MC, V. **Map** p311 H12.
A firm fixture on the scene, this frenetic flamenco bar plays a mixture of flamenco and rumba tunes, often to thundering effect.

★ Casa Patas

C/Cañizares 10, Lavapiés (91 369 04 96, www.casa patas.com). Metro Antón Martín. **Open** *Sept-July* 1-4.30pm, 8pm-midnight Mon-Thur; 1-4.30pm, 7.30pm-1am Fri; 7.30pm-1am Sat. *Aug* 8pm-midnight Mon-Thur; 7.30pm-1am Fri, Sat. *Performances* 10.30pm Mon-Thur; 9pm, midnight Fri, Sat. **Admission** (incl 1 drink) €34. **Credit** AmEx, DC, MC, V. **Map** p311 H14.
This is a plush and somewhat pricey place to savour traditional or nuevo flamenco. Recent headliners have included Chaquetón, Remedios Amaya and Niña Pastori. Casa Patas is deservedly proud of its reputation

and treats its loyal, knowledgeable and sometimes intimidating audience with respect. The same owners have a bar, Pata Chico, alongside for pre-flamenco drinks.

Corral de la Morería

C/Morería 17, Los Austrias (91 365 84 46, www.corraldelamoreria.com). Metro La Latina. **Open** 8pm-12.30am daily. *Performances* 9pm, 11pm daily. **Admission** (incl 1 drink) €47. **Credit** AmEx, DC, MC, V. **Map** p311 E13.
More serious and exacting than Las Carboneras, this longstanding *tablao* sports seemingly authentic Arab decor and an atmosphere to match. A relaxed mix of tourists, fans (Hemingway, Che Guevara and Picasso all paid a visit) and professionals enjoy a solid, expensive and sometimes exhilarating show.

Corral de la Pacheca

C/Juan Ramón Jiménez 26, North of centre (91 353 01 00, www.corraldelapacheca.com). Metro Cuzco. **Open** 8.30pm-midnight daily. *Performance* 10pm daily. **Admission** €30 (incl 1 drink); €15 if dining. **Credit** AmEx, MC, V.
This grand centre of popular and traditional flamenco boasts a history of star performers and even starrier punters. Built on the site of a 17th-century theatre, it began life as a *tablao* but has grown into an imposing venue with a large auditorium and stage.

Torres Bermejas

C/Mesonero Romanos 11 (91 532 33 22, www.torres bermejas.com). Metro Callao. **Open** 8.30pm-1.30am daily. *Performance* 9.30pm daily. **Admission** (incl 1 drink) €37. **Credit** AmEx, DC, MC, V. **Map** p311 H11.
Modelled somewhat kitschly on the Alhambra, this bar plays hosts to authentic Gypsy flamenco and a faithful in-crowd, managing to absorb the tour parties without spoiling the mood. The paella and Rioja veal are, like the flamenco, rich and satisfying.

Casa Patas.

Performing Arts

The city in stages, from Broadway blockbusters to home-grown operetta.

Madrid's cultural clout has steadily increased in recent years, with the city finally shaking off a reputation for producing stuffy composers, ensembles with limited scope, a lightweight contemporary classical scene and a reactionary public. Credit must go, too, to a city that depends predominantly on public funds to bring in top-class international musicians and ensembles to its worthy concert venues. Madrid's theatre scene is a polarised affair: while Gran Vía is littered with Broadway and West End hand-me-downs – Spain's fervent passion for the blockbuster musical has not wavered – little

theatres soldier on in the face of local government and city council limits on licences and funds. Still, the fighting spirit of the fringe makes up for the mainstream's old-fashioned outlook – although to some outsiders, the alternative scene here can seem fairly tame; bear in mind that until the late 1980s there was virtually no non-mainstream theatre here at all.

Classical & Opera

Traditionally, the scene orbits around three main venues: the modern and austere (and arguably best-quality classical venue in Europe) **Auditorio Nacional de Música** (*see p210*), the grand **Teatro Real** (*see p210*) hosting opera, and the **Teatro de la Zarzuela** (*see p211*) for a decent selection of classical concerts (as well as for *zarzuela*, Madrid's traditional operetta art form).

A word of advice if you're attending classical concerts in Madrid – make sure you get there early. The stereotypical Spanish tardiness is not a trait shared by classical music-lovers.

INFORMATION & TICKETS

Check venue websites for current and future seasons, as well as any last-minute changes or cancellations. You can pick up leaflets from most of the venues – often quicker than trying to get through by phone – or check the *Guía del Ocio* or daily newspapers. Tickets can usually be purchased over the phone, via the venue website or from **Telentrada** (902 10 12 12, www.telentrada.com) or **Ticketmaster** (www.ticketmaster.es). Tickets for state-run venues such as the Auditorio Nacional de Música and Teatro de la Zarzuela are sold at

the venue box offices, online at www.entradas inaem.es or by phone (902 22 49 49).

VENUES

The **Círculo de Bellas Artes'** classical and contemporary music programme has broadened immensely over the last decade or so (*see p43*). The **Teatro Español** (*see p214*) occasionally holds *zarzuelas* and performances by chamber and symphonic orchestras. A handful of cafés and restaurants around town offer an opera-accompanied dining experience. Try the **Café Viena** (C/Luisa Fernanda 23, 91 559 38 28, www.vienacapellades.com) for occasional Cenas Líricas (consisting of dinner and a short *zarzuela* or opera performance, all for €50 plus wine). Also, check out the professional singing waiters at **La Favorita** (*see p110*) and **La Castafiore** (C/Marqués de Monasterio 5, 91 319 42 21, www.lacastafiore.net). Another place to keep an eye on is the **Centro Asturiano** (C/Farmacia 2, 4°, 91 532 82 81, www.centroasturianomadrid.es), which runs a cycle called Lunes Musicales with concerts performed by small ensembles on Mondays. The Círculo de Bellas Artes also runs several concert cycles, including one dedicated to Bach and another, the Frontera Círculo, focusing on contemporary music. There are also regular concerts in a range of styles, from jazz to rock.

Auditorio Nacional de Música

*C/Príncipe de Vergara 146, Salamanca (info 91
337 01 40, www.auditorionacional.mcu.es; tickets
902 22 49 49, www.entradasinaem.es). Metro
Cruz del Rayo or Prosperidad.* **Open** *Box office*
4-6pm Mon; 10am-5pm Tue-Fri; 11am-1pm Sat.
Closed Aug. **Main season** Oct-June. **Tickets**
€9-€50. **Credit** MC, V.

This impressive concert hall has a main 2,000-
seater auditorium and a smaller chamber hall, the
Sala de Cámara. As well as being home to the OCNE,
the Auditorio also hosts the Comunidad de Madrid's
orchestra, ORCAM, and the Joven Orquesta
Nacional de España (JONDE, worth checking out for
their youth and enthusiasm). In addition, ensembles
such as the Universidad Politécnica de Madrid invite
orchestras to accompany the university's choir, performing on selected Friday and Saturday evenings
at 10.30pm. But the finest concerts are those by
invited international orchestras – which are, happily
enough, something the Spanish state likes to invest
its music budget in. The best seasons are the Grandes
Intérpretes, the Liceo de Cámara (Fundación Caja
Madrid), and Ibermúsica. Look out too for organ
recitals. Tickets for the Auditorio usually go on sale
about a fortnight before performances, and can be
hard to get hold of. Tickets are generally cheaper for
Sunday morning concerts.

Conde Duque

*C/Conde Duque 11, Malasaña (91 588 51 65,
www.condeduque.es). Metro Ventura Rodríguez
or Plaza de España.* **Concerts** Sept-June.
Tickets free-€20. **Credit** MC, V. **Map** p307 F8.

The Conde Duque cultural centre programmes a
wide range of events, including piano recitals in its
main auditorium on Tuesday nights, and concert
cycles such as the Baroque season. Chamber concerts, which often feature performers from prestigious international orchestras and choirs, are also
held here. Most are affordable, and some are free.

Real Academia de las Bellas
Artes de San Fernando

*C/Alcalá 13, Sol & Gran Vía (91 524 08 64,
www.realacademiabellasartessanfernando.com).
Metro Sevilla or Sol.* **Concerts** Sept-June noon
Sat. **Admission** free. **Map** p311 H11.

This beautiful building right in the heart of Madrid
is a must for a handsome concert experience. It
hosts three or four cycles of free concerts a year,
some organised through Radio Nacional de España
for broadcast with musicians from the Escuela
Superior de Música Reina Sofía. One annual highlight is the short baroque season, which usually
takes place in March.

Teatro Monumental

*C/Atocha 65, Lavapiés (91 429 12 81, box office
902 24 48 48, www.rtve.es/orquesta-coro). Metro
Antón Martín.* **Open** *Box office* 11am-2pm, 5-7pm

Conde Duque.

daily (until 8pm on performance days). **Concerts**
Oct-May 8pm Thur, Fri. **Tickets** €11-€25. **Credit**
AmEx, DC, MC, V. **Map** p312 H13.

Located in slightly seedy Antón Martín, the
Monumental has more character than most, but is
functional rather than beautiful. Its main purpose
is to record broadcast concerts by the RTVE
Orchestra and Choir – consequently it may not have
the glitz of the Teatro Real, but it does have excellent acoustics and high-quality performances. The
principal diet here is concerts, with a side order of
opera and *zarzuela*. The Monumental opens to the
public free of charge for rehearsals on Thursday
mornings and chamber music concerts around midday on Saturdays.

Teatro Real

*Plaza de Isabel II, Los Austrias (information
91 516 06 60, box office 902 24 48 48,
www.teatro-real.com). Metro Opera.* **Open** *Box
office* 9.15am-8pm Mon-Fri (10am-8pm Sat
performance days). *Visits* 10.30am-1pm daily.
Main season Sept-July. **Tickets** *Ballet* €9-
€106. *Opera* €9-€363.*Visits* €8; €6 reductions.
Credit AmEx, DC, MC, V. **Map** p311 F11.

Shaped like a compressed oval, the interior of the
city's opera house is breathtakingly ornate compared with its sombre façade, and one of the most
technologically advanced in Europe. Productions are

impressive, with complicated revolving sets and attention to detail in costumes and props, and enjoy funding from some of Spain's biggest companies, as well as the Comunidad de Madrid. Projection screens at either side of the stage show the full action, though this doesn't quite compensate for the lack of vision at the far ends of the top galleries (the *tribunas* and part of the *anfiteatro*). There's also a screen above the stage showing Spanish surtitles for non-Spanish operas. The acoustics are so good that quality of sound is practically the same everywhere in the hall.

The annual Festival de Verano runs alongside the theatre's regular programme in June and July but offers a more orchestra- and dance-orientated programme, as well as children's shows (tickets for these events are much cheaper and easier to obtain). Guided tours run daily and take visitors through the main dressing room and auditoria. Tours last 50 minutes, and a minimum of ten people are required for a tour to take place (call 91 516 06 96 for all tour enquiries/bookings).

Performances usually begin at 8pm, or 6pm on Sundays, with ballet and family opera matinées at noon. Tickets go on sale approximately ten days before the première and standby tickets are available on the day. With the cheapest tickets, for rows F and G, vision is seriously restricted; check the website for a detailed plan.

Teatro de la Zarzuela

C/Jovellanos 4, Huertas & Santa Ana (box office 91 524 54 10, http://teatrodelazarzuela.mcu.es). Metro Banco de España. **Open** *Box office noon-6pm daily (until 8pm on performance days).* **Main season** Sept-July. **Tickets** €5-€50. **Credit** AmEx, DC, V. **Map** p312 I11.

The Teatro de la Zarzuela, which served as an opera house for many years before the Teatro Real's renovation, is now principally devoted to its *raison d'être* – staging *zarzuela*, home-grown Spanish operetta. Despite *zarzuela*'s uncool image and lack of credibility among serious music-lovers, it retains considerable popularity, drawing decent audiences for the daily 8pm performances from October to July. Accompanying the Teatro's packed *zarzuela* programme are dance performances (often put on by the Ballet Nacional), concerts, plays, conferences and family-orientated shows. The annual Ciclo del Lied, which pays tribute to the lesser-known 19th-century German song form, has an excellent reputation. *Photo p213.*

Institutions

Institutions such as the **British Council** (www.britishcouncil.org/spain), the **Institut Français** (www.institutfrancais.es/madrid), the **Istituto Italiano di Cultura** (www.iicmadrid.esteri.it) and the **Goethe Institut** (www.goethe.de/ins/es/mad/esindex.htm) are also worth checking for classical music concerts and related activities.

Fundación Canal

C/Mateo Inurria 2, Chamartín (91 545 15 06, www.fundacioncanal.com). Metro Plaza de Castilla. **Concerts** 7.30pm Sun. **Main season** Oct-June.

Set up by Madrid's water company, Canal de Isabel II, this foundation has become active in all areas of the arts during the last few years, programming occasionally excellent exhibitions and concerts throughout the year. The foundation's music programming has included seasons of chamber music performed by musicians from the Orquesta de la Comunidad de Madrid.

Fundación Carlos Amberes

C/Claudio Coello 99, Salamanca (91 435 22 01, www.fcamberes.org). Metro Serrano. **Main season** Sept-July. **Map** p309 L7.

The Carlos Amberes Foundation dates back to 1594, when it was founded by a 16th-century Flemish

Teatro Real.

ARTS & ENTERTAINMENT

benefactor. Today, as well as exhibitions and conferences, it hosts an average of 15 concerts per year in three cycles (one at the beginning of the year, one in May and one at the end of the year), both in its rather dingy basement and sometimes upstairs in a converted church, which is pretty but has poor acoustics. The programme tends to focus on the music of the Low Countries.

Fundación Juan March

C/Castelló 77, Salamanca (91 435 42 40, www.march.es). Metro Núñez de Balboa. **Main season** Oct-June. **Map** p309 N7.
Set up in 1955, this charitable foundation and hive of musical, artistic and scientific activity was one of few such organisations in Spain for a good many years. These days the Fundación Juan March

remains a key player on Madrid's classical scene, putting on around 150-200 free concerts per year. These usually consist of soloists or chamber ensembles, and take place on Wednesday evenings from 7.30pm (the most popular slot, featuring better-known professional musicians and broadcast on Radio Nacional), themed cycles on Fridays at 8pm, as well as some Saturdays and Sundays at midday featuring performances ranging from jazz and classical to world music. Sundays are usually dedicated to young, up-and-coming musicians. The concert hall seats 300. When it fills up a second hall with a big screen is opened, and then the bar. The programme is pretty flexible as it doesn't depend on ticket sales, though there's a slant towards Spanish composers. Take in some good art exhibitions while you're there.

Music Beyond Madrid

Head out of the capital for these charming classical festivals.

Concert programmers in and around Madrid have woken up to the charms of the region, taking music out of the theatres and lighting up monasteries, palaces and gardens. What could be more inviting than a soirée of Rachmaninoff, Fauré and Schumann in one of the cool churches of the Sierra when the temperature is in the forties in Madrid?

The **Clásicos en Verano** (www.madrid.org/clasicosenverano) concerts may not feature the greatest musicians, but the range is broad. Come July and August, it seems every nook and cranny, every old church and town hall around Madrid, io filled with the sweet sounds of piano concertos, percussion groups, choirs, wind ensembles, string quartets, accompanied poetry and medieval music by local groups. The apparently random programming has led to Bach and Handel arias being performed at the San Andrés church in Rascafría, while in nearby Alameda del Valle young men climbed stepladders to read names and numbers from the phone book as if they were poetry.

Not only are these concerts widespread and plentiful (there are about 80 of them in 51 different towns), they're also free. Pass by a tourist information office or the Consejería de Cultura y Deportes on C/Alcalá 31 to pick up a full programme. Some of the more striking venues include the Castillo de los Mendoza in Manzanares el Real (*see p239*) and the Iglesia de los Arroyos in El Escorial (*see p230*).

Care for a turn about the charming gardens of the Aranjuez Palace (*see p243*)

Aranjuez Palace.

while being serenaded by *zarambeques, folías, marionas, fandangos* and *pasacalles*? The **Música Antigua Aranjuez** festival (www.musicaantiguaaranjuez.net) keeps the music alive in the place that inspired Joaquín Rodrigo's haunting *Concierto de Aranjuez*, with sounds from much earlier in the palace's history. At weekends during the months of May and June, the palace hosts concerts of medieval, renaissance and baroque music played on original instruments from the period. Many of the composers featured do not enjoy wide exposure today, although they were well known in their day. Concerts are held inside the palace (in the chapel and the Sala de Teatro), as well as in the palace grounds. The much-loved guided 'musical walks' feature pauses for concerts along the way. Tickets are around €20 for concerts and €18 for musical walks, and can be bought from Telentrada (902 10 12 12, www.telentrada.com).

Teatro de la Zarzuela. *See p211.*

ORCHESTRAS & ENSEMBLES

Orquesta y Coro de la Comunidad de Madrid (ORCAM)

www.orcam.org

Madrid's state-funded regional orchestra is one of the city's most highly regarded. It provides accompaniment for the shows at the Teatro de la Zarzuela, but also performs at the Auditorio Nacional. The orchestra's artistic director, José Ramón Encinar, provides an occasionally erratic programme of mainly Spanish composers.

Orquesta & Coro Nacionales de España (OCNE)

http://ocne.mcu.es

A certain element of instability has hounded Spain's national orchestra and choir over the years, with numerous strikes carried out by the state-employed members when asked to practise at home outside their set paid hours. They take to the stage every weekend at the Auditorio Nacional, occasionally performing world premières of contemporary pieces. Josep Pons is the current artistic director of the orchestra and choir, and is attempting to renovate programme content. He has even shown an interest in adding jazz, tango and ethnic music to the orchestra's traditionally classical and Romantic repertoire.

Orquesta y Coro de RTVE

www.rtve.es/rtve/orquesta-coro

The orchestra and choir of Spain's national state-run television and radio stations (Radio Televisión España) was originally founded for broadcasting purposes. Its home is in the Teatro Monumental, and concerts usually take place on Thursdays and Fridays at 8pm. Season tickets, running from October to late March, are reasonably priced and the programme is consistently good. Carlos Kalmar has been the artistic director since 2011.

Orquesta Sinfónica de Madrid (OSM)

www.osm.es

The *orquesta titular* of the Teatro Real and oldest existing symphonic ensemble in Spain has a reputation within classical music circles for proposing odd, irregular seasonal programmes. Recent years have looked more stable, however, with a proposed series of chamber concerts, *zarzuelas* and symphonic concerts. At the Teatro Real, the major operas are also usually complemented by related concerts put on by the orchestra and performed in a new concert space in one of the upstairs rooms. As well as all the top Spanish conductors, the OSM has also worked with international greats such as Peter Haag, Pinchas Steinberg and Kurt Sanderling.

Theatre

Look beyond the heavyweights, such as the **Teatro Español** (*see p214*) and the **Teatro María Guerrero** (*see p215*), and you'll find that Madrid has an active fringe scene, with key players the **Sala Triángulo** and **Cuarta Pared** (for both, *see pp216-217*) the oldest of the *salas alternativas*. Other theatres to look for include **Teatro Cofidis** (formerly the Alcázar, C/Alcalá 20, 91 532 06 16, www.teatrocofidis.com), **Teatro Caser Calderón** (C/Atocha 18, 902 00 66 17, www.teatrocalderon.com), **Teatro Lara** (Corredera Baja de San Pablo 15, 91 523

Sala Mirador.

90 27, www.teatrolara.com) for family entertainment along with other shows, and **Teatro de Cámara Chéjov** (C/Martires de la Ventilla 68, 91 527 09 54, www.teatrochejov. com) for major classics.

VENUES
Mainstream theatres

Sala Mirador
C/Doctor Fourquet 31, Lavapiés (91 539 57 67, www.cnc-eca.es). Metro Atocha or Lavapiés. **Open** *Box office* 1hr before performance Thur-Sun. Closed Aug. **Tickets** €8-€18. **Credit** MC, V. **Map** p312 I15.
Doubling as a theatre/dance school and performance space, the Sala Mirador is home to the Centro de Nuevos Creadores (Centre of New Creators). It is also the site of the long-running *La Katarsis del Tomatazo*, performed every Friday and Saturday night at 10.30pm. The audience are given tomatoes as they enter, which they can use to express their feelings on this singing and dancing cabaret.

Teatro de la Abadía
C/Fernández de los Ríos 42, Chamberí (box office 91 448 16 27, information 91 448 11 81, www.teatroabadia.com). Metro Quevedo. **Open** *Box office* 5-9pm Tue-Sat; 5-8pm Sun. Closed Aug. **Tickets** €12-€24; Wed reductions. **Credit** V. **Map** p307 F6.
Housed inside an abandoned church, the award-winning Abadia dabbles in music and dance as well as theatre. It participates in the Festival de Otoño en Primavera and Madrid en Danza festivals, and brings unusual one-offs to the regular schedule.

Teatro Alfil
C/Pez 10, Malasaña (box office 91 521 58 27, information 91 521 45 41, http://teatroalfil.com). Metro Callao or Noviciado. **Open** *Box office* 1hr before performance Tue-Sun. **Tickets** €14-€26. **Credit** MC, V. **Map** p309 G10.
Madrid's renegade theatre, the Alfil has been threatened with closure in previous years, but has battled on and produces increasingly radical plays – both *The Vagina Monologues* and *Puppetry of the Penis* have been staged here. It's also one of the few venues to host stand-up comedy, including Giggling Guiri English comedy nights (www.comedyinspain.com).

Teatro Fernán Gomez Centro de Arte
Jardines del Descubrimiento, Plaza de Colón, Salamanca (91 486 25 40, http://teatro fernangomez.esmadrid.com). Metro Serrano. **Open** *Box office* Oct-June 11am-1.30pm, 5-7pm daily or until performance. July-Sept 11.30am-3pm, 5-7pm daily. **Tickets** €10-€18. **Credit** AmEx, DC, MC, V. **Map** p308 K9.
The theatre in the city's purpose-built cultural centre shows an eclectic mix of concerts, opera, *zarzuela*, cinema, drama and dance. There are also jazz performances, workshops and children's puppet shows.

Teatro Español
C/Príncipe 25, Huertas & Santa Ana (box office 91 360 14 84, information 91 360 14 80, www. teatroespanol.es). Metro Sevilla or Sol. **Open** *Box office* 5-7pm Tue-Sun for advanced purchase; 11.30am-1.30pm for same-day tickets. **Tickets** €5-€25. **No credit cards. Map** p312 H12.
This grand theatre on Plaza Santa Ana dates back to 1745, but that doesn't mean it's old-fashioned – in fact, it has enjoyed some fairly radical programming

in recent years. The 2012-13 season included productions of Jean Anouilh's *Antigone*, David Hare's *Skylight* and *Unsound, Babylon, Demodé* by the Compañía Nacional de Danza (Spanish National Dance Company). Teatro Español also holds performances at the Matadero (*see p84*), a converted slaughterhouse with various performance spaces.

Teatro Fernando de Rojas

C/Alcalá 42, Sol & Gran Vía (91 360 54 00, www. circulobellasartes.com). Metro Banco de España or Sevilla. **Open** *Box office* 5.30-9pm Tue-Sun. Closed Aug. **Tickets** vary. **No credit cards. Map** p312 I11.

Housed in the Círculo de Bellas Artes, and not to be confused with the unconnected Teatro de Bellas Artes next door, the Fernando de Rojas stages three or four works a season, mixing contemporary and traditional, Spanish and international.

Teatro La Latina

Plaza de la Cebada 2, La Latina (box office 91 188 08 30, information 91 365 28 35, www.teatro lalatina.net). Metro La Latina or Tirso de Molina. **Open** *Box office* 5-8pm Tue; 11am-1.30pm, 5pm until performance Wed-Sun. **Tickets** €12-€22. **No credit cards. Map** p311 F13.

Previously known for its homespun comic theatre (plenty of star names in farcical situations and lots of banging of doors), this comfortable venue has undergone a slight shift of image in recent years. Although the programme now consists mainly of high-quality drama, the theatre also sometimes hosts less high-brow productions. *Photo p216.*

★ Teatro María Guerrero

C/Tamayo y Baus 4, Chueca (information 91 310 15 00, http://cdn.mcu.es). Metro Colón.

Open *Box office* noon-6pm or until performance daily. Closed Aug. **Tickets** €4-€20; reductions Wed. **Credit** AmEx, DC, V. **Map** p308 J10.

This beautiful late 19th-century theatre is home to the state-run Centro Dramático Nacional (CDN), and has retained much of its red velvet plushness after comprehensive renovations. The 2012-13 season ran the gamut from Pérez Galdós' *Doña Perfecta* and Chekhov's *Three Sisters* to Martin Crimp's *No One Sees the Video.*

Teatro Nuevo Apolo

Plaza de Tirso de Molina 1, Rastro & Lavapiés (91 369 06 37, www.summummusic.com). Metro Tirso de Molina. **Open** *Box office* 11.30am-1.30pm, 5-9pm Tue-Sat; 5-7pm Sun. Closed mid July-mid Aug. **Tickets** €15-€25. **No credit cards** (except for purchases exceeding €150). **Map** p311 G13.

This grand old theatre celebrated its 80th anniversary in 2013, and popular recent shows have included *De Carmen*, a homage to the great dancer Carmen Amaya, performed by the Compañía Tránsit Dansa. Its programme largely features musicals, classic ballet (*The Nutcracker, Swan Lake*) and musical extravaganzas such as *Abba Mania.*

Teatro Pavón

C/Embajadores 9, La Latina (91 528 28 19, http:// teatroclasico.mcu.es). Metro La Latina. **Open** *Box office* Sept-May 11am-until start of performance; June-July 10am-2pm Mon-Fri. Closed Aug. **Tickets** €3-€20. **Credit** MC, V. **Map** p311 G14.

The Compañía Nacional de Teatro Clásico moved here while its real home, the Teatro de la Comédia, is being restored. An impressive building that sat semi-derelict for many years, it currently stages classical productions by the Compañía Nacional, as well

Teatro Español.

as by a number of invited companies. Expect works by Spanish Golden Age greats, along with occasional Molière, Shakespeare and the like.

Teatro Valle-Inclán

Plaza de Lavapiés s/n, Rastro & Lavapiés (91 505 88 01, http://cdn.mcu.es; tickets 902 22 49 49, www.entradasinaem.es). Metro Lavapiés. **Open** *Box office* noon-6pm or until performance daily. Closed Aug. **Tickets** €12-€20; reductions Wed. **Credit** AmEx, DC, V. **Map** p311 H14.
The Valle-Inclán is the Centro Dramático Nacional's second venue after the María Guerrero. The main theatre, with 510 seats, is equipped with the latest technology and offers a programme of contemporary Spanish playwrights, as well as works by authors such as Pirandello, Ibsen and Jean Genet. In the adjoining Sala Franciso Nieva, which seats 150, you're more likely to find works by newer writers.

★ Teatros del Canal

C/Cea Bermúdez 1, Chamberí (91 308 99 50, www.teatrosdelcanal.com). Metro Canal. **Open** *Box office* 11am-1pm, 5.30-9pm Mon-Sat; 5.30-8pm Sun. **Tickets** €12-€34; 20% discount reductions. **Credit** AmEx, DC, V.
Consisting of two theatres – the Sala Roja (Red Room) and the Sala Verde (Green Room) – the Teatros del Canal performing arts centre opened in the *barrio* of Chamberí in 2009, to much excitement. The flashy avant-garde building has advanced audio-visual technology and impressive interiors. The centre also houses the Centro Danza Canal (CDC) dance school, and the Victor Ullate-Ballet-Comunidad de Madrid dance company. It hosts a range of performances in a variety of genres, including theatre, opera, dance and *zarzuela*.

Fringe/alternative spaces

The **Teatro de las Aguas** (C/Aguas 8, 91 366 96 42) occasionally has productions in English. Small, more alternative spaces include **DT Espacio Escénico** (C/Reina 9, 91 521 71 55, www.dtespacioescenico.com) for theatre, cabaret and dance productions on gay themes; **Nave de Los Locos** (C/Francisco Guzmán 28, 91 560 14 79, www.lanavedeloslocos.org), which hosts theatrical productions, workshops and forums in a bid to develop 'the creative imagination'; and **Lagrada** (C/Ercilla 20, 91 517 96 98, www.teatrolagrada.com) for kitchen-sink dramas and contemporary plays.

Cuarta Pared

C/Ercilla 17, South of centre (91 517 23 17, www.cuartapared.es). Metro Embajadores. **Open** *Box office* 1hr before performance Thur-Sun. Closed Aug. **Tickets** €14; €10 reductions. *Children's shows* €9. **No credit cards**.
Cuarta Pared plays a crucial role in training and production. The resident company turns out some excellent work, and it also hosts visiting productions, is a major dance venue and stages acclaimed children's theatre.

El Montacargas

C/Antillón 19, Puerta del Ángel, South of centre (91 526 11 73, www.teatroelmontacargas.com). Metro Puerta del Ángel. **Open** *Box office* 30mins before show Thur-Sun. **Tickets** €12; €9 reductions. *Children's shows* €8. **No credit cards**.
Programming favours contemporary Spanish work, but it also hosts the Clown Festival in September.

Teatro La Latina. *See p215.*

Sala Triángulo

C/Zurita 20, Lavapiés (91 530 68 91, www.teatro triangulo.com). Metro Antón Martín or Lavapiés. **Open** *Box office* 30mins before show. **Tickets** €10-€13. **No credit cards. Map** p312 I14.

The original and probably the best of Madrid's alternative theatres, Triángulo is fiercely independent. There are always several productions in rep, usually including new writing and cross-form collaborations. It works closely with other theatres during festivals.

Teatro Pradillo

C/Pradillo 12, Chamartín (91 416 90 11, www.teatropradillo.com). Metro Concha Espina. **Open** *Box office* 1hr before performance. *Sept-June* Thur-Sun; *July, Aug* Wed-Sat. **Tickets** €12; €6 concessions. **Credit** MC, V.

This fantastically intimate theatre, with just 120 seats, runs a varied programme throughout the year. A particular strength is dance – the Pradillo gave well-known dancers Manuel Liñan and Daniel Doña their big breaks, and runs a dance programme for young audiences – while another strong point is children's theatre, and in particular puppet shows. It's one of the principal organisers of the Escena Contemporánea festival (www.escenacontemporanea.com), and runs a flamenco festival in August.

SEASONS AND FESTIVALS

The **Festival de Otoño en Primavera** (*see p28*) is the biggest event for theatre, dance and puppetry, attracting major international names and sometimes putting on shows in English. More alternative theatre and dance is showcased in January and February in the original **Escena Contemporánea** (*photo p218*), the better-funded sibling to the slightly more avant-garde **La Alternativa** festival. The summer **Veranos de la Villa** offers even more outdoor performances. The Centro Cultural de la Villa's **Apuesta por la Danza** attracts prestigious companies such as Ibérica de Danza and the Companhia Portuguesa de Bailado Contemporâneo. And, for a summer trip out of town, don't miss the **Festival Internacional de Teatro Clásico** in Almagro every July. The event pays tribute to Lope de Vega, Molière, Shakespeare et al with plays, workshops and street performances (call 91 521 07 20 or visit www.festivaldealmagro.com for details). The **Madrid Sur** festival is organised by the Fundación Instituto Internacional del Teatro del Mediterráneo (91 355 58 67, www.institutodelmediterraneo.es) in the autumn.

Dance

Three major companies are based in Madrid: the contemporary, but far from radical, **Compañía Nacional de Danza**; the state

Festival de Otoño en Primavera.

ARTS & ENTERTAINMENT

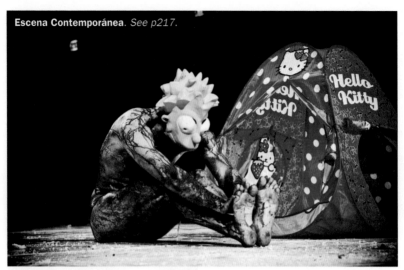

Escena Contemporánea. See p217.

Ballet Nacional de España, which specialises in Spanish styles of dance; and the **Ballet de la Comunidad de Madrid**, run by Victor Ullate.

As ever, contemporary dance teeters on an economic knife-edge, but spaces such as the **Pradillo** (*see p217*) continue to show good work. The two main contemporary dance companies are **10y10** (www.10y10danza.com), at the Centro de Nuevos Creadores, and **Provisional Danza** (www.provisionaldanza.com), one of the pioneers of contemporary dance in Spain since 1987, led by renowned choreographer Carmen Werner. The **Centro Danza Canal** (CDC) dance school and the **Víctor Ullate Ballet-Comunidad de Madrid** company are based in the **Teatros del Canal** performing arts centre (*see p216*). It's also worth noting that the **Teatro Real** (*see p210*) often stages dance productions, notably with the Ballet Nacional de España and the Compañía Nacional de Danza, as well as small pieces in its informal 'Café Danza'.

For flamenco, *see p207*.

ZARZUELA

Zarzuela is an ineffable part of *madrileño* culture, though tricky for the outsider to get a grip on. It was Spain's early answer to the Italian opera – shorter and funnier and incorporating elements of theatre, slapstick and dance. Golden Age playwrights Félix Lope de Vega and Pedro Calderón de la Barca were early pioneers of the genre, which was later developed by the likes of Ramón de la Cruz and composer Federico de Chueca and, moving into the 20th century, Amadeo Vives and Jacinto Guerrero. *Zarzuela* is full

of local jokes (usually rhyming and rattled off at speed) and traditional songs with which the public will sing along, so be prepared. Catch it in its home ground of the Teatro de la Zarzuela, in the Centro Cultural de la Villa in July or August, or at a summer open-air performance.

DANCE CLASSES

If you take more than a passive interest in flamenco, you might want to try classes. Below are some of the more established dance centres.

Centro de Danza Karen Taft

C/Libertad 15, Chueca (91 522 84 40, 91 522 20 87, www.karentaft.com). Metro Chueca. **Open** *Oct-June* 9am-10pm Mon-Fri. *July-Sept* 9.30am-10pm Mon-Thur. **Map** p312 I11.
One of the foremost dance schools in Spain, offering classes in classical and modern dance, and flamenco.

Estudios Amor de Dios

C/Santa Isabel 5, 1º, Lavapiés (91 360 04 34, www.amordedios.com). Metro Antón Martín. **Open** varies (call for details). **Map** p312 I13.
The world's most famous flamenco school is now over 60 years old. It sits (or rather stamps) above the Antón Martín indoor market building.

El Horno

C/Esgrima 11, Lavapiés (91 527 57 01, www.centroelhorno.com). Metro Tirso de Molina. **Open** 10am-11pm Mon-Fri; 10am-7pm Sat. **Map** p311 G13.
El Horno has a flamenco and *sevillana* leaning (but also offers classes from martial arts to singing).

Spoken Word

Check out Madrid's English-language productions.

Even hardened theatre buffs are daunted by a show in a language they don't understand and, of course, almost all Madrid theatre is staged in Spanish. English-speaking visitors might get lucky, though, and happen on a touring production during the Festival de Otoño en Primavera or Escena Contemporánea. The RSC has visited in recent years, and 2013 saw Cheek By Jowl's production of *'Tis Pity She's a Whore*, and the all-male Propeller Company's *Twelfth Night* and *The Taming of the Shrew*. But, best of all, English-language shows are on offer a few times a year courtesy of two local amateur groups, the Madrid Players and La Madrilera.

It would be easy to dismiss the former as expat ham-drams and frustrated thesps, but they firmly believe there is no such thing as an 'amateur performance' – especially for paying audiences. The **Madrid Players** (www.madridplayers.blogspot.com), with about 100 members of various nationalities, have been going for almost 50 years and now regularly perform in some of Madrid's better-known fringe venues, such as Teatro Triángulo. The staple earner, however, is the colourful, uproarious Christmas panto, which most years attracts total audiences of more than 2,000, many of them Spaniards.

Serious drama also has its place: recent seasons have seen performances of Alan Ayckbourn, Samuel Beckett,

Madrid Players.

Thornton Wilder, Michael Christofer, Chekhov and Shakespeare. Some members have worked professionally, others have not, but enthusiasm and sheer hard work ensure high standards. This fact has not been lost on the media; the group has featured several times in major dailies and has even made the national news on more than one occasion. It's worth pointing out that the idea of panto doesn't exist in Spain, and what local viewers make of a painted dame and several blokes in tights is anybody's guess.

Malasaña-based cultural association **La Madrilera** (www.lamadrilera.com) is a less formalised affair, but also puts on productions in English (as well as Spanish), and runs acting courses.

ARTS & ENTERTAINMENT

Propellor Company.

Sport & Fitness

From golf to Galácticos.

It has been a good few years for Spanish football, with Spain winning its first UEFA World Cup in 2010, as well as the European Championship in 2008 and 2012. The World Cup squad, although dominated by Barça players, included several Real Madrid stars, and the win was marked by night-long celebrations in this football-mad city. But the city's sporting scene is about more than just the beautiful game; Madrid is home to two of Spain's top basketball clubs, hosts one of Europe's most prestigious marathons, and is the setting for the finish of the famous Vuelta a España cycling race. The city is also now on the Tennis Masters circuit, held in the purpose-built, avant-garde Caja Mágica arena. Madrid failed in both its 2012 and 2016 Olympic bids, but is hoping to be more successful in its bid for the 2020 Olympics, which has led to the construction of new sports facilities in the city. Despite the summertime heat, *madrileños* are an active bunch. Head to the Parque del Canal de Isabel II to witness locals jogging, or playing football, golf or *padel* tennis – as with everything else in life, *madrileños* like to make keeping fit a sociable affair.

SPECTATOR SPORTS

Athletics/atletismo

Estadio Olímpico de Madrid
Avda de Arcentales s/n, Eastern suburbs.
Metro Las Musas.
This stadium, better known locally as Estadio La Peineta, was the centrepiece of Madrid's 2012 and 2016 Olympic bids, but after these failed, the city reached an agreement with Atlético de Madrid, who will be taking over the stadium from 2015. It is currently being renovated and expanded, and will eventually accommodate 75,000 spectators. In return, the city council will redevelop the area occupied by the *rojiblancos'* current ground, the Vicente Calderón, on the banks of the Manzanares river.

Maratón de Rock 'n' Roll Madrid
Information: MAPOMA, C/Galileo 74, Chamberí
(91 954 03 89, www.maratonmadrid.org).
Open 10am-2pm, 4.30-7.30pm Mon-Fri.
Map p307 F6.
Madrid's marathon, which is always held on a Sunday in late April, has grown year on year both in the number of participants and in prestige, and is now considered to be among the world's top ten. Since 2011, it has also been part of the international Rock 'n' Roll series, with live bands performing every mile or so to keep the runners motivated. The halfway mark is in the dead centre of the city; thousands of cheery folk collect in Puerta del Sol to egg on the tiring runners; an estimated one million spectators take to the city streets to catch the race. A week or two earlier there is a 20km race organised by Agrupación Deportiva Marathon (91 402 69 62, www.admarathon.es).

Palacio de Deportes de la Comunidad de Madrid
Avda Felipe II s/n, Salamanca (91 444 99 49,
www.palaciodedeportes.com). Metro Goya.
Map p309 O9.
This state-of-the-art 16,000-capacity sports venue was inaugurated in early 2005 and occupies the site where its predecessor stood until it was destroyed by fire four years previously. It is a multi-purpose arena that can host a wide range of indoor sports thanks to a system of retractable stands. As well as sports, you can catch spectacles such as *Disney on Ice* or any number of big-name concerts: Lady Gaga, Rihanna and J-Lo have all performed here.

Basketball/baloncesto

Basketball is Spain's second most popular sport, and Madrid has two of the country's top teams: **Estudiantes** is the city's best-supported club, while **Real Madrid**, affiliated to the football club of the same name, is traditionally the more successful. Both teams regularly qualify for the all-important league play-offs that run in May to eventually decide the national champions.

CB Estudiantes

Madrid Arena, Avda de Portugal s/n, Casa de Campo (91 722 04 00, www.madridarena. org). Metro Alto de Extremadura or Lago. **Map** p310 A11/12.

Since the beginning of the 2005-06 season, 'El Estu' has made the city council-owned Madrid Arena its home. The less successful of Madrid's clubs, Estudiantes nevertheless has passionate supporters. Among them, the most vociferous are a group known as 'La Demencia' who make for a great atmosphere home or away. You can order tickets (€10-€60) at www.clubestudiantes.com or through FNAC (www.fnac.es) or Marca Entradas (www.marcaentradas.com). Alternatively, buy tickets in person by visiting the club's student team venue, the Polideportivo Antonio Magariños (C/Serrano 127, 90 240 00 02, open 10am-2pm, 4-7pm Mon-Fri).

Real Madrid Baloncesto

Caja Mágica, C/Camino de Perales s/n, Parque Lineal de Manzanares, San Fermín (91 722 04 00, www.realmadrid.com). Metro San Fermín-Orcasur. **Tickets** €10-€75.

Real Madrid's hoop stars have a trophy record to match that of the football team, and after a few years in the doldrums look set to return to the top. The team lost its previous home when former club president Florentino Pérez sold the land to pay off the football team's huge debts, but since 2010 the team has had an official new home in the handsome Caja Mágica (*see p223*). Expect goals galore and exuberant professional cheerleaders.

Cycling/ciclismo

La Vuelta a España (www.lavuelta.com) is an enormous deal in the cycling world, with the best international cyclists competing with a ferocity and determination only surpassed by their efforts in the Tour de France. La Vuelta finishes in Madrid, where a knowledgeable crowd awaits the arrival of the time-triallers.

Football/fútbol

Madrid has four main clubs, the world-famous **Real Madrid** (known as 'El Madrid'), the sometimes-successful **Atlético de Madrid**

('El Atleti') and the modest **Rayo Vallecano** and **Getafe** clubs. While Real Madrid has historically been Spain's and Europe's most successful club, boasting a dazzling collection of silverware, the team has not won the Champions League since 2002 – despite lavish spending on a new generation of 'Galácticos', including Cristiano Ronaldo and the Brazilian Kaká. In 2013, Real Madrid reached the Champions League semi-final before being knocked out by Borussia Dortmund.

While El Atleti may not be considered among Europe's elite teams, it overshadowed Real Madrid in 2010 by winning the Europa League (and won the UEFA Super Cup in the same year, and again in 2012). Getafe has also had some glory in recent years, reaching the final of the Copa del Rey for the first time in its history in 2007, then repeating the feat the following year. Since promotion in 2004, it has also become a mainstay in the Primera Liga.

League matches are played on Saturday or Sunday evenings, from September to May or June; at least one of the teams plays in Madrid every weekend. Cup and European matches are held during the week. Tickets can be very hard to come by, especially for Real Madrid games; if you can't get one at the ticket office, you might have to resort to buying a *'reventa'* ('resale') from one of the touts outside the ground. For shirts and various bits of fan-junk, head to the Adidas shops in the stadium or at C/Carmen 3, or shop online. Atlético's shop, 1903 Football Megastore, is housed in the stadium.

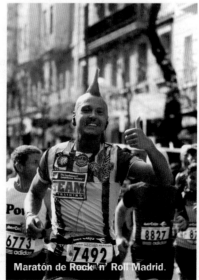

Maratón de Rock 'n' Roll Madrid.

Real Madrid's Estadio Bernabéu

Good coverage of Spanish football can be found weekly in Sid Lowe's column at www.guardian.co.uk/football.

Atlético de Madrid

Estadio Vicente Calderón, Paseo Virgen del Puerto 67, South of centre (91 366 47 07, shop 91 366 82 37, www.clubatleticodemadrid. com). Metro Pirámides. **Open** *Ticket office* 10am-2pm, 5-8pm day before match; from 11am till kick-off on match days. **Tickets** €20-€80. **Credit** MC, V.

Now back in the first division, 'El Atleti' won the UEFA Europa League in 2010, defeating Fulham in the final and overshadowing arch-rivals Real Madrid. The star player of the squad is currently the Colombian Radamel Falcao García Zarate, known as 'El Tigre'. The loyal '*rojiblanco*' faithful create a vibrant atmosphere in the 57,000-capacity Calderón stadium, and although the football itself can often leave more than a little to be desired, it is not uncommon for tickets to sell out entirely. When available, tickets can now be bought via the website or by phone (902 530 500). There's also a museum, located near Gate 23 (91 365 09 31, open 11am-7pm Tue-Sun, admission €3-€6, €5-€10 with a tour of the stadium included).

Getafe CF

Avda Teresa de Calcuta s/n, Getafe (91 695 49 63, www.getafecf.com). Metro Los Espartales. **Open** 10am-1.30pm, 5-8.30pm Mon-Fri in weeks before home games; 11am-half time match days. **Tickets** €40-€80. **No credit cards.**

With the current name dating only from 1983, after the merger of two locally based regional league clubs, Getafe CF reached the top flight for the first time in 2004. Against all expectations, not only has the '*azulón*' stayed there but, under the management of Luis García Plaza, it's also looking ever more like solid upper-mid table material, able to mix it with the best – although the team is having a hard time replicating its 2009-10 form when it finished sixth in La Liga. Getting tickets for the 14,000-capacity stadium isn't usually a problem as the fan base is relatively small, but it may be problematic when one of the bigger teams is visiting.

Real Madrid

Estadio Santiago Bernabéu, Paseo de la Castellana 144, Chamartín (91 398 43 00, www.realmadrid. com). Metro Santiago Bernabéu. **Open** (guided tours) 10am-7.30pm Mon-Sat; 10.30am-6.30pm Sun; tours close 5hrs before kick-off on match days. **Tickets** *Stadium tours* €19. *Match tickets* €65-€260. **Credit** AmEx, DC, MC, V.

After a few years blighted by infighting and power struggles, the Whites are thriving under the leadership of coach José Mourinho, although he has hinted he may be ready to move on at the end of the 2013 season after the team lost to Borussia Dortmund in the Champions League semi-final, having knocked out Manchester United in an earlier round. Tickets can be purchased online or at the stadium's ticket offices, but getting hold of one can be extremely difficult as 90% of tickets are taken up by club members. For more information on stadium tours, visit the Real Madrid website.

Motorsport

Circuito del Jarama
Ctra de Burgos (A-I), km 27, San Sebastián de los Reyes (91 657 08 75, www.jarama.org). Bus 171 from Plaza de Castilla to Ciudad Santo Domingo.
The last time the Jarama track hosted a Formula One race was way back in 1981, but it still has a full calendar of motorbike and truck racing.

Tennis

Caja Mágica
C/Camino de Perales s/n, Parque Lineal de Manzanares, San Fermín (91 718 55 62, www.madridcajamagica.com). Metro San Fermín-Orcasur.
The newest venue for top-level tennis, La Caja Mágica ('Magic Box') opened to much fanfare in 2008, replacing the Madrid Arena as the host venue for the Madrid Masters, the most prestigious event in the Spanish tennis calendar. Its retractable roofs are its most celebrated feature.

ACTIVE SPORTS
Bowling/boleras

Bowling Chamartín
Área recreativa, Estación de Chamartín, C/Agustín de Foxá (91 315 71 19, www.bowlingchamartin.com). Metro Chamartín.
Open 10am-12.30am daily. **Admission** (incl shoe hire) €3-€5. **No credit cards.**
This colourful 20-lane alley with neon-lit bar is the city's most central. It gets crowded on Saturdays. Prices rise after 5pm; university students can get a special deal on Friday afternoons.

Climbing

Indiana Parque Recreativo Natural
Apdo Correos 32, San Martín de Valdeiglesias (91 861 27 99, 663 871 143, www.indiana-sl.com). By bus 551 from Estación Príncipe Pío/by car A-5 then M501 (58.5km). **No credit cards.**

It may be a long schlep out of town, but this huge adventure park offers masses of activities, including climbing, archery and canoeing. Test your climbing skills on the popular adventure circuit through the trees, with rope bridges and zipwires.

Football/fútbol

FC Británico de Madrid
Originally made up of British expats, this men's football team, founded in 1972, is now multinational and plays against Spanish teams at weekends. They're always open to new players; if you're in Madrid for a while and want to get involved, training sessions start at 8.45pm on Wednesdays at Polideportivo Barrio del Pilar (Avenida de Monforte de Lemos 13, Northern Suburbs). For more information, call 91 234 33 87 or visit http://fcbritanico.com.

Golf

Golf clubs around Madrid tend to be exclusive, and expensive, affairs. A full list of all courses in the region is available on the website of the Federación de Golf de Madrid (www.fedgolfmadrid.com). Click on 'Campos' on the home page and choose from the options that appear.

Club de Campo Villa de Madrid
Ctra de Castilla, km 2 (91 550 20 10, www.clubvillademadrid.com). Bus 160 or 161 from Moncloa. **Open** *Sept-June* 9am-6pm Mon-Fri; 8.15am-6pm Sat. *July, Aug* 8.15am-9pm Mon-Sat. **Rates** *Mon-Fri* €17 club entry, plus €60.30 course fee. *Sat* €35 club entry, plus €75-€105 course fee. **No credit cards.**
Co-designed by Seve Ballesteros, this is considered the best and most difficult course near Madrid. As well as golf, there are squash and tennis courts, clay pigeon and range shooting, plus hockey pitches, polo facilities, horse riding and a pool. It can get crowded at weekends, with priority given to members.

Horse riding/hípica

Las Palomas
Club Hípico, Ctra de Colmenar Viejo, km 28.9 (91 127 21 28, mobile 670 972 150, http://personaltelefonica.terra.es/web/chlaspalomas). Bus 721, 724, 725, 726 from Plaza de Castilla. **Open** 5-8pm Mon-Fri; 10am-2pm, 5-7pm Sat, Sun. **No credit cards.**
Riding courses for all levels (€19 for a single one-hour lesson, €160 for ten lessons). Lessons are available in English on request.

Skiing

Before heading off to the ski resorts out of town, *madrileños* like to practise at the vast Xanadú indoor ski centre outside Madrid. *See also p178.*

ARTS & ENTERTAINMENT

Squash

Castellana Sports Club
Plaza Estación Chamartín (91 733 88 98, www. castellanasportsclub.com). Metro Estación de Chamartín. **Open** 6.30am-11pm Mon-Fri; 9am-10pm Sat; 9am-9pm Sun. **No credit cards.**
A fully equipped gym with seven squash courts. You can try the gym out for a day for free.

Swimming pools/piscinas

There are many open-air swimming pools in Madrid: see the 'Deportes' section of the website www.madrid.es or pick up a leaflet at any municipally run sports centre. The most accessible are listed below. There's also a popular rooftop pool at the **Hotel Emperador** (*see p157*), which non-guests can use for a fee (€33 Mon-Fri, €44 Sat & Sun). For Madrid's waterparks, *see p177*.

Open-air municipal pools
Piscinas Casa de Campo, Avda del Ángel s/n, Casa de Campo (91 463 00 50). Metro Lago. **Open** 11am-8.30pm daily. Closed Oct-May. **Admission** €5. **No credit cards.**
Landlocked Madrid gets stiflingly hot during the summer months, so at weekends half the city seems to turn up at this beautiful leafy complex with three open-air pools set in green meadows (expect queues on midsummer weekends). Topless bathing is tolerated and there's an informal gay area. Of the other municipal pools, the Francos Rodríguez has a beach volleyball court, and the Barrio del Pilar and La Elipa have nude sunbathing areas; the latter has water chutes. All have the same prices, but you should check the opening hours in advance at www.madrid.es/deportes.
Other pools Barrio del Pilar, C/Monforte de Lemos 13-15, Northern suburbs (91 314 79 43); Concepción, C/José del Hierro, Eastern suburbs (91 403 90 20); Francos Rodríguez, C/Numancia 1, Tetuán (91 459 98 71); Moratalaz, C/Valdebernardo s/n, Eastern suburbs (91 772 71 21).

Centro Deportivo Municipal del Canal de Isabel II
Avda Filipinas 54, Chamberí (91 533 17 91, www.cyii.es). Metro Canal or Rios Rosas. **Open** *Swimming pool* late May-early Sept 8am-10pm daily. **Admission** *Swimming pool* €5.50. **No credit cards.**
This long-established sports club features olympic-sized and children's swimming pools, tennis and basketball courts, and a bar and restaurant, all with good wheelchair access. The place can get very crowded on summer weekends. It also hosts a variety of competitive sports teams. Just over the road is the popular Parque del Canal de Isabel II outdoor sports complex.

Tennis

Tennis in Spain is accessible and reasonably priced, with numerous council-run clay and tarmac courts for hire. At municipal *polideportivos*, €6.90 gets you a court for an hour. The best city-run complex is the **Tenis Casa de Campo** in the Casa de Campo, close to the boating lake (91 464 96 17), which boasts 15 floodlit courts. The **Barrio del Pilar**, **Concepción** and **La Elipa** swimming pools (for all, *see left*) also have tennis courts, as does the **Canal de Isabel II** (*see p225*; book in advance).

The growing sport of *pádel* tennis (a kind of tennis/squash hybrid) is very popular in Spain; courts can be found around the city, including at the **Parque del Canal de Isabel II** (*see p225*).

FITNESS

Madrid has almost 70 city-owned and -run sports centres. For details, see www.madrid.es: click on 'Deportes', then 'centros deportivos municipals'. Otherwise, pick up a leaflet at any of the centres for information about other venues. Some are more basic than others, though the entrance fees are the same.

Runners should make a beeline for the **Parque del Canal de Isabel II** (*see p225*).

Gyms & sports centres/ gimnasios & polideportivos

Bodhidharma
C/Moratines 18-20, South of centre (91 517 45 28, www.bodhidharma-gym.com). Metro Acacias or Embajadores. **Open** *Sept-July* 8am-11pm Mon-Fri; 9am-2pm, 6-10pm Sat; 10am-3pm Sun. *Aug* 8am-11pm Mon-Fri; 9am-2pm Sat. **Rates** €66 per mth. **Credit** MC, V.
Bodhidharma is a well-equipped health club for men and women, with a sauna, free weights, machines and aerobics classes.

Centro Deportivo Municipal La Chopera
Calle Alfonso XII 48, Parque del Retiro (91 420 11 54). Metro Atocha or Retiro. **Open** 8.30am-9.30pm Mon-Fri; 9am-9pm Sat, Sun. Closed Aug. **Admission** varies. **Map** p313 L12/13.
Shaded by the trees of the Retiro park, La Chopera is a fine place to play tennis and five-a-side football (*fútbol sala*).

Paidesport Center
Parque de Ocio Barrio Art Decó, C/Sepúlveda 3-5, Virgen del Puerto, South of centre (91 470 00 00, www.paidesport.com). Metro Puerta del Ángel. **Open** *Sept-July* 9am-11pm Mon-Fri;

10am-8pm Sat; 10am-3pm Sun. *Aug* 9am-11pm Mon-Fri, Sun; 10am-3pm Sat. **Admission** *Squash* €15 per hr. *Swimming pool* varies. **No credit cards**.

A slick, privately run complex down near the river, open to non-members and generally rammed with earnest hardbodies pumping iron. It has racket courts, an open-air pool, a gym and weights room and an indoor sports hall. There are several other branches around the city; see website for details.

★ Parque del Canal de Isabel II

Entrance on Avda de las Islas Filipinas, Chamberí (91 533 17 91). Metro Canal or Ríos Rosas. **Open** 8am-10pm daily.

This lovely outdoor sports complex and park – located between Avenida de las Islas Filipinas, Calle de Santander and the Paseo de San Francisco de Sales – consists of a 1.5km running track and pedestrian pathway, a golf course, two football pitches and eight *pádel* courts, as well as a gym, tennis courts and outdoor pools. It is beautifully landscaped with lavender, rose bushes, cypress trees, water fountains, benches and shaded areas, and there's a great vibe on summer evenings when the park buzzes with runners, old folk on their evening strolls, families and more serious sporty types. Officially called the Centro de Ocio y Deportes Tercer Depósito del Canal de Isabel II, it's referred to by locals as simply Parque del Canal, or increasingly Parque Green Canal.

Yoga

Ashtanga Yoga

C/Juanelo 12, Lavapiés (91 369 00 33, www. ashtangayogamadrid.com). Metro Tirso de Molina. **Open** *Guided classes* 7pm Mon-Fri, Sun; 11am Sat. *Mysore self-practice* 8-10am, 8-10pm Mon, Tue, Thur; 8-10am Wed, Fri. **Admission** *1 class* €15. See website for deals. **Map** p311 G13.

An attractive Ashtanga studio. The guided classes are suitable for all levels, through a combination of instruction and Mysore-style (self-practice).

City Yoga

C/Artistas 43, Tetuán (91 553 47 51, www.city-yoga.com). Metro Cuatro Caminos or Nuevos Ministerios. **Open** See website for times of individual classes. **Admission** *1 class* €15 (joining fee €30); *3-month course* €240.

This large centre offers a range of classes, covering different styles. Pilates classes are also held.

DISABLED FACILITIES

The city sports authorities are slowly adapting their centres to allow full access for disabled users. The majority of indoor pools have been adapted, and many outdoor pools have ramps and full-access changing rooms. Those at Casa de Campo and Concepción (for both, *see p224*) have the best disabled facilities.

Bath Time

Get steamy at Madrid's finest hammam.

As work hours increase and the siesta diminishes, *madrileños* are turning to spas and alternative therapies with increasing frequency. The shining star of the city's current health and relaxation infatuation is the **Hammam Al Andalus**. An instant hit with locals from the minute the doors opened, the baths are still so popular that you sometimes need to call weeks in advance for a weekend booking. They are an oasis of calm, located just minutes from the bustling Puerta del Sol. A series of pools span out beneath arched ceilings, half-lit by flickering lamps. One shallow pool of warm water abuts another of hot water, with a deeper pool of cold water nearby for a chilly plunge.

The company behind the hammam, El Grupo Al Andalus, focuses on historic authenticity. Masons from Andalucía were hired to lay the stone floors, which replicate the streets of Granada's Albaicín (Moorish quarter). The mosaic walls at the entrance are designed in the red, blue and green tiles found in the Alhambra. Upstairs, a café/restaurant, La Colina de Almanzora, specialises in historic Arabic food.

Enthusiasts claim that the hammam provides relief for almost any ailment, from the common cold to arthritis and hangovers. The heat improves circulation, eliminates toxins and keeps the skin clean and supple. Most people feel suitably energised and refreshed after a visit, though for even deeper relaxation you can always book a 15-minute massage.

Hammam Al Andalus

C/Atocha 14 (91 429 90 20, www. hammamalandalus.com). Metro Sol or Tirso de Molina. **Open** 10am-2am (last entry midnight) daily. **Admission** *Baths* €30. *Baths & massage* €43-€73; before 4pm Mon-Fri €33; €31.50 reductions. **Credit** AmEx, DC, MC, V. **Map** p311 G12.

Escapes & Excursions

Escapes & Excursions

Head for the hills.

It's a tough call. Spend the entire long weekend in Madrid in order to fit in all three of the mandatory museums? Or take advantage of one of the city's extraordinary day trips? Three words: change your ticket. Because you'll want to do both. In summer, the cool mountain air of the sierras beckons, along with excellent hiking and some of the best campsites anywhere. In winter, what better than to hole up in a traditional *mesón* in the stately cities of Toledo or Segovia, with red wine, a log fire and some suckling pig? Year round, the palaces, monasteries and gardens at Aranjuez, La Granja, Riofrío and El Escorial make for a compelling visit.

The areas to the north and west of Madrid have the most spectacular landscapes, following the three main sierra ranges. The less dramatic country to the south and east – where dry tableland, tufty hillocks and fertile river basins gently intermingle – is full of fascinating towns.

ESCAPES & EXCURSIONS

GETTING THERE

By car

'National' roads, such as those formerly known as N-I and N-II, became A-1 and A-2 a few years back, except on toll paying roads (*peajes*), where the prefix is now AP. The six notorious major roads, numbered A-1 to A-6, can all be reached from the M-30 or the outlying M-40 ring road. The A-1 (Carretera de Burgos) leads to eastern Guadarrama and Sierra Pobre, the A-2 Barcelona road goes to Alcalá de Henares, and the A-3 Valencia road to Chinchón. The A-42 (formerly N-401) to Toledo can be reached from the M-30 or the A-4. The A-6 La Coruña road leads to El Escorial, Segovia, Ávila and Salamanca.

Expect bottlenecks at weekends, especially for the return trip on Sunday evenings: streets can be gridlocked until midnight. Traffic jams and accidents are also depressingly predictable during long holiday weekends (*puentes*). Don't even think about driving at the beginning or end of August, particularly on the A-3 Valencia road. For more on driving and car hire, *see pp278-281*.

By bus

Within the city, details of bus services are available by calling 012 (or 91 580 42 60 from outside Madrid), and you can get also get information from tourist offices and on the regional transport website – visit www.ctm-madrid.es. A large number of buses depart from Estación Sur de Autobuses (C/Méndez Álvaro, 91 468 42 00, www.estacionautobuses madrid.com, Metro Méndez Alvaro), but there are also five major interchange terminals (*intercambiadores*), where municipal bus services, regional bus services and Metro lines all converge. The Plaza de Castilla terminal, straddling Tetuán and Chamartín, serves destinations to the north west; the subterranean bus terminal at Moncloa in Chamberí feeds destinations mostly to the south and west of Madrid; the Avenida de America terminus serves the airport and destinations to the north east; the Príncipe Pío interchange handles over 20 interurban bus routes; while from the Plaza Elíptica station in the south of the city, you can catch buses to Toledo, among other destinations.

By train

The system of local trains (*cercanías*) runs to many interesting towns around Madrid: Alcalá de Henares, Aranjuez, El Escorial, Cercedilla and many more. The ageing but efficient single gauge extension line, the scenic C-9, wends its

Escapes & Excursions

© Copyright Time Out Group 2013

way up from Cercedilla through mountain pinewoods to Cotos, which adjoins ski slopes and a glacial lake. Services to other destinations leave from main-line stations Chamartín and Atocha, though many trains also stop between them at Nuevos Ministerios and Recoletos stations. It's also worth noting that the high-speed AVE and Talgo trains, from Atocha to Seville and Córdoba respectively, make a weekend or even a day trip to Andalucía a distinct possibility.

RENFE information

902 32 03 20, www.renfe.com. **Open** *Information* 24hrs. *Reservations* 5am-11.40pm daily. **Credit** AmEx, DC, MC, V.

RENFE central sales office

C/Alcalá 44, Huertas & Santa Ana (no phone). Metro Banco de España. **Open** 9.30am-8pm Mon-Fri. **Credit** AmEx, DC, MC, V. **Map** p312 H11.

Information and tickets for the AVE, Talgo and all other RENFE long-distance services are available from this office. It does not handle phone enquiries, which go through the central number above.

North & West

ÁVILA

It's an impressive sight; a forbidding stronghold encircled by thick 11th-century walls rising out of a boulder-strewn landscape. It is also the highest provincial capital in the country, with bitterly cold winters.

Despite its elegant buildings and well-to-do feel, there is something slightly sinister about Ávila's fortressed isolation; plaques around town celebrate Franco's victories and point out that this was the birthplace of Isabel 'la Católica' – the most powerful and merciless woman in the history of Spain. Proverbially a town of *cantos y santos* (stones and saints), it was also home to Spain's greatest mystic, Santa Teresa, the 16th-century religious reformer who founded 18 convents and revolutionised Catholicism, while living a life of spartan self-denial.

As well as a statue in the town centre, there are countless other reminders of her presence. The Baroque **Convento de Santa Teresa** (Plaza de la Santa 2, 920 21 10 30, admission free, museum €2, closed Mon) stands on the plot of the house in which she was born, while the nearby Convento de San José contains the **Museo Teresiano de Carmelitas Descalzas** (C/Madres 4, 920 22 21 27, admission €1.40) where you can see her manuscripts and relics. General Franco is said to have kept the saint's mummified arm by his bedside in his final years.

The medieval city is a timewarp of cobbled lanes, sleepy squares, family mansions and stately religious buildings. The highlight is undoubtedly the stark fortified 12th-century **cathedral** (Plaza de la Catedral 8, 920 21 16 41, admission €4), embedded in the city walls and rebuilt over the ages in Romanesque, Gothic and Renaissance styles. The **Basílica de San Vicente** (Plaza de San Vicente 6, 920 25 52 30, admission €2 Mon-Sat, free Sun and under-13s), located outside the walls, is a similar hybrid of styles. Built on the spot where St Vincent and his two sisters were martyred in the fourth century, it has gruesome scenes of their torture depicted in relief around Vicente's tomb. Nearby stand the Romanesque church of **San Andrés** and the palatial but melancholy 15th-century Gothic **Santo Tomás monastery**, containing the alabaster tomb of Ferdinand and Isabella's only son and heir, Don Juan, who died aged 19.

The city's wonderfully preserved **walls** (920 25 50 88, closed Mon, admission €5, €3.50 reductions), which were built after the knights had rid the city of the Moors, extend for one and a half miles and have nine gates and 88 watchtowers. For the best views go across the River Adaja to **Los Cuatro Postes**, a small Doric-columned monument perched on a knoll west of the city. The walls can be climbed at the Puerta del Alcázar just south of the cathedral and Puerta de San Vicente to the north.

Where to stay & eat

Among the major culinary delights to be found in Ávila are large steaks (*chuletones de Ávila*) from the fighting Iberian strain of black bulls, and delicious haricot beans (*judías* or *alubias*) from Barco de Ávila. Look out too for *cocido morañego*, a local variant on Madrid's famed winter stew; Ávila's own Castilian version of gazpacho, using fresh vegetables from the Tiétar Valley; roast lamb (*cordero asado*) and suckling pig (*lechona*). *Yemas de Santa Teresa* – rich sweets made from egg yolks and said to have been originally created by the saint herself in one of her rare moments of indulgence – are another of Ávila's specialities.

A good place to try them is the charming **Mesón del Rastro** (Plaza del Rastro 1, 920 21 12 19, mains €18-€22, set lunch €13-€24), which has all the trimmings of a traditional Castilian tavern (boars' heads, log fires and so on) without the traditionally high prices. **El Rincón** (Plaza de Zurraquín 3-4, 920 35 10 44, restaurant closed Mon & Feb, mains €10-€15, set lunch €10.50-€12.80) is another serving the same food as everywhere else, but at lower prices. **La Alcazaba** (Plaza Mosén Rubí 3, 920 25 62 90, closed 2wks Jan, mains €12-€22.90) is more creative – try monkfish in garlic and cream.

Many of the town's hotels are located in converted mansions and Renaissance palaces. The delightful **Parador Raimundo de Borgoña** (C/Marqués de Canales de Chozas 2, 920 21 13 40, www.parador.es, doubles €90-€140) serves an exceptional breakfast, available to non-residents as well as guests. **Palacio de Valderrábanos** (Plaza de la Catedral 9, 920 21 10 23, www.palaciovalderrabanoshotel.com, doubles €75-€125) is a grander hotel located on the plaza with splendid views of the cathedral.

Getting there

By bus

Avanzabus (902 02 00 52, www.avanzabus.com) from Estación Sur (91 468 42 00) runs 12 buses on weekdays, nine buses on weekends. Journey time is 1hr 30mins.

By train

There are 20 trains daily from Chamartín station, 8am-10.30pm. The last train back is at 9.10pm. Journey time is 1hr 15mins-2hrs.

Tourist information

Oficina de Turismo

C/San Segundo 17 (920 21 13 87, www.turismo castillayleon.com). **Open** *Oct-June* 9.30am-2pm, 4-7pm Mon-Sat; 9.30am-5pm Sun. *July-Sept* 9am-8pm daily.

EL ESCORIAL

The grand, austere monastery of San Lorenzo de El Escorial never fails to divide opinion, but is undoubtedly one of the most significant buildings in the history of Spain. Many people see it as the outward manifestation of its founding monarch's mind – Philip II was at once fanatically religious and wildly ambitious, and so his legacy in stone is both spartan and vast. The gloomy building is also symbolic architecturally, and it was the grey slate and spiky turrets of El Escorial that inspired decades of the 'Herreran' style (also known as Castilian baroque). Construction was completed in record time between 1563 and 1574, initially by Juan Bautista de Toledo – who died shortly after work started – and subsequently by Juan de Herrera. Everything here is on a grand scale: the main façade is 200 metres (700 feet) long, the overhead cupola measures 92 metres (302 feet), and there are 15 cloisters, 16km (10 miles) of corridors, 86 stairways, 88 fountains, 1,200 doors and 2,675 windows.

Philip conceived the palace as a mausoleum and contemplative retreat, built as a final resting place for his father, Charles I, and to celebrate the 1557 Spanish victory over the French at St

Quentin on St Lawrence's day (San Lorenzo). It's laid out to resemble the grid-iron on which the saint himself was martyred. The jasper, gold and marble **Panteón de los Reyes**, designed by Gian Battista Crescenzi in the 1620s, contains all but two of the sovereigns who reigned over four centuries (absentees being Philip V, who was buried at La Granja, and Ferdinand VI, whose remains are in Madrid). The Basilica, with its notable *Christ Crucified* in Carrara marble by Benvenuto Cellini, has no fewer than 45 altars.

The main galleries are located on what was the lower floor of Philip's own austere rooms, above the **Basilica**. There is a small jalousie window overlooking the high altar so he could participate in Mass even if he was ill and confined to his surprisingly small bed. His cherished Hieronymous Bosch triptych was just a tiny part of a huge Habsburg art collection that includes celebrated works by Velázquez, Ribera, Alonso Cano and individual masterpieces like El Greco's *Adoration of the Name of Jesus* and Titian's *Last Supper,* concentrated mainly in the museum, church, chapterhouse and the ornate barrel-vaulted library – whose 50,000 volumes rival the Vatican's holdings.

The most refreshing section of El Escorial is the **Palacio de los Borbones**, remodelled by Charles IV in a light neoclassical style that contrasts with the general austerity and gloom. Highlights here are the tapestries designed by Goya and his contemporaries. Guided tours can be arranged on Fridays and Saturdays.

Two other small palaces lie in the spacious gardens and parklands surrounding the monastery, and can be visited with a guided tour: the **Casita del Infante**, and the **Casita del Príncipe** (Prince's House), with paintings by Lucas Jordan and a charming garden. The park is open year-round (10am-6pm Tue-Sun).

Outside the monastery, El Escorial is really two separate towns. Down below, next to the train station, is **El Escorial de Abajo**, and at the top of the hill, alongside the monastery, is the grander **San Lorenzo**. Look out here for Charles III's 18th-century **Real Coliseo** theatre and the parish church of **San Bartolomé**. A couple of kilometres out on the road towards the Casita de Arriba is the **Silla de Felipe**, 'Philip's Seat', from where he used to watch progress on the building.

Real Monasterio de San Lorenzo de El Escorial

91 890 59 03/05, www.patrimonionacional.es. **Open** *Oct-Mar* 10am-6pm Tue-Sun. *Apr-Sept* 10am-8pm Tue-Sun. **Admission** *Monastery* €17 (incl guided tour Palacio de los Borbones & access to Casita del Príncipe & Casita del Infante); €10; €3-€4 reductions. Free Thur (EU citizens only). **No credit cards.**

Where to eat

Fonda Genara (Plaza San Lorenzo 2, 91 890 16 36, www.restaurantegenara.com, set lunch €15-€22, set dinner €25) is a pretty if slightly pricey restaurant with old theatre posters around the walls. **Parrilla Principe** (C/Floridablanca 6, 91 890 16 11, www.parrillaprincipe.com, doubles €40-€80, mains €15-€25, set menu €19) is a small, peaceful 18th-century palace with a hotel on the upper floors and a blend of Castilian and seafood cuisine available in the restaurant below. **Madrid Sevilla** (C/Benavente 1, 91 890 15 19, closed Mon, mains €10-€30, set menu €12.90-€18.90) has simple but reasonably priced food, while **La Chistera** (Plaza Jacinto Benavente 5, 91 890 37 26, closed Mon night, set lunch €7.50-€12, set dinner €14) is principally a tapas bar.

Up above the town in the Monte Abantos district, **Horizontal** (Camino Horizontal, 91 890 38 11, www.restaurantehorizontal.com, closed Tue-Wed dinner Nov-Mar, main courses €16) offers outdoor eating in summer and a seat by the fire in winter.

Where to stay

Designed by Herrera, the **Hotel Victoria Palace** (C/Juan de Toledo 4, 91 896 98 90, www.nh-hotels.com, doubles €61-€130) is an exquisite hotel with a charming garden just a couple of hundred yards from the monastery. **El Botánico** (C/Timoteo Padrós 16, 91 890 78 79, www.botanicohotel.com, doubles €88-€143) is a beautifully renovated summer house with a library, gardens and fine views of the monastery. A little cheaper, and right in the heart of San Lorenzo, the **Hotel Miranda & Suizo** (C/Floridablanca 18-20, 91 890 47 11, www.hotelmirandasuizo.com, doubles €50-€85) has reasonably appointed rooms looking out over the monastery and a bustling café.

Getting there

By bus
Herranz (91 890 41 00, www.autocaresherranz.com) buses 661 and 664 run from the Moncloa interchange (journey time 55mins), every 15-30mins 7am-11.30pm Mon-Fri, every 30-60mins 10am-10.15pm Sat, 8.45am-11pm Sun. Last return is at 10.30pm Mon-Fri, 9pm Sat, 10pm Sun.

By train
Cercanías from Atocha station (www.renfe.es). 27 trains daily Mon-Fri; hourly trains Sat, Sun. Trains run to El Escorial town, from where it's a 2km (1.25-mile) walk or bus ride uphill to San Lorenzo and the monastery.

Tourist information

Oficina de Turismo
C/Grimaldi 2 (91 890 53 13, www.sanlorenzo turismo.org). **Open** 10am-2pm, 3-6pm Tue-Sat; 10am-2pm Sun.

El Valle de los Caídos.

EL VALLE DE LOS CAÍDOS

Built between 1940 and 1959 by Civil War prisoners of the defeated Republican army, Franco's giant mausoleum, the 'Valley of the Fallen' (the fallen on Franco's side, at least) stands in a forested valley a few miles from El Escorial. It was the *generalísimo*'s grand project, and its stark, grandiose, authoritarian style is worthy of the likes of Mussolini or Ceaucescu. It is easily spotted from up to 50km (31 miles) away by a huge 150-metre (500-foot) high cross (said to weigh over 180,000 tons) which itself is placed 150 metres above the main esplanade.The monument was completed at great financial and human cost and many Republicans perished while quarrying the dense granite rock needed to build it. Ironically, and to the grief of their families, many of the Republican prisoners' bodies probably now lie side by side with those of their oppressors.

Like it or loathe it, its cold, atmospherically lit underground chambers, lined with eerie cowled figures, do exert a certain mesmerising aura. The mausoleum is basically a huge tunnel, driven 260 metres (867 feet) into the granite rock. At its entrance are 16th-century monoliths, 12 metres (40 feet) high, while deep in the interior you can see bright-coloured tapestries of the *Apocalypse of St John*; a cupola decorated with mosaics showing heaven-bound saints and martyrs of Spain, and an altar-bound polychrome wooden sculpture of Christ crucified. It contains a subterranean church, an ossuary of six chapels bearing the remains of Civil War dead and the tombs of two men – Franco himself and José Antonio Primo de Rivera, the rich young founder of the Falange who died in the early phases of the Civil War, thus conveniently leaving El Caudillo from El Ferrol unchallenged as leader. Both have fresh flowers placed on their graves daily, paid for by the state, to the disgust of most (though by no means all) of the Spanish population. The views are quite staggering, especially from the base of the cross, reached via a funicular (closed at the time of writing).

El Valle de los Caídos

91 890 56 11, www.patrimonionacional.es.
Open *Oct-Mar* 10am-5pm Tue-Sun. *Apr-Sept* 10am-6pm Tue-Sun. **Admission** €5; €2.50 reductions; Wed pm & Thur free for EU & Latin American citizens. **Credit** MC, V.

Getting there

By bus

Herranz (91 890 41 22, www.autocaresherranz. com) bus 660 runs hourly from San Lorenzo de El Escorial (*see p231*). Last return at 8.45pm. Journey time 15mins.

SIERRA DE GUADARRAMA

The Guadarrama range runs from El Escorial (*see p231*) in the south-west to Somosierra in the north-east, and separates the two Castilian *mesetas*, or plains: Castile to the north, and La Mancha to the south. For a selection of the many walks possible in the area, visit the information centre in the Plaza de Ayuntamiento in Guadarrama (*see p235*).

Until the 1970s, when a tunnel was built underneath it, the Puerto de Guadarrama pass was the only way out of Madrid to Segovia and Valladolid, and it would often be impassable for days on end in winter. Also known as the Alto de los Leones because of the lion that sits atop a plinth here (the lion is the symbol of the village of Guadarrama), the pass was the scene of bitter fighting during the battle for Madrid during the Civil War, and Hemingway set large parts of *For Whom the Bell Tolls* here. The remains of gun emplacements and bunkers from that era still litter the area.

A dirt road runs from the top of the pass, south-west for 30km (19 miles) to the charming and peaceful village of Peguerinos, from where there are buses and a fully paved road to El Escorial. Along the way there are several opportunities for camping. The track (signposted) veers off to the left from the Guadarrama direction, among a jumble of radio towers and satellite dishes. There is a restaurant called Alto de León on the side of the main road just at the turning. Coming the other way, the track is signposted 'Valle Enmedio'.

Another breathtaking walk, taking around three hours, runs from **Tablada** station. Walk up 2km (1.25 miles) – not all the way to the pass – to a post indicating km.56, and take a forestry track on the right, clearly marked with a stone sign, to the Peña del Arcipreste de Hita (1,527m/ 5,010ft). The track eventually descends again, to reach the station at Cercedilla.

Cercedilla is not an especially picturesque village, but it has managed to retain its own identity despite its popularity in summer, when the population swells from 5,000 to around 40,000. To find it at its most authentic, visit in winter, especially if you want to try any of the longer walks nearby. Additionally, rooms can be very difficult to find in summer. The village sits at the head of a valley that leads up to the **Puerto de la Fuenfría** (1,796m/5,895ft), a pass that in turn forms a route across the Sierra dating back to at least Roman times. Along the way there is a Calzada Romana (Roman Road), which dates back to the first century AD, with two fine Roman bridges still standing at El Descalzo and Enmedio. The pass is also an important junction of carefully developed modern footpaths.

Sierra de Guadarrama. *See p233.*

The most leisurely excursion from Cercedilla is aboard the old-world narrow-gauge *cercanías* line (C-9) that runs through fine scenery up to the Cotos ski station, a charming way to get up to and beyond the **Puerto de Navacerrada**, especially when it's snowing. Alternatively, from the *cercanías* station in Cercedilla, a 45-minute walk up the M-966 (the main road in front of you) will bring you to a stretch of open alpine woodland known as **Las Dehesas**, with an information centre that's an essential port of call for visitors to the valley, with good free maps. Las Dehesas is a very popular picnic spot with natural spring swimming pools – they're only open during summer and freezing even then.

The nearby town of **Navacerrada** is a lively place with a mountain village feel, and several decent restaurants serving appropriately Alpine food (expect to be dipping your bread into lots of raclettes and fondues), making it a fun base.

Where to stay & eat

Camping Valle Enmedio (91 898 31 76, www.vallenmedio.com, closed Mon-Thur mid Sept-June, call for rates), 11km (seven miles) along the track to Peguerinos, is an isolated, idyllic and well-equipped campsite with wooden bungalows, set in a forest. In Peguerinos itself, **La Flor** (C/Espinar 7, 91 898 30 40) is a basic but friendly *pensión* with a small restaurant downstairs. For food, another good bet is the no-frills **Alto del León** (91 854 12 27, mains €13), on the crest of the pass.

Choices are much greater in Cercedilla. **Casa Gómez** (C/Emilio Serrano 32, 91 852 01 46, mains €10-€16, set lunch €12, 1-4.30pm), opposite the railway station, specialises in wild mushrooms and game in season.

As you come out of the station, on the right is **Hostal Longinos – El Aribel** (C/Emilio Serrano 41, 91 852 15 11, www.hostalaribel. com, doubles €50). Make sure you book ahead in summer and at weekends.

In Navacerrada, one of the better hotels is the **Hotel Nava Real** (C/Huertas 1, 91 853 10 00, www.hotelnavareal.com, doubles €70, mains €12), which also has a more imaginative restaurant than most. **Restaurante Casa Paco** (Plaza Doctor Gereda 2, 91 856 05 62, mains €12, closed Wed) has tables outside overlooking the town square.

Getting there

By bus

The Larrea (91 851 55 92, www.autobuseslarrea. com) bus 684 from Moncloa to Cercedilla leaves every 30mins (journey time 50mins-1hr) 6.40am-11.30pm Mon-Fri, hourly 6.30am-11.45pm Sat, Sun. Last return is at 10.20pm. The Larrea bus 691 runs from Madrid to Navacerrada every 30mins, 7am-10.40pm Mon-Fri, hourly 8am-10.30pm Sat, Sun. Last return is at 10.35pm.

By train

For Cercedilla, take the train from Chamartín to Segovia. Trains depart seven times a day 6.16am-11.16pm Mon-Fri, and five times a day

7.15am-10.36pm Sat, Sun; the last train back from Cercedilla leaves at about 10.35pm.

Tourist information

Centro de Interpretación Turística
Plaza del Ayuntamiento, Guadarrama (91 849 47 03). Open June-Aug 9am-8pm daily. *Sept-May* 10am-2pm, 5-8pm Mon, Wed, Fri; 5-8pm Tue, Thur; 10am-2pm Sat, Sun.

Take a Hike

Mountain outings near Madrid.

As Madrid becomes more and more crowded, so its inhabitants have come to rely on escapes to the Guadarrama and Gredos mountain ranges to maintain their sanity. The mountains are within easy reach: whether by car, bus or train, one can soon be up in alpine landscapes, 1,000 metres above sea level. Most villages in the sierras now have some kind of information centre, and simple illustrated guides to a varied range of walks (often signposted) are available. The town hall is also a good place to look for information. Take plenty of water and clothes offering protection from the sun in summer, and warm waterproof gear in winter. Only experienced walkers should try the higher walks in winter. The weather in the mountains is notoriously changeable: check forecasts before you go. Buying food and water in Madrid before setting off is also a good idea.

Skiing around the Madrid region is a hit-and-miss affair. Of the resorts near Madrid, **Valdesquí** (902 88 64 46, www.valdesqui.es) usually has the best (and most) snow. **La Pinilla** (902 87 90 69, www.lapinilla.es) is directly north of Madrid near Riaza; the others are in the central Guadarrama. The only one with any accommodation is **Puerto de Navacerrada** (902 88 23 28, www.puerto navacerrada.com). All-in package trips to these resorts can be booked at any travel agency in Madrid. These ski stations offer limited skiing only and are of little interest to intermediate or advanced skiers, but do make for great day trips out of Madrid. Recorded information (in Spanish only) on snow conditions at ski resorts and out-of-season activities can be found on the Atudem phoneline (91 359 15 57) or check out www.esquiespana.org and www.atudem.org.

VALLE DE LOZOYA

The wide, flat Valle de Lozoya runs north-east from below the pass of Puerto de los Cotos (1,830 metres/6,006 feet), to the main A-1 Burgos road. There is little to detain you in the village of **Rascafría** at the western end of the valley. For the most part, it has been drearily overdeveloped, with one exception – the stunning **Monasterio de Santa María del Paular** (91 869 14 25, daily tours, closed Thur, admission €5) nearby. This Benedictine monastery, a short way south of the village, was founded in 1390 but was still being added to 500 years later. It is still partly occupied by monks, even though most of it is now an unobtrusive Sheraton hotel, and it remains a wonderful sight with its stunning backdrop of snow-capped peaks.

One of the many rewarding walks around here is along the GR-10 pathway from the monastery up to the Puerto de los Cotos, which winds its way through pine forests and a picturesque roe deer habitat. Heading in the other direction, the path runs two kilometres to some natural swimming pools at Las Presillas. In summer, there is a small kiosk there selling drinks. From the town itself, it's also possible to walk across the mountains to the palace of La Granja (*see p236*).

Where to stay & eat

Casa Briscas (Plaza España 13, 91 869 12 26, www.casabriscas.com, mains €16.50, set lunch €10, closed Thur) is undoubtedly the best eating option in Rascafría's main square, and also has a lively terrace area. The 44-room **Santa María del Paular** (91 869 10 11, www. sheratonelpaular.com, doubles €109-€200, mains €20, closed Jan) occupies the former monastery cloister and is delightfully peaceful. **Los Calizos** (Carretera Miraflores-Rascafría km 30.5, 91 869 11 12, www.loscalizos.com, doubles €88 incl breakfast, mains €20) is a stone house by the side of the Lozoya river, a short distance outside town.

Getting there

By bus
To get to Rascafría, take bus 194 (www.ctm-madrid.es), which leaves Madrid from the Plaza Castilla interchange at 10am, 2pm, 6pm Mon-Fri; 8am, 6pm Sat; 8am, 3pm Sun. The last bus back is at 5pm Mon-Fri; 8.30pm Sat; 6.30pm Sun.

By train
For Puerto de los Cotos, hourly from Chamartín in Madrid to Cercedilla, then four trains daily to Cotos. Last return is 5.43pm.

LA GRANJA

This palace, which started life as a hunting
lodge and was later converted by the Bourbons,
is about 11km (seven miles) from Segovia back
towards Madrid on the N-101. It was built on
the site of a former shrine, San Ildefonso, by
Philip V, homesick for his youth in Versailles.
His wife Isabel Farnese also added some
distinctive touches, not least of which are the
fountains. The result is perhaps the loveliest
of all the Bourbon palaces.

Work on the structure was carried out in
record time between 1721 and 1723 by Teodoro
Ardamans, and on the extensive gardens over
a longer period under the main supervision of
René Carlier. Amid all the formal hedgerows,
lawns and rows of trees you'll find voluptuous
statues, limpid pools and the famous fountains,
some of which spring to life three times a week
in the summer and then all of which are turned
on for one memorable evening each year, on
25 August. Water comes from an artificial lake
called El Mar, which is set in a woodland at the
end of the estate and backed by the dramatic
sheer wall of the Peñalara, the highest peak
in the Guadarrama.

The palace itself, which was restored after
a devastating fire in 1918, is an opulent maze
of elegant salons and chambers that abound in
classical frescoes, dazzling cut-glass chandeliers
(made in the palace's own glass factory, which
still functions today) and priceless *objets d'art*.
The tapestry selection, although representing
only a part of the Spanish and Flemish royal
collection, is among the finest you'll see

anywhere. Unfortunately visits are only via
guided tours of up to 45 people at a time.

The charming village of **San Ildefonso**
has long been a favourite resort for escaping
the oppressive Madrid summer heat; if you
have your own transport it offers a relaxing
alternative to staying in Segovia. Among its
imposing private houses is the **Casa de
Infantes**, which was built by Carlos III for
his sons Gabriel and Antonio.

Palacio Real de La Granja de San Ildefonso

921 47 00 19, www.patrimonionacional.es.
Open *Oct-Mar* 10am-5.30pm Tue-Sun. *Apr-
Sept* 10am-7pm Tue-Sun. Fountains operate
Apr-July at 5.30pm Wed, Sat & Sun. **Admission**
Palace €4.50; €5 guided tour; €2.50 reductions.
Wed, Thur free for EU citizens. *Gardens*
free. *Fountains* €3.40; €1.70 reductions.
Credit MC, V.

Where to stay & eat

It's essential to reserve ahead at the wildly
popular **Casa Zaca** (C/Embajadores 6, 921
47 00 87, www.casazaca.com, closed dinner &
Mon, mains €10); it offers home-style cuisine, so
instead of the standard roast lamb or *cochinillo*
there are gutsy casseroles and braised ox tongue.
Alternatively try the tapas, in front of a roaring
fire, at the colourful **La Fundición** (Plaza de
la Calandria 1, 921 47 00 46, closed lunch Tue-
Fri, dinner Sun & all day Mon June-Sept;
closed lunch Fri, dinner Sun & all day Mon-
Thur Oct-May). **Hotel Roma** (C/Guardas 2,

La Granja

Palacio de Riofrío.

921 47 07 52, www.hotelroma.org, doubles
€50-€70, restaurant closed Tue, set lunch €15)
is comfortable enough.

Getting there

By bus
There are around 20 daily buses run by La
Sepulvedana (902 11 96 99, www.lasepulvedana.
com) from the Príncipe Pío interchange in
Madrid to Segovia (journey time 1hr 15mins).
From Segovia there are frequent connecting
buses to La Granja (journey time 20mins).

RIOFRÍO

After the death of Philip V, Isabel Farnese could
not bear to stay on at La Granja with her stepson
Fernando VI, and so had another palace built at
Riofrío. She was to survive Fernando as well,
however, and Riofrío was never completely
finished. Later Alfonso XII came here to mourn
the death of his new bride, Mercedes, and the
whole palace still has a melancholy air, despite
the warm pinks and greens of its exterior.

It was built in the best deer-hunting country
near Madrid, and later sovereigns also came
to this beautiful estate to blast away to their
hearts' content. With this in mind, half the
palace has been turned into a hunting museum
– a mandatory and overlong part of the guided
tour. Unless row after row of antlers and stuffed
animals really rock your boat, it is probably best
admired from outside, particularly with a picnic.

Palacio de Riofrío
921 47 00 19, www.patrimonionacional.es.
Open *Oct-Mar* 10am-6pm Tue-Sun. *Apr-Sept*
10am-8pm Tue-Sun. **Admission** (two days) €9;
€4 reductions. Wed, Thur free for EU citizens.
No credit cards.

Getting there

By train
Segovia trains (*see p239*) stop at La Losa-Navas
de Riofrío, about 2km (1.25 miles) from Riofrío.

SEGOVIA

Segovia combines beautiful architecture with
visual warmth in a region more associated with
austerity. In contrast with the traditional grey
chill of Castile it glows, radiant and mellow.
Make the approach by road across vast plains
and it appears as if by witchcraft, rising on
a burnished hillock like an acropolis or ship
in full sail. The scene is dominated by the
Alcázar fortress, with its sharply angled
ramparts, spiky towers and high gables; a
fantastical fairytale vision.

Impregnably poised on the edge of a hair-
raising abyss into which a negligent 14th-century
nurse once accidentally dropped an heir to the
throne and then flung herself after him to avoid
punishment, it was originally built as a modest
stone fort 200 years earlier, and underwent
radical changes over the centuries. Most of the
world-famous fairy-castle architecture seen today
is a brilliant work of restoration carried out
after a disastrous fire in 1862. Though owned
by the army, the bastion's purpose is now purely
commercial and its chambers are open daily
for the public to inspect the weapons, armour,
tapestries and artworks on display.

Close by is the huge, airy and very light
Gothic **Cathedral de Segovia** (Plaza Mayor,
921 46 22 05, admission €3, free 9.30am-1.15pm
Sun). The current structure was built to replace
a predecessor destroyed in a 1521 revolt. Inside
there's a tiny museum that holds an interesting
collection of tapestries, paintings and a
wonderful 16th-century grandfather clock.

Segovia. *See p237.*

ESCAPES & EXCURSIONS

Very different, but just as extraordinary as the Alcázar, is the 728-metre (2,426-foot) Roman **aqueduct**, made of Guadarrama granite in rough-hewn blocks that mesh perfectly without mortar, although it no longer brings water from the Riofrío as it first did over 2,000 years ago. The **Plaza del Azoguejo** below, where markets are now held, was a rendezvous for thieves and vagabonds in Cervantes' day. Steps rise up the wall at the place where the aqueduct merges into the hill, or you can spiral up the streets channelling traffic up and down. A warren of intricate lanes criss-crosses the old town like a demented spider's web, weaving you past squares, gardens, mansions, palaces and museums. The town is never short of tourists but is still resolutely traditional: in the Plaza Mayor the atmosphere of the past blends with real-life bustle and you can still find plenty of bars and cafés filled only with locals.

Of its dozen or so churches and convents, all built between the 12th and 16th centuries, **San Esteban**, noted for its striking bell tower, and **San Millán**, with its Moorish-influenced decor and elaborately carved wooden ceiling, stand out. Among its secular buildings the **Casa de los Picos**, with waffle-iron studs on its façade, can be found in the shopping streets downhill from the cathedral. Also not to be missed is the **Monastery of El Parral**, founded by Henry VI and now a national monument. One of the best views is from 13th-century **Iglesia de Vera Cruz** built by the Knights Templars with spoils from the Crusades.

Alcázar de Segovia
Plaza de la Reina Victoria Eugenia (921 46 07 59). **Open** *Oct-Mar* 10am-6pm daily. *Apr-Sept* 10am-7pm daily. **Admission** €4.50; €3 reductions. **No credit cards.**

Where to stay & eat

The **Casa Duque** (C/Cervantes 12, 921 46 24 87, www.restauranteduque.es, mains €18) is a long-standing favourite, with colourfully decorated dining rooms on several floors serving excellent Castilian fare. **Restaurante José María** (C/Cronista Lecea 11, 921 46 11 11, mains €15-€25) is a traditionally styled *mesón* serving first-rate *cochinillo* (suckling pig) and probably the best lamb in town. It also has a good tapas bar. **Cuevas de San Esteban** (C/Valdelaguila 15, 921 46 09 82, www.lacuevadesanesteban.com, set lunch €10, mains €12-€18) is another place to avoid the tourist-trap market with reasonably priced Castilian food. For something different, **Narizotas** (Plaza Medina del Campo 1, 921 46 26 79, www.narizotas.net, closed dinner Sun, mains €16, set menu €12.30) has a selection of risottos and salads, as well as the usual parade of roast meats.

The **Acueducto** (C/Padre Claret 10, 921 42 48 00, www.hotelacueducto.com, doubles €110) is a comfortable, established hotel where some of the rooms overlook the Roman aqueduct. Alternatively, try **Las Sirenas** (C/Juan Bravo 30, 921 46 26 63, www.hotelsirenas.com, doubles €45-€75), a homely hotel in the old town near

Segovia

ESCAPES & EXCURSIONS

San Martín church. **Hostal Taray** (Plaza San Facundo 1, 921 46 30 41, www.hostaltaray.com, doubles €30-€40) is useful for those on a budget, while the colourful and recently refurbished **Hotel Condes de Castilla** (C/José Canalejas 5, 921 46 35 29, www.hotelcondesdecastilla.com, doubles €55-€120) is very central.

Getting there

By bus

There are around 20 daily buses run by La Sepulvedana (902 11 96 99, www.lasepulvedana.es) from the Príncipe Pío interchange in Madrid to Segovia (journey time 1hr 15mins).

By train

There are six trains Mon-Fri and four trains Sat, Sun from Chamartín to Segovia, but it's a slow journey (1hr 50mins). Alternatively, you can catch the fast train connecting Madrid and Valladolid, which stops at Segovia on the way. There are ten daily trains and the journey is quicker (30mins) but more expensive.

Tourist information

Oficina de Turismo

Plaza Mayor 10 (921 46 03 34, www.turismo castillayleon.com). **Open** *July, Aug* 9am-3pm, 4-7pm Mon-Fri; 10am-3pm, 4-6.30pm Sat; 9.30am-3pm, 4-6.30pm Sun. *Sept-June* 9am-2pm, 5-8pm daily.

MANZANARES EL REAL & LA PEDRIZA

La Pedriza is a rocky crag crisscrossed with paths. Birthplace of the Manzanares river, it is home to the Sierra's biggest colony of griffon vultures, protected in the Parque Regional de la Cuenca Alta del Manzanares. The area fills up on Sundays, but don't be fooled – many experienced climbers still get lost in La Pedriza, and fatalities have been known. The starting point for a hike is the town of **Manzanares el Real**, dominated by the almost cartoonish vision of a perfect 'Spanish' castle, the 15th-century **Castillo de Manzanares el Real**, once the stronghold of the Mendozas, one of the most powerful aristocratic clans of medieval Castile. Much of its interior is the product of recent restoration work, but the castle still retains a fascinating mix of late Gothic and Mudéjar features, especially in the courtyard and the beautiful upper gallery, which has a spectacular view over the valley.

Castillo de Manzanares el Real

91 852 86 85. **Open** 10am-4pm Tue-Fri; 10am-6pm Sat, Sun. **Admission** €3; €1.50 reductions. **No credit cards**.

Where to stay & eat

A kilometre or so out of town on the path to El Yelmo is the small but well-appointed **Hostal El Tranco** (C/Tranco 4, 91 853 04 23, doubles €50-€55, mains €12). Nearby are a couple of lively bars with outdoor terraces. Another option is **La Fresneda** campsite on the Carretera M-608 in Soto el Real (www.campinglafresnada.com, Sept-June open weekends only, rates €4.50 per person, including tent and car; €12 per pitch).

Getting there

By bus

Bus 724 from the Plaza de Castilla interchange, operated by Herederos de J Colmenarejo (91 845 00 51, www.hjcolmenarejo.com) runs every 30 mins 7am-11.30pm Mon-Fri, 8am-11.30pm Sat, Sun. The last return is at 10.25pm.

SIERRA NORTE

In contrast to the majestic alpine landscapes of the Guadarrama, this tract of rolling hills some 60km (37 miles) north-east of Madrid towards Guadalajara at first seems decidedly the poorer relative. Isolated until the 1980s, the Sierra Norte suffered from depopulation, with many villages being abandoned, until it was 'discovered' by *madrileños* looking for a more authentic, and cheaper, weekend retreat. The Sierra Norte is also host to the region's finest deciduous forests. Even during the height of the summer season the area never feels crowded.

The gateway to the area is **Buitrago de Lozoya**, just off the A-1. What remains of its walled medieval centre shows traces of Arab times, and its cool and dignified Gothic 15th-century **Iglesia de Santa María**, recently restored after fire swept through it in 1936, is also worth a visit. The real charm of Buitrago, however, is the quirky little **Museo Picasso** in the basement of its town hall (Plaza Picasso 1, 91 868 00 04, www.sierranorte.com/buitrago,

admission free), consisting of some 60 works, especially centred on bullfighting themes, and mostly from his later years. Picasso donated the pictures to his hairdresser and friend Eugenio Arias, a native of the town who met Picasso in Toulouse, where they were both living in exile. For 26 years Arias cut Picasso's hair in return for his paintings and sketches, and on his return to Spain he donated them to the town.

Among the first places of interest after Buitrago is **Montejo de la Sierra**, 16km (10 miles) to the north-east, and a good central point for excursions on foot. It has an interesting Renaissance church, but the jewel in its crown is a magnificent beech forest, 8km (5 miles) away at **El Chaparral**. It can be visited on guided tours, run from the **Centro de Recursos de Alta Montaña** information centre (C/Real 64, 91 869 70 58). It's a good idea to book places well ahead, especially from October to December. This is also popular mountain biking country, and the same centre has information on hiking routes.

An easy-to-follow bike route from Montejo, taking about three and a half hours, but which can also be walked in about twice the time, is along a dirt track that bends off the road to La Hiruela uphill towards the signposted Puerto de Cardoso and Cardoso de la Sierra, in the province of Guadalajara, before turning back to descend again to Montejo. On the way there are inspiring views north to the Ayllón mountains, and the 2,129-metre (6,985-foot) Peña Cebollera. Further south, at the bottom of a magnificent valley in the very heart of the Sierra Norte, lies **Puebla de la Sierra**. With a population of less than 100, this mountain hamlet has been almost entirely restored, and probably looks better now than it ever has. There are many houses to rent at weekends, and it makes an ideal base for walks to the surrounding reservoirs. Information on walks is available at the Parador de la Puebla – not an official parador – in the centre of the village.

About 25km (16 miles) south-west of Puebla (as the crow flies, not as the road winds) is **El Berrueco**, with a 13th-century church and the huge El Atazar reservoir. **El Atazar** village is the starting point for more walks, and a range of water sports are yours for the asking at the reservoir. The picturesque villages of **Patones de Arriba** and **Patones de Abajo** sit on the southern edge of the Sierra, and are reached via the Torrelaguna road off the A-1 from Madrid. The former is a cluster of slate houses and narrow, cobbled streets, reached by a steep, twisting road, though most live in the latter. A restoration project in recent years has been a mixed blessing, saving many of the villages' ancient houses from decay, but attracting rich second-homers from the city. Patones (as they are collectively known) is thought to have once been a peculiar enclave within Spain, a diminutive Visigothic kingdom which held its independence up until the 18th century. A road north-east from Patones leads 7km (4.5 miles) to the vast **Cueva del Reguerillo**, with prehistoric cave paintings around its underground lakes. The cave is unmarked, so be sure to ask directions before setting off, and a torch is helpful when you get there.

Where to stay & eat

Buitrago has the **Hostal Madrid-Paris** (Avda Madrid 37, 91 868 11 26, www.madrid paris.com, doubles €48, set meal €10-€19), an old stone house with 25 bargain rooms and a great-value restaurant. For old-fashioned food in surroundings to match, try **Asador Jubel** (C/Real 33, 91 868 03 09, mains €9.50). **Mesón del Hayedo** (C/Turco, 91 869 70 23, www. mesonelhayedo.es, rates €40 incl breakfast, restaurant closed dinner Mon-Thur, Sun & all Mon, mains €15-€20) is small, with a crowded and lively restaurant (it's not always open to non-guests). **Taberna de Teo** (Plaza de la Constitución 10, 91 868 05 12, closed lunch Tue, dinner Sun & Tue, Wed Oct-May) is a beautifully restored wine bar serving up an excellent tapas selection.

In upmarket Patones the restored five-room country house **Hotel del Tiempo Perdido** (Travesía del Ayuntamiento 7, 91 843 21 52, www.eltiempoperdido.com, weekends only, closed 2wks Aug & 2wks Dec, doubles €110-€131) is as good as it gets. And for food, you can't beat the old-world charm of **El Rey de Patones** (C/Asas 13, 91 843 20 37, www. reydepatones.com, closed dinner Sun-Thur Aug, mains €18).

Getting there

By bus

Alsa (91 177 99 51, www.alsa.es) bus 191 runs up to hourly from Plaza de Castilla to Buitrago (6am-10pm Mon-Fri, 8am-10.30pm Sat, Sun). Last bus from Buitrago back to Madrid is 9.30pm Mon-Fri; 10pm Sat, Sun. Many local microbus services run from Buitrago.

Tourist information

Centro de Turismo de la Sierra Norte

Avda del Cabrera 36, La Cabrera (91 868 86 98, www.sierranortemadrid.org). **Open** 9am-5pm daily.
The impressive tourist office in La Cabrera, which lies 18km (11 miles) south of Buitrago, covers tourist information for the whole sierra and features its own botanical gardens.

South & East

ALCALÁ DE HENARES & AROUND

After the horrific terrorist attacks of March 2004, Alcalá de Henares was descended upon by the world's camera crews and catapulted to fame for all the wrong reasons. Centuries before, all eyes were on Alcalá as Spain's centre of learning and culture, with a superb university, founded in 1498, and later as the birthplace of Cervantes. As far back as Roman times, Complutum, as it was known then, was a large and important city.

The university moved to Madrid in the 19th century, but there is still a strong sense of the city's educational history here today. The streets in the old quarter are lined with **Colegios Mayores** – student halls of residence in the 16th and 17th centuries, now converted into hotels and restaurants. One of the most impressive is the **Colegio de San Ildefonso**, famous for its stunning Plateresque façade and its three-tiered patio, which is still the setting for the solemn opening of university terms and for the presentation of the Cervantes Prize for Literature.

The main square, named after the city's most famous literary son, is a great spot to relax over a coffee and admire the buildings that line it, such as the **Casa Consistorial** (town hall) and the **Capilla de Oidor**, a 15th-century chapel now used for exhibitions. If you want to know more about the creator of Don Quixote, head to the author's birthplace, now the **Museo Casa Cervantes** (C/Mayor 48, 91 889 96 54, www.museo-casa-natal-cervantes.org, closed Mon, admission free). On the city's west side are the **Catedral Magistral** and the **Museo de Esculturas al Aire Libre**, an open-air museum with 50 or so sculptures.

One of the most entertaining ways to get to Alcalá is via the Tren de Cervantes (which runs weekends in autumn and spring, leaving Atocha station in Madrid at 11am, and returning at 7pm). Guides in Golden Age costume ply passengers with information about the city, and, on arrival, give them a tour of the town.

From Alcalá you can take a short excursion 17 kilometres (9.5 miles) down the M-204, to **Nuevo Baztán**. A peaceful little place, it was founded by a banker in the early 18th century and the entire village designed by renowned architect José de Churriguera, giving it a wonderfully harmonious feel.

Where to eat

Alcalá's best-known restaurant is the **Hostería del Estudiante** (C/Colegios 3, 91 888 03 30,

Alcalá de Henares. *See p241.*

www.parador.es, closed Aug, mains €20-€30, set menu €34.60), which occupies a stunning 16th-century *colegio* and specialises in hearty Castilian food – roast lamb and suckling pig, garlic soup and the Alcalá dessert speciality, *costrada*, which is something like a sweet millefeuille. **Mesón Don José** (C/Santiago 4, 91 881 86 17, closed Mon dinner, set lunch €8) is cheap and quite atmospheric. For good tapas washed down with draught *vermut*, check out the attractive, tiled bar **Cerveceria El Hidalgo** (C/El Bedel 3, 91 883 43 48, closed Wed).

In Nuevo Baztán, **Mesón El Conde** (Plaza la Iglesia 5, 91 873 53 27, closed 2wks Aug, mains €12-€20, set lunch €9) is a reasonably priced, traditional place with balconies over the square and tables outside in summer.

Getting there

By bus
Alsa (91 177 99 51, www.alsa.es) bus 223 leaves the Avda de América interchange every 15-20mins 6.15am-midnight Mon-Thur, and every 10-15mins 6.15am-11pm Sat, Sun. The journey time is approx 40 mins.

By car
On the A-2 it's approximately a 25min drive (31km/19miles).

By train
Cercanías C-2 and C-7 depart from Madrid's Chamartin station approx every 10mins (15-25min weekends), 5.30am-11.37pm daily. Journey time

49 mins. From the station it's a 10min walk to the centre (go straight down Paseo de la Estación).

Tourist information

Oficinas de Turismo
Callejón Santa María 1, Plaza de Cervantes (91 889 26 94, www.turismo alcala.es). **Open** 10am-2pm, 4-7pm daily. *Plaza de los Santos Niños s/n (91 881 06 34).* **Open** *Sept-May* 10am-2pm, 4-7pm daily. *June-Aug* 10am-2pm, 5-8pm daily.

CHINCHÓN & AROUND

Out of season Chinchón is a sleepy little town, famous for its *anís* liqueur and pretty, arcaded Plaza Mayor, overlooked by wooden balconies all the way around, and occasionally used for bullfights. This is where you'll find the town hall, tourist office and, most importantly, plenty of balcony restaurants and bars, where the traditional lunch is lamb cooked in a wood-burning oven, washed down with red from the *cuevas* (cellars) and finished off with a glass of the famous local brew.

The neoclassical **Iglesia de la Asunción** overlooking the plaza houses Goya's depiction of the Assumption. Just next door is the **Teatro Lope de Vega,** where the playwright wrote *El Blasón de los Chavos de Villalba* and which now doubles as a cinema. Just outside the town is the 16th-century castle, built on the site of the original 12th-century fortress. Sadly, only the ground floor remains, and it's home to sheep and the local outdoor drinking scene.

Chinchón hosts an open-air folk festival in the plaza at the beginning of June, and during the fiestas in August the bulls run the Avda del Generalisimo (or C/Huertos as some residents prefer), and there are fireworks, a fairground and bands performing near the castle.

It's worth driving to **Colmenar de Oreja**, five kilometres (three miles) away on the M-311. A quiet, untouristy place, it has an unspoilt Plaza Mayor, again ringed with wooden galleries, though on a smaller scale than Chinchón's, and a handsome 13th-century church, the **Iglesia de Santa María**. The tower is by Juan de Herrera.

Where to stay & eat

The balcony restaurants lining the Plaza Mayor all offer similar Chinchón fare – garlic soup and roasted red peppers, roast lamb and suckling pig. **La Casa del Pregonero** (Plaza Mayor 4, 91 894 06 96, www.lacasadelpregonero.com, closed Tue, set lunch €18, mains €18-€20), is slightly different – it uses local ingredients with some interesting twists, and has an attractive patio at the back. **Mesón Cuevas del Vino** (C/Benito Hortelano 13, 91 894 02 06, www.cuevasdelvino.com, closed Tue, mains €17-€26) is an atmospheric place, with an ancient oil press

Chinchón.

and some old carriages. For accommodation, try the delightful **Parador de Chinchón** (C/Los Huertos 1, 91 894 08 36, www.parador.es, doubles €130-€176), in a 17th-century former Augustinian convent, or the slightly less luxurious, but still very comfortable **Hostal Chinchón** (C/Grande 16, 91 893 53 98, www.hostalchinchon.com, doubles €50).

Getting there

By bus

Bus 337 operated by La Veloz (902 55 15 80, www.crtm.es) runs from Plaza Conde de Casal (Metro Conde de Casal, line 6). Buses leave every 30mins, 7am-11pm Mon-Fri; every hour, 8am-midnight Sat, and every 90mins, 9am-11pm Sun. The last return is at 9.55pm Mon-Thur, Sun; at 12.20am on Fri, Sat. Journey time approx 1hr.

ARANJUEZ

Aranjuez was the official spring residence of the Spanish monarchy and its hangers-on from the 17th to the 19th century. It was probably originally chosen for its setting and lush countryside – it is an oasis in the arid plains of central Spain, situated in a wide valley formed by the Jarama and Tajo (Tagus) rivers. The royals have long gone, but the Palacio Real is still the principal tourist attraction, along with the town's famous asparagus and strawberries.

Originally built as a hunting lodge for Charles I of Spain (Charles V of the Holy Roman Empire), the palace took its current shape under Philip II in the 1560s, and was extended in the 1770s by Charles III. It's a charming mix of Baroque and classical, and typical of the Bourbon palaces, with a sumptuous **throne room** and a cosy **ballroom**. It is the gardens, however, that provide the real attraction, particularly the 16th-century-designed **Jardín de la Isla** and **Jardín del Príncipe**. The gardens inspired Rodrigo's famous *Concierto de Aranjuez* (*see p245* **Garden Composition**) and the music continues today with a summer season of mostly open-air concerts and musical promenades, principally featuring Baroque music. It's in the gardens that you'll find the delightfully over-the-top **Casa del Labrador**, which was built for Charles IV. This early 19th-century folly – complete with painted ceilings, tapestry-lined walls, and porcelain and marble floors – is said to be one of the most important examples of neoclassicism in Europe.

In the town itself, **Museo del Toro** (Avenida Plaza de Toros s/n, 91 892 16 43, open Mon, Sat & Sun, admission €5, €2.50 reductions) aims to re-create the atmosphere of the bullfight and the traditions and entertainments of the court. If you're so inclined you can travel to Aranjuez on

Palacio Real de Aranjuez.

the Tren de la Fresa steam train, with hostesses in period costume (*see right*).

Palacio Real de Aranjuez

91 891 07 40, www.patrimonionacional.es. **Open** *Palace* Oct-Mar 10am-5.15pm Tue-Sun. Apr-Sept 10am-6.15pm Tue-Sun. *Gardens* Jan, Feb, Nov, Dec 8am-6.30pm daily. First 2wks Mar, Oct 8am-7pm daily. Last 2wks Mar 8am-7.30pm daily. Apr-mid June, mid Aug-Sept 8am-8.30pm daily. Mid June-mid Aug 8am-9.30pm daily. **Admission** *Palace* €9; €4 reductions. *Guide* €6. *Gardens* free. Free for EU citizens Wed pm, Thur pm. **Credit** MC, V.

Real Casa del Labrador

91 891 03 05, 91 891 07 40, www.patrimonio nacional.es. **Open** *Oct-Mar* 10am-5pm Tue-Sun. *Apr-Sept* 10am-7pm Tue-Sun. **Admission** €9; €4 reductions. **Credit** MC, V.

Where to stay & eat

Casa Pablo (C/Almíbar 42, 91 891 14 51, www. casapablo.net, closed Aug, mains €20) serves up superb seafood. To stay the night, the sleek **Príncipe de la Paz** (C/San Antonio 22, 91 809 92 22, www.nh-hotels.com, doubles €77-€135) has stylish rooms overlooking the palace.

Getting there

By bus

Bus 423 (www.redtransporte.com) from Estación Sur runs every 15-30mins, 6.30am-11.45pm Mon-Fri; every 30mins-1hr, 7am-midnight Sat, Sun. Last return 11.15pm Mon-Sat, 11pm Sun.

By train

Cercanías C-3 from Atocha, trains depart every 15-30mins 5.36am-11.50pm daily (last return 11.29pm). The steam-powered 'Strawberry Train' (Tren de la Fresa) runs on summer weekends and during holidays.

Tourist information

Oficina de Turismo

Plaza de San Antonio 9 (91 891 04 27). **Open** 9.30am-6pm daily.

TOLEDO

Once the imperial capital of Spain (1087-1561) and still the ecclesiastical heart of the country, 'Holy Toledo' represents two millennia of history and so holds incomparable cultural riches. Its impregnable hilltop position, tremendous fortified walls and the natural moat formed by the River Tagus have made this an important strategic stronghold for everyone from the Romans to the Visigoths, Muslims and Christians.

During the Middle Ages, Toledo was known as 'the city of three cultures' when the Jewish, Muslim and Christian population lived in a uniquely heterogeneous society; many religious buildings still bear a strange palimpsest of crucifixes, stars of David and Arab script. Over time, these religions blurred into one another, creating the Mozárabes (Christians who lived under Muslim rule with a semi-Arabic liturgy), and later the Mudéjars, Muslims who did the reverse after the Christian conquest. This air of tolerance also attracted many world-class

Garden Composition

Aranjuez was the inspiration for Rodrigo's famous Concierto.

Inspired by Aranjuez's vast palace gardens, the *Concierto de Aranjuez*, composed in 1939 by Joaquín Rodrigo (1901-99), is probably the best-known piece of Spanish music. Sneered at by classical snobs, it's nonetheless a 20th-century classic, covered by greats such as flamenco guitarist Paco de Lucia and, famously, Miles Davis, who used its 'Adagio' section as the cornerstone of his *Sketches of Spain* album. The *Concierto* has featured in commercials and World Championship-winning skating routines, and even inspired Jack Black to start his 'School of Rock'.

Blinded after a diphtheria attack aged three, Rodrigo wanted the piece to depict the aural and olfactory pleasures he experienced in the Bourbon monarchs' summer retreat: 'the fragrance of magnolias, the singing of birds and the gushing of fountains'. Rodrigo drew on Spain's musical heritage – the formality of 17th- and 18th-century Baroque composers, as well as more passionate folk styles – to conjure up the magical flow of nature, as well as the splendour and darkness of the palace's history.

Unusual for pitting a solo guitar against a full orchestra, the *Concierto* comprises three movements. The first, 'Allegro con spirito', feels like an alfresco jaunt and is built on a series of switching elements – between solos and the orchestra, between the flamenco-tinged strumming of the guitar and the melody. The famous second movement, 'Adagio', is based on an Andalucían lament. Guitar and cor anglais swap the same mournful refrain back and forth, until the whole orchestra deliver an aching climax. The third movement, 'Allegro gentile', reverts back to the opening jauntiness, a forthright mix of Baroque-like counterpoint and folk-dance melody.

'After listening to it for a couple of weeks I couldn't get it out of my mind,' said Miles Davis, in early 1959. He and collaborator Gil Evans set about reworking that haunting central 'Adagio' section for their third album together, *Sketches of Spain*. Rodrigo, reportedly, wasn't in the end all that impressed, but many other listeners were. In his autobiography, Davis recounts the story a woman had told him of a retired matador, now raising *toros* himself, who after hearing *Sketches of Spain* had got out of his chair, put on his old bullfighting gear, gone outside and fought and killed one of his bulls. 'He said that he'd been so moved by the music that he just had to fight the bull,' Davis remembered. 'It was hard for me to believe the story, but she swore that it was true.'

The *Concierto* had its premiere in 1940 in Barcelona and brought Rodrigo worldwide fame. It is Aranjuez, though, that best commemorates the composer, with a statue off C/Infantas and, set into the pavement nearby, an inscription that includes musical notation from the *Concierto*. King Juan Carlos awarded Rodrigo the hereditary title of Marquis of the Gardens of Aranjuez in 1992. Rodrigo died in 1999 and was buried in Aranjuez's cemetery.

Toledo. See p244.

scholars, and Toledo became a famous centre of learning with prominent schools of science, mathematics, theology and mysticism.

Now enjoying a Golden Age of tourism, Toledo is by far the most popular daytrip from Madrid, and the cobbled streets are mobbed with tour groups until the buses depart at sundown. The city is absolutely gridlocked for the duration of the Corpus Christi processions, during which the route is marked by white awnings over the streets and the cobblestones are strewn with rosemary, thyme and rose petals. Incense and chanting give the town an eerie medieval air, as do the period costumes and the priceless Flemish tapestries hung on the cathedral walls.

THE BISAGRA TO THE CATHEDRAL

If you come from Madrid by bus, car or train, the main point of entry to the old walled city is the imposing **Puerta de Bisagra**. This was built at the end of the reign of Emperor Carlos V to replace the original 11th-century Moorish gate and bears his imperial crest of the two-headed eagle, the symbol of Toledo. The **Museo de Tavera** (C/Duque de Lerma 2, 925 22 04 51, admission €4.50) is housed in the 1541 **Hospital de Tavera**, with a fine chapel and Renaissance courtyards; it has works by Tintoretto, Zurbarán and the city's adopted son, El Greco. Part of it may only be visited by guided tour.

To avoid the steep climb from here to the city, take the free escalator (7am-10pm Mon-Fri, 8am-10pm weekends). Alternatively, behind the gate, the superb Mudéjar church of **Santiago del Arrabal** stands out, with an impressive brick

tower and horseshoe arches. Part of it was once a mosque, but after the Christian reconquest it was rebuilt as a church. The maze of streets on either side as you head up C/Real del Arrabal was (as the name implies) the Arrabal – an area originally outside the Christian city. Off to the right on C/Cristo de la Luz are the gardens and stunning latticed brickwork of the **Mezquita del Cristo de la Luz** (925 25 41 91, admission €2.30). Built in 999, this mosque is the oldest surviving building in Toledo. According to legend, its name came from the fact that as Alfonso VI entered Toledo after the reconquest, his horse knelt at the door of the mosque, where, behind a stone in the archway, stood Christ, illuminated by the light of an oil lamp.

Dominating the skyline is the grim, black-turretted **Alcázar**, an enormous fortress built on the highest point of Toledo where Roman, Visigothic and Muslim forts stood before. Using the Alcázar as a landmark, head up C/Real de Arrabal and C/Cuesta de Armas to the social nerve centre of the city, **Plaza de Zocodover**. Originally known as the *suk-al-dawad,* or animal market, it became the site for *autos-da-fé* after the reconquest, but is now lined with restaurant and café terraces serving everything from partridge to Big Macs. Nearby, the Renaissance **Hospital de Santa Cruz** (C/Miguel de Cervantes 3, 925 22 10 36, admission free) is now a museum housing tapestries, and works by El Greco and Ribera.

C/Comercio, the old town's main street, leads from the Zocodover to the Plaza Mayor, dominated by the **Palacio Arzobispal** (the

Archbishop's Palace) and the jaw-dropping **Cathedral** (C/Cardenal Cisneros 1, Plaza del Ayuntamiento, 925 22 22 41, admission €8).

Spain's second-largest cathedral (after Seville) but for many the more beautiful of the two, Toledo's cathedral was completed in 1493 after 250 years of construction. A Christian church is said to have been founded here in the first century AD by Saint Eugene, the first Bishop of Toledo. Mainly Gothic in style with touches of Mudéjar, neoclassical and Baroque, the cathedral has 750 stained-glass windows, 70 cupolas and five naves, and is supported by 88 columns with 22 side chapels. You could easily spend a whole day exploring its dark interiors but some of its most extraordinary features include the sacristy's prestigious art collection (including El Greco's *The Disrobing of Christ*) the lavishly carved central choir and, behind the main altar, Narciso Tomé's unique 16th-century *Transparente,* a Baroque frenzy of bronze, stucco, coloured marble and painting lit by beams of light via a circular 'sunroof' dripping with alabaster putti.

SANTO TOMÉ AND THE SYNAGOGUES

Just around the corner from the cathedral, the narrow alleys that lead to **Plaza del Salvador** are the most visited parts of Toledo. They are lined with shops selling Toledo's artisan products: Toledan steel has been famous for its strength since Roman times and C/Santo Tomé is packed with shops selling everything from flick-knives to sabres. Equally ubiquitous is *damasquinado* – the Damascus style of decoration brought by the Moors, in which fine threads of gold and silver are hammered into blackened metal – which covers everything from chess sets to knife handles and jewellery. For the sweet-toothed, Toledan marzipan is sold in all shapes and flavours.

The first major building en route is the **Taller del Moro**, a Mudéjar workshop that used to house exhibitions of Toledo crafts; it remained closed for long-term renovations as we went to press. Behind the Taller, down C/San Juan de Diós, follow the crowds to the Mudéjar church of **Santo Tomé** (Plaza del Conde 4, 925 25 60 98, www.santotome.org, admission €2.50), which holds only one painting: El Greco's masterpiece, *El Entierro del Conde de Orgaz*.

Around the corner lies the **Casa-Museo de El Greco** (C/Samuel Leví s/n, 925 22 36 65, 925 22 44 05), although, despite the fanfare, it has never actually been confirmed that the artist lived here. The house – a reconstructed 16th-century Toledan home – holds an impressive collection of El Greco's later works.

In medieval times this area was Toledo's *judería*, the Jewish quarter, once the world's most important centre of Jewish scholarship. Many of its finest works of Jewish-Mudéjar architecture were restored in 1992 as an act of atonement for the 500th anniversary of the expulsion of Jews from Spain. The most recent beneficiary of the makeover is the **Sinagoga del Tránsito**, a richly decorated multicultural blaze of Hebrew inscriptions, Gothic carvings and Moorish columns. It was built in 1357 and its immense size is a testimony to the huge Jewish population that once lived in Toledo. Today, there is not even the minimum number of adult males (ten) to hold a service. After 1492, the synagogue was used as a church, but it now pulls in crowds with its fascinating museum of Sephardic Jewish culture, the **Museo Sefardí** (C/Samuel Leví s/n, 925 22 36 65, www.museo sefardi.net, admission €3, €1.50 reductions) where displays include crystal circumcision instruments and a 2,000-year-old ossuary.

Another surviving medieval synagogue, the **Sinagoga de Santa María la Blanca** (C/Reyes Católicos 4, 925 22 72 57, admission €2.50) lies at the opposite end of narrow C/Judería. Its small, plain interior, dominated by horseshoe arches, is extremely beautiful, in spite of the gaudy Baroque altar that was added later.

Spires and Tyres

Religious recycling.

You may think you're doing your bit for the environment with that weekly trip to the recycling bins, but the average person's attempts at recycling pale into insignificance compared to the efforts of Justo Gallego, a pensioner in the small town of Mejorada del Campo, to the east of Madrid.

In the early 1960s, Justo took it upon himself to start building a cathedral, using stuff other people had thrown away. Neither architect nor engineer, he was a farmer before entering the Convento de Santa María de Huerta, a Trappist monastery in Soria, northern Spain. He stayed there for seven years until he caught TB and the other monks asked him to leave.

He was at something of a loose end after that, until 12 October 1961 – the feast day of Our Lady of the Pillar – when it suddenly came to him that he had been put on this earth to construct a cathedral in his home town. Justo flogged his belongings and started right away, on a patch of land he'd inherited from his parents. Unsurprisingly, the money didn't go very far, and soon he was using whatever he could scavenge. More than 40 years later, he's still at it. Local firms sometimes donate supplies they no longer need, but otherwise he has recycled the most unlikely of materials, helped along by occasional contributions.

It's a curious sight, but the structure does somehow resemble a cathedral, and mass has even been held there. It is, however, a long way from completion.

Now in his seventies, Justo is desperate for more funds and materials to complete his mission while he is still able to do so. Local builders and architects are reluctant to take the project on because it never had planning permission – or, indeed, any kind of official authorisation. In fact, Justo himself readily admits he never drew up any sort of plans and there is no guarantee it won't fall down at any minute.

The structure could be described as neo-Romanesque, and is 40 metres (131 foot) high with 12 towers. It has a large nave, partly covered by a dome with a diameter of almost 12 metres (39 feet). There's also a crypt, along with cloisters, a library and various other as yet unspecified spaces. Columns are made from oil drums, arches constructed from piles of old tyres and towers built with bits of bricks and piping. Bicycle wheels have been transformed into pulleys to get materials up the structure. The main entrance is approached by mosaic steps and spiral staircases link different levels. The structure has become a symbol of the town and attracted global media attention. If and when it will ever be completed, though, only God knows.

Catedral de Nuestra Senora del Pilar
C/Antoni Gaudí, Mejorada del Campo.
By bus 341 (*www.redtransporte.com*)
from Conde de Casal every 30mins weekdays, every 90mins Sat, Sun.
By car *A-3, then M-203 (21km).*

The main street of the *judería* is now, ironically, called C/Reyes Católicos, and is topped by the very Catholic **Monasterio de San Juan de los Reyes** (C/Reyes Católicos 17, 925 22 38 02, www.sanjuandelosreyes.org, admission €2.50). Built by Ferdinand and Isabella, it was originally intended to be the royal pantheon and has a dramatic Gothic cloister and an exterior garlanded with grim black chains; during the reconquest, these chains were supposedly taken from Christian prisoners and used to hang Jewish dissidents.

Next to the monastery is a long stone balcony with impossibly romantic views over the River Tagus, the San Martín bridge and the typical *cigarrales* (Toledan country homes) on the hill opposite. For another great view, back over the whole city, head out of town over the River Tagus by the San Martín bridge, and turn right along the Carretera de Piedrabuena.

Where to eat

As Toledo province is the hunting centre of Spain, hearty game dishes dominate. Partridge (*perdiz*) is the most typical dish, and is usually served *a la toledana* – cooked slowly with onion, garlic and bayleaf – or else with *pochas* (succulent white beans) or pickled and eaten cold. Venison and wild boar stews are another speciality, along with roast suckling pig and *cuchifrito* (fricassée of lamb with egg and wine) and *tortilla a la magra* (cured ham omelette).

All these and more are on offer at traditional restaurants such as **La Abadía** (Plaza de San Nicolás 3, 925 25 07 46, www.abadiatoledo.com, mains €9-€14, set lunch €12) where a labyrinth of bars and dining rooms fill a 16th-century palace. **Restaurante Aurelio** (C/Sinagoga 6, 925 22 41 05, www.casa-aurelio.com, closed Mon dinner, Sun, mains €18) is in the heart of the Jewish quarter and filled with ancient farming tools. Part of a chain, it has two other branches in the city – check the website for details. After more than a century serving food, **Venta de Aires** (Paseo Circo Romano 35, 925 22 05 45, www.ventadeaires.com, set lunch €18-€21, mains €7-€17) must be doing something right. Particularly good at lunchtime when it's packed with locals feasting on excellent cod dishes and, naturally, partridge, is **La Perdiz** (C/Reyes Católicos 7, 925 25 29 19, closed dinner Sun, mains €12-€20, set lunch €12.90).

For a sophisticated twist on local staples – quail fried with ginger and lemon or pork with berries – **Los Cuatro Tiempos** (C/Sixto Ramón Parro 5, 925 22 37 82, www.restaurante loscuatrotiempos.com, closed Sun dinner, mains €18, set lunch €18.50) is located in a charming 16th-century National Heritage building. For a real treat, the famous **Adolfo Restaurante** (C/Granada 7, 925 22 73 21, www.adolfo restaurante.com, closed dinner Sun, mains €24) is worth a visit for its fantastic wine list and light cuisine such as tempura courgette flowers with saffron. When planning your visit, bear in mind that most of Toledo's restaurants close for a fortnight in July or August.

Where to stay

With unbeatable views of the city, the luxury **Parador de Toledo** (Cerro del Emperador s/n, 925 22 18 50, www.parador.es, doubles €135-€180) is about ten minutes' cab ride from the city. The splendid pool and top-notch restaurant make it worth allowing a day just to spend in the hotel. Right next to the Casa El Greco, the charming **Hotel Pintor El Greco** (C/Alamillos del Tránsito 13, 925 28 51 91, www.hotel pintorelgreco.com, doubles €70-€250) occupies a 17th-century bakery. More economical is the new, central **Hostal Santo Tomé** (C/Santo Tomé 13, 925 22 17 12, www.hostalsantotome. com, doubles €52-€65) with ten comfortable rooms in an old Toledan townhouse. **Hostal Descalzos** (C/Descalzos 30, 925 22 28 88, www.hostaldescalzos.com, doubles €49-€56) is also great value with air-conditioned rooms around a sunny patio with pool and jacuzzi.

Getting there

By bus
Around ten different Continental Auto buses (902 33 04 00, www.continental-auto.es, www. alsa.es, www.redtransporte.com) and bus 402 (www.redtransporte.com) go to Toledo, from the Plaza Elíptica interchange terminal in Madrid. They leave every 15-30mins 6am-10pm Mon-Sat, 8am-10pm Sun. Last return at 11pm. Journey time is around 50mins: 75mins on bus 402.

By train
There are 13 daily trains to Toledo from Atocha station. The first train leaves at 6.50am Mon-Fri, 9.20am Sat, Sun. The last train leaves at 9.50pm daily; returning, the last train is at 9.30pm daily. The average journey time is 30mins. From Toledo station, take bus 6 to the Puerta de Bisagra or you'll face a long uphill walk.

Tourist information

Oficina Municipal de Turismo
Plaza del Consistorio (925 25 40 30).
Open 10am-6pm Tue-Sun.

Oficina de Turismo
Puerta de Bisagra (925 22 08 43). **Open** *Oct-June* 9am-6pm Mon-Fri; 9am-7pm Sat; 9am-3pm Sun. *July-Sept* 9am-7pm Mon-Sat; 9am-3pm Sun.

ESCAPES & EXCURSIONS

In Context

History

From shanty town to cosmopolitan capital.

TEXT: NICK RIDER

Around 100 years after Madrid had become capital of the Spanish Empire on the whim of Philip II, an attempt was made to construct an ancient past for it, and writers developed the story of its descent from a Roman city called Mantua Carpetana. Though there were Roman towns nearby at Alcalá de Henares (Complutum) and Toledo (Toletum), and Roman villas along the valley of the Manzanares river, there is no real evidence that there was ever a local Mantua, or that any of these settlements was the origin of modern Madrid. The story of Mantua Carpetana, however, served to obscure the insignificance of Madrid before Philip II moved his court here in 1561, and, above all, the embarrassing fact that it was founded by Muslims: specifically, in about 860 AD, during the reign of Mohammed I, fifth Emir of Córdoba.

ARABIAN SIGHTS

Following their eruption into the Iberian peninsula in 711, the Arab armies did not occupy the inhospitable lands north of the Sierra de Guadarrama, but established a frontier more or less along the old Roman road linking Mérida, Toledo and Saragossa. The original *qasr* (a word absorbed into Spanish as Alcázar) or fortress of Madrid was one of a string of watchtowers built north of this line in the ninth century, as Christian raids into Al-Andalus became more frequent. The rocky crag on which it stood, where the Palacio Real is today, was ideal for the purpose, since it had a view of the main tracks south from the Guadarrama. It also had excellent water, from underground streams within the rock. Madrid's original Arabic name, Mayrit or Magerit, means 'place of many springs'.

Mayrit became more than just a fortress, with an outer citadel, the eastern wall of which ran along the modern C/Factor, and a wider town or *medina* bounded by the Plaza de la Villa and C/Segovia. A section of wall, the Muralla Arabe on Cuesta de la Vega, and the remains recently excavated next to the Palacio Real are the only remnants of Muslim Madrid visible in the modern city. Both citadel and *medina* consisted of a mass of narrow alleys, like the old quarters of North African cities today.

Mayrit was attacked by Christian armies in 932 and 1047, and in the 970s was used by the great minister of Córdoba, Al-Mansur, as a base for his celebrated 100 campaigns against the north. By the 11th century, it had a population of around 7,000.

CHRISTIAN CONQUEST

In the 11th century the Caliphate of Córdoba disintegrated into a mass of petty princedoms called *taifas*, and Mayrit became part of the Emirate of Toledo. In 1086, Alfonso VI of Castile (*photo p255*) took advantage of this situation to conquer Toledo, and with it Madrid. The town's main mosque became the church of Santa María de la Almudena, which would survive until the 19th century. For many years, however, Madrid would

'Medieval Castile did not have a fixed capital, but instead the Court followed the king around the country.'

remain on the front line. In 1109, it was again besieged, by a Moorish army that camped below the Alcázar in the place since known as Campo del Moro (Field of the Moor). A new wall was built, enclosing the area between the Alcázar and Plaza Isabel II, Plaza San Miguel and Plaza Humilladero.

Christian Madrid was a very rural town, and most of the population who worked did so on the land. Madrid did acquire large religious houses, notably the Friary of San Francisco, where the church of San Francisco el Grande still stands, supposedly founded by St Francis of Assisi in 1217. But it was still not entirely Christian. Many Muslims, known as Mudéjares, had stayed in the conquered areas, retaining their own laws and religion, and were prized by the Castilian monarchs for their skills as builders and masons; their work can still seen today in the towers of San Nicolás de los Servitas and San Pedro el Viejo. In Madrid they were confined to the area known as the Morería. Medieval Madrid also had a smaller Jewish population, concentrated outside the walls in Lavapiés.

Madrid did finally begin to play more of a role in the affairs of Castile in the 14th century. In 1309, the Cortes, or parliament, met here for the first time. Medieval Castile did not have a fixed capital, but instead the Court followed the king around the country. In the 14th and 15th centuries Castile was dogged by a series of social revolts and civil wars, between monarchs, the nobility and rival claimants from the royal family. Against this backdrop, Madrid began to gain popularity as a royal residence, a country retreat more than a centre of power.

IN CONTEXT

Political instability did not prevent substantial economic progress in 15th-century Castile, with Madrid becoming a reasonably prosperous trading centre for the first time. Trade outgrew the old market in Plaza de la Villa, and in the 1460s an area east of the 12th-century wall was built up as a ramshackle new market square, the origin of the Plaza Mayor. A new town wall was built, not for defence but so that taxes could be levied on people living in the new parts of the town. Its eastern entrance was a new gate, the Puerta del Sol.

Madrid retained a degree of royal favour and continued its modest growth, and at the end of the Middle Ages had a population of around 10,000-12,000.

On 11 May 1561, the small-time aristocrats who ran the town of Madrid received a letter from their king, Philip II, warning that he, the entire royal household and all their hundreds of hangers-on would shortly be coming to stay.

CAPITAL IDEA

Philip II (1556-98; *photo p256*) was the fundamental figure in Madrid's history. He was a deeply pious, shy, austere man. His father had travelled incessantly about his many dominions, and led his armies into battle. Philip, in contrast, ruled his inheritance from behind a desk, as a kind of king-bureaucrat, sometimes dealing with over 400 documents a day. This extraordinary exercise in paperwork naturally required a permanent base.

Why Philip chose a town without a cathedral, college or printing press as capital remains unclear. The fact that Madrid was near the centre of the Iberian peninsula probably appealed to him, as he was fascinated by geometry and Renaissance ideas of a king as the 'centre' of the state, but his choice made no economic sense at all, since it gave Spain the only major European capital not on a navigable river. Madrid – which for centuries would normally be referred to in Spain as 'La Corte', the Court, never as a city in its own right, which indeed it wasn't – would be a capital of the monarchy's own creation, a pure expression of royal power.

Having established his ideal capital, Philip did little to build or plan it. He had extended the Alcázar when he was still crown prince, then his attention shifted to El Escorial, where he increasingly spent his time. Royal piety was demonstrated by the endowment of new houses for religious orders, such as the Descalzas Reales. Philip II founded 17 convents and monasteries in Madrid, Philip III 14 and Philip IV another 17, and they would cover a third of the city until the 19th century. A wider city wall was put up in 1566, and the Puente de Segovia in the 1580s. Philip's favourite architect, Juan de Herrera, planned the rebuilding of the Plaza Mayor, but the only part that was built during his reign was the Casa de la Panadería in 1590.

The establishment of the Court and aristocracy – the great centres of consumption and patronage – in Madrid made it a magnet for people from all over Spain and abroad. The population went from under 20,000 in 1561 to 55,000 in 1584 and close to 85,000 by 1600. Building did not keep up with the influx, and a law decreed that in any house of more than one storey, the upper floor could be requisitioned to house members of the Court. In response, people simply put up houses with only one floor, and much of the new Madrid grew as a mass of shabby, low buildings.

This improvised capital did not impress foreign visitors. Lambert Wyts, a Flemish aristocrat who arrived in 1571, said that it was 'the foulest and filthiest town in Spain'. Thick mud made it impossible to ride a horse down the main streets in winter until a few cobbles were put down in the 1580s. There were no drains of any kind, and the streets were full of waste thrown out of the houses every night, producing an 'unbearable stench'.

Madrid had taken on a characteristic that would stay with it to this day – that it was a city of outsiders, in which at least 50 per cent of the population was from somewhere else. Another trait for which Madrid would be repeatedly condemned was that it was a city that consumed but did not produce anything. The trades that did develop in Madrid – shoe-making,

IN CONTEXT

Alfonso VI (left). See p253.

carpentry, jewellery-making, fan-making, laceworking – were overwhelmingly to service the Court and aristocracy.

THE COURT ADJOURNS

The greatest success of Philip II's reign was the defeat of the Turkish fleet off Lepanto in Greece in 1571. In 1580, he became King of Portugal and appeared to be at the height of his strength. However, suspensions of payment on his debts were becoming frequent, and in the 1560s a rebellion broke out in the Netherlands that would develop into a morass into which Spanish armies and wealth would disappear. Philip's dispute with England – leading to the Armada catastrophe – and interventions in France's religious wars were as costly.

As the number of unresolved problems mounted, a gnawing frustration spread through Castilian society, and scapegoats were sought. The former Muslims, nominally converted in 1502, were put under increasing pressure and then expelled from Spain in 1609, and the Inquisition – if not the all-pervading force of Protestant caricature – gained great powers to investigate deviations from Catholic orthodoxy.

Philip II died in 1598 at El Escorial, aged 71. His son Philip III (1598-1621) and grandson Philip IV (1621-65) had neither the intelligence, confidence or motivation to carry on with the awesome burden of work he'd set as an example. Philip III began the practice of ruling through a favourite or *valido*, in his case the Duke of Lerma. Spain's impoverished state, aggravated by a devastating plague in 1599, was impossible to ignore, and Lerma responded by making peace with England and the Dutch.

He also committed the ultimate injury to Madrid by moving the Court to Valladolid, in 1601. The stated reason was that this would revive the economy of northern Castile, although Lerma stood to benefit personally. He also argued that Madrid was so overrun with undesirables that it had become intolerable. The monarchy's purpose-built capital was out of control and it would be best to write it off and start again.

Within a few months Madrid was so deserted 'it appeared as if the Moors or the English had sacked and burnt it'. By 1605, the population had fallen back to just 26,000, little more than before Philip II's arrival in 1561. However, the Valladolid experiment did not work, and it became evident that Madrid had acquired a momentum that was difficult to ignore. In 1606, the Court returned amid huge rejoicing, and only a year later the population was already back to 70,000.

POMP AND CIRCUMSTANCE

It was after Madrid's definitive establishment as capital, with Philip III's brief declaration *Sólo Madrid es Corte* (Only Madrid is the Court), that more was at last done to give it the look of a grand city. Plaza Mayor (*photo p260*) was finally completed in 1619, followed by the Ayuntamiento or city hall and the Buen Retiro palace. The aristocracy, too, began to build palaces around the city once they were assured they wouldn't have to move on again, and Madrid acquired several much more elaborate baroque churches.

The Plaza Mayor was the great arena of Habsburg Madrid. Able to hold a third of the city's population at that time, it was the venue for state ceremonies, bullfights, executions, *autos-da-fé* (the ritual condemnation of heretics), mock battles, circus acts and carnival fiestas, as well as still being a market square.

Habsburg Madrid functioned rather like a giant theatre, a great backdrop against which the monarchy could display itself to its subjects and to the world. On either side were royal estates, which determined the shape of the city left in the middle and its peculiar north-south pattern of growth. Several times a year royal processions took place, with stops for various ceremonies, in the Plaza Mayor and High Masses in various churches. For the occasion, buildings were covered in garlands, and temporary arches were erected along the route with extravagant decoration extolling the virtues of the dynasty. As the Spanish monarchy slid towards economic collapse the lavishness of these ceremonies only increased, maintaining an illusion of power and opulence.

Away from this ceremonial route, the Habsburgs built few squares and no grand avenues, and old Madrid continued to develop along the tangled street plan it retains today. Even so, the opulence of the Court – and the poverty outside the capital – still attracted more people into the city, and in about 1630 Madrid reached its maximum size under the Habsburgs, with possibly as many as 170,000 inhabitants. In 1656, it was given its fifth and final wall, roughly surrounding the area now considered 'old Madrid', which would set the limits of the city for the next 200 years.

Philip II. *See p254.*

THE PRICE OF WAR

For many years the centre of all the Court pomp was King Philip IV. Throughout the 1620s and 1630s, while the Court maintained its image of grandeur, his *valido,* the Count-Duke of Olivares, struggled to maintain the Spanish empire against threats on every side. In the 1620s, Spain won a series of victories, and for a time it seemed the rot had been stopped. In 1639, though, a Spanish fleet was destroyed by the Dutch, and in 1643 the French crushed the Spanish army at Rocroi in Flanders. Naval defeats made it ever more difficult for Spain to import gold and silver from America. Olivares sought to extend taxation in the non-Castilian dominions of the crown, which led in 1640 to revolts in Portugal and Catalonia. Portugal regained its independence, and the Catalan revolt was only suppressed after a 12-year war.

By mid-century the effects of endless wars on Castile were visible to all, in abandoned villages and social decay. Even Madrid went into decline, so that by 1700 the population had fallen back to about 100,000. In the 1660s, the total collapse of the Spanish empire seemed an immediate possibility. Castile, the first world power, had been left poorer than many countries it had tried to dominate.

END OF THE HABSBURG LINE

In the Court, meanwhile, life became ever more of a baroque melodrama. Of Philip IV's 12 legitimate children by his two wives, only two girls had survived into adulthood – the youngest the Infanta Margarita, the little princess in Velázquez's *Las Meninas*. In 1661, however, when Philip was already prematurely aged, the queen, Mariana of Austria, had a son.

The new heir, the future King Charles II, was chronically infirm from birth and provided the dynasty with scant consolation. The Habsburgs' marked tendency to ill-health was accentuated by their habit of marrying cousins or nieces. The Habsburg jaw, the growth of which can be followed through family portraits, had in Charles become a real disability. He was unable to eat solid food. Because of this – or, more likely, the endless cures he was subjected to for his many ailments – he suffered uncontrollable diarrhoea, which detracted from the stately dignity of Court ceremonies.

In the meantime, the economy and the government continued to slide. Concern centred again on the need for an heir, and Charles was married off twice, despite a general belief that he was both impotent and sterile. As it became evident that the throne of the Spanish empire would soon become vacant, the Court was overrun with bizarre intrigues, with different factions and the agents of European powers all waiting for Charles' final demise. In 1695, the French ambassador reported that the king 'appeared to be decomposing', and could barely walk without assistance. Even so, Charles hung on until the age of 38. In 1700, though, with the pathetic last words, '*Me duele todo*' (It hurts everywhere), he finally died, and the Spanish Habsburg dynasty came to an end.

BOURBON MADRID

Philip V (1700-46), first Bourbon King of Spain, secured his throne in 1714, after the 12-year War of the Spanish

Succession. He was the grandson of Louis XIV of France and María Teresa, daughter of Philip IV of Spain. Castile, abandoning its more usual francophobia, gave him complete support. The alternative, Archduke Charles of Austria, was supported by Catalonia and the other Aragonese territories, to which he had promised a restoration of their traditional rights. Twice, in 1706 and 1710, Charles' British, Dutch, Portuguese and Catalan army took Madrid, but was unable to hold it.

Once victorious, Philip reformed his new kingdom along the lines laid down by his illustrious grandfather in France. In 1715, the remaining rights of the former Aragonese territories were abolished, so that it is from this date that Spain can formally be said to exist.

A French king brought with him other innovations. Philip V, raised at Versailles, and his Italian second wife Isabella Farnese were not taken with Madrid or its gloomy Habsburg palaces, and so built their own Franco-Italian villa at La Granja. They were not overly upset when the entire Alcázar burned down in 1734, and a new Palacio Real was commissioned from Italian architects. Philip V and his administrator of Madrid, the Marqués de Vadillo, also sponsored many buildings by a local architect, Pedro de Ribera.

Reform led to economic recuperation and a recovery in Madrid's population. People still came and went, but the city also acquired a more stable resident population, with a merchant community and an artisan and working class. Even so, in many ways Madrid had changed little. Its main function was still to serve the Court, the ceremonies of which set the calendar. These were as lavish as ever: until the 1770s the amount spent annually by the Crown in Madrid was greater than the entire budget of the Spanish navy.

Fernando VI (1746-59) was a shy but popular king who gave Spain its longest period of peace for more than 200 years. Childless, he was succeeded by his half-brother Charles III (1759-88). Previously King of Naples for 20 years, he too was less than impressed by

IN CONTEXT

Madrid. However, more than any of his predecessors he set about improving the city, becoming known as Madrid's Rey-Alcalde or 'King-Mayor'.

ENLIGHTENMENT STRIKES

Charles was fascinated by Enlightenment ideas of progress, science and applied use of reason. No democrat, he sought to bring about rational improvement from the top. Reforms were undertaken in the bureaucracy and armed forces, and to improve trade with Spanish America. He challenged the privileges of the religious orders, and expelled the Jesuits from Spain in 1767 for their refusal to co-operate.

In Madrid, Charles first undertook to do something about the mud in winter, suffocating dust in summer and foul smells at all times – which were noted by every visitor to the city. A 1761 decree banned the dumping of waste in the streets, and Charles' Italian engineer-architect Francesco Sabatini began building sewers and street lighting. A string of major buildings was erected, of which the Casa de Correos in Puerta del Sol and Puerta de Alcalá are the best-known. A later queen of Spain remarked that it sometimes seemed as if all the monuments of Madrid had been built by Charles III.

Charles III's grandest project was the Paseo del Prado. He sent scientific expeditions to every corner of his empire, and planned to exhibit the fruits of their varied researches in a Museum of Natural Sciences – now the Museo del Prado – and the adjacent Jardín Botánico.

Reform and improved trade did create a feeling of well-being in late 18th-century Madrid. Nevertheless, Spain was still a very feudal society, and the real economy remained backward and frail. And, in an absolute monarchy, a great deal depended on each monarch. Charles IV (1788-1808) had none of his father's energy or intelligence. Also, he chose as his minister the corrupt Manuel Godoy. After the French Revolution, Spain joined other monarchies in attacking the new regime; in 1795, however, Godoy made peace and then an alliance with France, leading to an unpopular war with Britain.

IN CONTEXT

Then, in 1808, when Godoy was vacillating over changing sides once again, he was forestalled by anti-French riots that proclaimed Charles IV's son Fernando as king in his place. Napoleon sent troops to Madrid, assuming this decrepit state would be as easy to conquer as any other. It was not to be, at least not initially, and the consequences were horrific (see p259 **In the Frame**).

Once victory was his, Napoleon made his brother, Joseph Bonaparte, King of Spain. In Madrid he tried in a well-meaning fashion to make improvements, among them some squares for which the city has since been very grateful, notably the Plaza de Oriente and the Plaza Santa Ana. However, this did nothing to overcome the animosity around him. In 1812, the Duke of Wellington and his army arrived to take the city, in a battle that destroyed much of the Retiro palace. The French were finally driven out of Spain in 1813. As well as the fighting itself, the year 1812 brought with it a catastrophic famine, which in Madrid killed over 30,000 people.

The shock of this upheaval initiated a period of instability that continued until 1874 – in fact, it could be said that the instability only really ended with the death of Franco in 1975. Spain withdrew into its own problems, with one conflict after another between conservatives, reformists, revolutionaries and other factions. Each struggled to impose its model on the state and create a political system that could accommodate, or hold back, the pressures for modernisation and some form of democracy.

In 1812, a Cortes had met in Cádiz and given Spain its first constitution. Yet when Fernando VII (1808-33) returned from French captivity in 1814, his only thought was to cancel the constitution and return to the methods of his ancestors. His absolute rule, though, was incapable of responding to the bankruptcy of the country. The regime was also struggling to hold on to its American colonies, which were by then in complete rebellion. In 1820, a liberal revolt in the army forced Fernando to reinstate the constitution. He was saved three years later, ironically

In the Frame The Third of May

Goya's extraordinary painting of the reality of war.

IN CONTEXT

More than 200 years old, this remains one of the world's most modern paintings. It marked a complete transformation in the portrayal of war. Previously, with very few exceptions, war paintings had presented war as a noble contest, glorifying heroic deeds and celebrating kings and commanders – a prime example, Velázquez's *Las Lanzas*, hangs near Goya's work in the Prado. In Goya's war images, in contrast – whether the *Tres de Mayo* or the *Desastres de la Guerra* – there is no glory, only misery, brutality and chaos. Death, mutilation and casual savagery are more prominent than victories. There are no generals or famous heroes, only faces in the crowd. There is heroism – again anonymous – but it seems wild, desperate, ultimately futile. It is this searingly honest, unblinking sense of the truth and horror of violence that makes the *Tres de Mayo* so permanently contemporary.

The events portrayed were very real. On 2 May 1808, Madrid awoke to learn that Napoleon had kidnapped the Spanish royal family, and that French troops were taking over the country. The French expected little resistance beyond skirmishes and some manageable grumbling. Instead, uncoordinated Spanish army units and, above all, the people of Madrid fought the invaders street by street, using knives or their bare hands. As the day wore on, the French gradually won control of Madrid, and in the early morning of 3 May – enraged that they had had to fight so hard against a mere street mob, rather than real soldiers – they set out to teach the city a lesson. Captured 'insurgents' were disposed of in mass executions on the hill of Príncipe Pío, which is now at the southern end of the Parque del Oeste.

Goya painted his *Dos de Mayo*, of the struggle in the Puerta del Sol, and *Tres de Mayo* in 1814, just after the French had been driven out of Spain. How much personal observation went into them is an unanswered question. Goya was in Madrid during those days, and one of his gardeners later claimed the artist had watched the executions through a telescope. However, this is impossible to confirm.

by a French army, sent to restore monarchical rule. Meanwhile, defeat at Ayacucho in Peru (1824) left Spain with only Cuba, Santo Domingo and Puerto Rico of its former American empire.

In 1830, Fernando VII's wife María Cristina gave birth to a daughter, soon to be Queen Isabel II (1833-68). Previously, the most reactionary sectors of the aristocracy, the Church and other ultra-conservative groups had aligned themselves behind the king's brother Don Carlos. When Fernando died in 1833, Carlos demanded the throne, launching what became known as the Carlist Wars. To defend her daughter's rights, María Cristina, as Regent, had no choice but to look for support from liberals, and so was obliged to promise some form of constitutional rule.

OLD ROMANTICS

For the next 40 years Spanish politics were a see-saw, as conservative and liberal factions vied for power, while the Carlists, off the spectrum for most people in Madrid, occasionally threatened at the gates. Madrid was the great centre for aspiring politicians, and the problems of Spain were discussed endlessly in its salons and new cafés, which multiplied around this time. This was the era of Romanticism, and writers such as the journalist Larra and poet José Espronceda were heavily involved in politics. Similarly, many of the politicians of the day were also writers.

Much of the time, though, these reformers were shepherds in search of a flock, for there were no true political parties. The only way a faction could hope to gain power was with the support of a general with troops at his disposal.

This political instability did not mean that life in Madrid was chaotic. Visitors in the early 1830s found a small, sleepy, shabby city, which seemed sunk in the past. Convents and palaces still occupied nearly half its area. It was around this time that Spain acquired its romantic aura. A growing number of foreigners visited, drawn by Spain's timeless, exotic qualities. One was the French writer Prosper Mérimée, who in 1845 wrote his novel *Carmen*, later put to music by Bizet, who himself never visited Spain at all.

EXPANSION AND TURMOIL

The 1830s, however, also saw the single most important change in Madrid

Plaza Mayor. *See p255.*

during the 19th century. In 1836, the liberal minister Mendizábal took advantage of the church's sympathy for Carlism to introduce his Desamortización or Disentailment law, which dissolved most of Spain's monasteries. In Madrid, the church lost over 1,000 properties. Most were demolished remarkably quickly, and an enormous area thus became available for sale and new building.

Some urban reformers saw this as an opportunity to build broad, airy avenues, following the always-cited example of Paris. Some major projects were undertaken, the most important being the rebuilding of the Puerta del Sol in 1854-62. However, most of the local traders who benefited from Desamortización lacked the capital to contemplate grand projects, and built separate blocks without ever challenging the established, disorderly street plan. The districts of old Madrid took on the appearance they have largely kept until today, with great numbers of tenement blocks. They allowed Madrid to grow considerably in population, without going outside its still-standing wall of 1656.

A few factories had appeared in the city, but for the most part the Industrial Revolution was passing Madrid by. Constitutional governments expanded the administration, and the ambitions of the middle class were focused on obtaining official posts rather than on business ventures. Two more major changes arrived in the 1850s. In 1851, Madrid got its first railway, to Aranjuez, followed by a line running to the Mediterranean. Railways would transform Madrid's relationship with the rest of the country, opening up a realistic possibility of it fulfilling an economic function. Equally important was the completion of the Canal de Isabel II, bringing water from the Guadarrama, in 1858. Madrid's water supply, still part-based on Moorish water courses, had been inadequate for years. The canal removed a crippling obstruction to the city's growth.

Madrid's population was by this time over 300,000. Steps were finally taken for it to break out of its old walls, and in 1860 a plan by Carlos María de Castro was approved for the Ensanche

(extension) of Madrid, in an orderly grid pattern to the north and east. However, as with earlier rebuilding, the plan came up against the chronic lack of large-scale local investors. The only major development undertaken quickly was the section of C/Serrano bought up by the flamboyant speculator the Marqués de Salamanca, whose name was given to the whole district.

Meanwhile, the political situation was deteriorating once again, after a long period of conservative rule that began in 1856. Isabel II had become deeply unpopular, surrounded by an aura of sleaze and scandal. In September 1868, yet another military revolt deposed the government and, this time, the queen as well.

There followed six years of turmoil. The provisional government invited an Italian prince, Amadeo of Savoy, to become king of a truly constitutional monarchy. However, in December 1870, General Prim, strongman of the new regime, was assassinated. Carlist revolts broke out in some parts of the country, while on the left new, more radical groups began to appear. At the end of 1868, a meeting in Madrid addressed by Giuseppe Fanelli, an Italian associate of Russian revolutionary Mikhail Bakunin, led to the founding of the first anarchist group in Spain. The Cortes itself was riven by factions, and Amadeo decided to give up the struggle and return to Italy.

On 12 February 1873, Spain became a republic. Rightist resistance became stronger than ever, while many towns were taken over by left-wing juntas, who declared them autonomous 'cantons', horrifying conservative opinion. To keep control, Republican governments relied increasingly heavily on the army. This proved fatal, and on 3 January 1874 the army commander in Madrid, General Pavía, marched into the Cortes, sent all its members home, and installed a military dictatorship.

THE BOURBONS RETURN

At the end of 1874, the army decided to restore the Bourbon dynasty, in the shape of Alfonso XII (1874-85), son of Isabel II.

IN CONTEXT

The architect of the Restoration regime, however, was a civilian politician, Antonio Cánovas del Castillo. He established the system of *turno pacífico,* or peaceful alternation in power (thus avoiding social tensions), between a Conservative Party, led by himself, and a Liberal Party which was made up of former progressives. The control of these 'dynastic parties' over the political system was secured by election-rigging and occasional repression.

In the late 1870s, the wealthy of Madrid set out on a building boom. They finally overcame their reluctance to leave the old city, and the Salamanca area became the new centre of fashionable life. Most of the district's new apartment blocks had lifts, first seen in Madrid in 1874. In earlier blocks upper floors had been let cheaply, so that rich and poor had often continued to live side by side. With lifts, however, a top floor could be as desirable as a first, and this kind of class mixing faded.

Government and official bodies, too, undertook a huge round of new building. The Banco de España, the Bolsa and the main railway stations are all creations of the 1880s. Madrid meanwhile acquired a larger professional middle class; it also attracted intellectuals from around the country.

At the same time, Madrid was receiving an influx of poor migrants from rural Spain, with over 200,000 new arrivals between 1874 and 1900. Economic growth was reflected in the appearance of yet more small workshops rather than factories. There were also many with next to no work, and the 1880s saw the beginning of a housing crisis, with the growth of shanty towns around the outskirts of the city.

THE EMPIRE STRIKES BACK

Just before the end of the century, however, the preconceptions on which Spanish political life had been based received a huge blow. The Restoration regime presented itself as having returned the country to stability and some prestige in the world. However, in the 1890s Spain was involved in colonial wars against nationalists in the Philippines and Cuba.

In 1898, the government allowed itself to be manoeuvred into a disastrous war with the United States. In a few weeks, almost the entire Spanish navy was sunk, and Spain lost virtually all its remaining overseas territories. Known simply as 'The Disaster', this was a devastating blow to Spain's self-confidence. The regime itself was revealed as decrepit and incompetent, based on a feeble economy. Among intellectuals, the situation sparked off an intense round of self-examination and discussion of Spain's relationship with the very concept of modernity. The problems of the regime were not due to the country being backward, however. Rather, they spiralled out of control because after 1900 the country entered an unprecedented period of change.

CITY WITHOUT LIMITS

Sudden economic expansion was set off by three main factors. One, paradoxically, was the loss of the colonies, which led to large amounts of capital being brought back to the country. Most important was World War I, which provided opportunities for neutral Spain in the supply of goods to the Allied powers. Then, during the worldwide boom of the 1920s, Spain benefited hugely from foreign investment.

Within a few years, Spain had one of the fastest rates of urbanisation in the world. The economic upheaval caused by the world war led to runaway inflation, spurring a huge movement into the cities. Madrid did not grow as rapidly as industrial Barcelona, which had become the largest city in the country. Nevertheless, after taking four centuries to reach half a million, it doubled its population again in just 30 years, to just under a million by 1930. Only 37 per cent of its people had been born in the city.

The most visible manifestation of this growth was a still-larger building boom. Bombastic creations such as the Palacio de Comunicaciones (now called the Palacio de Cibeles) were symptomatic of the expansive mood. Most important was the opening of the Gran Vía in 1910, a project that had first been discussed no less than 25 years previously, which would transform the heart of the old city

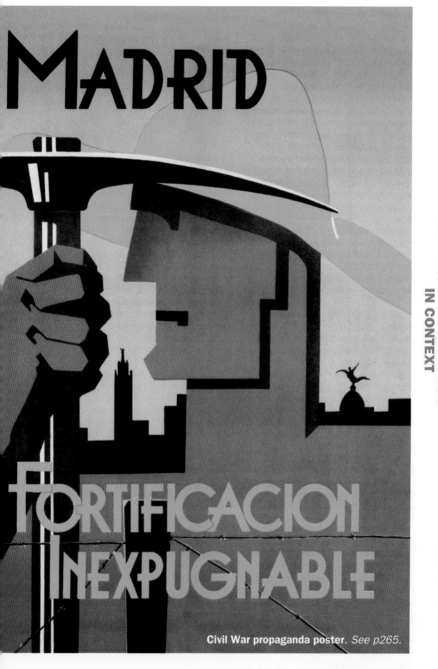

Civil War propaganda poster. *See p265*.

with a new grand thoroughfare for entertainment, business and banking. Another fundamental innovation was electricity. The city's trams were electrified in 1898, and the first metro line, between Sol and Cuatro Caminos, opened in 1919. Electricity allowed Madrid, far from any other source of power, finally to experience an industrial take-off in the years after 1910. At the same time, expansion in banking and office work was also reflected in the large number of white-collar workers.

Madrid was also, more than ever, the mecca for intellectuals and professionals from right across the country. This was the background to the enormous vigour of the city's intellectual life at this time, the so-called 'Silver Age' of Spanish literature. From writers of 1898, such as Antonio Machado and Baroja, to the famous poets of the 1927 generation, Rafael Alberti and García Lorca, the city welcomed a succession of literary talent, not to mention painters, historians and scientists. From the 1910s onward, Madrid's cafés were full of talk, forums for discussion multiplied, and a large number of newspapers and magazines were published.

In politics, this urban expansion made it impossible for the 'dynastic parties' to control elections in the way they were able to do in small towns and rural areas. In an attempt to move back towards some form of constitutional rule, the government decided to hold local elections on 12 April 1931. They were not expected to be a referendum on the monarchy. However, when the results came in it was seen that republican candidates had won sweeping majorities in all of Spain's cities.

THE SECOND REPUBLIC

On 14 April 1931, as the results of the local elections became clear, the streets of Spain's cities filled with people. In Madrid, a jubilant mass converged on the Puerta del Sol. It was these exultant crowds in the streets that drove the king to abdicate and spurred republican politicians into action, for they had never expected their opportunity to arrive so soon.

'Franco died in November 1975, closing a parenthesis of nearly 40 years in Spanish history.'

The second Spanish Republic arrived amid huge optimism, expressing the frustrated hopes of decades. Among the many schemes of its first government, a Republican-Socialist coalition, was a project for Madrid, the Gran Madrid or 'Greater Madrid' plan, intended to integrate the sprawling new areas around the city's edge. A key part of it was the extension of the Castellana, then blocked by a racecourse above C/Joaquín Costa. The racecourse was demolished, and the Castellana was allowed to snake endlessly northward, forming one of the modern city's most distinctive features. Also completed under the Republic was the last section of the Gran Vía, from Callao to Plaza de España, site of Madrid's best art deco buildings.

Possibilities of further change were to be entangled in the accelerating social crisis that overtook the Republic around this time. The new regime aroused expectations that would have been difficult to live up to at the best of times. Instead, its arrival coincided with the onset of the worldwide depression of the 1930s.

THE POLARISATION OF POLITICS

As unemployment and the gap between rich and poor increased, calls for the end of republican compromise in a second, social, revolution grew, especially from the anarchist CNT and the Communist Party. Even the Socialist Party was radicalised. On the right, similarly, the loudest voices – such as the fascist Falange, founded in 1933 by José Antonio Primo de Rivera, son of the former dictator – demanded authoritarian rule as the only means of preserving social order. The vogue for extremism was

IN CONTEXT

fed by the mood of the times, in which Nazism, Italian Fascism and Soviet Communism appeared as the most dynamic international models.

In 1933, the coalition between Socialists and liberal republicans broke up. With the left split, elections were won by conservative republicans backed by the CEDA, a parliamentary but authoritarian right-wing party. Reform came to a halt. In October 1934, the CEDA demanded to have ministers in the government, and a general strike was called in response. It was strongest in the mining region of Asturias, where it was savagely suppressed by a rising general called Francisco Franco.

Left-wing parties were subjected to a wave of repression that radicalised their supporters further. In new elections in February 1936, however, the left, united once again in the Frente Popular (Popular Front), were victorious. In Madrid, the Front won 54 per cent of the vote.

A liberal-republican government returned to power, with Manuel Azaña as president. By this time, however, the level of polarisation and of sheer hatred in the country was moving out of control. Right-wing politicians called almost openly for the army to save the country. The military had already laid their plans for a coup.

REVOLUTION AND WAR

On 18 July 1936, the generals made their move, with risings all over Spain, while German and Italian aircraft ferried Franco's colonial army from Spanish Morocco to Andalucia. In Madrid, troops failed to seize the city and barricaded themselves inside the Montaña barracks, the site of which is now in the Parque del Oeste.

The coup was the spark for an explosion of tension. Workers' parties demanded arms. On 20 July, as news came that the army had been defeated in Barcelona and many other cities, the Montaña was stormed and its defenders massacred, despite the efforts of political leaders to prevent it. Among left-wing militants the mood was ecstatic: factories, schools, the transport system and other public services were all taken over, and although the government

remained in place, it had little effective power. Ad-hoc militias and patrols were the only power on the streets, and, amid the paranoia and hatred that were the other side of revolutionary excitement, summary executions of suspected rightists were common.

Meanwhile, the war still had to be fought. Franco's troops were advancing from Seville preceded by stories of reprisals more terrible than anything done by the 'red terror' in Madrid. The militias seemed powerless to stop them. Defeat for the Republic seemed inevitable. German planes bombed the city. On 6 November, as Franco's advance guard arrived, the government left for Valencia, a move widely seen as desertion.

CITY UNDER SIEGE

Without a government, though, a new resolve was seen in the city. In the southern suburbs, troops were resisted street by street. Women, children and the elderly helped build trenches and barricades. On 9 November 1936, the first foreign volunteers, the International Brigades, arrived, doing wonders for morale. After savage fighting, Franco halted the frontal assault on Madrid later that month.

Madrid saw little more direct fighting. From the Casa de Campo, where the remains of trenches and bunkers still exist, the army settled in to a siege. Attempts to push them back north and south of Madrid were unsuccessful. The city was regularly bombed, and bombarded by artillery, who took their sights from the Gran Vía, 'Howitzer Avenue'.

General Franco, meanwhile, was advancing on other fronts. During 1937, his forces overran the Basque Country and Asturias, and in March 1938 they reached the Mediterranean near Castellón. In January 1939, they conquered Catalonia. In Madrid, fighting broke out behind Republican lines between the Communists, committed to fighting to the end, and groups that wanted to negotiate a settlement with Franco. Those in favour of negotiation won, but Franco had no intention of compromising. On 28 March 1939, the Nationalist army entered the Spanish capital.

IN CONTEXT

THE LONG DICTATORSHIP

Madrid emerged from the Civil War physically and psychologically battered. Hundreds of buildings stood in ruins. Buildings, however, could be rebuilt fairly quickly; healing the damage done to the city's spirit would take decades.

The Madrid of the 1940s was the sombre antithesis of the expansive city of ten years previously. A great many *madrileños* had lost someone close to them, to bombs, bullets, firing squads or prison camps. The black market, rather than art and literature, dominated café conversation, and the figures of earlier years were mostly in exile, or keeping indoors.

The existence of 'two Spains' (right–left, traditional–liberal, rich–poor) was all too apparent. As the victors marched in, they wasted no time in rounding up members (or just suspected sympathisers) of 'enemy' groups, anarchists, Communists, union members and liberals. Some were turned in by neighbours, creating a sordid atmosphere of bitterness and distrust. During the early '40s, while the rest of the world was wrapped up in World War II, thousands were executed in Spain. Others paid the price of defeat by serving as forced labour on fascist landmarks such as the Valle de los Caídos, Franco's victory monument and tomb.

Madrid's loyalty to the Republic almost led to it losing its capital status, as voices were raised calling for a more 'loyal' city to represent the country. Tradition and financial interests bore more weight, however, and the capital stayed put. The Falange, official party of the regime, produced extravagant plans to turn Madrid into a Spanish version of Imperial Rome, but a lack of funding and galloping inflation scotched most of these nouveau-Imperialist notions. The economy was in a desperate state, and Spain went through a period of extreme hardship, the *años del hambre* ('hunger years'); many remember not having eaten properly for ten years after 1936. This poverty also led to the phenomenon that would most shape the face of Madrid in the post-war decades: massive immigration from Spain's rural provinces. Madrid grew faster than any

other European capital in the 20th century. A 'big village' of just over half a million at the turn of the century, and 950,000 in 1930, it passed the three million mark by 1970.

Most European countries continued to shun the regime, at least in public, but in 1953, as the Cold War intensified, Franco was saved by the US government's 'our son-of-a-bitch' policy in choosing allies. A co-operation treaty gave the regime renewed credibility and cash in exchange for air and sea bases on Spanish soil, and later President Eisenhower flew in to shake the dictator's hand.

For those not devoted to the regime, life under Franco was a matter of keeping one's head down. Football and other forms of escapism played a huge part in people's lives.

The national Stabilisation Plan of 1959 gave the fundamental push to Madrid's development, and brought Spain definitively back into the Western fold. The plan revolutionised the country's economy, and especially that of the Madrid region. In the 1960s, tourism began to pump money into Spain, and Madrid trebled in size to become an industrial powerhouse. Quiet tree-lined boulevards were widened to make way for cars, and elegant Castellana palaces were replaced by glass-sheathed monoliths. Madrid took on much more of the look, and feel, of a big city.

LIFE AFTER FRANCO

The 1960s also saw the revival of opposition to the regime in the shape of labour unrest, student protests, and the rise of the Basque organisation ETA. The oil crisis of 1973 coincided with the assassination by ETA of Franco's prime minister, Admiral Carrero Blanco, when a bomb planted beneath a Madrid street launched his car right over a five-storey building. The regime, already challenged by political opposition, now had to deal with rising unemployment, inflation and a moribund Franco. The transition to democracy had begun.

Franco died in November 1975, closing a parenthesis of nearly 40 years in Spanish history. A new age, uncertain

In the Frame The Majas

Goya's portraits of the majas are clothed (or otherwise) with intrigue.

In the 18th century, ordinary people in European cities began to look increasingly similar, wearing more or less the same three-cornered hats, breeches and mop-caps. Not so in Madrid, where this was the era of the *majos* and *majas*. A *majo* wore embroidered shirts, a short jacket with a swathe of buttons and a hair-net, and carried a knife. *Majas* wore short, mid-calf skirts with a mass of petticoats, pearl-white stockings, embroidered bodices, an intricately braided hairstyle and a dramatic lace mantilla. They were drawn from trades such as coach-driving, dressmaking, cigarette-rolling or market trading, and most often came from Lavapiés. *Majas* especially were known for their wit, grace and verbal ferocity. In a capital that was still largely a city of servants, but whose servants were renowned for talking back, they deferred to no one.

They were mostly seen in all their finery at *fiestas* such as the Romería de San Isidro. Goya depicted them often. Also, their cocky elegance led to their style being taken up by the upper classes, so that even *grandes dames*

such as the Duchess of Alba would dress up as *majas*, which is what probably gave rise to the story that Goya's nude and clothed *majas* are portraits of the Duchess herself.

This theory has been discredited by scholars in recent years, but still has many subscribers; the woman depicted does bear a startling resemblance to the Duchess, and the large bow around her waist featured in several of Goya's portraits of her. And, yes, it is possibly true that the Duchess had an affair with the painter, with whom she holed up for several months on one of her country estates after her husband died. It is unlikely that she would allow herself to be painted in such a way, though, given her standing in society. Some critics suggest the head was painted on the body later, and this is certainly the visual effect. What is irrefutable, however, is that Goya was obsessed with Alba, and a more probable explanation for the likeness is simply that he tended to project her image on to an idealised form of female beauty. *Clothed Maja* and *Nude Maja* are both on display at the Prado.

but exciting, dawned. In July 1976, King Juan Carlos, chosen by Franco to succeed him, named a former Falange bureaucrat, Adolfo Suárez, as prime minister. Nobody, however, knew quite what was going to happen. To widespread surprise, Suárez initiated a comprehensive programme of political reform. Clandestine opposition leaders surfaced, parties were legalised and famous exiles began coming home. The first democratic elections since 1936 were held in June 1977, and a constitution was approved in late 1978. Suárez's centrist UCD (Centre-Democratic Union) won the national elections, but local elections in Madrid in 1979 were won by the Socialists, led by Enrique Tierno Galván as Mayor.

The 'other' Spain, however, had not disappeared. In fact, it was starting to feel nervous. Hardcore Francoists were horrified at the thought of Socialists and/or Communists coming to power. Significantly, many of the 'old guard' still held influential positions in the armed forces, and were not inclined to give them up easily.

On 23 February 1981, democrats' worst nightmares appeared to come true when a Civil Guard colonel called Tejero burst into the Cortes with a squad of men, firing his pistol into the air. A little after midnight, King Juan Carlos appeared on TV and assured the country that the army had sworn him its allegiance and that the coup attempt would fail. The next day, people poured out on to the streets to demonstrate support for freedom and democracy.

The wolf had shown its teeth, but they were not as sharp as had been feared. Moreover, the coup attempt significantly helped to win Felipe González and the socialist PSOE their landslide victory in the elections of November 1982.

SOCIAL REVOLUTION, CITY RENOVATIONS

The late 1970s and early '80s saw the arrival of democracy and free speech, the loosening of drug laws and the breakdown of sexual conventions. The compulsorily staid Madrid of earlier years gave way to an anything-goes, vivacious city:

Protests against austerity measures, March 2013

an explosion of art, counter-culture and nightlife, creativity and frivolity known as the Movida – very roughly translatable as 'Shift' or 'Movement'.

The Socialists used their control of Madrid's Ayuntamiento – led by the fondly remembered Tierno Galván – to renovate the city's weak infrastructure, with long-overdue facelifts in squares and parks. Mayor Tierno also provided unprecedented support for various progressive causes and for the arts, launching a whole string of new festivals.

If Tierno Galván's local administration was happy to be regarded as godfather to the Movida, the national government of Felipe González was more eager still to be seen as leaders of a reborn country. Decades of isolation ended with Spain's entry into the EU in 1986. This had a near-immediate effect on the economy, and in the late '80s the country was the fastest-growing member of the EU. The González governments achieved major improvements in some areas – among them health and the transport system – but also frustrated the expectations of many of their supporters, often giving the impression they believed modernisation would solve all Spain's problems more or less by itself.

The apotheosis of the country's transition was the 'Year of Spain' in 1992, with the Barcelona Olympics, Expo '92 in Seville and, with a somewhat lower profile, Madrid's year as Cultural Capital of Europe. Afterwards, a different mood became apparent. Spain's pre-'92 boom had postponed the effects of the international downturn at the end of the '80s, but it hit Madrid with a vengeance in 1993. Breakneck growth had created its own problems, and land speculation sent property prices spiralling.

Disenchantment with the Socialists and a newly cautious mood that followed the brash overconfidence of the boom years were major factors behind the rise of the re-formed right of the Partido Popular (PP). Even before Spain's great year, in 1991, the PSOE had lost control of the Madrid city administration to the PP.

THE POPULAR VOTE

The 1990s in Spain were markedly different in feel and content from the preceding decade. Led by the deliberately bland José María Aznar, the Partido Popular (PP) ably connected with the groundswell of discontent provoked by the later years of Socialist administrations. In the 1993 election Felipe González, long the great survivor of Spanish politics, lost his overall majority, but staggered on for another three years by means of a pact with Catalan nationalists. The next time, however, in 1996, the winners were the PP, even though they too still had to rely on pacts with minority parties to be able to form a sustainable government. The PSOE was sent into opposition for the first time in 14 years.

In Madrid, the PP had already made its mark on local life. Having rallied voters by denouncing the sleaze and corruption that overwhelmed the PSOE, and the Socialists' irresponsible – as many saw it – spending of taxpayers' money, the PP felt it had a clear mandate to cut back and balance the books. In Madrid, this meant cuts in budgets for arts festivals, a tightening up on licences for new bars

and clubs, and a general attack on the supposed excesses of the nightlife scene.

Despite harsh criticism for its perceived philistine approach to culture, un-liberal stance on issues such as immigration and gay rights, and Francoist origins, the PP won an absolute majority in the 2000 general elections, thanks mainly to its practical approach to the economy and the disarray of the opposition. Its second term in office was a different story, with the 2002 general strike, followed by the sinking of the *Prestige*, Spain's worst-ever ecological disaster. Aznar's flirtation with Bush and Blair led to Spain participating, albeit in a small way, in the Iraq war, against the wishes of 94 per cent of the Spanish people.

The 11 March bombings, and the subsequent media manipulation, were the last straw. The Socialists, under the mild-mannered José Luis Zapatero, had been carefully rebuilding and were now seen as an alternative. On taking power, Zapatero's government immediately brought the Spanish troops back from Iraq and embarked cautiously but firmly on a programme of modernisation of political structures and society. Steps were taken to redefine the nature of relationships between the autonomous regions and the Spanish state, gender issues were addressed with, among other things, a record number of women in the cabinet, and gay marriages were legalised. First steps were taken on the rocky road to peace in the Basque Country. In March 2006, ETA declared a 'permanent ceasefire', but later claimed responsibility for a bomb that exploded at Barajas airport, killing two, in December 2006.

Zapatero won a second term in the 2008 elections. However, with Spain's rate of unemployment rapidly increasing from eight per cent to 20 per cent, the rising cost of living, and the government's wildly unpopular labour and pensions reforms as part of its austerity drive, the PP's victory in November 2011, with Mariano Rajoy at the helm, came as no surprise. The PP's austerity measures have proven no more popular, though, and the party has been dogged by corruption scandals. *Plus ça change.*

IN CONTEXT

Architecture

The making of Madrid.

TEXT: HARVEY HOLTOM

Madrid's past, turbulent and grand in equal measure, is barely apparent from the capital's architecture. The city walls stayed up until the 1860s – longer than in most European cities – meaning that Madrid was forced to build on top of itself, replacing existing constructions at such a rate that by the late 19th century it was a surprisingly modern city.

Its history is, however, reflected in a highly individual, eccentric mixture of architectural styles. To a greater or lesser degree, traces of most of Madrid's past epochs and their influences – Moorish, Flemish, Italian, French and American – are to be found. A truly *madrileño* architectural identity is elusive, but the city can claim one, typically unusual, style as its own – neo-Mudéjar. Madrid also has many unique monuments.

The urban planning boom of the past decade, which saw building works blocking up squares and closing off streets for years, has now slowed with the recession, delaying projects such as the high-profile Campus of Justice. But its legacy is some hugely impressive new architecture (CaixaForum, Matadero Madrid) and a host of revitalised, more pedestrian-friendly public spaces.

IN THE BEGINNING

The first town wall was built by the Moors, and a segment of it (the **Muralla Arabe**) can be found on Cuesta de la Vega, near the Almudena cathedral. For centuries after their 're-conquest', Madrid and most of Castile continued to have large populations of Muslims living under Christian rule, the Mudéjares. The Castilian monarchs were greatly in thrall to their superior building skills, especially in bricklaying and tiling, and throughout the Middle Ages many of the country's important buildings incorporated techniques and styles that had originated in Muslim Andalucia. Hallmarks of the Mudéjar style are Moorish arches and intricate geometric patterns in brickwork, as seen in the 12th-century tower of Madrid's oldest surviving church, **San Nicolás de las Servitas**, built by Arab craftsmen (the body was later rebuilt). Madrid's other Mudéjar tower, on **San Pedro el Viejo**, was built 200 years later. Other medieval buildings in Madrid, such as the 15th-century **Torre de los Lujanes** in Plaza de la Villa, were much plainer in style, reflecting the town's humble status before 1561.

CAPITAL GAINS

Capital status, gained briefly in 1561 and definitively from 1606, transformed Madrid and its architecture. As royal seat, 'the Court', the tastes of successive rulers were especially important. Philip II's favourite architect, Juan de Herrera, was the first to leave a stamp on the city. He and his royal master had little idea of urban planning, but their major constructions – the **Puente de Segovia** (1584), the first stages of the Plaza Mayor, and the widening of Calles Atocha and Segovia – gave Madrid a shape that lasts to this day.

El Escorial, designed by Herrera and Juan Bautista de Toledo, firmly established the 'Herreran' or 'Court' style – austere, rigid and typically employing grey slate for rooftops and the ubiquitous pointed turrets – that became near-obligatory for major buildings in Madrid until the end of the Habsburg era in 1700, despite changes in fashion elsewhere in

Europe. Now a symbol of the 'Madrid of the Austrias', it is also known as Castilian baroque, but few of its features are especially 'Castilian': the slate pinnacles came from Flanders, which appealed to the Flemish-born Charles V.

Herrera's chief disciple, Juan Gómez de Mora, modified his master's legacy with a lighter and less monolithic style. He oversaw the completion of the **Plaza Mayor** in 1619 – his original plan is still recognisable in the slate spires, high-pitched roofs and dormer windows – and the 1630 **Casa de la Villa**, the City Hall. Gómez was also structurally innovative, as seen in the massive cellars and housing blocks along Cava San Miguel, which back on to and complete the Plaza Mayor. Because of the abrupt drop in the level of the land, he had to build up to eight storeys high for these blocks to meet the rest of the square, making them Madrid's tallest buildings until the 20th century.

His great rival in Madrid was Gian Battista Crescenzi, an Italian who adopted the 'Court style' – with some Italian flourishes – to please his Spanish masters. Both architects probably worked, at different times, on the **Palacio de Santa Cruz** near the Plaza Mayor, which was built in 1629-43 and is nowadays home to the Foreign Ministry. It shows clear Italian baroque influences, with a façade much more richly shaped than anything Herrera would have tried. Crescenzi also undertook the largest single building scheme of Habsburg Madrid, the **Palacio del Buen Retiro**, parts of which have survived.

Though the Habsburgs commissioned much that was noble and even palatial, 17th-century visitors to Madrid still saw haphazard growth, chaos and dirt rather than a city fit to be capital of the first worldwide empire. Much building was unimpressive owing to the rickety economy, which meant bricks and mortar were favoured over expensive stone.

BOURBON RENEWAL

The expiry of the Spanish Habsburgs with King Charles II in 1700 was followed by war and the arrival of the Bourbons, under Philip V. The new dynasty endeavoured to embellish and dignify Madrid. The

IN CONTEXT

Bourbons were French, and Philip V's second wife, Isabella Farnese, was Italian, and these two influences would long predominate in the dynasty's architectural tastes. Nevertheless, Philip V's administrator in Madrid, the Marqués de Vadillo, commissioned a local architect, Pedro de Ribera, for many projects, among them the 1722 Hospice (now the **Museo de Historia**), the **Cuartel Conde Duque** barracks (now the Centro Cultural Conde Duque), the **Puente de Toledo** and many churches. Ribera's buildings, while following the Herreran tradition, feature exuberant baroque façades centred on elaborately carved entrance porticoes. Many Ribera entrances still survive on buildings that have since been rebuilt,

as in the 1734 Palace of the Dukes of Santoña at C/Huertas 3, now occupied by the Cámara de Comercio.

The influence of French and Italian architects was more apparent elsewhere in 18th-century Madrid. After the old grey-spired **Alcázar** burnt down in 1734, Philip V commissioned a new **Palacio Real** from a group of mainly Italian architects led by Filippo Juvarra and Giambattista Sacchetti. Responsible for many projects was Charles III's 'chief engineer', Francesco Sabatini. The great exponents of the sober, 'pure' neoclassicism of the later years of Charles III's reign, though, were Spaniards: Ventura Rodríguez, who had also worked on the Palacio Real, and Juan de Villanueva, architect of the

Underneath the Arches

The Moorish origins of Madrid's very own architectural style.

Around 1870, an architectural style emerged in Madrid that the city can claim as its own: neo-Mudéjar. The first example was the new bullring to replace the plain 18th-century one that stood near Puerta de Alcalá. In the revivalist atmosphere of the 19th century, architects Ricardo Rodríguez Ayuso and Lorenzo Alvarez Capra decided not to look to Gothic or Egyptian traditions for inspiration, but searched instead for something to revive that was closer to home. They opted for the styles and superb bricklaying techniques that had been employed by the Muslim Mudéjar master builders of medieval Castile.

Neo-Mudéjar uniquely incorporated Moorish horseshoe arches, interlaced brickwork and arabesque tiling, together with a modern use of glass and cast iron. The 1870s bullring no longer stands, but the style became near-obligatory for *plazas de toros* throughout Spain, and Madrid's next ring at Las Ventas, completed in 1934, sports many neo-Mudéjar features. The style was extended to other buildings too. Perhaps the best example in Madrid is the Escuelas Aguirre, also by Ayuso

and Alvarez Capra, at the intersection of Calles Alcalá and O'Donnell on the north side of the Retiro. Its outstanding feature is a slim minaret-style tower, with a glass and iron lookout-gallery.

Another splendid Arab-inspired tower is the giant spire of the Santa Cruz church at the top of C/Atocha (No.6), built in 1899-1902. And the city's **Matadero Madrid** cultural centre (*see p84*) is a revamped neo-Mudéjar series of buildings that once housed the city abattoir. But the style was also used for more everyday buildings, as in the block of flats at C/Barquillo 21 in Chueca, which displays a façade combining diamond-pattern brickwork, neo-Moorish plaster details and ironwork balconies.

Museo del Prado and the **Observatorio**. Like the greatest project of the king's reign, the **Paseo del Prado** – of which these buildings were part – they clearly reflect Enlightenment ideals of architecture and urban planning.

RISE AND SPRAWL

Joseph Bonaparte's brief reign (1808-13) saw the first demolition of monasteries and convents, to be replaced by squares such as Plaza Santa Ana. Generally, though, the first half of the 19th century brought architectural stagnation to Madrid. After the great clearance of monasteries began in the 1830s, many of the buildings that replaced them were simple apartment and tenement blocks, such as the *corralas* (*see p50*). Public buildings of this time, such as the 1840s **Cortes** or the **Teatro Real**, were often conservative and neoclassical in style.

Greater changes came to Madrid after 1860, with the demolition of the walls and Carlos María de Castro's plan for the city's extension or '*ensanche*'. Areas covered by the plan are easy to spot on a map by their grid street pattern. Chief among them is the Barrio de Salamanca, still the most self-consciously grand *barrio* of the *ensanche*. Its wealthiest residents built in an eclectic mix of styles; some of their opulent mansions still stand on Calles Velázquez and Serrano. Other *ensanche* districts – like Chamberí and Argüelles – show rational urban layout, wide thoroughfares and regular-sized blocks.

Public buildings of the first years of the Bourbon Restoration were as eclectic as Salamanca mansions. Madrid's own revivalist style, neo-Mudéjar (*see p272* **Underneath the Arches**), was used for official buildings, bullrings, churches, homes and factories. In contrast, one of the most extraordinary constructions of the time, Ricardo Velázquez's **Ministerio de Agricultura** in Atocha, is a remarkable combination of Castilian brickwork and extravagant, French Beaux Arts-style sculpted decoration. This was also the great period of cast-iron architecture in Madrid, with fine structures such as the city markets and the **Estación de Atocha**.

Art nouveau (called '*modernismo*' in Spain), so characteristic of early 20th-century Barcelona, aroused little interest in Madrid, but there are some examples. The **Sociedad General de Autores** (1902), by Jose Grasés Riera, is the best known, but the **Casa Pérez Villamil** at Plaza Matute 6, off C/Huertas, is also impressive.

CUTTING A SWATHE

As the *ensanche* progressed and Madrid's economy boomed from the 1900s to the 1920s, the city's architects looked for inspiration forwards and backwards in time, and both inside and outside Spain. The **Gran Vía**, which celebrated its centenary in 2010, was born of this thinking. An all-modern thoroughfare through Madrid's old centre, the Gran Vía destroyed 14 old streets, becoming grander and more eccentric as it progressed. Writer Francisco Umbral claims it recalls New York or Chicago, but its first building of any standing, the 1905 **Edificio Metrópolis**, shows French inspiration. No.24 is neo-Renaissance, the 1930s **Palacio de la Música** cinema (No.35) has distinctly baroque touches, and the 1929 **Telefónica** building (on the corner of C/Fuencarral) is a New York skyscraper in miniature. The 1930 apartment block at Gran Vía 60 is a classic of *madrileño* cosmopolitanism by Carlos Fernández Shaw, who in 1927 also built a futuristic petrol station where C/Alberto Aguilera meets Vallehermoso. Also working at this time was the very original Antonio Palacios, main architect of the **Palacio de Cibeles** (1904-18) and the more subtle **Círculo de Bellas Artes**.

During its brief existence the Spanish Republic further encouraged rationalist, rather self-consciously modern architecture, as in the earliest parts of the **Nuevos Ministerios**. Art deco was in vogue, in office blocks such as the **Capitol** building on Gran Vía (corner of C/Jacometrezo) or the curious model housing district of **El Viso**.

Civil war and the arrival of the Franco regime brought much destruction, and had an immediate impact in architecture. Falangist architectural thinking was dominated by nostalgia for a glorious past, and so Madrid acquired monster

IN CONTEXT

constructions that looked straight back to imperial Spain's Golden Age, combined with ideas from German and Italian Fascist architecture. The results were often grandiose, bombastic and, probably unwittingly, kitsch. The foremost example is the **Ministerio del Aire**, at the top of C/Princesa. In Plaza de España is the manically colossal **Edificio España**, the work of brothers Joaquín and José María Otamendi, completed in 1953. Conceived along American lines to be a 'small city' in one huge block, with shops, offices, a hotel and apartments, the building acquired all sorts of neo-Herreran decorative touches outside.

By the 1950s, the regime's ideological enthusiasms were fading, although it still sought to impress. Built with no pretence at neo-baroque or anything similar is the tacky 32-floor 1957 **Torre de Madrid** on Plaza de España. These years, though, also saw the beginnings of real modernity in Madrid, most notably with Francisco Cabrero and Rafael Aburto's **Casa Sindical** at Paseo del Prado 18-20, built in 1948-49 for the Francoist labour unions and now the Health Ministry. Until the 1960s, the floundering Spanish economy still limited the scope for building. When it did improve, Madrid opened up to international influences, but many of its newest buildings were dreary apartment blocks, built for a rapidly growing population.

BACK TO THE FUTURE

As Spanish society and the economy opened up with the rebirth of democracy in the late 1970s, one effect of Francoist retro-obsessions was that Spanish architects – and the public – felt little inclination to look back with nostalgia or add neoclassical fronts to new buildings, and welcomed modernity with gusto. The most influential contemporary architects in Madrid have been Alejandro de la Sota and Francisco Sáenz de Oíza, both active since the 1950s, and Sáenz's gifted and original protégé Rafael Moneo.

An important factor in construction during the 1980s was the Socialist takeover of the city council in 1979, and the government in 1982. Mayor Tierno Galván's Ayuntamiento was committed

to the regeneration of public spaces, and so facilitated the emergence of one of the characteristic features of modern Madrid – daringly imaginative 'grand revamps' of long-decrepit historic buildings. An outstanding example is the **Estación de Atocha**, a run-down, filthy 1880s cast-iron railway terminal that Moneo transformed into a multi-purpose space. The **Reina Sofía** and **Thyssen** museums were also rebuilt, and the Centro Cultural Conde Duque was created out of Ribera's 1720s barracks.

Outside the public domain, the most vigorous contributions to Madrid since the mid 1980s have been the skyscrapers that line the upper Paseo de la Castellana: the superb white 1988 **Torre Picasso** by Minoru Yamasaki and the spectacular leaning towers of the **Puerta de Europa** at Plaza Castilla. With Madrid's expansion, much recent building has taken place on the city's edge, such as the **Feria de Madrid** complex, Manuel Delgado and Fernando Vasco's **Estadio de la Comunidad de Madrid** (a dramatic structure in the form of a tilted oval plate), and Richard Rogers' huge Barajas airport terminal with its undulating Chinese bamboo-insulated roofs, which opened in 2006.

The past few years have also seen some exciting new projects, including Moneo's Prado extension (2007), Herzog & de Meuron's **CaixaForum** (see p275 **Power to the People**), the remodelling of the old city abattoir for **Matadero Madrid** (see p84) and Lord Foster's **Torre Caja Madrid** skyscraper (2009). Foster is also behind the cylindrical structures that will form the High and Provincial Courts at the **Campus of Justice**, near the airport. This complex, also involving Richard Rogers and Zaha Hadid, is already semi-complete, but has been put on hold for the foreseeable future while funds are channelled to more pressing concerns. Architect Emilio Ambasz, meanwhile, has chosen Madrid – more specifically, the Paseo del Prado – to create his five-storey, foliage-covered **Museum of Art, Architecture, Design and Urbanism**. It will be paid for by his wealthy foundation, but no completion date has yet been decided.

IN CONTEXT

Power to the People

Herzog & de Meuron's striking CaixaForum exhibition space.

Sure to become one of the city's landmarks, the **CaixaForum** (*see p60*) is Madrid's stunning avant-garde cultural centre on the Paseo del Prado, designed by Herzog & de Meuron. The building is the result of a six-year conversion of the 1899 Mediodía Electrical Power Station, one of the few examples of industrial architecture in central Madrid.

The building is striking for its rusted metal appearance and its apparent defiance of the laws of gravity, with the front part of the structure appearing to float off the ground. Its adjacent 24m (79ft) 'vertical garden', designed in conjunction with French botanist Patrick Blanc, complements the building's intense red and is now one of Madrid's most photographed spots. Herzog has stated that the aim of the garden is to provide a connection with the botanical gardens opposite, and the leafy landscape of the Paseo del Prado.

The only material from the original power station that the architects were able to use was the building's brick shell, which needed to be fully restored and secured with cast iron. The extraneous parts of the building were removed with surgical precision – including the stone base, the removal of which opened up the new public square in front of the building, while simultaneously providing a sheltered space where summertime visitors can cool off.

The inaugural show at the seven-floor building included 37 contemporary works from the Caixa Foundation's collection, with Cindy Sherman and Georg Baselitz featuring. Since then, the centre has held a wide range of art exhibitions, film screenings, concerts and educational programmes, and has become one of Madrid's most-visited attractions – as much for its awe-inspiring appearance as for the cultural attractions within. The arts centre's name comes from sponsorship by Catalan savings bank 'La Caixa', whose Obra Social Fundacíon 'La Caixa' operates community and welfare projects in Spain and abroad.

Essential Information

Getting Around

ARRIVING & LEAVING

By air

Madrid's **Barajas Airport** is 14km (9 miles) north-east of the city on the A2 motorway. Thanks to the new terminal T4 (a further 6km away), the airport is used by around 50 million passengers per year. All airlines that are members of the OneWorld network (including BA, Iberia, Aer Lingus and American Airlines) share T4 for national and international flights. All other traffic is distributed between the three older terminals. In T1 and T2 there are 24-hour exchange facilities, ATM machines and hotel booking desks. There's a tourist office and rail reservations desk in T1, and there are two tourist offices in T4.

For airport information, call 91 321 10 00, 91 393 60 00 or check www.aena.es, which has updated flight info. Phone lines are open 24 hours a day.

Airport Express The city council's express airport bus runs a 24/7 service (every 15mins in the day and 30mins at night). The easily identifiable yellow buses – which run between T1, T2, T4 and, in town, O'Donnell, Cibeles and Atocha – take around 40 mins and the journey costs €5.
Aerocity *902 151 654, www.aerocity.com.* Provides shuttle services between the airport and city hotels. Handy for small groups and cheaper than taking several taxis. Prices vary (€17-€38) depending on group size. The company has two airport reservation desks.
Bus from the airport *Avda de América terminal (info 91 406 88 10 or 91 406 88 00).* Local buses 200 and 204 run between the public transport hub on the Avenida de América and T1, T2 and T4. A single ticket costs €1.50.
Metro from the airport The metro is another cheap way to get to central Madrid, though there is a €3 supplement for journeys to the airport, so a regular journey will cost between €4.50 and €5. Bear in mind that the Aeropuerto metro station is between T2 and T3, which means that if, as is very likely, you arrive at T1, you have a

10-15min walk to get there. From T4, take the shuttle to T2 (allow 20mins in total). From the airport it's four stops on metro line 8 (pink) and 12mins to Nuevos Ministerios. From here it's around 15mins to the centre of Madrid. You can save money by buying a Metrobús ticket at the airport station.
Taxis from the airport Taxi fares to central Madrid should be around €20-€25 (depending on traffic), including a €5 airport supplement (no luggage supplement). There are further supplements after 10pm and on Sundays (for both, 15¢ per km). There are lots of taxis at Barajas, but ignore drivers who approach you inside the building; use ones at the ranks outside the terminal. Check the meter is at the current minimum fare (€2.30-€3.10, depending on day/time) when you begin the journey; check a map first and have a landmark in mind in the area you're going to. For more on taxis, *see p279.*
Train from the airport The RENFE *cercanías* line from the airport will take you from T4 to Atocha in 26 minutes.

By bus

Almost all international and long-distance coach services to Madrid terminate at the Estación Sur de Autobuses, C/Méndez Álvaro (info 91 468 42 00, 91 468 45 11 from 6.30am to midnight, www.estacion autobusesmadrid.com). It's next to metro (line 6) and *cercanía* (local train lines C5, C7 and C10) stations, both also called Méndez Álvaro. Bus 148 also runs from there to the centre (Plaza del Callao and Plaza de España). Taxi fares from the bus station carry a €3 supplement.

By train

Spanish national railways (RENFE) has two main stations in Madrid. Trains from France, Catalonia and northern Spain arrive at **Chamartín**, on the north side of the city, some distance from the centre. High-speed AVE trains from Andalucía, Barcelona and Valencia, express services from Lisbon and trains from southern and eastern Spain arrive at **Atocha**, at the southern end of the Paseo del

Prado. There are exchange facilities at both stations, and a tourist office at Chamartín. Atocha is also the main hub of RENFE's local rail lines (*cercanías*) for the Madrid area (*see p279*).

Metro line 10 is the fastest from Chamartín to the city centre, and Atocha RENFE (the train station; not the same metro as Atocha) is four metro stops from Sol on line 1. A taxi fare to the centre from Chamartín should be around €14, including a €3 station supplement. There are extra supplements at night and on Sundays (15¢ per km). The same need for caution with cabs at the airport (*see left*) applies to drivers touting for fares at main rail stations. For more information on all Madrid local rail services, *see p279.*

RENFE Information
902 320 320 or 902 240 202, www.renfe.es. **Open** *Information* 24hrs daily. *Reservations* 5am-10.30pm daily.
Estación de Atocha
Glorieta del Emperador Carlos V. Metro Atocha Renfe. **Map** p312 J14.
Estación de Chamartín
C/Agustín de Foxá, Chamartín. Metro Chamartín.

PUBLIC TRANSPORT

To really get to know Madrid, it's best to explore on foot. Most of the main attractions are within walking distance of one another, and for orientation purposes think of Puerta del Sol as the centre. Street numbers in Madrid all run outwards from Sol. Public transport is cheap and efficient – both bus and metro will get you where you want to go within half an hour, although it's best to avoid the buses during rush hour. Note: all transport and taxi fares are subject to revision in January.

For transport outside Madrid, *see p228.* For transport for disabled travellers, *see* **Resources A-Z.**

Fares

Madrid's fare structure is based on a €1.50 minimum, valid for up to nine stops, and then 10¢ for each stop thereafter (excluding Barajas Airport, which carries a €3 supplement) within the capital, no matter how long the journey. On the metro you can change any number of times as long as you don't leave a station. The exceptions are trips to the stations Rivas Urbanizaciones, Rivas Vaciamadrid, La Poveda and Arganda del Rey (all Line 9), and all stations beyond Puerta del Sur on the new Metro Sur line, which circles the southern suburbs.

However, it's easier and more economical to buy a ticket for ten journeys (*billete de diez/Metrobús*), which can be used on the bus and metro, available at all metro stations and some *estancos* and *kioskos*, but not on the bus. You can share the ticket between two or more people and keep it for as long as you like (or until the prices go up). The current price of a Metrobús is €12.20.

On the metro, you simply insert the ticket into the machine at the gate that leads through to the platform, which cancels one unit for each trip – remember to collect it afterwards – and will reject expired tickets. There is no checking or collection of tickets at station exits. On buses, the Metrobús should be inserted arrow downwards into the blue and yellow machine just behind the driver.

Abonos – season tickets

If you're planning to stay much longer than a fortnight, a monthly season ticket is a good idea. Unlike the Metrobús, it is valid for *cercanías* trains as well as the metro and city buses, allowing you to use it on some trips out of town. Your first *abono* must be obtained with an identity card, available only from *estancos*, for which you will need two passport-size photos and must fill in a brief form. In subsequent months you can buy tickets to revalidate the card from metro stations and EMT kiosks as well as *estancos*. Note, though, that an *abono* is valid for an actual calendar month, not for 30 days from date of purchase, so that if your stay runs across two months, buying one may not be particularly economical unless you qualify for one of the different age discounts. Also, if you can, buy your *abono* before the start of the month to avoid the nightmare queues on the first of the month.

Unless you are intending to travel a lot outside the city, Zone A should cover everywhere you need to go. A standard one-month Zone A *abono* currently costs €54.60, and there are substantial reductions for

young people and for over-65s. It can be used on the buses to the airport, for which *see p278*.

Metro

The metro is the quickest and simplest means of travelling to most parts of the city. Each of its 13 lines (including the Metrosur and Ramal lines) is identified by a number and a colour on maps and at stations. The metro is open 6am-2am daily. Tickets are available at all stations from coin-operated machines and staffed ticket booths. Trains run every three to six minutes during weekdays, and every 10-15mins after 11pm and on Sundays. The metro can get packed in rush hours (7.30-9.30am, 1-2.30pm, 7.30-9pm).

Metro information

C/Cavanilles 58, Salamanca & the Retiro (902 44 44 03, www.metro madrid.es). Metro Conde de Casal. **Open** 6am-1.30am daily. There are customer service points at the airport, Atocha, Chamartín, Avenida de América, Nuevos Ministerios and Alto de Arenal stations.

Buses

Run by **Empresa Municipal de Transportes**. See p278 for information about fares and tickets.

Most run about 6am-11.30pm daily, with buses every 10-15mins (more often on more popular routes). Night buses then take over. You board buses at the front, and get off via the middle or rear doors. The fare is the same for each journey (€1.50), however far you go. Officially, there is a limit to how much luggage you can take on city buses, and trying to board with luggage during rush hours is almost impossible. Drivers are not obliged to give you the change if they don't have it (and if what you give them is more than five times the price of the ticket), nor will they allow you to travel for free. But they must write down your contact details for the bus company to send you the change later on.

For tourist buses, *see p281*.

Night buses

Between midnight and around 5am there are 24 night routes in operation – N1 to N24 – called Búho (Owl) buses. All begin from Plaza de Cibeles and run out to the suburbs, and are numbered in a clockwise sequence. Although the

Metro closes at nights, at the weekends special buses, called Metro Búho, cover the routes of the 11 central metro lines (L1-L11). The buses alight at the bus stop nearest to each metro station. The timetable for each line varies, but generally the buses run from 12.45am until 5.45am. L1-L11 buses run every 15 to 20 minutes. There are three buses that cover the L12 Metrosur route, which connects Alcorcón, Leganés, Getafe, Fuenlabrada and Móstoles. The L12 buses run every 30 minutes, from 1.15am to 5.30am.

EMT Information

C/Cerro de la Plata 4, Retiro (91 406 88 10, www.emtmadrid.es). *Metro Pacífico.* **Open** 8am-2pm Mon-Fri.

Cercanías/local trains

The highly efficient *cercanías* or local network of railways for the Madrid area has been expanding in recent years in order to link the suburbs with the centre more directly. It consists of 12 lines converging on Atocha, several of which connect with metro lines along their routes.

As well as the suburbs, *cercanías* trains are useful for trips to Guadarrama and towns near Madrid such as Aranjuez or El Escorial. Also, line C effectively forms a circle line within Madrid that is quicker than the metro for some journeys, and the RENFE line between Chamartín and Atocha is the fastest link between the two main stations. *Cercanías* lines run from 5-6am to 11pm-midnight daily, with trains on most lines about every 10-30mins. Fares vary with distance, but the lines are included in the monthly season ticket. For a map of the *cercanías* network, *see p320*.

TAXIS

Madrid taxis are white, with a diagonal red stripe on the front doors. The city has more than 15,000 taxis, so they are rarely hard to find, except late at night at the weekend or on days when it's raining heavily. When a taxi is free there is a 'Libre' (free) sign behind the windscreen, and a green light on the roof. If there is also a sign with the name of a district in red, it means the driver is on the way home, and is not obliged to take you anywhere that isn't near that particular route. There are taxi ranks, marked by a blue sign with a

ESSENTIAL INFORMATION

white T, throughout the centre of Madrid. At the airport and rail and bus stations, it's always best to take a taxi from the official ranks; within the city, however, those in the know flag cabs down in the street, thereby avoiding the risk both of scams, and of station supplements. To avoid being swindled by a non-official taxi, make sure the driver has their licence number visible on the front and a meter, and always ask for the approximate fare before getting in.

Fares

Official fare rates and supplements are shown inside each cab (in English and Spanish), on the right-hand sun visor and/or the rear windows. The minimum fare is €2.30-€3.10 (depending on the day/time), which is what the meter should show when you first set off. The higher rate applies at night (11pm-6am) and on Sundays and public holidays, and there are extra supplements for trips starting from the bus and train stations (€3); to and from the trade fair complex (€3), and to and from the airport (€5.50). Also, the fare rate is higher for journeys to suburban towns in the outer tariff zone (zone B). Drivers are not officially required to carry more than €20 in change, and some accept credit cards.

Receipts and complaints

To get a receipt, ask for '*un recibo, por favor*'. If you think you've been overcharged or have any other complaint, insist the receipt is made out in full, with details of the journey and the driver's signature, NIF number and licence plate, and the date. Make a note of the taxi number, displayed on a plaque on the dashboard. Take or send the receipt, keeping a copy, with a complaints form to the city taxi office at the address below. The form is included in the Taxi Information leaflet available from tourist offices.

Oficina Municipal del Taxi
C/Albarracín 31 3ª, Eastern suburbs (91 480 46 23). Metro García Noblejas. **Open** 8.30am-2pm Mon-Fri.

Phone cabs

You can call for a cab from any of the companies listed below. Operators will rarely speak much English, so if you aren't at a specific address give the name of the street and a restaurant or bar that makes a suitable place to wait, or position

yourself near a street corner and say, for example, 'San Agustín, *esquina* Prado' (San Agustín, corner of Prado). The operator will also ask you your name. Phone cabs start the meter from the point when a call is answered. Very few cabs will take credit cards.

Radio-Taxi Asociación Gremial
91 447 32 32, www.radiotaxigremial.com
Radio-Taxi Independiente *91 405 12 13, www.radiotaxiindependiente.com*
Radioteléfono Taxi *91 547 82 00, www.radiotelefono-taxi.com*
Teletaxi *91 371 21 31.*

CYCLING

Cycling in Madrid is only for the truly experienced (or the utterly insane) in view of the heavy traffic and lack of cycle lanes on any of the city's central streets (there are a few in parks and by the river). However, bike lanes are gradually improving, and bikes are a great idea for trips to the larger city parks (Retiro, Casa de Campo) and especially the Madrid Sierras. Bikes can be taken free of charge on some *cercanías* lines and on the metro at weekends. Cycle hire shops often ask that you leave proof of identity (take a photocopy to avoid having to leave your passport) as well as a cash deposit. There are an increasing number of companies and associations in Madrid that are dedicated to cycling, including Pedalibre (www.pedalibre.org) and Ciclos Otero (www.oterociclos.es).

DRIVING

Thanks to traffic jams, driving in the city is rarely a quick way of getting anywhere, and finding a parking space is another headache.

Signs & terms

cede el paso – give way
usted no tiene la prioridad – you don't have the right of way
único sentido – one way
cambio de sentido – indicates a junction that allows you to change direction
recuerde – remember
cinturón de seguridad – seat belt
ronda de circunnavegación – ring road

Car & motorbike hire

Car hire can be pricey, so shop around; there are often good weekend deals. Most companies

have a minimum age limit (usually 21) and require you to have had a licence for over a year. You will also need a credit card (as opposed to a debit card), or leave a big cash deposit (sometimes up to €500). Check if IVA (VAT), at 16 per cent, and unlimited mileage are included. All the companies listed require you to take out a *seguro franquicia* – a fixed amount you have to pay in the event of an accident or any damage caused to the vehicle, and which is put on your credit card when you take the car (usually around half the hire cost – it is only charged if you return the vehicle damaged).

Avis *Estación de Chamartín, C/Agustín de Foxa 25, Chamartín (902 090 343, www.avis.es). Metro Plaza de Castilla.* **Open** 8am-9pm Mon-Fri; 8am-2pm Sat, Sun. **Credit** AmEx, DC, MC, V. **Other locations** throughout the city.

Easycar *Barajas Airport (www.easycar.com).* **Credit** DC, MC, V.

Europcar *Paseo de la Castellana 193 (91 555 99 30, www.europcar.com). Metro Plaza de Castilla.* **Open** 7am-9pm Mon-Fri; 8am-2pm Sat. **Credit** AmEx, DC, MC, V. **Other locations** throughout the city.

BlaferMotos *C/Clara del Rey 17, Chamartín (91 413 00 47, www.blafermotos.com). Metro Alfonso XIII.* **Open** 8.30am-6.30pm Mon-Fri; 10am-1.30pm Sat. **Credit** AmEx, MC, V. Motorcycle specialists.

National-Atesa *Plaza de España car park (1st floor) (91 542 96 10, www.atesa.es). Metro Plaza de España.* **Open** 8.30am-7.30pm Mon-Fri; 9am-1pm Sat. **Credit** AmEx, DC, MC, V. **Other locations**: throughout the city

PlanCar
C/Mauricio Legendre 3, Chamartín (91 314 23 10, www.plancar.com). Metro Chamartín. **Open** 9am-2pm, 4.30-8pm Mon-Fri; 9am-2pm Sat. **Credit** MC, V.

Breakdown services

If you are planning to take a car to Spain it's advisable to join a motoring organisation such as the AA or RAC, which have reciprocal arrangements with their Spanish equivalent, RACE.

RACE (Real Automóvil Club de España)
Assistance 902 300 505, info

902 404 545, 91 592 74 00, www.race.es.

The RACE has English-speaking staff and will send immediate 24hr breakdown assistance. Repairs are carried out on the spot when possible; if not, your vehicle will be towed to the nearest suitable garage. Members of affiliated organisations abroad are not charged for call-outs, but non-members pay around €115 (on-the-spot membership) for the basic breakdown service.

Parking

For car-owning *madrileños* parking is a daily trauma. The city police (Policia Municipal) give out tickets readily (many locals never pay them). Be careful not to park in front of doorways with the sign *'vado permanente'*, indicating an entry with 24-hour right of access. The SER (Servicio de Estacionamiento Regulado) system now applies (*see below*) to the whole city centre. Residents park for free if they have an annual sticker.

SER

Non-residents must pay to park in zones painted in blue or green from 9am to 9pm Mon-Fri and 9am to 3pm Sat (9am-3pm Mon-Sat in August). Pay-and-display machines are located on pavements. Maximum validity of tickets is two hours in blue zones and one hour in green, after which a new card must be used, and the car parked in a new spot. Cars parked in the SER zone without a card can be towed away (*see below*). In the blue areas, tickets cost up to €2.90 for two hours and in the green areas, €2.25 for one hour, although there are controversial plans to start charging extra for older cars from 2014. All streets in this zone that have no additional restrictions posted are SER parking areas.

Car parks

Central car parks *Plaza de las Cortes, Plaza Santa Ana, C/Sevilla, Plaza Jacinto Benavente, Plaza Mayor, Plaza Descalzas, C/Tudescos, Plaza de España.* **Open** 24hrs daily. **Rates** €1.20 for 30mins; €4.40 for 90mins, €8.90 for 3hrs; €31.50 for 12 to 24hrs (the maximum).

There are some 50 municipal car parks around Madrid, indicated by a white 'P'-on-blue sign. It's especially advisable to use a car park if your car has foreign plates. Car parks have disabled access. See

also www.madridmovilidad.es for more details.

Towing away
Information 91 787 72 92, www.madridmovilidad.es. **Main pounds** *Plaza Colón. Metro Colón.* **Map** p308 K9. *C/Velázquez 87. Metro Nuñez de Balboa.* **Map** p309 M6. **Open** 24hrs daily.

If your car seems to have been towed away, call the central number and quote your number plate to be told which pound it has gone to. It will cost €147.55 to recover your car. You'll have to pay €1.85 per hour for the first ten hours, timed from the moment it was towed away. For each complete extra day in the pound it's €19.20. You can also locate your car by entering your registration plate number on the website. Bring your ID and all car papers when you pick it up.

TOURS

If you prefer to see the city independently, but need extra guidance, then the website www.descubremadrid.com has a large number of suggested routes and guided maps you can print out.

Bus & coach tours/trips

The following run city tours and/or trips focused on bullfights, flamenco and so on, as well as tours of the towns around Madrid.

Juliá Travel *Plaza de España 7 (91 559 96 05, www.juliatravel.com). Metro Plaza de España.* **Open** 8am-10pm daily. **Credit** MC, V. **Map** p307 E10.
Madrid City Tour *91 360 47 72, www.autobusturisticomadrid.com.* **Tickets** 1 day €21; €9 7-15s, over-65s. 2 days €25; €12 7-16s, over-65s. Free under-7s. **No credit cards.**
City-owned tour service with two routes. Includes guided walk.
Trapsatur *C/San Bernardo 5, Malasaña (91 541 63 21, www.trapsatur.com).* **Metro** *Santo Domingo.* **Open** booking 9am-6.30pm Mon-Fri. **Credit** AmEx, MC, V. **Map** p307 F10.

Segway & GPS-guided tours

GoCar *C/Ferraz 26, Sol & Gran Via (91 559 45 35, www.gocar tours.es/madrid). Metro Ventura Rodriguez.* **Cars available** July, Aug 10am-9pm daily. Sept-June 10am-7pm daily. **Hire** 1hr €35; 2hrs

€60; 3 hrs €80. 5hrs €99. **Credit** AmEx, MC, V. **Map** p311 F12.
Zip around Madrid in a little yellow GoCar – a computer-guided storytelling vehicle that allows you to sightsee at your own pace. The average tour is 2-3hrs.
Madsegs *Meeting point: Plaza de España (mobile 659 824 499, www.madsegs.com). Metro Plaza de España.* **Tours** 10am daily. **Price** €65 (plus €15 deposit). **Credit** DC, MC, V. **Map** p307 E10.
Madrid's oldest Segway tour company offers a two-wheeled way to see the city. Price includes a 3hr tour, helmet, refreshments and photo CD.

Walking, bike & alternative tours

Carpetania Madrid *C/Jesús del Valle 11, Malasaña (91 531 40 18, www.carpetaniamadrid.com). Metro Noviciado.* **Open** 11am-8pm Fri-Sun. **Tours** (2hrs) €9-€12. **Credit** AmEx, DC, MC, V. **Map** p307 G9.
All the guides here are art history specialists. As well as city routes, there are expert guided tours around art exhibitions.
Descubre Madrid *Centro de Turismo de Madrid, Plaza Mayor 27, Los Austrias (91 454 44 10, www.esmadrid.com/descubre madrid). Metro Sol.* **Open** 9.30am-8.30pm daily. **Tickets** *On foot* €5.90. *By bike* €6.90. Free under-5s. **No credit cards. Map** p311 G12.
With over 100 different itineraries (by bus and on foot), this service, run by the tourist board, offers tours focusing on architecture, literature and history.
MadWay to Madrid *Paseo de los Melancólicos 28E (mobile 650 575 756, www.madwaytomadrid.com). Metro Puerta de Toledo.* **Tours** *See website for details of times and prices.* **No credit cards. Map** p310 C14.
Alternative and eco-friendly tours on foot or by bike, in English, Dutch, Spanish, French or Italian.

TICKETS

Madrid Card *91 588 29 00, www.madridcard.com.* **Prices** (5% discount if you buy online) 1 day €44; 2 days €54; 3 days €64. Buy from tourist offices, train stations and travel agents.
Available for one, two or three days, this card offers free admission to up to 40 of the city's museums, and discounts on the Madrid Vision tour bus, shops, restaurants, clubs, theatres and so on.

ESSENTIAL INFORMATION

Resources A-Z

ESSENTIAL INFORMATION

ADDRESSES

Individual flats in apartment blocks have traditionally been identified by the abbreviations z '*izq*' (*izquierda*, left) or '*dcha*' (*derecha*, right) after the floor number (C/Prado 221, 5ª dcha) and occasionally '*int*' (interior, inward facing) or '*ext*' (exterior); in newer buildings they may be shown more simply (C/Prado 223, 4B). A building with no street number (usually huge places like stations or hospitals) has *s/n* (*sin número*) after the street.

AGE RESTRICTIONS

In Spain, you have to be 18 to drive a car, smoke or drink, but the age of consent is a startling 13, although this looks set to rise significantly from late 2013.

BUSINESS

Administrative services

A *gestoría* is a very Spanish kind of institution, combining the functions of lawyer, accountant, business adviser and general aid with bureaucracy. They can be very helpful in seeing short cuts that foreigners are often unaware of. English is spoken at the following *gestoría*.

Gestoría Calvo Canga
Plaza Tirso de Molina 12, Lavapiés (91 577 07 09). Metro Tirso de Molina. **Open** 9am-5pm Mon-Thur; 9am-3pm Fri. **Map** p311 G13.
This is a general *gestoría* that deals with the areas of labour law, tax and accounts, and residency. English spoken.

Conventions & conferences

IFEMA/Feria de Madrid
Recinto Ferial Juan Carlos I, Northern suburbs (902 22 15 15, www.ifema.es). Metro Campo de las Naciones. **Open** *Office* 8am-8pm Mon-Fri.
Madrid's lavish state-of-the-art trade fair centre has ten main pavilions, a 600-seater auditorium, a 10,000sq m convention centre and many smaller facilities, plus 20 catering outlets and no less than 14,000 parking spaces. By the entrance is the Palacio Municipal de Congresos, a 2,000-capacity conference hall.

Madrid Convention Bureau
Plaza Mayor 27, Los Austrias (91 588 29 00, www.munimadrid.es). Metro Opera or Sol. **Open** *Mid Sept-mid June* 9am-6pm Mon-Thur; 9am-3pm Fri. *Mid June-mid Sept* 9am-1pm Mon-Fri. **Map** p311 E12.
An office of the city council that assists those planning to hold a conference or similar event in Madrid. The Oficina de Congresos will facilitate contacts with venues and service companies.

Palacio de Congresos de Madrid
Paseo de la Castellana 99, Tetuán (91 337 81 00, www.palacio congresosmadrid.es). Metro Lima. **Open** 8am-8pm daily.
This venue has been established for longer than the Feria de Madrid (*see above*) and is used for several major international conferences. It has conference rooms and galleries of all sizes; the facilities are excellent.

Recintos Feriales de la Casa de Campo
Avda de Portugal s/n, Casa de Campo (91 722 04 00, www. madridespaciosycongresos.com/

recinto). Metro Lago. **Open** *Sept-July* 8am-3pm Mon-Fri. *Aug* 8am-2pm Mon-Fri.
An attractive site with various halls, auditoria and open-air space.

Courier services

DHL
Ground services 902 12 30 30, air services 902 12 24 24, www.dhl.es. **Open** *Phoneline* 24hrs daily. *Pick-ups & deliveries* 9am-7.30pm Mon-Fri.

Motorecado
Avda del Manzanares 202, Southern suburbs (91 476 71 61, www.motorecado.com). Metro Laguna. **Open** 8am-7pm Mon-Fri. **No credit cards.**

Trébol
C/Embajadores 29, Lavapiés (91 530 32 32, www.trebol.org). Metro Embajadores. **Open** *Sept-July* 9am-8pm Mon-Fri. *Aug* 9am-3pm Mon-Fri. **No credit cards.** **Map** p311 G15.

Office & computer services

Data Rent
C/Mesena 18, Northern suburbs (91 759 62 42, www.datarent.es). Metro Arturo Soria. **Open** *Sept-June* 9am-2pm, 4-7pm Mon-Fri. *July, Aug* 8am-3pm Mon-Fri. **Credit** MC, V.
PCs, printers, OHPs and more for rent by the day, week or month.

Translators

Lionbridge Solutions
Edificio Ofpinar 7º, C/Caleruega 102-104, North of Centre (91 791 34 43, www.lionbridge.com). Metro Pinar de Chamartín. **Open** 9.30am-5.30pm Mon-Fri.
A professional translation service.

Polidioma
C/Rio Rosas 54, Chamberí (91 554 46 20). Metro Canal. **Open** 10am-2pm Mon-Fri; 4-6pm Sat.
In Spain, official and other bodies often demand that foreign documents be translated by legally certified translators. Call for an appointment; rates are higher than for other translators. Some consulates (*see p284*) also provide these services or they can put you in contact with other translators.

Useful organisations

Bolsa de Comercio (Stock Exchange)
Plaza de la Lealtad 1, Retiro (91 709 50 00, www.bolsa madrid.es). Metro Banco de España. **Open** 9am-5.30pm Mon-Fri. **Map** p312 J11.

Cámara de Comercio e Industria de Madrid
C/Ribera del Loira 56, Campo de las Naciones (91 538 35 00, www.camara madrid.es). Metro Campo de las Naciones or Mar de Cristal. **Open** 9am-4pm Mon-Thur; 9am-1am Fri.
Offers a useful information service for foreign investors in Madrid. You will have to make an appointment first.

Instituto Español de Comercio Exterior
Paseo de la Castellana 14-18, Salamanca (91 349 61 00/902 34 90 00, www.icex.es). Metro Colón. **Open** *Sept-June* 9am-2pm, 3-5pm Mon-Thur; 9am-2pm Fri. *July, Aug* 9am-2pm Mon-Fri. **Map** p308 K8.
The state-run ICEX (Spanish Institute for Foreign Trade) has an excellent information service to aid small- to medium-sized businesses.

COMPLAINTS

If you have a complaint, ask for an official complaint form (*hoja de reclamación*), which most businesses, shops, bars and so on are obliged to have available for customers. Fill out the form, leaving the colour copy with the business. Then take this, and any receipts or other relevant paperwork, to the official consumer office, listed below.

Oficina Municipal de Información al Consumidor
C/Principe de Vergara 140, Chamartín (91 529 82 10/010). Metro Cruz del Rayo. **Open** 8.30am-5pm Mon-Thur; 8.30am-2pm Fri. **Map** p307 H11.

The official centre for consumer advice and complaint follow-up. You will need to make an appointment first.

CUSTOMS

If tax has been paid in the country of origin then EU residents do not have to declare goods imported into Spain from other EU countries for their personal use. However, customs officers can question whether large amounts of any item really are for your own use, and random checks are made for drugs. Quantities accepted as being for personal use include:
● up to 800 cigarettes, 400 small cigars, 200 cigars or 1kg of loose tobacco
● 10 litres of spirits (over 22% alcohol), 20 litres of fortified wine or alcoholic drinks with under 22% of alcohol, 90 litres of wine (under 22%) or 110 litres of beer.

Limits for non-EU residents and goods brought from outside the EU:
● 200 cigarettes or 100 small cigars or 50 cigars or 250g (8.82oz) of tobacco
● 1 litre of spirits (over 22% alcohol) or 2 litres of any other alcoholic drink with under 22% alcohol
● 50g (1.76oz) of perfume
● 500g coffee, 100g tea

There are no restrictions on cameras, watches or electrical goods, within reasonable limits, and visitors are also allowed to carry up to €10,000 in cash. Non-EU residents can also reclaim the VAT (IVA) they have paid on certain large purchases when they leave Spain. For details, *see p135.*

DISABLED TRAVELLERS

Madrid is still not a city that disabled people, especially wheelchair users, will find it very easy to get around. However, the situation is steadily improving as new buildings are constructed with accessibility in mind and old ones are gradually adapted: technically all public buildings should have been made accessible by law, although in practice a great deal still remains to be done. Access to public transport is also patchy.

There is an excellent guide, *Guía de Accesibilidad de Madrid*, which is published by the Ayuntamiento (city council) in collaboration with the disabled association FAMMA. Information is available from

the FAMMA office at C/Galileo 69 (91 593 35 50, www.famma.org), and can also be accessed via the city council website (www.esmadrid.com).

Access to sights

Most of the city's museums and cultural centres are now wheelchair-friendly – see www.esmadrid.com for the full list.

Buses

There are seats reserved for people with mobility problems behind the driver on most of the city's buses. Buses on many routes are now of the *piso bajo* (low floor) type, with low doors and spaces for wheelchairs. These are identified by the red on white stripes at the front and back of the bus and the slogan *'piso bajo pensado para todos'.*

Metro

All new metro stations have been built with access in mind, which means that those on newer lines (Line 8 to the airport, the Gregorio Marañón interchange, Line 7 to Pitis, the new Puerto del Sol stops) have good lifts. However, older stations in the city centre generally have a lot of steps, and although you may get on at a station with a lift, it may turn out to be impossible to get off at your destination. The metro map on pp318-319 of this guide and the free maps available at metro stations indicate stations with lifts.

RENFE & cercanías

Of the mainline rail stations, Atocha, Chamartín, Nuevos Ministerios and Príncipe Pío all have good access. Cercanías trains have very limited access, but some newer stations such as Méndez Alvaro (by Estación Sur coach station) have lifts connecting metro, train and bus stations. There are also good interchanges at Moncloa and Plaza Castilla.

Taxis

Special taxis adapted for wheelchairs can be called through Eurotaxi on 51 593 23 46 and Teletaxi on 91 371 21 31. Make it clear you want an adapted model (ask for a Eurotaxi). The number of such taxis in Madrid is still very limited and the waiting time can be as long as half an hour. Fares are the same as for standard cabs, but the meter is started as soon as a request is received, so the cost can be quite high.

DRUGS

Many people openly smoke cannabis, but its possession or consumption in public are illegal. It's theoretically OK to smoke cannabis in private, but not to possess it; this law is rarely enforced. There's been a recent crackdown in bars, however.

ELECTRICITY

The standard current in Spain is now 220V, but a few old buildings in Madrid still have 125V circuits, so it's a good idea to check before using electrical equipment in older hotels. Plugs are all of the two-round-pin type. The 220V current works fine with British 240V products, with a plug adaptor. With US 110V appliances you will need a current transformer.

EMBASSIES

For a full list look in the local phone book under *embajadas*. Lots of embassies have moved to the Torre Espacio at Paseo de la Castellana 259 in the past few years.

American Embassy
C/Serrano 75, Salamanca (91 587 22 00, www.embusa.es). *Metro Rubén Darío.* **Open** *Phoneline* 24hrs daily. *Office* 8.30am-5.30pm Mon-Fri. **Map** p309 L6.
The general switchboard will put you through to the consulate.

Australian Embassy
24th floor, Torre Espacio, Paseo de la Castellana 259D, Northern suburbs (91 353 66 00/visas 91 353 66 90/emergency phoneline 900 99 61 99, www.spain.embassy. gov.au). *Metro Begoña.* **Open** 8.30am-2pm, 2.30-4.30pm (visas 9am-noon) Mon-Fri.

British Embassy
Torre Espacio, Paseo de la Castellana 259D, Northern suburbs (91 714 63 00/visas 807 457 100/ passports 807 444 949, http://ukinspain.fco. gov.uk). *Metro Begoña.* **Open** 9am-5pm Mon-Fri.
General commercial, economic and other information about the UK. For information on British passports, call 807 429 026 (9.30am-5.30pm).

British Consulate
Torre Espacio, Paseo de la Castellana 259D, Northern suburbs (91 714 64 00). *Metro Begoña.* **Open** 8.30am-1.30pm (until 6pm for emergencies) Mon-Fri.
For queries relating to passports, visas and legal problems.

Canadian Embassy
Torre Espacio, Paseo de la Castellana 259D, Northern suburbs (91 382 84 00, www. canadainternational.gc.ca/spain-espagne). *Metro Begoña.* **Open** *Consular services* 8.30am-12.30pm Mon-Fri. *Emergency services* Sept-July 8.30am-2pm, 3-5.30pm Mon-Thur; 8.30am-2.30pm Fri. Aug 8.30am-2.15pm Mon-Fri. Emergency number for citizens (reverse charge calls accepted) is 00 613 996 8885.

Irish Embassy
Paseo de la Castellana 46 4°, Salamanca (91 436 40 93/visas 91 431 97 84, www.irlanda.es). *Metro Rubén Darío.* **Open** 10am-2pm Mon-Fri. *Visas* 11.30am-1.15pm Mon, Wed. **Map** p309 L6.

New Zealand Embassy
C/Pinar 7 3°, Chamberí (91 523 02 26, www.nzembassy.com/spain). *Metro Gregorio Marañón.* **Open** 9am-2pm, 3-5.30pm Mon-Fri. **Map** p305 L5.

EMERGENCIES

All EU countries now have a general number – 112 – to call for the emergency services (you can also dial this number from GSM mobiles). Some staff speak English, French and/or German.

ETIQUETTE

Some of the stereotypes are true. It's all much more vivacious than at home, and certainly more vocal. It's normal to say 'Hola' to all strangers, even when you're in a lift. Queues may look like free-form free-for-alls, but they're not. The first thing you must say, when taking your place in line, is '¿Quién es el último?' Who is last in line? Make a mental note of which four-foot-tall old lady comes before you and be sure not to push in.

Packed rush-hour metro trains are common, so *madrileños* have a set way of alighting from them. Rather than just push past people, only to find they are also getting off, it's usual to ask those in front: '¿Va a salir?' ('Are you getting off?'). If they are not, watch in wonder as a path opens up before you.

GAY & LESBIAN

COGAM
C/Puebla 9, Malasaña & Conde Duque (91 523 00 70, www.cogam.org). *Metro Gran Vía.* **Open** 10am-2pm, 5-9pm Mon-Fri; 6-9pm Sat. **Map** p307 H10.
The largest gay and lesbian organisation in Madrid, COGAM is one of the main organisers of Gay Pride and campaigns on various issues. The on-site café is a great place to chill and find out what's new on the scene.

Fundación Triángulo
C/Melendez Valdés 52 1°D, Chamberí (91 593 05 40, www. fundaciontriangulo.es). *Metro Argüelles.* **Open** 10am-2pm, 4-8pm Mon-Fri. **Map** p307 E7.
A gay cultural organisation that campaigns on equality issues. It also runs a helpline (91 593 05 40, same times as above) and offers legal help, health advice and AIDS prevention programmes.

HEALTH

EU nationals are entitled to free basic medical attention if they have the European Health Insurance Card (EHIC), which replaced the old E111 form in 2006. Travellers from the British Isles should apply for one online at www.dh.gov.uk (providing name, date of birth, and NHS or NI number) at least ten days before leaving home. Citizens of certain other countries that have a special agreement with Spain, among them several Latin American states, can also have access to free care. These arrangements won't cover all eventualities, so always take out private health insurance.

Accidents & emergencies

In a medical emergency go to the casualty department (*urgencias*) of any of the city's major hospitals (see p285). All are open 24 hours daily; Clínico or Gregorio Marañón are most central. If you have no EHIC or insurance, you can be seen at any casualty department (pay on the spot and get reimbursed back home by presenting the invoices and medical reports). In a non-emergency, pharmacists are very well informed.
For an ambulance call 112.

AIDS/HIV

Free advice is available on freephone 900 11 10 00 (10am-

SIZE CHARTS

WOMEN'S CLOTHES

British	Spanish	US
4	32	2
6	34	4
8	36	6
10	38	8
12	40	10
14	42	12
16	44	14
18	46	16
20	48	18

WOMEN'S SHOES

British	Spanish	US
3	36	5
4	37	6
5	38	7
6	39	8
7	40	9
8	41	10
9	42	11

MEN'S CLOTHES

British	Spanish	US
34	44	34
36	46	36
38	48	38
40	50	40
42	52	42
44	54	44
46	56	46
48	58	48

MEN'S SHOES

British	Spanish	US
6	39	7
7.5	40	7.5
8	41	8
8	42	8.5
9	43	9.5
10	44	10.5
11	45	11
12	46	11.5

8pm Mon-Fri; 9.30am-2.30pm
Sat & Sun).

Centro Sanitario Sandoval
*C/Sandoval 7, Chamberí (91
445 23 28, www.cruzroja.es/vih).
Metro Bilbao or San Bernardo.*
Open 8.45am-noon Mon-Fri.
Map p307 G/H7.
An official clinic that carries out
free, confidential HIV tests.

Hospitals

Hospital Clínico San Carlos
*C/Profesor Martín Lagos,
Moncloa (91 330 30 00).
Metro Moncloa.*
To get to the Accident and
Emergency Department, enter
from C/Isaac Peral, which is off
Plaza de Cristo Rey.
**Hospital General Gregorio
Marañón**
*C/Doctor Esquerdo 44-46,
Salamanca (91 586 80 00,
www.hggm.es). Metro O'Donnell.*
**Hospital Universitario
La Paz**
*Paseo de la Castellana 261,
Chamartín (91 727 70 00).
Metro Begoña.*
The hospital is in Plaza Castilla to
the north of the city.

Complementary medicine

**Instituto Homeopático y
Hospital de San José**
*C/Eloy Gonzalo 3-5, Chamberí
(91 446 6076). Metro Quevedo.*

Open 9am-2pm, 4-7pm Mon-Fri;
9am-2pm Sat. **No credit cards.**
Map p307 H6.
There are several English-speaking
practitioners at this clinic, which
provides treatments ranging from
homeopathy to acupuncture.

Contraception & women's health

Condoms (*profilácticos, condones*
or *preservativos*) are available from
most pharmacies, as well as vending
machines and supermarkets.

**Asociación de Mujeres
para la Salud**
*Avda Alfonso XIII 118, Chamartín
(91 519 56 78, 91 519 59 26,
www.mujeresparalasalud.org).
Metro Colombia.* **Open** 9am-2pm,
4-8pm Mon-Fri. Closed Aug.
A feminist medical association
offering free advice and
counselling.
Clínica Duratón
*C/Colegiata 4, Los Austrias (91
429 77 69, www.duraton.org).
Metro Tirso de Molina.* **Open**
10am-8pm Mon-Thur; 10am-
2pm Fri. **Map** p311 G13.
Family-planning centre run by
women doctors and staff.

Dentists

Dentistry is not covered by
EU reciprocal agreements,
so private rates will apply to
any treatment.

Clínica Dental Cisne
*C/Magallanes 18 1ª, Chamberí
(91 446 32 21, 24hr emergencies
mobile 661 857 170, www.clinica
dentalcisne.com). Metro Quevedo.*
Open 9am-1pm, 3-7pm Mon-
Thur; 9am-3pm Fri. Closed
Aug. **Credit** DC, MC, V.
Map p307 G6.
British dentist Dr Ian Daniel is
based at this clinic in Chamberí.
Hours may vary during the
summer, and the clinic sometimes
closes in August.

Doctors

Centros de salud are local health
centres with a few doctors and
various specialised clinics. Waiting
times can be long and consultations
brief, but if necessary you will be
referred to a hospital. Usually
open 8am-9pm Mon-Fri and 9am-
5pm Sat. These are some of the
most central:

Centro de Salud Alameda
*C/Alameda 5, Huertas & Santa
Ana (91 420 38 02). Metro Atocha.*
Map p312 J13.
Centro de Salud Argüelles
*C/Quintana 11, Argüelles (91
559 02 23). Metro Argüelles.*
Map p306 D11.
Centro de Salud Las Cortes
*C/San Jerónimo 32, Huertas &
Santa Ana (91 369 04 91). Metro
Sevilla.* **Map** p312 I11.

Opticians

See p152.

Pharmacies

Pharmacies (*farmacias*) are
signalled by large, green, usually
flashing crosses. Those within
the official system of the College
of Pharmacies are normally open
9.30am-2pm, 5-8pm Mon-Sat. At
other times a duty rota operates.
Every pharmacy has a list of the
College's *farmacias de guardia*
(duty pharmacies) for that day
posted outside the door, with
the nearest ones highlighted
(many now show them using
a computerised, push-button
panel). Duty pharmacies are
also listed in local newspapers,
and information is available on
the 010 phoneline (*see p292*)
and at www.cofm.es. At night,
duty pharmacies may look closed;
knock on the shutters to be served.
   There are two 24-hour
pharmacies in Madrid, which
are open every day; *see p152.*

ESSENTIAL INFORMATION

Private healthcare

Unidad Médica Anglo-Americana

*C/Conde de Aranda 1-1º izq,
Salamanca (91 435 18 23,
www.unidadmedica.com). Metro
Retiro.* **Open** *Sept-July* 9am-8pm
Mon-Fri; 10am-1pm Sat. *Aug*
10am-5pm Mon-Fri; 10am-1pm
Sat. **Credit** AmEx, MC, V.
Map p309 L10.
Offers full range of services,
including dentistry. Will make
house/hotel calls.

HELPLINES

Alcoholics Anonymous

*C/Juan Bravo 40 2º, Salamanca
(91 309 19 47, www.aamadrid.
com). Metro Diego de León.*
Map p309 N6/7.
English-speaking group meets
every evening.

Narcotics Anonymous

*C/Doctor Piga 4 (902 11 41 47,
www.narcoticosanonimos.es).
Metro Lavapiés.* **Map** p312 I14.
English-speaking meeting every
Sunday at 5.30pm.

ID

Foreigners should carry national
ID or a passport with them at all
times, although a photocopy is
usually OK. You'll be asked to
show the passport itself or a
driving licence when paying
by credit card in shops.

INSURANCE

EU nationals are entitled to use
the Spanish state health service,
provided they have a European
Health Insurance Card (*see p284*),
which must be applied for well in
advance of travel. This will cover you
for emergencies, but for short-term
visitors it's often simpler to avoid
dealing with the state bureaucracy
and take out private travel insurance
before departure, particularly as
this will also cover you for stolen
or lost cash or valuables.

Some non-EU countries have
reciprocal healthcare agreements
with Spain, but again, for most
travellers it will be best to take
out private travel insurance
before arriving. For more on
health services, *see p284*.

INTERNET

Despite relatively high costs, Spain
boasts a high concentration of
internet users, and there are

internet cafés all over Madrid.
Most libraries (*see below*) have
free internet points and wireless
access for public use, although you
may have to join the library first.
The city council provides free but
slow Wi-Fi access in an increasing
amount of public spaces, such as
the Plaza Mayor and the Plaza
Santo Domingo, and look out, too,
for the news kiosks advertising free
council-provided Wi-Fi (there's a
maximum of 30 minutes).

WORKcenter

*C/Alberto Aguilera 1, Malasaña
(91 121 76 28, www.workcenter.es).
Metro San Bernardo.* **Open** 24hrs
daily. **Credit** MC, V. **Map** p307 G7.
An office centre where you can send
or receive faxes and emails, access
the net, make copies or get ID photos.
Internet access is pricey, charged at
€3 for 30 mins.
Other locations Paseo de
Castellana 149, Salamanca (91 121
76 30); C/Conde de Peñalver 51,
Salamanca (91 121 56 60); C/María
de Molina 40, Salamanca (91 121
56 80) and throughout the city.

LEFT LUGGAGE

Barajas airport

*Terminals T1, T2 & T4
(information 902 40 47 04).*
Open 24hrs daily. **Rates** €5.80
per day.

RENFE train stations

Open *Chamartín* 7am-11pm daily.
Atocha 6.30am-10.30pm daily.
Rates €3-€5 depending on
locker size.

LIBRARIES

Madrid has a great number of
municipal public libraries, but few
are in the centre of the city and,
not surprisingly, they generally
have limited selections of books
in English. For a full list of
libraries, check '*bibliotecas*' in
the local *Páginas Amarillas*
(*Yellow Pages*), call 010 or visit
www.madrid.org/bpcm.

Biblioteca Nacional

*Paseo de Recoletos 20, Salamanca
(91 580 77 00, 91 580 78 23,
www.bne.es). Metro Colón.* **Open**
9am-9pm Mon-Fri; 9am-2pm Sat.
Map p308 K10.
Spain's national library has early
books and manuscripts on display
(in the Museo del Libro), and is
also the home of the Hemeroteca
Nacional, the national newspaper
library. To use the library
regularly you need accreditation

from a university or similar
institution, but a one-day pass
is quite easy to obtain (you
will need to take a passport
or residency card).

Biblioteca Pedro Salinas

*Glorieta de la Puerta de Toledo 1,
La Latina (91 366 54 07). Metro
Puerta de Toledo.* **Open** *Oct-June*
9am-8.45pm Mon-Fri; 9am-1.45pm
Sat. *July-Sept* 9am-9pm Mon-Fri.
Map p311 E15.
The most attractive and convenient
of Madrid's public libraries. Books
can be taken out on loan.

British Council

*Paseo del General Martínez Campos
31, Chamberí (91 337 35 00,
www.britishcouncil.es). Metro
Iglesia.* **Open** *Sept-June* 9.30am-
6.45pm Mon-Wed; 9.30am-8.45pm
Thur; 9.30am-5.45pm Fri. *July,
Aug* 9.30am-2.45pm Mon-Fri.
Membership Call for details.
Map p308 J6.
The best place for English-language
books in Madrid, the library in the
British Council study centre has a
massive selection of books and
videos in English, as well as
CD-Roms, internet access and
daily newspapers.

Hemeroteca Municipal

*C/Conde Duque 9-11, Conde
Duque (91 588 57 72/75,
www.munimadrid.es/hemeroteca).
Metro Noviciado.* **Open** *Sept-July*
9am-8.30pm Mon-Fri. *Aug* 9am-
1.30pm Mon-Fri. **Map** p307 F8.
If you just have to track down that
essential piece of information, the
city newspaper library in the Centro
Conde Duque is the place to do it.
You need a researcher's card to
get in, for which you must provide
a copy of your passport and two
ID photos.

LOST PROPERTY

Airport & rail stations

If you lose something before check-
in at Barajas Airport, report the
loss to the Aviación Civil office
(AENA) in the relevant terminal,
or call the lost property office in
T1 (91 393 61 19, 8am-9pm) or T4
(91 746 64 39, 7am-11pm). If you
think you've mislaid anything on
the RENFE rail service, look for
the Atención al Viajero desk or
Jefe de Estación office at the main
station nearest to where your
property went astray. The Centros
de Viajes in the Chamartín and
Atocha train stations are the official
lost property centres for the
municipal train network. Call 902
24 02 02 for both and ask for the

ESSENTIAL INFORMATION

Centro de Viaje or information on *objetos perdidos*.

EMT (city buses)

C/Cerro de la Plata 4, Salamanca (91 406 88 43, www.emtmadrid.es). Metro Pacífico. **Open** 8am-2pm Mon-Fri. *Phone lines* 8am-9pm Mon-Fri.

The lost property office for items that have been lost on Madrid's city or airport buses.

Oficina de Objetos Perdidos (Madrid City Council)

Paseo del Molino 7, South of centre (91 527 95 90). Metro Legazpi. **Open** 8.30am-2pm Mon-Fri.

This office mainly receives articles found on the metro or in taxis, but if you're lucky, something lost in the street may turn up here.

MEDIA

Newspapers

Spanish newspapers may come in tabloid size, but they are far from light-hearted, preferring heavy political commentary. Sensationalist, celeb-dominated stories are reserved for the *prensa de corazón* (press of the heart), such as *¡Hola!, Diez Minutos* or *¡Qué me dices!*. Free daily papers *Metro, 20 Minutos* and the gossipy *¡Qué!* are handed out outside most central metro stations. The plethora of other free newspapers now on offer includes *Latino*, aimed at the South American market, and *Gol!*, a round-up of the weekend's sport.

ABC

ABC's journalists have the highest professional reputation. Read by Madrid's most respectable citizens.

Marca & As

Sports-only (in fact, mostly football-only) papers. *Marca* is usually the country's bestselling daily paper.

El Mundo

This centrist, populist paper made its name by unearthing many corruption scandals under the Socialists during the 1990s. Friday's 'La Luna de Metrópoli' supplement is a good source of listings and information on the cultural agenda.

El País

The liberal *El País* is the established paper of record, and also carries excellent daily information on Madrid, with Friday's 'Tentaciones' supplement a great source for music and popular culture.

La Razón

Right-wing and sensationalist daily with much of its editorial coming from *ABC*.

English-language

Foreign newspapers are on sale in **FNAC** (*see p135*), all **Vip's** stores (*see p135*) and at most kiosks around Sol, Gran Vía, Calle Alcalá and the Castellana.

InMadrid

A free monthly aimed at English-speaking residents – you can pick it up in pubs, bookshops, universities, language schools and tourist offices. Good articles on the Madrid scene, plus listings information, events, reviews and small ads.

Listings & classifieds

Local papers carry daily film and theatre listings, and the Friday supplements of *El Mundo* (Metrópoli) and *El País* (Tentaciones) give fuller information, reviews and so on. For monthly music listings look out for the Barcelona-based magazines *Mondo Sonoro* and *Go* (in bars and music shops).

Segundamano

www.segundamano.es
'Second-hand' comes out three times a week and is the best place for small ads of all kinds.

Guía del Ocio

www.guiadelocio.com
A weekly listings magazine with cinema, arts, entertainment, concerts, nightlife and restaurant listings, and a good galleries section. It's handy, but can be inaccurate.

Music & style mags

Undersounds, Rockdelux, the Spanish version of *Rolling Stone* and the new *MTV* magazine are mainly sold in kiosks or music shops and at festivals. A few free mags to look out for are clubbers' zine *AB*, the smarter monthly *Cartel* and *Mundo Sonoro*.

Radio

The Spanish are avid radio fans; you'll hear radios blaring out in bars, cafés, buses and taxis.

Radio Nacional de España stations to listen for include RNE-2 (96.5 FM, classical music) and RNE-3 (93.2 FM, an excellent and eclectic mix of rock and world

music). There are dozens of other local stations. The main commercial broadcaster is **SER** (Sociedad Española de Radiofusión), which controls four networks: SER, a news network, and two music channels.

One specific English-language programme to look out for is Radio Círculo's *Madrid Live* on Tuesdays from 8.30pm to 9pm (repeated on Friday at 10pm), which can be found on 100.4FM. Produced and presented by radio journalist Ann Bateson, it focuses on the city's arts, entertainment and social scene.

The BBC World Service can be found in the evenings on 12095 kHz shortwave.

TV

There are seven main channels, which pump out an endless diet of tacky game shows, talk shows, really bad imported *telenovelas* (soaps) from South America and badly dubbed American movies. Just about the only redeeming feature is the news, although **Canal 2** does show some good documentaries and films. Non-Spanish films and shows on some channels can be seen in undubbed versions on stereo TVs; look for VO (*versión original*) in listings and a 'Dual' symbol at the top of the screen.

TVE 1 (La Primera)

The flagship channel of state broadcaster RTVE has a reputation for toeing the government line.

TVE 2 (La Dos)

The least commercial of all the TV channels, La 2 is good for documentaries and late-night movies (often in VO).

Antena 3

A private channel with an emphasis on family entertainment mixed with late-night salaciousness.

Tele 5

Another private channel. This celeb-obsessed station is the one to blame for the Spanish *Big Brother, El Gran Hermano*. It is also the Formula One channel, which has become a national obsession since the rise and rise of one Fernando Alonso.

Telemadrid

Madrid's own station. Good for live football on Saturday and the Megahit movie on Sunday nights, but bad for political bias.

digital +

A subscriber channel with a good selection of sport, movies

ESSENTIAL INFORMATION

ESSENTIAL INFORMATION

and US hits. Many hotels and bars receive it.

Cuatro

This channel filled the gap left by Canal+, and is aimed squarely at people in their twenties with its mixture of American imports, flashy news programmes and chat shows.

La Sexta

La Sexta focuses on a mixture of documentaries, films and the obligatory American imports.

MONEY

Spain is part of the euro zone. One euro is made up of 100 *céntimos*. One thing to remember is that the British/ US practice on decimal points and commas is reversed (so 1.000 euros means one thousand euros, while 1,00 euro is one euro). There are banknotes for €5, €10, €20, €50, €100, €200 and €500, in different colours and designs. Then there are three copper coins (five, two and one *céntimo*), three gold-coloured coins (50, 20 and 10 *céntimos*) and large coins for one euro (silver centre, gold rim) and two euros (gold centre, silver rim).

Banks & exchange

Banks and savings banks (*cajas de ahorros*) readily accept cash and travellers' cheques (you must show your passport). Commission rates vary, and it's worth shopping around before changing money (although banks usually give the best rates); also, given the rates charged by Spanish banks, it's often cheaper to get money from an ATM machine by credit or debit card rather than with travellers' cheques. It is almost always quicker to change money at larger bank offices than at local branches.

There are many small bureaux de change (*cambio*), particularly on Gran Via and Puerta del Sol. Exchange rates are usually worse than in banks.

Bank hours

Banks and savings banks normally open from 8am to 2pm Monday to Friday. From October to May many branches also open from 9am to 1pm on Saturday. Hours vary a little between different banks, and some have branches that stay open until around 5pm one day a week (usually Thursday). Savings banks often open late on Thursday afternoons, but are less likely to

open on Saturdays. Banks are closed on public holidays.

Out-of-hours services

Outside normal hours you can change money at the airport (terminals T-1 and T-2, open 24hrs daily), at main train stations (Atocha, 9am-9pm daily; Chamartín, 8am-10pm daily), in El Corte Inglés (*see p135*), in hotels, at private *cambios* and at the places listed below. At the airport, Chamartín and outside some banks in Gran Vía and Puerta del Sol there are automatic cash exchange machines that accept notes in major currencies, in good condition (be careful if you need to use these at night).

American Express

Plaza de las Cortes 2, Huertas (91 322 55 00). Metro Banco de España. **Open** 9am-7.30pm Mon-Fri; 9am-2pm Sat. **Map** p312 I12. The usual services are offered, including money transfer worldwide in 24 hours.
Other locations throughout the city.

Western Union Money Transfer

Change Express, Gran Vía 16, Sol & Gran Vía (90 063 36 33). Metro Callao. **Open** 8am-10.30pm daily. **Map** p308 G11.
The local Western Union agent. It's the quickest if not the cheapest way to have money sent from abroad.
Other locations throughout the city.

Credit cards

Major credit and charge cards are accepted in most hotels, shops and restaurants. You can withdraw cash with major cards from most bank ATMs, which provide instructions in different languages. Exchange rates and handling fees often work out more economical than exchanging cash or travellers' cheques. Banks will advance cash against credit cards over the counter, but prefer you to use an ATM.

Lost or stolen cards
American Express *freephone* 902 37 56 37.
Diners Club 902 40 11 12.
Mastercard *freephone* 900 97 12 31.
Visa 900 99 11 24.

Tax

There are different rates of sales tax (IVA – VAT): for hotels and

restaurants, the rate is ten per cent; in shops, it's generally 21 per cent, but on some items it's lower. IVA is generally included in listed prices – if not, the expression '*más IVA*' (plus tax) must be stated after the price. In shops displaying a 'Tax-Free Shopping' sticker, non-EU residents can reclaim tax on large purchases (*see p283*).

OPENING TIMES

Eating, drinking and shopping all happen late in Madrid. The siesta has faded to a myth, but *madrileños* do operate to a distinctive schedule. Most shops open from 10am to 2pm, and 5-5.30pm to 8-8.30pm Monday to Saturday, although many stay closed on Saturday afternoons. Food markets open earlier, around 8am. In July and especially in August most shops and services (such as the Post Office and administrations) close in the afternoon. August is also the time when most shops, bars and restaurants close for their annual holidays (from two weeks up to the whole month). Major stores and malls are open from 10am to 9pm without a break, Monday to Saturday (for the vexed question of Sunday shopping, *see pp134-135*). Big supermarkets (Al Campo, Carrefour) open from 10am to 10pm Monday to Saturday and the first Sunday of each month.

Madrileños still eat, drink, go out and stay out later than their neighbours in virtually every other European country. Most restaurants are open 1.30-2pm to 4pm, and 9pm to midnight, and many close on Sunday nights and Mondays, and for at least part of August. Many businesses finish at 3pm in the summer. Most museums (state ones) close one day a week, usually Monday.

POLICE

Spain has several police forces. In Madrid the most important are the local Policía Municipal, in navy and pale blue, and the Policía Nacional, in darker blue and white uniforms (or all-blue combat gear). Each force has its own responsibilities, although they overlap. Municipales are principally concerned with traffic and parking problems and local regulations. The force with primary responsibility for dealing with crime are the Nacionales. The Guardia Civil, in green, are responsible, among other things, for policing inter-city highways, and customs.

Reporting a crime

If you are robbed or attacked, you should report the incident as soon as possible at the nearest Policía Nacional station (*comisaría*), where you will be asked to make an official statement (*denuncia*). It is extremely unlikely that anything you have lost will ever be recovered, but you will need the *denuncia* in order to make an insurance claim. Very few police officers speak any English.

Comisaría del Centro
C/Leganitos 19, Sol & Gran Vía (information 060, station 91 548 79 85). Metro Santo Domingo or Plaza de España. **Map** p307 F10. The Policía Nacional headquarters for central Madrid, near Plaza de España. Some other police stations in the city centre are listed below; all are open 24hrs daily.
Chamberí
C/Rafael Calvo 33 (91 322 32 68). Metro Iglesia. **Map** p308 K6.
Huertas/Retiro
C/Huertas 76-78 (91 322 10 27). Metro Antón Martín. **Map** p312 J13.
Salamanca
C/Príncipe de Asturias 8 (91 444 81 20). Metro Manuel Becerra.

POSTAL SERVICES

If you just need normal-rate stamps (*sellos*), it's easier to buy them in an *estanco* (*see right*). Post offices now have automatic stamp dispensing machines (with a weighing system) but they do not always work.

Oficina Principal de Correos en Madrid
Paseo del Prado 1, Retiro (91 523 06 94, www.correos.es). Metro Banco de España. **Open** 8.30am-9.30pm Mon-Fri; 8.30am-2pm Sat. **Map** p312 J11.
The central post office relocated from the magnificent Palacio de Cibeles to this building nearby in 2008. All manner of postal services are available at separate windows. Faxes can be sent and received at all post offices, but rates are expensive, so use a private fax bureau. Not all services are available at all times. Mail sent poste restante should be addressed to Lista de Correos, 28080 Madrid, Spain. To collect, bring your passport. For express post, say you want to send a *'carta urgente'*.

Other city centre post offices are at El Corte Inglés, C/Preciados 1-4, Sol & Gran Vía; Carrera de San Francisco 13, La Latina; C/Mejía Lequerica 7, Chueca; C/Jorge Juan 20, Salamanca, and at Terminal 1 in the airport.

Postal rates & postboxes

Letters and postcards up to 20g cost 37¢ within Spain, 75¢ to Europe and North Africa, and 90¢ to the rest of the world. Note that you will pay more for 'irregular' shaped envelopes (basically, not rectangular). Cards and letters to other European countries usually arrive in 3-4 days, those to North America in about a week. Normal postboxes are yellow with two horizontal red stripes. There are also a few special red postboxes for urgent mail, with hourly collections.

Postal Exprés
Available at all post offices, this efficient express mail offers next-day delivery within Spain. Packages up to 1kg (2.2lb) are €7.90-€15, according to distance and dimension.

Estancos

The main role of the tobacco shop or *estanco* (look for a brown and yellow sign with the word *'tabacos'*) is, of course, to supply tobacco-related products. But they also sell stamps, phonecards and Metrobús and monthly *abono* tickets. *Estancos* are the only places to obtain official money vouchers (*papel de estado*), needed for dealings with Spanish bureaucracy.

QUEUING

Despite appearances, Spaniards have a highly developed queuing culture. People don't always bother standing in line, but they generally know when it is their turn. Common practice is to ask when you first arrive, to no one in particular, *'¿Quién da la vez?'* or *'Quién es el último/la última?'* ('Who's last?'); see who nods, and follow on after them. Say *'yo'* (me) to the next person who asks.

RELIGION

Anglican

St George's (British Embassy Church)
C/Núñez de Balboa 43, Salamanca (91 576 51 09, www.stgeorges

madrid.com). Metro Velázquez. **Open** 10am-1pm Mon-Wed. Consult the Grapevine section of the website for latest service times. **Map** p309 M8.

Catholic (in English)

Our Lady of Mercy
C/Drácena 23, Chamartín (91 350 34 49, www.ourladyofmercy. info). Metro Pío XII. **English Mass** 11am Sun.
No shortage of Spanish Masses, but this is the Catholic church for the English-speaking parish of Madrid.

Jewish

Sinagoga de Madrid
C/Balmes 3, Eastern suburbs (91 591 31 31). Metro Iglesia. **Open** 9am-7.30pm Mon-Thur; 9am-1.30pm Fri; 10am-1.30pm Sun. Call for prayer times.

Muslim

Centro Cultural Islámico de Madrid
C/Salvador de Madariaga 4, Eastern suburbs (91 326 26 10, www.ccislamico.com). Metro Barrio de la Concepción. **Open** 10am-8pm Mon-Thur, Sat, Sun; noon-4pm Fri.

RENTING A FLAT

The price of flats to rent in Madrid varies wildly. A room in a shared flat costs upwards of €400 a month, while a one-bedroom flat is around €800 or more. Places to look for flat ads are the papers *Segundamano* and *Anuntis* and English language magazine *InMadrid* (for all, *see p287*). Another option is to look for *'Se alquila'* (to rent) signs.
Contratos de alquiler (rental agreements) generally cover a five-year period, within which a landlord can only raise the rent each year in line with inflation, set in the official price index (IPC). Landlords usually ask for the equivalent of one month's rent as a *fianza* (deposit) and a month's rent in advance. Details of contracts (especially with regards to responsibility for repairs) vary a lot; don't sign a *contrato* unless you're fully confident of your Spanish and/or a lawyer or *gestor* has looked at it.

SAFETY

As in most major cities, street crime is a problem in Madrid and tourists are often targeted. One plus point is that pickpocketing and bag-snatching are more likely than any violent crime. Places to be especially on your guard are the Puerta del Sol, Gran Vía, the Plaza Mayor, the Plaza Santa Ana and, above all, the Rastro and Retiro park; watch out, too, on the metro. The area around the junction of Gran Vía and Calle Montera is a centre of street prostitution, and can feel uncomfortable at night. Recently, the Lavapiés district has acquired a reputation for street crime, which has developed alongside growing racial tension in the area, with robberies often attributed to young, homeless North African illegal immigrants, even though most thefts reported by *Time Out* readers and local media seem to involve teenage eastern European or gypsy girls.

Street criminals prey very deliberately on the unwary, and their chances of success can be limited greatly by taking the following simple precautions.

● When sitting in a café, especially at an outside table, never leave a bag or coat on the ground, on the back of a chair or anywhere you cannot see it clearly. If in doubt, keep it on your lap.

● Give the impression of knowing what's going on around you, and – without getting paranoid – be alert and watch out to see if you are being followed.

● Wear shoulder bags pulled to the front, not at your back, especially in the underground. Keep the bag closed and a hand on top of it.

● Avoid pulling out large notes to pay for things, especially in the street at night; try not to get large notes when changing money.

● Be aware that street thieves often work in pairs or groups; if someone hassles you for money or to buy something, or pulls out a map and asks for directions, keep walking, as this can be a ruse to distract you so that the thief's 'partner' can get at your bag. This is often done pretty crudely, and so is not hard to recognise.

● Be extremely careful when you withdraw money from ATMs. Don't let anyone distract your attention while putting in your PIN code.

● Beware of fake policemen: if someone asks to see your ID, ask to see their identification first.

SMOKING

Most Spaniards are keen smokers, but since 2011 smoking has been banned in enclosed public places. Some hotels still have smoking rooms, but there will only be a handful.

STUDY

Foreign students from the EU staying more than three months require a residency permit (Tarjeta de Residencia Para la Realización de Estudios); non-EU students may also need a visa. For more details, *see below* **Studying in Madrid**.

Accommodation

Room Services Madrid
C/Conde Duque 7, Malasaña (91 548 03 35, mobile 654 538 164). Metro Plaza España. **Open** 10am-8pm Mon-Sat. **Map** p307 E9.

STUDYING IN MADRID

There are plenty of learning opportunities for foreign adults at Madrid's universities and private institutions. Unsurprisingly, many of these are Spanish-language courses.

Language schools offer intensive summer courses in general Spanish (from beginner level to advanced) lasting from one week to four months or more. **EleMadrid** (www.elemadrid.com), **Alba Language Consulting** (www.albalanguage.com) and **International House** (www.ihmadrid.com) also run specialised courses for job-related Spanish (in fields including medicine, law, commerce and hotel management) and for those who plan to become Spanish teachers. Many of the schools, such as **Acento Español** (www.acentoespanol.com), **Academia Contacto** (www.academiacontacto.com), **Academia InHispania** (www.inhispania.com) and **Idiomas Plus** (www.madridplus.es), balance the tuition programme with leisure activities aimed at allowing students to learn about the city and Spanish culture. Schools can help with accommodation.

For those who already possess a reasonable level of Spanish, there are plenty of other interesting programmes on the market. **Universidad Complutense de Madrid**'s (*see p291*) prestigious annual summer lecture series have been taking place for the last 17 years in the mountain town of El Escorial. Lecturers have included luminaries such as poet Rafael Albertí, filmmakers Pedro Almodóvar and Carlos Saura, and sculptor Eduardo Chillida, along with international artists, politicians, economists and scientists. Subjects are usually related in some way to current events, and have drawn on disciplines as varied as economics, art, politics, literature, psychology, sociology and environmentalism. Places on the lecture series are limited and fees are quite high (for details and fees, see www.ucm.es/info/cv). Students can apply for a scholarship that covers costs of accommodation and meals.

The **Madrid Chamber of Commerce** offers a good range of vocational courses. There are classes throughout the year in subjects ranging from business Spanish for foreign executives to Spanish wine-tasting and oenology (you'll need a good level of Spanish for the latter). These courses have a very good reputation, both in Spain and abroad. Tuition fees are reasonable and class sizes limited, which means there can be some competition for places. Check out www.camaramadrid.es for more information (click on 'formación'). Or phone the Chamber of Commerce (91 538 35 00, 8.30am-8.30pm Mon-Fri).

Cooking courses are popular too. **Club Cooking** (www.club-cooking.com) is a fun and friendly school with classes in cookery for all standards (there are even courses for children). Courses cover topics such as cooking with cod, rice cooking, Moroccan food, and cakes and pastry.

This agency specialises in finding rooms in shared flats, with a minimum stay of one month in summer and three months from September to June. At busy times you'll need to make an appointment a few hours in advance. See the Facebook page for details.

Madrid Sal y Ven

C/Cochabamba 17 (91 457 47 79, www.salyven.net). Metro Colombia. **Open** 9.30am-2pm, 3.30-6pm Mon-Fri. **Map** p308 K10.

Finds rooms in shared flats or with local families, with a minimum stay of one week. The agency charges an inscription charge of €60 and commission on top of that.

Language learning

Carpe Diem

C/Fuencarral 13, 2°, Malasaña (91 522 31 22, www.carpemadrid.com). Metro Gran Vía. **Open** 10am-7pm Mon-Thur; 10am-3pm Fri. **Map** p307 H11.

A young, funky Spanish-language academy, with small groups and enthusiastic teachers.

Escuela Oficial de Idiomas

C/Jesús Maestro 5, Chamberí (91 533 58 02/03, www.eoidiomas. com). Metro Islas Filipinas. **Open** 9am-2pm, 3.30-8.30pm Mon-Fri. Closed 2wks Aug.

This government-run school offers courses in Spanish through the academic year. The school has several other centres in the Madrid area; call for a full list. Registration is in August/September and April/May; competition for places is extremely stiff.

International House

C/Zurbano 8, Chamberí (902 14 15 17, www.ihmadrid.com). Metro Alonso Martínez. **Open** 9am-10pm Mon-Fri; 8am-3pm Sat. **Map** p308 J8.

International House offers Spanish courses at all levels.

Other locations throughout the city.

Universidad Complutense de Madrid

Secretaría del Centro Complutense para la Enseñanza del Español, Facultad de Filología, Ciudad Universitaria (91 394 53 25, www.ucm.es). **Open** *Office* Sept-June 10am-1pm, 3-6pm Mon-Fri. July 10am-1pm Mon-Fri. Closed Aug.

Three-month Spanish courses for foreigners are held during the academic year. Higher-level students can study linguistics, literature and culture; there are also intensive language courses.

Universities

Erasmus, Socrates & Lingua programmes

Information in the UK: British Council, 1 Kingsway, Cardiff (0292 092 4311, www.britishcouncil. org/erasmus.htm).

The Erasmus student-exchange scheme and Lingua project (for language learning) are the main parts of the EU's Socrates programme to help students move freely between member states. To be eligible you must be studying at an exchange institution. Prospective students should contact their college's Erasmus co-ordinator.

Universidad de Alcalá de Henares

C/Escritorios, 4, Alcalá de Henares (91 881 23 78, www. alcalingua.com). **Open** *Office* 9am-2pm, 4-7pm Mon-Fri.

Offers Spanish courses for foreigners all year. Intensive month-long courses are offered between June and September and cost €680 for language-only courses or €850 for language and culture courses.

Universidad Autónoma de Madrid

Ciudad Universitaria de Cantoblanco, Ctra de Colmenar km15 (91 497 50 00, www.uam.es). **Open** *Office* 9am-2pm, 3-5pm Mon-Thur; 9am-1.30pm Fri.

The UAM now competes in prestige with the Complutense.

Universidad Carlos III

C/Madrid 126, Getafe (91 624 60 00, 91 624 95 00, www.uc3m.es). **Open** *Office* 9am-2pm, 4-6pm Mon-Thur; 9am-2pm Fri. Closed Aug.

One of Madrid's newest universities, with campuses in Getafe and Leganés.

Universidad Complutense de Madrid

Avda de Séneca 2, Moncloa (91 452 04 00, www.ucm.es). **Open** *Office* 9am-2pm, 4-6pm Mon-Thur; 9am-2pm Fri.

The prestigious Complutense is Madrid's main university. The largest and oldest in Spain, it is home to 98,000 students, 3,000 of them from abroad.

TELEPHONES

Since the Spanish national phone company (Movistar) was privatised, other companies – such as Jazztel and Yoigo – now compete with it in certain areas. Nevertheless, Movistar remains the main player in the field as far as infrastructure is concerned, though its prices are relatively high.

Dialling & codes

It is necessary to dial provincial area codes with all phone numbers in Spain, even when you are calling from within the same area. Hence, all normal phone numbers in the Madrid area are preceded by 91, and you must dial this whether you're calling within Madrid, from elsewhere in Spain or from abroad. Calls from numbers beginning 90 can only be connected if dialled from within Spain. Numbers beginning 900 are freephone lines; 901, 902 or 906 numbers are special-rate services and can be very pricey, especially if dialled from a mobile phone. Spanish mobile phone numbers have six digits and begin with a 6.

International & long-distance calls

To call abroad, dial 00 followed by the country code, then the area code (omitting the first zero in UK numbers) and number. To call Madrid from abroad, dial the international code (00 in the UK, 001 from the USA), then 34 for Spain.

Australia 61.
Canada 1.
Irish Republic 353.
New Zealand 64.
United Kingdom 44.
USA 1.

Mobile phones

The Spanish are mobile (*móvil*) mad and just about everybody has one (or two). You can pay each month or use rechargeable pre-paid cards. Call costs depend on the type of contract you have. Mobile phones from other countries can be used in Spain with a 'roaming' system, which you need to activate before leaving home.

Phone centres

For international calls it's often worth using a call centre (*locutorio*). You don't need change (you are charged when you've finished your call), and the booths keep out noise, and many offer international call rates cheaper than Movistar's. There are many phone centres around Lavapiés, Huertas and Malasaña. Often other services – fax, internet, currency exchange, money transfer – are available. There is a directory of *locutorios* at www.ocio latino.com in the 'Guía Latina'.

ESSENTIAL INFORMATION

Money Exchange
C/Infantas 1, Chueca (91 532 75 35). Metro Gran Vía. **Open** 10am-10pm daily. **Map** p308 H10.

Public phones

Payphones are plentiful in the city, although due to the traffic noise it's often worth using a phone in a bar or café, even though they often cost 50 per cent more than regular booths. Most models of payphone take coins (from five *céntimos* up), phonecards and credit cards, and have a digital display with instructions in English and other languages.

The first minute of a daytime local call costs around 20 *céntimos*; to a mobile phone around 55¢; to a 902 number, around 70¢. You are usually given credit to make more calls without having to insert more money.

Kioskos and *estancos* sell €5 (up to 70 minutes of communication) and €10 (up to 140 minutes) phonecards by various companies. Many of the cards give you a free number to call; an operator or automatic system then connects you with the number you want and can tell you how much is left on your card.

Operator services

Usually, operators will only speak Spanish, though most international operators speak basic English.

National directory enquiries 11811

International directory enquiries & operator 11825

National operator 1009

National operator for calls to Europe 1008

National operator for calls outside Europe 1005

Movistar telephone faults service 1002

Time 1212

TIME

Spain is on CET (Central European Time), an hour ahead of UK time, six hours ahead of US EST and nine hours ahead of PST. Daylight saving time runs concurrently with the UK.

TIPPING

There are no rules or percentages for tipping and in general Spaniards tip very little. It is usual to leave five or ten per cent for a restaurant waiter, rarely more than €4, and people often leave a few *céntimos* of small change in a bar. It's also usual to tip hotel porters, toilet and cinema attendants. In taxis the norm is around five per cent, although you can give more for longer journeys, or if a driver has been especially helpful.

TOILETS

Public toilets are rare, although there are some with an attendant in the Retiro, by the lake; at Chamartín and Atocha stations; and in the Paseo del Prado. However, proprietors usually don't mind if you pop into a bar or café (better, though, if you ask first), and big stores such as El Corte Inglés or fast-food restaurants are a good bet.

TOURIST INFORMATION

The Centros de Turismo run by the city council, and the tourist office run by the regional authority (Comunidad de Madrid) provide similar basic information on Madrid and the surrounding region, plus free maps. The city also runs a phone information line for locals, 010 (*see right*), that can be useful to visitors. Tourist offices do not make hotel bookings but can advise on vacancies; for booking agencies, *see p169* **Going Flat Out**.

Full information on what's on is in local papers, listings magazines and local English-language magazines (*see p287*). For useful websites, *see p295*.

Centro de Turismo de Madrid
Plaza Mayor 27, Los Austrias (91 454 44 10). Metro Sol. **Open** 9.30am-8.30pm daily. **Map** p311 G12.
Centro de Turismo Colón
Plaza de Colón, Salamanca (91 454 44 10). Metro Colón. **Open** 9.30am-8.30pm daily. **Map** p308 K9.
Located in the old pedestrian subway running under the Paseo de la Castellana, this is the largest tourist information office in the city. Smaller *puntos de información turística*, all connected to the same telephone number as the Centros de Turismo, are located at: the Plaza de Cibeles; the Plaza de Callao; just

off the Plaza del Emperador Carlos V on C/Santa Isabel; and at Barajas Airport Terminals 2 & 4.
Oficinas de Turismo de la Comunidad de Madrid
C/Duque de Medinaceli 2, Huertas (91 429 49 51, 902 10 00 07). Metro Banco de España. **Open** 8am-8pm Mon-Sat; 9am-2pm Sun. **Map** p312 I12.
Summer information officers
During July and August pairs of young information guides, in bright yellow and blue uniforms, are sent to roam the central area ready to answer enquiries in a courageous variety of languages (8am-8pm daily). They also staff information stands at Puerta del Sol, Plaza del Callao, Plaza Mayor, by the Palacio Real and by the Prado.
010 phoneline
Open 8am-9pm Mon-Fri; 9am-2pm Sat.
A city-run information line that will answer enquiries of any kind on Madrid, and particularly on events promoted by the city council. Calls are accepted in French and English. For now, the non-premium rate equivalent is 91 529 82 10.

VISAS & IMMIGRATION

Spain is one of the EU countries that is party to the Schengen Agreement (which includes all of the EU except the UK, Ireland or the countries that joined in May 2004). These countries share immigration procedures and have reduced border controls between one another. To enter Spain, nationals from countries party to the agreement need only show their national ID card, but British, Irish, those from the new EU countries and all non-EU citizens must have full passports.

Additional visas are not needed by US, Canadian, Australian, New Zealand or Israeli citizens for stays of up to three months. Citizens of South Africa and some other countries do need a visa to enter Spain. They can be obtained from Spanish consulates in other European countries as well as in your home country.

WATER

Madrid's tap water is good and safe to drink, with less of the chlorine taste that you get in some Spanish cities. There are occasional water shortages in summer, and signs posted in hotels urge guests to avoid wasting water.

THE LOCAL CLIMATE

Average temperatures and monthly rainfall in Madrid.

	High (°C/°F)	Low (°C/°F)	Rainfall (mm/in)
Jan	9 / 48	2 / 36	39 / 1.5
Feb	11 / 52	2 / 36	34 / 1.3
Mar	15 / 59	5 / 41	43 / 1.7
Apr	18 / 64	7 / 45	48 / 1.9
May	21 / 70	10 / 50	47 / 1.8
June	27 / 81	15 / 59	27 / 1.0
July	31 / 88	17 / 63	11 / 0.4
Aug	30 / 86	17 / 63	15 / 0.6
Sept	25 / 77	14 / 57	32 / 1.2
Oct	19 / 66	10 / 50	53 / 2.0
Nov	13 / 55	5 / 41	47 / 1.8
Dec	9 / 48	2 / 36	48 / 1.9

If you want tap rather than bottled water in a restaurant specify that you want *agua del grifo*.

WHEN TO GO

The climate of Madrid has justly been described as 'nine months of winter (*invierno*) and three months of hell (*infierno*)'. Many people can't cope with the summer heat, others love it – and the city is great fun during the *fiestas*.

Climate

Winter in Madrid can be very cold, although there's often bright, crisp sunshine and most rain falls in autumn and spring. Spring is unpredictable – February can often be freakishly warm, while in April, rain is likely. Summer temperatures range from hot to unbearably hot, although it's a dry heat with little humidity. In July and August it doesn't really cool down at night, making partying in the street great fun, but sleeping less so. Traditionally there's a mass exodus in August. Autumn weather is usually bright and warm and it's often possible to eat and drink outside well into October.

Holidays

On public holidays (*fiestas*), virtually all shops, banks and offices, and some bars and restaurants, are closed. There is a near-normal public transport service, though, except on Christmas Day and New Year's Day, and many museums do remain open, albeit with Sunday hours operating. When a holiday falls on a Tuesday or Thursday it's a common practice for people to take the day before or after the weekend off as well, in a long weekend called a *puente* (bridge). Many places are also closed for the whole of Easter Week. For the city's festivals, *see pp22-29*. The usual official holidays are:

New Year's Day/
Año Nuevo 1 Jan
Three Kings/
Reyes Magos 6 Jan
Good Friday/Viernes Santo
May (Labour) Day/**Fiesta del Trabajo** 1 May
Madrid Day/**Día de la Comunidad de Madrid** 2 May
San Isidro 15 May
Virgen de la Paloma 15 Aug
Discovery of America/
Día de la Hispanidad 12 Oct
All Saints' Day/**Todos los Santos** 1 Nov
Virgen de la Almudena 9 Nov
Constitution Day/**Día de la Constitución** 6 Dec
Immaculate Conception/
La Inmaculada 8 Dec
Christmas Day/**Navidad** 25 Dec

WOMEN

Instituto de la Mujer

C/Condesa de Venadito 34, Concepción (91 452 85 00, www. inmujeres.es). Metro Barrio de la Concepción. **Open** 9am-8pm Mon-Thur; 9am-5.30pm.
A government organisation with a useful information service (900 191 010, 24hrs). The Institute has a legal office that deals with cases of discrimination (91 700 19 10).

WORKING

There are a huge number of foreigners living and working in Madrid. Ninety-five per cent of those from the EU are teaching English. To get a job in one of the academies with better pay and conditions, it's advisable to have a relevant qualification such as TEFL. Private classes are also available, but bear in mind that work often dries up over the summer and holiday periods.

There is a lot of red tape involved in working in Madrid; you can ignore the bureaucracy for a while, but in the long run it's best to sort things out. If you come here contracted from your country of origin, papers should be dealt with by your employer. The quickest way to deal with the state's love of form-filling is to resort to *gestorías*.

Those who have lived here for more than three months should obtain a residency certificate – see the British Embassy's website (www.gov.uk/spain) and the Ministry of the Interior's (www.mir. es/SGACAVT/extranje) for details. First you must obtain the NIE (*número de identificación de extranjeros* – foreigners' identity number). The process is simple – go to the Comisaría de Extranjería or a police station that deals with foreigners' affairs with your passport and a photocopy of the important pages, fill out an application form and you will be sent your number by post. The number is used for all financial dealings and is necessary for opening bank accounts, tax declarations and so on.

Everybody in Spain, both nationals and foreigners, is obliged to carry a valid form of ID. In the case of those foreigners who do not have a national ID card, this means carrying your passport, which is risky. Technically not legal, but usually acceptable, is to carry a photocopy of the relevant pages.

Non-EU citizens have a tougher time. While in Spain on a tourist visa you are technically not allowed to work, though many do. If you are made a job offer while in Spain you must return to your home country and apply for a *visado de residencia* (residence visa). Without this you may not enter Spain to work. It can take time and applications aren't always successful. Once the visa has been issued, you can travel to Spain, take up the job and begin the lengthy application process for a resident's card and work permit (*permiso de trabajo*).

Comisaría de Extranjería

C/General Pardiñas 90, Salamanca (91 322 68 01, www.interior.gob.es). Metro Núñez de Balboa. **Open** 9am-2pm Mon-Fri. **Map** p309 M6.

Vocabulary

Like other Latin languages, Spanish has different familiar and polite forms of the second person (you). Many young people now use the familiar **tú** form most of the time; for foreigners, though, it's always advisable to use the more polite **usted** with people you do not know, and certainly with anyone over the age of 50. In the phrases listed here all verbs are given in the *usted* form. For help in making your way through menus, see *p94* and *p113*.

PRONUNCIATION

c, before an **i** or an **e**, and **z** are like th in thin. **c** in all other cases is as in cat. **g**, before an **i** or an **e**, and **j** are pronounced with a guttural **h**-sound that does not exist in English – like ch in Scottish lo**ch**, but much harder. **g** in all other cases is pronounced as in g**e**t. **h** at the beginning of a word is normally silent. **ll** is pronounced almost like a **y**. **ñ** is like **ny** in ca**ny**on. A single **r** is like **r** at the beginning of a word and **rr** elsewhere are heavily rolled.

BASICS

hello *hola;* **hello** (when answering the phone) *hola, diga;* **good morning, good day** *buenos días;* **good afternoon, good evening** *buenas tardes;* **good evening** (after dark), **good night** *buenas noches;* **goodbye/see you later** *adiós/hasta luego;* **please** *por favor;* **thank you** (very much) *(muchas) gracias;* **you're welcome** *de nada;* **do you speak English?** *¿habla inglés?;* **I don't speak Spanish** *no hablo español;* **I don't understand** *no entiendo;* **what's your name?** *¿cómo se llama?;* **speak more slowly, please** *hable más despacio, por favor;* **wait a moment** *espere un momento;* **Sir/Mr** *señor (sr);* **Madam/Mrs** *señora (sra);* **Miss** *señorita (srta);* **excuse me/sorry** *perdón;* **excuse me, please** *oiga* (the standard way to attract someone's attention, politely; literally 'hear me');* **OK/fine/**(or to a waiter) **that's enough** *vale;* **where is...** *¿dónde está...?;* **why?** *¿porqué?;* **when?** *¿cuándo?;* **who?** *¿quién?;* **what?** *¿qué?;* **where?** *¿dónde?;* **how?** *¿cómo?;* **who is it?**

¿quién es?; **is/are there any...** *¿hay...?* **very** *muy;* **and** *y;* **or** *o;* **with** *con;* **without** *sin;* **open** *abierto;* **closed** *cerrado;* **what time does it open/close?** *¿a qué hora abre/cierra?;* **pull** (on signs) *tirar;* **push** *empujar;* **I would like...** *quiero...* (literally, 'I want... '); **how many would you like?** *¿cuántos quiere?;* **I like** *me gusta;* **I don't like** *no me gusta;* **good** *bueno/a;* **bad** *malo/a;* **well/badly** *bien/mal;* **small** *pequeño/a;* **big** *gran, grande;* **expensive** *caro/a;* **cheap** *barato/a;* **hot** (food, drink) *caliente;* **cold** *frío/a;* **something** *algo;* **nothing** *nada;* **more/less** *más/menos;* **more or less** *más o menos;* **the bill/check, please** *la cuenta, por favor;* **how much is it?** *¿cuánto es?;* **do you have any change?** *¿tiene cambio?;* **price** *precio;* **free** *gratis;* **discount** *descuento;* **bank** *banco;* **to rent** *alquilar;* **(for) rent, rental** *(en) alquiler;* **post office** *correos;* **stamp** *sello;* **postcard** *postal;* **toilet** *los servicios*

GETTING AROUND

airport *aeropuerto;* **railway station** *estación de ferrocarril/estación de RENFE* (Spanish Railways);* **Metro station** *estación de Metro;* **entrance** *entrada;* **exit** *salida;* **car** *coche;* **bus** *autobús;* **train** *tren;* **a ticket** *un billete;* **return** *de ida y vuelta;* **bus stop** *parada de autobús;* **the next stop** *la próxima parada;* **excuse me, do you know the way to...?** *¿oiga, señor/señora/etc, sabe como llegar a...?;* **left** *izquierda;* **right** *derecha;* **here** *aquí;* **there** *allí;* **straight on** *recto;* **to the end of the street** *al final de la calle* **as far as** *hasta;* **towards** *hacia;* **near** *cerca;* **far** *lejos*

ACCOMMODATION

do you have a double/single room for tonight/one week? *¿tiene una habitación doble/para una persona para esta noche/una semana?;* **where is the car park?** *¿dónde está el parking?;* **we have a reservation** *tenemos reserva;* **an inside/outside room** *una habitación interior/exterior;* **with/without bathroom** *con/sin baño;* **shower** *ducha;* **double bed** *cama de matrimonio;* **with**

twin beds *con dos camas;* **breakfast included** *desayuno incluido;* **air-conditioning** *aire acondicionado;* **lift** *ascensor;* **swimming pool** *piscina*

TIME

morning *la mañana;* **midday** *mediodía;* **afternoon/evening** *la tarde;* **night** *la noche;* **late night/early morning** (roughly 1-6am) *la madrugada;* **now** *ahora;* **later** *más tarde;* **yesterday** *ayer;* **today** *hoy;* **tomorrow** *mañana;* **tomorrow morning** *mañana por la mañana;* **early** *temprano;* **late** *tarde;* **delay** *retraso;* **delayed** *retrasado;* **at what time...?** *¿a qué hora...?* **in an hour** *en una hora;* **the bus will take 2 hours (to get there)** *el autobús tardará dos horas (en llegar);* **at 2** *a las dos;* **at 8pm** *a las ocho de la tarde;* **at 1.30** *a la una y media;* **at 5.15** *a las cinco y cuarto;* **at 22.30** *a veintidós treinta;*

NUMBERS

0 *cero;* **1** *un, uno, una;* **2** *dos;* **3** *tres;* **4** *cuatro;* **5** *cinco;* **6** *seis;* **7** *siete;* **8** *ocho;* **9** *nueve;* **10** *diez;* **11** *once;* **12** *doce;* **13** *trece;* **14** *catorce;* **15** *quince;* **16** *dieciséis;* **17** *diecisiete;* **18** *dieciocho,* **19** *diecinueve;* **20** *veinte;* **21** *veintiuno;* **22** *veintidós;* **30** *treinta;* **40** *cuarenta;* **50** *cincuenta;* **60** *sesenta;* **70** *setenta;* **80** *ochenta;* **90** *noventa;* **100** *cien;* **1,000** *mil;* **1,000,000** *un millón*

DAYS, MONTHS & SEASONS

Monday *lunes;* **Tuesday** *martes;* **Wednesday** *miércoles;* **Thursday** *jueves;* **Friday** *viernes;* **Saturday** *sábado;* **Sunday** *domingo .*

January *enero;* **February** *febrero;* **March** *marzo;* **April** *abril;* **May** *mayo;* **June** *junio;* **July** *julio;* **August** *agosto;* **September** *septiembre;* **October** *octubre;* **November** *noviembre;* **December** *diciembre* **spring** *primavera;* **summer** *verano;* **autumn/fall** *otoño;* **winter** *invierno*

Further Reference

BOOKS

Art & architecture

Hugh Broughton *Madrid* The capital's architecture analysed for a lay audience.
Jonathan Brown *Velázquez: Painter and Courtier* The most comprehensive study in English.
JH Elliott & Jonathan Brown *A Palace for a King: The Buen Retiro and the Court of Philip IV* A vivid reconstruction of the life, culture and spectacle of the Habsburg Court, and the grandest of Madrid's palaces.
Robert Hughes *Goya* A dynamic biography of Madrid's favourite son.
Michael Jacobs *Madrid Observed* A lively survey by one of the best current foreign writers on Spain. A good walking companion.

Food & drink

Alan Davidson *Tio Pepe Guide to the Seafood of Spain and Portugal* An excellent pocket-sized guide, with illustrations, to Spain's fishy delights.
Sam and Sam Clark *Moro* The best modern cookbook in English for reproducing the tastes of Spain.

History, politics & culture

Phil Ball *Morbo* A fascinating history of Spanish football, with a good section on Real Madrid.
JH Elliott *Imperial Spain, 1469-1716* The standard history.
RA Fletcher *Moorish Spain* Varied account of a little-known period in European history.
Ronald Fraser *Blood of Spain* An oral history of the Spanish Civil War, the most vivid and human account of Spain's great crisis.
Juan Lalaguna *A Traveller's History of Spain* A handy introduction to the country.
John Hooper *The New Spaniards* The best survey of post-1975 Spain, updated to cover changes in the 1990s.
Paul Preston *Franco*; *Comrades!*; *Doves of War* Exhaustive portraits of the key players on both sides of the Spanish Civil War. The same author's *The Spanish Civil War* is a good concise account of the war.

Hugh Thomas, ed *Madrid, A Traveller's Companion* A great anthology of writing on Madrid from the Middle Ages to the 1930s, by the likes of Casanova, Pérez Galdós and the Duke of Wellington.
Giles Tremlett *Ghosts of Spain: Travels through a Country's Hidden Past* Now an essential read if you're interested in Spain's history and culture over the past century.

Literature

Pedro Almodóvar *Patty Diphusa Stories and Other Writings* Frothy, disposable, but full of the sparky, sexy atmosphere of the Madrid of La Movida.
Camilo José Cela *The Hive* Nobel Prizewinner Cela's sardonic masterpiece on Madrid in the aftermath of the Civil War.
Miguel de Cervantes *Don Quixote* The Golden Age classic, and still an entertaining read. Now available in an excellent and lively new translation by Edith Grossman.
Benito Pérez Galdós *Fortunata and Jacinta* The masterwork of Spain's great 19th-century realist novelist, a story of love and class of great depth set amid the political conflicts of 1860s Madrid. If you like *War and Peace*, you'll like this.
Antonio Múñoz Molina *Prince of Shadows* A psychological thriller based on the legacy of the recent past in modern Madrid.
Tim Parfitt *A Load of Bull: An Englishman's Adventures in Madrid* An entertaining memoir on *madrileños* and their customs.
Arturo Pérez Reverte *The Fencing Master*; *The Flanders Road*; *The Club Dumas* (also published as *The Dumas Club*) Elegant, unconventional mystery novels by one of the most lauded of current Spanish writers.
Benjamin Prado *Not Only Fire* Examination of post-Civil War intergenerational relationships by one of Spain's bright young hopes.
CJ Sansom *Winter in Madrid* An insightful portrait of life in Madrid following the Spanish Civil War.

MUSIC

Plácido Domingo *Romanzas de Zarzuelas* One of his several recordings of lush tunes from the

zarzuelas that have played a big part in the recent revival of Madrid's own comic operas.
El Gran Lapofsky *Spain is Different* A fantastic selection of Latin, bossa, nu-jazz and funk-infused tracks – some otherwise unavailable rarities – interspersed with skits from Spaniards telling us just why Spain is different.
Ray Heredia *Quien no corre, vuela* One of the most original new flamenco performers.
Los Jóvenes Flamencos Several CDs in this series, bringing together all the best *nuevo flamenco* artists of the last 20 years, have been issued by the Nuevos Medios label.
Carmen Linares *Antología* Classic flamenco themes sung by one of the best younger *cantaoras*.
Corazón Loco *40 Joyas del Pop Español* Excellent intro to the perky, occasionally daft and sometimes pretty cool soundtrack of modern Madrid.
Paco de Lucía *Luzía*, or any of the many recordings by the greatest of modern flamenco guitarists.

MADRID ONLINE

www.madrid.es The Madrid Ayuntamiento's functional website, with some information in English.
www.madrid.org Equivalent site of the Comunidad: information on local services, in Spanish only.
www.esmadrid.com Useful website with information on all visitor attractions.
www.ctm-madrid.es Madrid transport information.
www.lanetro.com Concerts, clubs, films and reviews.
www.lecool.com Weekly round-up of the quirkiest, coolest events.
www.renfe.com Spanish Railways' site, with online booking.
http://madrid.lanetro.com The hippest and best of local Spanish-language events and listings sites.

MADRID APPS

Madrid – Offline Map Useful, free street maps that won't incur roaming charges.
Metro de Madrid Oficial Interactive metro map.
Madrid Map & Walking Tours DIY walking routes.

Index

INDEX

Maps

Madrid by Area

AVDA MONFORTE DE LEMOS

M30

NORTHERN
SUBURBS

Chamartín
Station

PLAZA DE
CASTILLA

TETUAN

PLAZA DE
CUZCO

C/RANO MURILLO

C/CAPELLA NIETO

CORENSE

PASEO DE LA CASTELLANA

CHAMARTÍN

AVDA PÍO XII

M30

Dehesa
de la Villa

Santiago
Bernabéu
Stadium

ARGÜELLES &
MONCLOA

AVDA RAMÓN Y CAJAL

See p305

C/RDO. FDEZ VILLAVERDE

PASEO DE SERRANO

C/ SERRANO

Auditorio
Nacional

C/ZADOQUIN COSTA

PASEO DE SAN FRANCISCO DE SALES

C/BRAVO MURILLO

C/CEA BERMUDEZ

C/JOSÉ ABASCAL

C/MARÍA DE MOLINA

AVENIDA DE AMÉRICA

CHAMBERÍ

C/SANTA ENGRACIA

C/FRANCISCO SILVELA

See pp306-307

See pp308-309

Parque
del Oeste

C/PRINCESA

C/VELAZQUEZ

C/PRÍNCIPE DE VERGARA

Las Ventas
Bullring

Centro Cultural
Conde Duque

PASEO DE RECOLETOS

MALASAÑA &
CONDE DUQUE

C/FUENCARRAL

PLAZA DE
COLÓN

C/ SERRANO

C/GOYA

SALAMANCA
& RETIRO

CASA DE
CAMPO

Príncipe Pío
Station

PLAZA DE
ESPAÑA

C/HORTALEZA

CHUECA

PASEO DE

C/ALCALÁ

C/O'DONNELL

GRAN VÍA

GRAN VÍA

Palacio
Real

C/ARENAL

Puerta
del Sol

Museo
Thyssen

CALLE DOCTOR ESQUERDO

C/BAILEN

Campo
del Moro

C/MAYOR

PLAZA
MAYOR

HUERTAS &
SANTA ANA

Parque del
Buen Retiro

Parque de
la Elipa

LOS AUSTRIAS
& LA LATINA

C/HUERTAS

PASEO DEL PRADO

Museo del
Prado

C/ATOCHA

RASTRO &
LAVAPIÉS

C/TOLEDO

RONDA DE TOLEDO

Centro de Arte
Reina Sofía

Atocha
Station

AVDA DEL MEDITERRÁNEO

See pp310-311

See pp312-313

AVDA CIUDAD DE BARCELONA

N

Vicente
Calderón
Stadium

PASEO SANTA MARÍA DE LA CABEZA

PASEO DE LAS DELICIAS

C/MÉNDEZ ÁLVARO

M30

SOUTHERN
SUBURBS

SOUTH OF
CENTRE

Planetario

Rayo
Vallecano
Stadium

0   800 m

0   800 yds

Parque de
Tierno Galván

VALLECAS

© Copyright Time Out Group 2013

J **K** C/GUTIÉRREZ SOLANA **L** C/SEGRE **M**

C/SANTIAGO BERNABÉU

1

Monumento
Picasso

C/HERMANOS PINZÓN

Plaza de
Picasso

1 Restaurants pp88-110
1 Tapas pp111-120
1 Cafés & Bars pp121-133
1 Hotels pp155-171

CHAMARTÍN

C/A. PALACIO VALDÉS

C/FRAY JUAN GIL C/PISUERGA

C/TORMES
C/JARAMA
C/ARGA
C/CINCA

C/F. DE ASÍS M. CASARIEGO
C/DIAFRO
C/HENARES
C/TORMES
C/EBRO
C/TAJO

C/LUIS MURIEL
C/ÉREZ
C/LEIZARÁN

C/E. ALCÁNTARA
C/GUADIANA
C/MIÑO
C/BIDASOA

2 TETUÁN

C/BALBINA VALVERDE
C/DANIEL URRABIETA
C/ERESMA
C/URIA
C/URUMEA

C/TAMBRE
C/NERVIÓN

C/R. F. VILLAVERDE
C/GUADALQUIVIR
C/SERRANO

Plaza del Poeta
Manuel del Palacio

C/JOAQUÍN COSTA

Nuevos Ministerios
Metro

Escuela Politécnica
Superior del Ejército
San Agustín
AVENIDA DOCTOR ARCE
C/HELECHO

C/CARBONERO Y SOL
C/F. DEL DUERO
Metro República
Argentina

C/VELÁZQUEZ
C/A. R. MARÍN

Plaza de la
República
Argentina

C/A. R. VILLA

3
C/BELÁZAR
C/GRIJALBA
C/VITRUVIO
C/JOAQUÍN COSTA

C/JORGE MANRIQUE
C/R. MARÍN

C/JORGE MANRIQUE
C/SERRANO

C/JUAN DE LA CIERVA
C/A. PÉREZ

Instituto Ramiro
de Maeztu

Sanatorio
S. F. de Asis

Estado Mayor
del Ejército
C/PARTICULAR
C/PABLO ARANDA
C/F. LOBO

4
Instituto Ciencias
Físico Químicas
Espíritu
Santo

Plaza
San Juan de la Cruz
C/RÍO ROSAS

C/SAN JUAN DE LA CRUZ
C/OQUENDO

C/ESPRONCEDA
C/ZURBANO

Museo
de
Ciencias
Naturales
Escuela T. S. de
Ingenieros
Industriales
C/SERRANO
C/CASTELLÓN DE LA PLANA

C/BRETÓN DE LOS HERREROS

C/MÁLAGA
C/PEDRO DE VALDIVIA
C/PEDRO DE VALDIVIA

72
C/LÓPEZ DE HOYOS

5 C/JOSÉ ABASCAL
Monumento
al Marqués
del Duero

Gregorio Marañón
Metro
C/SALAS
C/MARÍA DE MOLINA

0 300 m
0 300 yds

© Copyright Time Out Group 2013

CHAMBERÍ
C/LÓPEZ DE HOYOS
Museo
Lázaro
Galdiano
Secretaría
General de
Turismo

C/GARCÍA DE PAREDES
C/HERMANOS BÉCQUER
C/SERRANO
SALAMANCA
& RETIRO

6
C/ZURBANO
C/GENERAL ORÁA
C/VELÁZQUEZ

Museo
Sorolla
Glorieta
de Emilio
Castelar
Monumento
a Castelar
45
C/CLAUDIO COELLO
Convento
P. Dominicos
Sanatorio
Fleming
C/NÚÑEZ DE BALBOA

PASEO GENERAL MARTÍNEZ CAMPOS
59
C/LAGASCA

See
p308
Edificio de la
Unión y El Fénix
See
p309
Time Out Madrid 305
C/DIEGO DE LEÓN

A **B** **C** **D**

6

Restaurants pp88-110
Tapas pp111-120
Cafés & Bars pp121-133
Hotels pp155-171

Plaza de la Moncloa
Monte Metro Moncloa

C/FERNANDO EL CATÓLICO

PASEO DE RUPERTO CHAPI

PASEO DE MORET

C/MARTIN DE LOS HEROS

Ministerio de Defensa (Aire)

C/PRINCESA

C/HILARIÓN ESLAVA

C/MELÉNDEZ VALDÉS

C/GAZTAMBIDE

Cuartel Infantería Don Juan

PASEO DE RUPERTO CHAPÍ

PASEO DE CAMOENS Y VALERO

C/LISBOA

C/ECIJA

C/FRAY

C/FRANCISCO LOZANO

C/SAN JUAN BOSCO

C/ROMERO ROBLEDO

C/JUAN ÁLVAREZ MENDIZÁBAL

C/MARTIN DE LOS HEROS

C/ALTAMIRANO

C/RODRÍGUEZ SAN PEDRO

Metro Argüelles

7

PASEO DEL PINTOR ROSALES

Sagrado Corazón

C/BENITO GUTIÉRREZ

Convento Trinitaria

C/TUTOR

55

Parque del Oeste

C/F Y JACINTO ALCÁNTARA

C/MARQUÉS DE URQUIJO

Buen Suceso

C/TUTOR

C/JACINTO ALCÁNTARA

Estación Teleférico a Parque de Atracciones

C/FERRAZ

C/MARTIN DE LOS HEROS

PUE DEPÓSITO BENE

C/BUEN SUCESO

C/JUAN ÁLVAREZ MENDIZÁBAL

8

ARGÜELLES & MONCLOA

C/FRANCISCO JACINTO ALCÁNTARA

PASEO DEL PINTOR ROSALES

C/QUINTANA

C/REY FRANCISCO

C/EVARISTO SAN MIGUEL

AVENIDA VALLADOLID

C/ROSALEDA

La Rosaleda

Plaza Marqués Cerralbo

C/LUISA FERNANDA

Glorieta San Antonio de la Florida

PASEO DEL REY

PASEO DEL PINTOR ROSALES

Jardines Cuartel de la Montaña

C/PROFESOR M. A. BASCH

9

Ermita de San Antonio de la Florida
70

C/ROSALEDA

Templo de Debod

Jardines Ferraz

C/FERRAZ

C/IBERA DEL MANZANARES

Río Manzanares

C/MOZART

C/ANICETO MARINAS

PASEO DE LA FLORIDA

PASEO DEL REY

C/IRÚN

C/E BENOT

C/PROFESOR M. A. BASCH

C/CADARSO

PASEO DEL MARQUÉS DE MONISTROL

10

CASA DE CAMPO

Estación de Príncipe Pío

C/E FIGUERAS

C/ARRIAZA

C/ILUSTRACIÓN

0   300 m
0   300 yds

© Copyright Time Out Group 2013

Glorieta San Vicente

Metro Príncipe Pío

CUESTA DE SAN VICENTE

11

PASEO DEL EMBARCADERO

See p310

PASEO DE LA VIRGEN DEL PUERTO

Campo del Moro

- ❶ Restaurants pp88-110
- ❶ Tapas pp111-120
- ❶ Cafés & Bars pp121-133
- ❶ Hotels pp155-171

A PASEO DEL EMBARCADERO **B** See p306 **C** **D**

11 CASA DE CAMPO

❶ Restaurants pp88-110
❶ Tapas pp111-120
❶ Cafés & Bars pp121-133
❶ Hotels pp155-171

Campo del Moro

Plaza de Almería

Ermita de la Virgen del Puerto

Catedral de la Almudena

Muralla de Madrid

12 C/SAAVEDRA FAJARDO C/SAN CRISPÍN PASEO DE EXTREMADURA C/ANTONIO ZAMORA C/CARAMUEL C/DOÑA URRACA C/DOÑA BERENGUELA C/MENDOZA

PASEO MARQUÉS DE MONISTROL

PASEO CIUDAD DE PLASENCIA

Parque de Atenas

C/SEGOVIA

Jardines del Emir Mohamed I

C/SEGOVIA

Jardines de las Vistillas

C/BENITO GALINDO

Plaza Gabriel Miró

C/SAN BUENAVENTURA

TRV/VISTILLAS

13 PUNTA DEL ÁNGEL C/JUAN TORNERO

PASEO ERMITA DEL SANTO

PASEO BAJO DE LA VIRGEN DEL PUERTO

PASEO DE LA VIRGEN DEL PUERTO

C/LINNEO C/JUAN DUQUE C/MANZANARES C/MAZARREDO

RONDA DE SEGOVIA

CUESTA DESCARGAS

Capilla del Cristo de los Dolores

Parque de las Vistillas

C/MORENO NIETO

C/JUAN DUQUE

C/FÓSFORO

C/JERTE

San Francisco El Grande

14 C/CARAMUEL C/PABLO CASALS

COLONIA DEL CARMEN C/DAIMIEL

C/TIZARRA

C/LINNEO C/JUAN DUQUE

PASEO LE LOS MELANCÓLICOS

C/SANTA MARÍA LA REAL DE NIEVA

C/ROSARIO

C/SAN BERNABÉ

RONDA DE SEGOVIA

C/RUY GONZÁLES CLAVIJO

C/JEMENUÑO

TRAVESÍA GIL IMÓN

C/GIL IMÓN

15 Parque de Caramuel

C/SEPÚLVEDA

PASEO DE LA ERMITA DEL SANTO

AVENIDA DEL MANZANARES

Río Manzanares

PASEO VIRGEN DEL PUERTO

C/CHULAPOS

C/COBOS DE SEGOVIA

C/BERCIAL

PASEO IMPERIAL

C/MERCADO

C/VILLOSLADA

C/MERCADO

C/SAN CONRADO

C/CAPRICHOS

Parque de la Cuña Verde

C/MÁRMOL

PASEO DE LOS MELANCÓLICOS

C/PARADINAS

Plaza Francisco Morano

PASEO DR VALLEJO NÁGERA

0 300 m
0 300 yds

© Copyright Time Out Group 2013

16 Parque de San Isidro

PUENTE ELEVADO DE SAN ISIDRO

C/SAN ALEJANDRO

PASEO PONTONES

C/JARDINES

CHUECA C/ALCALÁ

H Las Calatravas

C/VIRGEN DE LOS PELIGROS

I Círculo de Bellas Artes

See p308

J Plaza de la Cibeles

K CentroCentro

C/VALENZUELA

C/ADUANA

C/MARQUÉS DE CASA RIERA

SOL

Real Academia de Bellas Artes

27 C/ALCALÁ

Metro **Sevilla**

C/MADRAZO

C/SEVILLA

C/CEDACEROS

C/ZORRILLA

C/JOVELLANOS

C/JUAN DE MENA

PASEO DEL PRADO

Museo Naval

La Bolsa

C/MONTALBÁN

Museo de Artes Decorativas **45**

C/RUIZ DE ALARCÓN

C/ALFONSO XI

11

C/ARLABÁN

34

C/ECHEGARAY

C/ARIABÁN

Plaza Canalejas

36 **26**

Congreso

Carrera San Jerónimo

C/SANTA CATALINA

C/FERNANFLOR

C/PRADO

37

Museo Thyssen-Bornemisza

Plaza de la Lealtad

C/ANTONIO MAURA

Salón de Reinos (Prado)

C/VICTORIA

C/CRUZ

13

C/PRÍNCIPE

28

C/VENTURA DE LA VEGA

Ateneo de Madrid

C/SANTA CATALINA

18

Plaza Las Cortes

16

Plaza Cánovas del Castillo

C/FELIPE IV

Casón del Buen Retiro

C/NÚÑEZ DE ARCE

19

C/MANUEL F. GLEZ.

28

C/PRADO

Casa de Lope de Vega

25

C/SAN AGUSTÍN

i

PASEO DEL PRADO

Academia Española de la Lengua

C/ACADEMIA

Los Jerónimos

12

C/ECHEGARAY

Plaza Santa Ana

22

Teatro Español

C/LEÓN

14

C/CERVANTES

Plaza de Jesús

Jesús de Medinaceli

33

C/RUIZ DE ALARCÓN

C/CASADO DEL ALISAL

28

15 **16** **18** **19**

17

20

Plaza del Ángel

32

C/INFANTE

32

C/LOPE DE VEGA

27

C/JESÚS

C/LOPE DE VEGA

21

Museo del Prado

C/ALBERTO BOSH

58

31

Plaza Matute

14

31

C/HUERTAS

17

17

18

SANTA ANA

C/AMOR DE DIOS

C/SANTA MARÍA

19

C/SAN PEDRO

51

Plaza de Murillo

C/ESPALTER

C/CANIZARES

C/ATOCHA

C/MAGDALENA

C/LEÓN

C/MORATÍN

20

33

C/SAN PEDRO

Plaza Platería Martínez

PASEO DE ROJAS CLEMENTE

C/CABEZA

Metro **Antón Martín**

C/ATOCHA

C/VERÓNICA

CUESTA DESAMPARADOS

35

PASEO DE CARLOS III

Real Jardín Botánico

13

C/OLMO

C/TORRECILLA DEL LEAL

C/GOBERNADOR

C/ALMADÉN

C/SAN BLAS

Caixa Forum

C/CLAUDIO MOYANO

See p311

38

C/AVE MARÍA

C/TRES PECES

C/SAN EUGENIO

C/SAN ILDEFONSO

C/FÚCAR

C/ALAMEDA

C/CENICERO

C/SAN CARLOS

C/ESPERANZA

C/SANTA ISABEL

C/MARQUÉS DE TOCA

C/SANTA INÉS

Conservatorio de Música

C/ATOCHA

Metro **Atocha**

Ministerio de Agricultura, Pesca y Alimentación

23

14

29

C/PRIMAVERA

C/BUENAVISTA

C/ZURITA

C/SAN COSME Y SAN DAMIÁN

C/SALITRE

Convento de Santa Isabel

C/DR. MATA

C/S. BUSTILLO

Plaza del Emperador Carlos V

Museo de Etnología

Plaza Lavapiés

Metro **Lavapiés**

C/FE

C/DOCTOR PIGA

23

36

LAVAPIÉS

C/SANTA ISABEL

AVENIDA DE LA CIUDAD DE BARCELONA

C/TRIBULETE

C/ARGUMOSA

C/COMBRERERÍA

C/DOCTOR FOURQUET

C/SOMBRERERÍA

C/ARGUMOSA

26

Centro de Arte Reina Sofía

Vieja Estación de Atocha

C/MIGUEL SERVET

C/DOCTOR FOURQUET

C/MALLORCA

C/VALENCIA

C/AMPARO

RONDA DE ATOCHA

C/MARQUÉS DE LA VALDAVIA

Metro **Atocha Renfe**

15

C/ZURITA

C/MÉNDEZ ÁLVARO

Estación de Atocha

CANEÓN DE PAREDES

RONDA DE VALENCIA

Escuela de Ingeniería

RONDA DE ATOCHA

C/DOCE DE OCTUBRE

C/ANDRÉS

PASEO DE LAS DELICIAS

C/TORTOSA

la Casa Encendida

C/SEBASTIÁN ELCANO

C/MURCIA

C/MURCIA

Embajadores

Metro

16

C/EMBAJADORES

C/SEBASTIÁN HERRERA

Nuestra Señora de Las Angustias

C/DELICIAS

C/CRAFAEL DE RIEGO

C/GENERAL LACY

C/BATALLA DEL SALADO

C/PEDRO UNANUE

C/VIZCAYA

C/DELICIAS

Street Index

STREET INDEX

STREET INDEX

Schematic map of the subway network

Metro Lines

1 PINAR DE CHAMARTÍN / VALDECARROS
2 LAS ROSAS / CUATRO CAMINOS
3 VILLAVERDE ALTO / MONCLOA
4 ARGÜELLES / PINAR DE CHAMARTÍN
5 ALAMEDA DE OSUNA / CASA DE CAMPO
6 CIRCULAR
7 HOSPITAL DEL HENARES / PITIS
8 NUEVOS MINISTERIOS / AEROPUERTO
9 MIRASIERRA / ARGANDA DEL REY
10 HOSPITAL INFANTA SOFÍA / PUERTA DEL SUR
11 PLAZA ELÍPTICA / LA FORTUNA
12 METROSUR
R ÓPERA / PRÍNCIPE PÍO

Keys

● Metro Interchange station
● Interchange station with long walking distance
● Station with restricted opening times
● Change of trains
✈ Madrid–Barajas Airport
▨ Airport extra charge
✈ Renfe suburban railway station
▣ Travel information centre
▣ Public Transport Card Office
P Parking
▣ Suburban bus station
▣ Interregional bus station
▣ Terminal night bus line
✈ Railway station
⇆ Transfer Terminal
B1 Light Rail
B2 Change of fare
B3

Light Rail

ML1 PINAR DE CHAMARTÍN / LAS TABLAS
ML2 COLONIA JARDÍN / ESTACIÓN DE ARAVACA
ML3 COLONIA JARDÍN / PUERTA DE BOADILLA

En Madrid no hay distancias

Hay Cercaní

renfe
Cercanías Madrid ⊙

Plano esquemático   April 2012

Legend:
- Estación con plataforma — Station with raising platform
- Estación con ascensor — Station with lift
- Estación accesible — Accessible station
- B1 Corona Tarifaria — Fare limit for the RENFE Suburban Train Network
- CIVIS Tren con paradas limitadas — Train with limited stops
- (*) Para estas estaciones se precisa la Tarjeta E1 del Consorcio de Transportes — (en these stations Card E1 of the Madrid Transport is required)
- Conexión con Metro — Connection with Metro
- Conexión con Metro ligero — Connection with Light Metro
- Estación de autobuses — Bus station
- Aparcamiento — Car Park
- Zona Verde
- Continúa a — Continues to Sta. Mª de la Alameda

Comunidad de Madrid

CONSEJERÍA DE TRANSPORTES, INFRAESTRUCTURAS Y VIVIENDA
La Suma de todos